AF743796

INTERNATIONAL COURTS AND TRIBUNALS SERIES

General Editors: RUTH MACKENZIE, CESARE P.R. ROMANO, AND PHILIPPE SANDS

The Reception of International Law in the European Court of Human Rights

INTERNATIONAL COURTS AND TRIBUNALS SERIES

A distinctive feature of modern international society is the increase in the number of international judicial bodies and dispute settlement and implementation control bodies; in their case loads; and in the range and importance of the issues that they are called upon to address. These factors reflect a new state in the delivery of international justice. The International Courts and Tribunals series has been established to encourage the publication of independent and scholarly works which address, in critical and analytical fashion, the legal and policy aspects of the functioning of international courts and tribunals, including the institutional, substantive, and procedural aspects.

The Reception of International Law in the European Court of Human Rights

MAGDALENA FOROWICZ

OXFORD
UNIVERSITY PRESS

OXFORD
UNIVERSITY PRESS

Great Clarendon Street, Oxford OX2 6DP

Oxford University Press is a department of the University of Oxford.
It furthers the University's objective of excellence in research, scholarship,
and education by publishing worldwide in

Oxford New York

Auckland Cape Town Dar es Salaam Hong Kong Karachi
Kuala Lumpur Madrid Melbourne Mexico City Nairobi
New Delhi Shanghai Taipei Toronto

With offices in

Argentina Austria Brazil Chile Czech Republic France Greece
Guatemala Hungary Italy Japan Poland Portugal Singapore
South Korea Switzerland Thailand Turkey Ukraine Vietnam

Oxford is a registered trade mark of Oxford University Press
in the UK and in certain other countries

Published in the United States
by Oxford University Press Inc., New York

© M. Forowicz, 2010

The moral rights of the author have been asserted

Crown copyright material is reproduced under Class Licence
Number C01P0000148 with the permission of OPSI
and the Queen's Printer for Scotland

Database right Oxford University Press (maker)

First published 2010

All rights reserved. No part of this publication may be reproduced,
stored in a retrieval system, or transmitted, in any form or by any means,
without the prior permission in writing of Oxford University Press,
or as expressly permitted by law, or under terms agreed with the appropriate
reprographics rights organization. Enquiries concerning reproduction
outside the scope of the above should be sent to the Rights Department,
Oxford University Press, at the address above

You must not circulate this book in any other binding or cover
and you must impose the same condition on any acquirer

British Library Cataloguing in Publication Data
Data available

Library of Congress Cataloging-in-Publication Data
Data available

Typeset by Newgen Imaging Systems (P) Ltd., Chennai, India
Printed in Great Britain
on acid-free paper by
CPI Antony Rowe, Chippenham, Wiltshire

ISBN 978–0–19–959267–8 (Hardback)

3 5 7 9 10 8 6 4 2

Preface

This volume aims to provide a comprehensive overview of the reception of international law in the case law of the European Commission on Human Rights and the European Court of Human Rights (ECtHR). It evaluates whether the Strasbourg bodies have been able to create a coherent and comprehensive approach to the interpretation and evaluation of international law. A fresh look at the approach of the Commission and the Court to international law is now required amidst the fragmented realities of the international legal order. Their interactions with the international legal order and other special regimes reveal important lessons for the good functioning of the ECHR and some areas of international law. This volume probes whether the Strasbourg bodies were able to contribute to international law and to the resolution of the fragmentation problem. It assesses fragmentation in specific areas of international human rights law and general international law, as it manifests itself in the European public order. In this context, an important question to consider is the extent to which the Court behaves autonomously and/or falls back on international law, either special or general. Further, the volume discusses the question of whether the Court or the Commission have sufficiently recognized that international law is a system, whether they have integrated the ECHR into this framework or whether they have created their own autonomous regime.

Six international human rights special regimes and two other areas of general international law were chosen as representative samples for the study of this reception process. Each chapter evaluates the case law referring to a special or general regime, and each regime includes one or more international instrument. The assessment is conducted on several levels. Although each chapter contains a summary of the findings, there is also a general comparative synthesis which incorporates the research results of all chapters. The six special regimes covered include international civil and political rights,[1] international child rights,[2] international refugee rights,[3] international humanitarian law,[4] the prohibition against

[1] United Nations Covenant on Civil and Political Rights, 999 UNTS 171 (entered into force 23 March 1976).

[2] United Nations Convention on the Rights of the Child, 1577 UNTS 3 (entered into force 2 September 1990); Convention concerning the Prohibition and Immediate Action for the Elimination of the Worst Forms of Child Labour (ILO No 182), 38 ILM 1207 (entered into force 19 November 2000); The Hague Convention on Protection of Children and Cooperation in respect of Intercountry Adoption (1993) 32 ILM 1134 (entered into force 1 May 1995); The Hague Convention on the Civil Aspects of International Child Abduction, 1343 UNTS 89 (entered into force 1 December 1983).

[3] United Nations Convention Relating to the Status of Refugees, 606 UNTS 267 (entered into force 22 April 1954).

[4] Convention for the Amelioration of the Condition of the Wounded and Sick in Armed Forces in the Field, 75 UNTS 31 (entered into force 21 October 1950); Convention for the Amelioration

torture,[5] and state immunity. The two areas of general international law analysed here are the law of treaties and the case law and Statute of the International Court of Justice.[6]

The special and general regimes evaluated in this study were chosen due to the frequent references made to them in the Strasbourg case law. The starting premise was that frequently mentioned instruments would accurately reflect the trends in the approach of the Court and Commission to international law. In addition, the special regimes selected were preferred over others due to their similarities to the ECHR and to the fact that they belong to the same branch of international law. It was believed, however, that the analysis of general international law would provide a useful contrast to the evaluation of special regimes. It would thus be possible to verify whether the approach of the Strasbourg bodies has varied in accordance with the nature of international law considered.

It is important to note that the case law of both the Commission and the Court are evaluated. Further, while some implicit references to international law are analysed, the volume focuses on explicit references since these display a more definite intention on the part of the Strasbourg bodies to rely on these sources. An important limitation of this approach is that not all influential material is cited in the case law. For instance, some material may be part of the judges' general understanding or may be referred to in argument but not cited for various reasons in the judgment. These latent influences are not considered in this volume, but it must be kept in mind that they do exist. Due to limitations of space, the relations between the ECHR, the Council of Europe, and the EU are also excluded from the analysis. For the same reason, the role of general international law in the ECHR special regime is not examined in greater detail. Given that only two general regimes are considered, the conclusions regarding their function in the ECHR system are necessarily limited.

The research methodology used consists of empirical, analytical, comparative, and theoretical approaches. From the empirical perspective, the study evaluates references to international law in the Strasbourg case law in order to deduce trends in judicial reasoning. In this manner, it aims to verify whether the Commission and the Court have adopted a coherent approach to international law. As part of

of the Condition of the Wounded, Sick, and Shipwrecked Members of Armed Forces at Sea, 75 UNTS 85 (entered into force 21 October 1950); Convention relative to the treatment of prisoners of war, 75 UNTS 135 (entered into force 21 October 1950); Convention relative to the Protection of Civilian Persons in Time of War, 75 UNTS 287 (entered into force 21 October 1950); Protocol Additional to the Geneva Conventions of 12 August 1949, and Relating to the Protection of Victims of International Armed Conflicts (Protocol I), 1123 UNTS 3 (entered into force 7 December 1978); Protocol Additional to the Geneva Conventions of 12 August 1949, and Relating to the Protection of Victims of Non-International Armed Conflicts (Protocol II), 1125 UNTS 609 (entered into force 7 December 1978).

[5] United Nations Convention against Torture and Other Cruel, Inhuman or Degrading Treatment or Punishment, 1465 UNTS 85 (entered into force 26 June 1987).

[6] Statute of the International Court of Justice, 3 Bevans 1179; 59 Stat 1055; TS No 993 (entered into force 24 October 1945).

this process, several variables are evaluated, such as the nature of the case, the nature of the international instrument involved, the relevant ECHR article, and public policy considerations. Further, the volume evaluates decisions, reports, and judgments in order to get an all-encompassing view of the Strasbourg bodies' approach.

Using a comparative approach, the volume attempts to evaluate the reception of international law in the Strasbourg jurisprudence in light of the approaches taken by other international courts. Each chapter therefore sets the ECHR against the background of the relevant regime that it considers. This perspective makes it possible to establish whether the ECHR system is keeping up to speed with international law and whether there is a need to harmonize the Convention with the international standards. In addition, the final chapter compares the various special and general regimes in order to evaluate the differences in the reception process. Thus, the comparative method is used as a means of documenting and explaining the Court's approach to international law.

The analytical perspective assesses the current state of reception of international law in the Strasbourg case law in order to determine the extent to which the ECHR is open to external sources. The various policy reasons prompting references to international law are analysed with the aim of demonstrating that the reception process is greatly conditioned by them. The individual predisposition of judges and the self-conception of the Court also play an important role in this framework. Finally, taking a theoretical approach, the volume attempts to define more specifically the nature of the ECHR special regime. In this context, it aims to determine the extent to which the Court has affirmed its role in the context of the international legal order. Further, the study intends to establish whether the Court can act as an anti-fragmentation body in the future.

The subject of this volume is of interest to academics and practitioners alike. While it has an important theoretical focus on the recent evolution of fragmentation at the European level, it also provides practical information on the use of international law before the ECtHR. In addition, the study sits at the apex of ECHR and international law and explores both perspectives. Lawyers wishing to strengthen their argumentation can use the volume as a guide to the Court's practice. Academics interested in fragmentation at the European level will also find an analysis of the recent trends.

Magdalena Forowicz
31 January 2010

Acknowledgements

The completion of this book was a long process which was initiated four years ago with a doctoral proposal. This lonesome endeavour would not have been possible without the support, encouragement, and confidence of numerous people, whom I would like to warmly thank here.

First and foremost, I would like to express my utmost gratitude to my thesis director, supervisor, and mentor, Professor Helen Keller, who provided tremendous inspiration, encouragement, patience, and guidance throughout this long project. Since our first discussions, Professor Keller has imparted the required theoretical framework, academic freedom, and time-frame to enable me to complete my work. Her academic experience in the area I have researched supplied the roots from which my ideas later grew. Professor Keller has provided me not only with a firm academic basis, but also with personal support and tremendous professional challenges, which have shaped my career and will continue to do so for years to come.

Special thanks are also due to Professor Nina Vajic, Judge at the European Court of Human Rights, who has offered me significant guidance in the initial phase of my research. Her extensive practical experience has allowed me to define more clearly the conceptual framework of my thesis. I am also very much indebted to Professor John Merrills who reviewed my initial work and gave me precious advice on how to complete my thesis. His innovative research was a springboard for the development of my own ideas. His objective guidance and great knowledge have given me confidence in my own work. Personal thanks are also due to my wonderful colleagues, and now close friends, who were a source of great support and understanding throughout this long voyage. The numerous memories, discussions, and laughs we shared have become an integral part of this experience.

Furthermore, I would like to thank my parents who have demonstrated great patience and understanding during the various stages of my thesis. My mother has provided me with a beaten path which I could follow in my professional endeavours. My father has also been an avid commentator and reviewer of all my work. I have deeply appreciated all his advice and comments. Finally, I would like to thank Maciej Swietlik for reviewing all of my work, providing accurate advice, and believing in my project at the most stressful of times.

Magdalena Forowicz
31 January 2010

Contents

Table of Cases

COURT

Decisions

Judgments

COMMISSION

Decisions

Reports

INTERNATIONAL COURTS/BODIES

Committee Against Torture

Human Rights Committee

Inter-American Commission on Human Rights

International Court of Justice

Contentious cases

Advisory Proceedings

Permanent Court of International Justice

United Kingdom

List of Abbreviations

Am J Com L	American Journal of Comparative Law
Am J Int'l L	American Journal of International Law
Am U Int'l Rev	American University International Law Review
Barry L Rev	Barry Law Review
BYIL	British Yearbook of International Law
Buff Hum Rts L Rev	Buffalo Human Rights Law Review
Buff L Rev	Buffalo Law Review
Colum J Transnat'l L	Columbia Journal of Transnational Law
CAT	Convention Against Torture
CRC	Convention on the Rights of the Child
Cornell Int'l LJ	Cornell International Law Journal
CoE	Council of Europe
CLP	Current Legal Problems
EPIL	Encyclopaedia of Public International Law
ECPT	European Committee for the Prevention of Torture and Inhuman or Degrading Treatment or Punishment
ECHR	European Convention on Human Rights
ECtHR	European Court of Human Rights
ECJ	European Court of Justice
EHRLR	European Human Rights Law Review
Eur J Int'l L	European Journal of International Law
ESA	European Space Agency
EU	European Union
FRY	Federal Republic of Yugoslavia
GDR	German Democratic Republic
GYIL	German Yearbook of International Law
Harv Hum Rts J	Harvard Human Rights Journal
Harv Int'l LJ	Harvard International Law Journal
Hum Rts Brief	Human Rights Brief
HRC	Human Rights Committee
Hum Rts J	Human Rights Journal
HRLR	Human Rights Law Review
Hum Rts Qrtly	Human Rights Quarterly
IACtHR	Inter-American Court of Human Rights
IICLR	Indiana International and Comparative Law Review

ICRC	International Committee of the Red Cross
Int'l Comp LQ	International & Comparative Law Quarterly
ICJ	International Court of Justice
ICCPR	International Covenant on Civil and Political Rights
ICESCR	International Covenant on Economic, Social and Cultural Rights
ICTR	International Criminal Tribunal for Rwanda
ICTY	International Criminal Tribunal for the former Yugoslavia
IHL	International Humanitarian Law
IJRL	International Journal of Refugee Law
ILO	International Labour Organization
ILC	International Law Commission
ILM	International Legal Materials
Int'l Org L Rev	International Organizations Law Review
IRRC	International Review of the Red Cross
IYHR	Israel Yearbook on Human Rights
J Con & Sec L	Journal of Conflict and Security Law
J Int'l Crim Just	Journal of International Criminal Justice
KFOR	Kosovo Force (NATO)
PKK	Kurdistan's Workers Party
LJIL	Leiden Journal of International Law
Mich J Int'l L	Michigan Journal of International Law
MLLWR	Military Law and Law of War Review
Mil L Rev	Military Law Review
Mel J Int'l L	Melbourne Journal of International Law
NATO	North Atlantic Treaty Organization
NGO	Non-governmental organization
NILR	Netherlands International Law Review
NQHR	Netherlands Quarterly of Human Rights
NYUJ Int'l L & Pol	New York University Journal of International Law and Politics
OP	Optional Protocol
OAS	Organization of American States
PCIJ	Permanent Court of International Justice
RGDIP	Revue Générale de Droit International Public
Sask L Rev	Saskatchewan Law Review
SZIER	Schweizerische Zeitschrift für internationales und europäisches Recht

TLCP	Transnational Law and Contemporary Problems
TRNC	Turkish Republic of Northern Cyprus
Tul J Int'l & Comp L	Tulane Journal of International and Comparative Law
Tul L Rev	Tulane Law Review
UDHR	Universal Declaration of Human Rights
UC Davis L Rev	University of California, Davis, Law Review
UN	United Nations
UNHCR	United Nations High Commissioner for Refugees
UNMIK	United Nations Interim Administration Mission in Kosovo
UNSC	United Nations Security Council
UNTS	United Nations Treaty Series
VCLT	Vienna Convention on the Law of Treaties
Wayne L Rev	Wayne Law Review
WTO	World Trade Organization
YHRDLJ	Yale Human Rights & Development Law Journal
Yale LJ	Yale Law Journal
ZaöRV	Zeitschrift für ausländisches öffentliches Recht und Völkerrecht
ZöR	Zeitschrift für öffentliches Recht

Introduction

1. The Evolving Background of the European Convention

No man is an Island, entire of itself; every man is a piece of the Continent, a part of the main; if a clod be washed away by the sea, Europe is the less, as well as if a promontory were, as well as if a manor of thy friends or of thine own were; any man's death diminishes me, because I am involved in Mankind; And therefore never send to know for whom the bell tolls; It tolls for thee.[1]

If one were to be arrested by the police of a European country on suspicion of being a terrorist, where would one turn if all domestic avenues of justice had already been explored? Would the European Court of Human Rights (ECtHR) be the best solution? And if the European Convention on Human Rights (ECHR) did not deliver the desired result, would it be advisable to turn to another international body, such as the Human Rights Committee (HRC)? Would it be possible to apply simultaneously to the ECtHR and to the HRC? The choices available to the individual applicant often seem endless and complex. With several overlapping instruments applicable to a single claim, the international web of justice is becoming more and more entangled. In most situations, the ECHR would probably still provide the most efficient means to seek justice. Would this be the case for a person accused of terrorism? As convoluted as they may be, these are the new realities of the international adjudication of human rights violations. It is thus through their lens that the ECHR system and its institutions have to be seen.

The Convention, which entered into force in 1953, established an exhaustive catalogue of rights as well as two institutions (the ECtHR and the European Commission of Human Rights) responsible for its enforcement. The ECHR system quickly evolved into a complex and effective mechanism for the protection of human rights. Over time, the Contracting States have updated, expanded, and strengthened the ECHR's scope and objectives through subsequent treaty amendments. As part of these fundamental changes, new rights were included, further powers were attributed to the ECtHR, and the position of the individual applicant was strengthened. The previous European Commission of Human

[1] John Donne, *The Major Works including Songs and Sonnets and Sermons* (Oxford/New York: Oxford University Press, 1990), 344.

Rights ceased to exist and its functions were taken over by a permanent court. The ECtHR developed a creative, complex, and expansive case law which put flesh on to the Convention and further expanded its scope, thus allowing it to keep up to speed with evolving realities. The ECtHR became one of the most experienced and efficient human rights enforcement bodies, on to which other judicial or quasi-judicial bodies have looked for guidance. As an autonomous and authoritative court exclusively charged with the application of the ECHR, the Court may appear, at first, as a self-sufficient institution which does not need to refer to any other external non-ECHR sources.

However, as the jurisprudence of the Strasbourg bodies developed, it became increasingly clear that appearances were deceiving. The Strasbourg bodies have been compelled to look beyond the Convention as part of their case law. With the proliferation of international courts and tribunals and with the expansion of international law, external sources penetrated the ECHR system. Over time, international law started to regulate increasing fields of human activity. As a result of this expansion, international law necessarily became more specialized and compartmentalized. The international legal system became fragmented and appeared to foreclose any hope for unity, coherence, or certainty. It is needless to mention that in the past 50 years more treaties and courts have been established than ever before. Currently, a single human rights violation falls under a number of treaties. Cases have become intertwined with various treaty regimes and it was difficult for the Strasbourg bodies to consider them without referring to other instruments. Increasingly, more references to international law have appeared as the Strasbourg case law has exploded in recent years. This phenomenon, now fairly frequent yet not systematized, occurs in a wide variety of circumstances, involves cross-cutting issues, and relates to different international law instruments. This volume intends to rationalize and to elucidate the causes of this practice in order to facilitate the understanding of the relationship between European public order and other international special regimes and general international law.

The main purpose of the research is to evaluate how international law was received into the ECHR system. The concept of reception refers here to the means and methods through which the ECtHR judges and Commission members used and resisted or accepted international law.[2] The Strasbourg bodies used both positive and negative references[3] when considering international law;

[2] For further information on the reception concept, see Helen Keller, *Rezeption des Volkerrechts, Max-Planck-Institut für ausländisches öffentliches Recht und Völkerrecht, Beiträge zum ausländischen öffentlichen Recht und Völkerrecht* (Berlin/Heidelberg/New York/Barcelona: Springer, 2003), 3–44; Alec Stone Sweet and Helen Keller, 'The Reception of the ECHR in National Legal Orders' in Helen Keller and Alec Stone Sweet (eds), *A Europe of Rights: The Impact of the ECHR on the National Legal Systems* (Oxford/New York: OUP, 2008), 3, 4, 15–18.

[3] Nathan Miller, 'An International Jurisprudence? The Operation of "Precedent" Across International Tribunals' (2002) 15 LJIL 483, 490–492. However, in most reception cases considered in this volume, the Court and the Commission relied on positive reception and integrated international law in their reasoning as a result of its usefulness. Negative references or the instances where the Strasbourg bodies disagreed with international law were rare.

negative reception was used to distinguish the ECHR from other instruments or to disagree with another source, whereas positive reception was employed to support or to complement the reasoning of the Strasbourg bodies. In this context, the Strasbourg bodies' approach and predisposition towards international law will be analysed in order to determine whether they are inclined to receive international norms. Further, the study considers the Strasbourg bodies' self-perception and interpretation of the ECHR in order to define with greater precision the nature of their special regime. The level of reception of international sources is considered to be an indicator of the Strasbourg bodies' parochialism or cosmopolitanism. Thus, the study attempts to probe whether the ECHR is sufficiently integrated into the international legal system and whether the Court could be perceived as a harmonizing or anti-fragmentation body at the European level. It is a geographically limited court that did not have anti-fragmentation as part of its original mandate. Nonetheless, the ECHR is a system in mutation; as a living instrument, it must be adapted and tailored to the new fragmented legal realities. Furthermore, the ECtHR is an experienced and influential court; its anti-fragmentation case law could have an impact in numerous domestic and international jurisdictions. As such, it could potentially reduce fragmentation at European and international levels.

2. A Delicate Balance of Reception: The Interpretation Framework

The ECHR system is situated within a greater framework where numerous complex legal and political interactions take place. The ECHR is surrounded by a number of outer systems which can be subdivided in accordance with the Court's interactions with them. These systems comprise: (1) the Council of Europe; (2) the Contracting States; (3) the European Union; and (4) the international legal order, including special regimes and general international law. As part of the first level of interactions, the Court has very close relations with the Council of Europe and its treaties. The ECHR was prepared by the Council of Europe and is a crucial component of the Council of Europe framework. In addition to the Convention, the Council of Europe has established 202 treaties,[4] including numerous human rights treaties.[5] The Strasbourg case law is therefore replete with references to these instruments.

The second level of interactions concerns the Court's relations with the Contracting States. The Contracting States' respect of the Court's decisions and implementation of the Convention constitutes a cornerstone in the good

[4] Council of Europe, Complete List of the Council of Europe's Treaties, <http://conventions.coe.int/Treaty/Commun/ListeTraites.asp?CM=8&CL=ENG> (last visited 10 January 2010).

[5] Clare Ovey and Robin CA White, *The European Convention on Human Rights* (Oxford/New York: OUP, 4th edn, 2006), 17.

functioning of the ECHR system. In order to maintain its institutional credibility, the Court must refrain from interfering with the margin of appreciation granted to Contracting States and from imposing its will in areas in which it was not explicitly mandated to decide. Being subsidiary to national jurisdictions, the Court is often cautious when it considers cases relating to complex state interests and policies. Having certain expectations from the ECHR system, Contracting States exert an important influence on the Court's case law.

At the third level of interactions, the Court often refers to EU legislation and case law concerning human rights. The European Court of Justice (ECJ) has put into place a substantial judicial catalogue of human rights. Further, the adoption of the Charter of Fundamental Rights[6] has exerted a positive influence on the protection of human rights in the EU, even though it is not binding. The eventual enactment of the Treaty of Lisbon[7] will attribute further human rights competencies to the EU institutions. The ECtHR and the ECJ often interact with each other and their jurisdictions overlap in certain human rights areas. The EU's accession to the ECHR will improve the functioning of both systems with respect to the protection of human rights in Europe. As a result, the ties between the ECHR and the EU will also become tighter.

The fourth layer of interactions relates to the contact that the Court has with the international legal order. These relations concern the Court's reliance on general international law and special regimes. They also include the Court's interactions with the United Nations bodies, NATO, other international organizations, as well as regional human rights courts. International political tensions are often represented in the cases that reach Strasbourg; they have an important bearing on the reasoning of the ECtHR. Nonetheless, the heterogeneity of the actors on the international scene and the generality of international law often draw the Court toward self-centrism and introvertism.

This study focuses mainly on the second and fourth layers of interactions. The first and third layers are thus excluded from its scope.

The Court's consideration of external sources is dependent to a large extent on the ECHR interpretation process developed by the Court over the years. There is no single centrifugal force pulling the Court in one direction and driving it to refer to external sources. Rather, there are several issues pulling the Court in two different directions. These elements either hinder or enhance the level of reception of international law and can be subsumed into two different categories. Thus, the Court finds itself at the apex of two diametrically different judicial paradigms.

The paradigm at one end of the spectrum is usually characterized by a high level of judicial activism and unhindered references to international law; this will be referred to as the 'open paradigm'. At the other end of the spectrum, the Court's

[6] Charter of Fundamental Rights of the European Union [2001] OJ C364/01, 18 December 2000, 1–22.

[7] Treaty of Lisbon amending the Treaty on European Union and the Treaty establishing the European Community, signed at Lisbon [2007] OJ C306/01, 17 December 2007, 1–145.

reasoning is marked by judicial restraint and few references to international law; this will be referred to as the 'closed paradigm'. The closed paradigm essentially maintains the status quo with regard to the fragmentation between the ECHR and international law and does not allow for the penetration of external sources into the Court's case law. It is thus the open paradigm that is the most conducive to the reception of international law and to the reduction of fragmentation. In most cases, the Court must refer to international law in order to harmonize the ECHR with prevailing international standards. Thus, the Court's jurisdiction should remain open to external influences and cross-fertilization if it wants to integrate itself into the international legal system and to adjust its provisions to the surrounding regimes. Such an approach can improve the coherence, unity, and functioning of the international legal system as a whole. It would therefore be desirable for the Court to lean more towards the open paradigm than the closed one.

The reduction of fragmentation is not, however, always desirable in the context of the ECHR. Although it may improve the effectiveness of the international legal order, anti-fragmentation may not fulfil the aims and purpose of the ECHR system. Moreover, it can impair the special features of the ECHR. It is therefore not always advantageous to integrate certain international law provisions into the Strasbourg case law by relying on the open paradigm. There are numerous situations in which the closed paradigm can better fulfil the needs of the ECHR and further strengthen the European human rights system. This may, however, further isolate the ECHR system within the international legal order. Thus, the application of both paradigms is situated at the apex of two important considerations, namely the need to improve the ECHR system and the need to integrate into the international legal system. These considerations have proven to be mutually exclusive on occasion. The use of these paradigms is also conditioned by the Court's competence and willingness to intervene in certain international policy issues.

In addition to this, it is crucial to differentiate between appropriate and inappropriate reception of international law. The desirability of reception is analysed here through the lens of the ECHR system; it would be interpreted differently if it were viewed from the perspective of the international legal order. The reduction of fragmentation is generally desirable for the ECHR when the international law referred to complies with the aim, purpose, and special features of the ECHR. Usually, specialized human rights systems can fulfil these requirements and give rise to appropriate reception of international law. Overall, the reliance on the open paradigm is conducive to both the reception and dismissal of international law. It can also generate both fragmentation and anti-fragmentation between international law and Strasbourg case law. The closed paradigm, however, generally contributes to the disregard of external sources and to the deepening of fragmentation between the ECHR and international law. The choice of paradigm largely depends on the results that need to be achieved and on whether the external sources are compliant with the specific character of the ECHR. Although the

Strasbourg bodies never fully embrace one of the extremes of the spectrum, they tend to lean more towards one end than the other.

In the Court's reasoning, the closed paradigm has been couched in constitutional terms. The Court stated in the *Loizidou* case[8] that the ECHR is a 'constitutional instrument of European public order (ordre public)'.[9] On the other hand, the open paradigm has been articulated using more expansive vocabulary. In the *Banković* case,[10] the Court 'recalled that the Convention must be interpreted in the light of the rules of interpretation set out in the Vienna Convention of 23 May 1969 on the Law of Treaties and that Article 31 para. 3 (c) of that treaty indicates that account is to be taken of "any relevant rules of international law applicable in the relations between the parties" '.[11] In the Court's view, 'the principles underlying the Convention cannot be interpreted and applied in a vacuum. Mindful of the Convention's special character as a human rights treaty, it must also take into account any relevant rules of international law when deciding on disputes concerning its jurisdiction pursuant to Article 49 of the Convention.'[12] Generally, a mixture of these paradigms can be found in the Court's case law. The ECHR usually considers itself as being part of the community of international courts, albeit within the context of its constitutive treaty.[13]

Thus, the Court's approach is usually situated between these paradigms or extremes of the spectrum, and varies according to the nature of the violation at stake and the specific circumstances of the case. If the Court leans towards the closed paradigm, it reinforces the autonomous and self-contained character of the ECHR system. If the Court, however, reaches closer to the open paradigm, then it further demonstrates that the ECHR system is dependent on external sources. The level of autonomy of the ECHR system is conditioned to a greater extent by the level of reception of international law.

The level of reception of international law under the ECHR is dependent to a great extent on the interpretation methodology adopted by the Strasbourg bodies. In this context, international rules have provided, at least in part, the backbone for the development of numerous ECHR interpretation techniques. Naturally, the Convention is an international treaty and is bound to follow the rules of international law which determine the life of international conventions.[14] Although Articles 31 to 33 of the Vienna Convention on the Law of Treaties (VCLT)[15] were seldom cited in the Court's judgments, they may have been a constant source of

[8] *Loizidou v Turkey (Preliminary Objections)* (App No 15318/89), judgment, 23 March 1995, Series A, Vol 310.

[9] Ibid, para 75.

[10] *Banković and others v Belgium and 16 Other Contracting States* (App No 52207/99), judgment, 12 December 2001, Reports 2001-XII, 333.

[11] Ibid, para 43.

[12] Ibid.

[13] Jonathan I Charney, 'Is International Threatened by the Multiple International Law Tribunals?' (1998) 27 *Recueil des Cours* 101, 216.

[14] Christos L Rozakis, 'The European Judge as Comparatist' (2005) 80(1) Tul L Rev 257, 269.

[15] Vienna Convention on the Law of Treaties, 1155 UNTS 331, entered into force 27 January 1980. For more details, see ch I .

inspiration. They have only been explicitly mentioned in a few cases, but it can be argued that they were often part of the reasoning by implication.[16] Further, although the Strasbourg case law has been influenced by the ECHR's special characteristics, it is essentially grounded in the VCLT. Interestingly, it appears that that the VCLT rules have mostly assisted the Strasbourg bodies in shaping interpretation techniques which further the reception of international law.

2.1 Interpretation Hindering the Reception Process

2.1.1 Margin of Appreciation

The margin of appreciation is generally understood as the margin of manoeuvre or discretion that the Strasbourg bodies are willing to give to Contracting States with regard to the implementation of their obligations under the ECHR.[17] This notion is not defined in either the text of the Convention or the *travaux préparatoires*, but it appeared for the first time in 1958 in the Commission's report in *Greece v United Kingdom*.[18] The Strasbourg bodies have since relied very frequently on this concept, which has played an important role in the adjudication of cases relating to Articles 8 to 11, 14, and 15 of the ECHR and Article 1 of Protocol No 1. It is difficult to define the contours of this notion very precisely, as the Strasbourg bodies have applied it with great flexibility and in an unpredictable manner. The margin of appreciation has proven to be an elusive concept.

The reasoning prompting the creation of the margin of appreciation was aptly encapsulated by the Court in the *Handyside* judgment.[19] In this case, the Court examined whether the applicant's conviction for disseminating a publication considered to be obscene by English courts was a necessary restriction of his freedom of expression under Article 10(2) of the ECHR. The Court pointed out that:

> the machinery of protection established by the Convention is subsidiary to the national systems safeguarding human rights.... The Convention leaves to each Contracting State, in the first place, the task of securing the rights and liberties it enshrines. The institutions created by it make their own contribution to this task but they become involved only through contentious proceedings and once all domestic remedies have been exhausted (Article 26). These observations apply, notably, to Article 10 para. 2. In particular, it is not possible to find in the domestic law of the various Contracting States a uniform European

[16] François Ost, 'The Original Canons of Interpretation of the European Court of Human Rights' in Mireille Delmas-Marty and Christine Chodakiewicz (eds), (*The European Convention for the Protection of Human Rights: International Protection versus National Restriction* (Dordrecht/Boston/London: Martinus Nijhoff, 1992), 288; see Alastair Mowbray, 'The Creativity of the European Court of Human Rights' (2005) 5 HRLR 57, 59; John Graham Merrills, *The Development of International Law by the European Court of Human Rights* (Manchester/New York: Manchester University Press, 2nd edn, 1993), 69.

[17] Steven Greer, *La marge d'appréciation: Interprétation et pouvoir discrétionnaire dans le cadre de la Convention européenne des Droits de l'Homme*, Dossiers sur les droits de l'homme no 17, Editions du Conseil de l'Europe 2000, 5.

[18] *Greece v United Kingdom* (App No 176/56), Report, 26 September 1958, 2 YB 172.

[19] *Handyside v United Kingdom* (App No 5493/72), judgment, 7 December 1972, Series A, Vol 24.

conception of morals.... By reason of their direct and continuous contact with the vital forces of their countries, State authorities are in principle in a better position than the international judge to give an opinion on the exact content of these requirements as well as on the 'necessity' of a 'restriction' or 'penalty' intended to meet them.[20]

Thus, the Court on occasion defers to the Contracting States' determinations when it considers that it is not appropriate for it to decide a certain question.

The Court usually resorts to the margin of appreciation whenever a case raises an issue that requires a balancing of interests or when vague terms and expressions contained in ECHR provisions are being interpreted.[21] The margin of appreciation is also used when the review of a case requires the Court to assess the seriousness of a particular situation, especially where the domestic authorities would be in a better position to evaluate it and where national opinions may differ.[22] The scope of this concept tends to vary according to the importance of the rights, the nature of the interference, the text and aim of the ECHR provision, the context of the case,[23] or the general policies involved (social, economic, environmental, urban, and rural planning).[24] Moreover, the margin of appreciation tends to be narrower whenever there is a European common ground among the Contracting States.[25] If no such consensus can be found, the Court usually grants a wider margin of appreciation to the states.

The margin of appreciation doctrine limits the Court's jurisdiction in a number of areas where Contracting States have more competence, and indirectly restrains the Court's ability to refer to international law. The Court is often prevented from moving beyond the consensus which is prevalent among the Contracting States. It remains vulnerable to their criticism that it is not taking state practice into account. Further, its reliance on international law can be viewed by states as a non-mandated use of its jurisdiction. Thus, in order to preserve its authority, the Court takes a pragmatic approach to the setting of standards in its case law.[26] This aspect is of tremendous importance as the Convention's effectiveness is dependent on state cooperation in implementing the necessary changes into domestic law following a Court ruling.[27] For this reason, the Court may be unwilling to advance beyond the common ground among the Contracting States. In contrast to this, it should be pointed out that international human rights bodies have largely succeeded in avoiding a systematic recourse to the margin of appreciation (apart from a few cases where it was endorsed implicitly).[28] Thus, the influential Strasbourg

[20] Ibid, para 48. See also Pieter Van Dijk and Godefrious JH Van Hoof, *Theory and Practice of the European Convention on Human Rights* (The Hague/London/Boston: Kluwer Law International, 3rd edn, 1998), 83.

[21] Van Dijk and Van Hoof (n 20 above), 83.

[22] Ibid, 85–86.

[23] Greer (n 17 above), 7.

[24] Van Dijk and Van Hoof (n 20 above), 89.

[25] Ibid, 87; Ovey and White (n 5 above), 54.

[26] Ed Bates, 'The Al-Adsani Case, State Immunity and the International Legal Prohibition on Torture' (2003) 3(2) HRLR 193, 213.

[27] Ibid, 214.

[28] Eyal Benvenisti, 'Margin of Appreciation, Consensus, and Universal Standards' (1999) 21 NYUJ Int'l L & Pol 843, 844.

case law and its frequent use of the doctrine may compromise global efforts of other human rights bodies and national judges to set universal standards.[29]

2.1.2 Consensual Interpretation

Another important method which hinders the reception of international law is consensual interpretation. This method of interpretation allows the Court to deduce the content of rights guaranteed by the ECHR. When faced with difficulties regarding the agreed content of a right and practice of a state, the Court attempts to find a consensus among the various views held by Contracting States by evaluating whether there is common ground in their domestic law. Consensual interpretation originates from the Preamble to the ECHR, which stipulates that Contracting States have agreed on the ECHR, thereby '[r]eaffirming their profound belief in those fundamental freedoms which are the foundation of justice and peace in the world and are best maintained on the one hand by an effective political democracy and on the other by a common understanding and observance of the human rights upon which they depend'.[30]

As a legitimate interpretation technique, it is based on the norms which have been approved by states and which reflect the will of the majority. When the Court decides whether a certain measure taken by a Contracting State violates the ECHR, it often proceeds first to a comparative analysis of various national laws to determine the level of protection existing in different Contracting States.[31] While the Court does not apply domestic law, it uses it as a source of inspiration for its reasoning. The Commission, for instance, has used this comparative methodology as a guide to the scope of the ECHR when examining domestic laws relating to vagrancy, criminal procedure, age of criminal responsibility, or recognition of the gender identity of transsexuals.[32]

References to domestic law legitimize the Court's interpretative approach, which will then be better accepted by the Contracting States. Such an approach may seem surprising given that the Court, which has the duty to verify the conventionality of domestic law, refers to domestic law to justify this control.[33] In reality, this only occurs if there is an important convergence which then creates some sort of European common ground on the basis of which the Court could create or expand ECHR rights.[34] It appears, therefore, that it is the consensus among Contracting States which constitutes one of the bases for the elaboration of the ECHR. From the perspective of reception, this aspect can inhibit international law references as the strong consensus among Contracting States would then take priority and would render these references aimless.

[29] Ibid, 844–845.

[30] Ramona Toma, *La réalité judiciaire de la Cour européenne des droits de l'homme: Activisme et retenue judiciaires* (Baden-Baden: Nomos Verlagsgesellschaft, 2003), 31.

[31] Ibid.

[32] Ovey and White (n 5 above), 49.

[33] Toma (n 30 above), 33.

[34] Ibid.

2.1.3 Autonomous Interpretation

The Strasbourg bodies' autonomous interpretation or independent classification of words can inhibit the reception of international instruments under the ECHR. Some of the terms used in the Convention are considered to have a special, independent, or autonomous meaning.[35] As a result, the sense of certain words differs and does not necessarily correspond to the meaning of an identical term in domestic or international law.[36] For instance, the words 'civil rights and obligations' or 'criminal charge' under Article 6 of the ECHR have an autonomous meaning. The Court tries to diminish the risk that domestic authorities will depart from the specific meaning of the ECHR by attributing unilateral qualifications to its provisions.

There is thus a difference between traditional international treaty interpretation and the autonomous interpretation of the ECHR. In fact, attributing an independent meaning to words may lead to results which depart from the rule that a treaty should be interpreted according to ordinary meaning being given to its terms, as required by Article 31(1) of the VCLT.[37] Further, adopting a meaning which is approved by most Contracting States may deter references to international instruments. Most importantly, it can isolate the ECHR in its own regime by providing a vocabulary which is not used by any other international court. This contributes further to the fragmentation of international law and inhibits dialogue among international judges. Clearly, international judges speaking different legal languages may have difficulties understanding one another.

2.1.4 Judicial Restraint

Judicial restraint has affected the Strasbourg bodies' case law by limiting their margin of manoeuvre and impeding judges from referring to international law. This approach is premised on the idea that a judge's duty consists of applying the law and not in making it.[38] Naturally, this also means that when new cases and situations come before a court, new law will inevitably be made. However, judges using restraint try to limit themselves to applying the law as it exists, and leaving its development and modification to the legislature.[39] Advocates of this approach believe that law reform should be carried out as part of the political process and that judges are outsiders to this process. It is considered that judges should not behave as legislators. Moreover, cases are to be decided according to authoritative rules traditionally regarded as containing the relevant law.[40] For the Court, the relevant law is the ECHR and judges practising restraint rely exclusively on this instrument. In this context, referring to international sources is perceived as overstepping legitimate judicial duties.

[35] Van Dijk and Van Hoof (n 20 above), 77.
[36] Toma (n 30 above), 61.
[37] Van Dijk and Van Hoof (n 20 above), 77.
[38] Merrills (n 16 above), 230.
[39] Ibid.
[40] Ibid.

2.2 Interpretation Enhancing the Reception Process

2.2.1 Evolutive and Dynamic Interpretation

Undoubtedly, the meaning of the rights in the Convention has changed over time. In fact, the Convention was concluded for an indeterminate period of time and its meaning therefore needs to be updated according to current standards. Evolutive interpretation allows contemporary realities to be taken into account and a departure from the circumstances which prevailed at the time of the drafting of the Convention. It is based on the rule contained in Article 31(3)(b) of the VCLT, which stipulates that any subsequent practice in the application of the treaty shall be taken into account together with the context of the treaty. The Court affirmed this principle in the *Tyrer* case,[41] which concerned the question of whether corporal punishment of juvenile offenders amounts to degrading punishment under Article 3 of the ECHR. The Court found that standards considered to be acceptable previously may no longer be tolerable today: 'the Convention is a living instrument which ... must be interpreted in the light of present-day conditions. In the case now before it the Court cannot but be influenced by the developments and commonly accepted standards in the penal policy of the member States of the Council of Europe in this field.'[42] It therefore held that such a punishment infringed Article 3.

The principle of evolutive interpretation is also closely linked to consensual interpretation carried out on the basis of domestic or international law, which allows the Court to determine whether the European legal common ground has evolved.[43] For instance, in the *Marckx* case,[44] the Court admitted that, due to changes in international law and the domestic law of the majority of Council of Europe Member States, it was no longer permissible to draw a distinction between 'illegitimate' and 'legitimate' family members.[45]

Subsequently, evolutive interpretation allowed the Court to update several ECHR provisions by, *inter alia*, limiting the role of a government minister in determining the release of a prisoner,[46] recognizing the right not to be compelled to belong to a trade union,[47] and requiring the legal recognition of the new identity of transsexuals.[48] This method of interpretation has therefore enabled the Strasbourg bodies to distance themselves from older assessments, to stay abreast of changes in society, and to creatively expand the meaning of certain rights.

[41] *Tyrer v United Kingdom* (App No 5856/72), judgment, 25 April 1978, Series A, Vol 26.
[42] Ibid, para 31. [43] Van Dijk and Van Hoof (n 20 above), 78.
[44] *Marckx v Belgium* (App No 6833/74), judgment, 13 June 1979, Series A, Vol 31.
[45] Ibid, para 41.
[46] *Stafford v United Kingdom* (App No 46295/99), judgment, 28 May 2002, Reports 2002-IV, 115; see Mowbray (n 16 above), 69.
[47] *Sigurdur A Sigurjónsson v Iceland* (App No 16130/90), judgment, 30 June 1993, Series A, Vol 264.
[48] *Christine Goodwin v United Kingdom* (App No 28957/95), judgment, 11 July 2002, Reports 2002-VI, 1.

The Court did not provide justifications for the application of evolutive interpretation or further details as to its origins, advantages, and disadvantages. It has been suggested that this provides 'ammunition to critics who contend that the Court is prone to policy-making'.[49] Moreover, it procures further ground for arguing that the Court is engaging in judicial activism due to the lack of justification or elaboration of evolutive interpretation. In addition, it is very difficult to determine whether the Court modifies or interprets the ECHR when it resorts to this method of interpretation. Undoubtedly, evolutive interpretation enhances reception by providing the Court with a convenient tool to include international legal instruments in its reasoning.

2.2.2 Effectiveness Principle

Another important factor which has had a bearing on the Strasbourg bodies' reception of international law is the effectiveness principle. This allows the ECHR to be interpreted in a manner which seeks to ensure that its rights and freedoms are 'practical and effective' to complainants.[50] By looking beyond appearances and formalities, the Court and the Commission focus on the concrete position of the individual in order to ensure that ECHR rights are not theoretical and illusory. This may sometimes lead them to adopt an extensive interpretation of the rights contained in the relevant ECHR provisions. In this manner, the Strasbourg bodies also try to strengthen the ECHR and to provide an optimal effectiveness of the rights contained therein.

A representative example of the use of this principle can be found in the *Airey* case,[51] where the Court examined the question of whether the applicant had the right of access to court in order to seek a decree of judicial separation from her husband. The applicant alleged that she was unable to pay for a lawyer and no legal aid was available to assist her. She complained that there was a breach of Article 6(1) of the ECHR by reason of a denial of access to a court. The respondent government submitted that the applicant could have appeared in person without being represented by a lawyer. The Court found that it was unrealistic for the applicant to conduct her case effectively on her own and that there was a violation of Article 6(1). While the Court considered that free legal aid does not need to be provided for each dispute, Article 6(1) may sometimes compel the state to provide for the assistance of a lawyer when such assistance proves indispensable for effective access to court.[52]

The Court has also used this interpretation technique for holding that an ECHR right contained positive obligations for Contracting States, although this did not explicitly follow from the text.[53] In certain cases, it was not sufficient for Contracting States to adopt a passive approach to the fulfilment of their obligations under the

[49] Mowbray (n 16 above), 69; Franz Matscher, 'Methods of Interpretation of the Convention' in Ronald St J Macdonald, Franz Matscher, and Herbert Petzold (eds), *The European System for the Protection of Human Rights* (Dordrecht/Boston/London: Martinus Nijhoff, 1993), 63, 69–70.

[50] Mowbray (n 16 above), 72.

[51] *Airey v Ireland* (App No 6289/73), judgment, 9 October 1979, Series A, Vol 32.

[52] Ibid, para 26. [53] Van Dijk and Van Hoof (n 20 above), 74.

ECHR. Using the effectiveness principle, the Court has imposed positive obligations on to Contracting States, which include the duty to ensure that domestic law provides adequate recognition of family relationships,[54] the duty to protect the lawful exercise of freedom of assembly[55] and expression,[56] and the duty to conduct investigations into unlawful killings.[57] This interpretation technique has thus allowed the Strasbourg bodies to ensure that the ECHR can be meaningfully enforced.

2.2.3 Systemic Integration

The most influential principle in terms of reception of international law has been the rule contained in Article 31(3)(c) of the VCLT, which stipulates that in addition to the context 'any relevant rules of international law applicable in the relations between the parties' should be taken into account. This principle compels the Court to take into account other international instruments on the basis that the ECHR is part of the international legal system. As already mentioned, the Court reaffirmed in *Banković*[58] that the ECHR had to be interpreted according to the rules contained in the VCLT and that international instruments needed to be taken into account in this context. There are few explicit references to Article 31(3)(c) of the VCLT in the Court's case law. It can thus be argued that, once the Court incorporated this provision into its case law, it no longer felt the need to refer to it explicitly in subsequent decisions. Thus, the references to this principle of interpretation later became implicit. This rule is, nonetheless, far from being unequivocal and the Court has not fully engaged with its most problematic aspects. While it may have provided an important starting base to the Strasbourg bodies, it appears that Article 31(3)(c) has not been fully considered and integrated. This could be due to the fact that there are still numerous uncertainties associated with this rule. The Court's case law is thus marked by a partial reception of Article 31(3)(c). As a result, it is difficult to make any definite assessments with regard to the Court's reliance on the systemic integration rule contained in this provision.

2.2.4 Judicial Activism

The notion of judicial activism is an elusive concept and has been interpreted differently in various parts of the world. According to one interpretation, the approach of judicial activism consists in using and developing law to achieve

[54] *Marckx v Belgium* (App No 6833/74), judgment, 13 June 1979, Series A, Vol 31; Mowbray (n 16 above), 78.

[55] *Plattform 'Ärzte für das Leben' v Austria* (App No 10126/82), judgment, 21 June 1988, Series A, Vol 139.

[56] *Özgür Gündem v Turkey* (App No 23144/93), judgment, 16 March 2000, Reports 2000-III, 1.

[57] *McCann and others v United Kingdom* (App No 18984/91), judgment, 27 September 1995, Series A, Vol 324.

[58] *Banković and others v Belgium and 16 Other Contracting States* (App No 52207/99), judgment, 12 December 2001, Reports 2001-XII, 333, para 43.

certain results or objectives.[59] Those advocating judicial activism interpret the constraints imposed on the judicial role rather liberally and consider that it is part of a judge's duty to achieve the desired result. In this context, law becomes a means to achieve a certain end.[60] In addition, judges practising activism use interpretation as a method of expanding, updating, and modifying the scope of the relevant law. Advocates of this approach are, therefore, not afraid of judicial innovation and see new doctrines or ideas as an opportunity to develop the law.[61] This also prompts them to look beyond the instrument which has been traditionally considered to contain the relevant law. Judicial activism does not exclude the fact that courts have some legislative role to play. Thus, the act of judging is much more than simply the application of rules; it also involves developing and changing those rules.

The approach of judicial activism transcends numerous areas of the Strasbourg bodies' activity. As Strasbourg jurisprudence evolved, the Court developed an extensive range of interpretative methods to meaningfully enforce ECHR rights.[62] By resorting to evolutive and dynamic interpretation, the Court has continued to update and expand the meaning of the ECHR. It has determined common human rights standards for all Contracting States, requiring them to take active measures to remedy possible violations. Conscious that individuals needed to be given concrete means to exercise their rights, the Court enjoined the Contracting States to ensure that these were practical and effective. It was not sufficient to take a passive approach and to refrain from interfering with ECHR rights. The Court also required Contracting States to take positive steps in ensuring that these were enforced and respected.[63] Over time, the Court has put flesh on to the ECHR provisions, filling in gaps whenever this was necessary. Thus, it has transformed the ECHR into a 'constitutional instrument of European public order' and had become—in spite of its subsidiary nature—the supranational arbiter of European human rights. The Court has substantially and actively intervened in domestic legal orders by imposing human rights standards which have to be respected by all Contracting States. Such activism appears to have been necessary in order to attribute meaning to ECHR rights and to ensure that they are respected by Contracting States.

3. A Systemic Approach to the European Public Order

This volume was predicated on the basis that the European public order is not isolated from the realities dominating the international legal scene. It is in fact a component of a greater system—the international legal order—and, as such, is also affected by the phenomena which occur as part of this greater framework.

59 Merrills (n 16 above), 231. 60 Ibid. 61 Ibid, 232.
62 Toma (n 30 above), 29. 63 Ibid.

In recent times, the body of international law has expanded and reached areas never regulated before at this level. This trend was accompanied by the enactment of numerous treaties regulating very specific areas of activity and the creation of numerous judicial or quasi-judicial bodies which became competent in their own specialized domains. As a result, international law has become increasingly compartmentalized, fragmented, and divided. The increasingly disparate nature of expanding international law gave rise to questions relating to its unity and coherence. This added another level of complexity to the ECHR's context, which requires this volume to consider its international environment. As will be seen, these international tendencies have an important bearing on the international law references made by the Strasbourg bodies. Thus, this volume evaluates the reception of international law from a systemic perspective and attempts to analyse the phenomena in the ECtHR's jurisdiction through the lens of dilemmas affecting the international legal order in general.

3.1 An Operational System

While this statement may seem obvious and elementary, it must be emphasized and reiterated that international law constitutes a legal system.[64] This finding has been usefully restated by the International Law Commission (ILC), which has further underlined that the international legal system's 'rules and principles (i.e. its norms) act in relation to and should be interpreted against the background of other rules and principles'.[65] Further, 'international law is not a random collection of such norms. There are meaningful relationships between them. Norms may thus exist at higher or lower hierarchical levels, their formation may involve greater or lesser generality and speciality and their validity may date back to earlier or later moments in time.'[66] Indeed, international treaties do interact with one another and in a case of tensions between two treaties there is a presumption against conflict. Whenever possible, in order to resolve conflict through interpretation, it is necessary to read a treaty in a harmonious way with other treaties.

In fact, Article 31(3)(c) stipulates that when interpreting a treaty, account must be taken of 'any relevant rules of international law applicable in the relations between the parties'. This provision reflects further the systemic nature and the

[64] Bruno Simma and Dirk Pulkowski, 'Of Planets and the Universe: Self-Contained Regimes in International Law' (2006) 17 Eur J Int'l L 483, 499–500; Pierre-Marie Dupuy, 'The Danger of Fragmentation or Unification of the International Legal System and the International Court of Justice' (1999) 31 NYUJ Int'l L & Pol 791, 793–795. For further information, see Jean Combacau, '*Le droit international: bric-à-brac ou système?*' (1986) 31 *Archives de philosophie du droit* 85; Christian Dominicé, 'Methodology of International Law' in Rudolf Bernhardt (ed) (1997) 3 EPIL 354; James Crawford, *International Law as an Open System* (London: Cameron May, 2002); Karl Zemanek, 'The Legal Foundations of the International System' (1997) 266 *Recueil des Cours* 62.

[65] United Nations, *Conclusion of the work of the Study Group on the Fragmentation of International Law: Difficulties Arising from the Diversification and Expansion of International Law* (International Law Commission, 2006), para 1.

[66] Ibid.

relations thereby created between the different treaties. As previously mentioned, the Court has also recognized the systemic nature of international law and the fact that the ECHR is part of this system. In the *Banković* case,[67] it found that the ECHR could not be construed in a vacuum and that it needed to be interpreted in accordance with the VCLT, including Article 31(3)(c).[68] Thus, the Court confirmed that the ECHR is part of a greater system and that it needs to be interpreted against this background.

3.2 A Special Regime

As international law is a legal system, it is composed of smaller regimes or sub-systems. These sub-systems have often been referred to as special or self-contained regimes. It appears that there is no single definition of this concept. In its final report on fragmentation, the ILC Study Group listed three different definitions of 'self-contained regimes' that were used in the context of state responsibility. A 'self-contained regime' could be (1) 'a special set of secondary rules that determine the consequences of a breach of certain primary rules',[69] (2) 'any interrelated cluster (set, regime, subsystem) of rules on a limited problem together with the rules for the creation, interpretation, application, modification, or termination...of those rules',[70] or (3) the different branches of international law (human rights law, trade law, environmental law, etc).[71]

The ILC Study Group found, however, that the use of the term 'self-contained regime' is misleading as it implies that each sub-system is insular and isolated from the other sub-systems. Although there is a difference in the degree to which each sub-system is supplemented by international law, there is no support for the view that general international law would be completely excluded.[72] In fact, it would be conceptually impossible to isolate such sub-systems from international law. It was therefore suggested that the term 'self-contained regime' be replaced with 'special regime'.[73]

It is important to note that each special regime has its specific interests and objectives and that it applies its own rules on a *lex specialis* basis. As a result, there is a tendency on the part of special regimes to advance their own goals in order to better fulfil their respective missions. Problems arise when special regimes apply general international law, such as the VCLT, in order to reinforce their jurisdiction and the special nature of the relevant treaty. In attempting to buttress their own interest and objectives, these special regimes may deviate from the standard interpretation and

[67] *Banković and others v Belgium and 16 Other Contracting States* (App No 52207/99), judgment, 12 December 2001, Reports 2001-XII, 333.
[68] Ibid, para 43.
[69] Report of the Study Group of the International Law Commission, *Fragmentation of International Law: Difficulties Arising from the Diversification and Expansion of International Law*, finalized by Martti Koskenniemi, International Law Commission, 58th session, 1 May to 9 June and 3 July to 11 August 2006, UN Doc No A/CN.4/L.682, 13 April 2006, 81, para 152, (1).
[70] Ibid.
[71] Ibid.
[72] Ibid, 82, para 152, (5).
[73] Ibid.

thereby weaken its authority.[74] Thus, the application of general international law should ideally remain uniform throughout the different special regimes.

Against this background, it appears that the ECHR constitutes a special regime. This standpoint is further supported by the Strasbourg case law and the Court's perception of its own system. The Court has underlined that the ECHR should be interpreted differently from general international treaties.[75] The ECHR was also found to have a special nature given that it is a human rights treaty. The Court observed that, '[u]nlike international treaties of the classical kind, the Convention comprises more than mere reciprocal engagements between Contracting States. It creates over and above a network of mutual bilateral undertakings, objective obligations which in the words of the preamble benefit from a "collective enforcement".'[76] In expressing these findings, the Court has attempted to establish its own special regime.

The ECHR system appears to be a special regime of the second type, as defined in the final report of the ILC Study Group. It is geographically limited and is less extensive than the branch of international law of which it is part, namely human rights law. Furthermore, it contains rules relating to the creation, interpretation, application, and modification of standards contained therein. It could, however, also be argued that it is a special regime of the third type. For the benefit of unity of international law, it would be advantageous to adopt a wider definition and to include the ECHR as part of the human rights law special regime. Nevertheless, it appears that until now the Court has behaved as the second type of special regime. This definition thus appears to reflect most accurately its self-perception. Finally, the ECHR special regime has a strong institutional structure, and it has evolved, since its inception, into a quasi-constitutional or auto-constitutional system.[77]

The ECHR is not isolated from general international law or from other special regimes. As the Strasbourg case law evolved, international law started to penetrate into the Commission's and the Court's reasoning. Interestingly, the Strasbourg bodies did not require any conflict of laws provision or any explicit article allowing for the incorporation of international law. Several ECHR provisions do mention international law, namely Articles 7(1),[78] 7(2),[79] 15(1),[80] and

[74] Martti Koskenniemi and Päivi Leino, 'Fragmentation of International Law? Postmodern Anxieties' (2002) 15 LJIL 553, 561–562.

[75] *Loizidou v Turkey (Preliminary Objections)* (App No 15318/89), judgment, 23 March 1995, Series A, Vol 310, paras 83–85. In this volume, see ch II, 2.4.

[76] Ibid, para 70.

[77] See also Simma and Pulkowski (n 64 above), 504; Andreas Fischer-Lescano and Günter Teubner, 'Regime-Collissions: The Vain Search for Legal Unity in the Fragmentation of Global Law' (2004) 25 Mich J Int'l L 999, 1014–1015.

[78] 'No one shall be held guilty of any criminal offence on account of any act or omission which did not constitute a criminal offence under national or *international law* at the time when it was committed. Nor shall a heavier penalty be imposed than the one that was applicable at the time the criminal offence was committed' (italics added).

[79] 'This article shall not prejudice the trial and punishment of any person for any act or omission which, at the time when it was committed, was criminal according to the *general principles of law recognised by civilised nations*' (italics added).

[80] 'In time of war or other public emergency threatening the life of the nation any High Contracting Party may take measures derogating from its obligations under this Convention to

35(1)[81], and Article 1 of Protocol No 1.[82] However, international law references were not limited to these areas of the ECHR. Without further formalities, both the Commission and the Court supported their reasoning with international instruments in a wide variety of situations. The fact that the incorporation of international law did not have a formal basis gave the Court an important discretion in deciding when it would refer to non-ECHR sources. As a result, many references to international law appear to have been made on an ad hoc basis.

3.3 Fragmentation

The changing nature of international law has alerted practitioners and academics worldwide, leading them to question the consequences that could ensue from the increasingly fragmented international legal order. The United Nations General Assembly requested the ILC to give further consideration to these issues as part of a long-term programme. The Commission created a Study Group and requested it to prepare a study on the function and scope of the *lex specialis* and the question of 'self-contained regimes'. Subsequently, numerous additional studies were produced, and in 2006 the Group presented a consolidated report on the research conducted during the course of four years.[83]

The phenomenon of fragmentation at international level has been marked by the emergence of specialized and (relatively) autonomous rules, rule-complexes, legal institutions, and spheres of legal practice.[84] The areas once governed by 'general international law' have been divided into branches or areas, such as 'trade law', 'human rights law', 'environmental law', 'law of the sea', and 'European law'. Each one of these spheres possesses its own rules and institutions. The problem with such divisions appears to be that specialized legal domains and institutions exist in relative ignorance of the legislative and institutional activities taking place in the other legal branches and in general international law and practice.[85] As a result, conflicts between the different branches arise, leading possibly to a loss of an overall perspective on the law.[86]

The Study Group distinguished between three different types of fragmentation, namely fragmentation that occurs (1) through conflicting interpretations

the extent strictly required by the exigencies of the situation, provided that such measures are not inconsistent with its other obligations under *international law*' (italics added).

81 'The Court may only deal with the matter after all domestic remedies have been exhausted, according to the *generally recognised rules of international law*, and within a period of six months from the date on which the final decision was taken' (italics added).

82 'Every natural or legal person is entitled to the peaceful enjoyment of his possessions. No one shall be deprived of his possessions except in the public interest and subject to the conditions provided for by law and by the *general principles of international law*' (italics added).

83 Report of the Study Group of the International Law Commission (n 69 above).

84 Ibid, 11, para 8. 85 Ibid. 86 Ibid.

of general law, (2) through the emergence of special law as exception to the general law, and (3) through conflict between different types of special law.[87] As will become apparent in the following chapters, all three types of fragmentation are present in the Strasbourg bodies' case law. In addition, numerous overlapping legal regimes became available when a case arose, leading to an increasing trend of forum shopping. An important by-product of this trend was the problem of litispendence and *res judicata*. It became increasingly possible that two international judicial bodies would investigate the same legal question.

In its report, the ILC Study Group did not aim to set up definite priorities between the different international rules or rule-systems.[88] It was considered that such hierarchies could not be attained by a mere elucidation of the process of legal reasoning.[89] They would usually require international actors to agree upon certain political preferences. The Study Group, nonetheless, considered that the absence of hierarchies in international law did not entail that normative conflicts would lead to legal paralysis.[90] These hierarchies could be established on an ad hoc basis and in the context of specific problems. Thus, the Study Group tried to illustrate by examples, drawn from the practice of international courts and tribunals, techniques available for lawyers as they approach problems that appear to involve conflicts between rules or rule-systems.[91] An important emphasis was laid on the function that judicial interpretation and an increased use of the VCLT can play in this context.

The phenomenon of fragmentation undoubtedly exists and has exerted an important influence on the body of international law. Nonetheless, academics and practitioners have evaluated this tendency in different manners. Some authors have considered that fragmentation is not tremendously detrimental to the international legal system and that it has emerged as a result of its development and maturity.[92] It allows the development of better rules and, in case of need, it can be remedied through better judicial coordination.[93] Other commentators have seen fragmentation in a more negative light, suggesting that it leads to the erosion of general international law, the emergence of conflicting jurisprudence, the loss

[87] International Law Commission, *Report of its fifty-sixth Session*, 3 May to 4 June and 5 July to 6 August 2004, Supp No 10, UN Doc No A/59/10, 283–303.

[88] Report of the Study Group of the International Law Commission (n 69 above), 245, para 484.

[89] Ibid.

[90] Ibid, 245, para 485.

[91] Ibid.

[92] See, for instance, Pemmaraju Rao Sreenivasa, 'Multiple Judicial Forums: A Reflection of the Growing Strength of International Law or Its Fragmentations' (2004) 25 Mich J Int'l L 929; Charney (n 13 above); Jonathan I Charney, 'The Impact on the International Legal System of the Growth of International Courts and Tribunals' (1999) 31 NYUJ Int'l & Pol 697; Georges Abi-Saab, 'Fragmentation or Unification: Some Concluding Remarks' (1999) 31 NYU J Int'l L & Pol 919.

[93] United Nations General Assembly (n 83 above), 12, para 9.

of legal certainty, and forum shopping.[94] As a result, they have argued that it is necessary to improve the unity of international law.

Following the latter direction, this volume postulates that fragmentation in the field of human rights law reduces the standard of protection and effectiveness of human rights in most cases. It is submitted that the number of human rights bodies should not be reduced and international law instruments should not be merged or repealed. Rather, effective communications channels and methods of interpretation should be put into place in order to ensure that the different standards are harmonized, that judges respect each others' rulings, that they do not take on a case already before another court, and that they are aware of the standards employed by other judges. Furthermore, continuing education courses on international law should be dispensed to ECtHR judges who have not had direct contact with international law.

3.4 International Constitutionalism

Another important discourse has been developed in international law as a knee-jerk reaction to the phenomenon of fragmentation. An important number of critics of fragmentation, especially European ones, have proposed solutions of a constitutional nature, thereby creating a very fashionable doctrine called 'international constitutionalism'.[95] They reaffirmed the existence of a system or unity of international law in order to organize the numerous institutions and courts into a hierarchy. Some of the hierarchies envisaged by academics are based on the Charter of the United Nations or the UN Security Council, others on *jus cogens* norms or on the concept of global legal community. Constitutionalism is, however, a notion which is difficult to rationalize at the international level. There is no clear legislative or executive body as in domestic legal systems. Further, from

[94] Ibid. See, in general, Dupuy (n 64 above). A number of former Presidents of the International Court of Justice have also pleaded in favour of improving the unity of international law by enabling the ICJ to issue advisory opinions at the request of other international courts or tribunals. See 'Failure by Member States of the United Nations to pay their dues transgresses principles of international law, President Schwebel tells United Nations General Assembly', 26 October 1999, Press Release No 1999/46, <http://www.icj-cij.org/presscom/index.php?pr=133&pt=1&p1=6&p2=1> (last visited 11 January 2010); Judge Gilbert Guillaume, President of the International Court of Justice to the United Nations General Assembly, 26 October 2000, Press Release No 2000/36, <http://www.icj-cij.org/presscom/files/9/3069.pdf> (last visited 11 January 2010). For the advantages and disadvantages of fragmentation, see Gerhard Hafner, 'Pros and Cons Ensuing from Fragmentation of International Law' (2004) 25 Mich J Int'l L 849.

[95] For further information, see, for instance, Christian Tomuschat, 'International Law: Ensuring the Survival of Mankind on the Eve of a New Century, General Discourse on Public International Law' (2001) 281 *Recueil des Cours* 63; Armin Von Bogdandy, 'Constitutionalism in International Law: Comment on Proposal from Germany' (2001) 47 Harv Int'l LJ 223; Jan Klabbers, 'Constitutionalism Lite' (2004) 1 Int'l Org L Rev 31; Ronald St John Macdonald and Douglas M Johnston, *Towards World Constitutionalism: Issues in the Legal Ordering of the World Community* (Leiden: Martinus Nijhoff, 2005); Erika De Wet, 'The Emergence of International and Regional Value Systems as a Manifestation of the Emerging Constitutional Order' (2006) 19 LJIL 611.

the domestic perspective, constitutionalism refers in some sense to law as a shared project for a reasonably clearly defined (often historically informed) objective.[96] At the international level, there is no similar aim sought either in diplomacy or in positive law. Thus, constitutionalism is difficult to envisage at the international level due to the inherent differences between international and domestic law.

This volume adopts a sceptical view of international constitutionalism as a possible remedy to fragmentation and will not examine this doctrine in greater detail. Moreover, this notion is of limited significance in evaluating fragmentation of international law at the European level. Thus, only certain aspects of European constitutionalism based on the ECHR will be considered here. It has already been recognized that the ECHR is a constitutional instrument of European public order, and therefore a certain form of regional constitutionalism is certainly conceivable at the European level. Unfortunately, the case law of national constitutional courts and European Union law will not be evaluated here due to time and space limitations.

This volume postulates that the truth lies in between an international hierarchical set-up and a purely fragmented international legal order. It is believed that there is an operational international legal system which provides a diversified legal tool-box to judges, lawyers, academics, and others.[97] Due to the difficulties in reaching an agreement at the international level among non-homogeneous states and due to the lack of an international legislative body, it is often left to international judges to close the gap and to harmonize different international legal norms. In this context, as accurately re-stated by the ILC Study Group, the VCLT can play an important role by linking special regimes.[98] Thus, international judges need to adopt a systemic approach when evaluating cases in order to include the relevant international instruments in their reasoning and to preserve the coherence of the international legal order. At the same time, they should bear in mind the magnitude of the role attributed to them as part of the international legal order.

[96] Koskenniemi Martti, 'The Fate of Public International Law: Constitutional Utopia or Fragmentation', Chorley Lecture 2006, London School of Economics, 7 June 2006, available at <http://www.helsinki.fi/eci/Publications/MKChorley%20Text-06a.pdf> (last visited 13 June 2010), 24–25.

[97] Report of the Study Group of the International Law Commission (n 69 above), 115, para 222, 248–249, para 492, 250.

[98] Ibid, 15, para 17, 250.

I

The Law of Treaties

1. Preliminary Observations

The ECHR cannot be conceived independently from public international law and international human rights law, as it is an integral part of both systems. Being an international treaty, the ECHR clearly falls under the rules that govern the interpretation, scope, and validity of such instruments. In this context, the Vienna Convention on the Law of Treaties (VCLT) has played a considerable role in shaping the interpretation techniques used by the Strasbourg bodies. Further, it has set the general framework for the Commission's and the Court's references to international norms. As a springboard to external legal systems, the VCLT often facilitated the reliance on international law and provided greater legitimacy to the Strasbourg bodies in this task. The VCLT thus became an integral part of the international law reception process in Strasbourg case law.

The *Golder v United Kingdom* case,[1] a landmark judgment handed down by the ECtHR in 1975, set the tone of the interpretation framework that the Court would develop in subsequent years. The case contains the first, and the most exhaustive, discussion of the rules of interpretation contained in the VCLT.[2] At that time, none of the interpretation principles currently used by the ECtHR existed; the 'living instrument' principle was established in the *Tyrer* case[3] in 1978, the theory of autonomous concepts was inaugurated in the *Engel* case[4] in 1976, and the principle of effectiveness was thoroughly applied in the *Airey* case[5] in 1978.

It therefore appears that the Court used the VCLT as the backbone on which it implanted its interpretation framework. In a quasi-mythical statement, the Court announced that it 'is prepared to consider, as do the Government and

[1] *Golder v United Kingdom* (App No 4451/70), judgment, 21 February 1975, Series A, Vol 18.

[2] George Letsas, *A Theory of Interpretation of the European Convention on Human Rights* (Oxford: OUP, 2007), 61.

[3] *Tyrer v United Kingdom* (App No 5856/72), judgment, 25 April 1978, Series A, Vol 26; Letsas (n 2 above), 61.

[4] *Engel and others v Netherlands* (App Nos 5100/71; 5101/71; 5102/71; 5354/72; 5370/72), judgment, 8 June 1976, Series A, Vol 22; Letsas (n 2 above), 61.

[5] *Airey v Ireland* (App No 6289/73), judgment, 9 October 1979, Series A, Vol 32; Letsas (n 2 above), 61.

the Commission, that it should be guided by Articles 31 to 33 of the Vienna Convention of 23 May 1969 on the Law of Treaties. That Convention has not yet entered into force and it specifies, at Article 4, that it will not be retroactive, but its Articles 31 to 33 enunciate in essence generally accepted principles of international law to which the Court has already referred to on occasion.'[6] Furthermore, '[i]n the way in which it is presented in the "general rule" in Article 31 of the Vienna Convention, the process of interpretation of a treaty is a unity, a single combined operation; this rule, closely integrated, places on the same footing the various elements enumerated in the four paragraphs of the Article'.[7] Thus, the Court set the background for the upcoming cases establishing specific interpretation rules. It also initiated a more profound dialogue between the European and international human rights spheres, thereby arguably reducing the fragmentation divide.

Nonetheless, the Court's reliance on Articles 31 and 32 of the VCLT gives rise to difficult questions. The interpretation rules of the Vienna Convention do not provide standardized solutions to uncertain treaty interpretations and for decades scholars have grappled with the issues that they raise. The courts that resort to them are therefore faced with many options when interpreting a treaty. As was rightly observed, '[d]epending on many factors of which the court's perception of its own role is perhaps the most important one, a court may be inclined towards an interpretation which is focused on the "ordinary meaning" of the treaty terms or conversely, towards "an object and purpose"-oriented interpretation'.[8] The VCLT does not take any stand as to whether textual interpretation or teleological interpretation should be adopted.[9]

The pivotal centre around which the interpretation of the ECHR revolves therefore resides in the Strasbourg Court's self-perception in a given case. Indeed, the role that the Court has played in the different cases has had a variable geometry, one that was highly conditioned by the margin of appreciation granted to Contracting States and by the predisposition of the judges that composed the Court. Thus, it becomes difficult to deduce a single approach of the Court towards the VCLT; also, to require one on the part of the Court would perhaps be unrealistic. Arguably, the Court could have resorted more often to these interpretation rules. The Court has, nonetheless, always stressed that the ECHR has a number of special features and has thus resorted to its own principles. The Vienna Convention was, for the ECtHR, a starting point in interpretation, which over time seems to have become a complementary tool in this process.

[6] *Golder v United Kingdom* (n 1 above) para 29. [7] Ibid, para 30.

[8] Pieter Van Dijk and Godefrious JH Van Hoof, *Theory and Practice of the European Convention on Human Rights* (The Hague/London/Boston: Kluwer Law International, 3rd edn, 1998), 72.

[9] Report of the Study Group of the International Law Commission, *Fragmentation of International Law: Difficulties Arising from the Diversification and Expansion of International Law*, finalized by Martti Koskenniemi, International Law Commission, 58th session, 1 May to 9 June and 3 July to 11 August 2006, A/CN.4/L.682, 13 April 2006, para 427.

The interpretation rules of the VCLT were conceived over 50 years ago; while much academic ink has flown since then, the number of judges who took the rules into account was fewer than expected. In the last decades, the international legal architecture has witnessed a tremendous expansion and proliferation of legal norms, which have slowly led to complications as well as to the problem of fragmentation of international law. The nature of legal agreements between states has changed over time; we have moved from bilateral contractual agreements between states to multilateral human rights treaties which bestow rights and obligations upon the states' citizens. Thus, the role of the VCLT has been forever altered; it has had to be reinvented and 'operationalized'. The Vienna Convention was given a second chance to flourish in the context of fragmentation as one of the solutions to this problem. It is yet to be seen how international and domestic courts will resort to these rules in order to resolve interpretative dilemmas caused by fragmentation. The rules contained in Articles 31 and 32 of the VCLT constitute international customary law,[10] and thus the ratification record[11] of this Convention was less relevant for the Court in this particular context.

The following evaluation of the Strasbourg jurisprudence aims to demonstrate that the Court and the Commission became less responsive to the VCLT rules over the years. Initially, the Court resorted to the VCLT in order to mould its own autonomous means of interpretation. In subsequent years, the VCLT was used as a rubber stamp to legitimate references to various international law instruments. With time, the VCLT interpretation rules have survived in the Strasbourg case law and are currently applied, albeit infrequently, along with the autonomous concepts that the Court has created. The Strasbourg bodies' approach to these interpretation rules has not been entirely coherent, but it appears to have crystallized itself in certain areas. Such an analysis is compelling in the context of this study, as it demonstrates how the Strasbourg bodies have resorted to international law in a situation where there were no specific Convention rules available.

The rule contained in Article 31(3)(c) of the VCLT deserves particular attention in this context; it has been thoroughly analysed by the ILC Study Group as one of the possible solutions to alleviate the problems created by the fragmentation of international law. Indeed, if this rule were to be used systematically by international and domestic courts, the relationship between the various international treaties would certainly become clearer. International law could also be applied in a more coherent and harmonious manner. The Strasbourg bodies' reliance on Article 31(3)(c) may shed further light on the manner in which this rule ought to be used by other courts. Arguably, Article 31(3)(c) became an implicit basis of the Strasbourg bodies' reasoning in all cases referring to international law. Thus,

[10] Ibid.

[11] The VCLT was ratified by 38 of the 47 ECHR Contracting States. This information was verified on 13 June 2010: United Nations Treaty Collection, Status, <http://treaties.un.org/Pages/ViewDetailsIII.aspx?&src=IND&mtdsg_no=XXIII-1&chapter=23&Temp=mtdsg3&lang=en>.

this chapter attempts to evaluate whether the Court and the Commission have made any contributions to the 'operationalization' of this rule in the context of fragmentation of international law.

2. The Case Law of the Court Concerning the VCLT

2.1 The Ordinary Meaning of Words

The requirement of interpreting a treaty provision according to the ordinary meaning of its words lies at the heart of textual interpretation. This methodology has often been used by the Court as part of the consensual interpretation of the ECHR and as part of its deference to the states' margin of appreciation. While the term 'ordinary' is not defined in Article 31(1) of the VCLT, it is generally understood that it refers to the current, normal, and everyday usage of language.[12] According to the VCLT, this meaning needs to be considered in light of the context and purpose of the treaty. A term may nonetheless have a number of meanings which can change over time.[13] Unfortunately, the VCLT does not provide further guidance in this regard. Moreover, the requirement of ordinary meaning has a particular significance in the context of the ECHR. The ECtHR has frequently used words which do not have the same meaning as the one attributed to them in the Contracting States' domestic legal systems. The Court has used its own rules to determine the meaning of these terms, which then became more widely known as autonomous concepts.

The Court's case law referring to Article 31(1) of the VCLT relates mainly to three areas, namely the interference with property rights and the meaning of 'general principles of international law' under Article 1 of Protocol No 1, the scope of the rights to marry contained in Article 12 of the ECHR, and the meaning of the term 'alcoholics' under Article 5(1)(e) of the ECHR. Most of these cases were marked by an important margin of appreciation on the part of the Contracting States. The ECtHR's interpretative approach has slowly evolved over the decades as the Court became more familiar with the interpretation rules and adhered more literally to the VCLT requirements.

In the mid-1980s, the Court started using explicitly the 'ordinary meaning' rule contained in Article 31(1) of the VCLT in *James and others v United*

[12] Mark E Villiger, 'Articles 31 and 32 of the Vienna Convention on the Law of Treaties in the Case-Law of the European Court of Human Rights' in Jürgen Bröhmer (ed), *Internationale Gemeinschaft und Menschenrechte: Festschrift für Georg Reiss zum 70. Geburtstag am 21. Januar 2005* (Cologne: Carl Heymann, 2005), 317, 324. See also, in general, Mustafa Kamil Yaseen, '*L'interprétation des traités d'après la Convention de Vienne sur le Droit des Traîtés*' (1976) 151 *Recueil des Cours* 1. See, however, Ulk Linderfalk, 'On the Interpretation of Treaties: The Modern International Law as Expressed in the 1969 Vienna Convention on the Law of Treaties', Law and Philosophy Library 83, Springer, 2007, 61 *et seq.*

[13] Villiger (n 12 above).

Kingdom,[14] *Lithgow and others v United Kingdom*,[15] and *Johnston and others v United Kingdom*.[16] In the *James* case, the Court considered a claim concerning the long leasehold system of tenure in England and Wales, which permitted occupying tenants of dwelling houses to acquire the property on certain conditions specified in the Leasehold Reform Act 1967 (as amended). The applicants argued that the compulsory transfer of their property gave rise, *inter alia*, to a breach of Article 1 of Protocol No 1. The applicants also alleged that there was a violation under Articles 13 and 14.

The Commission had found unanimously that there was no violation on the basis of any of the grounds invoked. The Court followed this opinion and considered that there was no breach of the above-mentioned articles. The Court resorted to the VCLT when interpreting the expression 'general principles of international law' included in the second sentence of Article 1 of Protocol No 1. The applicants argued that the reference to the 'general principles of international law' meant that the international law requirement of adequate and effective compensation for expropriation of property of foreigners also applied to nationals. The Court agreed, however, with the Commission which had consistently held that the principles in question were not applicable to a state taking the property belonging to its own nationals. While the Court found that there was some force in the applicants' argument from a grammatical point of view, it nonetheless considered that the reasons for a different construction were more convincing. According to the Court, it was more natural to interpret the expression 'general principles of international law' as meaning that these principles are incorporated into Article 1 of Protocol No 1, but only as regards acts to which they normally apply, namely acts of state concerning non-nationals. Furthermore, 'the words of a treaty should be understood to have their ordinary meaning (see Article 31 of the 1969 Vienna Convention on the Law of Treaties), and to interpret the phrase in question as extending to the general principles of international law beyond their normal sphere of applicability is less consistent with the ordinary meaning of terms used, notwithstanding their context'.[17] The textual interpretation of the term 'general principles of international law' constituted naturally the first stage in the Court's construction. The Court then proceeded to examine the expression from a teleological point of view. In subsequent judgments, it became clear that this was the hierarchy of interpretation that the Strasbourg bodies wished to follow and that they would apply the principles of interpretation contained in the VCLT.

In *Lithgow*, the Court considered a case of nationalization of seven undertakings under the UK Aircraft and Shipbuilding Industries Act 1977. The

[14] *James and others v United Kingdom* (App No 8793/79), judgment, 21 February 1986, Series A, Vol 98-B.

[15] *Lithgow and others v United Kingdom* (App Nos 9006/80; 9262/81; 9263/81; 9265/81; 9266/81; 9313/81; 9405/81), judgment, 8 July 1986, Series A, Vol 102.

[16] *Johnston and others v Ireland* (App No 9697/82), judgment, 18 December 1986, Series A, Vol 112.

[17] *James and others v United Kingdom* (n 14 above), para 61.

applicants had been compensated but they complained that the amount that they had received was inadequate and discriminatory. Similarly to the *James* case they argued, *inter alia*, that the expression 'general principles of international law' in Article 1 of Protocol No 1 entailed that the compensation for deprivation of property for foreigners under international law also applied to nationals. They contended that there was a breach of Articles 6, 13, 14, 17 (prohibition of abuse of rights), and 18 (limitation on use of restrictions on rights) of the ECHR.

The Commission opined that there was no violation of any of the provisions invoked, and the Court followed the Commission's decision. With regard to the interpretation of the 'general principles of international law', the reasoning of the Court was almost identical to the one used in the *James* case. The Court noted that the Commission has consistently held that the principles in question are not applicable to a taking by a state of the property of its own nationals and that the Government had supported this opinion. While observing that the applicant's argument has some merit, the Court reiterated its arguments from the *James* case; it found that it is more natural to understand these principles as referring to acts to which they are normally applicable, namely acts of state concerning non-nationals. Moreover, it was recalled that the words of a treaty should be interpreted in accordance with their ordinary meaning.[18] As in the *James* case, the Court then examined the interpretation of the expression from the teleological perspective.

In both of the above cases, another important element played a role in the Court's interpretation, namely the wide margin of appreciation granted to Contracting States with regard to deprivation and nationalization of property. This consideration is absent from the VCLT. In the *Lithgow* case, the Court concluded that:

> [a] decision to enact nationalisation legislation will commonly involve consideration of various issues on which opinions within a democratic society may reasonably differ widely. Because of their direct knowledge of their society and its needs and resources, the national authorities are in principle better placed than the international judge to appreciate what measures are appropriate in this area and consequently the margin of appreciation available to them should be a wide one.... Accordingly, the Court's power to review in the present case is limited to ascertaining whether the decision regarding compensation fell outside the United Kingdom's wide margin of appreciation; it will respect the legislature's judgement in this connection unless that judgement was manifestly without reasonable foundation.[19]

In the *James* case, the Court also considered that the state has a wide margin of appreciation in determining what is necessary in the public interest due to its familiarity with society and its needs. The Court held that '[u]nder the system of protection established by the Convention, it is thus for the national authorities to make the initial assessment both of the existence of a problem of public concern

[18] *Lithgow and others v United Kingdom* (n 15 above), para 114.
[19] *James and others v United Kingdom* (n 14 above), para 122.

warranting measures of deprivation of property and of the remedial action to be taken'.[20] Moreover, the Court found it 'natural that the margin of appreciation available to the legislature in implementing social and economic policies should be a wide one',[21] and observed that it is bound to respect the legislature's judgment as to what may be in the public interest (unless it is manifestly unreasonable). Thus, both cases involved a wide margin of appreciation with respect to what may be 'in the public interest', which influenced the Court's interpretation of the expression 'general principles of international law' contained in the same provision. In this context, it is possible that the VCLT was used as a means to provide greater legitimacy to the interpretation adopted by the Court. Further, the Court may have felt particularly compelled to respect the ordinary meaning of the terms of the ECHR, given that it was bound by the wide margin of appreciation granted to the Contracting States in this particular area of the Convention.

In the same year, the Court gave judgment in *Johnston*, which concerned a couple's inability to obtain a divorce in Ireland. Before the Commission, the applicants complained about the absence of a provision in Ireland for divorce and recognition of the family life of persons who, after the breakdown of the marriage of one of them, are living in a family relationship outside marriage. While they alleged that there were violations of Articles 8, 9, 12, 13, and 14 (taken together with Articles 8 and 12) of the ECHR, the Commission only found a breach of Article 8 in that the legal regime concerning the status of the child born out of wedlock under Irish law failed to respect the family life of the applicants. The Court reached the same conclusion in its judgment.

As part of this case, the Court had to consider whether the applicants could derive a right to divorce under Article 12 of the ECHR. As in the two previous cases examined above, the Court started by examining the ordinary meaning of the words to be given to the terms of this provision, but this time it used the wording of Article 31(1) of the VCLT, which also refers to contextual and purposive interpretation. The Court observed that 'it will seek to ascertain the ordinary meaning to be given to the terms of this provision in their context and in the light of its object and purpose'.[22] Pursuant to this rule, the Court agreed with the Commission that the ordinary meaning of the words 'right to marry' is clear and that they only cover the formation of marital relationships and not their dissolution.[23] The Court then examined the context, object, and purpose, as revealed in the *travaux préparatoires*. According to its view, the *travaux préparatoires* confirmed this interpretation and evidenced no intention to include under Article 12 the right to divorce.[24] As is apparent from this judgment, the Court cited the wording of Article 31(1) of the VCLT and attempted to adhere fully to the rule

[20] Ibid, para 46. [21] Ibid. [22] *Johnston and others v Ireland* (n 16 above), para 51.

[23] Ibid, para 52.

[24] Ibid; *Collected Edition of the 'travaux préparatoires' of the European Convention on Human Rights*, Preparatory Commission of the Council of Europe, Committee of Ministers, Consultative Assembly, 11 May to 8 September 1949 (The Hague: Martinus Nijhoff, 1949), Vol I, 268.

contained therein. It is this formulation of the 'ordinary meaning' rule or the 'general rule of interpretation' that prevailed in later case law.[25]

In the 1990s, the Court had a further opportunity to consider this rule in the *Loizidou* case.[26] The applicant in this case was born in northern Cyprus where she owned land, but she married and moved to the Republic of Cyprus. As a result of the presence of the Turkish forces in Cyprus, she was prevented from accessing her property. The applicant took part in a march organized by a Greek Cypriot women's group which intended to cross the Turkish forces' cease-fire line with the aim of asserting the right of Greek Cypriot refugees to return to their homes. The applicant, together with a number of other women, succeeded in crossing the line. They were arrested and released the same day. The applicant claimed that her arrest and detention violated Articles 3 and 5(1) of the ECHR. Furthermore, there was a violation of Article 8 and Article 1 of Protocol No 1 because she was unable to access her property in northern Cyprus. The Commission found that there were no violations of the articles invoked by the applicant.

Before the Court, the Turkish Government submitted preliminary objections claiming, *inter alia*, that the case fell outside its jurisdiction because it related to events which occurred before Turkey's acceptance of the ECtHR's compulsory jurisdiction. Furthermore, in accordance with the declarations under former Articles 25 (Article 34) and 46 of the ECHR, Turkey did not accept the competence of the Commission or the Court to examine acts and events outside its territory. When examining the territorial validity of the restrictions attached by Turkey to former Articles 25 (Article 34) and 46, the Court stated that 'it will seek to ascertain the ordinary meaning to be given to the terms of these provisions in their context and in the light of their object and purpose'.[27] The Court declared that the restrictions *ratione loci* attached to Turkey's declarations under Articles 25 and 46 were invalid.

In the *Witold Litwa v Poland* case,[28] the Court held that there had been a violation of Article 5(1)(e) of the ECHR in that the detention of the applicant in a sobering-up centre was unlawful. The Court had to interpret the notion of 'alcoholics' included in the Article; it observed that the general rule contained in Article 31 of the VCLT

> places on the same footing the various elements enumerated in the four paragraphs of that Article.... The sequence in which those elements are listed in Article 31 ... regulates, however, the order which the process of interpretation of the treaty should follow. That

[25] See, for example, *Loizidou v Turkey (Preliminary Objections)* (App No 15318/89), judgment, 23 March 1995, Series A, Vol 310; *Witold Litwa v Poland* (App No 26629/95), judgment, 4 April 2000, Reports 2000-III, 289, para 59; *Bosphorous Hava Yolları Turizm ve Ticaret Anonim Şirketi v Ireland* (App No 45036/98), judgment, 30 June 2005, Reports 2005-VI, 107, para 100.

[26] *Loizidou v Turkey (Preliminary Objections)* (n 25 above).

[27] Ibid, para 73.

[28] *Witold Litwa v Poland*, (App No 26629/95), judgment, 4 April 2000, Reports 2000-III, 289, para 59.

process must start from ascertaining the ordinary meaning of the terms of a treaty—in their context and in light of its object and purpose, as laid down in paragraph 1 of Article 31. This is particularly so in relation to exceptions to a general rule which, for this very reason, cannot be given an extensive interpretation.[29]

With this statement, the Court confirmed again the order of interpretation that it would follow.

More recently, in the *Bosphorous* case,[30] the Court considered an application brought by an airline charter company, Bosphorous Airways, which had leased an aircraft from Yugoslav Airlines (JAT). This aircraft was seized under EU regulations (which had implemented UN sanctions against the Federal Republic of Yugoslavia) by the Irish authorities when it had been in Ireland for maintenance. Bosphorous Airways complained that the manner in which Ireland implemented the sanction regime to impound its aircraft was a reviewable exercise of discretion under Article 1 of the ECHR and a violation of Article 1 of Protocol No 1.

The Court had to determine, *inter alia*, the question of whether the important general interest of compliance with Community obligations could justify the impugned interference by the Irish State with the applicant company's property rights. The Court noted that the VCLT was a relevant instrument in its interpretation; it mentioned the 'general rule of interpretation' as it appears in Article 31(1) of the VCLT, quoting its full text.[31] The remaining references to the VCLT were, however, limited to the requirement contained in Article 31(3)(c).[32] This was also a case where the respondent State enjoyed, according to the Court, a wide margin of appreciation under Article 1 of Protocol No 1.[33] The Court found that the impounding of the aircraft fell within the jurisdiction of the respondent State under Article 1 of the ECHR and that it did not constitute a violation of Article 1 of Protocol No 1.

Thus, it appears that the Court's approach to the 'ordinary meaning of words' rule has crystallized itself over the years. The Court now appears to adhere scrupulously to the text of the 'general rule' contained in Article 31(1) of the VCLT. It has simply transposed the exact wording of this rule into its case law. Unfortunately, the cases in which Article 31(1) appeared were not numerous. Furthermore, the Court has used this provision only under certain circumstances which precluded an extensive interpretation, namely when the relevant state had a wide margin of appreciation or when the terms to be interpreted constituted an exception to the general rule.

2.2 The Object and Context

By including the treaty's object and purpose in the general rule, Article 31(1) of the VCLT entrenches the teleological method of interpretation. It is based on

[29] Ibid, paras 58–59.

[30] *Bosphorous Hava Yolları Turizm ve Ticaret Anonim Şirketi v Ireland* (App No 45036/98), judgment, 30 June 2005, Reports 2005-VI, 107, para 100.

[31] Ibid, para 100.

[32] Ibid, para 150.

[33] Ibid, para 149.

the consideration that treaty terms constitute a whole and that they include the treaty's aim and purpose. The particular aim of a treaty is especially important in the case of human rights conventions, such as the ECHR, as it allows the courts to ensure their effectiveness. The objective of human rights protection further entails that limitations imposed on certain rights must be narrowly construed. The use of this technique is also very important in the ECHR context, given that the Convention goes beyond reciprocal obligations; the ECHR effectively intervenes in domestic legal systems and the Court hands down judgments and decisions which are binding on the Contracting States. Moreover, teleological interpretation permits the adaptation of the ECHR to current conditions by using evolutive interpretation. It also allows the Court to harmonize different standards and interests. Article 31(1) of the VCLT does not, however, indicate where the object and purpose of a treaty may be found. Typically, the ECHR has resorted to the Preamble to the ECHR in order to elucidate its aim.

The Court has also used contextual interpretation as provided in Article 31(1) and (2) of the VCLT. The terms of the ECHR were not drafted in isolation and their meaning has to be considered in the context of the entire text. Article 31(2) of the VCLT stipulates that the context comprises, in addition to the text (including its Preamble and annexes), '(a) any agreement relating to the treaty which was made between all the parties in connection with the conclusion of the treaty; and (b) any instrument which was made by one or more parties in connection with the conclusion of the treaty and accepted by the other parties as an instrument related to the treaty'. In the context of the ECHR, the text of the respective provision includes the remaining terms of the sentence and of the paragraph, the entire provision at issue, and the remainder of the Convention, including the Preamble and the Protocols.[34]

There have been very few decisions in which the Court expressly referred to the teleological and contextual interpretation as included in the VCLT. Article 31 was invoked for the first time by the Court in 1975 in the *Golder* case,[35] where teleological interpretation was used to deduce a right of access to courts from Article 6(1) of the ECHR. It is interesting to note, however, that the Court had resorted to teleological interpretation before 1975 and, on this basis, referred to the Preamble to the Convention. For instance, in the *Austria v Italy* case,[36] the Commission considered, *inter alia*, whether Austria could lodge an application in relation to a matter which arose prior to the country's ratification of the ECHR.

In order to determine the extent of powers possessed by Austria with regard to the possibility of lodging an application in this case, the Commission referred to the Preamble to the Convention.[37] In addition, the Commission noted that the

[34] Villiger (n 12 above), 325.

[35] *Golder v United Kingdom* (n 1 above).

[36] *Austria v Italy* (App No 788/60), decision, 11 January 1961, (1962) 4 YB 116.

[37] Ibid, 138. The Commission reiterated that 'the aim of the Council of Europe is the achievement of greater unity between its Members and that one of the methods by which the aim is to be

Contracting States were 'resolved, as the Governments of European countries which are like-minded and have a common heritage of political traditions, ideals, freedom and the rule of law to take the first steps for the collective enforcement of certain of the Rights stated in the Universal Declaration'.[38] In the Commission's opinion, this meant that the Contracting States did not intend to grant themselves reciprocal rights and obligations for the pursuit of their national interests, but rather to carry out the objectives and ideals of the Council of Europe.[39] The Commission concluded on the basis, *inter alia*, of the Preamble that it had competence to examine the question raised by the application.

In the *Wemhoff v Germany* case,[40] the Court also used teleological interpretation in a very meaningful manner without referring to the VCLT; it clarified that the ECHR is a law-making treaty and that the right interpretation must be sought in order to achieve the object and purpose of this treaty. In that case, a question was raised regarding the period of detention covered by the requirement of a reasonable time in Article 5(3) of the ECHR. The German Government maintained, as did the Commission, that it is the time of appearance before the trial court that marks the end of the period with which Article 5(3) is concerned. The Court, however, disagreed with this stance, finding it to be too restrictive.

The Court analysed both linguistic versions of the text and found that the English version allowed for two possible interpretations while the French version permitted only one. The French version contained very broad language which, according to the Court, covered both the trial and the investigation. Subsequently, the Court resorted to teleological interpretation in the following words:

> Thus confronted with two versions of a treaty which are equally authentic but not exactly the same, the Court must, following established international law precedents, interpret them in a way that will reconcile them as far as possible. Given that it is a law-making treaty, it is also necessary to seek the interpretation that is most appropriate in order to realise the aim and achieve the object of the treaty, not that which would restrict to the greatest possible degree the obligations undertaken by the Parties. It is impossible to see why the protection against unduly long detention on remand which Article 5 seeks to ensure for persons suspected of offences should not continue up to delivery of judgment rather than cease at the moment the trial opens.[41]

The use of teleological interpretation in this case allowed the Court to clarify further the objective of the ECHR.

pursued is the maintenance and further realization of Human Rights and Fundamental Freedoms'. Furthermore, it was recalled that states have reaffirmed 'their profound belief in those Fundamental Freedoms which are the foundation of justice and peace in the world and are best maintained on the one hand by an effective political democracy and on the other by a common understanding and observance of the Human Rights upon which they depend'.

[38] Ibid. [39] Ibid.

[40] *Wemhoff v Germany* (App No 2122/64), judgment, 27 June 1968, Series A, Vol 8.

[41] Ibid, para 8.

The *Golder* case,[42] mentioned earlier, concerned an application lodged by a prisoner who had allegedly taken part in a prison disturbance and had assaulted a prison officer. He disputed this allegation and requested the Home Secretary to allow him to consult a solicitor in order to sue the prison officer for libel. This action was refused on the basis of the Prison Rules. The prisoner therefore claimed before the Commission that this refusal violated his rights under Articles 6 and 8 of the ECHR. The Commission found that both of these articles were violated and the Court followed this decision when the case was referred to it.

The Court had to decide whether Article 6(1) is limited to guaranteeing the right to a fair trial in legal proceedings which are pending or whether it secures in addition a right of access to courts for every person wishing to commence an action. In the latter eventuality, the Court had to consider whether there were any implied limitations on the right of access or on the exercise of this right in the instant case. When considering whether the right of access to court was included under Article 6(1), the Court found that the terms taken in their context gave reasons to think that this right was inherent in the guarantees contained therein.[43]

Subsequently, the Court relied on teleological interpretation to elucidate the meaning of Article 6(1). It was noted that, pursuant to 'Article 31 para 2 of the Vienna Convention, the preamble to a treaty forms an integral part of the context. Furthermore, the preamble is generally very useful for the determination of the "object" and "purpose" of the instrument to be construed.'[44] The Court considered that, in the instant case, the most significant passage in the ECHR Preamble was the Contracting States' declaration that they are 'resolved, as the Governments of European countries which are like-minded and have a common heritage of political traditions, ideals, freedom and the rule of law, to take the first steps for the collective enforcement of certain of the Rights stated in the Universal Declaration'.[45] Furthermore, it was emphasized that '[o]ne reason why the signatory Governments decided to "take the first steps for the collective enforcement of certain of the Rights stated in the Universal Declaration" was their profound belief in the rule of law'.[46] In the Court's view, it was therefore natural and in conformity with the principle of good faith (Article 31(1) of the VCLT) to bear in mind this consideration when interpreting Article 6(1) of the ECHR.

Judge Sir Fitzmaurice strongly disagreed with this teleological interpretation of Article 6(1) and advocated a more cautious approach based on the terms and intentions of the drafters.[47] According to him, this provision did not include a right of access to court. In his separate opinion, Judge Sir Fitzmaurice made it clear that, for reasons relating to legal certainty, the Court should have exercised

[42] *Golder v United Kingdom* (n 1 above).
[43] Ibid, para 29.
[44] Ibid, para 34. [45] Ibid. [46] Ibid.
[47] For a criticism of the Court's approach, see Ian Sinclair, *The Vienna Convention and Law of Treaties, Melland Schill Monographs in International Law* (Manchester: Manchester University Press, 1984), 133.

self-restraint. He argued that 'the parties cannot be expected to implement what would be an important international obligation when it is not defined sufficiently to enable them to know exactly what it involves—indeed is not defined at all because (in so far as it exists) it rests on an implication that is never particularized or spelt out'.[48] Furthermore, he considered that:

> it is for the States upon whose consent the Convention rests, and from which consent alone it derives its obligatory force, to close the gap or put the defect right by an amendment—not for a judicial tribunal to substitute itself for the convention-makers, to do their work for them. Once wide interpretations of the kind now in question are adopted by a court... considerations of consistency will, thereafter, make it difficult to refuse extensive interpretations in other contexts where good sense might dictate differently: freedom of action will have been impaired.[49]

According to Judge Sir Fitzmaurice, it would only be legitimate for a judge to substitute its intention for that of the drafters if it was proven that Contracting States unambiguously consented to grant this power to them. His reasoning was premised on the principle of contemporaneity, which entails that a treaty should be interpreted in accordance with the intention of the drafters, as expressed at the time when the treaty was concluded. This stance was, however, rejected by the majority of the Court in this case.[50]

The Court also took into account the context and the object of the ECHR provisions when deciding on the validity of the restrictions attached to Turkey's declarations under former Articles 25 (Article 34) and 46 of the ECHR in the *Loizidou* case,[51] analysed earlier.[52] This time, it did not resort to the Preamble to the Convention. The applicant in that case invoked international law principles relating to state responsibility[53] and the respondent Government referred to the VCLT.[54] Resorting to teleological interpretation, the Court observed that:

> [i]f, as contended by the respondent Government, substantive or territorial restrictions were permissible under these provisions, Contracting Parties would be free to subscribe to separate regimes of enforcement of Convention obligations depending on the scope of their acceptances. Such a system, which would enable States to qualify their consent under the optional clauses, would not only seriously weaken the role of the Commission and the Court in the discharge of their functions but would also diminish the effectiveness of the Convention as a constitutional instrument of European public order. Moreover, where the Convention permits States to limit their acceptance under Article 5, there is an express stipulation to this effect.... In the Court's view, having regard to the

[48] *Golder v United Kingdom*, Separate Opinion of Judge Sir Gerald Fitzmaurice (n 1 above), para 30.

[49] Ibid, para 37.

[50] For an interesting interpretation of the *Golder* case from the perspective of constitutional originalism, see Letsas (n 2 above), 60–65.

[51] *Loizidou v Turkey (Preliminary Objections)* (n 25 above). See also 2.1 above.

[52] See 2.1 above.

[53] *Loizidou v Turkey (Preliminary Objections)* (n 25 above), para 57.

[54] Ibid, para 67.

object and purpose of the Convention system as set out above, the consequences for the enforcement of the Convention and the achievement of its aim would be so far-reaching that a power to this effect should have been expressly provided for. However no such provision exists in either Article 25 or Article 46.[55]

In this powerful statement, the Court defined more specifically its role in the context of this case. By finding that the ECHR was a constitutional instrument of European public order, the Court seems to have likened itself to a constitutional court.

Further, the Court considered the context of former Articles 25 (Article 34) and 46 of the ECHR when it noted that:

Article 64 of the Convention enables States to enter reservations when signing the Convention or when depositing their instruments of ratification. The power to make reservations under Article 64 is, however, a limited one, being confined to particular provisions of the Convention 'to the extent that any law then in force in [the] territory [of the relevant Contracting Party] is not in conformity with the provision'. In addition, reservations of a general nature are prohibited. In the Court's view, the existence of such a restrictive clause governing reservations suggests that States could not qualify their acceptance of the optional clauses thereby effectively excluding areas of their law and practice within their 'jurisdiction' from supervision by the Convention institutions.[56]

Although not premised on self-restraint, these statements represent an illustrious example of the manner in which the Court stood as a guardian of the protection of human rights.

Undoubtedly, the teleological and contextual interpretations, as included in Article 31(1) and (2) of the VCLT, have played a detrimental role in the interpretation of the ECHR. They have both permitted the Court to adapt the Convention to present conditions and to keep up with the changes in society. Furthermore, they have allowed the Court to preserve the aim of the ECHR in situations where conflicting interests appeared. The Court has also been able to flesh out certain rights contained in the ECHR which were drafted with great generality.

As is often the case, the Court's approach has been met with intense criticism. It has been argued that the VCLT only allows the Court to apply teleological interpretation to the 'substantive' guarantees contained in the ECHR and not the 'procedural or structural' ones.[57] On this basis, it would be illegitimate for the Court to use the object and purpose of the ECHR to attribute a meaning to any procedural or structural provision that would be different from the subjective understanding of the Contracting States. Furthermore, whenever the need arose to modify these provisions, it was usually achieved by means of an amending

[55] Ibid, para 75. [56] Ibid, paras 76–77.

[57] Heribert Golsong, 'Interpreting the European Convention on Human Rights Beyond the Confines of the Vienna Convention on the Law of the Treaties?' in Ronald St J Macdonald, Franz Matscher, and Herbert Petzold (eds), *The European System for the Protection of Human Rights* (Dordrecht/Boston/London: Martinus Nijhoff, 1993), 147.

Protocol.[58] It was found that the Court had deviated from these rules and had used teleological interpretation to exceed the clear meaning of the text.[59] These criticisms appear nonetheless to be quite strict and rigid. They do not display the kind of flexibility that is necessary to adapt the ECHR to new realities. As such, they are bound to lead to an atrophy of the interpretation rules and techniques used thus far by the Court.

2.3 Subsequent Practice

Article 31(3)(b) of the VCLT provides that 'any subsequent practice in the application of the treaty which establishes the agreement of the parties regarding its interpretation' shall be taken into account as part of its context. Pursuant to this rule, all parties agree or accept the interpretation of treaty terms by means which are extrinsic to the treaty.[60] Article 31(3)(b) covers only subsequent practice common to all parties, and subsequent practice which does not fall within this definition may only constitute a supplementary means of interpretation.[61] No party should have raised an objection to this practice, as it must be common to all those that ratified the treaty. The value of such practice will depend on the extent to which it is concordant, common, and consistent.[62]

There is an inherent difficulty in fixing the dividing line between interpretation and a modification effected under the cover of interpretation. There is therefore a close link between the concept that subsequent practice is an element to be taken into account in the interpretation of a treaty and the concept that a treaty may be modified by subsequent practice of the parties.[63] However, it appears that the VCLT is silent on the modification of a treaty by subsequent practice, in spite of the fact that this mechanism is recognized in international law.[64] According to one view, subsequent practice may operate as a tacit or implicit modification of the terms of the treaty in international law.[65] Pursuant to Article 42(2) of the VCLT, a treaty can be modified 'only as a result of the applications of the provisions of the treaty or of the present Convention'. It has, however, been argued that this provision in itself does not preclude a modification of a treaty by subsequent practice.[66]

[58] Ibid, 150. [59] Ibid, 151–161. [60] Villiger (n 12 above), 326.

[61] Sinclair (n 47 above), 128. See also *Report of the International Law Commission on the Work of its Eighteenth Session* (Geneva, 4 May to 19 July 1966), 1966 (2) Yearbook of the International Law Commission 173, 222.

[62] Sinclair (n 47 above), 137. [63] Ibid, 138.

[64] Lucius Caflisch and Antônio Cançado Trindade, '*Les Conventions Américaine et Européenne des Droits de l'Homme et le Droit International Général*' (2004-I) 108 RGDIP 5, 18. [65] Ibid.

[66] Vladimir Degan, *Sources of International Law* (The Hague/Boston/London: Martinus Nijhoff, 1997), 251–252; Michael Akehurst, 'The Hierarchy of the Sources of International Law' (1974/1975) 47 BYIL 273, 277; Sinclair (n 47 above), 138; *Air Transport Services Agreement Arbitration* 38 ILR 182, 249; *Legal Consequences for States of the Continued Presence of South Africa in Namibia (South West Africa), Notwithstanding Security Council Resolution 276*, advisory opinion, 21 June 1971, 1971 ICJ Reports 16, 22, para 22.

In the context of the ECHR, the subsequent practice interpretation rule has been applied explicitly in several cases which concerned issues of central importance to the protection of human rights, namely the abolition of the death penalty in Europe, the binding nature of interim measures, and the validity of reservations entered by states. Beyond these literal uses, Article 31(3)(b) of the VCLT has also found expression in the Court's characterization of the ECHR as a 'living instrument' as well as part of the evolutive and dynamic interpretation. The Court has been rather cautious in its application of the subsequent practice rule, and it did not go as far as explicitly admitting that its application would entail a modification of the ECHR.

One of the most important uses of subsequent practice in the Strasbourg jurisprudence appeared in *Soering v United Kindgom*.[67] The case concerned the extradition of a person to a state where he could face the risk of being exposed to the death row phenomenon. The Court had to decide, *inter alia*, in that case whether the death penalty was inhuman. One of the aspects to be determined was the relationship between Articles 2(1) and 3 of the ECHR. There was no mention of the VCLT in the judges' reasoning. The Court reiterated that the ECHR had to be interpreted as a whole, which meant that the drafters did not intend to enact two contradictory rules. It was, however, emphasized that '[s]ubsequent practice in national penal policy, in the form of a generalised abolition of capital punishment, could be taken as establishing the agreement of the Contracting States to abrogate the exception provided for under 2 § 1 and hence to remove a textual limit on the scope of evolutive interpretation of Article 3'.[68] This passage was criticized by commentators who found that the Court should have required a proof of abolition of the death penalty by all Contracting States and a proof of an engagement not to reintroduce this punishment for a modification of the Convention's text.[69]

Later, in 2003, the Court referred once again to this judgment, noting that many changes had occurred in state practice since then. The *Öcalan v Turkey* case[70] concerned Abdullah Öcalan, the former leader of the Kurdistan Workers' Party (*Partiya Karkerên Kurdistan*, PKK), against whom the Turkish courts had issued seven arrest warrants. He was found guilty of carrying out actions aimed at the separation of part of the Turkish territory and of forming and leading an armed gang to achieve this end. He was sentenced to death, but later this sentence was commuted to life imprisonment. The applicant claimed, *inter alia*, that the imposition of the death penalty was or would be in violation of Articles 2, 3, and 14 of

67 *Soering v United Kingdom* (App No 14038/88), judgment, 7 July 1989, Series A, Vol 161.

68 Ibid, para 103.

69 Caflisch and Cançado Trindade (n 64 above), 19; John Graham Merrills, *The Development of International Law by the European Court of Human Rights* (Manchester/New York: Manchester University Press, 2nd edn, 1993), 82.

70 *Öcalan v Turkey* (App No 46221/99), judgment, 12 March 2003, not reported.

the ECHR. These complaints were, however, rejected because there were no longer substantial grounds to believe that the applicant would be executed.

The Court then went on to determine whether the imposition of the death penalty would give rise to a breach of the ECHR. The Court resorted again to the subsequent practice of states, but its reasoning did not explicitly acknowledge Article 31(3)(b) of the VCLT. The Court found that:

> the legal position as regards the death penalty has undergone a considerable evolution since the *Soering* case was decided. The... almost complete abandonment of the death penalty in times of peace in Europe is reflected in the fact that all the Contracting States have signed Protocol No. 6 and forty-one States have ratified it, that is to say, all except Turkey, Armenia and Russia.... Such a marked development could now be taken as signalling the agreement of the Contracting States to abrogate, or at the very least to modify, the second sentence of Article 2 § 1, particularly when regard is had to the fact that all Contracting States have now signed Protocol No. 6 and that it has been ratified by forty-one States.[71]

The Court noted, however, that the opening for signature of Protocol No 13 (concerning the abolition of the death penalty in all circumstances) indicated that the Contracting States had chosen a traditional method of amendment in the pursuit of the abolition policy. This Protocol was the final step in this process, as it attempted to extend the abolition of the death penalty to all circumstances (in times of peace and war). According to the Court, the Protocol 'can be seen as a confirmation of the abolitionist trend established by the practice of the Contracting States. It does not necessarily run counter to the view that Article 2 has been amended in so far as it permits the death penalty in times of peace'.[72] The Court further added that 'it cannot now be excluded, in the light of the developments that have taken place in this area, that the States have agreed through their practice to modify the second sentence in Article 2 § 1 in so far as it permits capital punishment in peacetime. Against this background it can also be argued that the implementation of the death penalty can be regarded as inhuman and degrading treatment contrary to Article 3.'[73] However, the Court had already found that there had been a violation of the applicant's right to a fair trial in Article 6(1) of the ECHR. Thus, it found it unnecessary to reach any firm conclusions about subsequent practice in the context of the abolition of the death penalty; it was sufficient to hold that it would run counter to the Convention to implement a death sentence following an unfair trial, even if Article 2 of the ECHR were to be construed as still permitting the death penalty.[74] It is deplorable that the Court did not take this opportunity to reach a more significant conclusion with regard to the abolition of the death penalty in its jurisdiction.

In the *Cruz Varas and others v Sweden* case,[75] the Court also referred to subsequent state practice in the context of interim measures. The applicants were

[71] Ibid, paras 195–196. [72] Ibid, para 197. [73] Ibid. [74] Ibid, para 198.

[75] *Cruz Varas and others v Sweden* (App No 15576/89), judgment, 20 March 1991, Series A, Vol 201.

Chilean citizens who came to Sweden in 1987. The National Immigration Board decided to expel the applicants and refused their request for refugee status. The first applicant claimed that he had worked in Sweden for a radical organization which had tried to kill General Pinochet and that he ran the risk of political persecution if he returned to Chile. He also claimed to have been tortured on several occasions in Chile. Before the expulsion took place, the Agent of the Government was informed that the Commission had decided, in accordance with Rule 36 of the Commission's Rules of Procedure, that it was desirable not to deport the applicants to Chile until the Commission had an opportunity to examine the application further. In spite of this warning, the first applicant was expelled to Chile on the same day. The applicants alleged that there were violations of Articles 3, 8, and former Article 25(1) (Article 34) of the ECHR as a result of the Government's failure to adhere to Rule 36 of the Commission's Rules. In its report, the Commission found that there had been no violation of Article 3 or 8, but that there had been a failure to comply with former Article 25(1) (Article 34) by not following the Commission's Rule 36 request not to expel the first applicant. The Court found, however, that there was no violation of either one of these articles.

When considering whether the respondent Government had violated former Article 25(1) (Article 34), the Court had to determine whether interim measures authorized by Rule 36 were obligatory for the Contracting States. The Court considered that:

> [t]he practice of Contracting Parties in this area shows that there has been almost total compliance with Rule 36 indications. Subsequent practice could be taken as establishing the agreement of Contracting States regarding the interpretation of a Convention provision... but not to create new rights and obligations which were not included in the Convention at the outset.... In any event, as reflected in the various recommendations of the Council of Europe bodies referred to above, the practice of complying with Rule 36 indications cannot have been based on a belief that these indications gave rise to a binding obligation.... It was rather a matter of good faith co-operation with the Commission in cases where this was considered reasonable and practicable.[76]

Thus, the Court found that no power to order binding interim measures could be inferred from former Article 25 (1) (Article 34) of the ECHR. It was pointed out that the Court has rightly distinguished between the interpretation of the ECHR on the basis of subsequent practice and the modification of the ECHR by such practice, the VCLT being silent with regard to the latter.[77] Such a view is, however, restrictive and the Court's interpretation of this principle can be criticized for being circumspect and traditional.

A further use of subsequent practice appeared in the *Loizidou v Turkey* case,[78] considered above,[79] where the Court expressed the opinion that the territorial

[76] Ibid, para 100.
[77] Caflisch and Cançado Trindade (n 64 above), 18.
[78] *Loizidou v Turkey (Preliminary Objections)* (n 25 above).
[79] See 2.1 and 2.2 above.

restrictions imposed on former Article 25 (Article 34) and Article 46 declarations by Turkey were not permitted under the Convention system. According to the Court:

> [t]his approach is confirmed by subsequent practice of Contracting Parties under these provisions. Since the entry into force of the Convention until the present day, almost all of the thirty parties to the Convention, apart from the respondent Government, have accepted the competence of the Commission and the Court to examine complaints without restrictions ratione loci and ratione materiae. The only exceptions to such a consistent practice appear in the restrictions attached to the Cypriot declaration under Article 25 . . . which have now been withdrawn . . . . The existence of such a uniform and consistent State practice clearly rebuts the respondent Government's arguments that restrictions attaching to Article 25 and Article 46 declarations must have been envisaged by the drafters of the Convention in the light of practice under Article 36 of the Statute of the International Court of Justice. Finally, no assistance can be derived from general principles of international law since, as observed by the Commission, the question whether interim measures indicated by international tribunals are binding is a controversial one and no uniform legal rule exists.[80]

The Court used subsequent practice in order to clarify the meaning of an ECHR provision in this case. In this context, it has clearly given more weight to the subsequent practice rule. This interpretation is therefore more expansive and less traditional than the one used in the *Cruz Varas* case.

The conclusion in the *Cruz Varas* case was nonetheless reversed in the *Mamatkulov and Abdurasulovic v Turkey* case[81] before the Chamber, and this was further confirmed in the *Mamatkulov and Askarov v Turkey* case[82] before the Grand Chamber. Following the *Mamatkulov* judgments, interim measures acquired a binding character under the ECHR. They concerned applications brought by two Uzbek nationals, Rustam Mamatkulov and Abdurasulovic Askarov, who were members of the ERK 'Freedom' Party (an opposition party in Uzbekistan). Mr Mamatkulov and Mr Askarov arrived in Turkey in 1998 and 1999 respectively; they were subsequently arrested and taken into police custody. Both men were suspected of murder, causing injuries by the explosion of a bomb in Uzbekistan, and an attempted terrorist attack on the President of the Republic. Uzbekistan requested their extradition under a bilateral treaty with Turkey. Despite the Court's indication to the Turkish Government not to extradite the applicants, they were sent to Uzbekistan, where they were found guilty and sentenced to 20 and 11 years' imprisonment respectively. Before the ECtHR, the applicants complained of breaches of Articles 2, 3, and 6 of the ECHR as well as Rule 39 (interim measures) of the Court's Rules. In the Chamber and

80 *Loizidou v Turkey (Preliminary Objections)* (n 25 above), paras 79–82.

81 *Mamatkulov and Abdurasulovic v Turkey* (App Nos 46827/99; 46951/99), judgment, 6 February 2003, not reported. See Introduction, 2.2.3; ch II, 2.6; ch IV, 2.2.8; and ch V, 3.2.1.

82 *Mamatkulov and Askarov v Turkey* (App Nos 46827/99; 46951/99), judgment, 4 February 2005, Reports 2005-I, 293.

the Grand Chamber judgments, the Court held there had been no violation of Article 3, that Article 6(1) was inapplicable to the extradition procedure, and that there had been a breach of Article 34 because Turkey had not complied with the interim measures indicated by the Court.[83] The Court did not find it necessary to consider separately the applicants' allegations under Article 2.

Despite the fact that the Court is heading towards a more expansive interpretation of the subsequent practice rule, some dissenting voices in the Grand Chamber judgment suggested that this rule should have been applied more strictly in the *Cruz Varas v Sweden* judgment. It was noted that in the *Cruz Varas* case, '[a]fter describing early unsuccessful attempts of the Convention institutions at adopting recommendations in the matter . . . , the Court found that the prevailing—but not complete—compliance with provisional measures was inspired by the desire of States Parties to cooperate. There was, in other words, no evidence that that practice, as is required by the Vienna Convention, "established the *agreement* of the Parties regarding its interpretation".'[84] It pointed out, however, that at the Committee of Experts for the Improvement of Procedures for the Protection of Human Rights (DH-PR) in 1994, the Commission and the Court considered that the new Court should have the power to issue interim measures with legally binding effect and that this should be provided for in the Convention. Nonetheless, all the proposals submitted, requesting consideration of whether interim measures had a mandatory character, were rejected by the government experts.[85] Furthermore, the Committee of Ministers declined to include a provision on interim measures in the Convention. Thus, the dissenting judges adhered strictly to the requirements of Article 31(3)(b) of the VCLT by pointing out that subsequent practice needed to have complete approval of the Contracting States.

It follows from the above analysis that the Court's interpretation of Article 31(3)(b) of the VCLT could have been more expansive and less traditional in certain cases, namely in the *Öcalan* and *Cruz Varas* judgments. In these instances, the Court's more rigid approach may have been caused by the fear that it would be seen as introducing new elements into the ECHR without the Contracting States' consent. Despite this, the remaining cases in which the Court considered the subsequent practice rule reveal that it has done so in a manner which complies with the text and the spirit of Article 31(3)(b), although perhaps not with the more progressive trend in international law.

[83] The Grand Chamber found in addition that there was no violation of Art 6(1) of the ECHR with regard to the criminal proceedings in Uzbekistan. The Grand Chamber and the Chamber did not, however, rely on the subsequent practice rule but rather on an interpretation based on other international rules enshrined in Art 31(3)(c) of the VCLT.

[84] *Mamatkulov and Askarov v Turkey*, joint partly dissenting opinion of Judges Caflisch, Türmen, and Kovler (n 82 above), para 18 (italics in original).

[85] Ibid, paras 18–19.

2.4 Other Relevant Rules of International Law

2.4.1 Renewed Interest in Article 31(3)(c) of the VCLT

Article 31(3)(c) of the VCLT has been read recently with renewed interest in the context of fragmentation and judicial interpretation of international law. This article provides only that '[t]here shall be taken into account together with the context... any relevant rules of international law applicable in the relations between the parties'. It has been found, nonetheless, that it contains a general principle of interpretation, namely the principle of systemic integration in international law.[86] Systemic integration implies that treaties are part of the international legal system; regardless of the extensiveness of their subject matter, international treaties are limited in scope and are dependent on this system for their existence and operation.[87] Thus, international rules must be interpreted as being part of a whole and in accordance with general principles of international law.

The renewed importance of this rule arises primarily from the fact that it has been considered by the International Law Commission (ILC) as one of the possible solutions to the problem of fragmentation of international law. The ILC did not fully explore the implications of Article 31(3)(c) when it instated the VCLT.[88] Nonetheless, when it took up the study of the fragmentation of international law, the Commission focused on the legal techniques which could be used to resolve conflicts of norms. Thus, the ILC Study Group also had the opportunity to analyse the rule enshrined in Article 31(3)(c) as one of the possible methods of averting such conflicts and harmonizing international rules.

Article 31(3)(c) was scarcely used in the past by international or domestic courts. As Sands noted, '[t]he reluctance to refer to Article 31(3)(c) seems endemic, even when clear opportunities present themselves'.[89] It has more often than not been criticized for the lack of clarity it introduces in the interpretative process. Indeed, some questions remain open, and judges and academics have not found any definite answers to them. Recent practice seems to demonstrate that Article 31(3)(c) has been resorted to by applicants and by the courts more often than before. The case law of the ECtHR was one of the main areas in which such references appeared.[90] Other references have appeared in the Iran-United States

[86] Campbell McLachlan, 'The Principle of Systemic Integration and Article 31(3)(c) of the Vienna Convention' (2005) 54 Int'l Comp LQ 279, 280. See also Mark E Villiger, *Commentary on the 1969 Vienna Convention on the Law of Treaties* (Leiden/Boston: Martinus Nijhoff, 2009), 432, para 24.

[87] Ibid.

[88] Ibid, 281.

[89] Philippe Sands, 'Treaty, Custom and the Cross-Fertilization of International Law' (1998) 1 YHRDLJ 85, 96.

[90] *Golder v United Kingdom* (n 1 above); *Loizidou v Turkey (Merits)* (App No 15318/89), judgment, 18 December 1996, Reports 1996-VI (No 26), 2216; *Fogarty v United Kingdom* (App No 37112/97), judgment, 21 November 2001, Reports 2001-XI, 157; *McElhinney v Ireland*, (App No 31253/96), judgment, 21 November 2001, Reports 2001-XI, 37; *Al-Adsani v United Kingdom* (App No 35763/97), judgment, 21 November 2001, Reports 2001-XI, 79; *Banković and others v Belgium*

Claims Tribunal,[91] arbitral tribunals,[92] the Appellate Body in the WTO Dispute Settlement System,[93] and the International Court of Justice.[94]

Due to this renewed interest, it has been proposed to reactivate or to 'operationalize' Article 31(3)(c). The ILC Study Group made several suggestions as to how this could be carried out. It was proposed that, as part of systemic integration, attention should be given to rules of customary international law and to general principles of law that are applicable in the relations between parties to the treaty. This principle subsumes two presumptions: (i) from a negative point of view, it is assumed that when the parties entered into a treaty, they did not intend to contravene customary international law or general principles of international law;[95] and (ii) from a positive point of view, parties are taken to refer to principles of general international law for questions which are not resolved by the treaty in express terms or otherwise.[96] Custom and general principles become very important when a treaty provision is unclear or open-ended, or when the terms used in the treaty have a recognized meaning in customary international law to which the parties may have referred.

The ILC Study Group in its 2004 report noted that '[a]s a general rule, there would be no room to refer to other rules of international law unless the treaty itself gave rise to a problem in its interpretation'.[97] Furthermore, '[a] need for the use of article 31(3)(c) specifically would arise normally if (a) the treaty rule

and 16 Other Contracting States (App No 52207/99), judgment, 12 December 2001, Reports 2001-XII, 333.

91 *Esphahanian v Bank Tejarat* (1983) 2 IUSCTR 157; *Case No A/18* (1984) 5 IUSCTR 251, 260; *Grimm v Iran*, 2 IUSCTR 78, 82 (dissent); *Amoco International Finance Corporation v Iran* (1987-II) 15 IUSCTR 189, 222.

92 See, for example, the Permanent Court of Arbitration, *Dispute concerning access to information under article 9 of the OSPAR Convention: Ireland v United Kingdom*, Final Award, 2 July 2003, (2003) 42 ILM 1118; the International Tribunal for the Law of the Sea: the *Mox Plant case (Ireland v United Kingdom)*, Request for Provisional Measures Order, 3 December 2001; the Permanent Court of Arbitration, *Mox Plant (Ireland v United Kingdom)*, Order No 3, 24 June 2003, (2003) 42 ILM 1187.

93 WTO Appellate Body Report, *United States—Import Prohibition of Certain Shrimp and Shrimp Products*, WT/DS58/AB/R, adopted 6 November 1998, DSR 1998:VII, 2755; WTO Appellate Body Report, *European Communities—Measures Concerning Meat and Meat Products (Hormones)*, WT/DS26/AB/R, WT/DS48/AB/R, adopted 13 February 1998, DSR 1998:I, 135.

94 *Oil Platforms (Islamic Republic of Iran v United States)*, judgment, 12 December 1996, 2003 ICJ Reports 161; *Gabčikovo-Nagymaros Project (Hungary v Slovakia)*, judgment, 25 September 1997, separate opinion of Judge Weeramantry, 1997 ICJ Reports 88, 114.

95 Report of the International Law Commission, 57th Session (2 May to 3 June and 11 July to 5 August 2005), United Nations General Assembly, Official Records, 60th Session, Supplement No 10 (A/60/10), 216, para 470; *Right of Passage over Indian Territory (Portugal v India) (Preliminary Objections)*, judgment, 26 November 1957, 1957 ICJ Reports 142.

96 Report of the International Law Commission (n 95 above); *Georges Pinson* case (France/United Mexican States), Award of 13 April 1928, UNRIAA, Vol V, 422.

97 Report of the Study Group on Fragmentation of International Law, *Difficulties Arising from the Diversity and Expansion of International Law*, International Law Commission, 56th Session, 3 May to 4 June 2004 and 5 July to 6 August 2004, A/CN.4/L.663/Rev1, 28 July 2004, 21, para 52.

is unclear and the ambiguity appears to be resolved by reference to a developed body of international law; (b) the terms used in the treaty have a well-recognized meaning in customary international law, to which the parties can therefore be taken to have intended to refer; or (c) the terms of the treaty are by their nature open-textured and reference to other sources of international law will assist in giving content to the rule'.[98]

There are a number of outstanding issues hindering the interpretation of Article 31(3)(c). Due to the limited scope of this chapter, it will only be possible to take some of these issues into account. One of the problematic aspects of Article 31(3)(c) is that it does not specify whether the international law source, being relied on as part of the interpretation, needs to be binding among all parties that have ratified the treaty. The meaning of a 'party' is defined in the VCLT as 'a State which has consented to be bound by the treaty and for which the treaty is in force'. The ILC Study Group found that there were four possible solutions to this question: (i) all parties to the treaty under interpretation should also be parties to any treaty relied upon for its interpretation; (ii) the parties in the dispute should be parties to the other treaty; (iii) the rule contained in a particular treaty should possess the status of customary international law; and (iv) the complete identity of treaty parties would not be required but the other rule relied upon could be said to have been implicitly accepted or tolerated by all parties to the treaty under interpretation.[99] The ILC Study Group abstained from taking any stand on this question and did not find that any of these stances were better than the rest. It was found that the task of choosing a position rested on the judge or administrator according to the nature of the treaty and the concrete facts in each case.[100] It was further considered that a fifth approach could be viable, namely that all the relevant rules applicable to relations between the parties be taken into account and be given the weight appropriate under the circumstances.[101]

Another problem which is unclear under Article 31(3)(c) is the issue of intertemporality, namely whether the interpreter who resorts to other relevant sources of international law as part of treaty interpretation is limited to those sources that existed at the moment when the treaty was concluded ('the principle of contemporaneity') or whether subsequent treaty developments can be taken into account.[102] Although there was support for the principle of contemporaneity, it was found that parties could stipulate that a treaty should follow subsequent

[98] Ibid.

[99] Report of the Study Group on Fragmentation of International Law, *Difficulties Arising from the Diversity and Expansion of International Law*, International Law Commission, 56th Session, 2 May to 3 June and 11 July to 5 August 2005, A/CN.4/L.676, 29 July 2005, 14–15, para 32.

[100] Ibid, 17–18, para 38.

[101] Ibid. For academic debate on this question, see Linderfalk (n 12 above), 178; McLachlan (n 86 above), 315; Duncan French, 'Treaty Interpretation and the Incorporation of Extraneous Legal Rules' (2006) 55 Int'l Comp LQ 281, 305–307.

[102] Report of the Study Group on Fragmentation of International Law (n 99 above), 15–16, para 33.

developments. It was considered that a safer guide to the interpretation of a treaty provision was the evaluation of the parties' intentions in relation to the sources in Articles 31 and 32 of the VCLT, namely object, purpose, context, and subsequent practice.

The Study Group did not consider that it was its task to adopt a firm position with regard to inter-temporality. Rather, it was felt that it was more appropriate to indicate which approaches were available to the judge or administrator charged with answering the question of whether the interpretation should be conducted in accordance with the law applicable at the time the treaty was concluded or otherwise.[103] The conclusions of the Study Group are broad and state that '[a] treaty may convey whether in applying Article 31(3)(c) the interpreter should refer only to rules of international law in force at the time of the conclusion of the treaty or may also take into account subsequent changes in the law. Moreover, the meaning of a treaty provision may also be affected by subsequent development in customary law or general principles of law.'[104]

The unresolved definitional problems and the generality of certain terms included in Article 31(3)(c) could hinder the interpretative process of judges or, vice versa, provide them with a wider discretion in the resolution of cases. Arguably, this uncertainty could be eliminated by providing stricter principles for judges to follow. Nonetheless, the ILC Study Group expressed doubt as to whether it is possible to make progress in this area by determining firm rules of interpretation.[105] It was found that '[s]uch interpretation was rather an "artistic" activity that could scarcely be grasped by firm rules or processes'.[106] Further, the ILC Study Group emphasized the flexibility inherent in Article 31(3)(c). It was accepted that the rules referred to in the provision included not only treaty rules, but also customary law and general principles of law.[107] Naturally, Article 31(3)(c) represents only one of the possible solutions to the fragmentation of international law. While it has an important contributory role to play, treaty interpretation cannot on its own promote harmonization and guarantee the unity of the entire international legal system.[108]

A very instructive use of Article 31(3)(c) was made in the *Oil Platforms* case,[109] where the ICJ shed further light on the difficulties inherent in the interpretation of this provision. The judgment further reinforced the idea that a myriad of views exist as to how this provision ought to be interpreted. In this case, the ICJ

[103] Ibid, 220, para 479.

[104] Report of the International Law Commission, 58th Session (1 May to 9 June and 3 July to 11 August 2005), General Assembly, Official Records, 60th Session, Supplement No 10 (A/61/10), 415, para 22. For academic debate on this question, see McLachlan (n 86 above), 317; French (n 101 above), 296, 298–299. See also the ICJ's approach in the *Gabčíkovo-Nagymaros Project (Hungary v Slovakia)*, judgment, 25 September 1997, 1997 ICJ Reports 7, 76–80.

[105] Report of the Study Group on Fragmentation of International Law (n 99 above), 17, para 36.

[106] Ibid. [107] Ibid, 220, para 477. [108] French (n 101 above), 302.

[109] *Oil Platforms (Islamic Republic of Iran v United States)*, judgment, 12 December 1996, 2003 ICJ Reports 161.

had to decide whether actions of the Iranian authorities were in breach of the 1955 Treaty of Amity, Economic Relations and Consular Rights between the United States and Iran.[110] The ICJ had to interpret two of the 1955 Treaty's provisions. One of the provisions provided that '[t]he present Treaty shall not preclude the application of measures: . . . (d) necessary to fulfil the obligations of the High Contracting Parties for the maintenance or restoration of international peace and security, or necessary to protect its essential security interests'.[111] The ICJ considered whether such measures could include the use of armed force and whether the conditions under which such force could be used in international law applied.

While a clear majority of judges refused to uphold Iranian and American claims, very divergent opinions were expressed as to how the 1955 Treaty ought to be interpreted. In his separate opinion, Judge Simma took the most expansive view of the interpretation of Article 31(3)(c) of the VCLT. Judge Higgins advocated a broad but more critical reading of this provision, whilst Judge Buergenthal's reasoning yielded the narrowest and least flexible construction. With extremely divergent academic and judicial opinions as to how Article 31(3)(c) ought to be interpreted, the ECtHR judges had a very difficult task on their hands. This may explain, in part, why the Strasbourg judiciary resorted so infrequently to this provision in its jurisprudence, even in cases where an obvious interpretation example presented itself. In cases where Article 31(3)(c) was raised, the Court usually construed it in an expansive way, and thus its approach resembled most closely the approach adopted by the ILC and Judge Simma in the *Oil Platforms* case. It must be noted, however, that the Court did not fully engage with the uncertainties of Article 31(3)(c) and thus any classification of its interpretative style remains difficult.

2.4.2 Case Law Relating to Article 31(3)(c) of the VCLT

In the Strasbourg case law, there are few explicit references to the principle enshrined in Article 31(3)(c) of the VCLT. Nonetheless, it has been argued that in most cases where the Court has incorporated international law into its reasoning, it has resorted to this provision indirectly.[112] The cases where the Court explicitly invoked Article 31(3)(c) can be sub-divided into four groups: (i) those concerning the right to a fair trial (Article 6 of the ECHR); (ii) those concerning the balance between the application of state immunity and the right to access

[110] Treaty of Amity, Economic Relations and Consular Rights between the United States and Iran, 284 UNTS 93, entered into force 16 June 1957.

[111] Ibid, Art XX(1)(d).

[112] François Ost, 'The Original Canons of Interpretation of the European Court of Human Rights' in Mireille Delmas-Marty and Christine Chodakiewicz (eds), *The European Convention for the Protection of Human Rights: International Protection versus National Restriction* (Dordrecht/Boston/London: Martinus Nijhoff, 1992), 283, 288; see also Alastair Mowbray, 'The Creativity of the European Court of Human Rights' (2005) 5 HRLR 57, 59; John Graham Merrills (n 69 above), 69.

to a court (Article 6(1) of the ECHR);[113] (iii) those concerning the compulsory nature of interim measures (Rule 39 of the Rules of the Court and Article 34 of the ECHR); and (iv) child abduction cases closely intertwined with the Hague Convention on the Civil Aspects of International Child Abduction. Thus, most cases concerned a substantive right enshrined in Article 6 of the ECHR and the remaining cases had a procedural character of fundamental importance to the Contracting States. There does not seem to be an apparent reason explaining why the Court may have resorted to Article 31(3)(c) only in these contexts.

The first explicit reference to Article 31(3)(c) appeared in the *Golder* case.[114] In that case, the Court used the provision as a means of referring to other provisions of international law. In addition, Article 31(3)(c) served as a mechanism to incorporate the right of access to the Court in the framework of Article 6(1) of the ECHR. Undoubtedly, the Court's reasoning was bold, as the provision did not explicitly refer to this right. As part of its examination as to whether Article 6(1) guarantees a right of access to the courts or tribunals, the Court first took into account the text, context, object, and purpose of Article 6(1). Following this analysis, it considered that 'in civil matters one can scarcely conceive of the rule of law without there being a possibility of having access to the courts'.[115] In support of this statement, the Court further stated that 'Article 31 para 3 (c) of the Vienna Convention indicates that account is to be taken, together with the context, of "any relevant rules of international law applicable in the relations between the parties"'.[116] The Court used Article 31(3)(c) as a means of referring to the Statute of the International Court of Justice. It then observed that '[a]mong those rules are general principles of law and especially "general principles of law recognized by civilized nations" (Article 38 para 1 (c) of the Statute of the International Court of Justice)'.[117]

Applying this reasoning to the *Golder* case, the Court resorted to a general principle that it considered to be recognized by most states. The Court observed that '[t]he principle whereby a civil claim must be capable of being submitted to a judge ranks as one of the universally "recognised" fundamental principles of law; the same is true of the principle of international law which forbids the denial of justice'.[118] This led the Court to conclude that '[i]t would be unconceivable... that Article 6 para 1 should describe in detail the procedural guarantees afforded to parties in a pending lawsuit and should not first protect that which alone makes it in fact possible to benefit from such guarantees, that is, access to a court. The fair, public and expeditious characteristics of judicial proceedings are of no value at all if there are no judicial proceedings.'[119] Thus, on the basis of the terms of the first sentence of Article 6(1) of the ECHR read in its context and with a due regard to the object and purpose of the Convention, the Court decided

113 See ch VII.
114 *Golder v United Kingdom* (n 1 above). 115 Ibid, para 34. 116 Ibid, para 35.
117 Ibid.
118 Ibid. 119 Ibid.

that the right of access to a court is inherent in this provision. In its report[120] in the *Golder* case, the Commission also took into account the VCLT interpretative principles as part of its examination of Article 6(1).[121] However, it did not analyse Article 31(3)(c) of the VCLT extensively. In substance, it noted that the treaties invoked by the United Kingdom to support the distinction between the right to a fair hearing and the right of access to courts were not relevant.[122]

Another important reference to Article 31(3)(c) appeared only 20 years later in the *Loizidou v Turkey* case.[123] In this judgment, the Court used the provision as a means of referring to the resolutions of the UN Security Council. As already mentioned,[124] the case concerned a Greek national who took part in a march organized by a Greek Cypriot women's group which intended to cross the Turkish forces' cease-fire line. The applicant succeeded in crossing the line, and was arrested and released the same day. She was born in northern Cyprus where she owned land, but she married and moved to the Republic of Cyprus. As a result of the presence of Turkish forces in Cyprus, she was prevented from accessing her property. Before the Court, in its judgment on the merits, the applicant claimed that the Turkish State was responsible for the continuing violations of Article 1 of Protocol No 1 and Article 8 of the ECHR. Furthermore, she submitted that the state had a duty to allow her to exercise her rights and to provide just satisfaction in accordance with former Article 50 (Article 41) of the ECHR. The applicant invoked international law in support of her application, but it is not apparent from the Court's judgment on which specific instruments she had relied.[125] In its report,[126] the Commission did not refer to the VCLT when interpreting the ECHR.

The Court revisited the preliminary objections raised by Turkey in previous proceedings. It was noted that, while the *ratione temporis* objection question had already been raised previously, there had been no discussion before the Strasbourg bodies as to whether the matters complained of involved a continuing situation or an instantaneous act. The Court clarified that this case concerned alleged violations of a continuing nature if the applicant could still be regarded as the legal owner of the land. The Turkish Government claimed that the process of taking property in Northern Cyprus started in 1974 and amounted to an irreversible expropriation pursuant to the 1985 Constitution of the Turkish Republic of Northern Cyprus (TRNC). This implied that the applicant had only lost ownership in 1985. However, the Court recalled that UN Security Council Resolution 541 (1983)[127] declared the proclamation of the establishment of the

[120] *Golder v United Kingdom* (App No 4451/70), report, 1 June 1973, Series B, Vol 16.
[121] Ibid, paras 44–64. [122] Ibid, para 63.
[123] *Loizidou v Turkey (Merits)* (n 90 above). [124] See 2.1, 2.2, and 2.3 above.
[125] *Loizidou v Turkey (Merits)* (n 90 above), para 36.
[126] *Loizidou v Turkey* (App No 15318/89), report, 8 July 1993, not reported.
[127] United Nations Security Council, Resolution 541 (1983) concerning Cyprus, 18 November 1983.

TRNC as legally invalid and called upon states not to recognize any Cypriot State apart from the Republic of Cyprus. The Court also stated that 'it is only the Cypriot Government which is recognised internationally as the Government of the Republic of Cyprus in the context of diplomatic and treaty relations and the working of international organisations'.[128]

The Court then 'recalled that the Convention must be interpreted in the light of the rules of interpretation set out in the Vienna Convention of 23 May 1969 on the Law of Treaties and that Article 31 para 3 (c) of that treaty indicates that account is to be taken of "any relevant rules of international law applicable in the relations between the parties"'.[129] It was the Court's view that 'the principles underlying the Convention cannot be interpreted and applied in a vacuum. Mindful of the Convention's special character as a human rights treaty, it must also take into account any relevant rules of international law when deciding on disputes concerning its jurisdiction pursuant to Article 49 of the Convention.'[130] Furthermore, it was evident 'from international practice and the various, strongly worded resolutions referred to . . . that the international community does not regard the "TRNC" as a State under international law and that the Republic of Cyprus has remained the sole legitimate Government of Cyprus—itself, bound to respect international standards in the field of the protection of human and minority rights'.[131] For these reasons, the Court did not regard the TRNC as being legally valid. The Turkish Government could not therefore claim that the applicant lost ownership of her property as a result of Article 159 of the TRNC. Thus, the *ratione temporis* objection failed given that, for the purpose of the ECHR, the applicant still remained the legal owner of the land.

In a trilogy of cases decided six years later, the ECtHR applied Article 31(3)(c) of the VCLT in order to refer to generally recognized rules of international law on state immunity.[132] In *McElhinney v United Kingdom*,[133] *Fogarty v United Kingdom*,[134] and *Al-Adsani v United Kingdom*,[135] the majority applied a proportionality test in order to verify whether the restriction imposed by state immunity was proportionate to the aim pursued. The Court reiterated that 'the Convention has to be interpreted in the light of rules set out in the Vienna Convention of 23 May 1969 on the Law of Treaties, and that Article 31 § 3 (c) of that treaty indicates that account is to be taken of "any relevant rules of international law applicable in the relations between parties". Thus, the Convention, including Article 6, cannot be interpreted in a vacuum.'[136] The Court further added that judges must

[128] *Loizidou v Turkey (Merits)* (n 90 above), para 42.
[129] Ibid, para 43. [130] Ibid. [131] Ibid, para 44.
[132] See ch VII discussing in detail the three cases.
[133] *McElhinney v United Kingdom* (n 90 above).
[134] *Fogarty v United Kingdom* (n 90 above).
[135] *Al-Adsani v United Kingdom* (n 90 above).
[136] *McElhinney v United Kingdom* (n 90 above), para 36; *Fogarty v United Kingdom* (n 90 above), para 35; *Al-Adsani v United Kingdom* (n 90 above), para 55.

be mindful of the special character of the Convention as a human rights treaty and that other relevant rules of international law should be taken into account. Most importantly, it was also noted that '[t]he Convention should so far as possible be interpreted in harmony with other rules of international law of which it forms part, including those relating to the granting of State immunity'.[137] For the majority, it followed that 'measures taken by a High Contracting Party which reflect generally recognised rules of public international law on State immunity cannot in principle be regarded as imposing a disproportionate restriction on the right of access to court as embodied in Article 6 § 1'.[138]

Thus, in these three cases, the Court decided to uphold the law of state immunity over the right of access to a court provided for in the ECHR. The Court reached this decision by determining first that the right of access to a court is not absolute and can be subjected to limitations, which must be proportionate to a legitimate aim. The Court then used the provision as a tool to resolve a conflict between a right guaranteed by the ECHR and a rule of international law.[139] It was surprising how far the Court would go to give primacy to traditional rules on state immunity over the *jus cogens* norm of prohibition of torture. As was previously explained by Higgins, the Court consciously chose 'to apply the immunity norm in that context',[140] although this was not necessarily required. Thus, the Court resorted to Article 31(3)(c) in order to be able to give more weight to international law pertaining to state immunity. Interestingly, the decisions of the Commission in the three cases did not contain any references to Article 31(3)(c).[141]

Article 31(3)(c) was also considered in the *Bankovic and others v Belgium and 16 Other Contracting States* case.[142] The case concerned an application brought by six Yugoslav nationals, living in Belgrade, concerning the bombing by the North Atlantic Treaty Organization (NATO) of the Radio-Television Serbia (*Radio Televizije Srbije*, RTS) headquarters in Belgrade as part of NATO's campaign of air strikes against former Yugoslavia during the Kosovo conflict. During this intervention, 16 people were killed and 16 others injured. The case was brought against 17 Member States of NATO, which were also ECHR Contracting States. The

[137] Ibid. The same statement was reiterated in a recent admissibility decision, *Sedelmayer v Germany* (App Nos 30190/06; 30216/06), decision, 10 November 2009, not yet reported, para 1.

[138] *McElhinney v United Kingdom* (n 90 above), para 37; *Fogarty v United Kingdom* (n 90 above), para 36; *Al-Adsani v United Kingdom* (n 90 above), para 56.

[139] See, for further details, McLachlan (n 86 above), 304–306.

[140] Rosalyn Higgins, 'A Babel of Judicial Voices? Ruminations from the Bench' (2006) 55 Int'l Comp LQ 791, 793.

[141] *McElhinney v United Kingdom* (App No 31253/96), decision, 9 February 2000, not reported; *Fogarty v United Kingdom* (App No 37112/97), decision, 1 March 2000, not reported; *Al-Adsani v United Kingdom* (App No 35763/97), decision, 1 March 2000, not reported.

[142] *Banković and others v Belgium and 16 Other Contracting States* (App No 52207/99), judgment, 12 December 2001, Reports 2001-XII, 333.

applicants complained that the bombardment of the RTS headquarters by NATO violated Articles 2, 10, and 13 of the ECHR. Noting that the impugned act was performed, or had effects, outside the territory of the respondent States, the Court considered that the essential question to be examined was whether the applicants and their deceased relatives were, as a result of that extraterritorial act, capable of falling within the jurisdiction of the respondent States. The main issues in the case therefore related to the question of whether the applicants fell within the jurisdiction of the respondent State within the meaning of Article 1 of the ECHR and to the meaning of the expression 'within their jurisdiction' in that article.

When considering the expression 'within their jurisdiction', the Court recalled that the ECHR must be interpreted in light of the rules contained in the VCLT. Thus, it stated that it would have regard to the object and purpose of the Convention, to any subsequent practice in its application, as well as to any relevant rules of international law. In support of this finding the Court stated more generally that:

> the principles underlying the Convention cannot be interpreted and applied in a vacuum. The Court must also take into account any relevant rules of international law when examining questions concerning its jurisdiction and, consequently, determine State responsibility in conformity with the governing principles of international law, although it must remain mindful of the Convention's special character as a human rights treaty.... The Convention should be interpreted as far as possible in harmony with other principles of international law of which it forms part.[143]

Relying on this reasoning, the Court was able to incorporate rules of international law into its findings. It determined that, from the standpoint of public international law, the 'ordinary meaning' of the term 'jurisdiction' in Article 1 is primarily territorial.[144] While international law did not exclude a state's exercise of jurisdiction extra-territorially, the suggested bases of such jurisdiction (including nationality, flag, diplomatic and consular relations, effect, protection, passive personality, and universality) were, as a general rule, defined and limited by the sovereign territorial rights of the other relevant states.[145] Furthermore, 'a State may not actually exercise jurisdiction on the territory of another without the latter's consent, invitation or acquiescence, unless the former is an occupying State in which case it can be found to exercise jurisdiction in that territory, at least in certain respects'.[146] The Court stated that Article 1 must therefore be considered to reflect this ordinary and essentially territorial notion of jurisdiction, other bases of jurisdiction being exceptional and requiring special justification in the particular circumstances of each case.[147] Given that this reasoning could entail detrimental consequences for the Contracting States, it is not surprising that the Court's construction of the notion of jurisdiction was restrictive and did not include any other types of jurisdiction. A more expansive interpretation of this

143 Ibid, para 57. 144 Ibid, para 59. 145 Ibid. 146 Ibid, para 60.
147 Ibid, para 61.

notion may have been met with strong opposition from the Contracting States, given that the Court could be seen as infringing the consensual jurisdiction upon which the ECHR is based.

Article 31(3)(c) of the VCLT constituted an integral part of the Court's reasoning in child abduction cases under Article 8 of the ECHR. These cases were very closely intertwined with the 1980 Hague Convention on the Civil Aspects of International Child Abduction, which was invoked and applied in the domestic proceedings. Most of the cases concerned the question of whether domestic decisions taken subsequent to a parent's abduction of a child to another country complied with the ECHR. The Strasbourg Court had no jurisdiction to examine direct complaints concerning the implementation of the 1980 Hague Convention. It could evaluate, however, whether the decisions taken by the domestic authorities in application of their margin of appreciation complied with the ECHR. In this context, the Court used Article 31(3)(c) of the VCLT as a means of referring to the 1980 Hague Convention.[148] It then established that the ECHR articles relevant to child abduction must be interpreted in light of the 1980 Hague Convention.[149] The Court's references in this context were mostly prompted by necessity, given that the 1980 Hague Convention was part of the facts of the case. Further, the Court's choice in relying on this instrument was not excessively controversial due to its generally procedural character. This trend in the Strasbourg jurisprudence is, however, discussed later in this volume and will not be examined in great detail here.[150]

Subsequently, the Court used Article 31(3)(c) in the *Mamatkulov and Abdurasulovic v Turkey*[151] and *Mamatkulov and Askarov v Turkey*[152] cases as a gateway, allowing it to resort to legal principles as well as approaches used by the treaty bodies and international courts. In the Chamber and in the Grand Chamber judgment in the *Mamatkulov* case, the Court considered, *inter alia*, the question of whether the power to order binding interim measures could be

[148] *Bianchi v Switzerland* (App No 7548/04), judgment, 22 June 2006, not reported, available in French only, para 81. See also *Streletz, Kessler, and Krenz v Germany* (App Nos 34044/96; 35532/97; 44801/98), judgment, 22 March 2001, Reports 2001-II, 409, para 90; *Al-Adsani v United Kingdom* (App No 35763/97), decision, 1 March 2000, not reported, para 55.

[149] *Ignaccolo-Zenide v Romania* (App No 31679/96), judgment, 25 January 2000, Reports 2000-I, 241, para 95; *Monory v Romania and Hungary* (App No 71099/01), judgment, 5 April 2005, not reported, para 73; *Guichard v France* (App No 56838/00), decision, 2 September 2003, Reports 2003-X, 419, 431–432; *Paradis v Germany* (App No 4783/03), decision, 15 May 2003, not reported; *Iglesias Gil and AUI v Spain* (App No 56673/00), judgment, 19 April 2003, Reports 2003-V, 275, para 51; *Iosub Caras v Romania* (App No. 7198/04), Judgment, 17 July 2006, not reported, para 33; *Karadzic v Croatia* (App No 35030/04), judgment, 12 December 2005, not reported, para 54; *HN v Poland* (App No 77710/01), judgment, 13 September 2005, not reported, para 75; *Sylvester v Austria (No 1)* (App Nos 36812/97; 40104/98), judgment, 24 April 2003, not reported, para 57.

[150] See ch III, 2.3.

[151] *Mamatkulov and Abdurasulovic v Turkey* (n 81 above).

[152] *Mamatkulov and Askarov v Turkey* (n 82 above).

derived from Article 34 of the ECHR, taken alone or in conjunction with Rule 39 of the Rules of the Court. The reasoning of the Court on this point in both judgments is very similar and thus this analysis will focus on the latest judgment. The Grand Chamber observed that in examining the case, it would 'also have regard to general principles of international law and the view expressed on this subject by other international bodies since *Cruz Varas and Others*'.[153] It further recalled that the Convention must be interpreted in the light of the rules set out in the VCLT, including Article 31(3)(c).[154] The Court decided that it would determine the responsibility of the states in accordance with the principles of international law governing this sphere while taking into account the special nature of the ECHR as an instrument of human rights protection.

The Court conducted a very thorough evaluation of the trends in the international legal landscape concerning interim measures.[155] Its analysis included the approaches taken by the UN Human Rights Committee, the UN Committee Against Torture, the Inter-American Court of Human Rights, and the International Court of Justice. It was noted that '[i]n a number of recent decisions and orders, international courts and institutions have stressed the importance and purpose of interim measures and pointed out that compliance with such measure was necessary to ensure the effectiveness of their decisions on the merits'.[156] Furthermore, the Court emphasized that 'the ICJ, the Inter-American Court of Human Rights, the Human Rights Committee and the Committee against Torture of United Nations, although operating under different treaty provisions to those of the Court, have confirmed in their reasoning in recent decisions that the preservation of the asserted rights of the parties in the face of the risk of irreparable damage represents an essential objective of interim measures in international law'.[157] Also, independently of the legal system in question, 'the proper administration of justice requires that no irreparable action be taken while proceedings are pending'.[158]

Applying this reasoning to the ECHR context, the Court noted that '[t]he notion of an effective remedy under Article 13 ECHR requires a remedy capable of preventing the execution of measures that are contrary to the Convention and whose effects are potentially irreversible'.[159] As in other international legal systems, interim measures play a fundamental role in averting such situations and allowing the Court to examine an application properly. Thus, under the ECHR system, a failure by a respondent state to comply with interim measures undermines the

[153] Ibid, para 110 (italics in original).

[154] Ibid, para 111; *Mamatkulov and Abdurasulovic v Turkey* (n 81 above), para 99.

[155] *Mamatkulov and Askarov v Turkey* (n 82 above), paras 112–117; *Mamatkulov and Abdurasulovic v Turkey* (n 81 above), paras 100–104.

[156] *Mamatkulov and Askarov v Turkey* (n 82 above) para 113; *Mamatkulov and Abdurasulovic v Turkey* (n 81 above), para 101.

[157] Ibid, para 124. See also Mark E Villiger, *Commentary on the 1969 Vienna Convention on the Law of Treaties* (Leiden/Boston: Martinus Nijhoff, 2009), 434, para 25.

[158] *Mamatkulov and Abdurasulovic v Turkey* (n 81 above), para 101.

[159] Ibid.

effectiveness of the right to individual petition guaranteed by Article 34 of the ECHR. According to the view expressed by the Court in the Grand Chamber and Chamber judgments, Turkey breached its obligations under Article 34 by failing to comply with the measures indicated under Rule 39 of the Rules of the Court.

The Court's reasoning in both *Mamatkulov* judgments[160] was very bold and courageous, as the Court decided that interim measures would be binding. Furthermore, the Court aided in the further consolidation of international law pertaining to interim measures. This development was strongly criticized by some of the dissenting judges in the case. It was argued, *inter alia*, that the Court imposed its views on the Contracting States without their consent.[161] The Court had relied on the case law of the ICJ based on Article 41 of the ICJ Statute, a provision which has been found to impose binding interim measures. The dissenting judges considered that there was no similar provision in the ECHR. It was further noted that 'there is a wide difference between the mere *interpretation* of a treaty and its *amendment*, between the exercise of judicial functions and international law-making'.[162] In its view, the Grand Chamber and the Chamber both exercised 'a *legislative function*, for the Convention as it stands nowhere prescribes that the State Parties to it must recognise the binding force of interim measures indicated by this Court'.[163]

The dissenting judges also applied Article 31(3)(c) of the VCLT in order to verify whether the Court could order interim measures on the basis of a rule of general international law or a general principle of law 'recognised by civilised nations'. With regard to the former, the dissenting judges noted that 'there may well be a widespread rule on obligatory interim measures on the domestic level, based on the rule of compulsory jurisdiction applicable on that level'.[164] This rule does not, however, prevail on the international level and this principle cannot be transposed to the context of an international court. Thus, the dissenting judges considered that power to order interim measures could not be derived from Article 34, Article 26(d), or from general international law. Furthermore, it was found that the subject-matter under examination was one which belonged to the sphere of legislation and not judicial action. These findings were indeed strong and demonstrate the amplitude of the Court's intervention and reliance on international law to determine the nature of interim measures under the ECHR.

Most recently, in the *Saadi v United Kingdom* case,[165] the Court used Article 31(3)(c) of the VCLT when interpreting for the first time a phrase contained in Article 5(1)(f) of the ECHR.[166] The *Saadi* case concerned an Iraqi doctor who

[160] Ibid.

[161] Ibid, joint partly dissenting opinion of Judges Caflisch, Türmen, and Kovler, para 11.

[162] Ibid (italics in original). [163] Ibid (italics in original). [164] Ibid, para 22.

[165] *Saadi v United Kingdom* (App No 13229/03), judgment, 29 January 2008, not yet reported. See ch VI, 2.2.5 and 2.2.6.

[166] See also the recent *Rantsev* case, where the Court used Art 31(3)(c) of the VCLT when it considered trafficking in human beings, a phenomenon which it has never encountered before as part of its case law. Using other rules of international law, it has deduced from Art 4 of the ECHR

belonged to the Iraqi Workers' Communist Party. He fled from his home country after having treated and helped to escape three fellow party members. When he arrived at London Heathrow Airport he claimed asylum and was initially granted temporary admission. He was taken into detention at the Oakington Reception Centre as part of a fast-tack procedure for determining asylum claims. He was detained there for seven days and was given reasons for his detention 76 hours after being taken in. The applicant alleged that the respondent Government had infringed Article 5(1) and (2) of the ECHR. In the Chamber and the Grand Chamber judgments, the Court found that there was no violation of Article 5(1), but held unanimously that there had been a breach of Article 5(2).[167]

In the Grand Chamber judgment, the Court analysed for the first time the meaning of the expression 'lawful . . . detention of a person to prevent his effecting an unauthorised entry' contained in Article 5(1)(f). The applicant had submitted that this expression should be interpreted in light of Articles 31 to 33 of the VCLT. He also referred to the case law of the Human Rights Committee[168] and suggested that similar principles should be applied under Article 5(1)(f). The Court observed that 'it will, as always, be guided by Articles 31 to 33 of the Vienna Convention on the Law of Treaties'.[169] Thus, it reiterated that the ECHR had to be interpreted according to the ordinary meaning of its words in their context and in light of their object and purpose (Article 31(1) of the VCLT).[170] It then referred to Article 31(3)(c) of the VCLT and stated that it would also take into account any relevant rules and principles of international law applicable in relations between the Contracting States.[171]

When applying these rules to the case, the Court emphasized that Article 5 of the ECHR enshrines a fundamental human right, namely the protection of the individual against arbitrary state interferences with his right to liberty.[172] Article 5(1)(f) provides an exception to this general rule by permitting the detention of foreigners in an immigration context. The Court recalled that states have the 'undeniable sovereign right to control aliens' entry into and residence in their territory'.[173] They are 'permitted to detain would-be immigrants who have applied for permission to enter, whether by way of asylum or not'.[174] The Court

a procedural obligation to investigate alleged trafficking, a positive obligation to put in place an appropriate legislative and administrative framework, and a positive obligation to take protective measures against trafficking: *Rantsev v Cyprus and Russia* (App No 25965/04), judgment, 7 January 2010, not yet reported.

[167] *Saadi v United Kingdom* (App No 13229/03), judgment, 11 July 2006, not reported. See ch VI, 2.2.5 and 2.2.6.

[168] *A v Australia*, Communication No 560/1993, CCPR/C/59/D/560/1993, 30 April 1997, Human Rights Committee; *C v Australia*, Communication No 900/1999, CCPR/C/76/D/900/1999, 28 October 2002, Human Rights Committee; *Celeri v Sweden*, Communication No 456/1991, CCPR/C/51/D/456/1991, 26 July 1994, Human Rights Committee; *Saadi v United Kingdom* (App No 13229/03), judgment, 11 July 2006, not reported, para 31.

[169] *Saadi v United Kingdom* (n 165 above).

[170] Ibid, para 62.

[171] Ibid.

[172] Ibid, para 63.

[173] Ibid, para 64.

[174] Ibid.

deferred to the findings of the House of Lords and the Chamber by holding that until a state authorizes entry into a country any entry remains unauthorized. Thus, persons who wish to enter the country but do not have the required authorization can be detained under Article 5(1)(f).[175]

The Court did not accept that, as soon as an asylum-seeker surrendered to the immigration authorities, he could be considered to be making an authorized entry. According to its view, interpreting Article 5(1)(f) only to permit detention of 'a person who is trying to evade entry restrictions would be to place too narrow a construction on the terms of the provision and on the power of the State to exercise its undeniable right of control'.[176] Moreover, such an interpretation would 'be inconsistent with Conclusion No. 44 of the Executive Committee of the United Nations High Commissioner for Refugees' Programme, the UNHCR's Guidelines and the Committee of Ministers' Recommendation..., all of which envisage the detention of asylum seekers in certain circumstances, for example while identity checks are taking place or when elements on which the asylum claim is based have to be determined'.[177] The Court went on to consider the meaning of the expression 'freedom from arbitrariness' contained in Article 5(1)(f). In this part of its judgment, it no longer relied on international law.

The Court was criticized by its own members in a joint partly dissenting opinion.[178] According to their view, the Court's finding that states are permitted to detain would-be immigrants who have applied for permission to enter did not comply with international law. It did not sit comfortably 'with the principle that asylum seekers who have presented a claim for international protection are *ipso facto* within the territory of a State, in particular for the purposes of Article 12 of the International Convention on Civil and Political Rights (liberty of movement) and the case-law of the Human Rights Committee, according to which a persons has duly presented an application for asylum is considered to be "lawfully within the territory"'.[179] Further, it was stated that the Court should have followed the finding of the Human Rights Committee that Article 9 of the International Covenant on Civil and Political Rights (ICCPR) prohibits detention on grounds of administrative expediency.[180] However, the most important question for the partly dissenting judges was whether it was 'permissible today for the European Convention on Human Rights to provide a lower level of protection than that which is recognized and accepted in the other organisations'.[181]

Thus, the Court invoked Article 31(3)(c) of the VCLT in order to legitimize its reliance on soft law documents issued by the UNHCR. Given that the applicants invoked Articles 31 to 33 of the VCLT before the Court, it was not surprising to find references to these articles in the judgment. Further, the Court stated that it

175 Ibid, para 65. 176 Ibid. 177 Ibid.

178 Ibid, joint partly dissenting opinion of Judges Rozakis, Tulkens, Kovler, Hajiyev, Spielmann, and Hirvelä. 179 Ibid (italics in original).

180 Ibid. *Van Alphen v The Netherlands*, Communication No 305/1988, CCPR/C/39/D/305/1988, 23 July 1990, Human Rights Committee. 181 *Saadi v United Kingdom* (n 165 above).

would be guided, as always, by these provisions in its reasoning. On this basis, it could be hypothesized that—even in the absence of the explicit references—the Court always uses Article 31(3)(c) when it invokes international law. In addition, the Court has used Article 31(3)(c) to rubber stamp its expansive interpretation of state powers under Article 5(1)(f) of the ECHR in light of UNHCR soft law instruments. This way, it has evaded the more restrictive ICCPR provisions and case law of the Human Rights Committee, which were favoured by the partly dissenting judges. The Court's interpretation of the UNHCR soft law instruments seems to be strained and incompatible with the meaning attributed to them by the UNHCR (intervening as third party in this case).[182]

From the foregoing survey of cases, it transpires that the Court has resorted to Article 31(3)(c) when substantive issues of fundamental importance for the protection of human rights have presented themselves. Most of the cases before the Court concerned crucial questions pertaining to the very nature of state immunity, reservations, access to court, jurisdiction, interim measures, and detention of asylum-seekers. Some also concerned certain procedural aspects of child abduction; these cases are analysed in Chapter III.[183] In all these fields, the margin of appreciation granted to states was wide. It does not appear, however, that this margin has played a constant role in the Court's reasoning. Indeed, the Court's findings seem to have been more dependent on the circumstances of each case.

Overall, the Court has used Article 31(3)(c) as a gateway to international instruments and as a means to support an expansive or restrictive reading of the ECHR provisions. In some cases, it appears that the Court needed Article 31(3)(c) as a rubber stamp legitimating its use of international law. It is, nonetheless, puzzling that the Court has not resorted to this provision in all the other cases referring to international law. In those instances, it could be argued that the references to Article 31(3)(c) were implicit in the Court's reasoning, given that the Court is always guided by the VCLT interpretation rules. These inferences are probably the only ones that can be drawn at present; further conclusions concerning the Court's resort to Article 31(3)(c) seem to be precluded, since the references made were not sufficiently numerous and substantiated to exhibit a more significant trend in the Court's approach.

2.5 *Travaux Préparatoires*

The *travaux préparatoires* or the preparatory works are included in Article 32 of the VCLT, which refers to supplementary means of interpretation. The International Law Commission chose not to define this term fearing that 'to do so might only lead to the possible exclusion of relevant evidence'.[184] The nature of preparatory

[182] Ibid, paras 54–57. [183] See ch III, 2.3.

[184] *Report of the International Law Commission on the Work of its Eighteenth Session* (Geneva, 4 May to 19 July 1966), 1966 (2) Yearbook of the International Law Commission 173, 223, para 20.

work of a treaty is extremely heterogeneous in character[185] and it should thus be understood in a broad sense as including all documents relevant to a forthcoming treaty and generated by the parties during a treaty's preparation until its conclusion.[186] These usually include memoranda, statements, and observations of governments transmitted to each other or to the drafting body, diplomatic exchanges between the parties, treaty drafts, negotiation records, and minutes of commission, and plenary meeting. Such documents, produced at different times and by different bodies, may sometimes contradict themselves. They can serve as aids in interpretation, but the extent to which they are used will depend on their cogency, accessibility, direct relevance, consistency among the means found, the number of parties involved in the evolution of the particular terms, and the reactions of other parties.[187] They are not the primary means of interpretation; Article 32 of the VCLT provides that they can be used to confirm the meaning resulting from the application of Article 31 or to determine the meaning when the interpretation according to Article 31 leaves it ambiguous or obscure. They can also be resorted to when the general rule in Article 31 leads to a result that is manifestly absurd or unreasonable.

Despite these narrow conditions, it appears that the *travaux préparatoires* can be invoked in a wide variety of circumstances.[188] As stressed by the International Law Commission, it is only logic that suggests that the supplementary means of interpretation should follow, and not precede, the previous paragraphs. Nonetheless, these means of interpretation 'are all of an obligatory character and by their very nature could not be considered to be norms of interpretation in any way inferior to those which precede them'.[189] Caflisch and Cançado Trindade have suggested that they can always be invoked in the context of general international law.[190] Similarly, Villiger expressed the view that it could be difficult to find instances where they are not applicable.[191] These perceptions seem to be more in tune with the ECHR practice than the view that recourse to *travaux préparatoires* 'is permissible in carefully controlled circumstances'.[192]

[185] Villiger (n 12 above), 328; Linderfalk (n 12 above), 241.

[186] Villiger (n 12 above). Interestingly, it has recently been proposed on the basis of doctrinal arguments to define the term 'preparatory work of the treaty' as 'representation, whether textual or non-textual, produced during the drafting of a treaty': Linderfalk (n 12 above), 241. This definition leaves a wide discretion to judges, but it does not necessarily entail a loss of legal certainty or promote judicial activism. While the discussion of the definition of *travaux préparatoires* is beyond the scope of this study, it is submitted that this expression should not be understood in a narrow sense, as it would deprive the judge of its legitimate interpretation duties. Interpretation conducted in accordance with *travaux préparatoires* should, nonetheless, be used with caution in the specific context of human rights treaties.

[187] *Report of the International Law Commission on the Work of its Eighteenth Session* (n 184 above), 223, paras 19–20.

[188] Caflisch and Cançado Trindade (n 64 above), 19–20.

[189] *Report of the International Law Commission on the Work of its Eighteenth Session* (n 184 above), 220, para 9.

[190] Caflisch and Cançado Trindade (n 64 above), 19–20.

[191] Villiger (n 12 above), 328.

[192] Sinclair (n 47 above), 142.

Ovey and White nonetheless rightly suggest that the *travaux préparatoires* should be invoked with some caution, due to their limited utility and reliability.[193] The authors found that 'because of the special features of the European Convention [they] should be invoked, if at all, as a guide to the general intentions of the Parties, rather than to delimit strictly the scope of particular articles'.[194] Moreover, given that the Court has confirmed that the ECHR is a living instrument and has used a dynamic interpretation in its reasoning, they found that caution is required with regard to the use of preparatory work. It could be argued that following the Court's finding that the ECHR is a 'living instrument', the ECtHR has rejected the rule contained in Article 32 of the VCLT with regard to preparatory work. This argument does not, however, accurately reflect the reality of the Court's practice. It appears that the Court has resorted to the rule enshrined in Article 32, albeit sparingly. It has used it on occasion and, in some instances, has either bypassed the article or demonstrated reticence towards using it. It therefore seems to have adopted a rather cautious approach towards this means of interpretation.

In *Lawless v Ireland*,[195] the Court declined to use the *travaux préparatoires* finding that Article 5 of the ECHR was sufficiently clear. The *Lawless* case concerned a state of emergency declared by the United Kingdom under Article 15 of the ECHR on 5 July 1957. The derogation was a response to the impending release of almost 100 Irish Republic Army (IRA) prisoners and general fears of the Irish Government as to the intensification of IRA terrorist activities. At this time, the applicant was arrested and charged with unlawful possession of arms; he was later acquitted of this charge. Lawless admitted that he had been a member of the IRA but that he had left the organization. Subsequently, he was arrested again on suspicion of engaging in unlawful activities and was convicted for possession of incriminating documents. He served his sentence and was released. He was re-arrested when about to embark on a ship for England. He was detained for 24 hours, being a suspected IRA member. Following this, he was sent to a military camp where he was informed that he would be released, provided that he gave an undertaking in writing to respect the Constitution and laws of Ireland and not to be a member of an unlawful organization. At first, Lawless declined to give this undertaking, but later changed his mind and was released. Before the Strasbourg bodies, the applicant complained that his detention without trial had breached Articles 5, 6, 7, and 15 of the ECHR. The Court found that Articles 5 and 6 provided no legal foundation for the detention without trial. It also considered that there was no violation of Article 7. Further, Lawless' detention was based on the right of derogation duly exercised by the Irish Government under Article 15.

[193] Clare Ovey and Robin CA White, *The European Convention on Human Rights* (Oxford/New York: OUP, 4th edn, 2006), 40.

[194] Ibid (text inserted by the author).

[195] *Lawless v Ireland* (App No 332/57), judgment, 1 July 1961, Series A, Vol 3.

In its judgment, the Court considered the question of whether Article 5(1)(c) and (3) prescribes that a person arrested or detained 'when it is reasonably considered necessary to prevent his committing an offence' shall be brought before a judge. The Court found that Article 5(1)(c) 'is sufficiently clear to give an answer to this question'.[196] Moreover, 'it is evident that the expression "effected for purpose of bringing him before the competent legal authority" qualifies every category of cases of arrest or detention referred to in that sub-paragraph'.[197] Therefore, this provision 'permits deprivation of liberty only when such deprivation is effected for the purpose of bringing the person arrested or detained before the competent judicial authority, irrespective of whether such person is a person who is reasonably suspected of having committed an offence, or a person whom it is reasonably considered necessary to restrain from committing an offence, or a person whom it reasonably considered necessary to restrain from absconding after having committed an offence'.[198] Thus, 'having ascertained that the text of Article 5, paragraphs 1 (c) and 3, is sufficiently clear in itself', the Court found that it 'cannot, having regard to a generally recognised principle regarding the interpretation of international treaties, resort to the preparatory work'.[199]

It is interesting to note that in its report[200] in the *Lawless* case, the Commission also referred to preparatory work, but in a different context. Several members of the Commission resorted to preparatory work in the framework of Article 15 of the ECHR in order to confirm that 'a public emergency threatening the life of the nation' was meant to bear the meaning which they considered to be natural and ordinary, namely 'a situation of exceptional and imminent danger or crisis affecting the general public, as distinct from particular groups, and constituting a threat to the organised life of the community which composes the State in question'.[201] Preparatory work was also used by another member[202] to validate, *inter alia*, his argument that this expression could be defined as 'an emergency of such magnitude that it affects not one section of the population, but the nation as a whole'.[203]

In the *Golder* case,[204] the Court considered the working papers of the ECHR Consultative Assembly in the context of its use of Article 31(3)(c) of the VCLT. As already mentioned, the Court examined the question of whether the right of access to the Court was inherent in Article 6(1) of the VCLT. Using Article 31(3)(c), the Court referred to Article 38(1)(c) of the ICJ Statute pertaining to 'the general principles of law recognised by civilised nations'. It further observed that 'the Legal Committee of the Consultative Assembly of the Council of Europe foresaw in August 1950 that "the Commission and the Court must necessarily apply such

[196] Ibid, para 14. [197] Ibid. [198] Ibid. [199] Ibid.
[200] *Lawless v Ireland* (App No 332/57), report, 19 December 1959, Series B, Vol 1.
[201] Ibid, opinion of MM Waldock, Berg, Faber, Crosbie, and Erim, para 90.
[202] Ibid, opinion of M Eustathiades.
[203] Ibid, para 92. See also, ibid, para 93, opinion of M Süsterhenn.
[204] *Golder v United Kingdom* (n 1 above).

principles" in the execution of their duties and thus considered it to be "unnecessary" to insert a specific clause to this effect in the Convention'.[205]

The relevant passage of the report of the Consultative Assembly to which the Court alluded provides the following:

> The Committee, while recognising the importance of the proposal that the European Commission and the Court should apply the general principles of law recognised among civilised states, as referred to in Article 38 of the Statute of the International Court, were of the opinion that the insertion of a specific clause to this effect was unnecessary, but wished to recommend to the Assembly that in transmitting the draft Convention to the Committee of Ministers the attention of the latter might be drawn to this point. It is anticipated that the Commission and the Court must necessarily apply such principles in coming to any decision.[206]

This old statement from the preparatory work confirms once more the idea that the ECtHR should resort to international law in its case law.

The Court went on to consider the relevant principles of international law which allowed it to conclude that the right of access to a court was inherent in Article 6(1) of the ECHR. It used international instruments as an aid in interpretation and as a means to confirm the interpretation resulting from the application of Article 31(3)(c) of the VCLT. Interestingly, the Court clarified that it reached the conclusion, 'without needing to resort to "supplementary means of interpretation" as envisaged at Article 32 of the Vienna Convention, that Article 6 para 1 secures to everyone the right to have any claim relating to his civil rights and obligations brought before a court or tribunal. In this way the Article embodies the "right to a court", of which the right of access, that is the right to institute proceedings before courts in civil matters, constitutes one aspect only.'[207] Despite this finding, it is nonetheless submitted that the Court has clearly relied on supplementary means of interpretation by using the working papers of the Consultative Assembly, which appear to constitute *travaux préparatoires*. Thus, the Court's interpretation of the term 'supplementary means of interpretation' was too narrow in this case.

In its report[208] in the *Golder* case, the Commission adhered strictly to the requirements of Article 32 of the VCLT when resorting to the preparatory work. It clarified that:

> according to Art. 32 of the Vienna Convention, preparatory works are only supplementary means to which recourse may be had (a) to confirm the meaning resulting from the application of the 'general rule', (b) to determine the meaning when this rule leaves it

[205] Ibid, para 35. See also Consultative Assembly of the Council of Europe, *Report on the Draft Convention for the Protection of Human Rights and Fundamental Freedoms*, Ordinary Session 1950, 24 August 1950, Doc 93, 983.

[206] Consultative Assembly of the Council of Europe, ibid.

[207] Ibid, para 36.

[208] *Golder v United Kingdom* (n 120 above).

ambiguous or obscure, or (c) to correct a manifestly absurd or unreasonable result but, in the Commission's reading of art. 32, not to depart from the result of the application of the general rule in other cases.[209]

Finding that the case at hand fulfilled condition (b) among those enumerated, the Commission thus decided to resort to the preparatory work.[210] In the context of the examination of Article 6(1) of the ECHR, it was found that 'those who drafted the Convention did not consider the question of the right of access to the courts nor was it mentioned during the discussion in the Consultative Assembly'.[211] The Commission noted that the first versions of the ECHR had resembled Article 10 of the Universal Declaration of Human Rights[212] and Article 13 of the International Covenant on Civil and Political Rights. It was at the last minute that the expression 'rights and obligations in a suit at law' was replaced in the English text by 'civil rights and obligations'. This may have been done in order to bring the French and English version of the text into line. According to the Commission, '[n]either the study of the history of the Convention itself, nor the texts and travaux préparatoires of related provisions in the United Nations instruments . . . contain anything which . . . contradicts the interpretation arrived at'.[213]

In *Lithgow v United Kingdom*,[214] discussed above,[215] the Court resorted to the preparatory work when it determined that the term 'general principles of international law' in Article 1 of Protocol No 1 was not applicable to a taking by a state of the property of its own nationals. In that case, the applicants asserted that treating the 'general principles of international law' as being inapplicable to this situation permitted differentiation on the ground of nationality. The Court considered that, while most ECHR provisions guaranteed the same protection to nationals and non-nationals, there were some legitimate reasons to introduce a distinction with regard to the taking of property. Subsequently, '[c]onfronted with a text whose interpretation has given rise to such disagreement',[216] the Court felt that it was proper to have recourse to the *travaux préparatoires* as a supplementary means of interpretation. It further found that the '[e]xamination of the travaux préparatoires reveals that the express reference to a right to compensation contained in earlier drafts of Article 1 was excluded, notably in the face of opposition on part of the United Kingdom and other States. The mention of the general principles of international law was subsequently included and was subject to several statements to the effect that they protected only foreigners.'[217]

[209] Ibid, para 46. [210] Ibid, para 60. [211] Ibid, para 61.

[212] Universal Declaration of Human Rights, adopted and proclaimed by United Nations General Assembly resolution 217 A (III) of 10 December 1948.

[213] *Golder v United Kingdom* (n 1 above).

[214] *Lithgow and others v United Kingdom* (n 15 above). [215] See 2.1 above.

[216] *Lithgow v United Kingdom* (n 15 above), para 117. [217] Ibid.

The Court noted that 'it was agreed, at the request of the German and Belgian delegation, that "the general principles of international law, in their present connotation, entailed the obligation to pay compensation to non-nationals in cases of expropriation" '.[218] It was then reiterated that the Committee of Ministers in Resolution 52(1) of 19 March 1952 approving the text of Protocol No 1 stated that the general principles of international law entailed the obligation to pay compensation to non-nationals in cases of expropriation. Ultimately, the Court determined that, having regard to the negotiating history, 'this Resolution must be taken as a clear indication that the reference to the general principles of international law was not intended to extend to nationals'.[219] In this case, the preparatory work was used in the last phase of the Court's interpretation, as an ultimate confirmation of the interpretation obtained following the application of Article 31 of the VCLT. The Court also underlined that general principles of international law were used as supplementary means of interpretation. Furthermore, it appears that the extent of the disagreement with regard to the question examined in the case may have prompted the Court to use this means of interpretation. It should also be noted that the Court made the same references to preparatory work in the *James* case,[220] discussed above,[221] as part of the examination of the same question in that case.

In its report in *Lithgow v United Kingdom*,[222] the Commission found that 'any ambiguity... can be conclusively resolved by reference to the travaux préparatoires which confirm that the intention of the Contracting States was not to extend the applicability of the principles of international law to cover the taking of the property of nationals'.[223] The preparatory work used by the Commission was the same as that relied on by the Court.[224] Interestingly, in the *James and others v United Kingdom* decision,[225] the Commission did not pay further attention to the preparatory work, although it was invoked and thoroughly analysed by the parties in that case.

In *Johnston and others v Ireland*,[226] as already mentioned,[227] the Court examined the question of whether the applicants could derive a right to divorce from Article 12 of the ECHR. First, the Court attempted to ascertain the ordinary meaning to be given to the terms in the provision by taking into account their context as well as the object and purpose of the provision.[228] The Court's examination of the *travaux préparatoires* was conducted as part of the teleological interpretation of Article 12; the Court considered that the ordinary meaning of the expression 'right to marry',

[218] Ibid. [219] Ibid.
[220] *James and others v United Kingdom* (n 14 above). [221] See 2.1 above.
[222] *Lithgow v United Kingdom* (App Nos 9006/80; 9262/81; 9263/81; 9265/81; 9266/81; 9313/81; 9405/81), report, 7 March 1984, Series B, Vol 85. [223] Ibid, para 364.
[224] Ibid.
[225] *James and others v United Kingdom* (App No 8793/79), decision, 28 January 1983, DR 30, 30. [226] *Johnston and others v Ireland* (n 16 above).
[227] See 2.1 above. [228] *Johnston and others v Ireland* (n 16 above), paras 51–52.

which covers only the formation of marital relations and not their dissolution, 'is consistent with its object and purpose as revealed by the travaux préparatoires'.[229] The Court then reminded that the wording of Article 12 is based on that of Article 16(1) of the Universal Declaration of Human Rights, which stipulates that men and women of full age 'are entitled to equal rights as to marriage, during marriage and at dissolution'. This was further supported by the contentions of Mr Teitgen, the Rapporteur of the Committee on Legal and Administrative Questions, who explained that the Consultative Assembly did not mention this sentence of Article 16(1) in Article 12, as it intended to guarantee only the right to marry.[230] Thus, the Court reached the conclusion that *travaux préparatoires* disclose no intention to have the right to divorce included in Article 12.

It appears that the Court's assessment of preparatory work intervened at a different stage in this decision; it was almost simultaneous to the evaluation of the purpose of Article 12. In fact, the examinations of both elements were closely intertwined to the extent that they mutually clarified each other. Thus, the preparatory work was not merely a confirmation of the interpretation carried out pursuant to Article 31 of the VCLT. Further, the Court's finding followed that reached earlier by the Commission in its report, which made an even more extensive use of preparatory work invoked by the parties.[231] Attaching particular attention to the fact that various Contracting States did not provide for the dissolution of marriage in their legislation, the Commission considered that Article 12 did not contain a right to divorce.[232]

In *Sigurdur A Sigurjonsson v Iceland*,[233] the Court found that the use of *travaux préparatoires* in the earlier *Young, James and Webster* case,[234] relating to a similar issue, was not decisive. The *Sigurjonsson* case concerned an Icelandic taxi driver living in Reykjavik who had refused to join an automobile association which protected taxi-cab drivers' rights. Membership of the association was, under Icelandic law, a prerequisite for the acquisition of a taxi-cab driver's licence. The applicant complained that the subsequent refusal by the relevant authorities to grant him a licence violated his right not to join an association, which he claimed was protected by Articles 9, 10, 11, and 13 of the ECHR. The Court found a violation of Article 11 and held that it was not necessary to examine the remaining articles.

As part of its examination of the question of whether the objection to take part in the association was covered under Article 11 of the ECHR, the Court

[229] Ibid, para 52.
[230] *Johnston and others v Ireland* (App No 9697/82), judgment, 18 December 1986, Series A, Vol 112, para 52.
[231] *Johnston and others v Ireland* (App No 9697/82), report, 15 March 1985, Series B, Vol 95, paras 93–99.
[232] Ibid, para 99.
[233] *Sigurdur A Sigurjonsson v Iceland* (App No 16130/90), judgment, 30 June 1993, Series A, Vol 264.
[234] *Young, James and Webstser v United Kingdom* (App Nos 7601/76; 7806/77), judgment, 13 August 1981, Series A, Vol 44.

found 'that although the [*Young, James and Webster v United Kingdom*] judgment took account of the travaux préparatoires, it did not attach decisive importance to them; rather it used them as a working hypothesis'.[235] Furthermore, when reviewing the current status of the right not to be compelled to join an association, the Court noted that '[a] growing measure of common ground has emerged in this area... at the international level'[236] and among the Contracting States. It thus held that 'the Convention is a living instrument which must be interpreted in the light of present-day conditions.... Accordingly, Article 11 must be viewed as encompassing a negative right of association.'[237] The Commission, in its report[238] and decision,[239] did not take the preparatory work into consideration. The *Sigurjonsson* case thus confirmed that the Strasbourg bodies' approach to *travaux préparatoires* was circumspect and cautious.

The *Young, James and Webster v United Kingdom* case[240] concerned three applicants who had been employed by British Rail before being dismissed because they refused to join the designated trade union under a closed shop agreement[241] concluded the previous year between their employer and three railway unions. The Court did not explicitly address the question of whether Article 11 of the ECHR included a right not to be compelled to join an association, although it did acknowledge that the *travaux préparatoires* explicitly suggested that this right had been deliberately excluded from the Convention. The respondent Government argued that the preparatory work revealed that the drafters considered it undesirable to introduce into the Convention a rule similar to Article 20(2) of the Universal Declaration of Human Rights, which stipulates that no one may be compelled to belong to an association.

Earlier, the Commission, in its report, referred to the preparatory work of Article 11, although it found it unnecessary to examine the question of whether this provision contained a 'negative right' of association.[242] Considering the argument put forward by the respondent government, the Commission found that it

> cannot attach decisive importance to this particular drafting history.... Art. 11 neither prohibits, nor allows, the system of 'closed shops' in general. Nor can it be deduced from the history that this was the intent or effect of the deletion of the clause concerned. What

[235] Ibid, para 35 (text inserted by author).

[236] *Sigurdur A Sigurjonsson v Iceland* (n 233 above), para 35.

[237] Ibid, para 35.

[238] *Sigurdur A Sigurjonsson v Iceland* (App No 16130/90), report, 15 May 1992, not reported.

[239] *Sigurdur A Sigurjonsson v Iceland* (App No 16130/90), decision, 10 July 1991, not reported.

[240] *Young, James and Webster v United Kingdom* (n 234 above).

[241] The Court defined a closed shop agreements as 'an undertaking or workplace in which, as a result of an agreement or arrangement between one or more trade unions and one or more employers or employers' associations, employees of a certain class are in practice required to be or become members of a specified union. The employer is not under any legal obligation to consult or obtain the consent of individual employees directly before such an agreement or arrangement is put into effect'. See *Young, James and Webster v United Kingdom* (n 234 above), para 13.

[242] *Young, James and Webster v United Kingdom* (App Nos 7601/76; 7806/77), report, 14 December 1979, Series B, Vol 39.

should have been the effect of including it had apparently not been examined. All that is recorded is a brief reference to the practice of 'closed shops'. The drafting history is not specifically related to the practice at issue, namely the dismissal for refusal to join specific unions.[243]

In the *Young, James and Webster v United Kingdom* judgment, the wording of the Court's reasoning indicated that its use of the preparatory work was laden with caution. The Court assumed

> for the sake of argument that, for the reasons given in the... travaux préparatoires, a general rule such as that in Article 20 par. 2 of the Universal Declaration of Human Rights was deliberately omitted from, and so cannot be regarded as itself enshrined in, the Convention, it does not follow that the negative aspect of a person's freedom of association falls completely outside the ambit of Article 11 and that each and every compulsion to join a particular trade union is compatible with the intention of that provision. To construe Article 11 as permitting every kind of compulsion in the field of trade union membership would strike at the very substance of the freedom it is designed to guarantee.[244]

It further argued that, '[a]ssuming that Article 11 does not guarantee the negative aspect of that freedom on the same footing as the positive aspect, compulsion to join a particular trade union may not always be contrary to the Convention'.[245] It was, however, found that 'a threat of dismissal involving loss of livelihood is a most serious form of compulsion and, in the present instance, it was directed against persons engaged by British Rail before the introduction of any obligation to join a particular trade union'.[246] In the Court's view, this constituted the very nature of the freedom of assembly and association and thus gave rise to a violation of Article 11 of the ECHR.

More recently, in the *Litwa* case,[247] the Court held that the detention of the applicant in a sobering-up centre was a breach of Article 5(1)(e) of the ECHR. The Court had to interpret the notion of 'alcoholics' included in that article. For this purpose, the Court resorted to a myriad of *travaux préparatoires*, including the work of the Consultative Assembly and of the Committee of Experts.[248] The respondent Government agreed with the result of the interpretation of the term 'alcoholics' reached by the Commission. In particular, it accepted that this term should be understood as covering not only persons with a defined psychiatric condition of alcohol dependency but also those occasionally intoxicated. The respondent Government objected, however, to the Commission's view (based on Article 31(1) of the VCLT) that the term 'alcoholics' had to be interpreted in accordance with its ordinary meaning. The Government considered that 'a special meaning', as referred to in Article 31(4) of the VCLT, had to be given to the

[243] Ibid, para 166.
[244] *Young, James and Webster v United Kingdom* (n 234 above) , para 52.
[245] Ibid, para 55. [246] Ibid.
[247] *Witold Litwa v Poland* (App No 26629/95), judgment, 4 April 2000, Reports 2000-III, 289, para 59. See 2.1 above. [248] Ibid, paras 33–39.

phrase in question. According to the Government, this had been recorded in the preparatory work on the Convention, which showed that the reason for permitting the lawful detention of alcoholics in Article 5 of the ECHR was to provide the Contracting States with the necessary measure to combat drunkenness.

The Court considered that, 'under Article 5 § 1 (e) of the Convention, persons who are not medically diagnosed as "alcoholics", but whose conduct and behaviour under the influence of alcohol pose a threat to public order or themselves, can be taken into custody for the protection of the public or their own interests, such as their health or personal safety'.[249] For the Court, this did not entail, however, that 'Article 5 § 1 (e) of the Convention can be interpreted as permitting the detention of an individual merely because of his alcohol intake'.[250] Furthermore, it found that this meaning is confirmed by the preparatory work invoked. More specifically, the Court clarified that 'in the commentary on the preliminary draft Convention it is recorded that the text of the relevant Article covered the right of the signatory States to take measures to combat vagrancy and "drunkenness" ("*l'alcoolisme*" in French). It is further recorded that the Committee of Experts had no doubt that this could be agreed "since such restrictions were justified by the requirements of public morality and order".'[251] Thus, the Court concluded that the applicant's detention fell within the ambit of Article 5(1)(e) of the ECHR. The Commission had also considered the meaning of the term 'alcoholic' in its report,[252] where the substance of the preparatory work considered was the same as that included in the Court's judgment.[253] The Commission, however, reached a different result with regard to the preparatory work, finding that it provided no substantial assistance in the interpretation of this term.[254]

Overall, the analysis of the Court's case law reveals that its use of preparatory work has rarely been premised on a strict adherence to the rule contained in Article 32 of the VCLT. Usually, the Court has applied Article 32 in a flexible manner and used its discretion to resort to the preparatory work when it felt that to do so would contribute to the resolution of a case. At the same time, the Court was not afraid to discard historical interpretations of the ECHR when it considered that they were not an aid to interpretation. It also displayed great caution when relying on the content of preparatory work. Beyond these findings, however, the Court does not seem to have adopted a coherent and rationalized approach to the *travaux préparatoires* of the ECHR. Rather, its methodology was adapted on case-by-case basis depending on the context of a given situation; and this seems to comply with the flexible approach advocated by the International Law Commission.

[249] Ibid, para 61. [250] Ibid, para 62. [251] Ibid, para 63.
[252] *Witold Litwa v Poland* (App No 26629/95), report, 4 December 1998, not reported.
[253] Ibid, paras 41–47. [254] Ibid, para 74.

3. Rationale of the Reasoning

The ECtHR's use of the interpretation rules contained in the Vienna Convention provides an instructive illustration of the reception of international law in a situation where there were no previous, clearly established guidelines. The Court appears to have used the VCLT rules as a starting point in its interpretation of the ECHR in a given case, but also as a stumbling block in the creation of ECHR-specific interpretation concepts. While the Court should be commended for being one of the few international courts to have used the VCLT interpretation rules, it is deplorable that it has not resorted to them more frequently. Undoubtedly, this would have provided an example to follow for national courts as well as for other international courts and bodies which often look to the ECtHR for guidance. The cases in which explicit references to the VCLT appear are therefore fewer than expected. The Court has applied Articles 31 and 32 of the VCLT in a diverse manner, which renders the task of deducing a single approach to the VCLT interpretation rules more difficult. The Court's reception of the VCLT appears, nonetheless, to have crystallized itself under certain specific interpretation rules. Several conclusions can thus be made in this context.

As regards the 'general rule' contained in Article 31(1) of the VCLT, the Court now appears to adhere scrupulously to the text of this provision. It has simply transposed the exact wording of this rule into the body of its case law. This applies also to the ordinary meaning rule, which the Court has followed faithfully in several cases. It needs to be emphasized, however, that the cases where this rule was applied explicitly are not numerous. Furthermore, the ordinary meaning rule was used under certain specific circumstances, namely when states had a wide margin of interpretation or when the terms to be interpreted constituted an exception to the general rule.

The teleological and contextual interpretation techniques, as included in Article 31(1) and (2) of the VCLT, have played a detrimental role in shaping the interpretation of the ECHR. They have permitted the Court both to adapt the Convention to present-day conditions and to keep up with the changes in society. They were used by the Court as a springboard for the creation of the 'living instrument' principle, and also as a way to distance itself from the original intention of the ECHR drafters. What is more, purposive interpretation allowed the Court to mould certain rights from the very general ECHR provisions. Textual and contextual interpretation was incorporated into the case law of the ECHR on the basis of the 'general rule' contained in Article 31(1). Thus, when the Court transposed Article 31(1) textually, it had also *ipso facto* embraced the teleological and contextual interpretation rule contained therein. Similarly to the ordinary meaning rule, teleological interpretation as enshrined in Article 31(1) was explicitly mentioned in very few cases.

The rule regarding subsequent practice contained in Article 31(3)(b) of the VCLT was marked on occasion by a cautious and traditional approach. The

Court could have interpreted this provision in a more expansive way in some of the cases. The Court was thus careful in interpreting the ECHR in light of subsequent practice in order not to impose a certain interpretation of the ECHR to which the states had not subscribed. Generally, however, the Court's use of subsequent practice was still situated within the acceptable scope of Article 31(3)(b). Furthermore, the use of such practice intervened in cases raising very fundamental questions, namely the abolition of the death penalty, interim measures, and reservations. The Court has thus decided to resort to subsequent practice in areas which had a tremendous significance for the protection of human rights.

The Court's use of the rule concerning 'other relevant treaties of international law' contained in Article 31(3)(c) of the VCLT mostly concerned substantive rights enshrined in Article 6 of the ECHR. Some cases also had a procedural character, which was of fundamental importance to the Contracting States. There does not seem to be an apparent reason why the Court may have resorted to Article 31(3)(c) only in these contexts. The Court applied this rule in a flexible manner, which seems to resemble the approach used by Judge Simma in the ICJ's *Oil Platforms* case.[255] Nonetheless, the Court never analysed this rule in great detail and never tried to address the uncertainties that are inherent in its interpretation. In all the cases where it was invoked, the Court used Article 31(3)(c) as a mechanism to refer to other rules of international law. It served as a rubber stamp legitimating the Court's resort to international law. Given that these references appeared in few cases, it remains unclear why the Court did not need this legitimation in other cases where it extensively used international law. It can be argued that, in those cases, the rule in Article 31(3)(c) was used implicitly. Nevertheless, it is unlikely that the Court's jurisprudence can provide any further guidance as to how this rule should be 'operationalized'. This is due to the fact that the Court did not address the unresolved interpretative problems contained in Article 31(1)(c), but rather bypassed them and applied the rule mechanically without further analysis.

The use of preparatory work by the ECtHR in its case law was rarely premised on a strict adherence to the rule contained in Article 32 of the VCLT. In contrast to the other VCLT interpretation rules, it is interesting to note that the Court applied Article 32 flexibly and used its discretion to resort to the preparatory work when it felt that this would contribute to the resolution of the dispute. At the same time, the Court was not afraid to discard historical interpretations of the ECHR when it considered that they would not aid interpretation. It does not appear to have adopted a very clear and coherent approach in this regard, but rather one which is dependent on the circumstances and result of a case.

The VCLT interpretation rules infiltrated the ECtHR's case law before it started shaping and moulding the ECHR's interpretative principles. At that time, there

[255] *Oil Platforms (Islamic Republic of Iran v United States)*, judgment, 12 December 1996, 2003 ICJ Reports 161.

were few interpretation principles in the Court's case law; the VCLT provided a crucial foundation on which to build the Court's unique, autonomous, and specific methodology. When these principles were established, the Strasbourg bodies continued to refer to the VCLT interpretation rules merely as a complementary tool or as a starting point in the construction of the ECHR. Overall, few references to these rules appeared in the Strasbourg case law. There are several reasons which could explain, at least in part, the Strasbourg bodies' reluctance to refer to Articles 31 and 32 of the VCLT. First, the Court has often underlined the specificity of the ECHR as a human rights treaty which goes beyond granting reciprocal engagements between states. Due to the ECHR's special character, it was sometimes inappropriate to rely on Articles 31 and 32, which are very general and contain numerous interpretative difficulties. This may have occurred particularly in cases where Contracting States had a wider margin of appreciation. Secondly, the uncertainty inherent in the VCLT interpretation rules may have further discouraged the Court and the Commission from using them. Thirdly, given that Articles 31 and 32 constitute international customary law, the Strasbourg bodies probably felt that it was no longer necessary to mention them explicitly in their reasoning. Overall, the Court and the Commission have leaned more towards the closed paradigm in this strand of their case law; this may have been necessary in order not to weaken the ECHR system by relying on general international law that may not be entirely adapted to its context.

Finally, it is not accurate to postulate that the references to the VCLT rules in the ECtHR's case law have outlived their utility and that they are on their way to becoming extinct. The fragmentation of international law has revived the interest in Article 31(3)(c). As a result, references to this provision are bound to resurface in the Court's jurisprudence and could be viewed as an important tool to overcome various discrepancies in human rights protection. Until now, Article 31(3)(c) has been used as a tool to legitimize the Court's and the Commission's references to international law; little attention has been paid by the Strasbourg bodies to the interpretative dilemmas inherent in this rule. Thus, if lawyers, academics, domestic courts, and international bodies are to look for guidance in the application of this provision, they will probably have to rely, at least for now, on other influential international sources.

II

International Court of Justice

1. Preliminary Observations

Created in 1920, the Permanent Court of International Justice (PCIJ) was for a long time the only player on the international judicial stage. Its replacement in 1945 by the International Court of Justice (ICJ) more or less coincided with the development of new judicial *fora*, initially at the regional level, then at the global level. In fact, the European Court of Human Rights was established only five years after the ICJ and both institutions benefit from a comparable amount of experience in handing down judgments and developing the relevant legal instruments. The ICJ benefits from a special status within the international legal system given that it is the principal judicial body of the United Nations.[1] Further, it is considered that the ICJ is competent to interpret the UN Charter. As such, it has contributed to the development of international law, including international human rights law,[2] as well as to the functioning of the United Nations. The ICJ benefits from a considerable reputation and all ECHR Contracting States, being UN Members, are also States Parties to the ICJ Statute.[3] All Contracting States are also parties to the UN Charter.[4]

[1] Charter of the United Nations, 1 UNTS XVI, entered into force 24 October 1945, Article 92.

[2] Raymond Goy, *La Cour internationale de justice et les droits de l'homme, Droit et justice 36, Collection dirigée par Pierre Lambert* (Brussels: Nemesis/Bruylant, 2002); Shiv RS Bedi, *The Development of Human Rights by the Judges of the International Court of Justice* (Oxford/ Portland, Oregon: Hart Publishing, 2007), 87–351; Rosalyn Higgins, 'The International Court of Justice and Human Rights' in Karl Wellens (ed), *International Law: Theory and Practice, Essays in Honour of Eric Suy* (The Hague/Boston/London: Martinus Nijhoff, 1998), 691. See also Stephen M Schwebel, 'Human Rights in the World Court' in Raghunandan Swarup Pathak and Romaa Prasad Dhokalia (eds), *International Law in Transition, Essays in Memory of Judge Nagendra Singh* (Dordrecht/Boston/London: Martinus Nijhoff, 1992), 267; Nigel S Rodley, *The Treatment of Prisoners under International Law* (Oxford/New York: OUP, 2nd edn, 1999), 19.

[3] United Nations Treaty Collection, Status, <http://treaties.un.org/Pages/ViewDetails.aspx?src=IND&mtdsg_no=I-3&chapter=1&lang=en> (last visited 13 June 2010).

[4] This information was verified on 13 June 2010: United Nations Treaty Collection, Status, <http://treaties.un.org/Pages/ViewDetails.aspx?src=IND&mtdsg_no=I-1&chapter=1&lang=en>.

Being the principal UN judicial body, the ICJ could be seen as a central body which could reduce fragmentation at the international level.[5] Eventually, it could also constitute an antidote to this problem at European level. In fact, by following the decisions of this anti-fragmentation body, the ECtHR may be able to reduce fragmentation at the regional level. Viewed from this perspective, the references to the ICJ framework in the Strasbourg case law gain in importance and could constitute an important factor in the harmonization of international and regional jurisprudence. Nonetheless, it is important to remember that substantial differences exist between the two courts, given that they are at the apex of two very different legal systems. Thus, not all ICJ rulings can be readily integrated into the ECHR framework.

One of the most important differences between the courts has been underlined by the ECtHR in its case law. It relates to the specific context of human rights, namely to the fact that the ECHR protects individual applicants from their governments and applies a vertical relationship between unequal parties. Disputes before the ICJ, on the other hand, concern the horizontal relationship between two theoretically equal states. Moreover, the ECHR grants rights to the individual applicant whereas the ICJ Statute only grants rights to states. Further, the ICJ can judge any legal dispute between states that might occur in any part of the globe with reference to principles of international law. The subject-matter of the dispute can relate to any area of international law. In addition, its role, unlike the one attributed to the ECtHR, is not exclusively limited to the supervision of a single law-making treaty. While both bodies appeal to common cultural and legal values, the ICJ's audience, membership, and work are significantly more varied. Thus, issuing authoritative and persuasive rulings may be much more difficult for the ICJ than for the ECtHR.[6]

In addition to these fundamental distinctions, both systems diverge in terms of the nature of jurisdiction conferred upon their respective judicial bodies. Neither the UN Charter nor the ICJ Statute provide for the direct compulsory jurisdiction of the ICJ over all states as a result of being parties to the ICJ Statute. The ICJ's jurisdiction is based upon the consent of the parties involved in the dispute. Under the ECHR, however, the acceptance of ECtHR jurisdiction became compulsory following the entry into force of Protocol No 11. Another important difference between both frameworks relates to the nature of reservations that states are allowed to enter. Article 36(3) of the ICJ Statute provides that Member States can issue reservations concerning their recognition of ICJ jurisdiction. These reservations can relate to the ICJ's *ratione temporis*, *ratione personae*, and *ratione materiae* jurisdiction. Article 57(1) of the ECHR, however, allows only substantive reservations with respect to a particular ECHR provision, to the extent that

[5] Pierre-Marie Dupuy, 'The Danger of Fragmentation or Unification of the International Legal System and the International Court of Justice' (1999) 31 NYUJ Int'l L & Pol 791, 798–801.

[6] John Graham Merrills, *The Development of International Law by the European Court of Human Rights* (Manchester/New York: Manchester University Press, 2nd edn, 1993), 31.

any law existing at the time of ratification does not conform to it. Reservations of a general character are also forbidden by this article. While there is no express provision with regard to the withdrawal of reservations, it is considered that it would be against the spirit and object of the Convention to maintain them and not to amend the laws that do not comply with the ECHR.[7] Reservations pertaining to the recognition of the ECtHR or to the right of individual petitions are no longer allowed. In addition, the opposability of reservations differs under both ICJ and ECtHR case law, given that those formulated under the ICJ Statute function on a reciprocal basis as between two states.

It needs to be emphasized that, in spite of these differences, the ICJ has been dealing more and more with human rights issues in its jurisprudence. This may not be surprising in so far as the subject-matter jurisdiction of the World Court is without limitation and in so far as human rights violations are also a breach of international law.[8] A review of ICJ decisions demonstrates that, although it is not a human rights court, the ICJ is engaged in the judicial protection and advancement of human rights.[9] Further, it appears that human rights law is increasingly penetrating the field of general international law. In this respect, there is certainly a *rapprochement* between the ICJ and the ECtHR. This could also explain, in part, the reasons prompting ECtHR references to the ICJ framework. Notwithstanding this trend, the fact remains—and the ECtHR has underlined it—that the ECHR system is substantially different from the international legal system under the ICJ's competence; it does not merely operate on a reciprocal basis between states and it includes an individual complaint mechanism. While ICJ case law can be of assistance with regard to certain ECHR rights and functional aspects, the ICJ's rulings need to be evaluated critically and integrated when they further the protection of human rights.

The aim of this chapter is to demonstrate that, in spite of the differences between the ICJ and ECHR systems, the Strasbourg bodies have referred for many years to the PCIJ and ICJ case law and Statute in order to interpret and develop the ECHR. While these references remain punctual and infrequent, they demonstrate that the Commission and Court were very receptive to the findings of this authoritative international judicial body. Lacking a coherent evolution, the reliance on the PCIJ and ICJ is crucial for the individual changes that these cases have introduced. Furthermore, the references to the ICJ framework occurred in fields of tremendous importance for international relations and the international community; they included, *inter alia*, the question of recognition of northern Cyprus and the review of UN actions in Kosovo. At a time when general international law is becoming further imbued with human rights standards, the Court may feel less inhibited to seek assistance from the ICJ. This step should

[7] Clare Ovey and Robin CA White, *The European Convention on Human Rights* (Oxford/New York: OUP, 4th edn, 2006), 452.

[8] Higgins (n 2 above), 691.

[9] Ibid, 691.

be welcomed, but it is yet to be seen whether it could reduce fragmentation of human rights standards at the regional level.

2. Case Law Concerning the ICJ's Decisions and Statute

There are relatively few cases, 20 at most, referring to PCIJ and ICJ decisions or to the ICJ Statute. Most concern issues that are of great importance to the international community or that are crucial for the development of the ECHR. The Court has rarely disagreed with the ICJ and has treated its case law as an authoritative source. When it has, on occasion, decided not to follow the case law of the ICJ, it seems to have been motivated by reasons which are specific to the human rights field, namely the need to protect the rights of the individual. The references to the PCIJ and ICJ case law and Statute have filled important gaps in the Court's case law and have constituted important milestones in the Court's interpretation and development of this living instrument. The cases analysed in this chapter do not follow a linear or logical evolution. Further, there is no general and coherent approach underpinning the Court's references to the ICJ's decisions and Statute. These punctual and spasmodic references have acquired great importance as a result of the individual developments they introduced.

2.1 The Initial Case Law

The Court and the Commission began referring early on to the case law of the PCIJ and ICJ. The initial references were nonetheless modest and did not constitute substantial parts of the reasoning of the Court or the Commission. As part of this phase, the Commission appears to have relied more than the Court on PCIJ and ICJ decisions. Distancing itself from the ICJ framework, the Court foreshadowed future case law by emphasizing the important differences between the ECHR and ICJ systems. As part of these initial references, PCIJ and ICJ case law was generally treated as an aid to interpretation, and the Court attributed to it a rank lower than that occupied by the ECHR.

In *Lawless v Ireland*,[10] the Commission referred to various PCIJ and ICJ decisions, but the Court did not subsequently engage with this case law. The *Lawless* case concerned a complaint where the applicant alleged that the authorities of the Republic of Ireland had violated the Convention by detaining him without trial for over five months in a military detention camp pursuant to the special powers of arrest and detention granted to ministers of the state. The applicant was not a party to the proceedings before the Court, and the Commission wished to submit to the Court the applicant's view on the main points of the proceedings. Furthermore, the Commission had invoked 'various precedents drawn from the

[10] *Lawless v Ireland* (App No 332/57), judgment, 14 November 1960, Series A, Vol 1.

advisory opinion procedure at the Permanent Court of International Justice and, subsequently at the International Court of Justice, where observations by individuals submitted through the international organisations who applied for the advisory opinions have been taken into consideration, although the Statutes of both these bodies provide that States alone may be represented in Court'.[11] The Court did not pursue this line of argument further and stated that it is 'not called to examine in detail the precedents invoked by the Commission with regard to the part to be played by the individual before an international judicial body'.[12] According to the Court, this was due to the fact that none of these decisions involved an individual appealing against the action of his/her own government, as was usually the case before the Strasbourg bodies.

The Court observed that the solution must be sought in the special nature of the ECHR procedure. This finding implies that the special features of the ECHR, at least with regard to its procedural aspects, take precedence over ICJ case law. The Court noted that while Contracting States and the Commission were the only ones capable of bringing a case before the Court, it nonetheless had to bear in mind that its duty was to safeguard the interests of the individual and that the whole proceedings in this case concerned the interests of the applicant. Thus, it was found that the Court should take into consideration, if need be, the applicant's point of view. However, given that the Court had not yet examined the merits of the case, it found that it was unable to pronounce itself on the Commission's request to consider his views. Overall, this case reveals that, since its initial references to the ICJ framework, the Court has been attentive to the differences in the procedure before the ICJ and the ECHR. This was necessary to ensure that the rights of the individual are adequately protected. Thus, the Court considered that individual rights have priority over important international decisions, including those of the PCIJ and the ICJ.

In the *Case 'Relating to Certain Aspects of the Laws on the Use of Languages in Education in Belgium' v Belgium*,[13] the respondent Government referred to PCIJ and ICJ case law to underline the similar consensual basis underpinning both systems. In this case, the Court was called to decide whether certain provisions of the Belgian linguistic legislation complied with Articles 8 and 14 of the ECHR, as well as Article 2 of Protocol No 1. The applicants, Belgian parents, complained that they spoke French and that they wanted their children to be educated in that language. They complained that the Belgian State did not provide French-language education in the municipalities where they lived outside the Greater Brussels district, withheld grants from any institutions which did not fulfil the linguistic requirements, refused to homologate certificates issued by such institutions, did not allow their children to attend French classes, and obliged the

[11] Ibid. [12] Ibid.

[13] *Case 'Relating to Certain Aspects of the Laws on the Use of Languages in Education in Belgium' v Belgium (Preliminary Objections)* (App Nos 1474/62; 1677/62; 1769/63; 1994/63; 2126/64), judgment, 9 February 1967, Series A, Vol 5.

applicants to enrol their children in local Dutch-speaking schools. The Belgian Government argued that the complaints did not fall under the Convention or a Protocol, as they formed part of the reserved domain of Belgian legal order. It was submitted that linguistic and educational legislation was to a large extent an integral part of the state's political and social structure and that the Convention was not concerned with the organization of governmental authorities.

At the preliminary objections phase, the respondent Government invoked PCIJ and ICJ decisions to support the argument that the Court must first examine whether the Convention is applicable before it pronounces itself on the merits. Furthermore, the Government submitted that the Court could not accept the system of provisional conclusion adopted by the PCIJ in the special context of Opinion No 4 on nationality decrees.[14] It should instead follow, if necessary, the method used by that Court in its judgment of 30 August 1924, when, before ruling on the merits of the case, it verified that the treaty provisions invoked applied to the case.[15] This submission was rooted in the principle of economy of proceedings, the logical sequence of the questions, and the fact that 'the European Court, like the World Court, has only an attributed jurisdiction derived purely from the consent of States'.[16] The Commission rejected this argument, finding that the idea of reserved domain had no place under the system of supervision created by the Convention. Further, according to the Commission, the legal provisions and practice relating to the jurisdiction of other international courts could in their entirety govern proceedings before the European Court due to the specific ECHR provisions. In a similar vein, the Court rejected the Government's contention that it could not proceed to the examination of the merits of the case. It found that the complaints raised by the applicants concerned questions of interpretation and application of the ECHR. Referring to a PCIJ case,[17] the Court held that considering these issues 'would amount, not only to encroaching on the merits, but to coming to a decision in regard to one of the fundamental factors of the case, that is to say in regard to questions of interpretation and application which are inseparable from the merits'.[18]

At the merits phase in the same case,[19] it was recalled that the Commission had cited PCIJ and ICJ decisions when it considered the scope of Article 14 of

[14] *Nationality Decrees Issued in Tunis and Morocco (French Zone) on November 8th, 1921,* advisory opinion, Permanent Court of International Justice, 7 February 1923, Series B, No 4.

[15] *The Mavrommatis Palestine Concessions (Greece v United Kingdom),* judgment, Permanent Court of International Justice, J, 30 August 1924, Series A, No 2.

[16] *Case 'Relating to Certain Aspects of the Laws on the Use of Languages in Education in Belgium' v Belgium* (n 13 above).

[17] *Electricity Company of Sofia and Bulgaria,* judgment, Permanent Court of International Justice, 4 April 1939, Series A/B, No 77, 83.

[18] *Case 'Relating to Certain Aspects of the Laws on the Use of Languages in Education in Belgium' v Belgium* (n 13 above).

[19] *Case 'Relating to Certain Aspects of the Laws on the Use of Languages in Education in Belgium' v Belgium (Merits)* (App Nos 1474/62; 1677/62; 1769/63; 1994/63; 2126/64), judgment, 23 July 1968, Series A, Vol 6.

the ECHR in its report.[20] The Belgian Government submitted that a violation of Article 14 was inconceivable without a simultaneous violation of another article protecting a right or freedom, unless that article imposes positive obligations. The Commission found that the applicability of Article 14 was not limited to cases in which there was accompanying violation of another article. Such a restrictive interpretation would deprive Article 14 of any practical utility and would conflict with the principle of effectiveness established by PCIJ and ICJ case law.[21] In the Commission's view, discrimination would then be limited to the aggravation of the violation of another ECHR provision. In its judgment, the Court did not explicitly refer to the same PCIJ and ICJ decisions, but it followed the Commission's reasoning, which had taken these into account under Article 14.

In the *Ringeisen v Austria* case,[22] PCIJ and ICJ cases did not form a substantial part of the Court's decision and were more relied on in a separate opinion. The case concerned an Austrian insurance agent who also negotiated loans and dealt in real estate. As part of a loan transaction, the applicant was given, *inter alia*, the option to purchase the property of the debtors. If the transfer of ownership was refused by the relevant administrative body, the debtors promised to stop acting as owners and to grant the right to exclusive obligation to the applicant. The applicant then concluded a contract with the debtors to purchase the property and started selling part of the property. The relevant administrative authorities refused to approve the contract of sale. The Government argued that not all of the remedies had been exhausted in the case. Parties to the case submitted exhaustive interpretations of former Article 26 (Article 13) of the ECHR; the Government observed that all remedies had to be exhausted before the application was received by the Secretary-General of the Council of Europe, while the Commission's delegates argued that the non-exhaustion of remedies did not prevent the lodging of the application but solely its examination by the Commission.

The Court observed that it would be excessive and contrary to the spirit of the rule on the exhaustion of remedies to allow an applicant to lodge a complaint before exercising domestic remedies. Nonetheless, it considered that 'international courts have on various occasions held that international law cannot be applied with the same regard for matters of form as is sometimes necessary in the application of national law'.[23] This argument was based on certain findings made

[20] *Case 'Relating to Certain Aspects of the Laws on the Use of Languages in Education in Belgium' v Belgium* (App Nos 1474/62; 1677/62; 1769/63; 1994/63; 2126/64), report, 24 June 1965, Series B, Vols 3 and 4 (available only in French).

[21] *Case 'Relating to Certain Aspects of the Laws on the Use of Languages in Education in Belgium' v Belgium (Merits)* (n 19 above), 374; *Case 'Relating to Certain Aspects of the Laws on the Use of Languages in Education in Belgium' v Belgium*, report (n 20 above).

[22] *Ringeisen v Austria* (App No 2614/65), judgment, 16 July 1971, Series A, Vol 13.

[23] Ibid, para 89; *The Mavrommatis Palestine Concessions Case* (n 15 above); *Lawless v Ireland* (App No 332/57), decision, 19 December 1959, Series B, No 1.

in the report in the *Lawless v Ireland* case,[24] where the Commission relied on the PCIJ's decision in *Mavrommatis Palestine*[25] in support of the same observation. The Court found that there is a need to apply the exhaustion of remedies rule with greater flexibility under certain circumstances. Thus, 'it must be left open to the Commission to accept the fact that the last stage of such remedies may be reached shortly after the lodging of the application but before the Commission is called upon to pronounce itself on admissibility'.[26] In the instant case, it was found that Ringeisen had exhausted all remedies in spite of the fact that the Austrian Constitutional Court delivered its judgment after the application had been lodged in Strasbourg.

In a separate opinion,[27] Judge Verdross disagreed, *inter alia*, with the Court's interpretation of former Article 26 (Article 13) of the ECHR. According to his view, all remedies had to be exhausted prior to the registration of an application by the Commission. Judge Verdross also observed that the examination of international judicial precedents by the Strasbourg bodies in this case was not necessary. Noting that Article 13 refers to the 'generally recognised rules of international law', he clarified that this reference was made within the framework of special provisions of this article; this could be done because the rules of general international law on the exhaustion of domestic remedies are not part of the *jus cogens*. Thus, the special conditions of Article 13 prevailed over the general rules of international law and it was superfluous to examine international practice in the matter. While being aware that it would be desirable to amend Article 13, Judge Verdross nonetheless found that the Strasbourg bodies should apply the Convention as it had been drafted by the High Contracting Parties. Quoting the ICJ's advisory opinion on the *Interpretation of the Peace Treaties*,[28] he observed that '[l]ike the International Court of Justice, "it is the duty" of our Court "to interpret the Treaties not to revise them"'.[29] In this case, however, the Court seemed to rely on ICJ case law as an aid to interpretation and did not appear to grant a higher status than the one attributed to the special provisions of Article 13. By the same token, the Court's interpretation did not entail an amendment of the ECHR.

2.2 Filling in Gaps

As the cases analysed in this section will demonstrate, the Court and the Commission have resorted selectively to the ICJ framework in order to resolve issues which are fundamental for the effective protection of rights under the

[24] Ibid.

[25] *The Mavrommatis Palestine Concessions Case* (n 15 above).

[26] *Ringeisen v Austria* (App No 2614/65), judgment, 16 July 1971, Series A, Vol 13, para 91.

[27] Ibid, Separate Opinion of Judge Verdross.

[28] *Interpretation of the Peace Treaties with Bulgaria, Hungary and Romania*, advisory opinion, 18 July 1950, 1950 ICJ Reports 221.

[29] Ibid.

ECHR. These innovations were a necessary evolution of the ECHR framework and allowed the Strasbourg bodies to push the limits of protection further. The ICJ framework constituted here an important part of the reasoning of the Court and Commission. When the specificity of the human rights context required it, the Strasbourg bodies either distanced themselves from the ICJ framework or used the case law and Statute to strengthen the ECHR. The reasons prompting the references to the ICJ framework seem to have been conditioned by the need to effectively protect human rights in the European context.

In *Golder v United Kingdom*,[30] the Court used Article 38(1)(c) of the ICJ Statute as a means to remedy an important lack under the ECHR. As part of this judgment, the Court decided that the right of access to court was inherent in the right enshrined in Article 6(1) of the ECHR. In support of this finding, the Court observed that 'Article 31 para. 3 (c) of the Vienna Convention indicates that account is to be taken together with the context, of "any relevant rules of international law applicable in the relations between the parties". Among those rules are general principles of law and especially "general principles of law recognized by civilized nations (Article 38 para. 1 (c) of the Statute of the International Court of Justice)".'[31] Furthermore, 'the Legal Committee of the Consultative Assembly of the Council of Europe foresaw in August 1950 that "the Commission and the Court must necessarily apply such principles" in the execution of their duties and thus considered it to be "unnecessary" to insert a specific clause to this effect in the Convention (Documents of the Consultative Assembly, working papers of the 1950 session, Vol III, no 93, p. 982, para. 5)'.[32] According to the Court, the principle whereby a civil claim must be capable of being submitted to a judge ranked among the universally 'recognized' fundamental principles of law. Further, the prohibition of denial of justice was another such principle of international law. The Court considered that Article 6(1) of the ECHR must be read in the light of these principles and based itself, *inter alia*, on these principles to determine that this provision contained the right of access to court. The ICJ Statute, therefore, served the vital purpose of filling in gaps in the ECHR and creating new rights which were not explicitly included therein.

In another landmark case, *Ireland v United Kingdom*,[33] the Court observed that the British Government had invited the Court to declare moot a complaint raised by the applicant under Article 3 of the ECHR and relied in this connection on decisions of the ICJ in the *Northern Cameroons*[34] and *Nuclear Tests*[35] cases. The case concerned the use of extra-judicial powers of arrest, detention, and

30 *Golder v United Kingdom* (App No 4451/70), judgment, 21 February 1975, Series A, Vol 18.

31 Ibid, para 35. 32 Ibid.

33 *Ireland v United Kingdom* (App No 5310/71), judgment, 18 January 1978, Series A, Vol 25.

34 *Northern Cameroons (Cameroon v United Kingdom) (Preliminary Objections)*, judgment, 2 December 1963, 1963 ICJ Reports, 15.

35 *Nuclear Tests Case (New Zealand v France)*, judgment, 20 December 1974, 1974 ICJ Reports, 457.

internment by the domestic authorities during the long-running terrorist campaign in Northern Ireland. The proceedings related to the scope and operation of those measures as well as to the ill-treatment of persons deprived of their liberty. The reference to ICJ judgments appeared in the context of the UK's preliminary questions on alleged violations of Article 3 of the ECHR. The United Kingdom did not contest the breaches of Article 3, as found by the Commission, nor doubt the Court's jurisdiction to examine them. However, relying on ICJ case law, the respondent Government argued that the Court had the power to decline to exercise its jurisdiction where the objective of an application had been accomplished or where adjudication on the merits would be devoid of purpose. It was submitted that the findings in question were not contested and did not give rise to problems of interpretation or application of the ECHR, which required a decision from the Court.[36] Furthermore, the subject-matter of those findings now belonged to the past given that the interrogation techniques found to contravene the ECHR were abandoned and that the United Kingdom undertook not to reintroduce them and to prevent the various violations from recurring.[37]

The Court acknowledged the efforts of the United Kingdom in preventing the recurrence of similar violations, but it nevertheless considered that the responsibilities assigned to it under the ECHR extended to pronouncing itself on the non-contested allegations of Article 3 violations.[38] It was clarified that the Court's judgments do not only serve to decide the cases before it, but also to elucidate, safeguard, and develop the ECHR. Thus, the Court held that the non-contested allegations under Article 3 could not be said to have become without object; it therefore had to rule upon them in spite of the measures taken by the United Kingdom. The Court put aside the ICJ's findings in order to favour and reinforce the ECHR supervision system. Relying on the ICJ's decision in this context may have entailed a weakening of the ECHR system. This reasoning seems to indicate that the Court resorts to ICJ judgments when these reinforce its reasoning and the functioning of the ECHR system.

More than a decade later, the Commission made an important distinction between the ECHR and ICJ frameworks, and thereby distanced itself from the ICJ case law and Statute. In *Chrystosomos, Papachrystosomos & Loizidou v Turkey*[39] an important schism was initiated between ECtHR and ICJ case law with regard to the opposability of reservations. The Commission reiterated that, in previous cases, the Court had already held that, unlike international treaties of the classical kind, the Convention creates more than mere reciprocal engagements between Contracting States: 'It creates, over and above a network of mutual, bilateral undertakings, objective obligations which, in the words of the Preamble,

[36] *Ireland v United Kingdom* (n 33 above). [37] Ibid. [38] Ibid, para 154.

[39] *Chrystosomos, Papachrystosomos & Loizidou v Turkey* (App Nos 15299/89; 15300/89; 15318/89), decision, 4 March 1991, DR 68, 216.

benefit from a collective enforcement.'[40] Moreover, it was emphasized that the 'character of the Convention, as a constitutional instrument of European public order in the field of human rights, excluded application by analogy, as suggested by the respondent Government, of State practice under Article 36 para. 3 of the Statute of the International Court of Justice'.[41] Furthermore, Article 36(3) of the ICJ Statute did not, like former Article 25 (Article 34) of the ECHR, concern applications brought by individuals but rather by states. Under the ECHR, every state could bring applications pursuant to former Article 24 (Article 33) without any further agreement and without fulfilling any condition of reciprocity.[42] The Commission considered that there was no legal basis in the Convention for restrictions under former Article 25 (Article 34) other than temporal limitations. As will be seen, the Court reaffirmed this approach in subsequent case law, thereby entrenching further a reasoning which differs diametrically from the one used by the ICJ with respect to the opposability of reservations.[43]

In *Cruz Varas and others v Sweden*,[44] the Court used the ICJ Statute to justify a narrow interpretation of the powers granted to the Strasbourg bodies, thereby strengthening its departure from the ICJ framework.[45] The issue in that case was the scope of the Commission's power to indicate interim measures under Rule 36 of its Rules of Procedure, and in particular whether such measures were binding. To answer this question the Court referred, *inter alia*, to the ICJ Statute. The Court noted that the Convention must be interpreted in the light of its special character as a treaty for the protection of individual human beings. While this approach argues in favour of granting power to the Strasbourg bodies to order interim measures to protect ECHR rights, the Court considered that, unlike other international treaties or instruments, the Convention does not contain a specific provision with regard to such measures, such as Article 41 of the ICJ Statute.[46] While it was first proposed to include in a draft Statute of the ECtHR an interim measures provision based on Article 41 of the ICJ Statute, the *travaux préparatoires* of the Convention are silent as to any discussion which may have taken place on this question.[47] Thus, the Commission found that, due to the absence of a specific provision, the Convention bodies cannot order binding interim measures. While this finding further distanced the Strasbourg system

[40] Ibid, para 21; *Ireland v United Kingdom* (n 33 above), para 239.

[41] *Chrystosomos, Papachrystosomos & Loizidou v Turkey* (n 39 above), para 22.

[42] Ibid, para 22. [43] See 2.4 below.

[44] *Cruz Varas and others v Sweden* (App No 15576/89), judgment, 20 March 1991, Series A, Vol 201.

[45] John Graham Merrills, *The Development of International Law by the European Court of Human Rights* (Manchester/New York: Manchester University Press, 2nd edn, 1993), 204.

[46] *Cruz Varas and others v Sweden* (n 44 above), para 94.

[47] Ibid, para 95; *Collected edition of the 'travaux préparatoires' of the European Convention on Human Rights*, Preparatory Commission of the Council of Europe, Committee of Ministers, Consultative Assembly, 11 May to 8 September 1949 (The Hague: Martinus Nijhoff, 1949), Vol I, 314.

from the ICJ framework, it was overturned in subsequent case law where the Court followed the ICJ Statute and evolving case law.[48]

2.3 The Clarification of Certain Commercial Aspects

In *Stran Greek Refineries and Stratis Adreadis v Greece*,[49] the Court relied on a PCIJ decision and on famous arbitral awards to support its finding that an arbitral clause in a contract with a private party cannot be modified by a state. The case concerned a Greek company which concluded a contract with the Greek State, at the time when it was ruled by a military junta, to construct a crude oil refinery. The project stumbled given that the Government failed to fulfil its promise to buy a plot of land suitable for the construction of the refinery. Once democracy was restored in Greece, the Government took the view that the contract was prejudicial to the national economy. Following an arbitration procedure, the applicant was found to be entitled to compensation from the Greek State and to the return of a cheque it had lodged with the Ministry of National Economy as security for the proper performance of the contract.[50] Judicial proceedings followed and the case made its way to the Court of Cassation, at which stage the legislature intervened by enacting a law which provided that, upon the termination of the contract in question, the arbitration clause and award were void.[51]

The Court recognized that it was necessary for the democratic Greek State to terminate a contract which it considered to be prejudicial to its economic interests.[52] It was noted that 'according to the case-law of international courts and of arbitration tribunals any State has a sovereign power to amend or even terminate a contract concluded with private individuals, provided it pays compensation'.[53] Further, the unilateral termination of a contract cannot 'take effect in relation to certain essential features, such as an arbitral clause'.[54] Relying on the decision of the PCIJ in *Losinger*,[55] as well as other arbitral awards, the Court decided that in order '[t]o alter the machinery set up by enacting an authoritative amendment to such a clause would make it possible for one of the parties to evade jurisdiction in a dispute in respect of which specific provision was made for arbitration'.[56] Thus, the state was obliged to pay the sum awarded to the applicants following the arbitration procedure.

[48] *Mamatkulov and Askarov v Turkey* (App Nos 46827/99; 46951/99), judgment, 4 February 2005, Reports 2005-I, 293; see 2.6 below; see also Introduction, 2.2.3; ch I, 2.3 and 2.4.2; ch IV, 2.2.8; and ch V, 3.2.1.

[49] *Stran Greek Refineries and Stratis Adreadis v Greece* (App No 13427/87), judgment, 9 December 1994, Series A, Vol 301-B.

[50] Ibid, paras 13–14.

[51] Ibid, para 20.

[52] Ibid, para 72.

[53] Ibid.

[54] Ibid.

[55] *Losinger & Co Case (Switzerland v Yugoslavia)*, Order, Permanent Court of International Justice, 27 June 1936, Series C, No 78, 110.

[56] *Stran Greek Refineries and Stratis Adreadis v Greece* (n 49 above), para 72.

In *Agrotexim and others v Greece*,[57] the Court invoked the ICJ *Barcelona Traction* case[58] to support its finding that the piercing of the corporate veil is only allowed under certain circumstances. In that case, it was held that shareholders could not achieve 'victim' status for matters that concern the corporate person and not them directly as human shareholders. The Court noted that, in its report, the Commission seemed to accept that where a violation of a company's rights protected by Article 1 of Protocol No 1 resulted in a fall in the value of its shares, there is automatically an infringement of the shareholders' rights under that provision.[59] According to the Court, such a stand could create difficulties in determining who is entitled to apply to the Strasbourg institutions. It could also cause substantial problems with regard to the requirement of exhausting domestic remedies.[60] The Court noted that in the majority of legal systems shareholders do not normally have the right to bring an action for damages in respect of an act or an omission that was prejudicial to their company. It was considered that 'the piercing of the corporate veil or the disregarding of a company's legal personality will be justified only in exceptional circumstances, in particular where it is clearly established that it is impossible for the company to apply to the Convention institutions through the organs set up under its articles of incorporation or—in the event of liquidation—through its liquidators'.[61] The Court also found that this principle had been confirmed with regard to the diplomatic protection of companies and cited in support the ICJ *Barcelona Traction* case. In the case at hand, it had not been clearly established that it was impossible for the applicants to lodge an application through the company's liquidators.

2.4 The Growing Differences Between the Systems

In *Loizidou v Turkey*,[62] the Court reinforced its stand with regard to the important differences existing between the ICJ and ECHR systems. In this case, referred by the Republic of Cyprus, the applicant owned certain plots of land in northern Cyprus and was prevented from gaining access to her properties as a result of the presence of Turkish forces in Cyprus who exercised overall control in the relevant area. At the preliminary questions phase,[63] the Court found that Turkey acted in its capacity as a High Contracting Party and was the respondent State in this case. With respect to the question of whether the facts alleged by the applicant were capable of falling within the jurisdiction of Turkey

[57] *Agrotexim and others v Greece* (App No 14807/89), judgment, 24 October 1995, Series A, Vol 330-A.

[58] *Barcelona Traction, Light and Power Company, Limited (Belgium v Spain)*, New Application: 1962, Second Phase, judgment, 5 February 1970, ICJ Reports 1970, 3, 39, and 41, paras 56–58 and 66.

[59] *Agrotexim and others v Greece* (n 57 above), para 64.

[60] Ibid, para 65.

[61] Ibid.

[62] *Loizidou v Turkey (Preliminary Objections)* (App No 15318/89), judgment, 23 March 1995, Series A, Vol 310; *Loizidou v Turkey (Merits)* (App No 15318/89), judgment, 18 December 1996, Reports 1996-VI, 2216.

[63] *Loizidou v Turkey (Preliminary Objections)* (n 62 above).

under Article 1 of the ECHR, the Court found that the concept of 'jurisdiction' was not restricted to the national territory of the High Contracting Parties. Responsibility could also arise when, as a consequence of military action (lawful or unlawful), a Contracting Party exercised effective control of an area outside its national territory. It was not disputed that the applicant was prevented by the Turkish troops from gaining access to her property. The Court concluded that the facts alleged were capable of falling within Turkish 'jurisdiction' within the meaning of Article 1.

In addition, the Court had to consider the validity of territorial restrictions claimed by Turkey with regard to the right of individual petition under former Article 25 (Article 34) of the ECHR and the acceptance of the Court's compulsory jurisdiction under former Article 46. The Court noted that, if former Articles 25 (Article 34) and 46 were to be interpreted as permitting restrictions (other than temporal ones), states would be able to qualify their consent under the optional provisions and exclude certain areas from the Court's jurisdiction. This would severely weaken the role of the Commission and the Court and would diminish the effectiveness of the ECHR as a constitutional instrument of European public order. In the Court's view, there were significant considerations supporting the view that such restrictions were not allowed under the ECHR system.[64]

Further, this approach was confirmed by the subsequent practice of Contracting States under former Articles 25 (Article 34) and 46 of the ECHR. It was also 'supported by the reactions of the Governments of Sweden, Luxembourg, Denmark, Norway and Belgium, as well as the Secretary General of the Council of Europe as depositary, which reserved their positions as regards the legal questions arising as to the scope of Turkey's first Article 25 declaration ... and the Government of Greece which considered the restrictions to Turkey's declarations under Article 25 and 46 to be null and void'.[65] It was found that the existence of such a uniform and consistent state practice clearly rebutted 'the respondent Government's arguments that restrictions attaching to [former] Article 25 and Article 46 declarations must have been envisaged by the drafters of the Convention in the light of practice under Article 36 of the Statute of the International Court of Justice'.[66]

According to the Court, it did not follow

> that such restrictions to the acceptance of jurisdiction of the Commission and Court must also be permissible under the Convention. In the first place, the context within which the International Court of Justice operates is quite distinct from that of the Convention institutions. The International Court is called on *inter alia* to examine any legal dispute between States that might occur in any part of the globe with reference to principles of international law. The subject-matter of a dispute may relate to any area of international law. In the second place, unlike the Convention institutions, the role of the International Court is not exclusively limited to direct supervisory functions in respect of a law-making treaty such as the Convention. Such a fundamental difference in the role and purpose of

[64] Ibid, para 78. [65] Ibid, para 81. [66] Ibid, para 67 (text inserted by author).

the respective tribunals, coupled with the existence of a practice of unconditional acceptance under [former] Articles 25 and 46, provides a compelling basis for distinguishing Convention practice from that of the International Court.[67]

This argument was rooted in the finding that the ECHR had a special character as a constitutional instrument of European public order and as a treaty for the collective enforcement of human rights and fundamental freedoms. In the Court's view, '[u]nlike international treaties of the classical kind, the Convention comprises more than mere reciprocal engagements between Contracting States. It creates over and above a network of mutual bilateral undertakings, objective obligations which in the words of the preamble benefit from a "collective enforcement".'[68] This part of the Court's reasoning exhibits the tensions that exist between general law and specialized law. It appears that it was sufficient for the Court to distinguish itself from the general regime as an exception to avoid applying an old rule.[69]

In a similar vein, Judge Pettiti accurately pointed out in his individual dissenting opinion that the ECHR 'is not an international treaty of the traditional type nor a synallagmatic convention, as legal writers, . . . have pointed out, since it is not based on reciprocity. It is based on the principle that all individual subjects of law are its beneficiaries, so that fundamental rights can be protected more securely. The Court is the guarantor of the Convention and must endeavour to extend its protection as far as possible.'[70] Finally, the Court found that the impugned restrictions could be separated from the remainder of the text, leaving intact the acceptance of the optional clauses. It was held that the territorial restrictions were invalid, but that the declarations under former Articles 25 (Article 34) and 46 of the ECHR contained valid acceptances of the competence of the Commission and the Court.

At the merits phase in the *Loizidou* case,[71] the Turkish Government claimed, *inter alia*, that the applicant's property had been irreversibly expropriated by virtue of Article 159 of the Turkish Republic of Northern Cyprus (TRNC) Constitution of 7 May 1985, prior to the Turkish Declaration of 22 January 1990 accepting the Court's jurisdiction. The Court found that it was evident from international practice and resolutions of various international bodies that the

[67] Ibid, paras 83–85 (text inserted by author).

[68] Ibid, para 70.

[69] Martti Koskenniemi, 'The Fate of Public International Law: Constitutional Utopia or Fragmentation', Chorley Lecture, London School of Economics, 7 June 2006, 6 <http://www.helsinki.fi/eci/Publications/MKChorley%20Text-06a.pdf> (last visited 13 June 2010); United Nations General Assembly, *Fragmentation of International Law: Difficulties Arising from the Diversification and Expansion of International Law*, Report of the Study Group of the International Law Commission, Finalized by Martti Koskenniemi, International Law Commission, 58th session, 1 May to 9 June and 3 July to 11 August 2006, A/CN.4/L.682, 13 April 2006, 33, para 53.

[70] *Loizidou v Turkey (Preliminary Objections)* (n 62 above).

[71] *Loizidou v Turkey (Merits)* (n 62 above).

international community did not regard the TRNC as a state under international law and that the Republic of Cyprus remained the sole legitimate Government of Cyprus. Applying judicial restraint, the Court confined itself to this statement and did not consider it desirable to elaborate a general theory concerning the lawfulness of legislative and administrative acts of the TRNC. It further found that Article 159 of the Constitution, relied on by Turkey, could not be considered as being legally valid under the ECHR. The Court did mention, however, basing itself on the advisory opinion on *Legal Consequences for States of the Continued Presence of South Africa in Namibia (South West Africa)*,[72] that 'international law recognises the legitimacy of certain legal arrangements and transactions in such a situation, for instance as regards the registration of births, deaths and marriages, "the effects of which can be ignored only to the detriment of the inhabitants of the [t]erritory"'.[73]

In the Court's view, the Turkish army exercised effective overall control given that a large number of troops were engaged in active duties in northern Cyprus. In the circumstances of the case, this entailed Turkey's responsibility for policies and actions in northern Cyprus. Thus, denying the applicant access to her property in northern Cyprus fell within the Turkish 'jurisdiction' for the purposes of Article 1 of the ECHR and was imputable to Turkey. The establishment of state responsibility did not require an examination of the lawfulness of Turkey's intervention in 1974. The Court held that the applicant remained the legal owner of land, but since 1974 effectively lost all control, use, and enjoyment of it, which amounted to a violation of Article 1 of Protocol No 1.

Following the *Loizidou* case, it appeared that the Court's reasoning differed from the reasoning of the ICJ with regard to the opposability of reservations.[74] Thus, the important schism between the ECHR and the ICJ standards which appeared in *Chrystosomos, Papachrystosomos & Loizidou v Turkey*[75] reinforced itself further in the instant case as well as in the *Belilos*[76] and *Weber*[77] cases. In this context, the Court confirmed that—unlike under traditional treaty law—a reservation could be severed and regarded as null and void only in those parts that were incompatible with the object and purpose of the treaty.[78] Thus, a reservation would not automatically lose all its effect when it did comply with the treaty itself or its object and purpose. This approach was premised on the idea that

[72] *Legal Consequences for States of the Continued Presence of South Africa in Namibia (South West Africa) Notwithstanding Security Council Resolution 276 (1970)*, advisory opinion, 21 June 1971, 1971 ICJ Reports, 16, 56, para 125.

[73] Ibid, para 45.

[74] Dupuy (n 5 above), 797–798.

[75] *Chrystosomos, Papachrystosomos & Loizidou v Turkey* (n 39 above).

[76] *Belilos v Switzerland* (App No 10328/83), judgment, 29 April 1988, Series A, Vol 132, para 60.

[77] *Weber v Switzerland* (App No 11034/84), judgment, 22 May 1990, Series A, Vol 177, paras 38–40.

[78] Antonio Cassese, *International Law* (Oxford: Oxford University Press, 2nd edn, 2005), 175.

human rights standards prevailed over the concerns of sovereign states.[79] Thus, in a conflict between the international community's need to maintain international human rights standards and the intent of one of the parties to evade them, the first requirement had priority over the second in the Strasbourg case law.[80]

A different approach was followed by the ICJ in its case law. Following the advisory opinion delivered in 1951 by the ICJ on *Reservations to the Convention on Genocide*[81] and the enactment of the VCLT, states can add reservations at the time of ratification or accession, unless the reservation is expressly prohibited by the treaty or is incompatible with the object and purpose of the treaty. States can also formulate objections to a reservation within 12 months after its notification. Such an objection has a limited effect as it entails that the provisions covered by the reservation do not apply as between the two states to the extent of the reservation.[82] This regime allows as many states as possible to take part in treaties that include provisions unacceptable to them. It may, however, impair the integrity of multilateral treaties, which could be split into a series of bilateral agreements. In addition, it leaves the question of object and purpose to be determined by a Contracting Party.[83] Thus, the ECtHR's intent not to follow ICJ case law was motivated by the specific human rights context, which gives priority to individual rights over state conveniences.

2.5 Certain Points of Interest

In *Papamichalopoulos and others v Greece*,[84] the Court considered a PCIJ decision in order to determine the criteria to be used in establishing the reparation owed by the respondent State following an unlawful expropriation. When dictatorship was established, the Greek State transferred to the Navy Fund a large area of land in Attica. It then appeared that part of the land transferred consisted of agricultural land belonging to the applicants. Three of the applicants obtained orders for the return of their property, but the Navy retained the whole area, on which it built a naval base and a holiday village for naval officers. The instant case concerned a claim for just satisfaction submitted by 14 applicants whom, in an earlier judgment,[85] the Court had held to be victims of a breach of Article 1 of Protocol No 1. The Court clarified that the act of the Greek Government was not an expropriation, which would have been legitimate but for the failure to pay fair compensation: it was the taking by the State of land belonging to private

[79] Ibid. [80] Ibid.

[81] *Reservations to the Convention on the Prevention and Punishment of the Crime of Genocide*, advisory opinion, 28 May 1951, 1951 ICJ Reports, 15, 26–30.

[82] Cassese (n 78 above), 174. [83] Ibid.

[84] *Papamichalopoulos and others v Greece (Just Satisfaction)* (App No 14556/89), judgment, 31 October 1995, Series A, Vol 330-B.

[85] *Papamichalopoulos and others v Greece (Merits)* (App No 14556/89), judgment, 24 June 1993, Series A, Vol 260-B.

individuals that lasted 28 years, during which the authorities ignored the courts' decisions and their own promises to the applicants. According to the Court, the unlawful character of this dispossession affected the criteria to be used for determining the reparation owed by the respondent State, given that the pecuniary consequences flowing from lawful expropriation differ from those resulting from unlawful expropriation.[86]

As a source of inspiration for these criteria, the Court relied on the PCIJ's decision in the *Chorzów* case.[87] In that case, the PCIJ noted that:

> reparation must, as far as possible, wipe out all the consequences of the illegal act and re-establish the situation which would, in all probability, have existed if that act had not been committed. Restitution in kind, or, if this is not possible, payment of a sum corresponding to the value which a restitution in kind would bear; the award, if need be, of damages for loss sustained which would not be covered by restitution in kind or payment in place of it—such are the principles which should serve to determine the amount of compensation due for an act contrary to international law.[88]

Thus, applying this reasoning, the Court found that the compensation to be awarded was not limited to the value of the applicants' properties at the date on which the Navy had occupied them. Further, it was held that the land in issue had to be returned and that the existing buildings had to be awarded to the applicants in order to compensate for the consequences of loss of enjoyment.[89]

In *Akdivar and others v Turkey*,[90] the respondent Government invoked an ICJ judgment in support of the argument that the principle of exhaustion of remedies applied, unless it could be shown that the remedy was ineffective or that there was no remedy at all. According to the applicants, soldiers entered the village and instructed the mayor to evacuate all the inhabitants immediately as part of their fight with the Kurdistan's Workers Party (PKK). In the meantime, the soldiers set fire to houses, including those belonging to some of the applicants. Three villagers were killed and three others wounded. The Government submitted that the application should be rejected for failure to exhaust domestic remedies. It was argued on the basis of the ICJ *Interhandel* case[91] and other arbitral awards that 'the exhaustion requirement applied unless the applicant could show that the remedy provided was manifestly ineffective or that there was no remedy at all'.[92] In the Government's view, the applicants had failed to provide any

[86] *Papamichalopoulos and others v Greece (Just Satisfaction)* (n 84 above), para 36.

[87] *Factory at Chorzów*, judgment, Permanent Court of International Justice, 13 September 1928, Series A, No 17.

[88] Ibid, para 47; *Papamichalopoulos and others v Greece (Merits)* (n 84 above), para 36.

[89] Ibid, para 38.

[90] *Akdivar and others v Turkey* (App No 21893/93), judgment, 16 September 1996, Reports 1996-IV, 1192.

[91] *Interhandel (Switzerland v United States of America)*, judgment, 21 March 1959, 1959 ICJ Report, 6.

[92] *Akdivar and others v Turkey* (n 90 above), para 58.

evidence that there were insurmountable obstacles to taking proceedings before the Turkish courts.

The Court did not mention the ICJ *Interhandel* case in its reasoning. Instead, it was more lenient and favourable to the applicants by requiring that they demonstrate that 'the remedy advanced by the Government was in fact exhausted or was for some reason inadequate and ineffective in the particular circumstances of the case or that there existed special circumstances absolving... [them] from the requirement'.[93] The Court referred to the decisions of the Commission and the Inter-American Court of Human Rights in support of this finding.[94] Thus, it was held that, in the exceptional circumstances of this case, the applicants could address themselves directly to Strasbourg. The Court appears to have applied a lower threshold than that advocated by the respondent Government with regard to the necessity of exhausting domestic remedies. Thus, the Court did not have the chance to consider the ICJ *Interhandel* case cited by the respondent Government in this context. This could have been prompted, once again, by the need to strengthen the ECHR system and to ensure that the individual applicant was better protected.

2.6 Issues of Fundamental International and Regional Importance

References to the ICJ framework also appeared in cases which related to controversial international policy issues, such as the lack of recognition of northern Cyprus. In this context, the Court adopted a courageous and pragmatic, albeit questionable, approach based on the reasoning of the Commission and ICJ. It considered fundamental legal questions relating to northern Cyprus and bypassed the fact that this entity lacked international recognition. For the Court, the crux of the issue lay in the effective protection of human rights and not in the legal denomination to be attributed to this part of Cyprus. It is undeniable, however, that in this context the Court actively intervened in the field of international policy and went against the policy adopted by Contracting States with regard to northern Cyprus.

In the *Cyprus v Turkey* case,[95] the Court relied on the ICJ's advisory opinion in the *Namibia* case[96] to argue that the obligation to disregard de facto regimes was far from being absolute. The case concerned the situation that prevailed in northern Cyprus since the conduct of military operations by Turkey in July and August 1974 and the continuing division of Cypriot territory. With regard to this state of affairs, Cyprus maintained that Turkey had continued to violate the ECHR in northern Cyprus after the adoption of two earlier reports by the

[93] Ibid, para 68. [94] Ibid.

[95] *Cyprus v Turkey* (App No 25781/94), judgment, 10 May 2001, Reports 2001-IV, 1.

[96] *Legal Consequences for States of the Continued Presence of South Africa in Namibia (South West Africa) Notwithstanding Security Council Resolution 276 (1970)*, advisory opinion, 21 June 1971, 1971 ICJ Reports, 16.

Commission. Cyprus contended that Turkey was accountable for the alleged violations notwithstanding the proclamation of the Turkish Republic of Northern Cyprus (TRNC). In the view of Cyprus, the TRNC was an illegal entity from the standpoint of international law, and it referred to the international community's condemnation of the establishment of the TRNC. Turkey, on the other hand, maintained that the TRNC was a democratic and constitutional state, which was politically independent of all other sovereign states. Turkey claimed that it was not accountable as the violations alleged by Cyprus were solely imputable to the TRNC.

The Court held, *inter alia*, in that case that for the purposes of the exhaustion requirements under former Article 26 (Article 35(1)) of the ECHR, remedies available in the TRNC may be regarded as 'domestic remedies' of the respondent State. The question of their effectiveness had to be considered in the context of the specific circumstances, on a case-by-case basis. The majority of judges considered—in line with the Commission's view based on the ICJ's advisory opinion in the *Namibia* case—that in situations such as in the instant case, the obligation to disregard de facto regimes, as the TRNC, was far from being absolute. According to the Court, life carried on in the territory of the TRNC, and the lives of its inhabitants needed to be rendered tolerable and protected by the de facto authorities. In the interest of the inhabitants, the acts of those authorities could not simply be ignored by states or international bodies. Otherwise, the inhabitants of the territory would be deprived of their rights whenever their situation was discussed in an international context, and this would deny them the minimum standard of rights to which they were entitled.[97] For this reason, the Court found that it could not disregard the judicial organs set up by the TRNC. Thus, the applicants could be required to exhaust domestic remedies, unless their inexistence or ineffectiveness could be proven. Following the Commission's reasoning based on the ICJ *Namibia* case, the Court also rejected Cyprus' argument that the TRNC courts failed to satisfy the criteria laid down in Article 6 of the ECHR.

Interesting points were made by the judges in their partly dissenting opinions, which advocated a much narrower approach than that used by the majority of the Court. For instance, Judges Palm, Jungwiert, Levits, Pantîru, Kovler, and Marcus-Helmons argued that the Court should have demonstrated some judicial restraint and avoided examining areas of particular complexity and delicacy concerning an unlawful regime.[98] Further, it was not necessary to elaborate a general theory of remedies in the TRNC constructed upon the brief remarks of the ICJ in its advisory opinion on Namibia. According to the judges' view, the Court had undermined the firm position taken by the international community with regard to the TRNC. In this inter-state case, where issues having implications for the

[97] *Cyprus v Turkey* (n 95 above), para 96.

[98] Ibid, partly dissenting opinion of Judge Palm, joined by Judges Jungwiert, Levits, Pantîru, Kovler, and Marcus-Helmons, 107.

international community at large arose, the Court should have followed the position indicated by international practice.

Judge Marcus-Helmons,[99] in a separate dissenting opinion, considered that the Court erred in finding, based on the ICJ's decision, that the courts established by the TRNC could constitute domestic remedies to be exhausted. In his view, the *Namibia* case was misinterpreted by the Commission and the Court. In that case, the ICJ recognized exceptionally certain elements of de facto regimes when their effects could only be ignored to the detriment of the inhabitants. Here, requiring the applicants to exhaust remedies known to be ineffective would constitute an additional obstacle and would be to their detriment.[100] Further, the advisory opinion did not concern the exhaustion of domestic remedies or the validity of the courts established by an illegal regime.[101] The situation in Namibia and northern Cyprus are also completely different. Moreover, in the *Loizidou* case,[102] the Court did not refer to the *Namibia* case when considering the issue of the exhaustion of remedies under former Article 26 of the ECHR. Therefore, by using the ICJ advisory opinion with regard to this provision, the Court attributed an unduly wide interpretation to the ICJ's reasoning, for which there was no basis and which the ICJ never intended. He further emphasized that '[t]he Convention is a *lex specialis* whose special features must be respected and which is amenable to reasoning by analogy only in situations that are on all fours with each other (which is evidently not the case with the Advisory Opinion in the case of Namibia)'.[103] In his view, the courts established illegally in northern Cyprus did not fulfil the requirements of Article 6 of the ECHR. Judge Marcus-Helmons, nevertheless, found that the Court and the Commission treated with undue caution certain of the UN documents adduced by the applicant Government, which demonstrated that important ECHR violations occurred in northern Cyprus.[104]

References to the ICJ framework further allowed the Court to strengthen the ECHR by reversing former case law and ruling that interim measures were binding. In *Mamatkulov and Askarov v Turkey*,[105] the Court relied, *inter alia*, on the change in the ICJ's case law to support its finding that interim measures had an obligatory character. The Court recalled that the ICJ had found in the *LaGrand (Germany v United States of America)* case[106] that interim measures were binding and that this finding had been followed in subsequent case law. Relying on Article 31 of the VCLT, the ICJ used the following words:

[99] Ibid, partly dissenting opinion of Judge Marcus-Helmons, 125.
[100] Ibid, 126. [101] Ibid, 126, para 2.
[102] *Loizidou v Turkey (Merits)* (n 62 above).
[103] *Cyprus v Turkey* (n 95 above), partly dissenting opinion of Judge Marcus-Helmons, 127.
[104] Ibid, 132. [105] *Mamatkulov and Askarov v Turkey* (n 48 above).
[106] *LaGrand (Germany v United States of America)*, judgment, 27 June 2001, 2001 ICJ Reports, 466.

[i]t follows from the object and purpose of the Statute, as well as from the terms of Article 41 when read in their context, that the power to indicate provisional measures entails that such measures should be binding, inasmuch as the power in question is based on the necessity, when the circumstances call for it, to safeguard, and to avoid prejudice to, the rights of the parties as determined by the final judgment of the Court. The contention that provisional measures indicated under Article 41 might not be binding would be contrary to the object and purpose of that Article.[107]

This position was later confirmed in subsequent case law, and thus the ICJ attributed an obligatory character to provisional measures under the ICJ Statute.

Relying on the ICJ's finding, the ECtHR stated that 'the ICJ, [and other international bodies], although operating under different treaty provisions to those of the Court, have confirmed in their reasoning in recent decisions that the preservation of the asserted rights of the parties in the face of the risk of irreparable damage represents an essential objective of interim measures in international law. Indeed it can be said that, whatever the legal system in question, the proper administration of justice requires that no irreparable action be taken while proceedings are pending'.[108] Thus, the change in the ICJ's jurisprudence was reflected at the European level, in spite of the dissident's criticism that the Court was exercising a legislative function in this case.[109]

In *Blečić v Croatia*,[110] the respondent Government invoked an ICJ decision arguing that it was not the date on which the dispute arose that was important to establish jurisdiction *ratione materiae*, but the date on which facts giving rise to the dispute occurred. The case concerned a Croatian national who acquired a specially protected tenancy of a flat in Zadar. She went to stay with her daughter in Rome for a summer and asked a neighbour to pay the bills in her absence and to take care of the flat. Due to the war in Croatia, the lack of financial means, and poor health, the applicant stayed longer with her daughter in Rome. In the meantime, the Zadar Municipality brought a civil action against the applicant for termination of her tenancy, on the ground that she had been absent from the flat for more than six months without justification. The applicant alleged that her rights with regard to respect for her home and peaceful enjoyment of her possessions had been infringed under Article 8 of the ECHR and Article 1 of Protocol No 1. Croatia ratified the ECHR on 5 November 1997, and difficulties arose in the instant case given that the facts relied on fell partly within and partly outside the period of the Court's competence.

[107] Ibid, para 102.

[108] *Mamatkulov and Askarov v Turkey* (n 48 above), para 124 (text inserted by author); see also Christos L Rozakis, 'The European Judge as Comparatist' (2005) 80(1) Tul L Rev 257, 267–268, 275–276. See also *Paladi v Moldova* (App No 39806/05), judgment, 10 March 2009, not yet reported, where the Court also referred to the *LaGrand* judgment.

[109] *Mamatkulov and Askarov v Turkey* (n 48 above), joint partly dissenting opinion of Judges Caflisch, Türmen, and Kovler, 351.

[110] *Blečić v Croatia* (App No 59532/00), judgment, 8 March 2006, not reported.

The respondent Government raised a preliminary objection arguing that the Court lacked temporal jurisdiction. As part of the relevant international sources, the Croatian Government invoked the decision of the PCIJ in *Phosphates in Morocco*[111] and the ICJ case concerning *Certain Property (Lichtenstein v Germany)*.[112] The PCIJ found in *Phosphates in Morocco* that 'situations and facts which form the subject of the limitation *ratione temporis* have to be considered from the point of view of both of their date in relation to the date of ratification and of their connection with the birth of the dispute. Situations or facts subsequent to the ratification could serve to found the Court's compulsory jurisdiction only if it was with regard to them that dispute arose'.[113] The ICJ, however, reasoned that it was not the date on which the dispute arose that was important for establishing jurisdiction *ratione temporis*, but rather the date on which the facts or situations that led to the dispute occurred.[114] The applicant argued that the Government's reference to the ICJ's decision was irrelevant because the case law of the Court was significantly different from that of the ICJ due to the special nature of the Convention. Moreover, the Court, unlike the ICJ, recognized continuing violations, and the termination of the applicant's tenancy had resulted in a continuing situation (she was prevented at all times from returning to her home).[115]

The Court did not explicitly cite the decisions of the PCIJ and ICJ, but it appears to have followed the ICJ's reasoning by finding that jurisdiction *ratione temporis* is to be determined on the basis of the facts constitutive of the alleged interference.[116] The Court only explicitly mentioned its own case law to support this reasoning, which nonetheless appears generally to converge with the decisions of the ICJ. The Court found that the termination of the applicant's tenancy had been the fact constitutive of the alleged interference. Thus, it was held that this event had occurred before Croatia ratified the ECHR and that it fell outside the Court's temporal jurisdiction.

2.7 Judicial Review of the UN's Actions

A crucial reference to the ICJ framework appeared in *Behrami and Behrami v France* and *Saramati v France, Germany and Norway*,[117] where the ECtHR declined to review the actions conducted by the United Nations in Kosovo and enforced the principle of the primacy of the UN Charter over conflicting international instruments (in this case, the ECHR). The UN's administration of Kosovo

[111] *Phosphates in Morocco (Italy v France)*, judgment, Permanent Court of International Justice, 14 June 1938, Series A/B, No 74.

[112] *Certain Property (Lichtenstein v Germany) (Preliminary Objections)*, judgment, 10 February 2005, 2005 ICJ Reports 6.

[113] *Phosphates in Morocco (Italy v France)* (n 111 above), 24.

[114] *Certain Property (Lichtenstein v Germany)*, paras 48–49.

[115] *Blečić v Croatia* (n 110 above), para 57.

[116] Ibid, para 77.

[117] *Behrami and Behrami v France* and *Saramati v France, Germany and Norway* (App Nos 71412/01; 78166/01), judgment, 2 May 2007, not yet reported.

was a result of the ongoing armed conflict between Serbian and Kosovar forces in the then Federal Republic of Yugoslavia (FRY) that prompted international action. The North Atlantic Treaty Organization (NATO) conducted strategic air strikes on Serbian installations. The FRY agreed to the presence of an international peace-keeping force, to be established by UN Security Council Resolution 1244. This resolution called, *inter alia*, for the deployment to Kosovo of a NATO security force (KFOR) and the creation of the UN Interim Administrative Mission in Kosovo (UNMIK).

The applicants in the *Behrami and Behrami* case complained about the inaction of KFOR troops with regard to undetonated cluster bombs, which had been dropped when NATO bombed the FRY. The applicant's sons had played with such a bomb, which later detonated killing one son and injuring the other. The applicants claimed that France violated Article 2 of the ECHR, because French troops failed to mark or defuse known unexploded ordnance. The applicant in the *Saramati* case complained that he had been arrested by UNMIK police officers for attempted murder and unlawful possession of weapons. He successfully appealed and was released. Subsequently, he was arrested again and taken to a KFOR camp. The KFOR assumed authority to detain the applicant under Resolution 1244 of the UN Security Council to maintain a 'safe and secure environment'. Saramati was detained by order of the KFOR throughout his trial. He was convicted of murder, but his conviction was quashed; he was then released and a retrial was ordered. His complaint was against France, Germany, and Norway under Articles 5, 6(1), and 13 of the ECHR concerning his extra-judicial detention and the obligation of Contracting States to provide a fair trial. The respondent Governments submitted that the applications were incompatible *ratione loci* and *personae* with the ECHR provisions because the applicants did not fall within their jurisdiction as laid down in Article 1 of the ECHR. The Governments also maintained that, in accordance with the ICJ's *Monetary Gold* principle,[118] the Court could not decide the merits of the case as it would be determining rights and obligations of non-Contracting Parties.[119] The Court issued a joint decision holding that it was incompetent *ratione personae* to review complaints when the impugned conduct was attributable to the United Nations.

The Court considered that the question raised by the cases was whether it was competent to examine under the ECHR the Contracting States' contribution to the relevant civil and security presence having control in Kosovo. At the outset, the Court noted that it was not part of 'its role to seek to define authoritatively the meaning of provisions of the UN Charter and other international instruments: it must nevertheless examine whether there was a plausible basis in such

[118] *Monetary Gold Removed from Rome in 1943 (Italy v France, United Kingdom of Great Britain and Northern Ireland and United States of America)*, Preliminary Question, judgment, 15 June 1954, 1954 ICJ Reports, 19.

[119] *Behrami and Behrami v France* and *Saramati v France, Germany and Norway* (n 117 above), para 67.

instruments for the matters impugned before it'.[120] Referring to Article 31(3)(c) of the VCLT, the Court found that the ECHR could not be interpreted and applied in a vacuum, as account had to be taken of the relevant rules of international law.

The Court determined that the issuing of detention orders fell within the mandate of the KFOR and the supervision of de-mining into the mandate of the UNMIK. It also found that the impugned action of the KFOR and the inaction of the UNMIK could be attributed to the UN. This finding was rooted in the fact that Chapter VII of the UN Charter provided a framework for the delegation of the UN Security Council's security powers to the KFOR and of its civil administration powers to the UNMIK. Nonetheless, it was recalled, on the basis of the ICJ *Reperations* case,[121] that the UN had a separate legal personality from that of its Member States and that it was not a Contracting Party to the ECHR.

The Court then considered whether it was competent to review the acts of states carried out on behalf of the UN and, more generally, as to the relationship between the Convention and the UN's actions under Chapter VII of the UN Charter. The Court noted that the great majority of Contracting States had joined the UN before ratifying the ECHR and that all Contracting States were members of the UN. In fact, one of the aims of the ECHR was the collective enforcement of the Universal Declaration of Human Rights. Further, it was found that the Convention had to be interpreted in light of any rules and principles applicable in relations between the Contracting Parties. Pursuant to this requirement, the Court had regard to two complementary provisions of the UN Charter, Articles 25 and 103, as interpreted by the ICJ.[122] It is significant that in this context the Court entrusted the interpretation of the Charter to the ICJ, which is not an assumption that can readily be made. The Charter was drafted without any reference to any organ responsible for its interpretation.[123] A survey of ICJ case law demonstrates that the International Court of Justice has affirmed its power to interpret the UN Charter.[124] While the position of the ICJ has been disputed, it appears that a majority of international lawyers would be in favour of empowering it with such a function.[125]

The Court then emphasized that the primary objective of the UN was the maintenance of international peace and security:

> While it is equally clear that ensuring respect for human rights represents an important contribution to achieving international peace (see the Preamble to the Convention), the

[120] Ibid, para 122.

[121] *Reparation of Injuries Suffered in the Service of the United Nations*, 11 April 1949, 1949 ICJ Reports 174; *Behrami and Behrami v France* and *Saramati v France, Germany and Norway* (n 117 above), para 144.

[122] *Reparation of Injuries Suffered in the Service of the United Nations* (n 121 above), para 147.

[123] Mohamed Sameh M Amr, *The Role of the International Court of Justice as the Principal Judicial Organ of the United Nations, Legal Aspects of International Organisation* (The Hague/London/New York: Kluwer Law International, 2003), 124.

[124] Ibid, 127–128.

[125] Ibid, 124–125.

fact remains that the UNSC has primary responsibility, as well as extensive means under Chapter VII, to fulfil this objective, notably through the use of coercive measures. The responsibility of the UNSC in this respect is unique and has evolved as a counterpart to the prohibition, now customary international law, on the unilateral use of force.[126]

Thus, given that the operations established by UN Security Council Resolutions under Chapter VII are fundamental to this mission of the UN and that they rely for their effectiveness on the support of Member States, 'the Convention cannot be interpreted in a manner which would subject the acts and omissions of Contracting Parties which are covered by UNSC Resolutions and occur prior to or in the course of such missions, to the scrutiny of the Court'.[127] The Court considered that to do so would interfere with the fulfilment of the UN's key missions in the field, including the effective conduct of its operations. It would also amount to imposing conditions on the implementation of a UNSC Resolution which was not provided for in the text itself.[128]

This reasoning was rooted in the primacy principle of the UN Charter over other conflicting international treaties, as interpreted by the ICJ. The World Court had previously found that, pursuant to Article 103 of the UN Charter, the Charter obligations of UN Member States prevailed over conflicting obligations from another international treaty, regardless of whether the latter treaty was concluded before or after the UN Charter or was only a regional arrangement.[129] The Court also based itself on the ICJ's finding that, pursuant to Article 25 of the UN Charter, the UN Member States' obligations under a UN Security Council Resolution prevailed over obligations arising under any other international agreement.[130] In addition, the Court determined that the present case was clearly distinguishable from its earlier judgment in the *Bosphorous* case,[131] which the applicants referred to.

In the *Bosphorous* case, the Irish authorities impounded an aircraft in application of a UN Security Council Resolution, under the UN Charter (and a subsequent decision of the European Union). Taking this factor duly into account, the Court noted that:

State action taken in compliance with such legal obligations is justified as long as the relevant organisation is considered to protect fundamental rights, as regards both the substantive guarantees offered and the mechanisms controlling their observance, in a manner which can be considered at least equivalent to that for which the Convention provides... 'equivalent'... means 'comparable'; any requirement that the organisation's

[126] *Behrami and Behrami v France* and *Saramati v France, Germany and Norway* (n 117 above), para 148.

[127] Ibid, para 149.

[128] Ibid.

[129] *Military and Paramilitary Activities in and against Nicaragua (Nicaragua v United States of America)*, judgment, 26 November 1984, 1984 ICJ Reports 392, paras 107, 27.

[130] *Questions of Interpretation and Application of the 1971 Montreal Convention arising from the Aerial Incident at Lockerbie (Libyan Arab Jamahiriya v United States of America) (Preliminary Objections)*, 14 April 1992, 1992 ICJ Reports 114, 126, para 42.

[131] *Bosphorous Hava Yolları Turizm ve Ticaret Anonim Şirketi v Ireland* (App No 45036/98), judgment, 30 June 2005, Reports 2005-VI, 107.

protection be 'identical' could run counter to the interest of international cooperation pursued.... However, any such finding of equivalence could not be final and would be susceptible to review in the light of any relevant change in fundamental rights protection.[132]

Thus, it was found that the protection of fundamental rights through EU law could be considered 'equivalent' to that of the ECHR. Consequently, a presumption arose that Ireland did not depart from the requirements of the ECHR when it implemented legal obligations flowing from its EU membership. Such a presumption could be rebutted if, in a particular case, it was considered that the protection of Convention rights was manifestly deficient. In such cases, the interest of international cooperation would be outweighed by the Convention's role as a 'constitutional instrument of European public order' in the field of human rights. Thus, the Court's approach in the *Behrami* case departs from the approach in the *Bosphorous* case, given that the Court did not attempt to verify whether the UN Charter was 'equivalent' to the ECHR and simply gave priority to the former.

In addition, the Court's reasoning in the *Behrami* case differed diametrically from the reasoning adopted by the International Criminal Tribunal for the former Yugoslavia (ICTY) in the *Tadić* case.[133] The ICTY considered that, while it could not act as a constitutional tribunal to review UN acts, the power of the Tribunal did not disappear, 'particularly in cases where there might be a manifest contradiction with the Principles and Purposes of the Charter'.[134] In that case, the ICTY found that it had jurisdiction to examine the legality of its own establishment. Against this background, the ECtHR's finding in the *Behrami* case becomes even more surprising. It could be argued that the Court has treated the UN Charter as a constitutional instrument overriding ECHR rights, and thereby seems to have relied in its reasoning on a strand of the international constitutionalism which identifies the UN Charter as the constitution and attaches great importance to its primacy enshrined in Article 103. It seems, however, more plausible that the Court exercised judicial restraint in order not to interfere with the good functioning of the UN. Additionally, given the complexity of the international issues at stake, the Court may have wanted to avoid any further conflict and decided, prudently, to declare the case incompatible *ratione personae* with the provisions of the ECHR.

The *Behrami* reasoning was later followed in *Kasumaj v Greece*[135] and *Gajic v Germany*[136]—decisions dealing with issues of property occupied or used by KFOR contingents in Kosovo. The Court recalled, in both cases, that KFOR

[132] Ibid, para 155.

[133] *The Prosecutor v Duško Tadić*, Decision on the Defence Motion for Interlocutory Appeal on Jurisdiction, Case No IT-94-1, A Ch 2, October 1995, paras 20–22. See also Martti Koskenniemi and Päivi Leino, 'Fragmentation of International Law? Postmodern Anxieties' (2002) 15 LJIL 553, 563.

[134] *The Prosecutor v Duško Tadić* (n 133 above), para 22.

[135] *Kasumaj v Greece* (App No 6974/05), decision, 5 July 2007, not yet reported.

[136] *Gajic v Germany* (App No 36357/04), decision, 28 August 2007, not yet reported.

actions were in principle attributable to the UN, which had a legal personality separate from that of its Member States and which was not a Contracting Party to the ECHR. Relying on the *Behrami* case, the Court further held that it was not competent *ratione personae* to review the acts of the respondent States carried out on behalf of the UN. The same line of reasoning was followed in *Dušan Berić and others v Bosnia and Herzegovina*.[137] In this case, the High Representative removed the applicants from their public and political party positions and indefinitely barred them from holding any such positions and from running for election. The Court extended the *Behrami* reasoning to 'the acceptance of an international civil administration in its territory by a respondent State'[138] and found that the actions of the High Representative were, in principle, attributable to the UN.[139] Again, the Court reiterated that it was incompetent *ratione personae* to review the case in line with its previous decisions.

It is important to note that the ECtHR's reasoning often has, as in this case, a spill-over effect into domestic as well as international jurisdictions. Recently, the House of Lords has made substantial references to the *Behrami* judgment in a case concerning the acts of the Multi-National Force (MNF) in Iraq.[140] In dissenting from the majority view, Lord Rodger of Earlsferry considered that the differences between the situation in Iraq and that in Kosovo were not crucial; they supported the analogy between the *Behrami* case and the instant case. He further found that if the ECtHR had considered the case, it would have held 'that the action of the British troops, as members of the MNF, . . . was in principle attributable to the United Nations in terms of article 3 of the draft articles on the Responsibility of International Organisations'.[141]

The Court's decision in the *Behrami* case gave rise to criticism on the part of the academic community. Recently, Watson found that the ECtHR had weakened the extra-territorial reach of the Convention. Further, it was noted that the case clarified the ECHR's role vis-à-vis the UN Security Council at the expense of previous efforts to create a balance between facilitating international cooperation and ensuring the effective protection of human rights.[142] According to Watson, the Court relied more on the attributability (of responsibility) approach

[137] *Dušan Berić and others v Bosnia and Herzegovina* (Application Nos 36357/04; 36360/04; 38346/04; 41705/04; 45190/04; 45578/04–45580/04; 91/05; 97/05; 100/05; 101/05; 1121/05; 1123/05; 1125/05; 1129/05; 1132/05; 1133/05; 1169/05; 1172/05; 1175/05; 1177/05; 1180/05; 1185/05; 20793/05; 25496/05), decision, 16 October 2007, not yet reported, para 29.

[138] Ibid, para 30. [139] Ibid, para 28.

[140] *R (Al-Jedda) v Secretary of State for Defence* [2007] UKHL 58. See also Alexander Orakhelashvili, 'The Interaction between Human Rights and Humanitarian law: Fragmentation, Conflict, Parallelism, or Convergence?' (2008) 19 Eur J Int'l L 161.

[141] *R (Al-Jedda) v Secretary of State for Defence* (n 140 above), para 105; *Draft Articles on Responsibility of International Organisations*, Report of the International Law Commission on the work of its fifty-ninth session, 7 May to 5 June and 9 July to 10 August 2007, UN Doc No A/62/10, 2007, 184–199, paras 343–344.

[142] William Watson, '*Behrami v. France*: Constructive Blue Helmets Protect KFOR Nations From Accountability' (2008) 16 Tul J Int'l & Comp L 575, 587.

in *Bankovic*[143] than on the jurisdictional approach, as used in the *Loizidou*[144] and *Bosphorous*[145] cases. Thus, the Court's reasoning focused on the functionality of the United Nations and on recognizing the ECHR's place in international law, rather than on ensuring practical and effective protection of ECHR rights. It was emphasized that the protection of human rights should not take a backseat to collective security, as both fields are not mutually exclusive.[146] In addition, this case was not able to find a balance between international cooperation and the protection of European Convention rights.[147]

In a different comment on the same decision, Sari found that the most fundamental objections in relation to the decision concerned the ECtHR's identification of the legal issues raised by the complaints.[148] It was argued that the ECtHR rightly underlined that one of the relevant matters in the case concerned its competence to review the conduct of national contributions to the KFOR and UNMIK. This finding did not entitle it, however, to disregard the question of whether the applicants came within the jurisdiction of the respondent States under Article 1 of the ECHR.[149] The approach used by the Court was thus found to be unsatisfactory because it sidestepped the central issue raised by the case.[150] In addition, it was considered that the ECtHR confused the legality of delegation of Chapter VII powers by the UN Security Council with the attribution of wrongful conduct to an international organization.[151] More fundamentally, Sari also found that the Court set the wrong precedent for the protection of human rights in peace support operations, as it impeded the review of the conduct of national contingents performed in a national capacity during the course of operations established or authorized by the UN Security Council. This could potentially complicate the work of the International Law Commission on the responsibility of international organizations. Furthermore, the Court's argument did not seem to be based on legal conclusions but rather on policy arguments relating to the effective fulfilment of the UN Security Council's Chapter VII mandate and the UN's mission. Thus, in Sari's view, the Court's decision 'constitutes an unnecessary act of self-censorship motivated by an excessive deference to the primary responsibility of the Security Council in maintaining international peace and security'.[152]

In yet another comment regarding the *Behrami* case, it was considered that the Court's reliance on the ILC Draft Articles on the Responsibility of International

[143] *Bankovic, Stojadinovic, Stoiamenovski, Joksimovic and Sukovic v Belgium, the Czech Republic, Denmark, France, Germany, Greece, Hungary, Iceland, Italy, Luxembourg, the Netherlands, Norway, Poland, Portugal, Spain, Turkey and the United Kingdom* (App No 52207/99), decision, 12 December 2001, Reports 2001-XII, 333.

[144] *Loizidou v Turkey (Preliminary Objections)* (n 62 above).

[145] *Bosphorous Hava Yolları Turizm ve Ticaret Anonim Şirketi v Ireland* (n 131 above).

[146] Watson (n 142 above), 590.

[147] Ibid.

[148] Auriel Sari, 'Jurisdiction and International Responsibility in Peace Support Operations: The Behrami and Saramati Cases' (2008) 8 HRLR 151, 158.

[149] Ibid.

[150] Ibid, 159.

[151] Ibid, 169.

[152] Ibid, 170.

Organisations was questionable.[153] For instance, in denying the existence of a sufficient jurisdictional link between the applicants and the respondent States within the meaning of Article 1 of the ECHR, the Court relied on the concept of 'attribution' as reflected in the ILC Draft Articles, but its reasoning was potentially inconsistent with the ILC's own criteria.[154] Furthermore, the Court did not comment on the legal status of Draft Articles 3[155] and 5.[156] Although Draft Article 3 reflects customary international law, Draft Article 5 is specific to the responsibility of international organizations and its character was not addressed by the Court.[157] Further problems appeared in the Court's reasoning, given that it did not consider the possibility of dual or multiple attribution of responsibility.[158]

The criticism evoked by the academic community rightly demonstrates that the Court did not contribute to the advancement of human rights in this case. Rather, it was deferent to the ICJ's position and to the principles contained in the UN Charter which are aimed at protecting and rendering more effective the UN's mission to maintain peace and security. While the Court contributed to some extent to the reduction of fragmentation at the regional level by following the ICJ's reasoning concerning the primacy of the UN Charter, it distanced itself from its previous case law, especially the *Bosphorous* case, where the reasoning was grounded in human rights considerations. While reducing fragmentation may be a desirable goal for the coherence of international law, its achievements may sometimes be costly for the ECHR, as in the instant case, when principles of general international law take over more specific standards protecting individual rights.

3. Rationale of the Reasoning

Although the ICJ is an international body separate from the ECHR system, it has nonetheless played an important role in the case law of the Strasbourg bodies. The ICJ benefits from a considerable reputation which reaches beyond the UN system to the ECtHR's docket. The ICJ Statute provides that the ICJ is the principal judicial organ of the United Nations, and it is considered that the ICJ has the power to authoritatively interpret the UN Charter. Through this power, the ICJ has contributed to the progressive development of UN law and taken part

[153] Pierre Bodeau-Livinec, Gionata P Buzzini, and Santiago Villalpando, 'Agim Behrami & Bekir Behrami v. France; Ruzhdi Saramati v. France, Germany & Norway. Joined App. Nos. 71412/01 & 78166/01' (2008) 102 Am J Int'l L 323, 326–331; n 141 above. See also Pasquale De Sena and Maria Chiara Vitucci, 'The European Courts and the Security Council: Between Dédoublement Fonctionnel and Balancing of Values' (2009) 20 Eur J Int'l L 193, 203–209.

[154] Bodeau-Livinec, Buzzini, and Villalpando (n 153 above), 326–331.

[155] This Draft Article contains the general principles on the attribution of responsibility.

[156] This Draft Article regulates the conduct of bodies or agents placed at the disposal of an international organization by a state or another international organization.

[157] Bodeau-Livinec, Buzzini, and Villalpando (n 153 above), 326.

[158] Ibid, 328–329.

in achieving the objectives of the UN.[159] All ECHR Contracting States are also parties to the ICJ Statute and UN Charter. It is therefore not unusual that the ECtHR seldom disagreed with the findings of the ICJ and PCIJ. When it refused to follow the direction indicated by the latter bodies, this decision was usually justified by the need to reinforce and not weaken the protection of human rights within its special regime. This occurred in spite of the ICJ's increasing tendency to consider human rights issues.

The Strasbourg bodies' occasional unwillingness to follow the ICJ could also be attributed to the fact that the ICJ, like the UN treaty bodies, is composed of a less-homogenous group of states than the ECHR Contracting States. Given the generality of findings relating to such a wide group of states, the Court and the Commission were cautious and hesitant in integrating them into the regional human rights context. In most cases, however, the Court treated the ICJ as an authoritative body and important source of inspiration for the development of the ECHR and the resolution of difficult questions. The Court's approach was probably grounded, at least in part, in the fact that the ICJ renders binding decisions (between the parties to the dispute). This allowed the Court to give the decisions greater weight and to refer to them in a less-inhibited manner.

Initially, the Strasbourg bodies referred modestly to the ICJ framework and did not integrate it into their reasoning. They attributed a lower rank to the case law of the PCIJ and ICJ and treated it only as an aid to interpretation. References to the PCIJ's and the ICJ's findings were, since the beginning, selective, and followed only when they advanced the protection of ECHR rights. When the ICJ framework favoured states' needs over individual rights in certain circumstances, the Strasbourg bodies emphasized the differences between the ICJ and ECHR systems in order to distance themselves from the former. For instance, in the *Loizidou*,[160] *Weber*,[161] and *Belilos*[162] cases, the Court reached a diametrically different conclusion from the ICJ with regard to the opposability of reservations. Thus, an important schism, grounded in the specificity of human rights law, appeared between the standards applied by the ICJ and the ECtHR. These differences strengthened the fragmentation of treaty law concerning reservations. Such an evolution was, however, required in order to preserve the specific nature of human rights treaties.

The decisions of the PCIJ and ICJ, as well as the ICJ Statute, regulate issues of crucial importance for the advancement of international law. As such, they were of great assistance to the Court and to the Commission in the development

[159] Amr (n 123 above), 174.

[160] *Loizidou v Turkey (Preliminary Objections)* (n 62 above); *Loizidou v Turkey (Merits)* (n 62 above).

[161] *Weber v Switzerland* (n 77 above), paras 38–40.

[162] *Belilos v Switzerland* (n 76 above), para 60.

of ECHR rights. In fact, the Strasbourg bodies have greatly benefited from the experience of the PCIJ and ICJ in dealing with certain crucial questions. They have on occasion fully relied on the open paradigm, but overall their reasoning has coalesced around the closed paradigm. Often, the references to the case law or the Statute were prompted by the importance of the issue at stake, such as in the *Cyprus v Turkey* case.[163] The ICJ's judgments were also used by the Court to fill in gaps in the ECHR as part of the *Golder*[164] and *Mamatkulov*[165] cases. In those cases, the Court substantially developed the ECHR and was criticized for exercising a legislative function. Further, the Court relied on ICJ judgments to clarify certain aspects of commercial and compensation law. In several decisions containing references to the ICJ framework, the Court considered controversial international policy issues, such as the status of northern Cyprus. Although northern Cyprus was not recognized by ECHR Contracting States, the Court nevertheless bypassed this requirement and examined important legal questions pertaining to northern Cyprus' institutions. Despite much criticism, the Court demonstrated that it was not willing to defer to the Contracting States' position when important human rights issues were at stake.

As Strasbourg case law evolved, the Commission and the Court continued to underline the differences that existed between the systems and to draw clear limits to the references that could be made to the ICJ framework. In this way, they continued to distance themselves from the PCIJ and ICJ case law and Statute when these did not advance the effective protection of human rights law. However, when there were no relevant decisions or provisions to rely on under the ECHR, the Strasbourg bodies integrated the relevant aspects of these external sources into their case law. In filling gaps and advancing ECHR rights, the Strasbourg bodies felt compelled to rely on the ICJ framework.

The Strasbourg case law reached a critical point in the *Behrami* case,[166] where the Court attributed to the UN Charter and the corresponding ICJ decisions a rank higher than that occupied by the ECHR. In applying the primacy principle of the UN Charter over conflicting international treaties, the Court declined to exercise jurisdiction over UN actions conducted in Kosovo, emphasizing that this would tamper with the UN's mission in maintaining international peace and security. This finding was prompted, at least in part, by the fact that the Court was not created to resolve these kinds of dispute. It therefore felt incompetent to decide complex issues which could hinder the good functioning of the UN. The Court used judicial restraint in order not to interfere with controversial international policy issues under the competence of the UN.

[163] *Cyprus v Turkey* (n 95 above).
[164] *Golder v United Kingdom* (n 30 above).
[165] *Mamatkulov and Askarov v Turkey* (n 48 above).
[166] *Behrami and Behrami v France* and *Saramati v France, Germany and Norway* (n 117 above).

The *Behrami* reasoning could also be rooted in the Court's previous groundbreaking, albeit controversial, case law. For instance, in the *Cyprus v Turkey* inter-State complaint and the *Loizidou*[167] and *Bosphorous*[168] cases, the Court actively intervened in international policy issues and with the position of ECHR Contracting States. The Court's bold reasoning in these cases provoked strong reaction, which may have influenced the Court's return to a cautious and deferential approach in the *Behrami* case. Thus, the Court may have preferred to avoid any active interference in international issues, in order to reinforce its institutional credibility as an impartial court.

The reasoning in the *Behrami* case was nonetheless criticized for treating collective security and human rights as being mutually exclusive. Undoubtedly, this case constitutes one of the strongest and most important references to international sources; the Court simply applied—without further consideration—a fundamental principle of the UN Charter as part of its case law, thereby providing an important leeway to the UN and rendering much more difficult the review of the conduct of national contingents in peace support operations. Thus, the Court's references to the ICJ's findings in this case did not advance human rights, but they did contribute to regional anti-fragmentation of general international law and to the harmonization of the ECtHR's jurisprudence with ICJ decisions.

Undoubtedly, the ICJ represents a tremendous potential for the international community in terms of reducing fragmentation of international law.[169] It has been proposed to strengthen the Court's functions in respect of its role as the central judiciary body of the international community.[170] A wide range of means and procedures for achieving this goal have been suggested by various scholars and institutions.[171] In all likelihood, these changes have not been implemented because they would require a formal revision of the ICJ Statute pursuant to the strict conditions set out in Articles 108 and 109 of the UN Charter.[172] The ECtHR could represent a similar potential at the European level for reducing fragmentation of human rights standards. This prospect is, however, overshadowed by the expansion of the ECJ's jurisdiction in the human rights field. Furthermore, with the entry into force of the EU Treaty of Lisbon, this potential will become further compromised, as two bodies will be sharing competence over human rights at the European level. It is therefore doubtful whether in the distant future the ECtHR can play a dominant role as regards anti-fragmentation at the regional level.

167 *Loizidou v Turkey (Preliminary Objections)* (n 62 above).

168 *Bosphorous Hava Yolları Turizm ve Ticaret Anonim Şirketi v Ireland* (n 131 above).

169 Dupuy (n 5 above), 798–801.

170 Ibid, 798–802; Francisco Orrego Vicuña and Christofer Pinto, *The Peaceful Settlement of Disputes: Prospects for the Twenty-First Century*, Preliminary Report Prepared for the 1999 Centennial of the First International Peace Conference (The Hague, 1999).

171 Dupuy (n 5 above), 799.

172 Ibid, 800.

Another interesting aspect of the fragmentation problem is revealed by the analysis of the ECtHR's references to the PCIJ and ICJ case law and Statute. These constitute, in effect, references from a special regime to the general international legal order. The Court followed the dichotomy of special and general regimes in the *Loizidou* case[173] when it distinguished itself from the ICJ on the basis of its role and purpose. Although the ICJ framework does not tower over the international legal pyramid, it is a general international procedural system which transcends the other more restrained and special regimes. The ICJ is also capable of authoritatively interpreting primary international law, such as the UN Charter. Arguably, it would be easier for the Court to refer to this overreaching and more general international legal sphere than to other specialized legal domains. It is, however, more plausible that the ECtHR feels inhibited by the important differences that still exist between the ECHR and ICJ systems. It is therefore more convenient for the ECtHR to rely on other specialized international human rights systems. These regimes are much closer to the ECHR than the ICJ framework, as they concern a similar area and have similar objectives.

Finally, it appears that Strasbourg references to the ICJ framework are grounded in an older and more common question, namely the relationship between human rights law and general international law. While still mostly concerned with state relations and sovereignty, general international law has substantially evolved in the last decades. In fact, the human rights doctrine has created an important shift in traditional international law based on reciprocal legal relations and geared to the pursuit of states' interests.[174] As a result, international law has increasingly become imbued with human rights standards to the extent that it is no longer limited to regulation between states but also extends to the treatment of individuals within states.[175] Strasbourg references to the ICJ framework support this trend by demonstrating that it is possible for regional human rights bodies to rely on ICJ jurisprudence, which is becoming more sensitive to human rights standards.

Nonetheless, in spite of the ICJ's expanding treatment of human rights, it still remains doubtful whether the development of authoritative anti-fragmentation human rights jurisprudence will be possible under its auspices. At present, the differences between the systems still disallow the Court to fully integrate ICJ rulings into its case law. Unlike the ECtHR, the ICJ's jurisdiction remains grounded in reciprocity between states and is unavailable to individual applicants. Thus far, these references to the ICJ framework have contributed mostly towards reducing fragmentation of general international law and less towards harmonizing international human rights standards. Reducing fragmentation at

[173] *Loizidou v Turkey (Preliminary Objections)* (n 62 above), paras 84–85.

[174] Cassese (n 78 above), 396.

[175] Arnold Pronto, '"Human-Rightism" and the Development of General International Law' (2007) 20 LJIL 753, 754.

the regional level may have a substantial price for ECHR rights, if the international law being referred to does not enshrine the same human rights standards. Thus, ensuring that international law is not fragmented is not always a relevant consideration for the ECtHR when it is expounding human rights. For these reasons, the Strasbourg bodies have been compelled to rely on the closed paradigm in most of the cases assessed in this chapter.

III

Child Rights

1. Preliminary Observations

It is paramount in the international community that children's rights are taken seriously.[1] States across the globe have become more and more aware of the need to recognize the individuality and autonomy of children, who, like everybody else, have a status under international law. In the last decades, the United Nations and various NGOs have spoken emphatically of the inadequate situation of children throughout the world and of the need to improve their living conditions. It is believed that our future is inextricably linked to the childhoods of today, as children are the future hope of the current generation. Their situation today may reflect the nature of the developments that will take place in the years to come. For this reason, it is believed necessary to provide children with the right means to develop adequately and to grow up in the most favourable of conditions. As a response to these concerns, international child rights law is premised on the idea that law is an important tool to improve the lives of children.

In contrast, the ECHR contains very few explicit references to children and lacks any firm recognition of their rights. There is, however, some protection granted to children in very specific areas.[2] From a textual point of view, the ECHR affirms the dominance of parents in contexts relating to children. This situation evolved over time, as the European Court of Human Rights (ECtHR) adapted the ECHR to the changing standards in Contracting States. The objective of rendering the ECHR more child-friendly penetrated the ECtHR's reasoning and resulted in an extremely interesting and prolific case law, characterized by a very attentive approach to international developments.

This chapter will focus on four basic international instruments which significantly improved the situation of children around the globe, and found their way into the case law of the ECtHR, namely the Hague Convention on the Civil Aspects of International Child Abduction, the Hague Convention on Intercountry Adoption, the United Nations Convention on the Rights of the Child, and the International Labour Organization Convention concerning the Prohibition and

[1] Michael Freeman, 'Taking Children's Rights More Seriously' in Philip Alston, Steven Parker, and John Seymour (eds), *Children, Rights and the Law* (Oxford: Clarendon Press, 1992), 52.

[2] ECHR, Arts 5 and 6; Protocol No 1, Art 2; and Protocol No 7, Art 5.

Immediate Action for the Elimination of the Worst Forms of Child Labour (ILO Convention No 182). These four instruments are very well adapted to be considered within the ECHR framework, given that they have been ratified by most ECHR Contracting States. Nonetheless, the levels of reception with respect to each vary and the aim of this chapter is to uncover the factors which played a role in adapting the ECHR to international child rights law.

2. The Hague Convention on International Child Abduction

2.1 Strasbourg Case Law

After many years of deliberation, the Hague Conference on Private International Law decided to enact a treaty that regulates private international law remedies on child abduction. The Convention on the Civil Aspects of International Child Abduction was adopted on 24 October 1980 at the Fourteenth Session of the Hague Conference on Private International Law in Plenary Session by a unanimous vote of the states present.[3] It was initially signed by four states (France, Canada, Switzerland, and Greece). The number of Contracting States to the Convention has since risen to 79, which includes 42 ECHR Contracting States.[4] Andorra, Armenia, Azerbaijan, Liechtenstein, and Russia never signed the Hague Convention. Despite this, it appears that the Hague Convention has a high popularity among the ECHR Contracting States.

The Hague Convention on International Child Abduction has a mostly procedural character and is not an instrument dealing with the substantive aspects of custody. In general, its field of application is limited to providing practical measures 'to combat the illicit transfer and non-return of children abroad'. Its primary objective is to secure the prompt return of children wrongly removed or retained in any Contracting State and to ensure that the rights of custody and access under the law of one Contracting State are respected in other Contracting States.[5] It is also intended to re-establish the status quo that existed before the abduction took place, and to serve as a deterrent to parents engaging in forum shopping.[6] The Convention established central authorities, namely domestic governmental offices, to administer the operations under the Convention. These offices act, *inter alia*, as transmittal bodies ensuring the return of children.

[3] Elisa Pérez-Vera, *Explanatory Report*, The Hague Conference on Private International Law (HCCH Publications, 1982), 428.

[4] This information was verified on 13 June 2010: The Hague Conference on Private International Law, Status Table, <http://hcch.e-vision.nl/index_en.php?act=conventions.status&cid=24#nonmem>.

[5] Hague Convention, Art 1.

[6] Michael Walshand and Susan Savard, 'International Child Abduction and the Hague Convention (2006) 6 Barry L Rev 29.

The 1980 Hague Convention became the legal *modus operandi* in situations involving international child abduction. It was implemented at the domestic level by most Contracting States. Despite this, there are still several problems associated with the enforcement of the Convention. Domestic courts do not always interpret the Convention uniformly in the 79 Contracting States, which gives an uneven application of the Convention at the domestic level. Problems also arise with respect to the lack of constructive cooperation on the part of national authorities and courts, and the slow pace at which the return orders are enforced. Other issues of enforcement relate to the substance of the Convention, namely the short period of time during which it is possible to bring a return action and the defences or exceptions to return that can be invoked.[7]

In most of the ECHR Contracting States, a central authority has been put into place to deal with the abduction of children from one Hague Convention State to another. Although this has not prevented the ECtHR from examining complaints relating to child abduction, the existence of a proper forum has served to reduce the number of such complaints before the Court.[8] In this context, the ECtHR became an important body within the framework of the 1980 Hague Convention by reinforcing its application in ECHR Contracting States. Nonetheless, the lack of consensus at the European level regarding childcare and the legitimate nature of state interference have complicated the task of the Court even further.[9] In the past, the Court has recognized that national authorities are better placed to make an assessment of the circumstances in each case, being closer to the sensitive and complex issues involved.[10] Thus, Contracting States enjoy a certain degree of discretion in the determination of issues dealing with respect of family life. However, this degree of discretion is not constant, and varies in accordance with the seriousness of the issues and interests at stake; Contracting States have a greater margin of appreciation in cases dealing with the necessity of taking a child into care and a smaller margin with regard to restrictions on parental contact or any legal safeguards implemented to protect the right to family life.[11]

Most ECtHR judgments pertaining to the 1980 Hague Convention concern the question of whether the domestic decisions taken subsequent to a parent's abduction of a child to another country comply with the ECHR. In the jurisprudence of the ECtHR, this issue seems to have required stricter scrutiny than more complex family questions, where Contracting States have greater discretion. Although the Strasbourg Court has no jurisdiction to examine direct

[7] Linda Silberman, 'Interpreting the Hague Abduction Convention: In Search of a Global Jurisprudence' (2005) 38 UC Davis L Rev 1049, 1051.

[8] Ursula Kilkelly, *The Child and the European Convention on Human Rights* (Dartmouth/Aldershot/Brookfield/Singapore/Sydney: Ashgate, 1999), 259.

[9] Ibid, 204.

[10] Ibid. See also *Olsson v Sweden (No 2)* (App No 13441/87), judgment, 27 November 1992, Series A, Vol 250, para 90.

[11] Kilkelly (n 8 above), 204.

complaints concerning the implementation of the 1980 Hague Convention, it is able to evaluate whether the decisions made by domestic authorities pursuant to their obligations under that Convention comply with the ECHR. Significantly, the ECtHR has also established that the ECHR articles relevant to child abduction must be interpreted in light of the 1980 Hague Convention. In addition, it has granted greater protection to children than that afforded by the 1980 Hague Convention, thereby updating and expanding its scope of application.

It is also important to note that substantial differences exist between the ECHR and the 1980 Hague Convention. The former is a general human rights treaty enacted at the regional level and dealing with both procedural and substantive aspects of human rights. The latter is a mostly procedural treaty, enacted at the international level, dealing with a very specific aspect of child rights. The nature, scope, and level of enforcement of the two treaties are substantially different. This aspect, however, has not prevented the ECtHR from resorting to the 1980 Hague Convention when necessary. The Commission and Court have gradually developed considerable case law in the field of child abduction. These cases are usually closely intertwined with the 1980 Hague Convention, which was either invoked or applied in the decisions taken at the domestic level.

The Hague domestic proceedings appear before the Commission and Court in the form of complaints filed under Article 8 of the ECHR (right to respect for private and family life). Given that there is no special article dealing with child abduction under the ECHR, Article 8 has been used as a catch-all provision in this context. Article 8 protects the right to private and family life and prohibits public authorities from interfering with this right. Exceptionally, limitations of the right are allowed if they comply with the law and are necessary in a democratic society for certain legitimate interests.[12] In addition, Article 8 imposes positive obligations upon Contracting States, requiring them to take affirmative action to respect family life. The notion of positive obligation is, however, vague and the determination of its scope has been considered on the basis of a balancing exercise between the general interests of society and the interests of the individual applicant.[13]

2.2 The Case Law of the Commission

The Commission considered only six cases during the 15 years from the entry into force of the 1980 Hague Convention to the abolition of the Commission in

[12] These legitimate interests are national security, public safety or the economic well-being of the country, the prevention of disorder or crime, the protection of health or morals, and the protection of the rights and freedoms of others. See Art 8(2) of the ECHR.

[13] Kilkelly (n 8 above), 198.

1998.[14] It is interesting to note that in the early case law, important references were already being made to the 1980 Hague Convention.

In the Commission's first case (decided in 1993) pertaining to the 1980 Hague Convention, it was found that a complaint filed by a father for a violation of his right to a fair trial during return proceedings was inadmissible.[15] The applicant alleged that Article 6(1) of the ECHR had been breached, as a Norwegian court had ordered the return of his son to the mother without hearing the father. The domestic proceedings were conducted pursuant to the 1980 Hague Convention. The Commission found that there was no determination of a 'criminal charge' or of 'civil rights and obligations' involved in the case. Hence, it was decided that the 1980 Convention did not deal with a determination of 'civil rights and obligations', but rather a determination of fact.[16] This seems to be accurate as the 1980 Convention deals, as discussed above, with procedural issues and not substantive rights. Despite this, the issue was not taken up further in subsequent case law and Article 6 was either applied with no further arguments[17] or it was determined that the 1980 Hague Convention concerned the applicant's 'civil rights'.[18]

The next direct reference to the 1980 Hague Convention occurred in the *Laylle v Germany* decision,[19] which concerned a mother whose application for the return of her sons, retained unlawfully by their father, had been rejected by German courts. It was previously agreed between the parents that the children would stay with their mother in the United Kingdom during the school year and that they would spend their holidays with their father in Germany. In English domestic proceedings, it was decided that the retention of the children by their father was a wrongful retention within the meaning of Article 3 of the 1980 Hague Convention. In German proceedings, however, the mother's request for the return of her children was refused, and the German court based its decision on the views of the children.

Before the Commission, the applicant submitted that there was a violation of Articles 6, 8, and 14 of the ECHR. She alleged that the German court, which heard her two sons, aged seven and nine, did not hear her and thus violated her right to a fair hearing. In addition, the Court made no reference to the fact that she had not seen the boys for over four months by the time of the decision and

[14] Andrea Schulz, 'The 1980 Hague Child Abduction Convention and the European Convention on Human Rights' (2002) 12 TLCP 355, 356; *S v Norway* (App No 19992/92), decision (Commission), 5 May 1993, not reported; *Laylle v Germany* (App No 26376/95), decision (Commission), 4 September 1996, not reported; *Sogn Koutsofotinos v Norway and Greece* (App No 27095/95), decision (Commission), 10 September 1997, not reported; *Olsson v Norway* (App No 20592/92), decision (Commission), 5 April 1995, not reported; *Larson v Sweden* (App No 33250/96), decision (Commission), 22 October 1997, not reported; *Herron v United States* (App No 36931/97), decision (Commission), 3 December 1997, not reported.

[15] *S v Norway* (n 14 above).

[16] Schulz (n 14 above), 360.

[17] *Laylle v Germany* (n 14 above); Schulz (n 14 above), 360.

[18] *Larson v Sweden* (n 14 above); Schulz (n 14 above), 360.

[19] *Laylle v Germany* (n 14 above).

that they must have been influenced by the father. In her view, the children were too young for the case to be wholly decided on their own statements. The Commission held that the applicant's rights had not been violated.

Mrs Laylle had invoked the 1980 Hague Convention at the domestic level and the domestic courts had applied it in their decisions. She also invoked the 1980 Hague Convention before the European Commission of Human Rights. Thus, the Commission applied the 1980 Hague Convention directly when it considered whether there was a legitimate interference with the applicant's right to respect for her family life:

> The Commission considers that, on the basis of the intention and wording of the Child Abduction Convention and the wrongful retention of the children by their father, the applicant could reasonably expect that the children would be returned and that custody and access proceedings (if any were necessary) would then take place in England. The decisions of the German courts not to order the children's return can therefore be regarded as an interference with her right to respect for her family life.[20]

Even more explicitly, the Commission found that 'the Child Abduction Convention clearly and unambiguously permits, by the second paragraph of its Article 13, a refusal to order the return of a child where the child objects to being returned and has attained the age of maturity at which it is appropriate to take account of its views'.[21]

The Commission also underlined the lack of clarity of Article 13 of the 1980 Hague Convention (although it did not resolve the question):

> It is not clear whether the provisions of the third paragraph of the Child Abduction Convention require, as the applicant claims, the obtention of information from the relevant Central Authority or other competent authority when a decision is being taken under the second paragraph, whether that paragraph only applies in connection with the first paragraph, or whether it only applies where such information has been received.[22]

It did not, however, attempt to clarify the meaning of Article 13 of the 1980 Hague Convention, given that the applicant had not referred to this part of the article in the domestic proceedings. The Commission determined that the question of whether children were heard during proceedings and what weight should be attributed to their views was a matter of domestic law. It was, however, acceptable for a domestic court to hear children in absence of the parties and to base a decision solely upon the children's views. Mrs Laylle's application was thus rejected.

It is interesting to note that the 1980 Hague Convention is vague, as it does not explicitly state how the views of children should be taken into account and seems to leave the question to the domestic law. Article 13(2) merely states that '[t]he judicial or administrative authority may also refuse to order the return of the child if it finds that the child objects to being returned and has attained an age and degree of maturity at which it is appropriate to take account of its views'. The

[20] Ibid. [21] Ibid. [22] Ibid.

Commission's application of the ECHR therefore seems to fall within the scope of application of the 1980 Hague Convention.

The 1980 Hague Convention was also directly referred to in *Larson v Sweden*,[23] where the daughter of the applicant had been wrongfully retained by her mother. In this case, the applicant, an American citizen, and his Swedish wife decided to establish their residence in Utah, in the United States. The mother abducted the daughter twice (in 1991 and 1992) and remained with her in Sweden. She instituted divorce and custody proceedings there: a Swedish court ordered the dissolution of the marriage, gave her the temporary custody of the daughter, and granted the applicant visiting rights.

Subsequently, on a visit to Sweden, the applicant abducted his daughter. The mother instituted proceedings against him in Utah, and the court ordered the return of the daughter to the mother pending a hearing scheduled at a later date. The order prohibited the mother from removing the daughter from Utah. The applicant complied with the order and delivered the daughter to the mother who fled with her to Sweden (in 1994). Soon afterwards, a US court found the mother guilty of contempt of court and issued an arrest warrant against her. At the same time, the court also requested the return of the daughter to the father, but this was not complied with. As part of a different set of proceedings initiated in Utah by the father, it was also found that the removal of the daughter by her mother was wrongful and that, pursuant to the 1980 Hague Convention, the daughter had been habitually resident in the United States. The court further ordered that the daughter be immediately returned. However, in Swedish proceedings initiated earlier by the applicant for the return of his daughter, the Swedish Supreme Administrative Court (*Regeringsrätten*) concluded that the most recent removal of the daughter by the mother to Sweden in 1994 was not wrongful and that Sweden was her place of 'habitual residence'.

Before the Commission, the applicant complained, *inter alia*, of the fact that the Swedish courts failed to respect and to recognize the outcome of the Hague Convention proceedings in the United States. He also objected to the finding of the Swedish Supreme Administrative Court that his daughter's residence was in Sweden. Further, he argued that the proceedings before the Swedish and US courts lasted too long. In his view, these circumstances constituted violations of Articles 6 and 8 of the ECHR. The 1980 Hague Convention constituted the basis of the domestic proceedings in Sweden and the United States. In the end, the Commission found the application inadmissible.

The Members of the Commission considered that when applying the 1980 Hague Convention to determine the child's 'habitual residence', '[t]here is nothing to show that the court acted arbitrarily when evaluating the facts of the case or that it failed to strike a fair balance between the different interests at stake'.[24] Furthermore, although the proceedings under the 1980 Hague Convention must be conducted expeditiously, the Commission did not find that their length was

[23] *Larson v Sweden* (n 14 above). [24] Ibid.

excessive.[25] The Court stated that the applicant himself had requested a stay of the Swedish proceedings until the proceedings in the United States were decided. There was no breach of the ECHR in this case.

Another direct reference to the 1980 Hague Convention appeared in *Sogn Koutsofotinos v Norway and Greece*,[26] where the applicant complained, *inter alia*, that a Norwegian court's order to return her children to Greece violated her right to respect for family life and was not in the best interests of the children. She complained further that access to the children was denied to her. The 1980 Hague Convention was invoked and applied in domestic proceedings in Norway and Greece. The Commission evaluated whether the domestic courts' application of the 1980 Hague Convention complied with Article 8 of the ECHR: 'The question arises whether the Norwegian courts, in ordering that the applicant's children be returned to Greece in accordance with the 1980 Convention, showed a lack of respect for the applicant's family life.'[27] The Commission found that 'the Norwegian courts had carefully assessed whether the conditions for the applicant's children's return to Greece pursuant to the 1980 Convention were met'.[28] It then concluded that there was no violation of the ECHR in this case.

Although national authorities have an important discretion in deciding how to strike a balance between the competing interests involved in abduction cases, the Commission must evaluate under Article 8 of the ECHR whether they have taken all the necessary steps. In practice, and especially in these types of cases, this often translates into evaluating how the domestic courts have applied the 1980 Hague Convention.

It is difficult to determine whether the Commission has indeed established a jurisprudential trend, as there are only three cases where a brief, yet direct application of the Hague Convention was made. In the remaining cases, the Commission did not make any further substantive references to the 1980 Hague Convention. It must also be kept in mind that the three cases were closely intertwined with the 1980 Hague Convention, as it was previously applied in domestic proceedings that formed the basis of the application to the Commission. The Commission then had little choice but to also examine the 1980 Hague proceedings. Thus, these references are not extraordinary or unusual. Rather, they are important for the fact that they have aided in shaping an important trend in the ECtHR's jurisprudence within the framework of its reception of international law.

2.3 The Case Law of the ECtHR

In comparison to the Commission, the ECtHR established more elaborate case law and resorted to a more receptive approach in relation to the 1980 Hague Convention. As is apparent from the above discussion, in all the cases relating

[25] Ibid. [26] *Sogn Koutsofotinos v Norway and Greece* (n 14 above). [27] Ibid.
[28] Ibid.

to Hague proceedings considered by the Commission no violation of the ECHR was found. In contrast, the Court found numerous violations of Article 8 of the ECHR in the subsequent years. These findings allowed it to create a dynamic jurisprudential trend, closely intertwined with the 1980 Hague Convention, which mostly concerned the right of contact with the child, the right of custody of the child, and the enforcement of return orders. A clear epitome of this trend appeared in the *Bianchi v Switzerland* case,[29] where the Court finalized its standard approach based on the 1980 Hague Convention. On occasion, the Court was less receptive when the relevant Contracting State did not ratify the international instrument. It did not hesitate, however, to intervene in domestic law and rely on other external sources apart from the 1980 Hague Convention. At the same time, the lack of invocation and application of the Convention at the domestic level did not constitute a relevant factor in the level of reception applied in the case law.

2.3.1 An Archetypal Case

The Court's debut in relation to the reception of the 1980 Hague Convention within the framework of Article 8 of the ECHR was marked by the *Ignaccolo-Zenide* case,[30] where the Court considered that Article 8 must be interpreted in light of the 1980 Hague Convention. However, the climax of this trend became apparent in the *Bianchi v Switzerland*[31] judgment. The application concerned a boy who lived with his parents until they separated in 2002, when he was taken to Switzerland by his mother. The applicant (the father of the boy) entered claims before a Swiss court for the return of his child. Following a judgment of the Federal Supreme Court issued in April 2003, the boy and the mother returned to Italy. However, during a contact visit in December of the same year, the mother took the child back to Switzerland. The father filed a criminal complaint against the mother, which resulted in a fine of Sfr 300. A court of appeal in Lucerne, overturning a decision of a court in Willisau, ordered once again the return of the boy to Italy. Following an order emitted by the Willisau prefecture, the mother visited a police station and refused to divulge the whereabouts of the child. The police did not detain her, although an arrest warrant was subsequently issued against her. The Court ruled unanimously that Switzerland breached Article 8 of the ECHR in failing to take adequate measures to give effect to the aims and objectives of the 1980 Hague Convention after the abduction took place.

When considering the general principles contained in Article 8, the Court stated that the domestic authorities have a certain margin of appreciation and

[29] *Bianchi v Switzerland* (App No 7548/04), judgment, 22 June 2006, not reported, available in French only.

[30] *Ignaccolo-Zenide v Romania* (App No 31679/96), judgment, 25 January 2000, Reports 2000-I, 241.

[31] *Bianchi v Switzerland* (n 29 above).

that it cannot substitute itself for them in order to regulate questions pertaining to custody and visiting rights.[32] It can, however, evaluate whether the decisions taken by the domestic authorities in application of their margin of appreciation comply with the ECHR.[33] The Court also reiterated that the state has the obligation to take positive measures within the framework of Article 8. These positive measures include a right of parents to measures that will enable them to be reunited with their children and an obligation on national authorities to take such measures.[34]

With regard to international law, the Court stated that the Convention cannot be interpreted in isolation and that, pursuant to Article 31(3)(c) of the Vienna Convention on the Law of Treaties (VCLT) (of which Articles 31 to 33 are part of international customary law), it is necessary to take into account any rules of international law which apply to the Contracting Party.[35] As a consequence, the positive obligations contained in Article 8 of the ECHR must be interpreted in light of the Convention on the Rights of the Child and the 1980 Hague Convention. This was found to be even more the case here, given that Switzerland is party to the latter instrument (since 1 January 1984).[36] The Court recalled that in the Preamble to the 1980 Convention, the Signatory States underlined their conviction that 'the interests of children are of paramount importance in matters relating to their custody' and emphasized their desire 'to protect children internationally from the harmful effects of their wrongful removal or retention and to establish procedures to ensure their prompt return to the State of their habitual residence, as well as to secure protection for rights of access'.[37] The Court further added that, pursuant to Article 31(1) of the VCLT, these considerations, together with the requirements in Article 7 of the 1980 Hague Convention, constitute its object and purpose.[38] The Court then applied the 1980 Hague Convention to the case directly within the framework of Article 8 of the ECHR.[39]

[32] Ibid, paras 76–77. The judgment was not translated into English. The original passage in French provides the following:

La Cour n'a point pour tâche de se substituer aux autorités compétentes pour réglementer les questions de garde et de visites, mais d'apprécier sous l'angle de la Convention les décisions que ces autorités ont rendues dans l'exercice de leur pouvoir d'appréciation.

[33] Ibid, para 77.

[34] Ibid, para 78.

[35] Ibid, para 81. See also *Streletz, Kessler, and Krenz v Germany* (App Nos 34044/96; 35532/97; 44801/98), judgment, 22 March 2001, Reports 2001-II, 409, para 90; *Al-Adsani v United Kingdom* (App No 35763/97), judgment, 12 December 2001, Reports 2001-XI, 79, para 55.

[36] *Bianchi v Switzerland* (n 29 above), para 82.

[37] Ibid.

[38] Ibid, para 83.

[39] Ibid, paras 86–100. For other direct applications of the 1980 Hague Convention, see also *Iosub Caras v Romania* (App No 7198/04), judgment, 27 July 2006, not reported, paras 34–35; *Karadzic v Croatia* (App No 35030/04), judgment, 15 December 2005, not reported, paras 55 and 60; *Monory v Romania and Hungary* (App No 71099/01), judgment, 5 April 2005, not reported, paras 79 and 81; *Ignaccolo-Zenide v Romania* (n 30 above), para 116.

2.3.2 *Non-ratification as a Relevant Factor*

It is interesting to note that the *Bianchi v Switzerland* case,[40] as well as most of the other cases (considered in this section) containing references to the 1980 Hague Convention, concerned Contracting States which had adhered to the 1980 Hague Convention. One case, however, implicated a Contracting State which was not party to the 1980 Hague Convention. In *Bajarmi v Albania*,[41] the respondent State had not ratified the instrument at the time of the judgment, namely on 16 December 2006. Albania acceded to the 1980 Hague Convention only on 4 May 2007. The fact that Albania was not a party at the time seems to have constituted a relevant factor in the Court's reasoning.

First, the Court reiterated its standard position (included in most of the other cases referring to the 1980 Hague Convention) according to which 'Article 11 of the Hague Convention on the Civil Aspects of International Child Abduction of 25 October 1980 (to which Albania is not a State Party) requires the judicial or administrative authorities concerned to act expeditiously in proceedings for the return of children and any inaction lasting more than six weeks may give rise to a request for a statement of reasons for the delay'.[42] It continued that 'the Convention must be applied in accordance with the principles of international law, in particular with those relating to the international protection of human rights'[43] and 'the positive obligations that Article 8 of the Convention lays on the Contracting States in the matter of reuniting a parent with his or her children must be interpreted in the light of the Hague Convention of 25 October 1980'.[44]

The Court emphasized that Albania was not a state party to the 1980 Hague Convention. It was argued that 'the European Convention on Human Rights does not impose on States the obligation to ratify international conventions. However, it does require them to take all necessary measures of their choosing to secure the individual's rights guaranteed by Article 8 ECHR and, in particular, to secure the reunion of parents with their children in accordance with a final judgment of a domestic court.'[45] The Court found, however, that '[i]rrespective of the non-ratification by Albania of relevant international instruments in this area, ... the Albanian legal system, as it stands, has not provided any alternative framework affording the applicant the practical and effective protection that is required by the State's positive obligation enshrined in Article 8 of the Convention'.[46] By resolving the matter on the basis of the ECHR, the Court appears to have been less receptive than in *Bianchi v Switzerland*. It found itself unable to impose an interpretation of the 1980 Hague Convention on a state that had not ratified it at the time of the judgment.

40 *Bianchi v Switzerland* (n 29 above).
41 *Barjami v Albania* (App No 35853/04), judgment, 12 December 2006, not reported.
42 Ibid, para 53. 43 Ibid, para 55. 44 Ibid. 45 Ibid, para 66.
46 Ibid, para 67.

2.3.3 Other Sources External to the ECHR

In addition to the 1980 Hague Convention, the Court also resorted to other interpretation guides in its case law. For instance, in the *Monory v Romania and Hungary* case,[47] the Court referred to the domestic practice in other European states and to the Explanatory Report on the 1980 Hague Convention.[48] In this case, the Romanian Ministry (the central authority in Romania) had agreed to act upon the applicant's request for the return of his child, but had argued that their duties were limited to bringing a lawsuit for the return of a child before the competent courts (including representing the applicant and availing themselves of all possible appeals against the court decisions that were unfavourable to him).[49] In their view, no further obligations were incumbent upon them, given that no court had granted the applicant the right to exercise sole parental responsibility or any other right superior to that of the mother.[50] The ECtHR did not agree with this line of argument and recalled

> that joint custody, exercised by parents who are not divorced, is recognised by Article 3 paragraph (b) of the Hague Convention. This is supported by the Explanatory Report on the Hague Convention.... There is nothing in the Convention excluding married couples. Moreover, the Hague Convention has been interpreted by domestic courts of other European States as being applicable prior to the proceedings on divorce and child custody.[51]

By resorting to other relevant interpretation guides, the Court reinforced the reception of the 1980 Hague Convention.

2.3.4 Direct Intervention in Domestic Law

The most striking aspect of the *Monory v Romania and Hungary* case,[52] however, is the fact that the Court intervened in the domestic application of the 1980 Hague Convention, finding that the domestic courts had misinterpreted the instrument. In fact, the ECtHR noted that, in relation to the interpretation given in light of Hungarian law, all courts dealing with the case dismissed from the outset the applicability of Article 3 of the 1980 Hague Convention.[53] The courts found 'that, according to Hungarian law, the applicant did not have the right to have the child returned to him'.[54] However, it appeared 'that the child had been removed from her usual place of residence in breach of the formalities under Hungarian law. Moreover, the applicant had not been successful in his attempt to have the legality of the situation restored, despite his joint custody rights over the child.'[55] The ECtHR concluded that 'this interpretation by the Romanian courts

[47] *Monory v Romania and Hungary* (n 39 above). [48] Pérez-Vera (n 3 above), 428.
[49] *Monory v Romania and Hungary* (n 39 above), para 64. [50] Ibid, para 65.
[51] Ibid, para 76. See also *Iosub Caras v Romania* (n 39 above). In this case, the Court also referred to the Explanatory Report. [52] *Monory v Romania and Hungary* (n 39 above).
[53] Ibid, para 80. [54] Ibid, para 81. [55] Ibid.

contradicts the obvious meaning of the Hague Convention which transpires from its very text, its Explanatory Report and recognised common practice.... It deprives Article 3 and, therefore, the Hague Convention itself, of much of its useful effect.'[56] It also added that 'as Article 8 of the European Convention was examined in the light of the Hague Convention, the national courts' interpretation and application of the latter weakened the guarantees of Article 8'.[57] In the opinion of the ECtHR, 'the matter went beyond the simple matter of interpretation and application of domestic legislation falling within the exclusive competence of the national authorities'.[58] Thus, the Court clearly limited the Contracting States' margin of appreciation within the framework of Article 8 of the ECHR. The domestic misuse of the 1980 Hague Convention was therefore considered as falling under the Court's competence.

The *Monory* judgment aptly demonstrates that Article 8 enquiries are closely interwoven with the 1980 Hague Convention. From 2006 onwards, domestic courts dealing with 1980 Hague Convention proceedings (having their equivalent in the ECHR and in ECtHR case law) can clearly expect that the ECtHR will perform a judicial review of their interpretation in light of both the 1980 Hague Convention and the ECHR. This development represents a substantial expansion of the ECtHR's discretion in reviewing domestic application of international law.

2.3.5 Lack of Invocation and Application at the Domestic Level

The reception of the 1980 Hague Convention in these type of cases is impressive, especially given the fact that the ECtHR applied the Convention even when it was not invoked or applied at the domestic level. In *Iglesias GIL and AUI v Spain*,[59] the applicant did not refer to the 1980 Hague Convention in the domestic proceedings, nor was the 1980 Hague Convention applied by the domestic courts. Instead, the applicant relied on the Spanish Constitution, the United Nations Convention on the Rights of the Child, and the ECHR.[60] The ECtHR, however, reiterated that the obligations with regard to the return of a child under Article 8 of the ECHR must be interpreted in light of the 1980 Hague Convention.[61] The reference by the Court to the 1980 Hague Convention was favourable to the applicant.

In *Maire v Portugal*,[62] the 1980 Hague Convention had been invoked before the domestic authorities but was not taken into consideration later on in the proceedings. In spite of this fact, the ECtHR relied on the 1980 Hague Convention in its reasoning. The applicant lodged an application for the return of her child

[56] Ibid. [57] Ibid. [58] Ibid.

[59] *Iglesias GIL and AUI v Spain* (App No 56673/00), judgment, 29 April 2003, Reports 2003-V, 275. [60] Ibid, paras 11–26. [61] Ibid, para 56.

[62] *Maire v Portugal* (App No 48206/99), judgment, 26 June 2003, Reports 2003–VII, 333.

with the French Ministry of Justice (the French Central authority) on the basis of the 1980 Hague Convention and the Convention on Judicial Cooperation between France and Portugal for the Protection of Minors of 20 July 1983.[63] The application was referred to a Portuguese prosecution service which then applied to a court for the judicial return of the child only on the basis of Portuguese legislation and the Franco-Portuguese Convention.[64] The ECtHR reiterated that the positive obligations contained in Article 8 of the ECHR must be interpreted in light of the 1980 Hague Convention.[65] It then invoked Article 11 of the 1980 Hague Convention, recalling that the administrative authorities concerned must act expeditiously in proceedings for the return of children and that any failure to act for more than six weeks may give rise to a request for a statement of reasons for the delay.[66] This reference was courageous given that the 1980 Hague Convention had not been taken into account by the domestic authorities.

3. The Hague Convention on Intercountry Adoption

3.1 An International Treaty with Strong European Support

As the adoption of children from other countries has been on the rise, the response at the international level has been commensurate with the enactment of the European Convention on the Adoption of Children[67] and the Hague Convention on Intercountry Adoption.[68] Since the adoption of these instruments, the international legal landscape has been shifting—especially following the enactment of the Convention on the Rights of the Child—to a child-oriented adoption

[63] Ibid, para 14. [64] Ibid, para 15. [65] Ibid, para 72. [66] Ibid, para 74.

[67] The European Convention on the Adoption of Children, 634 UNTS 256, entered into force on 26 April 1968. It should be noted that in 1965, the Hague Conference promulgated the Hague Convention on Jurisdiction, Applicable Law and Recognition of Decrees relating to Adoptions (1965) 4 ILM 338, which entered into force on 23 October 1978. It was approved by only three countries (Austria, Switzerland, and the United Kingdom) which later withdrew from it. The 1965 Hague Convention provided for important safeguards in relation to intercountry adoption, as it sought to establish uniform jurisdictional rules to regulate consent and abandonment issues in intercountry adoptions. However, it still contained certain substantive problems. This information was verified on 13 June 2010: The Hague Conference on Private International Law, Status Table, <http://www.hcch.net/index_en.php?act=conventions.status&cid=75>.

[68] Providing 'that the best interests of the child shall be the paramount consideration', the Convention committed states to specific procedural protections (supervision, information, and informed consent); to '[r]ecognize that inter-country adoption may be considered as an alternative means of child's care, if the child cannot be placed in a foster or an adoptive family or cannot in any suitable manner be cared for in the child's country of origin'; to apply to international adoption the same 'safeguards and standards equivalent to those existing in the case of national adoption'; to '[t]ake all appropriate measures to ensure that, in inter-country adoption, the placement does not result in improper financial gain for those involved in it'; and to '[p]romote, where appropriate, the objectives of the present article by concluding bilateral or multilateral arrangements or agreements, and endeavour, within this framework, to ensure that the placement of the child in another country is carried out by competent authorities or organs'. See the Preamble to the Convention.

procedure, as opposed to an adoption procedure of children for adults. Despite the fact that these instruments establish important standards with respect to the administrative process of adoptions, they lack a strong enforcement mechanism.[69] As part of this important lacuna of international law, the ECtHR has been able to play a fundamental role by enforcing these instruments within the framework of the ECHR. The ECHR does not, however, include any provisions on domestic or intercountry adoption of children. Thus, until now, challenges to such adoptions have been considered under Article 12 of the ECHR, which enshrines the right to marry and to start a family, and Article 8, which protects the right to respect for family life.[70] These articles are not entirely adequate, as they do not replicate all the safeguards found at the international level.[71] Furthermore, the ECtHR's case law still seems to envisage the adoption procedure from an adult's perspective.[72] The Hague Convention on Intercountry Adoption was ratified by 42 of the 47 ECHR Contracting States.[73] It therefore benefits from very strong approval among the ECHR Contracting States, and the ECtHR refers to it in case of need.[74]

3.2 The *Pini and Others v Romania* Case

An important judgment with respect to intercountry adoption was handed down in *Pini and others v Romania*.[75] This case concerned the inability of two Italian couples (the applicants) to enforce decisions allowing them to adopt Romanian children because of Romania's objection. The applicants complained of an infringement of their right to family life under Article 8 of the ECHR and of the infringement of their right to a fair trial under Article 6. The Hague Convention on Intercountry Adoption was applied in the domestic proceedings.[76] In addition,

[69] Kilkelly (n 8 above), 295.

[70] Ibid. For instance, Art 20 of the Convention on the Rights of the Child, guaranteeing to a child the right to a replacement family, does not have an equivalent in the ECHR. Article 12 of the ECHR can be interpreted as including a right to adopt a child, but it is still subject to numerous limitations.

[71] Kilkelly (n 8 above), 296.

[72] Ibid; Geraldine Van Bueren, *The International Law on the Rights of the Child, International Studies in Human Rights, Vol 35* (Dordrecht/Boston/London: Martinus Nijhoff, 1995), 90.

[73] Armenia, Bosnia and Herzegovina, Montenegro, Greece, and Serbia did not ratify the Convention. This information was verified on 13 June 2010: The Hague Conference on Private International Law, Status Table, <http://www.hcch.net/index_en.php?act=conventions.status&cid=69>.

[74] It is interesting to note that when the Court invokes the Hague Convention on Intercountry Adoption, it also often refers to the European Convention on the Adoption of Children (n 67 above). This instrument, however, was only ratified by 18 of the 47 ECHR Contracting States. This information was verified on 13 June 2010: Council of Europe, Chart of signatures and ratifications, <http://conventions.coe.int/Treaty/Commun/ChercheSig.asp?NT=058&CM=&DF=&CL=ENG>.

[75] *Pini and Betrani and Manera and Atripaldi v Romania* (App Nos 78028/01; 78030/01), judgment, 22 June 2004, Reports 2004-V, 297.

[76] The Romanian Committee for Adoption considered that the adoption of Florence and Marianna was conducted in conformity with the Hague Convention on Intercountry Adoption: ibid, paras 19 and 24. See also para 161.

there were numerous references to international law made by the parties to the case before the ECtHR. The third parties observed that both the Convention on the Rights of the Child and the European Convention on the Adoption of Children permitted intercountry adoptions only where the child could not be adopted or cared for in a suitable manner in his or her own country.[77] They further submitted that, pursuant to the Hague Convention on Intercountry Adoption, adoption orders should be made with due regard to the wishes and views of those being adopted, which had not occurred in this case.[78] The applicants also relied on international law in their submissions; they pointed out that all the international treaties on children's rights stated unequivocally that the family provided the best environment for the development of the child's personality.[79] In addition, they referred to a report of the European Parliament that one of the areas given priority by the Romanian Government with a view to European Union accession was the question of children in institutions.[80]

As part of the enquiry under Article 8, the Court noted, as it did previously in the 1993 Hague Convention on Abduction proceedings, that 'the Convention must be applied in accordance with the rules of international law, in particular those concerning the international protection of human rights'.[81] More specifically, the Court considered that 'the obligations imposed by Article 8 of the Convention on the Contracting States in the field of adoption, and... the effects of adoption on the relationship between adopters and those being adopted,... must be interpreted in the light of the Hague Convention of 29 May 1993 on Protection of Children and Cooperation in respect of Intercountry Adoption, the United Nations Convention of 20 November 1989 on the Rights of the Child and the European Convention on the Adoption of Children, opened for signature in Strasbourg on 24 April 1967'.[82] The Court assumed that the adoption orders complied with domestic legislation and with the relevant international treaties.[83] While the Court noted that the children had not been asked to consent to the adoption because they had not reached the statutory age, it emphasized that, pursuant to Article 4(d) of the Hague Convention on Intercountry Adoption, national authorities are given some discretion as to the age at which children are to be regarded as sufficiently mature for their wishes to be taken into account.[84]

Applying the relevant international instruments to the situation at hand, the Court noted that 'particular importance must be attached to the best interests of the child in ascertaining whether the national authorities have taken all the necessary steps that can reasonably be demanded to facilitate the reunion of the

[77] Ibid, para 132. [78] Ibid, para 134. [79] Ibid, para 111.

[80] Ibid, paras 101 and 111. See also Baroness Nicholson of Winterbourne, *Report to the European Parliament on Romania's application for membership of the European Union and the state of negotiations* (COM (2000) 710—C5–0610/2000—1997/2172(COS)), 24 July 2001, A5–0259/200.

[81] *Pini and Betrani and Manera and Atripaldi v Romania* (n 75 above), para 138.

[82] Ibid, para 139. [83] Ibid, para 144. [84] Ibid, para 145.

child and his or her parents'.[85] When balancing the competing interests in the case, the Court noted that in such matters the child's interests may (depending on their nature and seriousness) override those of the parent. More specifically, 'it is even more important that the child's interests should prevail over those of the parents in the case of a relationship based on adoption, since, as it has previously held, adoption means "providing a child with a family, not a family with a child"'.[86] As the children concerned objected to the idea of being adopted, the Court concluded that there was no breach of Article 8 of the ECHR. The Court found, however, that there was a violation of Article 6 because the State had not taken sufficient action to ensure that the decisions were respected, in particular by failing to impose any sanctions on those responsible for the private institution (where the children had been placed) which had in effect thwarted all attempts to enforce the court decisions.

In this case, the Court's reception method resembled that applied in relation to the 1980 Hague Convention on International Child Abduction. The ECtHR repeated the same key phrases, stressing the need to rely on international law in a situation where the ECHR does not provide any guidance. In addition, the 1993 Hague Convention allowed the Court to close a very important gap in the ECHR. In return, reliance on the 1993 Hague Convention within the framework of the ECHR provided a stronger enforcement mechanism to the former.

4. The United Nations Convention on the Rights of the Child

4.1 An International Treaty with Unanimous European Support

Since its adoption in 1989, after more than 60 years of advocacy, the United Nations Convention on the Rights of the Child (CRC) has been ratified more quickly and by more governments than any other human rights instrument. There are 193 states parties to the Convention, which includes all 47 ECHR Contracting States.[87] The Convention, therefore, enjoys widespread support at European and international levels. It has also acquired the status of most highly ratified instrument in international law.[88] This quasi-universal approval of the Convention sends an important signal to the Strasbourg bodies with regard to the Contracting States' approval of the standards contained therein.

Shortly after the enactment of the CRC, both the Commission and the Court started referring to its provisions. These references occurred in varied contexts and were not confined to a single article, as was the case with the 1980 Hague Convention. The CRC has certainly benefited from this alternative enforcement,

[85] Ibid, para 155. [86] Ibid, para 156.

[87] This information was verified on 13 June 2010: United Nations Treaty Collection, Status, <http://treaties.un.org/Pages/ViewDetails.aspx?src=TREATY&mtdsg_no=IV-11&chapter=4&lang=en>.

[88] Kilkelly (n 8 above), 309.

which is more powerful than that set up by the United Nations. At the same time, the ECHR system was able to benefit from using the detailed and specific provisions of the CRC, given that most of the ECHR provisions are very general. Once again, it is important to note here the difference in approach between the Strasbourg bodies. Overall, the Commission, although older, used a more progressive and more receptive approach to the CRC than the Court (although this was not the case with the 1980 Hague Convention). Given that the areas and categories of rights considered are more diversified than in cases relating to the two Hague Conventions, the following section has been organized in function of the nature of rights concerned.

4.2 Corporal Punishment and Abuse

The CRC contains very detailed requirements with regard to corporal punishment and abuse. Article 19 enshrines the child's right to be protected from all forms of violence, abuse, and mistreatment. Under the ECHR, the Court has resorted to Article 3 (prohibition on inhuman and degrading treatment) and Article 8 (right to respect for private and family life) in situations of alleged corporal punishment, abuse, and neglect of children. The Court's references to the CRC gave shape to and adapted these articles to new contexts involving children.

In *Costello-Roberts v United Kingdom*, the Commission[89] and the Court[90] considered the situation of a seven-year-old boarder who had been given three 'whacks' on the bottom by the headmistress of a private school. The applicant complained that his rights under Articles 3 and 8 of the ECHR had been infringed. There was no violation found under either article by the Court. In its decision, the Commission did not make any mention of the CRC. The Strasbourg Court, however, referred explicitly to it.

When considering the scope of the state's obligation under Article 1 to secure ECHR rights and freedoms in its domestic legislation, the ECtHR held that the State had the duty to ensure that Articles 3 and 8 of the ECHR were enforced in independent schools.[91] It was then emphasized that the provisions of the ECHR and its Protocols must be read as a whole. Moreover, '[f]unctions relating to the internal administration of a school, such as discipline, cannot be said to be merely ancillary to the educational process'.[92] According to the Court, the fact that 'a school's disciplinary system falls within the ambit of the right to education has also been recognised, more recently, in Article 28 of the United Nations Convention on the Rights of the Child of 20 November 1989 which entered into force on 2 September 1990 and was ratified by the

[89] *Costello-Roberts v United Kingdom* (App No 13134/87), decision (Commission), 13 December 1990, not reported.

[90] *Costello-Roberts v United Kingdom* (App No 13134/87), judgment, 25 March 1993, Series A, Vol 247–C.

[91] Ibid, para 26.

[92] Ibid, para 27.

United Kingdom on 16 December 1991'.[93] The Court cited here the text of Article 28(2) of the CRC.

The judgment is also important for the fact that the Court used dynamic interpretation to update the scope of the ECHR. Although the Court found that there was no breach of Article 3 of the ECHR and did not explicitly disapprove of corporal punishment, it did make the following statement: 'While the Court has certain misgivings about the automatic nature of the punishment and the three day wait before its imposition, it considers that minimum level of severity not to have been attained in this case.'[94] It therefore appears that, while the CRC has outlawed corporal punishment altogether, the Court was at that time still lagging behind, and trying to catch up with, the international standards.

In relation to the complaint under Article 8 of the ECHR, the Court made the following explicit reference to its equivalent under the CRC (albeit more specific): 'In the applicant's submission, the aim of the punishment was to exercise coercion through force and fear and this constituted an interference with moral integrity as well as physical integrity. At school a child was in the public world where he had to learn to respect the privacy of others and was entitled to have his own private life respected, as was recognised by Article 16 of the United Nations Convention on the Rights of the Child of 20 November 1989, and to be treated with dignity.'[95] The Court's continued references to the CRC indicate its willingness to adapt the ECHR to international standards in areas where it does not provide for detailed requirements.

Another telling reference to the CRC was made in the case of *A v United Kingdom*.[96] The applicant was a boy who had been repeatedly caned by his stepfather, causing significant bruising. The stepfather was prosecuted in the United Kingdom for causing actual bodily harm but was found not guilty on the grounds that the punishment was 'reasonable chastisement'. In its report regarding the case, the Commission referred to the CRC and to the observations of the United Nations Committee on the Rights of the Child.[97] The Commission distinguished[98] the case from *Costello-Roberts v United Kingdom* and determined that it fell well within the ambit of Article 3 of the ECHR.[99] It then went on to enquire whether the State could be held responsible for such treatment when it was administered, not by an agent of the State or a teacher, but by the applicant's father. While it was determined that it was not the duty of the State to ensure that such treatment was not inflicted by a private individual on to another, the Commission did find that Contracting Parties were responsible under

[93] Ibid. [94] Ibid, para 32. [95] Ibid, para 35.

[96] *A v United Kingdom* (App No 25599/94), judgment, 23 September 1998, Reports 1998–VI, 2692.

[97] *A v United Kingdom* (App No 25599/94), report, 18 September 1997, Reports 1998–VI, 2703. See also Kilkelly (n 8 above), 316.

[98] *A v United Kingdom* (n 97 above), para 39. [99] Ibid, para 41.

Articles 1, 3, and 8 of the ECHR to ensure a legal system which provides adequate protection to children's physical and emotional integrity.[100] In deciding whether the United Kingdom had provided such protection, the Commission attached 'importance to the international recognition of the need of protection against all forms of physical ill-treatment of children, who by reason of their age and vulnerability are not capable of protecting themselves'.[101] The Commission mentioned in particular Article 19 of the CRC, which provides that states are enjoined to take all appropriate measures 'to protect the children from all forms of physical or mental violence, injury or abuse'.[102] According to the Commission, the protection provided by English law to children within the home is significantly reduced by the defence open to parents that the acts in question are legal because they constitute moderate and reasonable physical punishment of the child.[103] In addition, the Commission was not convinced by the Government's argument that the criteria applied by the domestic courts in determining whether the punishment is reasonable are very similar to those applied under the ECHR to determine whether punishment is inhuman or degrading.[104] In support of this finding, the Commission cited the Concluding Observations of 15 February 1995 of the United Nations Committee on the Rights of the Child, where the Committee showed concern regarding the legal provisions dealing with 'reasonable chastisement' within the family. The Commission found that '[t]he imprecise nature of the expression of reasonable chastisement as contained in these legal provisions may pave the way for it to be interpreted in a subjective and arbitrary manner'.[105]

In contrast to the Commission, the Court's approach was much less receptive, as it included very few references to international child rights law. The ECtHR judges unanimously found that the punishment violated Article 3 of the ECHR. Referring to Articles 19 and 37 of the CRC, the Court emphasized that '[c]hildren and other vulnerable individuals, in particular, are entitled to State protection, in the form of effective deterrence, against such serious breaches of personal integrity'.[106] It was concluded that English law did not provide sufficient protection to the child and there were no further references to the CRC. Thus, it is clear that the Commission used more innovative methods in interpreting the ECHR in this case.

[100] Ibid, para 45. The Court did note, however, in para 48 that 'the obligation under Article 1 ... cannot be interpreted as requiring the State to guarantee through its legal system that inhuman or degrading treatment is never inflicted by one individual or another or that, if it is, the perpetrator will be subject to criminal sanctions'.

[101] Ibid, para 49.

[102] Ibid. The statements of the Court cited here and below (n 106) appeared again in a similar statement in: *Z and others v United Kingdom* (App No 29392/95), report, 10 September 1999, not reported, para 93.

[103] *A v United Kingdom* (n 97 above), para 50.

[104] Ibid, para 52.

[105] Ibid. See also United Nations, Concluding Observations of the Committee on the Rights of the Child: United Kingdom of Great Britain and Ireland, 15 February 1998, CRC/C/15/Add.34, para 16.

[106] *A v United Kingdom* (n 96 above), para 22.

4.3 Children in Conflict with the Law and Juvenile Justice Issues

The administration of justice resorts to different guidelines in cases involving minor offenders from those that are used in adult offenders cases. Certain specific factors need to be taken into account in juvenile cases, namely the offender's situation in life, his/her limited ability to understand certain things, and the corresponding limited ability to assume full responsibility for his/her social behaviour. The special needs of juveniles gave rise to the creation, at the domestic level, of juvenile courts with special procedural rules aimed at correction and re-education rather than punishment of the minor.

The ECHR contains no specific provisions in relation to juvenile offenders or children in conflict with the law. However, despite its generality, it was found that Article 6 would apply to such situations. It was also thought that the homologue to this provision—Article 4 of the CRC—can be used to interpret Article 6 of the ECHR. Article 4 of the CRC requires that children be treated in a manner that promotes their sense of dignity and worth. It also requires that a child's age as well as the desirability of promoting the reintegration and constructive role of the child in society be taken into account.[107] In a more exhaustive manner than Article 6 of the ECHR, Article 40 of the CRC further enumerates specific procedural guarantees for children who have to undergo judicial proceedings. The Commission and the Court have used both Articles 4 and 40 of the CRC as interpretation tools to incorporate further rights under Article 6 of the ECHR.

4.3.1 The Nortier v The Netherlands *Case*

In the early case law, only several members of the Strasbourg bodies made references to minors' special needs and the corresponding international law.[108] In *Nortier v The Netherlands*,[109] the applicant complained that he had not received a hearing before an 'impartial tribunal' in the sense of Article 6 of the ECHR because his case had been reviewed, in the pre-trial and trial phases, by the same judge.[110] The fifteen-year-old, just released from a youth custody centre after serving a sentence for rape, had been arrested again on suspicion of attempted rape. The Court did not make any references to international child rights law and unanimously found that there was no breach of Article 6 of the ECHR. However, in a concurrent separate opinion, Judge Morenilla, agreeing with Mr Trechsel[111] joined by other members of the Commission, considered that minors are entitled to the same protection as adults, but that their developing personality

[107] CRC, Art 40. [108] Kilkelly (n 8 above), 95.

[109] *Nortier v The Netherlands* (App No 13924/88), judgment, 24 August 1993, Series A, Vol 267. [110] Ibid, paras 30–31.

[111] *Nortier v The Netherlands* (App No 13924/88), report, 9 July 1992, not reported, separate concurring opinion of Mr Trechsel, joined by Mm JA Frowein, HG Schermers, and Sir Basil Hall.

and consequential limited social ability should be taken into account under Article 6.[112] He supported this statement with a passage from the Preamble to Article 40(3) of the CRC:

States, therefore, should afford... [children] the 'necessary protection and assistance so that they can fully assume their responsibilities within the community', and prepare them 'to live an individual life in society'...by promoting 'the establishment of laws, procedures, authorities and institutions applicable to children alleged as, accused of, or recognised as having infringed the penal law'.[113]

Nonetheless, Judge Morenilla considered that the competence of the ECtHR in this field was limited, as 'the protection of children is a matter about which national authorities are better prepared to plan in accordance with the demands of their society. The Convention is meant to be interpreted in the sense of giving the member States a margin of appreciation as to the organisation of their system of penal justice to protect both the interests of the child and those of society.'[114]

4.3.2 The T v United Kingdom *and* V v United Kingdom *Cases*

The Strasbourg bodies were faced with two highly publicized and particularly cruel cases where a variety of international instruments pertaining to juvenile justice were used. In *T v United Kingdom*[115] and *V v United Kingdom*[116] two boys, aged 10 and 11, abducted a two-year-old boy from a shopping area, took him for a journey of over two miles, battered him to death, and left him on the railway line to be run over. With some procedural exceptions, the two boys were prosecuted and tried in public in an ordinary adult criminal court.[117] The two applicants were convicted of murder and sentenced to be detained indefinitely 'at her Majesty's pleasure'. In English law, young offenders must serve a 'tariff' established by the Home Secretary to satisfy the requirements of retribution and deterrence. They can be released subsequently unless the Parole Board decides that they represent a danger to the public. In this case, the Home Secretary set

112 *Nortier v The Netherlands* (n 109 above), concurring opinion of Judge Morenilla, para 2.

113 Ibid (text inserted by author).

114 Ibid, para 3.

115 *T v United Kingdom* (App No 24724/94), judgment, 16 December 1999, not reported; *T v United Kingdom* (App No 24724/94), report, 4 December 1998, not reported.

116 *V v United Kingdom* (App No 24888/94), judgment, 16 December 1999, not reported; *V v United Kingdom* (App No 24888/94), report, 4 December 1998, not reported.

117 'The trial was conducted with the formality of an adult criminal trial. The judge and counsel wore wigs and gowns. The procedure was, however, modified to a certain extent in view of the defendants' age. They were seated next to social workers in a specially raised dock. Their parents and lawyers were seated nearby. The hearing times were shortened to reflect the school day (10.30 a.m. to 3.30 p.m., with an hour's lunch break), and a ten-minute interval was taken every hour. During adjournments the defendants were allowed to spend time with their parents and social workers in a play area. The judge made it clear that he would adjourn whenever the social workers or defence lawyers told him that one of the defendants was showing signs of tiredness or stress. This occurred on one occasion': see *T v United Kingdom*, judgment (n 115 above), para 9; *V v United Kingdom*, judgment (n 116 above), para 9.

a tariff of 15 years for each applicant, which was later quashed by the House of Lords. There was no new tariff set at the time of the judgment.

The applicants complained that, given their young age, their public trial in an adult criminal court and the punitive nature of their sentence constituted inhuman or degrading treatment or punishment under Article 3 of the ECHR. In this respect, the applicants also invoked Rule 4 of the Standard Minimum Rules for the Administration of Juvenile Justice ('The Beijing Rules'),[118] together with its commentary. They submitted that according to those standards a child aged 10 cannot be considered to be fully responsible for his actions. They further alleged that they had been denied a fair trial in breach of Article 6 of the ECHR and had suffered discrimination in violation of Article 14 of the ECHR. In addition, they argued that the sentencing system in England which allows detention 'at her Majesty's pleasure' infringed their rights under Articles 3 and 5(1) of the ECHR. Further, the fact that a minister, rather than a judge, sentenced them violated Article 6 of the ECHR. They also invoked Article 37(b) of the CRC and Rules 16 and 17.1(a) and (b) of the Beijing Rules to emphasize that the detention of children should be for the shortest appropriate time and should be governed by the well-being of the individual and not retribution.[119] Finally, they complained under Article 5(4) of the ECHR that they did not have the possibility to have the continuing lawfulness of their detention reviewed by a judicial body.[120] The Commission found in its report that there was no violation under Article 3 of the ECHR with respect to the trial and the sentence, and under Articles 5(1) and (4) with respect to the review of the sentence. There had been, however, a violation of Article 6 with respect to the trial and sentence. No separate issue arose under Article 14 of the ECHR.[121]

With respect to the minimum age of criminal responsibility, the Commission looked beyond the ECHR legal landscape; it observed that there is no commonly accepted standard among countries and in international legal instruments. It was further noted that '[t]he United Nations texts have regard to the differing considerations that can apply and recommend the fixing of an age consonant with children's emotional, mental and intellectual development, without specifying what it could be'.[122] The Commission also took into account a fundamental principle enshrined in international child rights instruments and in the Strasbourg case law, which provides 'that law should protect children's welfare and afford them the protection necessitated by their vulnerability and lack of maturity'.[123]

[118] United Nations Standard Minimum Rules for the Administration of Juvenile Justice ('The Beijing Rules'), adopted on 29 November 1985, UN Doc A/40/53 (1985).

[119] *T v United Kingdom*, judgment (n 115 above), para 101; *V v United Kingdom*, judgment (n 116 above), para 102.

[120] For the complaints of the two applicants, see *T v United Kingdom*, judgment (n 115 above), para 49; *V v United Kingdom*, judgment (n 116 above), para 51.

[121] *T v United Kingdom*, report (n 115 above), para 4; *V v United Kingdom*, report (n 116 above), para 52.

[122] *T v United Kingdom*, report (n 115 above), para 82; *V v United Kingdom*, report (n 116 above), para 90.

[123] *T v United Kingdom*, report (n 115 above), para 83; *V v United Kingdom*, report (n 116 above), para 91.

In the Commission's view, this principle was reflected in the domestic law of Contracting States providing for social protection. Given the silence of the ECHR on this topic, the Commission felt compelled to look beyond it.

The Commission also referred to international law when it considered the applicants' complaints about the location in which they would be required to serve their sentence when they were older. It noted that this complaint could raise issues with regard to the CRC's primary consideration that offenders should be given the opportunity of reintegrating into society.[124] It avoided reaching any conclusion regarding this issue, as any change in the location and conditions of detention seemed speculative at that point. There was also a brief reference to the Beijing Rules when the Commission considered the length of the sentence given to the applicants. It reiterated in this context 'the principle identified in the Beijing rules that sentences of detention should be set at the minimum'.[125] In the Commission's view, only a short sentence, not an indeterminate one (as in the case of detention 'at her Majesty's pleasure'), would be compatible with Article 5(4) of the ECHR. In addition, a Member of the Commission considered, in his separate concurring opinion, that the public interest should give way here to the well-being of the defendants. In support of his argument, he cited Article 40 of the CRC, Article 14(4) of the United Nations Covenant on Civil and Political Rights (which provides that in the case of juvenile offenders the procedure must take into account the age and desirability to promote their rehabilitation), and the Beijing Rules (which emphasize the importance of protecting the privacy of the child at all stages).[126] These references to international child rights law were not numerous in this case, but signalled that the Commission will look beyond its own regime to find an answer which is lacking under the ECHR.

In its judgment, the Court reached the same verdict as the Commission regarding the alleged violations of the ECHR: it found that there was no breach of Article 3 with respect to the trial and the sentence, that there was no violation of Article 5(1) and (4) with respect to the review of the sentence, that no separate issue arose under Article 14, and that Article 6 had been breached with regard to the trial and sentence. In contrast to the Commission, however, the Court made more references to international child rights law. For instance, in the part of the judgment containing the relevant international texts, the following were mentioned: the Beijing Rules, the CRC, the Committee on the Rights of the Child report on the United Kingdom,[127] the International Covenant on Civil and Political Rights, and the Committee of Ministers of the Council of Europe Recommendation

[124] *T v United Kingdom*, report (n 115 above), para 111; *V v United Kingdom*, report (n 116 above), para 119.

[125] *T v United Kingdom*, report (n 115 above), para 135; *V v United Kingdom*, report (n 116 above), para 143.

[126] *T v United Kingdom*, report (n 115 above), concurring opinion of Mr N Bratza; *V v United Kingdom*, report (n 116 above), concurring opinion of Mr N Bratza.

[127] United Nations, Concluding Observations of the Committee on the Rights of the Child (n 105 above).

No R (87) 20.[128] In relation to the CRC, the Court emphasized the fact that it has binding force on all Member States of the Council of Europe. There was also a separate section (only one paragraph) on the age of criminal responsibility in Europe where the Court referred to the various age-limits used in numerous ECHR Contracting States.[129] The Court relied on these to determine that domestic practice is varied and there is no consensus.[130] This finding seems to have impacted on the Court's increased reliance on international law in this case.

Another important aspect of the judgment is the Court's consideration of international legal trends. The Court surveyed international tendencies when it considered the complaint under Article 3 of the ECHR regarding the fact that the trial took place in public and in an ordinary criminal adult court. The Court noted that:

> one of the minimum guarantees provided by Article 40 § 2 (b) of the UN Convention to children accused of crimes is that they should have their privacy fully respected at all stages of the proceedings. Similarly, Rule 8 of the Beijing Rules states that 'the juvenile's privacy shall be respected at all stages' and that 'in principle, no information that may lead to the identification of a juvenile offender shall be published'. Finally, the Committee of Ministers of the Council of Europe recommended in 1987 that Member States should review their law and practice with a view to avoiding committing minors to adult courts where juvenile courts exist and to recognising the right of juveniles to respect for their private lives.[131]

According to the Court, this constituted evidence of an international tendency in favour of protecting the privacy of juvenile defendants.[132] The Court noted in particular that the CRC was binding on the United Kingdom and on all the other Member States of the Council of Europe.[133] Reasoning with caution, it indicated, however, that this trend—despite being a significant factor—could not be determinative of the question whether the trial in public constituted ill-treatment falling under Article 3 of the ECHR.

The Court made another important reference to international child rights law when it considered the applicants' complaint that detention 'at her Majesty's pleasure' was severely disproportionate and in breach of Article 3 of the ECHR. The Court found that in deciding whether this type of detention constitutes ill-treatment under Article 3, it must consider Article 37 of the CRC, which prohibits life imprisonment without the possibility of release and provides for the use of

[128] Council of Europe, Committee of Ministers Recommendation No R (87) 20 to Member States on Social Reactions to Juvenile Delinquency. Adopted by the Committee on 17 September 1987, Ministers' Deputies 410th Meeting.

[129] *T v United Kingdom*, judgment (n 115 above), para 48; *V v United Kingdom*, judgment (n 116 above), para 50.

[130] *T v United Kingdom*, judgment (n 115 above), para 64; *V v United Kingdom*, judgment (n 116 above), para 66.

[131] *T v United Kingdom*, judgment (n 115 above), para 74; *V v United Kingdom*, judgment (n 116 above), para 76.

[132] *T v United Kingdom*, judgment (n 115 above), para 75; *V v United Kingdom*, judgment (n 116 above), para 77.

[133] *T v United Kingdom*, judgment (n 115 above), para 75; *V v United Kingdom*, judgment (n 116 above), para 77.

detention only as a measure of last resort. In addition, the Court found it useful to refer to Rule 17.1(b) of the Beijing Rules, which recommends that restriction on personal liberty of minors should be limited to a minimum.[134] At the time of the judgment, the applicants had been detained for six years, they had not reached the stage in their sentence to have their detention reviewed, and no new tariff had been set. The Court observed that an unjustified and persistent failure to fix a tariff could also amount to a violation of Article 3 of the ECHR. However, here, it considered that there was a relatively short period of time during which no tariff had been in force. The Court, finally, found it impossible to draw any conclusions with regard to this matter and determined that no issue arose under Article 3.[135]

Lord Reed, in his separate concurring opinion, also made several references to international child rights law. In his view, there was nothing in Article 6 of the ECHR to indicate that there could be any derogation, in cases involving children, from the principle that the trial process should provide for the effective participation of the accused. In order to respect this principle, the conditions under which the trial is held must effectively allow such participation. Further, the child's age, level of maturity, as well as intellectual and emotional capacity must be taken into account in this context. He determined that:

> [t]his interpretation of Article 6 is also in accordance with developments in international law: a number of relevant texts, including treaties accepted as binding by the United Kingdom and other member States (such as the UN Convention on the Rights of the Child, Article 40, and the International Covenant on Civil and Political Rights, Article 14(4)), require child offenders to be treated in a manner which takes account of their age and the desirability of promoting their rehabilitation.[136]

He noted, however, that there are a variety of ways in which these factors can be accounted for. Contracting States organized their criminal systems in a variety of ways in order to protect the interests of the individual and the wider public. Thus, Lord Reed determined that Article 6 provides a wide margin of appreciation to Contracting States with regard to their procedures for dealing with young offenders. Furthermore, in determining whether the length of the tariff is compliant with Article 3 of the ECHR:

> it is appropriate to have regard to the UN Convention on the Rights of the Child, which is accepted by all of the member States, including the United Kingdom. Article 3(i) of the UN Convention requires that in all actions concerning children the best interests of the child shall be a primary consideration. Article 40(1) requires the child offender

[134] *T v United Kingdom*, judgment (n 115 above), para 96; *V v United Kingdom*, judgment (n 116 above), para 97.

[135] For arguments in this paragraph, see *T v United Kingdom*, judgment (n 115 above), paras 96–99; *V v United Kingdom*, judgment (n 116 above), paras 97–100.

[136] *T v United Kingdom*, judgment, concurring opinion of Lord Reed; *V v United Kingdom*, judgment (n 116 above), concurring opinion of Lord Reed.

to be treated in a manner which takes into account the child's age and the desirability of promoting the child's reintegration and the child's assuming a constructive role in society. These general requirements are reflected in Article 37(b) of the UN Convention, which requires that the imprisonment of a child be used only as a measure of last resort and for the shortest appropriate period of time.[137]

Lord Reed concluded that there was no violation of Article 3 of the ECHR with respect to the imposition of the original tariff.

The decision of the majority of the Court with regard to Article 3 was criticized by the dissidents. In the joint partly dissenting opinions of Judges Pastor Ridruejo, Ress, Makarczyk, Tulkens, and Butkevych in both judgments, it was noted that 'the Court recognises that there is an international tendency in favour of the protection of the privacy of juvenile defendants. It nevertheless finds that a lack of privacy cannot be decisive for the question whether the trial in public amounted to treatment attaining the minimum level of severity necessary to bring it within the scope of Article 3 of the Convention.'[138] The dissenters emphasized that, according to Article 40 of the CRC, privacy had to be respected at all stages of the proceedings and that it constituted a crucial element in minimizing suffering and humiliation of children. It was observed that the United Kingdom continues to violate this requirement. Thus, the dissenters concluded that the trial in this case reached the minimum level of inhuman and degrading treatment.

4.4 Ill-treatment of Illegal Immigrant Children

The ECHR does not guarantee any specific rights to immigrants or refugees, and the same can be asserted, *mutatis mutandis*, with regard to immigrant and refugee children. Although the Court developed a considerable body of case law concerning the compatibility of immigration and asylum measures with the Convention,[139] the situation of detained refugee children remains fragile. There appears to be an international agreement that refugee children should not be detained,[140] but the ECHR does not seem to prohibit such treatment. In fact, Article 5(1)(f) permits detention in order to prevent entry into a Contracting State or prior to deportation. It is only recently that the Court decided to limit the scope of this article by referring to international law in the context of refugee children.

In *Mubilanzila Mayeka and Kaniki Mitunga v Belgium*,[141] the Court reviewed the case of a mother with refugee status in Canada attempting to be reunited

[137] *T v United Kingdom*, judgment (n 115 above), concurring opinion of Lord Reed; *V v United Kingdom*, judgment (n 116 above), concurring opinion of Lord Reed.

[138] *T v United Kingdom*, judgment (n 115 above), joint partly dissenting opinions of Judges Pastor Ridruejo, Ress, Markarczyk, Tulkens, and Butkevych, para 2; *V v United Kingdom*, judgment (n 116 above), joint partly dissenting opinions of Judges Pastor Ridruejo, Ress, Makarczyk, Tulkens, and Butkevych.

[139] Kilkelly (n 8 above), 214. See also ch VI, 2.1–2.3.

[140] Kilkelly (n 8 above), 233.

[141] *Mubilanzila Mayeka and Kaniki Mitunga v Belgium* (App No 13178/03), judgment, 12 October 2006, not reported.

with her daughter in the Democratic Republic of Congo. She had asked her brother, a Dutch national, to collect her daughter from Congo and to look after her until she was able to join her. The brother arrived in Belgium with his niece, but he did not have the required travel and immigration documents for her. The then five-year-old girl was refused leave to enter Belgium and was detained in a transit centre for two months. A lawyer was appointed and applied on her behalf for refugee status. His request was, however, declared inadmissible. In the meantime, the mother of the child initiated procedures to allow her daughter to join her in Canada. Before the outcome of these procedures was known, the Belgian authorities decided to deport the child to Congo, as they had found out that she had an uncle there.

The day before her deportation the *chambre du conseil* of the Brussels Court of First Instance held that the daughter's detention was incompatible with Article 3(1) and (2) of the CRC and ordered her immediate release. The girl was deported to Congo, but no one came to meet her, and she waited until an improvised arrangement was made for her to stay with a person from the domestic governmental authorities. She was then granted refugee status by the Canadian authorities and arrangements were made for her to join her mother. The two applicants in the case were the mother and her daughter and they complained that the daughter's detention and deportation breached Articles 3, 5, and 8 of the ECHR. The Court found unanimously that there was a violation of Article 3 with respect to both applicants' rights as a result of the girl's detention and deportation. There was also violation of Article 8 of the ECHR with respect to both applicants' rights as a result of the girl's detention and deportation. The Court also found that the girl's rights under Articles 5(1) and (4) were violated.

With respect to the applicants' complaint under Article 3 concerning the girl's detention, the Court made references to the CRC when discussing the measures taken by the Belgian authorities. The girl was detained for two months in the same conditions as adults in a centre which was initially meant for them. The Court found that the measures taken by the domestic authorities were inadequate given their obligation to take care of the child and the numerous alternatives at their disposal. It was recalled that under Articles 1 and 3 of the ECHR, states must take measures to ensure that individuals in their jurisdiction, especially children and other vulnerable members of society, are not subjected to torture or inhuman treatment. The Court noted, *inter alia*, that the decision of the *chambre du conseil* requested the girl's immediate release under the CRC. It stated that the Commissioner-General for Refugees and Stateless Persons had warned the Minister of Interior of the fact that the girl was a minor and that she was entitled to be reunited with her family under Article 10 of the CRC. It was also observed that the Committee on the Rights of the Child recommended that the Belgian State should expedite efforts to establish special reception centres.[142] In relation

142 Ibid, para 57.

to the complaint under Article 8 of the ECHR, the Court also made a brief reference to the CRC when it found that the child's detention in the closed centre was unnecessary. According to the Court, there were other measures to be taken which would have been more conducive to the higher interest of the child guaranteed in Article 3 of the CRC.[143]

4.5 Sexual Abuse and Rape

The ECHR does not contain any references to the prohibition of sexual abuse of adults or children. The Convention on the Rights of the Child, on the other hand, contains an express provision (Article 34), the relevant part of which provides that 'States Parties undertake to protect the child from all forms of sexual exploitation and sexual abuse. For these purposes, States Parties shall in particular take all appropriate national, bilateral and multilateral measures to prevent: (a) The inducement or coercion of a child to engage in any unlawful sexual activity.' However, despite the existence of this specific prohibition on sexual abuse of children, the Court relied on other external domestic and international legal sources in its case law. It is possible that these sources were more adapted to the interpretation framework that the Court chose in relation to this offence under the ECHR.

The ECtHR initially characterized rape as a violation of the right to privacy (Article 8 of the ECHR), then as torture (Article 3), and as ill-treatment (Article 3). In *X and Y v The Netherlands*,[144] decided in 1985, the ECtHR considered a case of a 16-year-old mentally handicapped girl who had been seriously sexually abused by the son-in-law of the head of a privately run home where she resided. The Strasbourg Court determined that rape infringes the right to privacy by finding that Article 8 of the ECHR 'covers the physical and moral integrity of the person, including his or her sexual life'.[145] Although the perpetrator was not an agent of the Dutch Government, the ECtHR held the Dutch Government responsible because it failed to provide an adequate remedy at the national level. It was found that the State would not have an excessive amount of discretion in this case, given that the right involved in this case was of vital importance and effective deterrence was indispensable.[146] There were no references to international law in this case.

In *Aydín v Turkey*,[147] decided in 1997, the ECtHR found that rape can also constitute a violation of Article 3 of the ECHR, given that it can amount to torture in certain situations. In *Aydín*, the ECHR considered a complaint regarding the behaviour of a local Turkish gendarme who raped a 17-year-old Kurdish girl while

[143] Ibid, para 83.
[144] *X and Y v The Netherlands* (App No 8978/80), judgment, 26 March 1985, Series A, Vol 91.
[145] Ibid, para 22. [146] Ibid, paras 24 and 27.
[147] *Aydín v Turkey* (App No 23178/94), judgment, 25 September 1997, Reports 1997-VI, 1866.

she was illegally detained. In her final submissions to the Court, the applicant did not invoke international law provisions.[148] However, Amnesty International made written submissions,[149] where it noted that the rape of a female detainee by an agent of the state for purposes of extraction of information or confessions or the humiliation, punishment, or intimidation of the victim was considered to be an act of torture under current interpretations of international human rights standards. In support of this, Amnesty International referred to the *Fernando and Raquel Mejia v Peru*[150] decision (which did not concern sexual abuse of a child but of an adult) of the Inter-American Commission on Human Rights taken under Article 5 of the American Convention on Human Rights,[151] to the reports published by the United Nations Special Rapporteur on Torture, and to the fact that the International Criminal Tribunal for the former Yugoslavia had approved bills of indictment against individuals for torture based on allegations that they had raped female detainees. The NGO also drew the Court's attention to current international legal standards on the investigation of allegations of rape made by detainees, in particular Articles 11 and 12 of the Convention Against Torture. The Convention Against Torture was ratified by all ECHR Contracting States.[152]

The ECHR considered that state action constitutes a crucial factor in meeting the severity requirement of the standard under Article 3 of the ECHR. It was noted that '[r]ape of a detainee by an official of the State must be considered to be an especially grave and abhorrent form of ill-treatment given the ease with which the offender can exploit the vulnerability and weakened resistance of his victim'.[153] The ECHR continued to explain that 'rape leaves deep psychological scars on the victim which do not respond to the passage of time as quickly as other forms of physical and mental violence'.[154] This was in addition to the acute physical pain suffered by the victim in this case. It was held that 'having regard to her sex and youth and the circumstances under which she was held',[155] the accumulation of physical and mental violence together with the especially cruel act of rape amounted to torture under Article 3 of the ECHR.[156] Although the Court did take notice of the child's age and sex, it did not seem to portray the victim as a girl or as a child throughout the judgment. Moreover, it did not make any references to the CRC, which could be considered as an appropriate instrument

[148] Ibid, para 54. [149] For the submissions of Amnesty International, see ibid, para 51.

[150] *Fernando and Raquel Mejia v Peru*, IACommHR Decision, 1 March 1996, Report No 5/96, Case 10, 970. In this case, the Inter-American Commission on Human Right held that rape could constitute torture. The Commission did not refer in this case to the United Nations Convention Against Torture, although it did rely on a report of the United Nations Rapporteur Against Torture.

[151] American Convention on Human Rights, OAS Treaty Series No 36, 1144 UNTS 123, in force 18 July 1978.

[152] This information was verified on 13 June 2010: United Nations Treaty Collection, Status, <http://treaties.un.org/Pages/ViewDetails.aspx?src=TREATY&mtdsg_no=IV-11&chapter=4&lang=en>. See ch V, 1, and ch VI, 3.

[153] *Aydín v Turkey* (n 147 above), para 83. [154] Ibid. [155] Ibid, para 84.

[156] Ibid, para 86.

to include among the other external sources. The only references to international law in the judgment were those to the Convention Against Torture.[157] Thus, the Court did not refer to the most specific legislation on the topic, which would have allowed it to pay sufficient attention to the special needs of the teenage girl in this case.

In *MC v Bulgaria*,[158] in contrast to the *Aydín* case, the Court refrained from qualifying rape as torture, and found instead that it was a form of ill-treatment falling under Article 3 of the ECHR.[159] In this case, the ECtHR concluded that positive obligations in Articles 3 and 8 of the ECHR require Contracting States to enact legislation to punish, investigate, and prosecute rape. In this case, a girl alleged that she was raped by two men aged 20 and 21 when she was 14 years old (the age of sexual consent in Bulgaria). She went into a club with two men and a friend and then agreed to go to another club only with the men. On the way back, one of the men wanted to stop at a reservoir for a swim. The girl alleged that she stayed behind until one of the men came back and forced her to have sexual intercourse with him. She was then taken to a private home and once again forced to have sex. The two men denied this version of the facts and claimed that they did not rape her. The criminal investigation found insufficient evidence that the applicant had been compelled to have sex with the two men, and the case was closed. The applicant complained that Bulgarian law and practice did not provide effective protection against rape and sexual abuse, as cases were only prosecuted when the victim resisted. She submitted that Bulgaria had a positive obligation to protect the individual's physical integrity and private life and to provide for an effective remedy. She relied on Articles 3, 8, 13, and 14 of the ECHR,[160] on Bulgarian law and practice,[161] on developments in international and comparative law,[162] and on a psychiatric and psychological expert opinion.[163] The Court concluded unanimously that there was a violation of Articles 3 and 8. The Court did not make reference to the CRC, but made extensive references to other domestic and international legal sources.

The Court reviewed the Bulgarian legislation on rape and then turned to the external sources to ascertain whether there was a convergent standard in relation to the offence. As part of its enquiry, the Court found the following sources relevant: the legislation on rape in some European countries, the Recommendation of the Committee of Ministers of the Council of Europe on the protection of women against violence,[164] the case law of the International Criminal Tribunal

[157] Ibid, para 103.

[158] *MC v Bulgaria* (App No 39272/98), judgment, 4 December 2003, Reports 2003-XII, 1.

[159] Cesare Pitea, 'Rape as a Human Rights Violation and a Criminal Offence: The European Court's Judgment in M.C. v. Bulgaria' (2005) 3 J Int'l Crim Just 447, 456–457.

[160] *MC v Bulgaria* (n 158 above), paras 109–110.

[161] Ibid, paras 111–114.

[162] Ibid, para 112.

[163] Ibid, paras 69–71 and 112.

[164] Recommendation Rec (2002) 5 of the Committee of Ministers of the Council of Europe on the protection of women against violence, adopted by the Committee of Ministers on 30 April 2002 at the 794th meeting of the Ministers' Deputies.

for the former Yugoslavia,[165] and General Recommendation No 19 of 29 January 1992 on violence against women of the United Nations Committee on the Elimination of Discrimination against Women.[166] Subsequently, it also analysed a submission (composed of reports) of an international NGO based in London, Interights, where the definition of rape in several civil and common law jurisdictions as well as in international law had been reviewed.

The Court noted that states enjoy a wide margin of discretion in choosing the means to ensure adequate protection against rape. This margin is nonetheless circumscribed by ECHR provisions which must be adapted by the Court to the changing conditions within the Contracting States.[167] The Court observed that proof of use of physical force and resistance is sometimes required, but this requirement seems now to have been rejected.[168] In most European countries influenced by continental legal traditions, the definition of rape contains references to the use of violence or threats of violence by the perpetrator.[169] However, in case law and legal theory, it is the lack of consent, and not force, which is the constituent of rape. The Court also noted that Member States of the Council of Europe, urging further reforms in this area of law, had agreed that penalizing non-consensual sexual acts was necessary for the effective protection of women against violence.[170] Furthermore, in international criminal law, any sexual penetration without the victim's consent constitutes rape, which reflects a universal trend towards regarding lack of consent as an essential element of rape and sexual abuse.[171] As a result, positive obligations under Articles 3 and 8 of the ECHR require Contracting States to penalize and prosecute non-consensual sexual acts, even when the element of force is lacking.

The Court did not refer to the CRC in the three cases analysed above, despite the fact that this instrument provides the more specific standard with regard to sexual abuse of children. There are several reasons which could explain this absence of reference. First, in two of the cases, the applicants referred to other external international legal sources, and therefore the Court may have felt constrained to pay attention only to the sources that were invoked. Secondly, the Court's references were conditioned by the qualification and interpretation framework that it chose to adopt. As there was no reference in the ECHR to sexual abuse or rape, the Court decided to include these offences under Articles 3 and 8 of the ECHR. Ultimately, it appears that Article 3, the prohibition on torture, was retained as the main provision for complaints regarding rape. In this way, the Court also followed the path indicated by its regional counterpart, the

165 *Prosecutor v Anto Furundžija*, Trial Chamber II, 10 December 1998, IT-95–17/1; *Prosecutor v Kunarac, Kovač and Vuković*, Trial Chamber I, 22 February 2001, IT-96–23&23/1.

166 United Nations, General Recommendation No 19 of 29 January 1992 on violence against women of the United Nations Committee on the Elimination of Discrimination against Women, 11th Session, CEDAW Gen Rec No 19, A/47/38.

167 *MC v Bulgaria* (n 158 above), paras 154–155.

168 Ibid, paras 156–158.

169 Ibid, para 159.

170 Ibid, para 163.

171 Ibid, para 166.

Inter-American Commission on Human Rights, which considered that rape can amount to torture. In this context, the closest international equivalent, in the eyes of the ECtHR, may have been the Convention Against Torture. Thirdly, the CRC does not contain a definition of torture, whereas the Convention Against Torture obviously contains a very specific definition. For this reason, the Court may have preferred to rely on the latter rather than the former. Fourthly, the changing conditions in the Contracting States' legal systems constituted an important factor in the Court's reasoning and this may have diverted its attention from the CRC.

5. ILO Convention on Worst Forms of Child Labour (No 182)

5.1 An International Treaty Neglected in the ECtHR's Case Law

The international legal instruments prohibiting forced labour grew out of an older initiative aimed at eradicating slavery, which subsumes to a certain extent the practice of forced labour. In 1927, the League of Nations adopted the Slavery Convention,[172] which was the first international agreement to define slavery and the slave trade. At the time, there was no consensus with regard to the question of whether forced labour could be treated analogically to slavery and whether it should be prohibited. Only in 1956 was an additional treaty clarifying the situation adopted. The aim of this treaty—the Supplementary Convention on the Abolition of Slavery, the Slave Trade, and Institutions and Practices Similar to Slavery[173]—was to augment the scope of the 1926 Slavery Convention and 'to intensify national as well as international efforts towards the abolition of slavery, the slave trade and institutions and practices similar to slavery'.[174] Thirty-seven ECHR Contracting States ratified the Supplementary Convention.[175]

The international treaties relating to forced labour were enacted under the auspices of the International Labour Organization (ILO), which worked on this issue following the date of its inception. The first human rights treaty it adopted was the Convention concerning Forced or Compulsory Labour (ILO Convention No 29).[176] This instrument pays particular attention to the forms of forced labour practised for economic purposes under colonialism and exempts five forms of

[172] Slavery, Servitude, Forced Labour and Similar Institutions and Practices Convention of 1926 ('1926 Slavery Convention'), 60 LNTS 253, entered into force on 9 March 1927.
[173] Supplementary Convention on the Abolition of Slavery, the Slave Trade, and Institutions and Practices Similar to Slavery, 226 UNTS 3, entered into force on 30 April 1957.
[174] Ibid, Preamble.
[175] This information was verified on 13 June 2010: United Nations Treaty Collection, Status, United Nations Treaty Collection, Status, <http://treaties.un.org/Pages/ViewDetailsIII.aspx?&src=TREATY&mtdsg_no=XVIII-4&chapter=18&Temp=mtdsg3&lang=en>.
[176] Convention concerning Forced or Compulsory Labour (ILO Convention No 29), 39 UNTS 55, entered into force on 1 May 1932.

forced or compulsory labour from the otherwise absolute prohibition on its use. In an effort to complement this initiative, the ILO endorsed the Convention on the Abolition of Forced Labour (ILO Convention No 105),[177] which reflects a post-Second World War concern about the use of forced labour for political coercion. Both instruments were ratified by 44 of the ECHR Contracting States.[178]

In relation to children, the ILO adopted the Convention concerning the Prohibition and Immediate Action for the Elimination of the Worst Forms of Child Labour (ILO Convention No 182). The Convention is enjoying the fastest pace of ratification in the ILO's history, and was ratified by 44 of the 47 ECHR Contracting States.[179] In 1999 it was supplemented with the Worst Forms of Child Labour Recommendation No 190.[180] Surprisingly, neither of these instruments has permeated into the ECtHR's case law concerning child forced labour.

5.2 Early Forced Labour Case Law

The prohibition on forced labour is enshrined in Article 4(2) of the ECHR, which provides that '[n]o one shall be required to perform forced or compulsory labour'. As in the international treaties, the concept of forced labour in the ECHR is delimited. Pursuant to Article 4(3), any work imposed during detention, during conditional release, any military service (or any service exacted instead of compulsory military service), any service exacted in case of an emergency, and any work being part of normal civic obligations does not constitute forced labour. These requirements serve, however, as aids in interpretation and not as limitations.[181]

The expression 'forced or compulsory labour' in Article 4 has been taken from ILO Convention No 29 (discussed above).[182] It has been considered that, in interpreting Article 4, it is reasonable to rely on the work of the ILO bodies in defining the term for the purposes of the ILO Conventions.[183] Indeed, in *Iversen v Norway*,[184] the first case on the topic, four Commission members considered that forced labour cannot be solely understood on the basis of its literal meaning. In international law and practice, it has been regarded as evidenced in the provisions and application of ILO Conventions and Resolutions on Forced Labour.[185] In

[177] Convention on the Abolition of Forced Labour (ILO Convention No 105), 320 UNTS 291, entered into force on 17 January 1959.

[178] This information was verified on 13 June 2010: International Labour Organization, ILOLEX, <http://www.ilo.org/ilolex/english/convdisp1.htm>.

[179] This information was verified on 13 June 2010: International Labour Organization, ILOLEX, <http://www.ilo.org/ilolex/english/convdisp1.htm>.

[180] Worst Forms of Child Labour Recommendation No 190, adopted on 17 June 1999, <http://www.ilo.org/ilolex/cgi-lex/convde.pl?R190> (last visited 13 June 2010).

[181] *Karlheinz Schmidt v Germany* (App No 13580/88), judgment, 18 July 1994, Series A, Vol 291–B, para 22.

[182] Clare Ovey and Robin CA White, *The European Convention on Human Rights* (Oxford/New York: OUP, 4th edn, 2006), 113.

[183] Ibid.

[184] *Iversen v Norway* (App No 1468/62), decision, 17 December 1963, 6 YB 278.

[185] Ibid, 328.

these instruments, forced labour is composed of two fundamental elements: first, the work or service is performed by the worker against his will; and, secondly, the work or service performed is unjust, oppressive, or involves avoidable hardship.[186] This case concerned a law passed in Norway in 1956 which provided that dentists might be required to work for a public dental clinic for a period of up to two years. With this reference, the Commission signalled early on that it would adopt an approach which is inclusive of international law when interpreting the prohibition on forced labour in Article 4.

In subsequent case law, the Court seems to have followed in the Commission's footsteps by using a very receptive approach. In *Van der Mussele v Belgium*[187] it was evident to the Court 'that the authors of the European Convention—following the example of the authors of Article 8 of the draft International Covenant on Civil and Political Rights—based themselves, to a large extent, on an earlier treaty of the International Labour Organisation, namely Convention No 29 concerning Forced or Compulsory Labour'.[188] Despite the substantive differences between the ILO Conventions and the ECHR,[189] the Court decided that it would nevertheless

> take into account... [ILO Conventions Nos 29 and 105] which are binding on nearly all the member States of the Council of Europe,... and especially Convention No 29. There is in fact a striking similarity, which is not accidental, between paragraph 3 of Article 4... of the European Convention and paragraph 2 of Article 2 of Convention No 29. Paragraph 1 of the last-mentioned Article provides that 'for the purposes' of the latter Convention, the term 'forced or compulsory labour' shall mean 'all work or service which is exacted from any person under the menace of any penalty and for which the said person has not offered himself voluntarily'. This definition can provide a starting-point for interpretation of Article 4 of the European Convention.[190]

The ECtHR decided not to use the two-prong test established by the Commission in *Iversen v Norway*. According to its interpretation of ILO Convention No 29, a different approach needed to be taken. Thus, the Court considered that the test should be composed of three criteria, namely whether there was 'the menace of a penalty', whether there was 'prior consent', and whether all the circumstances in the case viewed in light of the objectives of Article 4 of the ECHR indicated that the practice could be considered as forced labour under that provision.[191] The ECtHR's reasoning in this case constitutes a telling example of the fact that it is very conscious of the interrelations between the ECHR and other international instruments.

[186] Ibid.

[187] *Van der Mussele v Belgium* (App No 8919/80), judgment, 23 November 1983, Series A, Vol 70.

[188] Ibid, para 32.

[189] Ibid (text inserted by author). The Court clarified that ILO Convention No 29 undertook to suppress forced labour progressively. It was supplemented by ILO Convention No 105 which provided for the immediate abolition of forced labour in certain specified cases. The ECHR, however, contains a general and absolute prohibition of forced labour.

[190] Ibid.

[191] Ibid, paras 35–37.

5.3 The *Siliadin v France* Case

In spite of the exemplary reception of the ILO Conventions (existing at the time) in previous cases, the more recent case law of the ECtHR evidences a certain difficulty with regard to the Court's choice of international instruments used in its reasoning. As seen above, in 1999 the ILO adopted the Convention concerning the Prohibition and Immediate Action for the Elimination of the Worst Forms of Child Labour (ILO Convention No 182), which constituted the most specific legislation on the topic. It is curious that in a recent case, *Siliadin v France*,[192] the ECtHR decided to bypass this Convention in order to refer to older international instruments.

In the *Siliadin* case, a Togolese national (the applicant), who was then 15 and a half years old, arrived in France in 1994 with a French national of Togolese origin, Mrs D. The latter had undertaken to regularize the girl's immigration status and to arrange for her education, while the applicant was to do housework for Mrs D until she had earned enough to pay her back for her air ticket. The applicant effectively became an unpaid servant to Mr and Mrs D, and her passport was taken away from her. In the second half of 1994, she was then 'lent' to a couple of friends, Mr and Mrs B, who made her work from 7.30 am until 10.30 pm every day with little time off. The applicant slept in the children's bedroom on a mattress on the floor and wore old clothes. She was never paid, but received a little money from Mrs B's mother. A neighbour, in whom the applicant confided, informed the Committee against Modern Slavery, which reported the matter to the prosecuting authorities at an unspecified date.

In 1998, criminal proceedings were brought against Mr and Mrs B for wrongfully obtaining, between July 1995 and July 1998, unpaid or insufficiently paid services from a vulnerable or dependent person and for subjecting that person to working or living conditions incompatible with human dignity. The defendants were convicted at first instance but were acquitted on appeal. Following a referral by the Court of Cassation, another court found Mr and Mrs B guilty of making the applicant work unpaid for them, but considered that her working and living conditions did not violate her human dignity.

Before the ECtHR, the applicant relied on Article 4 of the ECHR (prohibition of forced labour) and on several international instruments. She submitted that French criminal law did not afford her sufficient and effective protection against the servitude in which she had been held, or at the very least against the forced

[192] *Siliadin v France* (App No 73316/01), judgment, 26 July 2005, Reports 2005-VII, 333. See also the recent *Rantsev* case, where the Court used Art 31(3)(c) of the VCLT when it considered trafficking in human beings, a phenomenon which it had never encountered before as part of its case law. Using other rules of international law, it has deduced from Art 4 of the ECHR a procedural obligation to investigate alleged trafficking, a positive obligation to put in place an appropriate legislative and administrative framework, and a positive obligation to take protective measures against trafficking: *Rantsev v Cyprus and Russia* (App No 25965/04), judgment, 7 January 2010, not yet reported.

and compulsory labour she had been required to perform. She argued that importance had to be attached to the criteria laid down by both the United Nations and the Council of Europe for identifying modern forms of slavery and servitude. She pointed out that her situation had corresponded to three of the four servile situations referred to in Article 1 of the Supplementary Geneva Convention, namely serfdom, debt bondage, and the delivery of a child to a third person for the exploitation of his or her labour.[193] She also referred to the documentation published by the Council of Europe and noted that it included passport confiscation as an important factor in this context.[194] In addition, she emphasized that developments in international law favoured granting special protection to children.[195] The applicant did not rely on ILO Convention No 182 before the Court.

The Court found that Article 4 of the ECHR enshrines one of the basic values of domestic societies. It does not suffice for a Contracting State to claim that it refrained from infringing this provision, as it imposes positive obligations on to states which consist of adopting effective criminal law implementing the prohibition of Article 4 of the ECHR. In support of this assertion, the Court noted that Article 4 of ILO Convention No 29 provides that the competent authority shall not impose forced or compulsory labour for the benefit of private individuals, companies, or associations. It then found that 'limiting compliance with Article 4 of the Convention only to direct action by the State authorities would be inconsistent with the international instruments specifically concerned with this issue and would amount to rendering it ineffective'.[196] Thus, it followed from this that Article 4, as Article 3 of the ECHR, imposes positive obligations, such as the adoption of criminal law provisions which penalize the practices referred to therein and their application in practice.

The Court also noted that 'in addition to the Convention, numerous international conventions have as their objective the protection of human beings from slavery, servitude and forced or compulsory labour'.[197] It was pointed out that the Parliamentary Assembly of the Council of Europe reported that, while slavery was abolished 150 years ago, 'domestic slavery' persists in Europe and concerns thousands of people, the majority of whom are women.[198] The Court asserted that '[i]n interpreting Article 4 of the European Convention, ... [it] has in a previous case already taken into account the ILO Conventions, which are binding on almost all of the Council of Europe's member States, including France, and especially the 1930 Forced Labour Convention'.[199] It considered that 'there is in fact a striking similarity, which is not accidental, between paragraph 2 of Article 4 of the European Convention and paragraph 2 of Article 2 of Convention No 29'.[200] It was found that the applicant had been subjected to forced labour in breach of Article 4 of the ECHR.

[193] *Siliadin v France* (n 192 above), para 91. [194] Ibid, para 93. [195] Ibid, para 97.
[196] Ibid, para 89. [197] Ibid, para 111. [198] Ibid, para 116.
[199] Ibid, para 115; *Van der Mussele v Belgium* (n 187 above) (text inserted by author).
[200] *Siliadin v France* (n 192 above), para 116.

It then remained to be determined whether the applicant had been subjected to slavery or servitude. The Court noted that the Convention is a living instrument which must be interpreted in light of present-day conditions. As increasingly high standards are being required for the protection of human rights, the Court found that greater firmness is required in assessing fundamental values breaches in democratic societies.[201] It then referred to the 1927 Slavery Convention, which provides that slavery is the status or condition of a person over whom all of the powers attaching to the right of ownership are exercised.[202] There was no evidence of slavery found in the case, given that Mr and Mrs B did not exercise a genuine right of ownership over the applicant. As to servitude, the Court noted that under the ECHR case law, where the Commission referred to the Convention on the Abolition of Slavery, it is to be regarded as an obligation to provide one's services under coercion, and it is linked to slavery. Under the Supplementary Convention on the Abolition of Slavery, Slave Trade, and Institutions and Practices Similar to Slavery, Member States must take all practicable and necessary legislative and other measures to end any practice by which a child or young person under the age of 18 is delivered, by natural parents or a guardian, to another person with a view to exploitation of his or her labour, for reward or not.[203] In the Court's view, the circumstances of the case indicated that the applicant had not chosen to work for Mr and Mrs B. Left at their mercy, she was afraid of being arrested and did not have any freedom of movement or free time. This constituted, according to the Court, servitude within the meaning of Article 4 of the ECHR.

Subsequently, the Court had to determine whether French legislation afforded sufficient protection to the applicant in light of France's positive obligations under Article 4. It noted that the Parliamentary Assembly regretted, in its Recommendation 1523 (2001), that none of the Council of Europe Member States had expressly made domestic slavery an offence in their criminal codes.[204] Slavery and servitude were not classified as criminal offences in the French criminal law. While the prosecution of Mr and Mrs B was conducted under criminal law provisions, their conviction was made under civil law. Furthermore, the relevant provisions of the French Criminal Code were open to varying interpretations. The Court emphasized that it has previously stated in its case law that children and other vulnerable individuals are entitled to state protection against serious breaches of personal integrity.[205] In support of this assertion, it cited, among others, Articles 19 and 37 of the CRC. Finally, it concluded that the French criminal legislation in force at the time did not provide sufficient protection to the applicant against the circumstances of this case.

As was recently noted, this decision marks the first recognition by the Court that Article 4 of the ECHR imposes positive obligations on states with regard

[201] Ibid, para 121. [202] Ibid, para 122. [203] Ibid, para 125.

[204] Ibid, para 133; Parliamentary Assembly of the Council of Europe Recommendation 1523 (2001), adopted on 26 June 2001.

[205] *Siliadin v France* (n 192 above), para 143.

to slavery, servitude, and forced labour.[206] Thus, the Court appears to be catching up with the international standards prevailing in this field. The Court's reliance on international law with regard to forced labour could be due to the fact that there is little domestic law in the Council of Europe States on the subject.[207] It is, however, surprising and disappointing that the Court relied on ILO Convention No 29, which predates ILO Convention No 182. It is noteworthy that ILO Convention No 29 contains language similar to Article 4 of the ECHR and includes a comprehensive definition of forced labour. ILO Convention No 29 is also well established and has a large body of interpretation. The same cannot be asserted in relation to ILO Convention No 182. In spite of these deficiencies, however, ILO Convention No 182 does contain specific examples of slavery-like practices including trafficking and debt bondage, which were potentially involved in the case.[208] Thus, the Court should have referred to this instrument—even if it was not invoked in the ECHR proceedings—in order to grant greater protection to the victim, who was a child at the time of the offence.

Another problematic element of the *Siliadin* case lies in the Court's finding that there was forced labour and servitude, but no slavery. In its reasoning, the ECtHR relied on the 1927 Slavery Convention and identified as relevant the element of ownership. It was, however, observed recently that the concept of ownership in the legal sense to which the Court refers has not always been applied strictly.[209] The International Criminal Tribunal for the Former Yugoslavia previously asserted that ownership was an essential element of slavery, but also found that it could just as easily be described as control rather than ownership.[210] In this respect, the Court's reasoning could have been more attentive to recent legal developments.

6. Rationale of the Reasoning

The receptiveness of the ECtHR's approach to international child rights law has been impressive. The Court has resorted to both the CRC and the two Hague Conventions whenever it was necessary to elucidate the meaning of the ECHR. As indicated above, the ECHR contains few specific references to child rights. Its general provisions had to be adapted by the Court in order to meet the changing international standards marked by a need to recognize child rights. At the international level, the field of child rights has been generally pre-empted by the enactment of very specific legislation. Thus, the Court, especially following the enactment of the CRC, had a voluminous and specialized legal base for

[206] Holly Cullen, '*Siliadin v France*: Positive Obligations under Article 4 of the European Convention on Human Rights' (2006) 6 HRLR 585.

[207] Ibid, 591.

[208] Ibid.

[209] Cullen (n 206 above), 592.

[210] Ibid; *Prosecutor v Kunarac, Kovač and Vuković* (n 165 above), paras 542–543.

developing child rights at the regional level. While it has been acknowledged that Contracting States have an important margin of appreciation in matters dealing with family law and juvenile justice, the Court did not shy away from intervening in the domestic legal domain when it felt that this was necessary. Given that there was a considerable lacuna in the protection of children and minors at the European level, the Court remedied the situation by using receptive case law. Giving less priority to the reinforcement of its own system, it has thus leaned more towards the open paradigm.

The Court's approach has been the most responsive to the Hague Conventions. The Court constantly resorted to its standard interpretation formula, according to which the ECHR cannot be interpreted in isolation and relevant rules of international law must be taken into consideration. As a consequence, it was found that the ECHR provisions had to be interpreted in light of the Hague Conventions. In effect, the Court has not merely interpreted the Hague Conventions, but seems to have applied them directly to the situation at hand. Interestingly, in all of the cases involving the Hague Conventions, the Court also invoked the CRC in support of its interpretation.

The ratification record seems to have played a less important role in this strand of Strasbourg case law. At times, the Court was prepared to invoke the relevant instrument even if the state involved had not ratified it.[211] Furthermore, the Court applied the 1980 Hague Convention when it was not invoked or applied at the domestic level.[212] Even more surprisingly, the Court once intervened in the domestic application of the 1980 Hague Convention finding that the courts had misinterpreted the instrument.[213] These references are perhaps less impressive when one considers the fact that the Hague Conventions have been ratified by most ECHR Contracting States, and that they have become the *modus operandi* in matters they regulate. Thus, the proceedings that came before the ECHR were so closely intertwined with the Hague Conventions that the Strasbourg Court may not have had any other choice but to refer to them. On the other hand, a very fundamental development has ensued from this strand of the Court's case law in that Contracting States can now expect to be subjected to a judicial review by the Court in relation to their application of the 1980 Hague Convention.

The fact that the CRC is an international instrument with a universal reach did not play a prominent role in this area of the Strasbourg case law. As with other international treaties, the CRC has been adapted to cover issues appearing in all existing countries. Further, the CRC Signatory States constitute an extremely diverse and heterogeneous group. Unlike the CRC, the ECHR is made up of a relatively homogeneous group of states with comparable economic, social,

211 *Barjami v Albania* (n 41 above).

212 *Iglesias GIL and AUI v Spain* (n 59 above).

213 *Monory v Romania and Hungary* (n 39 above).

political, and legal cultures.[214] Further, certain issues covered by the CRC do not directly concern ECHR Contracting States. In other areas discussed in this work, these considerations seem to have impeded further references to international sources.[215] They do not constitute, however, overwhelmingly important factors in the context of child rights issues.

In relation to the CRC, ratified by all ECHR Contracting States, the responsiveness of the ECtHR has been more moderate, but still very impressive in comparison to the other areas.[216] The Court was able to take the CRC into account in a wide variety of situations, given that this instrument is an all-encompassing code of substantive children's rights. The Court did not reiterate here, however, its standard position used in cases regarding Hague proceedings, that the ECHR should be interpreted in light of international law. With respect to corporal punishment, the Court mentioned the relevant CRC article to support its finding, without explicitly outlawing this practice as the CRC would have required. In relation to juvenile justice cases, the Court referred to various articles of the CRC (and to other international instruments), noting simultaneously that there was an international trend aimed at protecting the privacy of juvenile offenders. In relation to the ill-treatment of an illegal immigrant girl, the Court relied heavily on the relevant provisions of the CRC. In all these cases, the Court frequently invoked the recommendations of the Committee on the Rights of the Child.

Curiously, in relation to the sexual abuse of children, the Court relied on the Convention Against Torture—instead of the CRC—which also applies to children, but is nonetheless more general. This reliance on the Convention Against Torture could have been prompted by the interpretation framework the ECtHR chose to adopt under the ECHR (it qualified rape as torture). In this context, it is plausible that, in the eyes of the Court, the most useful instrument to elucidate the meaning of the ECHR was the CAT and not the CRC. In fact, the CAT contains a precise definition of torture, whereas the CRC does not define this offence.

A similar trend is apparent in the case law on forced labour, where the Court resorted to older instruments on the subject instead of more recent and specific ones. While the Court had at its disposition ILO Convention No 182, which provided very specific examples of prohibited forced labour imposed on children, it resorted to an older convention on forced labour which applies to all, namely ILO Convention No 29. The use of this approach was mainly due to the fact that the latter instrument had been relied on when Article 4 of the ECHR was drafted. There were many textual and substantive parallels in this respect between the ECHR and ILO Convention No 29. Nonetheless, ILO Convention

[214] Liz Hefferman, 'A Comparative View of Individual Petition Procedures under the European Convention on Human Rights and the International Covenant on Civil and Political Rights' (1997) 19(1) Hum Rts Qrtly 78, 84.

[215] See ch IV, 1.2 and 3; ch V, 4; and ch VI, 4.

[216] See Conclusion, 4.2.1 and 4.2.2.

No 182 contains certain offences specific to children which were not included in ILO Convention No 29.

Thus, in contrast to the Hague Conventions cases marked by an exemplary reception, the Court was moderately attentive to the CRC and completely unreceptive to ILO Convention No 182. This moderation or lack of reception could be due to the fact that the CRC and ILO Convention No 182 contain very substantive and comprehensive provisions, many of which are still evolving in international law. Therefore, the Court may have been more at ease and more receptive towards purely technical and procedural provisions devoid of controversy. The international instruments considered in this chapter have been ratified by almost all the ECHR Contracting States and therefore the Court could have safely referred to them. Hence, the difference in the approach adopted with regard to each instrument does not lie in the ratification record, but rather in the degree to which a case is intertwined with international law, the fact that an international text was invoked in domestic proceedings or before the ECtHR, the fact that an international text contains more specific definitions or guidelines than the ECHR, the similarity of language between the ECHR and international law provisions, as well as the interpretation framework chosen.

The foregoing analysis reveals that the Court has relied on the open paradigm in its case law referring to international child rights. This approach has allowed the Court to prevent and to reduce fragmentation between the ECHR and international child rights law. As already noted, the ECHR contains few specific child rights provisions and the Court was able to elucidate its meaning by relying on international law. As a result, the Court was also able to consolidate various child rights provisions and to apply them coherently to a specific case. This approach was very beneficial for this area of international law, given that international child rights instruments do not include strong enforcement mechanisms and depend largely on the will of the domestic authorities for their application. In future cases, the Court will also be able to intervene and rectify the application of treaties if they have been misinterpreted at the domestic level. Finally, the reception of international law was desirable in this strand of the Strasbourg case law; it has maximized the potential of international treaties in order to protect and promote children's rights.[217] This tendency is particularly justified in the context of children, who constitute one of the most vulnerable groups in society and deserve to be granted greater protection.

[217] Kilkelly (n 8 above), 326.

IV

Civil and Political Rights

1. Preliminary Observations

The historical enactment of the United Nations Covenant on Civil and Political Rights and its First Optional Protocol[1] ('First OP') provided additional options to the individual applicant seeking redress for wrongs suffered. At the same time, this innovation marked the beginning of a troublesome coexistence between the Strasbourg bodies and the United Nations Human Rights Committee (HRC). While there are many divergences between the systems, an applicant usually has the choice to apply either to the HRC or the European Court of Human Rights for resolution of a given violation. This state of affairs multiplies the various avenues of justice and further exacerbates the problem of forum shopping.[2] Moreover, it contributes to the fragmentation of international law and the isolation of the human rights special regimes. At present, all the ECHR Contracting States are bound by the International Covenant on Civil and Political Rights (ICCPR) and 44 out of 47 of them are also bound by the First OP.[3] It is therefore not surprising that the Court has made substantial references to the ICCPR framework. As will be seen, the Court's approach to the ICCPR has reduced the insularity between the systems to some extent.

1.1 The Coexistence of Both Systems

While the ECHR was the first to come into existence, the preparatory work leading up to the adoption of the ICCPR began earlier than that of its European counterpart. It appears nonetheless that the historical divergences in their creation did not have a substantial bearing on their relationship vis-à-vis one another. The United Nations Commission commenced its work on the enactment of an

[1] Optional Protocol to the International Covenant on Civil and Political Rights, 999 UNTS 302, entered into force 23 March 1976.

[2] Forum shopping occurs when an applicant brings the same claim with different instances in an attempt to obtain a favourable verdict.

[3] This information was verified on 13 June 2010: United Nations Treaty Collection, Status, <http://treaties.un.org/Pages/ViewDetails.aspx?src=TREATY&mtdsg_no=IV-4&chapter=4&lang=en>; <http://treaties.un.org/Pages/ViewDetails.aspx?src=TREATY&mtdsg_no=IV-5&chapter=4&lang=en>.

international human rights charter in the late 1940s. This process eventually culminated in the entry into force of the ICCPR and the International Covenant on Economic, Social and Cultural Rights[4] in 1976. It is questionable whether this early start had a significant bearing on the Strasbourg experience. In the early decades of their existence, the Strasbourg bodies were relatively inactive. Only in the 1970s did a proliferation of cases emerge and the Strasbourg docket become increasingly overburdened. Despite this, various questions relating to the coexistence of both bodies necessitated the taking of further measures which were included in both the UN Covenants and the ECHR.[5]

In order to avoid the duplicity of procedures, the First OP specifies in Article 5(2)(a) that the HRC 'shall not consider any communication from an individual unless it has ascertained that... the same matter is not being examined under another procedure of international investigation or settlement'. The ECHR, however, states in Article 35(2)(b) that the Strasbourg bodies 'shall not deal with any petition submitted under Article 34 which... is substantially the same as a matter that has already been examined by the Court or has already been submitted to another procedure of international investigation or settlement and contains no relevant new information'.

From both of these provisions, it follows that if a matter comes before the Court after having been considered by the HRC, the Court is prevented from considering it further. Moreover, an individual cannot lodge an application before the HRC if the Court is in the process of examining the application and has not yet rendered a judgment on the matter. However, once the Court has judged in a given case, there are no apparent obstacles for the claimant to bring the case before the HRC.

The Council of Europe chose to maintain the coexistence of both bodies and to provide the applicant with a choice as to the means available to him. However, it sought to avoid situations where the HRC acted as an instance of appeal following ECHR proceedings which were unfavourable to the applicant. In Resolution 70(17), it was suggested that Member States of the Council 'should normally utilise the procedures established by the European Convention relating to an alleged violation of a right which is in substance covered both by the European Convention (or its protocols) and by the UN Covenant on Civil and Political Rights, it being understood that the UN procedure may be invoked in relation to rights not guaranteed in the European Convention (or its protocols or in relation to States which are not Parties to the European Convention)'.[6]

[4] United Nations Covenant on Economic, Social and Cultural Rights, 993 UNTS 3, entered into force 3 January 1976.

[5] Liz Hefferman, 'A Comparative View of Individual Petition Procedures under the European Convention on Human Rights and the International Covenant on Civil and Political Rights' (1997) 19(1) Hum Rts Qrtly 78, 82–83.

[6] Consultative Assembly, Resolution (70) 17, 'UN Covenant on Civil and Political Rights and the European Convention on Human Rights: Procedure for dealing with inter-state complaints', Adopted by the Ministers' Deputies, 15 May 1970.

In addition, a Committee of Experts was established to study the problems of coexistence and the differences between the UN Covenants and the ECHR system.[7] Furthermore, it was emphasized in Resolution 552 (1973) that 'the programmes of the United Nations and of the Council of Europe for the protection and promotion of human rights are complementary and not competitive, and that all necessary steps should be taken to ensure their effective co-ordination'.[8] It was considered that, if Contracting States adopted reservations to the First OP preventing successive applications, part of the problem could be alleviated. The Committee of Ministers observed in May 1970 that 'member States of the Council of Europe which sign or ratify the Optional Protocol might wish to make a declaration, at the moment of signing or ratifying, whose effect would be that the competence of the U.N. Human Rights Committee would not extend to receiving and considering individual complaints relating to cases which are being or already have been examined under the procedure provided for by the European Convention'.[9] The Committee of Ministers transmitted to the Contracting States a text drafted by the Committee of Experts which could be used by their governments as an interpretative declaration or as a reservation.[10]

Thus, 19 states adopted a reservation or interpretative declaration which specified that the HRC would be prevented from considering communications from individuals if the same matter had already 'been considered under another procedure of international investigation or settlement'.[11] It is not entirely surprising that only three of the states issuing reservations were not Contracting States of the ECHR; most of the ECHR Contracting States wanted to prevent individuals, whose case had already been examined by the ECtHR, from submitting the same case to the HRC.[12] It is, nonetheless, possible that the HRC has recently dimin-

[7] Council of Europe, *Problems Arising from the Co-existence of the United Nations Covenants on Human Rights and the European Convention on Human Rights: Differences as regards the Rights Guaranteed*, Report of the Committee of Experts on Human Rights to the Committee of Ministers, Doc H (70) 7, September 1970.

[8] Consultative Assembly, Resolution 552 (1973) concerning the 25th Anniversary of the Universal Declaration of Human Rights and the 20th Anniversary of the European Convention on Human Rights, 27 September 1973.

[9] Consultative Assembly, 22nd Session, Doc No 2795, 22–23, 4 Docs (1970–1971), reproduced in Marc-André Eissen, 'The European Convention on Human Rights and the United Nations Covenant on Civil and Political Rights: Problems of Coexistence' (1972–1973) 22 Buff L Rev 181, 204–205.

[10] Ibid.

[11] Austria, Croatia, Denmark, France, Germany, Iceland, Ireland, Italy, Luxembourg, Malta, Norway, Poland, Romania, Slovenia, Spain, Sri Lanka, Sweden, Turkey, and Uganda. El Salvador, using weaker wording in its reservation than the other states, merely noted that the HRC is not competent 'to examine communications and/or complaints which have been submitted to other procedures of international investigation or settlement': United Nations Treaty Collection, Status, <http://treaties.un.org/Pages/ViewDetails.aspx?src=TREATY&mtdsg_no=IV-5&chapter=4&lang=en > (last visited 13 June 2010).

[12] Catherine Phuong, 'The Relationship Between the European Court of Human Rights and the Human Rights Committee: Has the "Same Matter" Already Been "Examined"?' (2007) 7/2 HRLR 385, 386.

ished the effect of these reservations and interpretative declarations by interpreting the notions of 'same matter' and 'examined' in Article 5(2)(a) of the First OP restrictively.[13] Following this line of reasoning, it thus appears that the HRC's approach complicates the relationship between the ECHR and the ICCPR systems even further.

Significant safeguards have been put into place to avoid cases of litispendence between the ECtHR and the HRC. Nevertheless, a large part of the ECtHR's case law referring to the ICCPR relates to their difficulties of coexistence.[14] In fact, cases in which an applicant introduced a complaint before the HRC before applying to the ECtHR were numerous, and provided an opportunity for the Court to further define its relationship with the ICCPR. They also allowed judges to refer to the ICCPR provisions and to use them as part of their reasoning. Thus, the Court's references to the ICCPR were prompted, at least in these cases, by complicated coexistence issues as well as by previous HRC proceedings.

1.2 The Differences Between the Systems

There are significant similarities between the ICCPR and the ECHR, as both instruments cover an exhaustive catalogue of civil and political rights, provide for an individual complaint procedure, and strive to achieve similar goals. Despite this, there are also many substantive differences in their mandates, membership, and operation.[15] The ECHR, a regional instrument, is made up of a relatively homogeneous group of states which have similar economic, social, political, and legal cultures.[16] The ICCPR, however, is an international treaty, and its Signatory States have diverse legal cultures. This renders the prospect of reaching a consensus in this framework much more difficult.[17] The ECHR is very central to the operation of the Council of Europe and its membership has become almost a precondition for Council of Europe membership. In contrast, the ICCPR benefits from greater independence within the UN system and its operation is under the sole competence of the HRC.[18]

Another significant difference between the systems is the role the individual complaint procedure plays in each. Under the ECHR, the complaint procedure is the very essence of the Strasbourg system. It represents most of the ECtHR's activity, and it is generally with this procedure that the ECtHR has been identified. The individual complaint mechanism does not have such a prominent role in the ICCPR system. Although the HRC is becoming increasingly more

[13] Ibid.

[14] See also Pieter Van Dijk, Fried Van Hoof, Arjen Van Rijn, and Loe Zwaak, *Theory and Practice of the European Convention on Human Rights* (Antwerp/Oxford: Intersentia, 4th edn, 2006), 89–93.

[15] Hefferman (n 5 above), 84.

[16] Ibid. See ch III, 6; ch V, 4; and ch VI, 4.

[17] Hefferman (n 5 above), 83–85.

[18] With the exception of the role of the UN Secretary General in transmitting individual complaints and the general supervisory power of the General Assembly. Ibid.

court-like,[19] the compulsory reporting system of the ICCPR still constitutes most of its work. This system also gave rise to another practice on the part of the HRC, namely the publication of General Comments. Initially, these were intended to provide interpretative guidance to governments, but now they also assist NGOs in drafting alternative reports for individuals in formulating their complaints.[20] Most importantly, the ECHR differs from the ICCPR in that it has a concrete enforcement mechanism. Unfortunately, compliance with the ICCPR is still reliant on the goodwill of states.

From a substantive point of view, both instruments cover similar territory, but the ICCPR appears to provide more extensive protection to the individual applicant in many contexts. Unlike the ECHR, the ICCPR also provides for the right of all peoples to self-determination (Article 1), the right of detainees to be treated with humanity and dignity (Article 10), the right to recognition as a person before the law (Article 16), the prohibition of propaganda for war and of incitement to national, racial, and religious hatred (Article 20), equality of rights and responsibilities of spouses in relation to marriage and at its dissolution (Article 23(4)), the rights of children (Articles 23(4) and 24), protection of the family (Article 23(1)), the right to participate in the conduct of public affairs in so far as this goes beyond the right to free elections (Article 25), equality before the law (Article 26), and the rights of minorities (Article 27).[21] There are also substantial differences in the formulation of certain rights, which appear to indicate that the ICCPR provides greater protection than the ECHR. This is the case with the formulation of the right to life, the prohibition of torture and slavery, the rights to liberty and fair trial, the rights of aliens, the right to an effective remedy, and the right to freedom of expression.[22]

In addition, both instruments impose limitations on the exercise of most rights. These rights can be limited by restrictions which are provided by law, serve one of the enumerated objectives (ie national security, public order, protection of health, morals, public safety, etc), and are necessary for achieving this objective.[23] In general, it appears that the Strasbourg Convention contains less-far-reaching limitations than the ICCPR. While the ECtHR affords an important margin of appreciation to the Contracting States, it also stipulates that the restrictions imposed be necessary in a democratic society. The ICCPR, however, imposes this requirement only with regard to restrictions on the publicity of trials and freedom of assembly and association (Articles 14(1), 21, and 22(2)), and not on the freedom of movement, religion, and expression (Articles 12(3), 18(3), and

[19] Laurence R Helfer and Anne-Marie Slaughter, 'Toward a Theory of Effective Supranational Adjudication' (1997) 107 Yale LJ 273, 344, 388–389.
[20] Ibid, 86–87.
[21] For further details, see Council of Europe (n 7 above); Manfred Nowak, 'The Interrelationship Between the Covenant on Civil and Political Rights and the European Convention on Human Rights' in Stavròula Vassilouni (ed), *Aspects of the Protection of Individual and Social Rights* (Hestia: Marangopoulos Foundation for Human Rights, 1995), 131.
[22] Ibid, 131, 153–159, 161.
[23] Ibid, 160.

19(3)).[24] Exceptionally, there are certain limitations under the ECHR which are more restrictive than those imposed by the ICCPR, namely in the case of Article 16, which imposes restrictions on the political activity of aliens. It is also important to emphasize that a number of rights in the ECHR are not covered at the international level. For instance, unlike the ICCPR, the ECHR covers the right to peaceful enjoyment of possessions (Article 1 of Protocol No 1), the right to education (Article 2 of Protocol No 1), and the prohibition of the collective expulsion of aliens (Article 4 of Protocol No 4).[25]

Interestingly, the individual complaint procedure under the First OP has not frequently been used by Europeans. The Strasbourg system remains more popular in ECHR Contracting States. Further, the ECtHR's authority in rendering binding judgments is certainly greater than that of the HRC. It has been argued, however, that there are still many valid reasons for applying to the HRC when a violation occurs. For instance, numerous civil and political rights are only covered by the ICCPR and not by the ECHR. Furthermore, certain rights are better protected by the former than by the latter. In addition, some limitations on human rights are more extensive under the ECHR. Finally, the ICCPR procedure is less complicated than that used in Strasbourg, and the HRC's case law under certain common provisions is more developed.[26]

2. International Civil and Political Rights

References to the ICCPR in Strasbourg case law can be sub-divided into two trends. The first deals with references which were prompted by structural or procedural reasons, namely the coexistence of both systems. These cases were generally marked by a high reception level and an uninhibited approach to international law on the part of the Strasbourg bodies. They were also closely intertwined with HRC proceedings and required a reference to HRC case law or the ICCPR as a prerequisite to resolving the case. The second trend includes cases where the Strasbourg bodies referred to the ICCPR in order to clarify or harmonize the ECHR with the Covenant. This strand of the Strasbourg case law followed an uneven evolution. In the 1980s and early 1990s, the Strasbourg bodies referred regularly to ICCPR provisions. Subsequently, both the Commission and the Court distanced themselves from the ICCPR framework and adopted a more circumspect approach. Nonetheless, in 2001 the Court made unusually extensive use of the ICCPR by applying it to a case where the relevant country had not incorporated it in its domestic law. Most recently, the Court's approach systematized itself and became more balanced and harmonious.

[24] Ibid. [25] Ibid, 136–139. [26] Ibid, 164.

2.1 Case Law on the Coexistence of the Strasbourg Bodies with the HRC

2.1.1 Definition of the Relationship

Despite the safety guards put into place, many coexistence problems persist between the Geneva and Strasbourg systems. In the 1990s, the Commission and the Court were able to further define this relationship when they examined cases concerning the same matter introduced both in Strasbourg and in Geneva. In *CW v Finland*,[27] the Commission found that it was not required to decide whether or not the facts submitted by the applicant disclosed any evidence of violation of ECHR rights, given that pursuant to Article 35(2)(b) of the ECHR (former Article 27(1)(b)) it should not deal with a case that had been submitted to another procedure of international investigation. In this case, the applicant stated that he had submitted a complaint to the HRC, and the Commission considered that it was substantially the same as the previous complaint.

In *Calcerrada Fornieles v Spain*,[28] the applicants, imprisoned militants of the First of October Antifascist Resistance Group (GRAPO), claimed that the decision of Spanish authorities to feed them against their will constituted a violation of Articles 3, 9, 10, and 14 of the ECHR. The applicants were deliberately on hunger strike. They had previously instituted proceedings before the HRC which they decided to suspend until the Commission decided the case at hand. The Commission found that the application was inadmissible because the same matter had been presented to the HRC. It was observed that Spain had ratified the First OP and had recognized the competence of the HRC in examining individual communications. In the Commission's view, the fact that two international instances judged simultaneously in the same case was not consonant with the letter and spirit of former Article 27(1)(b) (Article 35(2)(b)) of the ECHR. While the applicants had asked for a suspension of the proceedings before the HRC, the Commission considered that this did not entail that they had abandoned the case. It was noted that in the past the Court only decided to judge a case when proceedings before another international instance had been completely abandoned. Hence, it was found that the application was inadmissible.

2.1.2 Proceedings Raising Different Issues

In subsequent years, the Commission and the Court were brought to examine further proceedings initiated in both Geneva and Strasbourg. In contrast to the earlier case law, both the Commission and Court found that the issues brought before the HRC were not substantially the same as the issues before them. This strand in the case law allowed the Court and Commission to define further their

[27] *CW v Finland* (App No 17230/90), decision, 9 October 1991, not reported.

[28] *Calcerrada Fornieles and Cabeza Mato v Spain* (App No 17512/90), decision, 6 July 1992, not reported.

role vis-à-vis the HRC and international human rights law. Moreover, it has allowed both Strasbourg bodies to affirm their authority and impose their views on the similarity of issues brought before the HRC. On occasion, the HRC did not agree with the ECtHR on whether the issues were similar, but this did not entail further problems, given that both bodies appeared to consider different aspects of the complaint.

In 1995 the Commission considered the *Peltonen v Finland* case,[29] where the applicant, a Finnish citizen who resided permanently in Sweden, had been denied the issuance of his passport as he failed to attend the call-up for military service in Finland. The applicant had complained that this had interfered with his rights under Article 2(2) of Protocol No 4 as well as Articles 6(1) and 7(1) of the ECHR. The respondent Government submitted, *inter alia*, that the applicant's brother had brought a communication with contents similar to those of the present case to the HRC.[30] The brother had also been denied the delivery of his passport in Sweden on grounds that he had failed to report for military service in Finland; he complained that this limitation constituted a disproportionate punishment, a punishment not prescribed by law, and a violation of his right to leave any country under Article 12 of the ICCPR (right to freedom of movement).[31] The HRC found that the communication was admissible and that the restrictions placed on the applicant's right to leave any country were in accordance with Article 12(3) of the ICCPR. One member of the HRC (Mr Bertil Wenergren), issued an individual opinion in which he considered that Finland had violated Article 12(2).

The Commission recalled that pursuant to former Article 27(1)(b) (Article 35(2)(b)) of the ECHR it was not able to review a complaint which was substantially the same as a matter already submitted to another international investigation procedure and where it contained no relevant new information. It was acknowledged 'that the freedom guaranteed by Article 2 para. 2 of Protocol No 4 resembles that protected by Article 12 of the International Covenant on Civil and Political Rights, which entered into force with regard to Finland in 1976'. However, the Commission observed that 'if the complainants before the Commission and, for instance, the United Nations Human Rights Committee are not identical, the complaint to the Commission cannot be considered as being substantially the same as the communication to the Committee'. The Commission therefore dealt with the complaint and found that there was no apparent violation of Article 2(2) of Protocol No 4 and that Articles 6 and 7 of the ECHR were not applicable. The application was rejected on grounds that it was manifestly ill-founded and incompatible *ratione materiae* with the ECHR provisions in the meaning of former Article 27(2) (Article 35(3)).

[29] *Peltonen v Finland* (App No 19583/92), decision, 20 February 1995, not reported.

[30] *Peltonen v Finland*, Communication No 492/1992, CCPR/C/51/D/492/1992, 26 July 1994, Human Rights Committee.

[31] Ibid, para 3.

In the same year, the Commission considered the *Pauger v Austria* case,[32] which concerned a refusal of the applicant's request for a widower's pension. Domestic legislation provided that only widows could be recipients of this benefit. Before the Commission, the applicant complained that the administrative authorities which had considered his claim could not be deemed to be courts, that the Constitutional Court did not hold a hearing concerning his complaint, and that the proceedings were not fair and conducted within a reasonable time in violation of Article 6(1) of the ECHR. The applicant had also introduced a communication with the HRC alleging a violation of Article 26 of the ICCPR (equality and prohibition of discrimination).[33] The HRC found that it was competent to examine the case as it did not concern 'the same matter' and addressed other legal issues, although it did stem from the same factual situation. The HRC found that there was a violation of Article 26.[34]

Following the HRC communication, the Commission was brought to consider the case. The respondent Government alleged that the Commission was prevented by virtue of former Article 27(1)(b) (Article 35(2)(b)) of the ECHR from dealing with the application because the matter had already been submitted to a different international investigation procedure. The Commission recalled that this provision 'aims at avoiding the plurality of international procedures concerning the same case'.[35] Nonetheless, in this case it found that 'the applicant did not submit substantially the same matter as raised in his application before the Commission to the Human Rights Committee, because the complaints raised in the respective proceedings were different. While before the Human Rights Committee he complained of discrimination against him, before the Commission he complains about issues related to the proceedings before the Austrian authorities and courts.'[36] Thus, it was held that the applicant's complaint concerning the lack of a hearing before the Constitutional Court was admissible and that the remaining complaints were inadmissible. Subsequently, the Court considered the case and held that there was no violation of Article 6(1) of the ECHR with regard to the right to a hearing.[37] It also held that it was unnecessary to examine the complaint under former Article 27(1)(b) (Article 35(2)(b)) of the ECHR as the respondent Government did not raise it again before the Court.[38]

In 2002 the Court examined another case where proceedings were initiated before the HRC. In *Smirnova v Russia*,[39] the two applicants were convicted of large-scale fraud and sentenced to eight years' and six years' imprisonment,

[32] *Pauger v Austria* (App No 16717/90), decision (Commission), 9 January 1995, DR 80–A, 24.

[33] *Dietmar Pauger v Austria*, Communication No 716/1996, CCPR/C/65/D/716/1996, 30 April 1999, Human Rights Committee.

[34] Ibid, para 11.

[35] *Pauger v Austria* (n 32 above), 32.

[36] Ibid.

[37] *Pauger v Austria* (App No 16717/90), judgment, 28 May 1997, Reports 1997-III, 881, para 63.

[38] Ibid, para 66.

[39] *Smirnova and Smirnova v Russia* (App Nos 46133/99; 48183/99), decision, 3 October 2002, not reported.

respectively, and the confiscation of their property. They were both remanded in custody four times during criminal investigations. The Moscow City Court set aside their conviction and discharged them from serving their sentence because the time limit for establishing their criminal liability had expired. The first applicant's identity card was taken from her when she was arrested and withheld for over four years. As a result, the Moscow Social Security Service and a law firm both refused to employ her because she did not have her identity documents. A Moscow clinic informed her that free medical care could only be provided if she presented an insurance certificate and her identity card. For the same reason, the Moscow Telephone Company refused to install a telephone line in her home. The Moscow City Notary Office notified her that she needed to prove her identity if she wished to obtain notarial deeds. She was also refused the registration of her marriage. Moreover, she was stopped by a police patrol for an identity check. As she was unable to produce the identity card, she was taken to a police station and had to pay an administrative fine.

The first applicant submitted a communication to the HRC complaining, pursuant to Articles 7, 9, 10, and 14 of the ICCPR, about the arbitrariness of her arrest, the lack of effective judicial control surrounding her arrest, and the conditions in the remand prison. The HRC declared the case admissible and the proceedings were pending at the time the Commission examined the case.[40] The first applicant later submitted a further communication requesting that the Committee examine additional alleged violations of her rights by the State Party. This communication did not address the same matters as the original communication. Later, she submitted another communication, insisting that the State Party had not explained why genuine access to a court had not been provided.[41]

Before the Court, both applicants complained that their repeated detention on remand was unjustified and unlawful, and that the domestic courts took an unreasonably long time to determine the criminal charge upon them contrary to Article 6(1) of the ECHR. The first applicant complained under Articles 1, 8, and 12 of the ECHR and Articles 2 and 3 of Protocol No 1 that the withholding of her passport had prevented her from living a normal citizen's life. Furthermore, she claimed under Articles 6 and 13 of the ECHR that no appeal had been available against the decision to seize her identity card. It also constituted a violation of Article 7 of the ECHR, given that she was once fined for not carrying her passport with her.

The respondent Government claimed that the Court should not deal with the first applicant's complaint because it had been submitted to the HRC. The applicant contested this argument, indicating that her application to Geneva in 1995 concerned events that predated the application (ie the impossibility to

[40] *Yelena Pavlovna Smirnova v Russian Federation*, Communication No 712/1996, CCPR/C/81/D/712/1996, 18 August 2004, Human Rights Committee.

[41] Ibid, paras 7.1–7.6.

obtain a judicial review of her arrest) and therefore could not touch upon facts which occurred afterwards and were submitted to the Court in 1998. The Court found that this application was not the same as the proceedings pending before the HRC, because 'the scope of the factual basis for the first applicant's application to the Court, although going back to the arrest of 26 August 1995, is significantly wider. It extends to the whole of the proceedings which terminated in 2002, and includes the first applicant's arrest on three more occasions since 26 August 1995.'[42] It therefore followed that the matter before the HRC was not substantially the same as the one before the Court. In its decision, the Court declared that the applicants' complaints regarding their pre-trial detention and the length of criminal proceedings and the first applicant's complaint about the withholding of her passport were admissible, whereas the remaining complaints were declared inadmissible.

Subsequently, the ECtHR held in its judgment that there were violations of Articles 5, 6, and 8 of the ECHR and ordered compensation.[43] The HRC issued its communication when the ECtHR had already handed down its judgment in the case. The HRC took due notice of the outcome of the previous ECHR proceedings.[44] Further, it disagreed with the Strasbourg Court, finding that '[i]nsofar as the matters raised in the authors' communications to the Committee relate to circumstances occurring after the date of her initial communication to the Committee, these matters appear to the Committee to be the "same" as matters which were before the European Court'.[45] However, the HRC also found that the author's case before the Court had been determined, and that the matter was no longer 'being examined' under another international procedure.

The declaration of the Russian Federation issued under the First OP did not, unlike the reservations of other States Parties, preclude the HRC from considering the same matter which had been the subject of another international procedure.[46] Nevertheless, the fact that the Court had considered the case was relevant with regard to the question of whether the author was a victim of a violation by a State Party in accordance with Article 1 of the First OP. Given that the applicant was no longer in detention and that the Court had ordered compensation for matters arising after the introduction of the first communication, the HRC concluded that the applicant could no longer be perceived as a 'victim' under Article 1 of the First OP.[47] The HRC therefore found that the communication,

[42] *Smirnova and Smirnova v Russia* (n 39 above).

[43] *Smirnova v Russia* (App Nos 46133/99; 48183/99), judgment, 24 July 2003, Reports 2003-IX, 241.

[44] *Yelena Pavlovna Smirnova v Russian Federation* (n 40 above), paras 8.1–8.3.

[45] Ibid, para 9.2.

[46] Ibid. The Russian declaration mentions only that 'the Committee shall not consider any communications unless it has been ascertained that the same matter is not being examined under another procedure of international investigation or settlement': United Nations Treaty Collection, Status (n 11 above).

[47] Ibid, para 9.3.

to the extent that it concerned events which occurred after the date of introduction of the first communication before the Committee, was inadmissible under Article 1 of the First OP. Finally, with respect to the other events which occurred before this date, the HRC found that Russia had violated Articles 9(3), (4), and 10(1) of the ICCPR.

2.1.3 Differences in ECtHR and HRC Rulings on Identical Issues

The situation can become problematic when both the ECtHR and the HRC rule differently on identical issues. This occurred, for instance, in *Correia de Matos v Portugal*[48] where the applicant claimed that his right to defend himself in court without a lawyer had been violated. The ECtHR found that there was no breach of Article 6(3)(c) of the ECHR. The applicant then lodged an application concerning the same case with the HRC. Portugal had not formulated reservations to Article 5(2)(a) of the First OP. The Committee found that there had been a violation of the applicant's right to defend himself in person in breach of Article 14(3)(d) of the ICCPR.[49] Curiously, the HRC barely referred to the judgment of its European counterpart.[50] The Committee found that neither Article 5(2)(a) of the ICCPR nor Article 1 of the First OP impeded the examination of the communication.[51]

While neither the ECtHR nor the HRC is bound by the other's rulings, it is nonetheless regrettable that conflicting international jurisprudence exists in relation to the same issues.[52] This may compel European claimants to seek justice before the HRC instead of the ECtHR. It may also develop or reinforce a tendency of forum shopping on the part of applicants. Of the 42 ECHR Contracting States that signed the First OP, only 19 issued reservations or interpretative declarations with regard to Article 5(2)(a) of the First OP. This leaves 23 ECHR Contracting States that can be sued before the HRC once the ECtHR issues a judgment that is not in favour of the applicant. In other words, the *Correia de Matos* case[53] was probably not an isolated event, and if the dialogue between the HRC and the ECtHR does not improve, further contradictory cases could be handed down.

Naturally, the situation of Contracting States that have issued reservations or declarations with respect to Article 5(2)(a) of the First OP is different; in cases involving these states, the dialogue between the HRC and the ECtHR appears to be more structured and without any apparent encroachments on their respective competencies. Recently, in a communication concerning Spain—a State which

[48] *Correia de Matos v Portugal* (App No 48188/99), decision, 15 November 2001, Reports 2001-XII, 161.

[49] *Correia de Matos v Portugal*, Communication No 1123/2002, CCPR/C/86/D/1123/2002, 18 April 2006, Human Rights Committee.

[50] Phuong (n 12 above), 392–394.

[51] *Correia de Matos v Portugal* (n 49 above), paras 6.2–6.3.

[52] Phuong (n 12 above), 393.

[53] *Correia de Matos v Portugal* (n 49 above).

had issued a reservation to Article 5(2)(a) of the ICCPR—where the ECtHR found no evidence of violation,[54] the HRC decided that it was prevented from considering the matter any further because the Strasbourg Court had gone beyond the pure examination of admissibility criteria.[55]

2.1.4 An Improvement in the Relationship

There may, however, be hope that the Geneva-Strasbourg relationship has already started improving, as the Strasbourg Court seems to be more willing to follow the conclusions of the HRC (although this does not necessarily occur vice versa). Recently, the ECtHR was brought to consider a matter in the *Folgerø and others v Norway* case[56] which had been previously decided by the HRC. The Grand Chamber found that the matter examined by the HRC was not the same as the one before the Court, given that the applicants were not identical. Nonetheless, it appears that the issues raised by both cases were the same. This may have prompted the ECtHR to follow the HRC's conclusion that there was a violation in this case.

The *Folgerø* judgment concerned an application brought by three sets of parents whose children were at primary school at the time of the events complained of. In the autumn of 1997, the Norwegian primary school curriculum was changed, with two separate subjects—Christianity and philosophy of life—being replaced by a single subject covering Christianity, religion, and philosophy, known as KRL (*kristendomskunnskap med religions- og livssynsorientering*). Under the previous system, parents had been able to apply for their child to be exempted from Christianity lessons; however, it was only possible to request exemption from certain parts of KRL. During the school year 1999–2000, KRL was introduced at all levels in schools. The applicants and other parents made unsuccessful requests to have their children entirely exempted from KRL. The applicants complained, *inter alia*, that the refusal violated their rights under Articles 8 and 9 of the ECHR as well as Article 2 of Protocol No 1, taken together with Article 14 of the ECHR. In addition to these proceedings, four sets of parents (different from the ECtHR applicants) and their children lodged a communication on 25 March 2002 with the HRC.[57] The Committee found, in the applicants' case, that KRL, with its rules on exemptions, violated the Covenant.[58]

When the case reached the Court, the majority found that there was a preponderant weight attributed to Christianity as part of the KRL dispensed by Norwegian schools. It was noted that '[i]n view of the place occupied by Christianity in the national history and tradition of the respondent State, this

[54] *Rivera Fernández v Spain* (App No 9527/03), decision, 11 May 2004, not reported.

[55] *Rivera Fernández v Spain*, Communication No 1396/2005, CCPR/C/85/D/1396/2005, 22 May 2005, Human Rights Committee, para 6.2.

[56] *Folgerø and others v Norway* (App No 15472/02), judgment, 29 June 2007, not yet reported.

[57] *Leirvag and others v Norway*, Communication No 1155/2003, CCPR/C/82/D/1155/2003, 23 November 2004, Human Rights Committee.

[58] Ibid.

must be regarded as falling within the respondent State's margin of appreciation in planning and setting the curriculum'.[59] However, given the clear imbalance in the KRL to teaching Christian and other religious or philosophical beliefs, it was not clear to the Court how the aim of promoting understanding and respect and maintaining dialogue between people with different perceptions could be achieved. The Court then examined whether the possibility that the parents' request for a partial exemption from the KRL could counter the imbalance under Article 2 of Protocol No 1. A number of limitations imposed on the right to request a partial exemption rendered its practical operation problematic. The Court found accordingly that the system of partial exemption was capable of subjecting parents to a heavy burden, with a risk of undue exposure of their private life, and that the potential for conflict was likely to deter them from making such requests. It was recalled that the Convention was designed to guarantee rights that are practical and effective rather than theoretical. As a result, the respondent Government had violated Article 2 of Protocol No 1. It appears from this finding that the ECtHR was not swayed by deferent tendencies and actively intervened in a field where a state had a substantial margin of appreciation. Furthermore, the ECtHR's reasoning followed the previous HRC finding of violation.

In their separate opinion, Judges Zupančič and Borrego Borrego made interesting comments regarding the coexistence of the HRC and the Strasbourg Court.[60] They both considered that the application at hand was inadmissible and that the Court should have rejected it. It was recalled that the Commission had previously declared an application inadmissible on grounds that the parties could be regarded as being essentially identical, although the applicants before the Commission and the bodies of the International Labour Organization were not the same.[61] In the case at hand, however, '[n]otwithstanding the common features between the application lodged under the Convention in Strasbourg and the communication filed under the UN Covenant in Geneva',[62] the Court held that the parties before the HRC and the ECtHR were not identical.[63]

[59] *Folgerø and others v Norway* (App No 15472/02), judgment, 29 June 2007, not reported, para 89.

[60] Ibid, separate opinion of Judge Zupančič and Borrego Borrego.

[61] *Cereceda Martin and others v Spain* (App No 16358/90), decision, 12 October 1992, not reported.

[62] *Folgerø and others v Norway* (n 56 above).

[63] This finding was supported with numerous decisions where the Commission had previously clarified that Article 35(2)(b) of the ECHR was not infringed if the parties before the two international bodies were not the same. Cases concerning HRC proceedings: *Smirnova and Smirnova v Russia* (n 39 above) (not identical case); *Peltonen v Finland* (n 29 above) (not identical case); and *Calcerrada Fornieles and Cabeza Mato v Spain* (n 28 above) (identical case). Cases concerning ILO proceedings: *Council of Civil Service Unions and others v United Kingdom* (App No 11603/85), decision, 20 January 1987, DR 50, 228 (not identical case); *Cereceda Martin and 22 others v Spain* (App No 16358/90), decision, 12 October 1992, not reported (identical case).

Both judges rejected the reasoning of the HRC and ECtHR according to which:

> the key issue was not whether there had been a single set of domestic proceedings, or whether the single judgement had been examined by two different international bodies, or whether the facts submitted before the two organs were identical.... What really mattered was the fact that, as the applicants were a group of individuals, some of them had opted to petition the Human Rights Committee and some of them had submitted an application to the European Court of Human Rights. To put it briefly, different applicants of the same party had addressed different international bodies.[64]

In their view, it followed that the complaint, previously submitted to the HRC, should have been rejected because it concerned the same parties.

Judges Zupančič and Borrego Borrego further stated that international litispendence exists when the case concerns 'the same matter', 'the same judgement', 'the same complaint', 'the same party', and other similar issues. The interpretation of the majority in the *Folgerø* case means, however, that international litispendence ceases to exist when different individuals of the original group of applicants decide to separate in two groups to submit the same matter before different international organs.[65] In the judges' view, the risk of contradictory decisions persists and it is precisely the result which the ECHR and the First OP tried to avoid. The strong opinion of Judges Zupančič and Borrego Borrego warns the Court that Article 35(2)(b) of the ECHR should be not interpreted too narrowly.

2.1.5 The ECtHR following HRC Case Law

In recent times, the ECtHR has followed the HRC's findings and used them to support its own reasoning. In *Py v France*,[66] the Court considered a case where the applicant, a French national, was appointed to a post at the French University of the Pacific in Nouméa in New Caledonia. At his request, he was registered in the general electoral roll in respect of Nouméa, but was refused registration on the special electoral roll which would have enabled him to take part in the 1998 self-determination referendum. Subsequently, the Ordinance of 19 March 1999 on the institutional organization of New Caledonia introduced a 10-year residence condition for participating in elections to the Congress and provincial assemblies. In accordance with that law, the applicant's registration on the special electoral roll in respect of Nouméa, which would have enabled him to participate in the elections to Congress, was refused. Before the Strasbourg bodies, the applicant claimed that the restrictions imposed on his right to take part in the elections to the Congress and provincial assemblies of New Caledonia had violated the right to free elections guaranteed by Article 3 of Protocol No 1 of the

[64] *Folgerø and others v Norway* (n 56 above), separate opinion of Judge Zupančič and Borrego Borrego.

[65] *Cereceda Martin and 22 others v Spain* (n 63 above).

[66] *Py v France* (App No 66289/01), judgment, 1 November 2005, Reports 2005-I, 23.

ECHR and constituted discrimination on grounds of national origin, in breach of Article 14 of the ECHR.

Given the powers attributed to Congress by the 1999 Ordinance, the Court considered that it was sufficiently associated with the legislative process to be regarded as part of the 'legislature' of New Caledonia within the meaning of Article 3 of Protocol No 1 (right to free elections). According to the French Government, the reason for bringing in a residence condition was to ensure that the consultations would reflect the will of 'interested' persons and that the result would not be altered by a massive vote cast by recent arrivals to the territory who had no solid links with it. It was possible that Mr Py had established links with New Caledonia, but the law could not take account of every individual case. Mr Py, who had subsequently returned to metropolitan France, could not argue that he was targeted by the acts of political bodies to the same extent as resident citizens.

The respondent Government relied on the findings of the HRC, which, when the same problem had been referred to it, had expressed the view on 15 July 2002 that the facts before it did not disclose any violation of the ICCPR. Thus, the Court in the *Py* case had the benefit of hindsight and some guidance imparted by the HRC. In *Marie-Hélène Gillot v France*,[67] the HRC found that the requirements imposed on the author's right to vote in the referendums of 1998 and from 2014 onwards in New Caledonia did not violate any ICCPR rights, as the criteria were based 'on objective grounds for differentiation that are reasonable and compatible with the provisions of the Covenant'.[68]

The Strasbourg Court found that New Caledonia's current status amounted to a transitional phase prior to the acquisition of full sovereignty and was part of a process of self-determination. After a tormented political and institutional history, the 10-year residence condition had been a key factor in appeasing this conflict. In support of its reasoning, the Court quoted a passage from the HRC's communication where it was found that:

> the cut-off points set for the referendum of 1998 and referendums from 2014 onwards are not excessive inasmuch as they are in keeping with the nature and purpose of these ballots, namely a self-determination process involving the participation of persons able to prove sufficiently strong ties to the territory whose future is being decided. This being the case, these cut-off points do not appear to be disproportionate with respect to a decolonization process involving the participation of residents who, over and above their ethnic origin or political affiliation, have helped, and continue to help, build New Caledonia through their sufficiently strong ties to the territory.[69]

In the Court's opinion, the history and status of New Caledonia were such that they could be regarded as amounting to 'local requirements' of a kind warranting

[67] *Marie-Hélène Gillot v France*, Communication No 932/2000, A/57/40, 15 July 2002, Human Rights Committee.

[68] Ibid, para 13.18.

[69] Ibid, para 14.7.

the restrictions imposed on the applicant's right to vote. This led the Court to conclude that there had not been a violation of Article 3 of Protocol No 1 and that, having regard to this finding, it was not necessary to examine the complaint based on Article 14. Thus, the Court was guided to a large extent by the HRC's reasoning in a similar case.

2.2 Case Law Referring to the ICCPR

2.2.1 The Council of Civil Service Unions *Case*

The Commission showed a willingness in the late 1980s to use the ICCPR as a potential aid to interpretation. It also explicitly acknowledged that it had previously made references to international law in its case law. In *Council of Civil Service Unions and others v United Kingdom*,[70] the applicants complained against a measure introduced in 1984 by the then Prime Minster ordering government employees at the General Communications Headquarters (GCHQ) to cease belonging to a trade union. GCHQ has the function of ensuring the security of the UK's military and official communications and to provide signals intelligence for the Government. The employees were informed that disciplinary action might be undertaken against anyone involved in industrial action. Staff not wishing to remain at GCHQ were to be given the opportunity to seek a transfer elsewhere in the civil service. At the time of the decision, the seven applicants submitting the application were either former civil servants or still employed as civil servants. The applicants complained under Article 11 of the ECHR that the UK Government had deprived GCHQ employees of the right to belong to a trade union and deprived the trade unions of any role in industrial relations at GCHQ. It was submitted that the Government's actions were not 'prescribed by law' in the sense of Article 11(2) of the ECHR. They considered that the expression 'members of the administration of the State' contained in Article 11(2) should not be construed as covering all employees of GCHQ. Furthermore, they complained under Article 13 of the ECHR that there was no effective remedy under domestic law for the breach of Article 11 of the ECHR. They invoked numerous international instruments, including the ICCPR. A similar complaint had also been submitted by the General Council of the Trades Union Congress to the Director General of the International Labour Organization (ILO). It was alleged that the United Kingdom was in breach of Articles 2–5 and 11 of ILO Convention No 87 on Freedom of Association.[71] The ILO Committee of Freedom of Association reported that the Government's actions did not comply with ILO Convention No 87.[72]

[70] *Council of Civil Service Unions and others v United Kingdom* (n 63 above).

[71] Freedom of Association and Protection of the Right to Organise Convention, 68 UNTS 17, entered into force 4 July 1950.

[72] *Council of Civil Service Unions and others v United Kingdom* (n 63 above).

When examining the complaint under Article 11(2), the Commission found that the applicants had placed much reliance on the various international instruments as support for their interpretation of this provision. The Commission also recalled that it 'has occasionally had recourse to other international instruments under international law'.[73] Further, it noted that 'Article 22 para. 1 of the International Covenant on Civil and Political Rights of 1966 ensures the right to form and join trade unions' and that '[t]he second sentence of Article 22 para. 2 is similar to the second sentence of Article 11 para. 2 of the Convention, while only mentioning "the armed forces and . . . the police" but not the administration of the State'.[74] In addition, 'Article 8 para. 1 (a) of the International Covenant on Economic, Social and Cultural Rights of 1966 also guarantees the right to form and join trade unions'.[75] However, 'Article 8 para. 2 which resembles the second sentence in Article 11 para. 2 of the Convention now expressly includes the "members . . . of the administration of the State" '.[76]

In the Commission's opinion, 'these differences sufficiently demonstrate that there can be no settled view under international law as to the position of members of the "administration of the State" in respect of trade union rights, and that these instruments can not therefore be of assistance to the Commission in the present case'.[77] As the meaning of these words was uncertain, the Commission decided that it would not attempt to define them in detail. It was noted, however, that the expressions 'members of the administration of the State' and 'members of the armed forces and of the police' appeared in the same sentence in Article 11(2). The function of GCHQ was similar to that of the armed forces and the police, given that GCHQ staff fulfilled vital functions in protecting national security. Thus, the Commission found that GCHQ staff could be considered as 'members of the administration of the Staff'. In addition, it emphasized that Contracting States enjoyed a wide margin of appreciation in the protection of national security. Finally, it was found that the Government's action was drastic, but that it was not unlawful within the meaning of Article 11(2). Moreover, effective remedies were available to the applicants and Article 13 of the ECHR was, therefore, not violated.

The Commission demonstrated that it was willing to consider the ICCPR in an uninhibited manner. This was partly due to the fact that the ICCPR had been relied upon by the applicants and that international law had been used in previous cases. Interestingly, the Commission did not evade the fact that it had resorted to international instruments. It appears to have acknowledged that this flowed naturally from its role. Nonetheless, the attempt to use the ICCPR as a means to clarify the meaning of the ECHR failed. The Court did not consider that the Covenant could assist in this case, as the status of the relevant rule remained unsettled in international law. Thus, the most compelling element in this case remains the fact that the Commission was open to the reception of the ICCPR and that it further clarified its role vis-à-vis international law.

[73] Ibid. [74] Ibid. [75] Ibid. [76] Ibid. [77] Ibid.

2.2.2 *The* Groppera Radio *Case*

Following in the steps of the Commission, the Court used the ICCPR in the early 1990s to clarify the meaning of the ECHR. In *Groppera Radio AG v Switzerland*,[78] the Court considered the case of a limited company under Swiss law, Groppera Radio, which used powerful transmitters in Italy to broadcast radio programmes to listeners in Switzerland. The programmes were received by owners of private radio sets, to begin with, and by cable-network companies subsequently, which retransmitted them. An Ordinance adopted by the Federal Council came into force, prohibiting Swiss cable companies which had a community-antenna licence from re-broadcasting programmes from transmitters that did not satisfy the requirement of the international agreements on radio and telecommunications. It was found that Groppera Radio did not satisfy these requirements. The company, together with others, brought an appeal, which was subsequently dismissed. It was found that, since the transmitter in Italy had been destroyed by lightning, the applicants no longer had any legal interest in taking proceedings. Before the Commission, the applicants contended that the ban on cable transmissions in Switzerland of their broadcasts from Italy infringed their right to impart information and ideas under Article 10 of the ECHR. They also claimed that there was an infringement of their right to an effective remedy under Article 13 of the ECHR. The Commission declared the claim admissible and considered that there was only a violation of Article 10.

The Court held that the broadcasting of programmes over the air and their cable retransmissions were covered by the right enshrined in the first two sentences of Article 10(1) of the ECHR. Further, it held that the third sentence of Article 10(1) ('This Article shall not prevent States from requiring the licensing of broadcasting, television or cinema enterprises') was applicable, and it went on to determine its exact meaning. The Court noted that national licensing systems were required not only for the orderly regulation of broadcasting enterprises at national level, but also in large part to give effect to international rules. There was no equivalent of the third sentence in Article 10(1) in Articles 8(1), 9(1), and 11(1), although their structure was similar to that of Article 10. However, the wording of Article 10(1) was similar to Article 11(2), and a comparison of both articles indicated that the third sentence of Article 11(2) had limited scope.[79]

The Court then observed that Article 19 of the ICCPR concerning the freedom of expression did not include a provision corresponding to the third sentence of Article 10(1) of the ECHR. Moreover:

> [t]he negotiating history of Article 19 shows that the inclusion of such a provision in that Article had been proposed with a view to the licensing not of the information imparted but rather of the technical means of broadcasting in order to prevent chaos in the use of

[78] *Groppera Radio AG and others v Switzerland* (App No 10890/84), judgment, 28 March 1990, Series A, Vol 273.

[79] Ibid, para 61.

frequencies. However, its inclusion was opposed on the ground that it might be utilised to hamper free expression, and it was decided that such a provision was not necessary because licensing in the sense intended was deemed to be covered by the reference to 'public order' in paragraph 3 of the Article.[80]

According to the Court, this view supported the conclusion that the purpose of the third sentence of Article 10(1) was to clarify that states are permitted to control, by means of a licensing system, the way in which broadcasting is organized in their territories. This did not mean, however, that licensing measures could be exempted from Article 10(2) requirements. Thus, it was found that the interference was in accordance with the third sentence of Article 10(1) and that it satisfied the conditions of Article 10(2).

In his concurring opinion, Judge Pinheiro Farinha agreed with the result of the judgment but did not find that the use of international law made by the majority was appropriate. His judicial self-restraint was expressed in the following words:

> In my opinion, it is unacceptable to reason on the basis of the drafting history of a later instrument drawn up within a different community (the UN), not within the Council of Europe. The third sentence is there; it has a meaning and authorises the methodical regulation of broadcasting in Switzerland.... The fact that the sentence was not included in the International Covenant on Civil and Political Rights is of no importance when interpreting paragraph 1 of Article 10 of the European Convention on Human Rights, in which it does not occur.[81]

The approach to international law used by Judge Pinheiro Farinha differs to a large extent from that used by the majority of judges. The majority demonstrated that it was willing to refer to the ICCPR and its drafting history in order to clarify the meaning of the ECHR. This was an important step towards recognizing the ICCPR as a source of inspiration and affirming the Court's receptive approach. If Judge Farinha's approach were to be followed, it would preclude any references to international law on the basis that it was not part of the Council of Europe framework. However, this opinion was formulated almost 20 years ago. It appears that the ECtHR and the Convention system have both moved beyond such orthodox insularity.

2.2.3 *The* TH and SH v Finland *Case*

In 1993 the Commission used the ICCPR and the HRC's case law as an aid in the interpretation of a reservation to the ECHR. The *TH and SH v Finland*[82] case concerned a Finnish farmer and his child—both applicants in the case—whose wife and mother, respectively, had committed suicide. The father had agreed with the child's maternal grandparents that they would provisionally take care of the child until he resolved the problems caused by his wife's death and reorganized

[80] Ibid. [81] Ibid, concurring opinion of Judge Pinheiro Farinha, para. 4.
[82] *TH and SH v Finland* (App No 19823/92), decision, 9 February 1993, DR 74, 228.

his farming activities. The maternal parents then refused to return the child to the father. Following lengthy domestic proceedings, the care and the control of the child were transferred to the grandparents. The father was granted certain visiting rights and was allowed to remain the child's guardian.

Before the Commission, the applicants complained of a violation of the right to respect for family life under Article 8 of the ECHR and Article 5 of Protocol No 7. Invoking Article 6(1) of the ECHR, the applicants argued that the domestic proceedings were unfair in that no oral hearing took place before the Court of Appeal and the Supreme Court. The applicants also complained of the length of the custody proceedings and of the absence of reasoning in the Supreme Court's decision. They alleged that they have been deprived of an effective remedy under Article 13 of the ECHR, given that the authorities had failed to take the necessary measures for the man and child to be reunited.

When evaluating the complaint of unfair proceedings, the Commission considered in greater detail Finland's ratification of the ICCPR, which had an impact on the reservation it had issued under Article 6(1) of the ECHR. The Government submitted that this complaint was incompatible *ratione materiae* with the ECHR, given that Finland had issued a reservation according to which it could not guarantee an oral hearing in proceedings before the courts of appeal and the Supreme Court. The applicants argued that Finland's reservation only applied in so far as the current Finnish legislation did not provide a right to an oral hearing. However, the ICCPR, to which Finland had made no reservation, had been incorporated in the form of an Act of Parliament. The reservation, therefore, had to be interpreted in light of Article 14(1) of the ICCPR which stipulates that everyone is entitled to a fair and public hearing. Thus, the Commission examined the question whether the reservation to Article 6(1) of the ECHR also covered any right to an oral hearing which the ICCPR might guarantee. The Commission relied on an HRC communication in support of its evaluation of this question.

According to the Commission, it appeared from 'the interpretation of Article 14 para. 1 of the Covenant that the right to an oral hearing before appellate courts is not guaranteed in that provision to the same extent as by Article 6 para. 1 of the Convention. Thus, in a published decision rendered in 1989 regarding the absence of an oral hearing in criminal proceedings before a Finnish court of appeal, the Human Rights Committee "believe[d] that the absence of oral hearings in the appellate proceedings raises no issue under Article 14..." (Communication No 301/1988, 1989 Annual Report, Doc. A/44/40, p. 300, para. 6.4.).'[83] The Commission found that, under certain circumstances, the ICCPR had been interpreted to require an oral hearing before an appellate court. Nonetheless, it considered that it could not 'speculate whether the present case belongs to that category of exceptional cases, but rather has to proceed from the main principle that "the absence of oral hearings in the appellate proceedings raises no issue

[83] Ibid, 230.

under Article 14 [of the Covenant]". Therefore, no right to an oral hearing under Finnish law, circumventing Finland's reservation to the Convention, can be derived from the Covenant.'[84] The Commission concluded that the Finnish reservation covered the applicant's complaint regarding the absence of an oral hearing before the Court of Appeal and the Supreme Court. In the end, the application was declared inadmissible.

The reception of the ICCPR and the case law of the HRC in this decision follows in the footsteps of previous cases. The Commission relied on both sources in order to clarify the meaning of the ECHR and the Finnish reservation. Furthermore, the views expressed by the HRC constituted an authoritative benchmark against which the Commission measured the legality of the reservation. The Court paid deference to the HRC's findings and transposed them to the context of the ECHR. This approach further confirmed the Strasbourg bodies' friendly attitude towards the ICCPR and the HRC.

2.2.4 The Brannigan and McBride *and* JS, PB and Others *Cases*

In 1993 the Court issued its judgment in the *Brannigan and McBride v United Kingdom*[85] case where it examined Article 4 of the ICCPR in the context of Article 15 of the ECHR. Although McBride died in 1992, Brannigan still lived in Downpatrick, Northern Ireland, at the time of the judgment. Brannigan was arrested at his home by police in accordance with the temporary provisions on the prevention of terrorism. He was not allowed access to books, newspapers, or writing materials, and was denied access to a solicitor for 48 hours. The second applicant, McBride, was arrested at his home by police officers pursuant to the same temporary measures. He was detained for a total period of four days, six hours, and 25 minutes. He received two visits from his solicitor. McBride was shot dead on 4 February 1992 by a policeman who had run amok and attacked the *Sinn Fein* headquarters in Belfast. Both applicants were Irish citizens. They complained that, as a result of anti-terrorism measures enforced by the United Kingdom, they were not brought promptly before a judge as required by Article 5(3) of the ECHR. They also alleged that they did not have an enforceable right to compensation under Article 5(5) and that they had no effective remedy under Article 13. Moreover, they complained that the public emergency derogation entered into by the United Kingdom did not comply with Article 15.

While the Court noted that the UK Government had not respected Articles 5(3) and 5(5), it found that the situation had to be assessed in light of the validity of the derogation issued by the United Kingdom. The Court clarified that the Contracting States possessed a wide margin of appreciation in assessing public emergency situations on their territory. It was found that, given the nature of

[84] Ibid, 231 (text inserted by author).

[85] *Brannigan and McBride v United Kingdom* (App Nos 14553/89; 14554/89), judgment, 25 May 1993, Series A, Vol 258-B.

the terrorist threat in Northern Ireland, the limited scope of the derogation, the reasons advanced in support of it, and the existence of basic safeguards against abuse, the United Kingdom did not exceed its margin of appreciation by proclaiming a public emergency.[86]

The Court then went on to consider whether under Article 15(1) the measures taken by the State were consistent 'with its other obligations under international law'. The Court referred to Article 4 of the ICCPR which had been invoked by the applicants. It was noted that the United Kingdom had ratified the ICCPR. The applicants contented that it was an essential requirement for a valid derogation under Article 4 that a public emergency must have been 'officially proclaimed'. For the UK Government, it was not fully certain that an official proclamation was necessary for the purposes of Article 4, as the emergency existed before the ratification of the Covenant by the United Kingdom and had continued until the time of the judgment. The Court observed 'that it is not its role to seek to define authoritatively the meaning of the terms "officially proclaimed" in Article 4 of the Covenant',[87] but that nevertheless it had to examine whether the applicants' argument was plausible. The Court found that the statement of the Secretary of State for the Home Department to the House of Commons, 'which was formal in character and made public the Government's intentions as regards derogation, was well in keeping with the notion of an official proclamation'.[88] Further, it was held that the derogation issued by the United Kingdom satisfied the requirements of Article 15 of the ECHR and that the applicants could not validly complain of a violation under Article 5(3). As a result, there was no obligation under Article 5(5) to provide applicants with an enforceable right to compensation.[89] Lastly, the Court found that there was no violation of Article 13 concerning the right to an effective remedy.

In this complex legal situation, the Court unsuccessfully tried to maintain its distance vis-à-vis the ICCPR framework. Despite its limited role, the Court was nonetheless compelled to examine the applicants' arguments concerning the ICCPR under Article 15 of the ECHR. Given the express mention in this provision of 'other obligations under international law', the Court had to evaluate whether the derogations used by the United Kingdom were compatible with other international instruments. Overall, the Court's references to the ICCPR were not very surprising given that the Covenant had been invoked by the applicants and that Article 15 of the ECHR expressly mentioned international law as a requirement for the validity of public emergency derogations. The references to the ICCPR which appeared in the judgment were facilitated by the wording of Article 15 of the ECHR and by the fact that the case was intertwined with international law. As a result, they were not solely prompted by the Court's willingness to receive the ICCPR in its jurisprudence. Rather, the reliance on international law seems to have been necessary for the resolution of this case.

[86] Ibid, para 68. [87] Ibid, para 72. [88] Ibid, para 73. [89] Ibid, para 74.

In 1995 the Commission examined the case of *JS, PB and others v The Netherlands*,[90] where the applicants, all Dutch dairy farmers, complained that they did not have access to an independent tribunal for the determination of their civil rights as provided in Article 6(1) of the ECHR. Many of the applicants also alleged that they had not received a fair hearing as required by that provision. The claims arose in the context of the implementation by the Netherlands of Council Regulation (EEC) 857/84 on the Super Levy[91] which provided that dairy farmers were allowed to produce a certain amount of milk on the basis of their production capacity prior to 1 April 1984 (the 'reference quantity'). For any surplus, a levy would have to be paid. A group among the applicants complained that proceedings on their request for a 'reference quantity' constituted mental torture contrary to Article 3 of the ECHR and violated Articles 7 and 14 of the ICCPR, Article 3(2) and (3) of the EEC Regulation, and section 43 of the Statute of the Kingdom of the Netherlands.

Considering the group's complaint under Article 3 of the ECHR, the ICCPR, the EEC Regulation, and the Statute of the Kingdom of the Netherlands, the Commission observed that it could 'only examine a complaint on the basis of the provisions of the European Convention on Human Rights. Insofar as the applicants also refer to the International Covenant on Civil and Political Rights, the EEC Council Regulation No 857/84 and the Statute of the Kingdom of the Netherlands, these complaints fall outside the competence of the Commission.'[92] Under Article 3 of the ECHR, the Commission found that this complaint had not attained the minimum level of severity and that it was manifestly ill-founded under Article 27(2). Finally, the case was found to be partly admissible and partly inadmissible.

Thus, the Commission expressed its self-restraint and clarified that it was not prepared to examine the complaint pertaining to the ICCPR. This approach stands in great contrast to that adopted by the Court in *Brannigan and McBride*. In that judgment, the Court observed that it was not its duty to examine in detail the terms contained in the ICCPR, but it was nonetheless compelled to evaluate the plausibility of the applicants' arguments. In contrast, the Commission clearly excluded any analysis of the ICCPR in the *JS, PB and others* case. It is interesting to note that the ICCPR had been invoked in both cases by the applicants. Nonetheless, the *Brannigan and McBride* case concerned Article 15 of the ECHR, which requires that measures taken by the state are consistent 'with its other obligations under international law'. Thus, the Court used this expression as a means to refer to the ICCPR. In the *JS, PB and others* case, however, none of the ECHR

[90] *JS, PB and others v The Netherlands* (App Nos 14561/89; 14657/89; 15105/89; 15343/89; 15712/89; 15908/89; 15988/90; 16118/90; 16513/90; 16583/90; 16843/90; 16896/90; 16897/90; 17001/90; 17241/90; 17252/90; 17675/90), decision, 7 September 1995, not reported.

[91] Council Regulation (EEC) 857/84 of 31 March 1984 adopting general rules for the application of the levy referred to in Article 5c of Regulation (EEC) No 804/68 in the milk and milk products sector [1984] OJ L90/13.

[92] *JS, PB and others v The Netherlands* (n 90 above).

articles invoked referred directly to international law, and the Commission may have felt less compelled to refer to the ICCPR. Further, the Commission was not explicitly mandated to rule on the merits of a case, and this could explain why its analysis was less exhaustive than that of the Court in *Brannigan and McBride*. While these characteristics elucidate in part the difference in the Strasbourg bodies' behaviour, they do not account for the shift in approach to international law vis-à-vis previous case law. Indeed, the attitude of the Court and Commission towards the ICCPR was far less open and receptive in the *Brannigan and McBride* and *JS, PB and others* cases than in the cases analysed above.

2.2.5 The Kurt *Case*

In 1998 the Court considered the case of *Kurt v Turkey*,[93] where the applicant's son, Üzeyir Kurt, disappeared in Turkey and had last been seen surrounded by members of the security forces. She made an application before the Commission against the Turkish authorities which refused to admit that her son had been taken into custody and had not been seen since. The Turkish authorities argued that her son was kidnapped by the Kurdistan Workers' Party (PKK). She was thereafter pressed by the Turkish authorities to withdraw her application. The applicant claimed that her son's disappearance was the responsibility of the State and that there was a violation of Articles 2, 3, 5, 13, 14, and 18 of the ECHR.

The applicant and Amnesty International (intervening in the case) invoked in their written submissions international material pertaining to enforced disappearances, including the case law of the HRC, material from the Organization of American States, and case law of the Inter-American Court of Human Rights. The Commission had also referred to this material and had concluded that the respondent State had violated Article 5 of the ECHR. It did not find it necessary to examine issues raised under Articles 2 and 3 of the ECHR.

Amnesty International found in its written submissions that:

> [t]he gravity of the violations of the rights attendant on a disappearance has led the United Nations Human Rights Committee to conclude in relation to Article 6 of the International Covenant on Civil and Political Rights that State Parties should take specific and effective measures to prevent the disappearance of individuals and should establish facilities and procedures to investigate thoroughly cases of missing and disappeared persons which may involve a violation of the right to life.... The Human Rights Committee later affirmed this statement in its Mojica v Dominican Republic decision of 15 July 1994 with respect to the need to safeguard disappeared persons against the risks of ill-treatment.[94]

Furthermore, Amnesty International stated that '[i]n its Mojica v Dominican Republic decision of 15 July 1994, the United Nations Human Rights Committee

[93] *Kurt v Turkey* (App No 15/1997/799/1002), judgment, 25 May 1998, Reports 1998-III, 1152.

[94] Ibid, para 69.

considered that the disappearance of a person is inseparably linked to treatment that amounts to a violation of Article 7 of the International Covenant on Civil and Political Rights which mirrors Article 3 of the European Convention on Human Rights'.[95] In line with the approach taken by the HRC and the Inter-American Court of Human Rights to the phenomenon of disappearances, the applicant urged the Court 'not to confine its consideration of her son's plight to the issues raised under Article 5 of the Convention but to have regard also to those raised under Articles 2 and 3'.[96]

Examining the applicant's complaint under Article 2 of the ECHR, the Court decided not to take the line of reasoning employed by the HRC. It noted the Commission's finding that, 'in the absence of any evidence as to the fate of Üzeyir Kurt subsequent to his detention in the village, it would be inappropriate to draw the conclusion that he had been a victim of a violation of Article 2'.[97] It was also relevant that the Commission had disagreed with the applicant's argument that it could be inferred that her son had been killed. As a result, the applicant's allegations regarding the forced disappearance of her son and the failure of the authorities to protect him were considered under Article 5 of the ECHR.[98] The Court found that, like the Commission, it would have to evaluate whether there was concrete evidence indicating, beyond reasonable doubt, that the applicant's son was killed by the State authorities. Further, in cases where it was found that a Contracting State had a positive obligation under Article 2 of the ECHR to conduct an effective investigation into the circumstances of an alleged killing by state authorities, there had to exist evidence of a fatal shooting. In the Court's view, however, the case at hand was entirely based on presumptions deduced from the victim's initial detention. Thus, the Court followed the Commission's finding and held that the applicant's claims under Articles 2 and 3 of the ECHR should be considered from the point of view of Article 5. Lastly, it was held that there had been a particularly grave violation of Article 5.

The applicant had also complained that she was a victim of a violation under Article 3 of the ECHR on account of her son's disappearance. She invoked in support of her argument a decision of the HRC in the case of *Quinteros v Uruguay*[99] affirming that the next-of-kin of a disappeared person must also be considered as a victim. The Commission had found that the applicant had been subjected to inhuman and degrading treatment in the sense of Article 3 of the ECHR. The Court observed that the applicant had been left in anguish of knowing that her son had been detained and that there was a complete absence of official information as to his fate. Finding that there had been a violation of Article 3, the Court appears to have followed the reasoning of the Commission and the HRC. Although it could be argued that the Court was influenced by the HRC in this case, it is more plausible

[95] Ibid, para 70. [96] Ibid, para 84. [97] Ibid, para 105. [98] Ibid.

[99] *María del Carmen Almeida de Quinteros et al v Uruguay*, Communication No 107/1981, CCPR/C/OP/2, 21 July 1983, Human Rights Committee.

that it simply adopted the findings of the Commission. Further, it is also unlikely that the reliance by the applicant and Amnesty International on HRC case law imbued the Court's reasoning with the approach used by the Committee. The convergence between the Court's findings and the HRC's approach was incidental. As a result, the Court's reasoning in this case was marked by prudent self-restraint and has remained within the confines of the ECHR.

2.2.6 The Streletz *and* K-H W *Cases*

In 2001 the Court made more extensive use of the ICCPR in the *Streletz, Kessler and Krenz v Germany*[100] and *K-H W v Germany*[101] cases concerning the German Democratic Republic's (GDR's) border-policing practice. The *Streletz* case involved three senior members of the GDR Government, the ruling Socialist Unity Party, and the National Defence Council. Following the unification of Germany, these members were convicted for incitement to commit intentional homicide on the grounds that they shared responsibility for the deaths of a number of young people aged between 18 and 28 who were killed by East German border guards or anti-personnel mines when they attempted to flee the GDR between 1971 and 1989. The *K-H W* case concerned a member of the GDR National People's Army who was stationed as a guard on the border between the two German States. After unification, he was convicted for intentional homicide on grounds that he and another guard had shot a fugitive trying to swim away from East Berlin, after shouting to him and firing warning shots.

The applicants alleged that their actions, at the time when they were committed, did not constitute offences under the law of the GDR or international law and that their convictions by the German courts breached Article 7(1) of the ECHR. They also relied on Articles 1 and 2(2) of the Convention. The Government submitted that the applicants could easily have realized that killing unarmed fugitives as part of the GDR's border-policing regime might have given rise to a criminal prosecution. Moreover, the German courts had applied GDR law in a legitimate way. If the GDR authorities had applied their own relevant legal provisions, taking account of the GDR's international obligations flowing from the ratification of the ICCPR, they would have arrived at the same interpretation. In the Government's view, the question of whether or not the ICCPR had been transposed into the GDR's domestic law was not important in this regard. It was significant, however, that the ICCPR had also been invoked in the domestic proceedings. Due to the similarities in the Court's reasoning in the *Streletz* and *K-H W* judgments, both cases will be analysed simultaneously in this section.

The Court considered that it had to examine whether at the time the relevant acts were committed they were defined with sufficient accessibility and

[100] *Streletz, Kessler and Krenz v Germany* (App Nos 34044/96; 35532/97; 44801/98), judgment, 22 March 2001, Reports 2001-II, 409.

[101] *K-H W v Germany* (App No 37201/97), judgment, 22 March 2001, Reports 2001-II, 495.

foreseeability under GDR law. It was found that the applicants' conviction based on the GDR's Constitution and other legal provisions did not appear, at first sight, to have been either arbitrary or contrary to Article 7(1) of the ECHR. The Court also pointed out that the GDR's reasons of state invoked in favour of its border policy had to be limited by the need to preserve human life, enshrined in the GDR Constitution, the People's Police Act, and the State Borders Act. It was noted that at the material time the right to life was already, internationally, the most important right in the hierarchy of human rights.[102]

With regard to the foreseeability of the convictions, the Court found in the *Streletz* case that the applicants had been directly responsible for the situation that had persisted at the border between the two German States from the beginning of the 1960s until 1989. In the *K-H W* case, the Court considered that a private soldier could not show total, blind obedience to orders which flagrantly infringed the GDR's legal principles and internationally recognized rights. While the applicant was in an especially difficult situation given the political context of the GDR, the Court established that such orders could not justify firing on unarmed persons trying to flee the country. Moreover, the German courts had exhaustively examined the extenuating circumstances in the applicant's favour. In both judgments, the Court considered that it was part of its duty to examine the case from the point of view of international law principles, especially those relating to human rights protection, since the arguments of the German courts were rooted in these principles.[103] Thus, the Court had to establish whether, at the time when they were committed, the applicants' actions constituted offences under international human rights law.

The GDR ratified the ICCPR on 8 November 1974, but did not incorporate its provisions into domestic law.[104] Under Article 51 of the GDR Constitution, the Parliament was required to approve international treaties in so far as these would amend domestic laws. Thus, Articles 6 (right to life) and 12 (freedom of movement) of the ICCPR were not transposed at the national level by an Act of Parliament. The ratified and unincorporated ICCPR could not have had any bearing on the domestic legal regime.[105] It is also unlikely that the limitations imposed on the right to life and freedom of movement could have amounted at the time to customary law. Further, the GDR was supported in its practice by other communist states.[106] It is therefore plausible that the international system

[102] *Streletz, Kessler and Krenz v Germany* (n 100 above), paras 72 and 94; *K-H W v Germany* (n 101 above), paras 66 and 96.

[103] *Streletz, Kessler and Krenz v Germany* (n 100 above), para 90; *K-H W v Germany* (n 101 above), para 92.

[104] Brad Roth, 'Retrospective Justice or Retroactive Standards? Human Rights as a Sword in the East German Leaders Case' (2004) 50 Wayne L Rev 37, 56–63; Micah Goodman, 'After the Wall: the Legal Ramifications of the East German Border Guard Trials in United Germany' (1996) 29 Cornell Int'l LJ 727, 751–756; Peter Quint, 'The Border Guard Trials and the East German Past—Seven Arguments' (2000) 48 Am J Com L 541, 554; Fred Reineke, 'Treaty and Non-Treaty Human Rights Agreements: A Case Study of Freedom of Movement in East Germany' (1986) 24 Colum J Transnat'l L 647, 659.

[105] Roth (n 104 above), 60; Quint (n 104 above), 554.

[106] See also Roth (n 104 above), 61.

lacked the necessary mechanisms to generate an authoritative interpretation of the ICCPR or customary law.[107] For this reason, it will become apparent that the findings of the Court in these cases regarding the ICCPR were surprising and legally questionable.

With regard to the protection of life, the Court noted that 'in the course of the development of that protection the relevant conventions and other instruments have constantly affirmed the pre-eminence of the right to life'.[108] In support of this, the Court mentioned Article 3 of the Universal Declaration of Human Rights and Article 2 of the ICCPR. It was further found that '[t]he convergence of the above-mentioned instruments is significant: it indicates that the right to life is an inalienable attribute of human beings and forms the supreme value in the hierarchy of human rights'.[109] The Court considered that the defence raised by the applicants—that their conduct was justified because it constituted a use of force which was absolutely necessary—could not be justified under Article 2(2) of the ICCPR.

With regard to the protection of the freedom of movement, the Court observed that, like Article 2(2) of Protocol No 4 of the ECHR, Article 12(2) of the ICCPR provided that '[e]veryone shall be free to leave any country including his own'. This right can only be restricted where it is provided by law, where it is necessary to protect national security, public order, public health or morals, or the rights and freedoms of others, and where it is consistent with the other rights recognized by the ICCPR. The applicants in the *Streletz* case invoked these grounds to justify their behaviour, but the Court found that none of the exceptions applied. In the Court's view, 'the acts in issue were orders, given and executed, which were not compatible with either the Constitution or statute law'.[110] Furthermore, it could not be argued that 'a general measure preventing almost the entire population of State from leaving was necessary to protect its security, or for that matter other interests mentioned'.[111] In addition, the way in which the prohibition of leaving was put into practice contravened the right to life enshrined in Article 6 of the ICCPR.

The Court then considered that, if the GDR still existed, it would be responsible under international law for the acts concerned.[112] Furthermore, the applicants also bore criminal responsibility at the material time. The Court stated that '[e]ven supposing that such responsibility cannot be inferred from the above-mentioned international instruments on the protection of human rights, it may be deduced from those instruments when they are read together with Article 95 of the GDR's Criminal Code, which explicitly provided, and moreover from as long ago as 1968, that individual criminal responsibility was to be borne by those who violated the GDR's international obligations or human rights and fundamental

[107] Ibid.

[108] *Streletz, Kessler and Krenz v Germany* (n 100 above), para 92; *K-H W v Germany* (n 101 above), para 94.

[109] *Streletz, Kessler and Krenz v Germany* (n 100 above), para 94; *K-H W v Germany* (n 101 above), para 96.

[110] *Streletz, Kessler and Krenz v Germany* (n 100 above), para 100.

[111] Ibid.

[112] *Streletz, Kessler and Krenz v Germany* (n 100 above), para 104; *K-H W v Germany* (n 101 above), para 103.

freedoms'.[113] Article 95 of the GDR Criminal Code states that '[a]ny person whose conduct violates human or fundamental right, international obligations or the national sovereignty of the German Democratic Republic may not plead [*kann sich nicht berufen auf*] statute law, an order or written instruction in justification; he shall be held criminally responsible'.[114] The Court seems to have reasoned that the ICCPR was therefore incorporated through this provision. Thus, the Court considered that at the time they were committed the applicants' acts constituted offences defined with sufficient accessibility and foreseeability by the rules of international human rights law.[115] In addition, the Court found that the applicants' convictions did not breach Article 7(1) of the ECHR and that there was no need to consider whether the convictions were justified under Article 7(2).

The Court's reliance on Articles 6 and 12 of the ICCPR is surprising, given that this Convention had not been transposed into GDR domestic law. Thus, the Covenant had a dubious status at the national level and could not have been interpreted as invalidating the defences that existed under GDR law at the time. What is more, the relevant act in the *K-H W* case took place before the ICCPR had been ratified by the GDR. Similarly, a part of the acts committed by the applicants in the *Streletz* case took place before the ratification of the ICCPR. The Court's reference to Article 95 of the GDR Constitution was also problematic, as it assumed that the ICCPR could have been incorporated by means of its reference to fundamental rights and international obligations.

Overall, the Court's application of Articles 6 and 12 of the ICCPR is strained and dubious from a legal point of view. While the Court is usually circumspect when referring to international law, here it used an unduly open and receptive approach to the ICCPR. It simply applied the two ICCPR provisions without further consideration. This approach stands in great contrast with the other cases in which the ICCPR was invoked. The Court's reliance on the Covenant was also rooted in the fact that the case was intertwined with some of its provisions at the domestic level. The German courts had referred to the ICCPR, and since the Court was considering the merits of these decisions, it may have felt the need to do so itself. Moreover, the importance of the issue at stake may have prompted the Court not to use a very traditional approach to international law and to refer to the relevant ICCPR provisions when necessary.

In addition to these legal arguments, it is essential to take into account the political climate of these cases. While the first individuals to have been tried in the reunified Germany were East German border guards,[116] the Germans soon

[113] *Streletz, Kessler and Krenz v Germany* (n 100 above), para 104; *K-H W v Germany* (n 101 above), para 103.

[114] *Streletz, Kessler and Krenz v Germany* (n 100 above), para 30; *K-H W v Germany* (n 101 above), para 24 (italics in original).

[115] *Streletz, Kessler and Krenz v Germany* (n 100 above), para 105; *K-H W v Germany* (n 101 above), para 105.

[116] Adrienne Quill, 'To Prosecute or Not To Prosecute: Problems Encountered in the Prosecution of Former Communist Officials in Germany, Czechoslovakia, and the Czech Republic' (1996) 7 IICLR 165, 178–180.

grew weary of trials of people who had carried out orders. They began requesting that those who gave the orders also be tried. Thus, Germany brought charges against high-ranking East German officials, but these trials were affected by numerous problems and rendered the prosecution unsatisfactory. While charges were brought against Erich Honecker for his role in the GDR's border policy, they were dropped in 1993 because he was terminally ill with cancer. At that time, both eastern and western Germans felt that Honecker had dodged the punishment that he deserved. There was nonetheless a sentiment that there was a need to let him go due to his terminal illness.[117] Furthermore, the trial in 1993 of Erich Mielke, the former *Stasi* director, gave rise to a murder conviction, but not on the basis of the GDR's border policy. He was sentenced to six years' imprisonment for the murder of two policemen in 1931. Given the outcome of these trials, there was strong pressure to bring the remaining officials of the former GDR to trial. This has exerted an important influence over the reasoning of the German courts and of the ECtHR. Thus, the determination of the German courts to convict the applicants and the ECtHR's willingness to respect at all costs their findings is reflected in the artificial and strained legal arguments used.

2.2.7 The Gatzinger *and* Polacek *Cases*

In 2002 the Court reinstated its cautious approach to the ICCPR in the *Polacek and Polackova v The Czech Republic*[118] and the *Gratzinger and Gratzingerova v The Czech Republic*[119] decisions. These cases concerned the applicants' inability, as US nationals, to recover property confiscated by the former Czechoslovak Socialist Republic. After fleeing the communist regime, the applicants were convicted *in absentia*; they were sentenced to imprisonment and had all their property confiscated. Having settled in the United States, they acquired American nationality and lost their Czech nationality. In 1990 their convictions and the decisions to confiscate their property were quashed by the Czech courts with retrospective effect. However, actions subsequently brought by the applicants for recovery of the property were dismissed under the Extrajudicial Rehabilitation Act (Law No 87/1991), which provides that restitution claims may only be submitted by Czech nationals. They complained that the Czech courts' refusal to return their former property contravened Article 1 of Protocol No 1 of the ECHR. They also alleged that they were discriminated against on the basis of their nationality in violation of Article 26 of the ICCPR.[120] The applicants suggested that the Court should

[117] Ibid, 181.

[118] *Polacek and Polackova v The Czech Republic* (App No 38645/97), decision, 10 July 2002, not reported.

[119] *Gratzinger and Gratzingerova v The Czech Republic* (App No 39794/98), decision, 10 July 2002, not reported.

[120] *Polacek and Polackova v The Czech Republic* (n 118 above), paras 43–44; *Gratzinger and Gratzingerova v The Czech Republic* (n 119 above), para 47.

follow the HRC's communication of 19 July 1995,[121] in which it was established that the requirement of Czech nationality for persons lodging restitution claims was unreasonable and violated Article 26 of the ICCPR.[122] In addition, the applicants in the *Gratzinger* case alleged that their rights under Articles 6 and 8 of the ECHR had been violated.

Evaluating the complaint under Article 26, the Court noted that 'its jurisdiction extends only to applying the European Convention on Human Rights and not to applying other international treaties. However, in interpreting the provisions of the Convention, it may find it helpful to be guided by provisions of other international legal instruments'.[123] While the Court held that it could not consider the complaint under Article 26, an examination under Article 14 of the ECHR was nonetheless found to be appropriate, since both provisions prohibit discrimination.[124] The Court noted that there were differences between these two provisions: 'while Article 26 of the Covenant may be applied independently and also guarantees the equality of all persons before the law, Article 14 of the Convention may only be applied in conjunction with another Article of the Convention or of its Protocols'.[125] It was considered, however, that these differences did not prevent the applicants' complaints from being examined under Article 14 of the ECHR, together with Article 1 of Protocol No 1.[126]

On the basis of this reasoning, the Court observed that the applicants had not shown that their claim was sufficiently established to be enforceable. Thus, they could not argue that they had a 'possession' in the sense of Article 1 of Protocol No 1 and that their complaint fell under this provision.[127] Further, due to the non-autonomous nature of Article 14 of the ECHR and the non-applicability of Article 1 of Protocol No 1, the Court considered that Article 14 could not be applied to the case at hand. Thus, the Court was prevented from pronouncing itself on the allegation of violation under Article 14. At the same time, it did not have the opportunity to consider in greater depth HRC case law on the same subject. It appears that the Court missed a good opportunity to harmonize the Strasbourg jurisprudence with the decisions of the HRC on the same topic. It is

[121] *Alina Simunek and others v The Czech Republic*, Communication No 516/1992, CCPR/C/54/D/516/1992, 19 July 1995, Human Rights Committee. See also other communications invoked: *Josef Frank Adam v The Czech Republic*, Communication No 586/1994, CCPR/C/57/D/586/1994, 25 July 1996, Human Rights Committee; *Karel Des Fours Walderode and Johanna Kammerlander v The Czech Republic*, Communication No 747/1997, CCPR/C/73/D/747/1997, 2 November 2001, Human Rights Committee. See *Polacek and Polackova v The Czech Republic* (n 118 above), paras 41–42; *Gratzinger and Gratzingerova v The Czech Republic* (n 119 above), paras 45–46.

[122] *Polacek and Polackova v The Czech Republic* (n 118 above), paras 41–43, 60; *Gratzinger and Gratzingerova v The Czech Republic* (n 119 above), paras 45–46, 67.

[123] *Polacek and Polackova v The Czech Republic* (n 118 above), para 45; *Gratzinger and Gratzingerova v The Czech Republic* (n 119 above), para 50.

[124] Ibid.

[125] *Polacek and Polackova v The Czech Republic* (n 118 above), para 46; *Gratzinger and Gratzingerova v The Czech Republic* (n 119 above), para 51.

[126] Ibid.

[127] *Polacek and Polackova v The Czech Republic* (n 118 above), para 67; *Gratzinger and Gratzingerova v The Czech Republic* (n 119 above), para 74.

nonetheless not surprising that, when there is an equivalent ECHR provision to the ICCPR article invoked by the applicants, the Court will prefer to use the ECHR equivalent. Further, as there was no ambiguity or gap under the ECHR, the Court did not find it necessary to rely on Article 26 of the ICCPR. The Court was thus, incidentally or willfully, absolved from considering the ICCPR and HRC case law.

2.2.8 The Mamatkulov *Cases*

In 2003 and 2005 the Court delivered two landmark cases where it referred, inter alia, to HRC case law in order to strengthen the ECHR system. In the *Mamatkulov and Abdurasulovic v Turkey* case[128] and the *Mamatkulov and Askarov v Turkey* case,[129] the Court held that interim measures had an obligatory character under the ECHR. The *Mamatkulov* cases concerned applications brought by Uzbek opposition party members who were arrested in Turkey on suspicion of murder and causing injuries by a bomb explosion in Uzbekistan and an attempted terrorist attack on the President of the Republic. Uzbekistan requested their extradition under a bilateral treaty with Turkey. Despite the Court's indication to the Turkish Government not to extradite the applicants, they were sent to Uzbekistan, where they were found guilty and sentenced to imprisonment.

In support of its finding that interim measures were binding, the Court relied on various international sources, including two decisions handed down by the HRC. The Court noted that under HRC jurisprudence 'a failure to comply with interim measures constitutes a breach by the State concerned of its legal obligations under the International Covenant on Civil and Political Rights and the Optional Protocol thereto, and of its duty to cooperate with the Committee under the individual-communications procedure'.[130] The Court's observation was rooted in the *Glen Ashby v Trinidad and Tobago*[131] and *Dante Piandiong, Jesus Morallos and Archie Bulan v The Philippines*[132] cases. In a decision issued on 26 July 1994 in the *Glen Ashby* case,[133] the Committee considered the State Party's refusal to comply with its request to stay an execution of the petitioner. The Committee

[128] *Mamatkulov and Abdurasulovic v Turkey* (App Nos 46827/99; 46951/99), judgment, 6 February 2003, not reported. See Introduction, 2.2.3; ch I, 2.3 and 2.4.2; ch II, 2.6; and ch V, 3.2.1.

[129] *Mamatkulov and Askarov v Turkey* (App Nos 46827/99; 46951/99), judgment, 4 February 2005, Reports 2005-I, 293.

[130] *Mamatkulov and Abdurasulovic v Turkey* (n 128 above), para 102; *Mamatkulov and Askarov v Turkey* (n 129 above), para 114.

[131] *Glen Ashby v Trinidad and Tobago*, Communication No 580/1994, CCPR/C/54/D/580/1994, 21 March 2002, Human Rights Committee.

[132] *Dante Piandiong, Jesus Morallos and Archie Bulan v The Philippines*, Communication No 869/1999, CCPR/C/70/D/869/1999, 19 October 2000, Human Rights Committee; *Mamatkulov and Abdurasulovic v Turkey* (n 128 above), para 46; *Mamatkulov and Askarov v Turkey* (n 129 above), para 42.

[133] Human Rights Committee, *Annual Report to the UN General Assembly*, A/49/40, Vol 1 (1994), 74–75, paras 410–411; *Mamatkulov and Abdurasulovic v Turkey* (n 128 above), para 45; *Mamatkulov and Askarov v Turkey* (n 129 above), para 41.

recalled that 'the State party, upon ratifying the Optional Protocol, undertook to cooperate with the Committee under the procedure, and... [emphasized] that the State party has failed to comply with its obligations, both under the Optional Protocol and under the Covenant'.[134]

In the *Dante Piandiong* case, the Committee found that, by adhering to the First Optional Protocol, States Parties undertook to cooperate with the Committee. It was therefore 'incompatible with these obligations for a State Party to take any action that would prevent or frustrate the Committee in its consideration and examination of the communication, and in the expression of its Views'.[135] According to the Committee, interim measures taken under the Committee's rules and the ICCPR 'are essential to the Committee's role under the Protocol. Flouting of the Rule, especially by irreversible measures such as the execution of the alleged victim or his/her deportation from the country, undermines the protection of Covenant rights through the Optional Protocol'.[136] These two decisions and other international sources[137] constituted important stumbling blocks in the Court's finding that interim measures under the ECHR were binding. They enabled the Court to put more flesh on to Rule 39 of the Court's Rules and aided in strengthening the ECHR system as a whole.

2.2.9 The Riener *and* Bartik *Cases*

In 2006 the Court used the ICCPR in order to further clarify the meaning of the ECHR. The *Riener v Bulgaria* case[138] concerned an applicant with Austrian and Bulgarian citizenship who had been found by a Bulgarian court to owe the equivalent of approximately US$1 million in unpaid excise tax and interest. The police passport department issued an order imposing a travel ban on the applicant and that her travel documents be seized. The applicant appealed, claiming that she was a Bulgarian citizen and that such measures did not apply to her. The courts rejected her appeals, finding that her obligation to pay the outstanding taxes, as established by the court, was a sufficient ground in law to seize any passport used for international travel. The travel ban was lifted when the Ministry of the Interior repealed the prohibition at the request of the Sofia tax authority, since the statute of limitations for the applicant's debt had expired. The applicant wished to renounce her Bulgarian citizenship. Although this request was initially denied, it was granted subsequently. Before the Court, she complained about the ban preventing her from leaving Bulgaria, the refusal of her request to renounce Bulgarian citizenship, and the alleged lack of effective remedies in relation to those events. She relied on Articles 8 and 13 of the ECHR and Article 2 of Protocol No 4.

[134] Ibid, para 411 (text inserted by author).

[135] *Dante Piandiong, Jesus Morallos and Archie Bulan v The Philippines* (n 132 above), para 5.1.

[136] Ibid, para 5.4.

[137] See Introduction, 2.2.3; ch I, 2.3 and 2.4.2; ch II, 2.6; and ch V, 3.2.1.

[138] *Riener v Bulgaria* (App No 46343/99), judgment, 23 May 2006, not reported.

The Court noted that any restriction of Article 2 of Protocol No 4, guaranteeing the right to freedom of movement, must pursue a legitimate aim and strike a fair balance between the public interest and the individual's rights. It further found that the prohibition against the applicant leaving Bulgaria constituted interference by a public authority with her right to leave the country. The Court was satisfied that the prohibition had a basis in Bulgarian law and that it had a legitimate aim, namely to recover tax debt. Nonetheless, the Court concluded that the authorities had failed to give due consideration to the principle of proportionality in their decisions. It was found that 'States have a certain margin of appreciation to frame and organise their fiscal policies and make arrangement to ensure that taxes are paid'.[139] The Court noted, however, that the prohibition against the applicant leaving the country had been in place for more than five years when Protocol No 4 entered into force in Bulgaria. It had remained unaltered for nearly four years. The Court found that, even when a restriction imposed on an individual's freedom of movement was initially justified, maintaining it automatically over a lengthy period of time could become disproportionate.[140]

In support of this finding, the Court observed that a similar position was reached in the HRC Communication in *Miguel González del Río v Peru*.[141] In this case, the HRC found that 'pending judicial proceedings may justify restrictions on an individual's right to leave his country. But where the judicial proceedings are unduly delayed, a constraint upon the right to leave the country is thus not justified. In this case, the restriction on Mr. González' freedom to leave Peru has been in force for seven years, and the date of its termination remains uncertain. ... this situation violates the author's rights under article 12, paragraph 2.'[142] The Court recalled that Article 12 of the ICCPR had served as a basis for drafting Article 2 of Protocol No 4 of the ECHR, and thus found it justified referring to HRC case law.[143] The Court also noted that the General Comment No 27 (1999), containing some observations on the interpretation of Article 12, constituted relevant international material to consider in this context.

In the Court's view, it followed that a restriction to leave one's country on grounds of unpaid debt could only be justified as long as it served the aim of recovering the debt. In the applicant's case, it did not appear that the fiscal authorities actively sought to collect the debt, either before or after the entry into force of Protocol No 4 in Bulgaria. Furthermore, the Court considered that the travel ban was an automatic measure of indefinite duration. It could only be lifted on grounds of payment, submission of security, or extinction of the debt by prescription. Moreover, the applicable law treated as irrelevant the question of whether or not the fiscal authorities made efforts to secure payment by others, the debtor's

139 Ibid, para 119. 140 Ibid, para 120.

141 *Miguel González del Río v Peru*, Communication No 263/1987, CCPR/C/46/D/263/1987, 2 November 1992, Human Rights Committee. 142 Ibid, para 5.3.

143 *Riener v Bulgaria* (n 138 above), para 81.

attitude, and his or her potential ability to pay.[144] It was also noted that, under the domestic law of a number of Contracting States, travel bans for unpaid taxes can only be imposed when there are concrete reasons to believe that the person concerned will evade payment if allowed to travel. Thus, the Court held that the automatic nature of the travel ban, the failure to respect the principle of proportionality, and the lack of clarity in the relevant law and practice constituted violations of Article 2(2) of Protocol No 4. In view of that finding, the Court held that it was unnecessary to examine the same facts and decisions with regard to Article 8 of the ECHR. The Court further considered that the scope of review afforded to the applicant under Bulgarian law was too limited and that it constituted a violation of Article 13 of the ECHR. However, no violations of Articles 8 and 13 were found with regard to the refusal of the authorities to grant the applicant's request to renounce her citizenship, as those decisions did not interfere with her right to respect for private life.

In the same year, the Court made a very similar reference to Article 12 of the ICCPR in *Bartik v Russia*.[145] In this case, the applicant's right to travel abroad was forfeited for five years because he had had access in the past to state secrets. The restriction was imposed by means of a general provision of Russian law prohibiting persons who have had access to classified information from leaving Russia. The applicant complained that he was prevented from visiting his elderly ailing father who was receiving treatment in Germany. He alleged that the Russian authorities' refusal to issue him with a passport to travel abroad violated Article 2 of Protocol No 4.

The Government's argument that there were no legal grounds to apply the ECHR as the applicant was a permanent US resident was rejected. The Court noted that the Explanatory Report on Protocol No 4[146] indicated that the Committee of Experts on Human Rights set up by the Committee of Ministers endorsed the changes bringing the text of Article 2 of Protocol No 4 into conformity with Article 12 of the ICCPR.[147] The Court then reiterated that Article 2 of Protocol No 4 was intended to secure to any person a right to liberty of movement within a territory and to leave that territory. Any restrictions imposed on this right had to be 'necessary in a democratic society' in the pursuit of the legitimate aims mentioned in Article 2(3) of Protocol No 4.[148] It had been found previously that a measure denying the use of an identity document which would

[144] Ibid, para 127.

[145] *Bartik v Russia* (App No 55565/00), judgment, 21 December 2006, not reported.

[146] Protocol No 4 to the Convention for the Protection of Human Rights and Fundamental Freedoms, securing certain rights and freedoms other than those already included in the Convention and the First Protocol thereto (ETS No 46), Explanatory Report, Council of Europe, Strasbourg, <http://conventions.coe.int/Treaty/EN/Reports/Html/046.htm> (last visited 13 June 2010).

[147] *Bartik v Russia* (n 145 above), para 26.

[148] These legitimate aims include the interests of national security or public safety for the maintenance of *ordre public*, for the prevention of crime, for the protection of health or morals, and for the protection of the rights and freedoms of others.

have permitted an individual to leave the country amounted to interference.[149] The Court clarified this statement further by referring to General Comment No 27,[150] where the HRC examined the scope of the obligation included in the identically worded Article 12 of the ICCPR. The HRC found that 'the right to leave a country must include the right to obtain the necessary travel documents'.[151] Thus, the Court found that there had been an interference with the applicant's right to leave his own country.

Subsequently, the Court proceeded to verify whether the restriction was 'in accordance with the law', whether it was 'necessary in a democratic society', and whether it pursued one of the legitimate aims mentioned in Article 2(3) of Protocol No 4. It found that the restriction was applied pursuant to Russian law and that it fulfilled the legitimate aim of national security. The Court then considered whether the measure interfered with the pursuit of this aim no more than was necessary to achieve it. It was reiterated that the principle of proportionality required that restrictive measures be appropriate to achieve their protective function.[152] In support of this statement, the Court referred to HRC General Comment No 27,[153] where the Committee explained that 'it is not sufficient that the restrictions serve the permissible purposes; they must also be necessary to protect them. Restrictive measures must conform to the principle of proportionality; they must be appropriate to achieve their protective function; they must be the least intrusive instrument amongst those which might achieve the desired result; and they must be proportionate to the interest to be protected'.[154]

The restriction imposed upon the applicant was unqualified and the Government did not indicate how the applicant's ability to travel served the interests of national security.[155] The Court considered, however, that what was missing specifically was the link between the restrictive measure at issue and its protective function. Previously, the protective function of the measure served to prevent the disclosure of classified information concerning state secrets. The State controlled the transmission of information through the control of correspondence, travel and emigration bans, and the prohibition of unsupervised contacts with foreigners. However, since the control of correspondence and the ban on contacts with foreigners were removed, the necessity to restrict international travel for private purposes became less obvious. Thus, in a contemporary democratic society the measure failed to achieve the function ascribed to it. The Court supported this

[149] *Napijalo v Croatia* (App No 66485/01), judgment, 13 November 2003, not reported, paras 69 and 73; *Baumann v France* (App No 33592/96), judgment, 22 May 2001, Reports 2001-V, 207, para 62; *Timishev v Russia* (App Nos 55762/00; 55974/00), decision, 30 March 2004, not reported.

[150] United Nations, Human Rights Committee, General Comment No 27: Freedom of movement (Art.12), CCPR/C/21/Rev1/Add.9, 2 November 1999, <http://www.unhchr.ch/tbs/doc.nsf/0/6c76e1b8ee1710e380256824005a10a9?Opendocument> (last visited 13 June 2010).

[151] Ibid, para 9.

[152] *Bartik v Russia* (n 145 above), para 46.

[153] Ibid.

[154] United Nations Human Rights Committee (n 150 above), para 14.

[155] *Bartik v Russia* (n 145 above), para 49.

finding with a statement from General Comment No 27,[156] where it was found that 'the test of necessity and the requirements of proportionality... would not be met, for example, if an individual were prevented from leaving a country merely on the ground that he or she is the holder of "State secrets"'.[157] The Court also noted that Russia had not fulfilled its undertaking to abolish the restrictions on travel for persons with knowledge of 'State secrets'. Finally, the restriction in the instant case was imposed over a considerable time period and its impact on the applicant was great as he had not been able to travel since the beginning of his employment in 1977. The Court found that the restriction was not 'necessary in a democratic society' and violated Article 2 of Protocol No 4.[158]

In the *Riener* and *Bartik* cases the Court referred to the ICCPR in a relatively unhindered manner. This was due to the textual resemblance between Article 12 of the ICCPR and Article 2 of Protocol No 4 of the ECHR, and the fact that the former served as a basis on which to draft the latter. Thus, the Court probably felt that its references to the ICCPR would not have been opposed or contested by Contracting States. These references to the ICCPR served to support its reasoning and to further clarify the meaning of the requirements under Article 2 of Protocol No 4. The Court therefore used international law as an aid in interpretation and as a means to harmonize its case law with Article 12 of the ICCPR.

3. Rationale of the Reasoning

Generally, the Strasbourg bodies were much more receptive to the ICCPR framework than to most other regimes considered in this book. Their responsiveness to the ICCPR situated itself between a moderate and high level of reception. The Strasbourg case law referring to the ICCPR can be divided into two strands. The first relates to a structural or procedural need to prevent the same case from reaching both bodies. The second provides a more compelling insight into the Court's reception of and approach to the ICCPR, as it does not concern procedural issues slipping beyond the ECtHR's control. This strand of the Strasbourg jurisprudence relates to the substantive references made by the Strasbourg bodies as a result of the similarities and differences between both systems in cases never brought before the HRC.

The level of reception in the first strand of case law was conditioned by the fact that the cases were intertwined with the ICCPR and that the outcome of the cases before the ECtHR required a reference to the former instrument. These references were necessary and made outside the Court's sphere of influence. As such, mention of the ICCPR in this context was less instructive with regard to the Court's approach to international law. Nonetheless, the coexistence of the Court

[156] Ibid. [157] United Nations Human Rights Committee (n 150 above), para 16.
[158] *Bartik v Russia* (n 145 above), para 52.

and HRC is extremely important for the coherence of international human rights protection. The above analysis has demonstrated that the Court previously ruled differently from the HRC in an identical case. However, it appears that—for the moment at least—this episode in the case law of the Court has come to an end. Undoubtedly, the procedural framework regulating the relationship between both systems has an important bearing on the fragmentation of international human rights law. If both bodies are aware of the other's case law, they can render harmonious communications and judgments and thereby contribute to the unity of international human rights law.

As part of the second strand of case law, the references to the ICCPR arose in contexts where the applicant had invoked the ICCPR in support of his complaint, where the case law of the HRC was more developed under a given provision, or where the ICCPR provided more extensive protection to the claimant. It has, however, also been the case that the ECtHR referred to the ICCPR in a situation where it was interpreting a provision common to both instruments and that the HRC provided further guidance as to its construction. Given the resemblances in the catalogue of human rights covered by both instruments and given that certain members of the ECtHR are experts in international and European human rights law, it is only natural that certain interactions and cross-fertilization exist between HRC and ECtHR jurisprudence, and vice versa.[159] It remains, nonetheless, difficult to trace exhaustively the various relations which arise between both sets of case law, as they are often indirect and informal.[160]

As already seen, the second strand of case law was marked in the 1980s and early 1990s by the willingness of the Court and the Commission to refer to the drafting history of the ICCPR, HRC case law, and ICCPR provisions as aids in interpretation and as a means of clarifying the extent of the ECHR. Moreover, these sources constituted an important benchmark in the examination of the applications that came to Strasbourg. In 1993, however, both the Commission and the Court adopted a more traditional and circumspect approach to the ICCPR and HRC case law, announcing that it was not part of their duty to consider these in the framework of the ECHR. Both bodies then exercised self-restraint and did not refer extensively to the ICCPR regime.

Surprisingly, the Court made very extensive use of the ICCPR in 2001 as part of the cases concerning the GDR's border-policing practice. These cases appear to constitute the apogee of reception in Strasbourg case law referring to the ICCPR. The Court's reliance on the ICCPR in these cases was startling, as it applied an instrument which had been ratified but not implemented by the GDR at the time. This approach stands in great contrast with the other cases in which the

[159] Marc Bossuyt and Olivier Lins, '*La prise en considération de la jurisprudence de Strasbourg par le Comité des droits de l'homme des Nations Unies*' in Gérard Cohen-Jonathan and Jean-François Flauss, (eds), *Le rayonnement international de la jurisprudence de la Cour européenne des droits de l'homme, Droit & Justice 64* (collection directed by Pierre Lambert) (Brussels: Bryulant/Nemesis, 2005), 83, 84.

[160] Ibid, 85.

ICCPR was invoked. Nonetheless, it could be explained by the importance of the issue at hand and by the political pressure put on judges with regard to punishment of former GDR authorities. This strand of case law was followed by a swing in the opposite direction: as part of two decisions in 2002, the Court avoided referring to the ICCPR on the basis that there was an ECHR equivalent, and distanced itself from the findings of the HRC in similar cases.

Recently, the Court's interactions with the ICCPR framework appear to have become more balanced and harmonious. The Court began once more to refer to the provisions of the ICCPR and to HRC case law in a less-restrictive manner. This was due, at least in part, to the textual similarities of the ICCPR and ECHR. The Court's references were not controversial and the Court may have felt that they would not have been opposed or contested. These references to the ICCPR served to support the Court's reasoning and to clarify further the meaning of the requirements under the ECHR. Thus, the Court used international law as an aid to interpretation and as a means to harmonize its case law with the ICCPR. These references did not, however, come close to the level of reception reached by the Court in the GDR border-policing cases.

The Strasbourg bodies' reasoning was not completely deprived of reluctance to refer to the ICCPR. In some cases, the Court and the Commission displayed significant caution and self-restraint. Naturally, it is normal for a jurisdictional body rendering binding decisions to avoid referring to non-binding conclusions handed down by a quasi-jurisdictional body. The unwillingness to reach beyond the ECHR could also be due to the fact that the ICCPR is an instrument with a universal reach; its provisions have been adapted to all existing countries and may have a different meaning in different parts of the world. Moreover, European states constitute a minority of the ICCPR members, and some HRC case law may concern issues that do not arise in Europe. Thus, the Strasbourg bodies probably considered that referring to the ICCPR and HRC case law would not necessarily contribute to the interpretation of ECHR rights, which are based on a relatively homogenous legal and political culture.[161] While these considerations need to be taken into account, they should not dominate judges' reasoning. It is important to remember that human rights have a universal value and that they are not merely a Western creation.[162] The Court should therefore not be unduly swayed by the issues enumerated here.

Overall, the Strasbourg bodies have leaned more towards the open paradigm in this strand of their jurisprudence. This tendency has been accompanied by the need to prevent fragmentation between the ECHR and the ICCPR. The reception of international law was therefore an appropriate step to take in this context. The approach of the Strasbourg bodies was the most receptive in the first strand

[161] Hefferman (n 5 above). See ch III, 6; ch V, 4; and ch VI, 4. See also 1.2 above.

[162] Rosalyn Higgins, 'Ten Years of the UN Human Rights Committee: Some Thoughts upon Parting' (1996) 6 EHRLR 574.

of the case law, where the references to the ICCPR were prompted by necessity and procedural reasons. The second strand of the case law, involving substantive references to the ICCPR, was marked by an uneven and lower level of reception. The result of this assessment is not surprising, as it is more legitimate for the Court to use the ICCPR when a certain reference is required or necessary. It is also less controversial to rely on the ICCPR when there are no complex international policy issues involved in the case. The Court's treatment of the ICCPR has not been exemplary, but it was what could have been reasonably expected under the circumstances. Further, the interaction between the HRC and the ECtHR became tremendously problematic when both bodies ruled differently in an identical case. Fortunately, this troublesome episode in the Court's case law seems to have ended, thereby hopefully giving way to a more balanced approach to the ICCPR.

Thus, while the Court's approach towards the ICCPR could have been more coherent and harmonious, it has nonetheless contributed towards reducing the isolation of the ICCPR and ECHR systems. In future cases, further effort should be channelled into systematizing the Court's approach towards the ICCPR and ensuring that there is an efficient dialogue between the HRC and the ECtHR. It has been proposed that the HRC should actively seek convergence with the ECtHR's reasoning in cases concerning rights and freedoms which are either identical or substantially similar under both instruments.[163] Undoubtedly, a similar initiative should also be taken under the auspices of the ECtHR. By linking the case law of both bodies, the inception of a concrete dialogue would render the coordination between the institutions more viable and strengthen the protection of the rights enshrined in the ECHR and ICCPR.

[163] Laurence R Helfer and Anne-Marie Slaughter, 'Toward a Theory of Effective Supranational Adjudication' (1997) 107 Yale LJ 273, 373–390.

V

Prohibition on Torture and Other Ill-treatment

1. Preliminary Observations

While torture once constituted a valid method of law enforcement, it was largely outlawed in the nineteenth century in all European states.[1] The practice, however, returned to Europe and was widely used during the first half of the twentieth century by totalitarian regimes, such as those created by Hitler and Stalin.[2] After the Second World War, the Allies declared that torture was morally unacceptable and not in accordance with international law. War criminals were tried and held personally accountable for their crimes in the Nuremberg and Tokyo trials. During those trials, judges applied certain standards which flow from the current international and regional instruments prohibiting torture and cruel, inhuman, or degrading treatment. Further, in order to prevent such cruelty from occurring again, states drew up human rights instruments to ban this cruel practice.

While considerable progress has been made towards criminalizing torture since the Second World War, certain states have tried to circumvent the international legal instruments put into place. As part of the fight against terrorism that has swept the world, numerous states have adopted anti-terrorism measures which have been found to infringe human rights standards. Some of these measures have often bordered on torture and cruel, inhuman, or degrading treatment. Nonetheless, states have attempted to justify their actions by invoking the emergency of the situation or by arguing that their actions did not constitute torture or ill-treatment. Thus, there is currently a renewed and enduring interest in ensuring that the prohibition against torture is fully respected and that states do not try to circumvent it in the context of the fight against terrorism.

The roots of the international prohibition on torture lie in Article 5 of the Universal Declaration of Human Rights (UDHR), which states that '[n]o one shall be subjected to torture or to cruel, inhuman or degrading treatment or punishment'. Article 3 of the ECHR essentially repeats the content of Article 5 of the UDHR using very similar language. It provides that '[n]o one shall be subjected

[1] Chris Inglese, *The U.N. Committee Against Torture: An Assessment* (The Hague/London/Boston: Kluwer Law International, 2001), 29.

[2] Ibid, 30.

to torture or to inhuman or degrading treatment or punishment'. The drafters of this provision took the UDHR as their model and the provision was hardly debated. Article 3 belongs to the hard core of rights protected under Article 15(2) of the ECHR, which entails that neither the prohibition on torture nor the prohibition on cruel, inhuman, or degrading treatment can be limited by law or deviated from on grounds of a state of emergency. Thus, the prohibition of this type of behaviour is absolute and the ECHR framework provides a powerful mechanism for its enforcement.

In addition, on 26 November 1987 the Member States of the Council of Europe adopted the European Convention for the Prevention of Torture and Inhuman or Degrading Treatment or Punishment,[3] which was subsequently ratified by all ECHR Contracting States. This instrument provides for non-judicial preventive machinery to protect detainees. It is based on a system of visits by the European Committee for the Prevention of Torture and Inhuman or Degrading Treatment or Punishment, set up under the same Convention. The Committee visits all places of detention of the Council of Europe's Member States to see how persons deprived of their liberty are treated and, if necessary, recommends improvements to states. The European Convention for the Prevention of Torture and Inhuman or Degrading Treatment or Punishment will not be analysed as part of this chapter because it is a regional instrument; this study focuses on the response of the Strasbourg bodies to international instruments.

When the United Nations began evaluating the possibility of enacting a convention against torture, they were able to draw upon substantial experience and material. It was found, however, that a prohibition as found in the ECHR was not sufficient. In 1975 the General Assembly adopted the Declaration on the Protection of All Persons from Being Subjected to Torture and Other Cruel, Inhuman or Degrading Treatment or Punishment.[4] This Declaration was not legally binding and merely constituted a recommendation of the General Assembly. However, it contained very detailed rules and formed the first far-reaching guidelines for the existing prohibition on torture and cruel, inhuman, and degrading treatment.[5] Moreover, it was the first international document to include a detailed definition of torture.[6] Gradually, however, consensus grew to develop a convention against torture, and the Declaration constituted the blueprint for this document.

The United Nations Convention Against Torture and Other Cruel, Inhuman or Degrading Treatment or Punishment ('CAT') was adopted by the United Nations General Assembly on 10 December 1984 and came into force on 26 June

[3] European Convention for the Prevention of Torture and Inhuman or Degrading Treatment or Punishment, CETS No 126, adopted on 26 November 1987, entered into force 1 February 1989.

[4] Declaration on the Protection of All Persons from Being Subjected to Torture and Other Cruel, Inhuman or Degrading Treatment or Punishment, Resolution 3452 (XXX), adopted by the General Assembly of the United Nations, 2433rd Plenary Meeting, 9 December 1975.

[5] Inglese (n 1 above), 70. [6] Ibid.

1987. The CAT was ratified by all ECHR Contracting States.[7] While the prohibition on torture existed in other treaties, the CAT clarified this requirement further by explicitly obliging states (after ratification) to take specific effective measures to prevent and combat torture. Further, the CAT provided a more detailed definition of torture, introduced the obligation of *non-refoulement* in the event of a threat of torture, provided for a system of universal jurisdiction, and established the principle of *aut dedere aut judicare* in relation to this crime.[8] As with the ECHR, the prohibition on torture under the CAT is absolute and non-derogable. In the CAT, however, the absolute prohibition refers only to torture, whereas under the ECHR it also applies to inhuman and degrading treatment. Nevertheless, according to Manfred and McArthur, the CAT also forbids any derogation to cruel, inhuman, or degrading treatment.[9]

The CAT established a Committee Against Torture, which constitutes one of the seven UN human rights treaty bodies. All State Parties are obliged under the Convention to submit regular reports to the Committee on how the rights under the CAT are being implemented. In addition to this reporting obligation, the Convention establishes three mechanisms through which the Committee performs its monitoring functions: the inquiry procedure, the examination of inter-state complaints, and the examination of individual complaints. However, as with other UN human rights treaty bodies, the Committee Against Torture cannot impose sanctions against states for failing to carry out their obligations and it cannot hand down legally binding decisions. In comparison to the ECtHR, the Committee Against Torture lacks the teeth necessary for enforcement.[10]

As an important addition to this system, the European Convention for the Prevention of Torture and Inhuman or Degrading Treatment or Punishment was adapted and generalized by the United Nations through the adoption of the Optional Protocol to the Convention Against Torture and other Cruel, Inhuman

[7] This information was verified on 13 June 2010: United Nations Treaty Collection, Status, <http://treaties.un.org/Pages/ViewDetails.aspx?src=IND&mtdsg_no=IV-9&chapter=4&lang=en>. See ch III, 4.5 and ch VI, 3.

[8] Inglese (n 1 above), 70.

[9] Nowak and McArthur accurately point out that '[t]he revised Swedish draft on which the final text of Article 2(2) CAT is based no longer contained any reference to cruel, inhuman or degrading treatment which means that there is no explicit provision in the Convention that prohibits any derogation from the prohibition on cruel, inhuman or degrading treatment. However, since the Preamble of the Convention clearly refers to the existing standards under the CCPR and the 1975 Declaration and affirms the desire of the drafters to make more effective (and not less effective) the struggle against torture and cruel, inhuman or degrading treatment, one should not give too much weight to this retrogressive provision. In addition, Article 16(2) CAT contains an explicit savings clause in relation to other treaty provisions prohibiting cruel, inhuman or degrading treatment': Manfred Nowak and Elizabeth McArthur, *The United Nations Convention Against Torture: A Commentary* (Oxford/New York: OUP, 2008), 118–119, para 59.

[10] Ahcene Boulesbaa, *The U.N. Convention on Torture and the Prospects for Enforcement, International Studies in Human Rights* (The Hague/Boston/London: Martinus Nijhoff, 1999), 293.

or Degrading Treatment or Punishment.[11] This Optional Protocol seeks to prevent torture and other forms of ill-treatment through the establishment of a system of regular visits by independent international and national bodies to places of detention. This system is overseen by a Subcommittee on Prevention of Torture and Other Cruel, Inhuman or Degrading Treatment or Punishment, which cooperates with the relevant international, regional, and national institutions or organizations. The Optional Protocol was signed by 20 ECHR Contracting States and ratified by 15 of them.[12]

It is also important to note that the then UN Commission on Human Rights (now the Human Rights Council) created its own mechanism on torture. Pursuant to Resolution 1985/33,[13] the Commission appointed an expert, a Special Rapporteur, to examine questions relevant to torture. The mandate of the special rapporteur covers all countries, irrespective of whether a state has ratified the CAT. His or her mandate comprises three main activities: transmitting urgent appeals to states with regard to individuals reported to be at risk of torture (as well as communications on past alleged cases of torture); undertaking fact-finding country visits; and submitting annual reports on activities, the mandate, and methods of work to the Human Rights Council and the General Assembly. The findings of the Special Rapporteur have often been relevant in cases brought before the Commission and the Court.

Important inroads into the law of ECHR Contracting States have been made with regard to the use of torture and cruel, inhuman, or degrading treatment. The prohibition of this behaviour has an absolute character and no derogation thereto is permitted. Thus, the margin of appreciation with regard to the prohibition on torture and other ill-treatment is considerably reduced, if not inexistent. The European framework has had an undeniable influence on the implementation of the prohibition of torture and other ill-treatment at the international level. Nonetheless, this dynamic reversed itself when the CAT was adopted in 1984. The Court began to refer to its provisions and to the case law of the Committee Against Torture. While the Court has not completely overtaken the approach of the CAT and the Committee Against Torture, it is fair to observe that both have made a permanent and substantial imprint on its reasoning. Article 1 of the CAT now constitutes an important element of the Court's approach to the distinction between torture and cruel, inhuman, or degrading treatment. Further, there is an increasing convergence between the ECHR and the Committee's case law. In some cases, however, the Court referred less to the UN Committee's findings due

[11] Optional Protocol to the Convention Against Torture and other Cruel, Inhuman or Degrading Treatment or Punishment, GA Res A/RES/57/199, adopted on 18 December 2002, entered into force 22 June 2006.

[12] This information was verified on 13 June 2010: United Nations Treaty Collections, Status, <http://treaties.un.org/Pages/ViewDetails.aspx?src=IND&mtdsg_no=IV-9-b&chapter=4&lang=en>.

[13] Resolution No 1985/33, aimed at appointing a Special Rapporteur on Torture, E/CN.4/1985/SR.55, Commission on Human Rights, 55th meeting, 13 March 1985.

to the existence of the European Committee for the Prevention of Torture. As it could rely on its regional sibling, the Court did not feel that it was necessary to reach outside the family circle to support its findings in relation to the CAT or the case law of the Committee.[14]

2. Case Law Concerning the CAT Framework and Beyond

2.1 Case Law Referring to the Convention Against Torture

Overall, the case law relating to the reception of the CAT is characterized by an increasing tendency on the part of the Court to follow the requirements of Articles 1 and 16 of the CAT. This statement, however, needs to be qualified. The initial pre-CAT case law is marked by the tendency of the Commission to follow a purpose-oriented approach to the distinction between torture and inhuman or degrading treatment. During this time, the Court's approach was based on the 'severity of pain' requirement. The Court's reasoning undeniably marked the evolution of subsequent case law. When the CAT was enacted, its drafters followed the purpose-oriented approach indicated previously by the Commission. With the enactment of the CAT, the approach of the Court also unfastened itself and the CAT gradually penetrated its reasoning. This marked a slow, albeit incomplete, return to the Commission's initial case law. The Court's initial approach fixed an endurable imprint on Strasbourg reasoning, thereby preventing it from coming full circle.

2.1.1 Pre-CAT Case Law

The Strasbourg bodies appear to have been the first to apply a prohibition of torture based on a statute. Article 3 of the ECHR contains three components, namely torture, inhuman treatment, and degrading treatment. A complicated jurisprudential trend focused on the definition of these terms. The roots of the Court's approach to Article 3 of the ECHR lie in the opinion adopted by the European Commission on Human Rights in the *Greek Case*[15] in 1969. This was the first decision to consider the definition of torture and cruel, inhuman, or degrading treatment. In that case the Governments of Denmark, Norway, Sweden, and the Netherlands brought allegations that the Greek Government had committed acts that infringed, *inter alia*, Article 3 of the ECHR. The Commission found that '[t]he notion of inhuman treatment covers at least such treatment as deliberately causes severe suffering, mental or physical, which, in the particular situation is unjustifiable'.[16] It was considered that '[t]reatment or punishment of an individual may be said to be

[14] It should be noted that the role of the Committee and of the CAT in the protection of refugees will not be considered here, but rather as part of the chapter on refugee rights. See ch VI, 3.

[15] *The Greek Case (Denmark, Norway, Sweden and The Netherlands v Greece)*, report, 5 November 1969, 12 YB 1.

[16] Ibid, 186.

degrading if it grossly humiliates him before others or drives him to act against his will or conscience'.[17] Torture was found to constitute 'inhuman treatment which has a purpose such as the obtaining of information or confessions, or the infliction of punishment, and it is generally an aggravated form of inhuman and degrading treatment'.[18] Thus, an important distinction between torture and other types of treatment was the purpose for which such conduct was carried out.[19]

According to the Commission, the Greek Government had inflicted torture and ill-treatment on several individuals in custody. The purpose of the torture had been the extraction of information, including confessions concerning the victims' political activities and associations.[20] The Commission's analysis of inhuman treatment has been criticized due to its reference to treatment which could be unjustifiable in a particular situation. In fact, this definition appears to be misleading, as it suggests that torture and inhuman treatment could be justifiable.[21] Despite this failure in the approach of the Commission, it appears that the *Greek Case* may have influenced the development of the 1975 UN Declaration and, as a consequence, the 1984 UN Convention Against Torture.[22] The idea of aggravation made its way into the definition of torture used in the Declaration, which stipulates that '[t]orture constitutes an aggravated and deliberate form of cruel, inhuman or degrading treatment or punishment'.[23] The Declaration, in turn, directly influenced and made its way into Strasbourg case law.[24]

In the *Ireland v United Kingdom* case,[25] the Commission (1976) and the Court (1978) considered the allegations of torture and inhuman treatment in the conflict in Northern Ireland. In that case, 14 people had been arrested, singled out, and taken to unidentified interrogation centres. There, they were submitted to a number of interrogation techniques which consisted of: wall-standing; hooding; subjection to noise; deprivation of sleep; and deprivation of food and drink.

[17] Ibid. [18] Ibid.

[19] Manfred Nowak, 'What Practices Constitute Torture?: US and UN Standards' (2001) 28 Hum Rts Qrtly 809, 820; Nowak and McArthur (n 9 above), 67, para 94, 68, paras 96–97; Christian De Vos, 'Mind the Gap: Purpose, Pain, and the Difference Between Torture and Inhuman Treatment' (2007) 14(2) Hum Rts Brief 4; Pieter Van Dijk, Fried Van Hoof, Arjen Van Rijn, and Loe Zwaak, *Theory and Practice of the European Convention on Human Rights* (Antwerp/Oxford: Intersentia, 4th edn, 2006), 406–407. [20] *The Greek Case* (n 15 above), 504.

[21] Clare Ovey and Robin CA White, *The European Convention on Human Rights* (Oxford/New York: OUP, 4th edn, 2006), 76.

[22] Malcolm D Evans and Rod Morgan, *Preventing Torture: A Study of the European Convention for the Protection of Torture and Inhuman or Degrading Treatment or Punishment* (Oxford: Clarendon Press, 1998), 74; Hans Danelius, 'Protection Against Torture in Europe and the World' in Ronald St J Macdonald, Franz Matscher, and Herbert Petzold, *The European System for the Protection of Human Rights* (Dordrecht: Martinus Nijhoff, 1993), 267; De Vos (n 19 above), 821; Nigel S Rodley, 'The Definition(s) of Torture in International Law' (2002) 55 CLP 467, 471; Declaration on the Protection of All Persons From Being Subjected to Torture and Other Cruel, Inhuman or Degrading Treatment or Punishment, Resolution 3452 (XXX), adopted by the General Assembly of the United Nations, 2433rd Plenary Meeting, 9 December 1975. [23] Ibid, Art 1.

[24] Rodley (n 22 above), 471.

[25] *Ireland v United Kingdom* (App No 5310/71), report, 25 January 1976, Series B, Vol 23; *Ireland v United Kingdom* (App No 5310/71), judgment, 18 January 1978, Series A, Vol 25.

The Irish Government alleged that the United Kingdom had infringed Articles 1–3, 5, 6, and 14 of the ECHR. In its report, the Commission considered that the purpose of the techniques was to obtain information from the persons subjected to them and unanimously held that the techniques amounted to torture. More specifically, it was held that 'the systemic application of the techniques for the purpose of inducing a person to give information shows a clear resemblance to those methods of systemic torture which have been known over the ages'.[26] Thus, the Commission seems to have followed the approach indicated previously in the *Greek Case.*

The Court disagreed with the Commission's reasoning; while it held that the interrogation techniques used constituted inhuman treatment, it also considered that they did not fulfil the requirements of torture. The Court stated that a minimum severity threshold had to be attained before the provision could be applied. In its view, '[t]he assessment of this minimum is, in the nature of things, relative; it depends on all the circumstances of the case, such as the duration of the treatment, its physical or mental effects and, in some cases, the sex, age and state of health of the victim, etc'.[27] Furthermore, the Court noted that '[t]he Convention prohibits in absolute terms torture and inhuman or degrading treatment or punishment, irrespective of the victim's conduct. Unlike most of the substantive clauses of the Convention and of Protocols Nos. 1 and 4, Article 3 makes no provision for exceptions and, under Article 15 para. 2, there can be no derogation therefrom even in the event of a public emergency threatening the life of the nation.'[28]

In order to determine whether these interrogation techniques constituted torture, the Court considered that it had to have regard to the distinction, embodied in Article 3 of the ECHR, between this notion and that of inhuman or degrading treatment. In its view, this distinction derived principally from a difference in the intensity of the suffering inflicted.[29] Moreover, it emphasized that 'it was the intention that the Convention, with its distinction between "torture" and "inhuman or degrading treatment", should by the first of these terms attach a special stigma to deliberate inhuman treatment causing very serious and cruel suffering'.[30] In order to support this statement, the Court resorted to the torture definition contained in Article 1 of the Declaration on the Protection of All Persons from Being Subjected to Torture and Other Cruel, Inhuman or Degrading Treatment or Punishment adopted by the General Assembly of the United Nations on 9 December 1975. The Court found that '[a]lthough the five techniques, as applied in combination, undoubtedly amounted to inhuman and degrading treatment, although their object was the extraction of confessions, the naming of others and/or information and although they were used systematically,

[26] *Ireland v United Kingdom*, report (n 25 above), 402.
[27] *Ireland v United Kingdom*, judgment (n 25 above), para 162. [28] Ibid.
[29] Ibid, para 167. [30] Ibid.

they did not occasion suffering of the particular intensity and cruelty implied by the word torture as so understood'.[31] Thus, it was held that the use of the interrogation techniques constituted inhuman and degrading treatment and violated Article 3 of the ECHR.

The Court's finding has given rise to intense criticism from legal scholars. One commentator argued, for instance, that the majority opinion presented a very narrow view of torture and failed to develop Article 3 to meet the challenges of refined repression methods.[32] In his view, the Court was influenced by the idea that 'the common understanding of torture must be limited to mean extreme barbary' and excluded 'the systematically researched and applied subtle techniques of psychological manipulation which nullify the human will'.[33] Despite the accuracy of this criticism, the *Ireland v United Kingdom* case[34] constitutes a very important episode in the Court's case law under Article 3 of the ECHR, as it sets the tone for the Court's reasoning in subsequent cases. The criteria used by the Court to distinguish between torture and cruel, inhuman, and degrading treatment were applied in numerous cases that followed.[35] The Court, unlike the Commission in the *Greek Case*, grounded the distinction between torture and cruel, inhuman, or degrading treatment in the difference between the intensity of suffering inflicted. Although the Commission seems to have accepted that the severity of pain could distinguish both types of act, its analysis appears to have focused more on the purpose of the conduct.[36]

Thus, in *Tyrer v United Kindgom*[37] in 1978 the Court applied the reasoning set out in the *Ireland* judgment with regard to the distinction between torture and inhuman punishment. The applicant, a British citizen, pleaded guilty before the local juvenile court to an unlawful assault occasioning actual bodily harm to a senior pupil at his school. He was sentenced on the same day to three strokes of the birch in accordance with the relevant legislation. He complained in his application that judicial corporal punishment constituted a breach of Articles 1, 3, 8, 13, and 14 of the ECHR. In deciding whether the applicant's punishment amounted to torture under Article 3, the Court found that the facts of the case did not reveal that he underwent suffering of the level inherent in this notion, as it was interpreted and applied in the *Ireland* judgment.[38] The Court decided that there was no torture or inhuman treatment in this case. It nonetheless found that

[31] Ibid.

[32] See, for example, Robert J Spjut, 'Torture Under the European Convention on Human Rights' (1979) 73 Am J Int L 267, 272.

[33] Ibid, 271.

[34] *Ireland v United Kingdom* (n 25 above), para 167.

[35] Winston P Nakan and Lucie Atkins, 'The International Law of Torture: From Universal Proscription to Effective Application and Enforcement' (2001) 14 Harv Hum Rts J 87, 115.

[36] De Vos (n 19 above), 4; Nowak (n 19 above), 820; Nowak and McArthur (n 9 above), 67, para 94.

[37] *Tyrer v United Kingdom* (App No 5856/72), judgment, 25 April 1978, Series A, Vol 26.

[38] Ibid, para 29; *Ireland v United Kingdom* (n 25 above), paras 167 and 174.

the judicial corporal punishment inflicted on the applicant constituted degrading treatment as enshrined in Article 3 of the ECHR.

From this early Strasbourg case law, it is apparent that the Commission and Court have taken different approaches to the definition of torture and cruel, inhuman, or degrading treatment. The reasoning used by the Court appears to have been based on the severity of treatment inflicted. The approach taken by the Commission, however, was based on the purpose element of the treatment, and thus was closer to the approach taken by the United Nations in the CAT. It also flows from the opinions of the Commission that states have no margin of appreciation in applying Article 3 given that it allows no derogation.[39] The interpretation used by the Commission further demonstrates that it does not accept a too-narrow construction favouring state sovereignty. Instead, the Commission has tried to promote the protection of the individual. The Court's approach was more restrictive as it resorted to a narrower interpretation of the notion of torture. Overall, the Court's approach appears to have made an endurable imprint on Strasbourg case law. Nonetheless, the approach used earlier by the Commission in the *Greek Case*, later reflected in the CAT, has been an important influence and was also later included in the Court's reasoning. Although a number of renowned experts maintain that the distinction between torture and other inhuman acts is grounded in the purpose,[40] it has been accurately pointed out that the debate is actually divided, with some authors leaning towards the purpose-oriented approach and others supporting the severity-oriented theory.[41] It does appear, in fact, that the practice and the doctrine are not unequivocal with regard to the approach that should be adopted towards this distinction. Against this background, it is easier to assess the evolution in the reasoning of the Strasbourg bodies which followed both approaches and did not take a stand with regard to either one of them. Most recently, however, the Court has resorted to a mixed approach based on purpose and severity of pain.

2.1.2 Post-CAT Case Law

In 1984 the UN General Assembly adopted the CAT, which contained a new definition of torture. The biggest difference between the definition contained in the CAT and that in its predecessor (the Declaration Against Torture) was that it left out the notion that torture constituted an aggravated form of ill-treatment. As previously discussed, this change in the definition appears to indicate that the

[39] Love Kellberg, 'The Case-Law of the European Commission of Human Rights' in Antonio Cassese (ed), *The International Fight Against Torture: La lutte internationale contre la torture* (Baden-Baden: Nomos, 1991), 119.

[40] Evans and Morgan (n 22 above), 73–79; Nigel S Rodley, *The Treatment of Prisoners under International Law* (Oxford/New York: OUP, 2nd edn, 1999), 29–31 and 75–106; Rodley (n 22 above), 481, 489–493; Nowak (n 19 above), 821–822, 830–831 and 839; Nowak and McArthur (n 9 above), 68, paras 96–97.

[41] Walter Kälin and Jörg Künzli, *Universeller Menschenrechtsschutz* (Basle: Helbing & Lichtenhahn/Nomos, 2008), 365–368.

UN wished to follow the approach taken by the Commission in the *Greek Case*[42] rather than that of the Court in the *Ireland* case.[43] Similarly, one commentator noted that the language of Article 16 of the CAT (regarding cruel, inhuman, or degrading treatment) represented a compromise between non-governmental organizations that wanted the total elimination of the idea of the intensity of pain or suffering and those parties, including the United Kingdom, that wanted to preserve what they saw as the benefits of the *Ireland* judgment.[44] The agreed language appears, however, to have left the issue open.[45] It could be hypothesized that the enactment of the CAT would have a substantial impact on the subsequent practice concerning torture and that it would perhaps become an important benchmark.[46] However, the ECtHR was initially reluctant to move away from its traditional position. Only much later did it begin to refer more to the CAT; the Court even integrated its definition into its case law, stressing the purposive element of torture. Overall, however, it repeated like a mantra its standard formula that it was the intention that the Convention should attach a special stigma of torture only to deliberate inhuman treatment causing very serious and cruel suffering.[47] Thus, as will be seen below, the Court has reaffirmed, at least in part, the reasoning used in the *Ireland* judgment.[48]

2.1.2.1 Post-Ireland Case Law and its Enduring Influence

It appears that between 1978 and 1996 there were no findings of torture before the ECtHR.[49] The Strasbourg bodies did, however, refer to the CAT in their case law. In 1989, in *Soering v United Kingdom*,[50] a landmark case concerning the extradition of a person to a state where he risked being exposed to the death row syndrome, the Court used the CAT (invoked by the respondent Government) to support its reasoning. The Court considered the question whether the extradition of a fugitive to another state, where he could be subjected to torture or inhuman or degrading treatment, would engage the responsibility of a Contracting State under Article 3 of the ECHR.[51] It was noted that Article 3 of the CAT recognizes the abhorrence of such treatment and provides that no State Party should extradite a person where there are reasonable grounds to believe that he could be subjected to torture. Nonetheless, in the Court's view, '[t]he fact that a specialised treaty should spell out in detail a specific obligation attaching to the prohibition of torture does not mean that an essentially similar obligation is not already inherent

[42] *The Greek Case (Denmark, Norway, Sweden and The Netherlands v Greece)*, report, 5 November 1969, 12 YB 1.

[43] *Ireland v United Kingdom*, judgment (n 25 above). See Nowak (n 19 above), 821. See also n 22 above and accompanying text.

[44] Rodley (n 22 above), 475. [45] Ibid. [46] Ibid, 474. [47] Ibid, 475.

[48] Ibid.

[49] Louis-Philippe F Rouillard, 'Misinterpreting the Prohibition on Torture Under International Law: The Office of Legal Council Memorandum' (2005) 21 Am U Int'l Rev 9, 30.

[50] *Soering v United Kingdom* (App No 14038/88), judgment, 7 July 1989, Series A, Vol 161.

[51] Ibid, para 88.

in the general terms of Article 3 of the European Convention'.[52] In the Court's view, it would be incompatible with the underlying values of the Convention for a Contracting State to knowingly surrender a fugitive to another state if there were substantial grounds to believe that he could be subjected to torture, independently of the gravity of the crime committed. The Court's stated that '[e]xtradition in such circumstances, while not explicitly referred to in the brief and general wording of Article 3, would plainly be contrary to the spirit and intendment of the Article, and...this inherent obligation not to extradite also extends to cases in which the fugitive would be faced in the receiving State by a real risk of exposure to inhuman or degrading treatment or punishment proscribed by that Article'.[53] It should be noted that the Commission took the same approach in its report and cited Article 3 of the CAT in support of its reasoning.[54] Thus, the Strasbourg bodies used the CAT as an interpretation aid which allowed them to read into the ECHR an obligation not to extradite under Article 3 of the ECHR.

In 1996 the Court handed down its judgment in the *Aksoy v Turkey* case,[55] which is a representative example of the post-*Ireland* case law as well as the first case in which the Court found that torture had been inflicted by a state on to a person.[56] In the *Aksoy* case, the applicant was arrested and taken into police custody. He further alleged that the police had subjected him, *inter alia*, to a form of torture known as 'Palestinian hanging' which involved being stripped naked and hung up by his arms. He also alleged to have been electrocuted in his genitals, kicked, slapped, and verbally abused whilst in this position. He stated that as a result of the hanging he lost the use of his arms and hands. Furthermore, the reports of international organizations (the European Committee for the Prevention of Torture, the Committee Against Torture, the Special Rapporteur on Torture) showed that torture of detainees continued to be widespread and systematic in Turkey and raised questions about the commitment of the state to end this practice.[57] He also invoked reports of international organizations (Amnesty International, the European Committee for the Prevention of Torture, and the Committee Against Torture) to support his argument that the safeguards contained in the Turkish Criminal Code were inadequate and routinely ignored.[58] The applicant complained that the treatment to which he was subjected violated Articles 3, 5(3), 6(1), and 13 of the ECHR. Later, the Commission was informed by the applicant's representatives that he had been murdered.

The Court faithfully followed the previous judgment in *Ireland v United Kingdom*[59] and reiterated that: 'In order to determine whether any particular

[52] Ibid. [53] Ibid.

[54] *Soering v United Kingdom* (App No 14038/88), report, 19 January 1989, not reported, paras 96–97.

[55] *Aksoy v Turkey* (App No 21987/93), judgment, 18 December 1996, Reports 1996-VI, 2260.

[56] Van Dijk et al (n 19 above), 407.

[57] *Aksoy v Turkey* (n 55 above), para 46. See also *Aksoy v Turkey* (App No 21987/93), report, 23 October 1995, not reported, para 52.

[58] Ibid, para 80.

[59] *Ireland v United Kingdom*, judgment (n 25 above).

form of ill-treatment should be qualified as torture, the Court must have regard to the distinction drawn in Article 3 between this notion and that of inhuman or degrading treatment. As it has remarked before, this distinction would appear to have been embodied in the Convention to allow the special stigma of "torture" to attach only to deliberate inhuman treatment causing very serious and cruel suffering.'[60] According to the Court, the 'Palestinian hanging' had been deliberately inflicted on to the applicant. Furthermore, it appeared to have been administered with the aim of obtaining admissions or information from the applicant. The Court also observed that it had caused severe pain and caused a temporary paralysis of the applicant's arms. Thus, it was found that this treatment was of such a cruel and serious nature that it could only constitute torture in breach of Article 3 of the ECHR.

As part of its examination of Article 13 of the ECHR, the Court held that where an individual has an arguable claim that he has been tortured by agents of the state, the notion of an effective remedy entails, in addition to payment of compensation where appropriate, the conduct of a thorough and effective investigation capable of leading to the identification and punishment of the culprits. In support of this, the Court noted that the nature of the protection enshrined in Article 3 of the ECHR had implications for Article 13. Given the fundamental importance of the prohibition against torture, Article 13 imposes an obligation on states to carry out a thorough and effective investigation of incidents of torture. In order to support this conclusion, the Court observed that:

> [i]t is true that no express provision exists in the Convention such as can be found in Article 12 of the 1984 United Nations Convention Against Torture and Other Cruel, Inhuman or Degrading Treatment or Punishment, which imposes a duty to proceed to a 'prompt and impartial' investigation whenever there is a reasonable ground to believe that an act of torture has been committed. However, in the Court's view, such a requirement is implicit in the notion of an 'effective remedy' under Article 13.[61]

Thus, the Court used the CAT to support its interpretation of the ECHR and to provide a stronger, albeit still insufficient, legal base to this duty.

In 1997 the Court issued its judgment in the *Aydín v Turkey* case,[62] where it also followed the *Ireland* judgment and used the CAT to provide a legal basis for the obligation contained in Article 13 of the ECHR. The *Aydín* case concerned the alleged torture and rape of a 17-year-old Kurdish girl while in the custody of the State security forces. The victim claimed that a violation of Article 3 of the ECHR had occurred, and also that she had no access to a court or effective remedy in this respect (Articles 6(1) and 13 of the ECHR). It is noteworthy that the applicant invoked reports of the European Committee for the Prevention of

[60] *Aksoy v Turkey* (n 55 above), para 63.

[61] Ibid, para 98. See also *Aydín v Turkey* (App No 23178/94), judgment, 25 September 1997, Reports 1997-VII, 1866, para 103. See ch III, 4.5 and 4.6.

[62] *Aydín v Turkey* (n 61 above).

Torture and the United Nations Committee Against Torture.[63] Furthermore, Amnesty International intervened in the case and drew attention to current legal standards on the investigation of rape allegations, in particular in Articles 11 and 12 of the CAT.

When evaluating the claim under Article 3 of the ECHR, the Court reiterated its stand on the distinction between torture and other inhuman treatment. It was recalled that the ECHR attaches the special stigma of torture only to deliberate inhuman treatment causing very serious and cruel suffering (as observed in *Ireland v United Kindgom*). As the ECHR did not contain any references to rape, the Court decided to characterize this behaviour as torture under Article 3. It was found that the accumulation of physical and mental violence inflicted on the applicant and the especially cruel act of rape amounted to torture in breach of Article 3. Surprisingly, the Court resorted in this child rights case to the CAT instead of the Convention on the Rights of the Child (CRC). Using the CRC would have been more appropriate in this context, given that this instrument is more specific than the CAT and prohibits sexual abuse of children. However, having classified rape as torture, the Court probably preferred to refer to the CAT which, unlike the CRC, contains a precise definition of torture.[64]

When examining Article 13 of the ECHR, the Court reaffirmed that there is a positive obligation to conduct an investigation under this provision. Referring to the *Aksoy* judgment,[65] the Court noted once again that 'no express provision exists in the Convention such as can be found in Article 12 of the 1984 United Nations Convention Against Torture or Other Cruel, Inhuman or Degrading Treatment or Punishment, which imposes a duty to proceed to a "prompt and impartial" investigation whenever there is a reasonable ground to believe that an act of torture has been committed'.[66] In the instant case, the Court found that there was a breach of Article 13 of the ECHR since the authorities had carried out an incomplete enquiry and there had been no meaningful measures taken to establish the veracity of the allegations. Thus, as in the *Askoy* case, the Court reaffirmed its willingness to use the CAT as an interpretative tool to strengthen the legal base of the positive obligation inherent in Article 13 of the ECHR. Nonetheless, in *Assenov and others v Bulgaria*,[67] in a judgment handed down a year later, the Court departed from this tendency and grounded the obligation to investigate in Article 3 of the ECHR read in conjunction with Article 1.[68]

63 *Aydín v Turkey* (App No 23178/94), report, 7 March 1996, not reported, para 193; *Aydín v Turkey* (n 61 above), para 122.

64 See ch IV, 4.5 and 6.

65 *Aksoy v Turkey* (n 55 above).

66 *Aydín v Turkey* (n 61 above), para 103.

67 *Assenov and others v Bulgaria* (App No 24760/94), judgment, 28 October 1998, Reports 1998-VIII, 3264, para 102.

68 Ibid, para 32. This reasoning was later followed in *Sevtap Verznedargolu v Turkey* (App No 32357/96), judgment, 11 April 2000, not reported, para 32.

2.1.2.2 A Shift Away from the Ireland Judgment

In 1999 the Court began to depart from its reasoning in *Ireland v United Kingdom*,[69] and this tendency has continued until the present day; however, the Court has not completely moved away from the judgment. In the *Selmouni v France* case,[70] the Court considered an application brought by a Netherlands and Moroccan national, who was held in police custody in Bobigny for four days and questioned by police officers in connection with drug-trafficking proceedings. An expert medical report ordered by the investigating judge concluded that the injuries visible on the applicant's body had been sustained at a time which corresponded to the applicant's detention in police custody.

Before the Court, the applicant alleged that, due to the ill-treatment he had suffered in police custody and the length of the domestic proceedings, there had been a violation of Articles 3 and 6(1) of the ECHR. According to the applicant, the severity and cruelty of the suffering inflicted justified classifying the acts as torture within the meaning of Article 3. The Commission had previously held that the treatment must have been inflicted on the applicant deliberately and with the aim of obtaining a confession. Moreover, it was found that the treatment was of such a serious and cruel nature that it could only be described as torture.[71]

As part of the complaint under Article 3 of the ECHR, the Court made substantive references to the CAT and even applied some of its principles to the case at hand. Its approach seems to have originated from the Commission's reasoning in the same case. In fact, the Commission had referred in its report to the CAT in the context of Article 3 of the ECHR. When it drew a distinction between torture and inhuman treatment, the Commission relied on both the *Ireland* judgment and the CAT. The Commission maintained that it was the intention that the Convention should attach the special stigma of torture only to deliberate inhuman treatment causing very serious and cruel suffering.[72] In support of this, the Commission also referred to the definition of torture enshrined in Article 1 of the CAT.[73] It was found that torture had been committed in the instant case and that a violation of Article 3 of the ECHR had occurred.[74] A dissenting Member criticized the Commission for resorting to Article 1 of the CAT on grounds that it was exterior to the ECHR, did not contribute to the understanding of Article 3 of the ECHR, and allowed the Commission to bypass previous case law.[75]

The Court followed the Commission's approach and reiterated that the Convention attached the special stigma of torture only to deliberate inhuman

[69] *Ireland v United Kingdom*, judgment (n 25 above).
[70] *Selmouni v France* (App No 25803/94), judgment, 28 July 1999, Reports 1999-V, 149.
[71] *Selmouni v France* (App No 25803/94), report, 11 December 1977, not reported, para 70.
[72] Ibid, para 67. [73] Ibid.
[74] Ibid, para 70. A member of the Commission dissented from this finding on grounds that the purposive element of torture enshrined in Article 1 of the CAT had not been demonstrated: ibid, separate concurring opinion of MK Herrdl.
[75] Ibid, separate concurring opinion of MJ-C Soyer, para 6.

treatment causing very serious and cruel suffering. It supported this statement by referring to Articles 1 and 16 of the CAT, which in its opinion made the same distinction.[76] It has been pointed out, however, that despite the reference to these articles, the Court insisted on its traditional distinction; in effect, it had overlooked the definition of torture in the CAT, reading Articles 1 and 16 of the CAT to corroborate its traditional approach.[77]

The Court went on to consider whether the treatment inflicted could constitute inhuman and degrading treatment. It was found that the various medical certificates as well as the applicant's statements established that he had undergone physical and mental suffering. In the Court's view, it was also demonstrated 'that the pain or suffering was inflicted on the applicant intentionally for the purpose of, *inter alia*, making him confess to the offence which he was suspected of having committed'.[78] These acts could arouse feelings of fear, anguish, and inferiority capable of humiliating and debasing the applicant, thereby possibly breaking his physical and moral resistance. Referring to the *Ireland* judgment, the Court therefore found that the suffering was sufficiently serious to render the treatment inflicted in the instant case inhuman and degrading.[79]

It remained to be established whether the pain and suffering inflicted on the applicant could be defined as severe within the meaning of Article 1 of the CAT. According to the Court, the 'severity' in Article 1 of the ECHR was the same as the 'minimum severity' requirement in Article 3 of the ECHR, that is relative.[80] It depended on all the circumstances of the case, such as the duration of the treatment, its physical or mental effects, as well as the sex, age, state of health of the victim, etc.[81] The Court noted that it had previously concluded in the *Aksoy*[82] and *Aydín*[83] cases that there had to be treatment which could only be described as torture.[84] Nonetheless, given that the Convention is a 'living instrument', the Court considered 'that certain acts which were classified in the past as "inhuman and degrading treatment" as opposed to "torture" could be classified differently in future'.[85] Furthermore, the Court emphasized that 'the increasingly high standard being required in the area of the protection of human rights and fundamental liberties correspondingly and inevitably requires greater firmness in assessing breaches of the fundamental values of democratic societies'.[86] The Court considered that 'the physical and mental violence, considered as a whole, committed on the applicant's person caused "severe" pain and suffering and was particularly serious and cruel'.[87] Thus, it was found to constitute torture in the sense of Article 3 of the ECHR. Clearly, the language and reasoning used in this

[76] Ibid, para 97. [77] Rodley (n 22 above), 477.
[78] *Selmouni v France* (n 70 above), para 98 (italics in original). [79] Ibid, para 99.
[80] Ibid, para 100. [81] Ibid. [82] *Aksoy v Turkey* (n 55 above).
[83] *Aydín v Turkey* (n 61 above). [84] *Selmouni v France* (n 70 above), para 101.
[85] Ibid. [86] Ibid. [87] Ibid, para 105.

part of the judgment were intended to mark a departure from the *Ireland* line of reasoning.

It is also noteworthy that, as part of his complaint under Article 6(1) of the ECHR, the applicant contended that an obligation to investigate was expressly laid down in Article 12 of the CAT.[88] The Court, however, handled this issue as part of the preliminary objection entered by the Government that the applicant's complaint under Article 3 of the ECHR could not be examined because he had not exhausted the remedies. In the Court's view, the issue was not so much whether there was an enquiry (it appeared that there was one), but rather whether it was effective. The Court reiterated that, if an individual has an arguable claim that a violation of Article 3 occurred, the notion of effective remedy entails that an investigation must be conducted.[89] While the Court did not invoke the CAT in this part of its reasoning, it did recall its previous case law where substantial references to this instrument were made.[90] It therefore appears that the legal basis used by the Court to entrench the duty to investigate torture allegations was different from the one used in previous case law.[91]

A year later, the Court made several findings of torture in cases against Turkey.[92] These cases demonstrate that the Court was more willing to classify certain behaviour as torture. In addition, the Court referred to the CAT and integrated the definition of torture in Article 1 into its case law. Although the Court was not willing to depart completely from its reasoning in the *Ireland* judgment, it nonetheless laid much emphasis on the purpose of the definition of torture. In *Dikme v Turkey*[93] the Court considered the case of a Turkish citizen who was arrested on 10 February 1992 and taken into custody by the Anti-Terrorist Brigade of the Istanbul Security Police on suspicion of having carried out a number of attacks in the name of an extreme left-wing armed group *Devrimci Sol* (revolutionary left). After being brought before a judge, he was examined by the prison doctor who noted in his medical report signs of approximately 20 abrasions, cuts, and grazes, mainly on the arms and legs. Before the Court, the applicant complained of violations under Articles 3, 5(2), 5(3), and 6(3)(c) of the ECHR.

When assessing the complaint under Article 3, the Court reiterated that the Convention was a living instrument and that certain acts which had been classified as inhuman and degrading as opposed to torture might be classified differently in

[88] Ibid, para 108. [89] Ibid, para 79.

[90] Here, the Court referred to *Aksoy v Turkey* (n 55 above), and *Assenov and others v Bulgaria* (n 67 above).

[91] *Aksoy v Turkey* (n 55 above); *Aydín v Turkey* (n 61 above).

[92] *Salman v Turkey* (App No 21986/93), judgment, 27 June 2000, Reports 2000-VII, 365; *İlhan v Turkey* (App No 22277/93), judgment, 27 June 2000, Reports 2000-VII, 267; *Dikme v Turkey* (App No 20869/92), judgment, 11 July 2000, Reports 2000-VIII, 223; *Akkoç v Turkey* (App Nos 22947/93; 22948/93), judgment, 10 October 2000, Reports 2000-X, 389.

[93] *Dikme v Turkey* (n 92 above).

the future. Thus, the Court went on to distinguish between torture and inhuman or degrading treatment and to examine whether the treatment inflicted upon the applicant could constitute torture.[94] The Court reiterated its standard view that the distinction between both types of conduct was drawn in the Convention in order to attach a special stigma to deliberate inhuman treatment causing very serious and cruel suffering.[95] In support of this statement, the Court noted that a similar distinction was made in Article 1 of the CAT and cited the definition of torture therein. It is noteworthy that the Government had invoked the CAT at the hearing in support of its argument that the medical reports, relied on by the applicant, did not certify any form of ill-treatment within the meaning of the CAT.[96] The Court concluded that the violence inflicted on the applicant, taken as a whole and having regard to its purpose and duration, was particularly serious and cruel and amounted to torture in breach of Article 3 of the ECHR.[97] Thus, in this judgment the Court treated the definition of the CAT as an interpretation aid as well as an integral part of its reasoning.

In the other cases,[98] where findings of torture were made that year, the Court used a different language as well as taking a slightly different approach under Article 3 of the ECHR. These cases concerned allegations of torture which were inflicted by state agents on applicants whilst they were detained. As part of its assessment of the applicants' complaints under Article 3, the Court recalled that the Convention intended to attach a special stigma to torture.[99] It cited here the *Ireland* judgment[100] as a source of this reasoning, and reaffirmed its willingness to continue following this case. At the same time, however, the Court noted that:

> [i]n addition to the severity of the treatment, there is a purposive element, as recognised in the United Nations Convention Against Torture and Other Cruel, Inhuman or Degrading Treatment or Punishment, which came into force on 26 June 1987, and which defines torture in terms of the intentional infliction of severe pain or suffering with the aim, *inter alia*, of obtaining information, inflicting punishment or intimidating.[101]

Thus, the Court combined its approach in the *Ireland* case with the approach taken under the CAT. It therefore appears to have reaffirmed that the CAT

[94] Ibid, paras 92–96. [95] Ibid, para 93. [96] Ibid, para 94. [97] Ibid, para 96.

[98] *Salman v Turkey* (n 92 above); *İlhan v Turkey* (n 92 above); *Akkoç v Turkey* (n 92 above).

[99] *Salman v Turkey* (n 92 above), para 114; *İlhan v Turkey* (n 92 above), para 85; *Akkoç v Turkey* (n 92 above), para 114.

[100] *Ireland v United Kingdom*, judgment (n 25 above), para 167.

[101] *Salman v Turkey* (n 92 above), para 114 (italics in original); *İlhan v Turkey* (n 92 above), para 85; *Akkoç v Turkey* (n 92 above), para 114. Although these three cases involved findings of torture, the same reasoning was also used in a case giving rise to a finding of inhuman and degrading treatment: see *Mahmut Kaya v Turkey* (App No 22535/93), judgment, 28 March 2000, Reports 2000-III, 149.

constitutes an important benchmark in the assessment of allegations of ill-treatment under the ECHR.

In 2001 the Court pointed out, in addition, that the severity of suffering was not always an important element to consider, and thereby appeared to distance itself further from its reasoning in the *Ireland* judgment. In the *Keenan v United Kindgom* judgment,[102] the Court considered the application of a British national whose son had died in prison from asphyxia caused by self-suspension. The applicant alleged that her son died from suicide in prison due to a failure to protect his life by the prison authorities, that he had suffered inhuman and degrading treatment due to the conditions of detention, and that she had no effective remedy in respect of her complaints. As part of its assessment of the complaint under Article 3 of the ECHR, the Court considered that, '[w]hile it is true that the severity of suffering, physical or mental, attributable to a particular measure has been a significant consideration in many of the cases decided by the Court under Article 3 of the ECHR, there are circumstances where proof of the actual effect on the person may not be a major factor'.[103] For instance, in respect of a person deprived of his or her liberty, recourse to physical force which has not been made strictly necessary by his or her own conduct diminishes human dignity and is in principle an infringement of the right set out in Article 3. Similarly, it was observed that treatment of a mentally ill person may be incompatible with the standards imposed by Article 3, even though that person may not be able, or capable of, pointing to any specific ill-effects.[104]

One commentator has accurately pointed out that the Court's findings in the *Keenan* and *Selmouni* cases 'suggest that the level of pain inflicted is increasingly a less determinate factor, as acts it once considered only "inhuman" could now rise to the level of torture, depending on the context and purpose for which physical force is employed'.[105] Indeed, with an increasing case law and a widening range of situations falling under Article 3 of the ECHR, the Court seems to have opted for a more flexible and nuanced approach to the distinction between torture and cruel or inhuman treatment.[106] It remains the case, however, that the Court has continued to distinguish both concepts and has not completely moved away from its traditional standpoint.

In the same year (2001), the Court handed down a landmark case on state immunities—analysed in Chapter VII[107]—where it considered the *jus cogens* nature of the prohibition on torture. In *Al-Adsani v United Kindgom*,[108] the Court examined the case of a British and Kuwaiti national, who was allegedly tortured in Kuwait in 1991 by order of a Kuwaiti Sheikh. In British civil proceedings, the

[102] *Keenan v United Kingdom* (App No 27229/95), judgment, 3 April 2001, Reports 2001-III, 149.
[103] Ibid, para 113. [104] Ibid. [105] De Vos (n 19 above), 7.
[106] See also Malcolm D Evans, 'Getting to Grips with Torture' (April 2002) 51 Int'l Comp LQ 365, 373. [107] See 2.2 and 3.
[108] *Al-Adsani v United Kingdom* (App No 35763/97), judgment, 12 December 2001, Reports 2001-XI, 79.

applicant sought compensation against the Sheikh and the State of Kuwait and, later, against two other individuals. The British Court of Appeal granted immunity to Kuwait on the basis that the circumstances of the case did not constitute an exception to the immunity principle under the terms of the British State Immunity Act 1978. The applicant argued that the British courts, by granting immunity from suit to the State of Kuwait, failed to secure enjoyment of his right not to be tortured and denied him access to a court, contrary to Articles 3, 6(1), and 13 of the ECHR.

The Court found (by 9 to 8) that there was no violation of Articles 3 and 6 of the ECHR. It appears to have agreed only in part with the applicant's argument that the prohibition on torture constitutes a *jus cogens* norm, which takes precedence over treaty law and other rules of international law. The majority emphasized that the prohibition on torture is one of the fundamental values of a democratic society and that there is a 'growing recognition of the overriding importance of the prohibition of torture'.[109] As evidence of this trend, the Court referred, *inter alia*, to Articles 2 (obligation on part of state to prevent torture) and 4 (obligation to implement the offence of torture in domestic criminal law) of the CAT.

The majority further quoted a statement from the *Furundzija* judgment,[110] where the International Criminal Tribunal for the former Yugoslavia observed that the prohibition of torture had become a *jus cogens* norm and that it had attained the status of a peremptory norm. However, according to the Court, the case at hand did not concern 'as in *Furundzija* and *Pinochet*, the criminal liability of an individual for alleged acts of torture, but the immunity of a State in a civil suit for damages in respect of acts of torture within the territory of that State'.[111] The Court observed that none of the international legal instruments it had enumerated earlier related to civil proceedings and state immunity. Thus, in its view, it was not established in international law that there should be an exception to the application of the rule on state immunity in civil proceedings for damages of torture committed outside the forum state. Following this reasoning, it would appear that the *jus cogens* norm of prohibition on torture only prevails in criminal proceedings.

It is important to note that the Court was the first international court to address the trumping effect of *jus cogens* over state immunity at the level of international law.[112] Despite this, the majority's reasoning was artificial and contained contradictions. While the Court recognized that the prohibition of torture has the status of a *jus cogens* norm and precedes other norms of international law, it also accepted that—given the absence of an established rule of international law—it

[109] Ibid, para 60.

[110] *Prosecutor v Anto Furundzija*, judgment, ICTY, 10 December 1998, IT-95–17/1-T (1999) 38 ILM 317.

[111] *Al-Adsani v United Kingdom* (n 108 above), para 61.

[112] Ed Bates, 'The Al-Adsani Case, State Immunity and the International Legal Prohibition on Torture' (2003) 3(2) HRLR 193, 221.

does not have this status in civil proceedings. It is difficult to imagine that a *jus cogens* norm changes its status from one situation to the next and is selectively peremptory. Indeed, if this were the case, the norm would no longer be peremptory. The Court's reasoning with regard to the effect of *jus cogens* norms was therefore strained and legally dubious.[113]

2.1.2.3 More Recent Case Law

In subsequent case law, the Court resorted, as it did in the Turkish cases outlined above, to a combination of purpose and severity of suffering requirement, basing itself on the *Ireland* judgment[114] and the CAT. In *Ilaşcu and others v Moldova and Russia*,[115] handed down in 2004, the Court reiterated that the Convention attaches the special stigma of torture to deliberate inhuman treatment causing very serious and cruel suffering. Further, it noted once again that the same distinction is drawn in Article 1 of the CAT and recalled the definition of torture.[116] It also reiterated that the requirement of severity is relative and relates to all the circumstances of the case.[117]

A year later, in the *Sükeyla Aydin v Turkey* judgment,[118] the Court's reasoning concerning the distinction between torture and other inhuman treatment was textually identical to the Turkish torture cases discussed above.[119] In the *Sükeyla Aydin* case, the applicant claimed that she and her husband had suffered harassment from the Turkish security forces and the police due to their trade union activities. While she had been released, her husband never returned and was subsequently found dead. The applicant claimed that she had been subjected to inhuman and degrading treatment and that her husband was tortured. She also claimed that her husband had been killed by State agents and that the authorities failed to carry out an investigation. In her view, he had been killed for his trade union activities. As previously, the Court observed that torture carried with it a special stigma and that both the severity of the treatment and the purposive element (recognized in the CAT) needed to be considered when distinguishing between torture and other ill-treatment.[120] The Court also recalled the definition of torture in Article 1 of the CAT. It reaffirmed its intention to use this reasoning as its standard formula, at least in this type of case. Although the Court found that there was insufficient evidence to conclude that torture had occurred, it nonetheless considered that the treatment inflicted on the applicant's husband amounted to inhuman treatment in breach of Article 3

[113] See ch VII, 3.2.2.
[114] *Ireland v United Kingdom*, judgment (n 25 above).
[115] *Ilaşcu and others v Moldova and Russia* (App No 48787/99), judgment, 8 July 2004, Reports 2004-VII, 179.
[116] Ibid, para 426; *Selmouni v France* (n 70 above), para 97.
[117] *Ilaşcu and others v Moldova and Russia* (n 115 above), para 427.
[118] *Sükeyla Aydin v Turkey* (App No 25660/94), judgment, 24 May 2005, not reported.
[119] *Salman v Turkey* (n 92 above); *İlhan v Turkey* (n 92 above); *Akkoç v Turkey* (n 92 above). See nn 92–101 above, together with accompanying text.
[120] *Sükeyla Aydin v Turkey* (n 118 above), para 195.

of the ECHR. As regards the treatment of the applicant, there was no evidence to support her complaint.

Most recently, in the *Jalloh v Germany* judgment,[121] the dissenting judges resorted more to the CAT than the majority. The *Jalloh* case concerned a Sierra Leone national who was arrested on suspicion of drug-trafficking in Germany. Plain clothes policemen had seen the applicant taking small plastic bags out of his mouth and handing them over for money. He was taken to a hospital where he was forced to take emetics (medication causing vomiting) through a tube inserted in his nose. The applicant claimed that he had been given emetics by force and that the evidence had been obtained illegally. Further, he alleged that the German authorities had violated Articles 3, 6, and 8 of the ECHR. The Court found that he had been subjected to inhuman and degrading treatment in breach of Article 3 of the ECHR. Although the Court did not refer to the CAT as part of its examination of this provision, it did refer to the Convention as part of its assessment of the claim under Article 6 of the ECHR.

Considering the complaint under Article 6, the Court noted that the evidence had been obtained in a manner that violated Article 3. This raised serious issues as to the fairness of the proceedings. It was reiterated that pursuant to Article 15 of the CAT statements which are established to have been made as a result of torture shall not be used as evidence in proceedings against the victim of torture.[122] Although the treatment inflicted on the applicant did not amount to torture, the Court did not conclude that evidence obtained through inhuman and degrading treatment could render a trial unfair; this question was left open. It was crucial in the case that the evidence was obtained through a measure which breached one of the ECHR rights and that it was a decisive element in securing the applicant's conviction. Moreover, according to the Court, the public interest in securing the applicant's conviction did not have such weight as to allow the use of the evidence at trial. Thus, it was found that the use of evidence obtained by forced administration of emetics in this case rendered the trial unfair under Article 6(1) of the ECHR.

The dissenting judges in this case made certain comments which clarified further the Court's use of the CAT in its case law. Judge Zupančič observed that in *Selmouni v France*[123] the Court integrated Article 1 of the CAT into its own case law. Using the definition of torture enshrined in that provision, he found that torture is composed of four elements. First, it is a *delictum proprium* (it can only be committed by a public official); secondly, it requires a specific intent; thirdly, it occurs as a consequence of the conduct of public officials; and, fourthly, it causes severe physical or mental pain.[124] According to his view, the decisive question in the case at hand was whether the particular conduct had caused severe pain and suffering. He observed that torture is an aggravated form of inhuman and

[121] *Jalloh v Germany* (App No 54810/00), judgment, 11 July 2006, not reported.

[122] Ibid, para 105.

[123] *Selmouni v France* (n 70 above).

[124] *Jalloh v Germany* (n 121 above), concurring opinion of Judge Zupančič.

degrading treatment, and whether it had actually occurred was a question of fact. Thus, the distinction between torture and other treatment described here differs from the CAT, as it puts more emphasis on the severity of pain requirement.

Subsequently, Judge Zupančič considered the question of using extracted drug packages as evidence in order to obtain the applicant's conviction. Using Article 15 of the CAT as a benchmark, he commented on the Court's case law relating to the exclusion of evidence under the ECHR. In his view, the Court came to the conclusion in *Saunders v United Kingdom*[125] that only audible words extracted from the mouth of a suspect constituted inadmissible evidence. In his opinion, this was in clear contradiction of Article 15, which mandates the strict exclusion of all evidence if it is obtained through torture, independently of whether it is verbal or non-verbal.[126] Judge Zupančič's reasoning in the instant case was courageous because it resorted extensively to the CAT as a benchmark in the assessment the Court's previous case law.

An interesting point was also made with regard to Article 15 of the CAT by Judges Ress, Pellopnää, Baka, and Sikuta in their joint dissenting opinions. While they agreed with the principle enshrined in this provision, they nonetheless expressed their reservation as to its extension to other violations of the Convention (as in this case). They observed that '[t]he case-law according to which the admissibility of evidence is primarily a matter for regulation under domestic law... is an important expression of the principle of subsidiarity, exceptions to which should be construed narrowly'.[127] They did not consider it necessary to pursue the matter further, given that the majority indicated that it would leave open the question of whether evidence obtained as a result of inhuman and degrading treatment automatically rendered a trial unfair. While the judges' observations in this dissenting opinion were rather traditional, they have contributed towards understanding the reasons why the Court abstained from considering this issue further.

Although lacking any explicit references to the CAT, another very important judgment was issued by the Court in *Saadi v Italy*.[128] In this case, the Court reaffirmed the absolute nature of Article 3 of the ECHR, holding that the previously established test for *non-refoulement* was not subject to alteration or balancing on the basis of the perceived dangerousness of the individual concerned. This case concerned a Tunisian national who was to be deported to his homeland where he had been sentenced to 20 years' imprisonment for membership of a terrorist organization. The applicant argued, *inter alia*, that his deportation would expose him to the risk of being subjected to treatment contrary to Article 3 of

[125] *Saunders v United Kingdom* (App No 54810/00), judgment, 17 December 1996, Reports 1996-VI, 2044.

[126] For the arguments in this paragraph, see *Jalloh v Germany* (n 121 above), concurring opinion of Judge Zupančič.

[127] *Jalloh v Germany* (n 121 above), joint dissenting opinion of Judges Ress, Pellopnää, Baka, and Sikuta.

[128] *Saadi v Italy* (App No 37201/06), judgment, 28 February 2008, not yet reported.

the ECHR. The Court crucially reiterated that, in order to determine whether there was a risk of ill-treatment, it had to examine the general situation in the receiving country. In the past, it had 'often attached importance to the information contained in recent reports from independent international human-rights-protection associations such as Amnesty International, or governmental sources, including the US State Department'.[129] When the sources available described a general situation, the applicant's specific allegations in a given case needed to be corroborated by other evidence. In this case, the international reports mentioned numerous and regular cases of torture and ill-treatment of persons accused of terrorist activities. Using this information, the Court found that the applicant belonged to a group at risk of ill-treatment.

The Court also observed that it could not underestimate the danger of terrorism and noted that states were facing considerable difficulties in protecting their communities from terrorist violence. However, that should not call into question the absolute nature of Article 3 of the ECHR. Contrary to the argument of the United Kingdom as third-party intervener, the Court considered that it was not possible to weigh the risk that a person might be subjected to ill-treatment against his dangerousness to the community.[130] The prospect that he might pose a serious threat to the community did not diminish in any way the risk that he might suffer harm if deported. Thus, the Court reaffirmed the principle stated in the *Chahal v United Kingdom* judgment[131] that it is not possible to weigh the risk of ill-treatment against the reasons put forward for the expulsion in order to determine whether the responsibility of a state is engaged under Article 3. While the Court made no references to the CAT framework, it nonetheless upheld a principle enshrined in Article 2(2) of the CAT and in the decisions of the Committee Against Torture. In addition, Judge Zupančič reiterated, in his separate concurring opinion, that the *non-refoulement* rule in Article 3 of the ECHR (forbidding the expulsion of someone to another country if there are substantial grounds to believe that she/he would be subjected to torture or to inhuman or degrading treatment) had been used by the UN Committee Against Torture when applying the CAT.[132]

Overall, the Court has resorted in recent times to a mixed approach to the distinction between torture and other inhuman treatment. This approach has been based on the severity of pain and purpose elements. Both components appear to have been granted equal weight in the Court's latest assessments. It has been argued, however, that the 'severity of pain, although constituting an essential element of the definition of torture, is not a criteria distinguishing torture from cruel and inhuman treatment'.[133] Thus, following this line of reasoning, the question of whether cruel or inhuman treatment can also be classified as torture

129 Ibid, para 131. 130 Ibid, para 138.

131 *Chahal v United Kingdom* (App No 22414/93), judgment, 15 November 1996, Reports 1996-V, 1831, para 81.

132 *Saadi v Italy* (n 128 above), concurring opinion of Judge Zupančič.

133 Nowak (n 19 above), 821–822. See also Rodley (n 22 above), 491; De Vos (n 19 above), 7.

depends on the fulfilment of the requirements contained in Article 1 of the CAT, namely whether it corresponds to one of the purposes mentioned. Arguably, the Committee Against Torture has recently been leaning more towards a purpose-oriented approach.[134]

Despite the merits of this criticism, it appears that the current understanding of torture in the doctrine and in practice is still not unequivocal; numerous uncertainties remain as to the approach to be adopted towards the distinction between torture and other inhuman treatment.[135] Thus, it seems that the Court, which has not taken a stand on which approach should be followed, may have been influenced by the uncertainty of the debate at the international level. At the same time, however, the Court has contributed to the debate by using a mixed approach—or a compromise position—to the distinction between torture and other inhuman acts. This approach has important advantages for the protection of human rights, as it embraces a wide array of situations and allows the Court to proceed on a case-by-case basis. Further, using this type of assessment may be desirable with regard to torture that is difficult to evaluate and continues to evolve rapidly in the context of the fight against terrorism.

3. Case Law Referring to the Committee Against Torture

The decisions and judgments referring to the case law of the Committee Against Torture did not follow as clear an evolution as those referring only to the CAT. They can nonetheless be sub-divided into (1) cases relating to the relationship between the Committee and the Strasbourg bodies, (2) cases where the Court referred to the Committee's case law, and (3) cases where the reports of the Committee or of the Special Rapporteur were invoked. The first aspect of this case law is mainly procedural and explores the coexistence of the Committee and the Strasbourg framework. In these cases, there were few meaningful references which could teach us more about the reception process. The second and third aspects of this jurisprudence are more substantive and were prompted by the Court's need to support its interpretation of the ECHR or of the facts in a given case. These strands of the Strasbourg jurisprudence were generally marked by the Court's implicit tendency to follow the case law of the Committee. Overall, the Court's findings, especially in the area of refugee protection, appear to be converging with the standards set by the Committee Against Torture.

[134] Nowak (n 19 above), 822–829; De Vos (n 19 above), 7–8. See *Dragan Dimitrijevic v Serbia and Montenegro*, Communication No 207/2002, CAT/C/33/D/207/2002, 24 November 2004, Committee Against Torture, para 5.3; *Jovica Dimitrov v Serbia and Montenegro*, Communication No 171/2000, CAT/C/34/D/171/2000, 3 May 2005, Committee Against Torture, para 7.1; *Danilo Dimitrijevic v Serbia and Montenegro*, Communication No 172/00, CAT/C/35/D/172/2000, 16 November 2005, para 7.1.

[135] See nn 40 and 41 above and accompanying text.

3.1 Case Law on the Coexistence with the Committee

The provisions regulating concurrent jurisdiction are very similar under the CAT and the ECHR. They both efficiently reduce the likelihood of litispendence from occurring between bodies. Article 22(5)(a) of the CAT prevents the Committee Against Torture from considering a matter which is simultaneously being examined or has been previously examined under another procedure of international investigation or settlement. The substance of this provision is similar to Article 35(2)(b) of the ECHR which provides that the Court cannot examine a matter that 'has already been submitted to another procedure of international investigation or settlement and contains no relevant new information'. As has already been noted, this differs from Article 5(2)(a) of the First Optional Protocol to the ICCPR, which prevents the Human Rights Committee only from considering a complaint which is simultaneously being examined under another comparable procedure. Thus, the coexistence problems which characterize the relationship between the HRC and the Court do not occur as part of the relationship between the Committee Against Torture and the Court. Thus far, there have been no difficulties in the Strasbourg case law concerning the coexistence between the HRC and the Court. It should be noted, however, that the Strasbourg case law relating to the relationship between both bodies is scarce and the findings are limited. Thus, they provide little guidance regarding the Court's use of international law in this context.

In *Paez v Sweden*,[136] the Court considered a case where the applicant's brother had previously brought a very similar petition before the Committee Against Torture. The applicant was a Peruvian citizen who had claimed asylum in Sweden on grounds that he was a member of the Communist Party of Peru—Shining Path (*Partido Comunista del Perú-Sendero Luminoso*, PCP-SL). His asylum request was rejected and his expulsion ordered. Before the Commission, the applicant claimed that his expulsion to Peru would expose him to ill-treatment contrary to Article 3 of the ECHR. The decision to expel him was stayed following an indication to this effect by the Commission. The applicant's brother also claimed asylum, but his request was rejected and the decision to expel him was also stayed. The applicant lodged a fresh asylum request with the Swedish authorities. In the meantime, the Commission concluded, by 15 votes to 14, that the applicant's expulsion to Peru would not violate this provision.[137]

Subsequently, the Committee Against Torture examined a petition lodged by the applicant's brother.[138] The Committee found that Sweden had an obligation

[136] *Paez v Sweden* (App No 29482/95), judgment, 30 October 1997, Reports 1997-VII, 2436.

[137] *Paez v Sweden* (App No 29482/95), report, 6 December 1996, not reported, para 84. As part of its report, the Commission examined in detail the Committee's assessment of Peru's initial report, which was submitted as evidence by the parties. The Committee had noted that torture was being used extensively in connection with the investigation of acts of terrorism: ibid, para 36.

[138] *Gorki Ernesto Tapia Paez v Sweden*, Communication No 39/1996, 28 April 1997, CAT/C/18/D/39/1996, 28 April 1997, Committee Against Torture.

under the CAT to refrain from forcibly returning him to Peru. Having regard to these findings, the Swedish authorities granted the brother permanent residence in Sweden. Given that the applicant's case was in their view similar, the applicant was also granted a permanent residence permit. Taking the decisions of the Committee Against Torture and the Swedish authorities duly into consideration, the Court noted that the applicant had been granted permanent residence in Sweden and that the expulsion order against him had been revoked.[139] Further, the Court observed that the threat of potential violation had however been removed by virtue of the decision to grant him permanent residence in Sweden and the lifting of the expulsion order. In addition, there was no apparent public policy reason for continuing proceedings. Thus, the case was struck out of the list of cases and the Court was prevented from considering further the decision of the Committee. This case nonetheless demonstrates how the jurisdiction of the Court can overlap with that of the Committee Against Torture. While both the Court and the Committee are precluded from considering cases which were or are being considered by either one of them, it is yet to be demonstrated how this will be carried out.

The situation was similar in the *Hamid Ovihangy v Sweden* decision[140] handed down by the Court in 2004. The case concerned an Iranian national who claimed asylum in Sweden on grounds that he was of Kurdish descent and that he had taken part in anti-regime activities for which he had been detained and tortured. His request was rejected by the Swedish authorities who found that ethnic minorities were not regularly discriminated against in Iran and that the applicant's fears of reprisals on the part of Iranian authorities were exaggerated. He then filed a petition under the CAT which was rejected by the Committee.[141] The Committee Members found that 'the political activities that the petitioner claims to have carried out prior to and during the demonstrations in February 1999 are not of such a nature as to lead to the conclusion that he risks being tortured upon his return'.[142] The applicant claimed before the ECtHR that his expulsion would constitute, *inter alia*, inhuman treatment in breach of Article 3 of the ECHR. The Swedish authorities' attempt to enforce the expulsion order proved to be unsuccessful due to the applicant's fits of violence during the trip. Following the ECtHR's decision to apply Rule 39 of the Court's Rules, the domestic authorities stayed the enforcement of the expulsion order. The applicant was subsequently granted a permanent residence permit in Sweden, and he decided that he would not pursue his complaints before the Court. The case was therefore struck out of the list of cases, and the Court did not pronounce itself on the decision handed down earlier by the Committee Against Torture.

[139] *Paez v Sweden* (n 136 above), para 29.

[140] *Hamid Ovihangy v Sweden* (App No 44421/02), decision, 9 March 2004, not reported.

[141] *HO v Sweden,* Communication No 178/2001, CAT/C/27/D/178/2001, 13 November 2001, Committee Against Torture.

[142] Ibid, para 14.

From the foregoing analysis, it transpires that the cases relating to the coexistence of the Court and the Committee are scarce and largely inconclusive. They demonstrate that there is a certain structural interaction between the Court and the Committee. They were nonetheless prompted by the necessity to note that a similar, or the same, case had been introduced before the Committee Against Torture. As such, these references belong to the realm of necessary procedural or structural references, rather than to the realm of references which are based on the Court's discretion and which teach us more about its willingness to refer to international sources. Given that these two cases were struck out of the list, the Court has not yet had the opportunity to pronounce itself on a case which has also been brought before the Committee Against Torture. Thus, it still remains to be seen how the coexistence of the two bodies will be articulated in practice.

It appears, however, that there may be few cases of this type as claimants originating from the ECHR Contracting States may prefer to present their application before the ECtHR, which offers better prospects of enforcement. In addition, certain rights are better protected under the ECHR than the CAT. For instance, the prohibition against cruel, inhuman, or degrading treatment is more far-reaching under the ECHR than under the CAT. Article 3 of the CAT, which enshrines the principle of *non-refoulement*, applies as a general rule only to torture,[143] whereas Article 3 of the ECHR, containing the same principle, applies in addition to cruel, inhuman, or degrading treatment. Further, Article 1 of the ECHR stipulates that Members States shall take 'effective legislative, administrative, judicial or other measures to prevent acts of torture in any territory under its jurisdiction', while Article 16(1) of the CAT states only that a State Party 'shall undertake to prevent in any territory under its jurisdiction other acts of cruel, inhuman or degrading treatment or punishment which do not amount to torture as defined in article 1'. In fact, the requirements of *aut dedere au judicare* and establishing jurisdiction under the CAT (Articles 4, 5, and 7) do not apply to acts of cruel, inhuman, or degrading treatment. Thus, Article 1 of the ECHR goes further than the CAT by providing that '[t]he High Contracting Parties shall secure to everyone within their jurisdiction the rights and freedoms defined in Section I of this Convention'. These differences in the protection against cruel, inhuman, or degrading treatment may encourage those who have been mistreated but not tortured to lodge a complaint before the Court rather than the Committee.

143 Nowak and McArthur (n 9 above, 574–575, para 76) clarify that 'in exceptional cases a removal *per se* may amount to a violation of a State party's obligation to prevent acts of cruel, inhuman or degrading treatment in any territory under its jurisdiction. In such a case it could be assumed that Article 16(1) would be taken standing alone. However, in cases where a person might be subjected to cruel, inhuman or degrading treatment or punishment in the country of return, the Committee would not find a violation of Article 3 as this provision only applies to torture as defined in Article 1' (italics in original). However, see Art 16(2) of the CAT referring to expulsion and extradition, which would allow the application of the *non-refoulement* principle to cruel, inhuman, or degrading punishment on the basis of Art 3 of the ECHR and Art 7 of the ICCPR. Nowak and McArthur (n 9 above), 575, para 78.

Until now, this strand of the case law, marked by procedural and structural references, teaches little about the Court's tendency to refer to case law of the Committee Against Torture. Further, if more cases of this type reach the Court, there should not be excessive complications, given that the CAT and the ECHR regulate the coexistence of the two bodies in a similarly clear and coherent manner. Thus, unlike the relationship between the HRC and the Court, the interaction between the Committee Against Torture and the Court should be a harmonious one.[144]

3.2 Case Law Referring to the Committee's Activities

In this strand of the case law, the Commission and the Court resorted to the case law and the reports of the Committee Against Torture as well as to the reports of the Special Rapporteur on Torture. In most of the cases where the decisions of the Committee were invoked, the Court did not explicitly apply them but ruled in the same direction as the Committee, thereby maintaining the same standards in its reasoning. Further, in cases where the reports of the Committee and Special Rapporteur were relied on by the parties, the Court used them in the majority of cases in support of its findings and reasoning. Most of these cases concerned violations of rights of homosexuals, Roma, immigrants, and prisoners. Overall, this trend in the Strasbourg jurisprudence demonstrates that the Commission and the Court have resorted to standards which converge with those used by the Committee Against Torture.

3.2.1 Case Law Concerning the Committee's Jurisprudence

Most of the references to the jurisprudence of the Committee appeared in the decisions of the Commission. Nonetheless, some very substantial references to this jurisprudence can also be found in the judgments of the Court. In *X v The Netherlands*,[145] the Commission referred to the Committee's case law but did not rely on it as such. The case concerned a Turk of Kurdish origin who feared that, if expelled to Turkey, he could be killed or ill-treated given that he had been politically active and that he sympathized with the Kurdish people. His fears were also prompted by the fact that his brother was a public figure as a result of his political activities for the Kurdish people. Without success, the applicant had tried to obtain asylum and a residence permit in the Netherlands.

The Commission noted that the Committee Against Torture had found in *Ismail Alan v Switzerland*[146] that the practice of torture was still systematic in Turkey. Despite this observation, the Commission concluded that the applicant's

[144] See ch IV, 1.1 and 2.1.

[145] *X v The Netherlands* (App No 331247/96), report, 9 July 1998, not reported.

[146] *Ismail Alan v Switzerland*, Communication No 21/1995, CAT/C/16/D/21/1995, 8 May 1996, Committee Against Torture; *X v The Netherlands* (n 145 above), para 73.

submissions concerning his background and situation did not disclose that his personal position exposed him to special risks as a member of the Kurdish community in Turkey. Thus, it appears that the findings of the Committee were not so decisive in this case. The most important element for the Commission was the fact that the applicant's fears were not substantiated. The case was found to be admissible and the Commission expressed the opinion that the applicant's expulsion to Turkey would not infringe Article 3 of the ECHR.

In 2004, however, the Court appears to have followed the Committee's case law in the *F v United Kingdom*[147] and *IIN v The Netherlands*[148] decisions. These two cases concerned individuals who complained, *inter alia*, that if returned to Iran they would face a real risk of treatment contrary to Article 3 of the ECHR on grounds that they were homosexuals. Without success, they had applied for asylum in the Netherlands. In both cases, the Court cited the decision of the Committee Against Torture in *KSY v The Netherlands*.[149] In this case, the Committee had rejected an Iranian petitioner's case where he complained that the Netherlands would expel him to his home country where he had previously been detained and tortured for his homosexuality. The Committee also noted from different and reliable sources that there was no active policy of prosecution of charges of homosexuality in Iran.[150] The Court observed in *F v United Kingdom* and *IIN v The Netherlands* that the materials which it had examined did not disclose a situation of active persecution by the authorities of adults involved in consensual and private homosexual relationships. There were no recent substantiated instances of trials solely on the basis of such relationships. Further, the Court noted that the majority of sources demonstrated that in practice there was a certain tolerance of homosexuals. The few sources referring to trials or execution for homosexual offences were found to be vague and unspecific. While the Court acknowledged that the general situation in Iran did not foster the protection of human rights, it expressed the opinion that the applicant had not established that in his case there were substantial grounds to believe that he would be exposed to a real risk of being subjected to treatment contrary to Article 3 of the ECHR. Both applications were found to be inadmissible. In reaching its conclusion with regard to Article 3, the Court seems to have followed previous CAT case law. This indicates that the Court's decisions are converging with those of the Committee in this area.

In the same year (2004) the Court resorted once more to the Committee's case law and appears to have ruled in the same direction. In *F v United Kindgom*,[151] the Court considered the case of a Libyan national who had arrived in the United Kingdom with a short-term visitor's visa. He was given leave to enter for a month

[147] *F v United Kingdom* (App No 17341/03), decision, 22 June 2003, not reported.
[148] *IIN v The Netherlands* (App No 2035/04), decision, 9 December 2004, not reported.
[149] *KSY v The Netherlands*, Communication No 190/2001, CAT/C/30/D/190/2001, 26 May 2003, Committee Against Torture.
[150] Ibid, para 7.4.
[151] *F v United Kingdom* (App No 36812/02), decision, 31 August 2004, not reported.

after he stated that he was looking at colleges with a view to studying English. Subsequently, he was convicted for theft and sentenced to 14 days' imprisonment. He was also convicted for dishonest handling and again sentenced to imprisonment. He married a British citizen, had a child with her, and later separated. The applicant claimed asylum and said that, while he had never been politically active, a magazine published in the Middle East had indicated that he was wanted by the Libyan authorities. His request was rejected and a deportation order was issued against him. Before the Court, he alleged that, as a failed asylum-seeker, he would run a real risk of treatment contrary to Article 3 of the ECHR upon his return to Libya.

The Court referred to the Committee's decision in *FFZ v Denmark*,[152] which concerned the deportation to his home country of a Libyan national and alleged supporter of an Islamic movement. His asylum request had been previously turned down by the Danish authorities. The Committee rejected his complaint on the basis that the political activities in which he was involved were not of such nature as to conclude that he ran a real risk of being tortured upon his return. Further, he did not seem to have been particularly exposed to persecution by the Libyan authorities. The State Party in that case had noted, *inter alia*, that none of the arrests of the applicant related to his political activities and that an Amnesty International report provided no objective indication that he was subjected to gross violations. In the same vein, the Court did not find that there were any substantial grounds to believe that the applicant would run a real risk of treatment contrary to Article 3 of the ECHR on expulsion to Libya.

The tendency of the Court to rely on the Committee's decision continued in *Nachova and others v Bulgaria*.[153] In this judgment, the Court considered the case of Bulgarian nationals of Roma origin whose relatives had been killed by a military policeman whilst trying to arrest them. The relatives who were killed were two conscripts in a division of the army dealing with the construction of apartment blocks and other civilian projects. They had been arrested for repeated absences without leave and sentenced to several months' imprisonment. Later, they escaped from a construction site where they were working and went to the home of a relative. Four military policemen were subsequently sent to arrest them. The two men attempted to escape but, following a warning, they were shot and killed by the policeman.

The applicants complained that their relatives had been deprived of their lives in violation of Article 2 of the ECHR and that the prejudice and hostile attitudes towards persons of Roma origin had played a decisive role in the events leading up to their deaths in breach of Article 14. The Court recalled a decision of the

[152] *FFZ v Denmark*, Communication No 180/2001, A/57/44, 30 April 2002, Committee Against Torture.

[153] *Nachova and others v Bulgaria (Preliminary Objections)* (App Nos 43577/98; 43579/98), judgment, 26 February 2004, not reported.

Committee Against Torture, *Hajrizi Dzemajl and others v Yugoslavia*,[154] where it was found that a mob action by Montenegro residents who destroyed a Roma settlement in the presence of police officers was committed with a significant level of racial motivation.[155] Moreover, the policemen, who were informed of the risk faced by the complainants and were present on the scene, had acquiesced to the acts; this was found to constitute an act of cruel, inhuman, or degrading treatment in violation of Article 16(1) of the CAT. In addition, the Committee was of the view that the investigation conducted by the authorities in the case did not satisfy the requirements of Articles 12 and 13 of the CAT.

In relation to the complaint under Article 14 of the ECHR, the Court recalled that states have a general obligation under Article 2 to conduct an effective investigation in cases of deprivation of life. Further, when investigating violent incidents, in particular deaths at the hands of state agents, state authorities have the additional duty to take all reasonable steps to uncover racist motives and to establish whether ethnic hatred played a role in the events.[156] The Court found that in the instant case the burden of proof shifted to the respondent Government which had to demonstrate, on the basis of additional evidence or explanation, that the relevant events were not induced by discriminatory attitudes on the part of State agents. The Government had not, however, offered any such explanation. The Court further observed that there were repeated cases of alleged police brutality against Roma in Bulgaria in which it had found that law enforcement officers had subjected Roma to violence resulting in death. It was also noted that many other incidents of alleged police brutality against Roma in Bulgaria had been reported, *inter alia*, by the UN bodies.[157] Finally, the Court found that a violation of Article 14 of the ECHR (prohibition on discrimination), taken together with Article 2, had occurred in relation to the shootings themselves and in the absence of any investigation into whether discriminatory attitudes had played a role. Thus, the Court appears to have ruled in the same direction as the Committee Against Torture in *Hajrizi Dzemajl and others v Yugoslavia*, where it was considered that the action against Roma residents was motivated by racial attitudes. This has ensured that the standards available under the ECHR are the same as those under the CAT.

The Grand Chamber, however, delivered a more subtle judgment a year later and departed from the Committee's reasoning.[158] While the Grand Chamber had referred briefly to the *Hajrizi Dzemajl and others v Yugoslavia* decision, as a relevant source of international practice, it did not follow this case. Unlike the Court, the Grand Chamber found that there had been no violation of Article 14

[154] *Hajrizi Dzemajl and others v Yugoslavia*, Communication No 161/2000, CAT/C/29/D/161/2000, 21 November 2002, Committee Against Torture; *Nachova and others v Bulgaria* (n 153 above), para 72.

[155] *Hajrizi Dzemajl and others v Yugoslavia* (n 154 above), para 9.2.

[156] *Nachova and others v Bulgaria* (n 153 above), para 158.

[157] Ibid, para 174.

[158] *Nachova and others v Bulgaria* (App Nos 43577/98; 43579/98), judgment, 6 July 2005, Reports 2005-VII, 1.

of the ECHR, taken in conjunction with Article 2, in respect of the allegation that the events leading to the deaths of two conscripts constituted an act of racial violence. According to the Grand Chamber, it was not established that racial attitudes had played a role in the killing of the two conscripts.[159] Nonetheless, like the Court previously, it also held that there had been a violation of Article 14 of the ECHR, taken in conjunction with Article 2, in that the authorities had failed to investigate possible racist motives behind the events that had led to the deaths of the two men.[160] Thus, the Grand Chamber distanced itself from the Chamber's previous approach (inspired by the Committee Against Torture) by finding that the acts in themselves were not racially motivated.

Around the same time, the ECtHR delivered two landmark cases where it also substantially relied on various international sources, including the case law of the Committee. Following the *Mamatkulov and Abdurasulovic v Turkey* case[161] before the Chamber, and the *Mamatkulov and Askarov v Turkey* case[162] before the Grand Chamber, interim measures acquired a binding character under the ECHR. These cases concerned applications brought by Uzbek opposition party members who were arrested in Turkey on suspicion of murder, causing injuries by a bomb explosion in Uzbekistan and an attempted terrorist attack on the President of the Republic. Uzbekistan requested their extradition under a bilateral treaty with Turkey. Despite the Court's instruction to the Turkish Government not to extradite the applicants, they were sent to Uzbekistan, where they were found guilty and sentenced to imprisonment. Before the Court, the applicants complained of breaches of Articles 2, 3, and 6 of the ECHR as well as Rule 39 (interim measures) of the Court's Rules. In the Chamber and the Grand Chamber judgments, the Court held that there had been no violation of Article 3, that Article 6(1) was inapplicable to the extradition procedure, and that there had been a breach of Article 34 of the ECHR because Turkey had not complied with the interim measures indicated by the Court. In both cases, the Court resorted to the Committee's case law and Rules of Procedure in support of its finding regarding the binding character of interim measures under the ECHR.

The Court relied on, *inter alia*, Rule 108(9) of the Committee's Rules of Procedure which allowed interim measures to be adopted in proceedings brought by individuals alleging a violation of the CAT.[163] The Court also invoked two decisions of the Committee, namely the *Cecilia Rosana Núñez Chipana v*

[159] Ibid, para 157. [160] Ibid, para 168.

[161] *Mamatkulov and Abdurasulovic v Turkey* (App Nos 46827/99; 46951/99), judgment, 6 February 2003, not reported. See Introduction, 2.2.3; ch I, 2.3 and 2.4.2; ch II, 2.6; and ch IV, 2.2.8.

[162] *Mamatkulov and Askarov v Turkey* (App Nos 46827/99; 46951/99), judgment, 4 February 2005, Reports 2005-I, 293.

[163] *Mamatkulov and Abdurasulovic v Turkey* (n 161 above), para 40; *Mamatkulov and Askarov v Turkey* (n 162 above), para 43.

Venezuela[164] and *TPS v Canada*[165] cases. The *Chipana* case concerned a Peruvian citizen residing in Venezuela who was extradited to Peru in spite of the fact that interim measures had requested a stay of the extradition. The Court recalled the view expressed by the Committee Against Torture which found that '[c]ompliance with the provisional measures... in cases it considers reasonable is essential in order to protect the person in question from irreparable harm, which could, moreover, nullify the end result of the proceedings before the Committee'.[166] The *TPS* case concerned the extradition of an Indian citizen residing in Canada to his home country despite the indication of interim measures requesting Canada to stay the extradition. There, the Committee reiterated that the failure to comply with the requested interim measures 'could... nullify the end result of the proceedings before the Committee'.[167]

Against this background, the Court interpreted the ECHR and found in a language similar to that used by the Committee that 'any State Party to the Convention to which interim measures have been indicated in order to avoid irreparable harm being caused to the victim of an alleged violation must comply with those measures and refrain from any act or omission that will undermine the authority and effectiveness of the final judgment'.[168] The Grand Chamber put it even more forcefully and found that '[a] failure by a Contracting State to comply with interim measures is to be regarded as preventing the Court from effectively examining the applicant's complaint and as hindering the effective exercise of his or her right and, accordingly, as a violation of Article 34'.[169] Thus, by using the Committee's case law as one of the interpretation aids, the Court was able to attribute a binding character to the interim measures used under the ECHR.

3.2.2 Reports of the Committee and Special Rapporteur

In numerous cases brought to Strasbourg, the Commission and the Court relied on other documents, normally reports, originating from the Committee Against Torture and the Special Rapporteur on torture and cruel, inhuman, or degrading treatment. Cited as authoritative sources, these were generally used in support of the findings of the Commission or Court. For instance, in the *Chahal v United Kingdom* judgment[170] (discussed above), the Court took into account the report

164 *Cecilia Rosana Núñez Chipana v Venezuela,* Communication No 110/1998, CAT/C/21/D/110/1998, 10 November 1988, Committee Against Torture.

165 *TPS v Canada*, Communication No 99/1997, CAT/C/24/D/99/1997, 16 May 2000, Committee Against Torture.

166 *Cecilia Rosana Núñez Chipana v Venezuela*, para 8 (n 164 above); *Mamatkulov and Abdurasulovic v Turkey* (n 161 above), para 47; *Mamatkulov and Askarov v Turkey* (n 162 above), para 44.

167 *TPS v Canada*, para 15.6; *Mamatkulov and Abdurasulovic v Turkey* (n 161 above), paras 48 and 102; *Mamatkulov and Askarov v Turkey* (n 162 above), paras 45 and 115.

168 *Mamatkulov and Abdurasulovic v Turkey* (n 161 above), para 110.

169 *Mamatkulov and Askarov v Turkey* (n 162 above), para 128.

170 *Chahal v United Kingdom* (n 131 above); see ch VI, 2.1.3, 2.2.1, and 2.2.6.

of the Special Rapporteur. The case concerned a Sikh applicant from India, who entered the United Kingdom illegally, and later brought his Indian wife, who gave birth to two children. He was granted indefinite leave to remain in the United Kingdom and later became a leading Sikh militant. He was arrested on suspicion of involvement in a conspiracy to assassinate the Indian Prime Minister and moderate Sikhs in the United Kingdom. When the Home Secretary decided that he should be deported, the complainant applied for asylum. His application was rejected, and he lodged a claim with the ECtHR noting that his deportation would infringe Articles 3, 5(1), 5(4), 8, and 13 of the ECHR.

As part of the evidence available to the Court, the 1995 Report of the Special Rapporteur on Torture indicated that 'few incidents, in what is credibly alleged to be a widespread, if not endemic phenomenon, are prosecuted and even fewer lead to conviction of the perpetrators.... very many cases that come to the attention of the Special Rapporteur are those that result in death, in other words, those where torture may have been applied with the most extreme results.'[171] Considering this report, the Court noted that 'Mr. Chahal, if returned to India, would be most at risk from the Punjab security forces acting either within or outside State boundaries'.[172] Further, the Court observed that 'the United Nations' Special Rapporteur on torture has described the practice of torture upon those in police custody as "endemic" and has complained that inadequate measures are taken to bring those responsible to justice'.[173] Thus, the Court was not persuaded by the assurances of the Indian Government that the applicant would benefit from the same legal protection as other Indian citizens and that he would not be mistreated. Among other findings, the judges concluded that the applicant's deportation would violate Article 3 of the ECHR.

In the *Gerard Magee v United Kingdom* decision,[174] handed down in 1999, the Court examined the conclusions and recommendations of the Committee Against Torture. In that case, the applicant was arrested in connection with an attempted bomb attack on military personnel. He was taken to Castlereagh Police Office, where he was refused access to a solicitor for two days and was questioned intensely by rotating teams of detectives about his part in the bombing incident. Before the Court, he invoked, *inter alia*, the conclusions and recommendations of the Committee Against Torture contained in its report of 17 November 1995.[175] The Committee had found that the detention regime in the Castlereagh

[171] Report of the Special Rapporteur, Mr Nigel S Rodley, submitted pursuant to Commission on Human Rights Resolution 1992/32, United Nations Commission on Human Rights, 50th Session, 12 January 1995; *Chahal v United Kingdom* (n 131 above), para 51.

[172] Ibid, para 104.

[173] Ibid, para 104.

[174] *Gerard Magee v United Kingdom* (App No 28135/95), decision, 14 September 1999, not reported.

[175] Committee Against Torture, Summary record of the first part of the 234th meeting: United Kingdom of Great Britain and Northern Ireland, held at the Palais des Nations, Geneva, on Friday, 17 November 1995, at 10 am CAT/C/SR.234, 22 November 95; Comité contre la torture, Compte rendu analytique de la premiere partie de la 235ème seance: United Kingdom of Great Britain and

Police Office was intended to be coercive in order to break the will of the detainee to remain silent. Thus, the Committee found that it contravened international human rights norms.[176] While the Court noted that criticism had been directed against the detention conditions in the Castlereagh Police Office, it found that its task in the case was to determine whether the applicant had substantiated his claim that he was a direct victim of a breach of Article 3 of the ECHR and whether the treatment inflicted reached the minimum level of severity. In the judgment in the *Magee* case,[177] the applicant invoked the same Committee report, but the Court paid greater attention to a report of the European Committee for the Prevention of Torture (also invoked by the applicant) concerning the Castlereagh Holding Centre.[178]

In decisions of the Court, many references to the reports of the Committee and Special Rapporteur remain unexplored due to technical reasons. Mainly, this is caused by the fact that a case was struck out of the list, that it was found to be inadmissible, or that the judges refrained from expressing an extensive opinion on the alleged violations. For instance, in the *Yang Chun Jin alias Yang Xiaolin v Hungary* decision,[179] handed down in 2001, the respondent Government invoked a report of the Committee, but the Court did not analyse it further. In that case, a national of China and Sierra Leone alleged that, if extradited to China, he risked having an unfair trial, being detained under harsh conditions, being subjected to torture, or being sentenced to death. The respondent Government noted, *inter alia*, that the Committee Against Torture appreciated its efforts in amending legislation and implementing a number of the Committee's recommendations.[180] However, these were not considered further by the Court. The case was declared admissible and was brought before the Court. In its judgment,[181] the Court did not make any references to the Committee's report. Noting that the Hungarian Minister of Justice had decided to refuse the applicant's extradition to China and that the applicant had left Hungary for Sierra Leone, the Court found that the matter was resolved. The case was therefore struck out and the Court did not have the opportunity to consider the Committee's findings.

Northern Ireland, tenue au Palais des Nations, à Genève, le vendredi 17 novembre 1995, à 15 heures, CAT/C/SR.235, 27 novembre 1995; Committee Against Torture, Concluding observations of the Committee against Torture: United Kingdom of Great Britain and Northern Ireland, A/51/44, 9 July 1996, paras 58–65.

[176] Ibid.

[177] *Gerard Magee v United Kingdom* (App No 28135/95), judgment, 6 June 2000, Reports 2000-VI, 159.

[178] Ibid, paras 30 and 43.

[179] *Yang Chun Jin alias Yang Xiaolin v Hungary* (App No 58073/00), decision, 8 March 2001, not reported.

[180] Ibid; Summary record of the second part of the 423rd meeting: China, CAT/C/SR.423/Add.1, 9 May 2000, Committee Against Torture.

[181] *Yang Chun Jin alias Yang Xiaolin v Hungary* (App No 58073/00), judgment, 11 January 2001, not reported.

Similarly, in another decision in 2004, *Viorel Carabulea v Romania*,[182] the Court did not refer extensively to a report of the Special Rapporteur invoked by the applicants. This could have been due to the fact that it abstained from expressing an opinion on the alleged violations and only focused on the admissibility of the case. The application was filed by Mr Carabulea, a Romanian of Roma origin, whose brother died in police custody under suspicious circumstances. The applicant alleged that violations of Articles 2, 3, 6(1), and 14 of the ECHR had occurred. In support of his claim, the applicant invoked the report of the Special Rapporteur on Torture, Sir Nigel Rodley (at the time), where he observed that:

> the system of investigation in which the military prosecutors have the exclusive authority to investigate and prosecute is ineffective. At a minimum, there is a perception that the military prosecutors lack independence and impartiality. While there have been a few cases in which police officers have been prosecuted and sentenced, in most cases the investigations result in decisions not to prosecute. It is also of concern that the military prosecutors are assisted by the police in these investigations.[183]

The Court did not comment further on this report or on the alleged violations, but found instead that the complaint required an examination of the merits.[184]

Most recently, in the *Ismoilov and others v Russia* case,[185] the Court paid more attention than in previous cases to the findings of the Special Rapporteur on Torture. The case concerned a complaint lodged by a Kyrgyz national and 12 Uzbek nationals regarding the Russian authorities' decision to extradite them to Uzbekistan, where they could be ill-treated and face an unfair trial. In 2005 armed men attacked Andijan's prison (Uzbekistan) and freed prisoners who had been arrested on suspicion of involvement with an extremist religious and terrorist organization. The applicants were subsequently arrested and detained in Russia, pending extradition, on suspicion of having financed the rebellion in Andijan. Under Rule 39 of the Rules of Court (interim measures), the ECtHR asked Russia to stay the applicants' extradition until further notice. The Uzbek authorities had given assurances that they would not persecute the applicants and that the applicants would not be ill-treated or subjected to the death penalty in Uzbekistan.

The applicants alleged that their rights under Articles 3, 5(1), 5(4), 6(1), and 6(2) of the ECHR had been infringed. In support of their claims, they invoked, *inter alia*, reports of the Special Rapporteur on Torture.[186] Thus, the Court examined,

[182] *Viorel Carabulea v Romania* (App No 45661/99), decision, 21 September 2004, not reported.

[183] Report of the Special Rapporteur on the question of torture, Sir Nigel S Rodley, submitted pursuant to Commission on Human Rights Resolution 1999/32, Addendum: Visit of the Special Rapporteur to Romania, E/CN.4/2000/9/Add.3, United Nations Commission on Human Rights, 56th Session, 23 November 1999.

[184] At the time of writing, there was no judgment in the case.

[185] *Ismoilov and others v Russia* (App No 2947/06), judgment, 24 April 2008, not yet reported.

[186] Ibid, para 64.

as part of the relevant sources, the report of the Special Rapporteur on Torture, Theo van Boven (at the time), where he noted that torture or similar treatment was systemic in Uzbekistan.[187] Another report of the Special Rapporteur considered by the Court concerned the use of diplomatic assurances.[188] In this report, the Special Rapporteur on Torture, Manfred Nowak (current), observed generally that 'diplomatic assurances are unreliable and ineffective in the protection against torture and ill-treatment... States cannot resort to diplomatic assurances as a safeguard against torture and ill-treatment where there are substantial grounds for believing that a person would be in danger of being subjected to torture or ill-treatment upon return'.[189]

With regard to the specific torture situation in Uzbekistan and the reliance upon the Uzbek authorities' diplomatic assurances, the Court recalled the Special Rapporteur's statement that there was strong and credible testimony that the Uzbek military and security forces committed grave human rights violations during the Andijan incident.[190] The Special Rapporteur was deeply concerned that the Government had rejected an international inquiry into the Andijan events and that there was no internationally accepted account of the situation. Thus, the Special Rapporteur reiterated that diplomatic assurances were not legally binding and undermined the existing obligations of states to prohibit torture.[191] It should be noted that the third party in the case, Human Rights Watch and the Advice on Individual Rights in Europe (AIRE) Centre, had also invoked a decision of the Committee where it was found that the procurement of diplomatic assurances did not suffice to protect against a manifest risk of ill-treatment.[192]

When considering these documents, the Court noted that:

> [t]he evidence from a number of objective sources demonstrates that problems still persist in Uzbekistan in connection with the ill-treatment of detainees. In particular, in 2002 the UN Special Rapporteur on Torture described the practice of torture upon those in police custody as 'systematic' and 'indiscriminate'. His successor in this post announced in 2006 that his mandate continued to receive serious allegations of torture by Uzbek law enforcement officials.... Although the Uzbek government adopted certain measures designed to combat the practice of torture..., there is no evidence that those measures returned any positive results.[193]

[187] Ibid, para 74; Report of the Special Rapporteur on the question of torture, Theo van Boven, submitted in accordance with Commission Resolution 2002/38, Addendum: Mission to Uzbekistan, E/CN.4/2003/68/Add.2, United Nations Commission on Human Rights, 59th Session, 3 February 2003, paras 66–68.

[188] *Ismoilov and others v Russia* (n 185 above), para 97; Report of the Special Rapporteur on torture and other cruel, inhuman or degrading treatment or punishment, A/60/316, United Nations General Assembly, 60th Session, 30 August 2005.

[189] *Ismoilov and others v Russia* (n 185 above), para 97; Report of the Special Rapporteur on torture (n 188 above), para 51.

[190] *Ismoilov and others v Russia* (n 185 above), para 98.

[191] Ibid.

[192] Ibid, para 112; *Agiza v Sweden*, Communication No 233/2003, CAT/C/34/D/233/2003, 20 May 2005, Committee Against Torture.

[193] *Ismoilov and others v Russia* (n 185 above), para 121.

Basing itself on the reports of the Special Rapporteur, the Court was thus persuaded that ill-treatment of detainees was a pervasive and enduring problem in Uzbekistan.

With regard to the personal situation of the applicants, the Court noted, *inter alia*, that the UN High Commissioner for Refugees as well as the Special Rapporteur on Torture had urged the Governments to refrain from transferring persons accused of involvement in the Andijan incident to Uzbekistan where they could be tortured. It was also significant that the UN High Commissioner for Refugees granted the applicants refugee status after determining that they each had a well-founded fear of being persecuted and ill-treated upon return.[194] The Court cited additional material from the United Nations and international NGOs in support of its finding that the applicants could face torture or other inhuman treatment if extradited to their country of origin.

Most recently, in *Saadi v Italy*,[195] the Court recalled that, in assessing the general situation in the receiving country, 'it has often attached importance to the information contained in recent reports from independent international human-rights-protection associations such as Amnesty International, or governmental sources, including the US State Department'.[196] When the sources available described a general situation, the applicant's specific allegations in a given case needed to be corroborated by other evidence. These reports constituted an important source of information in the Court's reasoning.

In addition to the Court's references to the reports of the Committee and Special Rapporteur, it is also important to mention that there are substantial approximations between the ECHR and the CAT case law concerning refugee protection, even in the absence of any mention of the case law of the CAT or Committee. For instance, in the *Hatami v Sweden* judgment,[197] the Commission considered that 'complete accuracy is seldom to be expected by victims of torture. Furthermore, ... the inaccuracies which may exist are not due to the applicant's presentation of facts and do not raise doubts about the general veracity of his claims.'[198] Similarly, in *Aemei v Switzerland*,[199] the Committee opined that 'even though there may be some remaining doubt as to the veracity of the facts adduced by the author of a communication, it must ensure that his security is not endangered. In order to do this, it is not necessary that all the facts invoked by the author should be proved; it is sufficient that the Committee should consider them to be sufficiently substantiated and reliable.'[200] In *Tala v Sweden*,[201] the

[194] Ibid, para 125.

[195] *Saadi v Italy* (n 128 above); discussed at 2.1.2.3 above.

[196] Ibid, para 131.

[197] *Hatami v Sweden* (App No 32448/96), report, 23 April 1998, not reported, para 106.

[198] Ibid.

[199] *Aemei v Switzerland*, Communication No 34/1995, CAT/C/18/D/34/1995, 29 May 1997, Committee Against Torture.

[200] Ibid, para 9.6.

[201] *Tala v Sweden*, Communication No 43/1996, CAT/C/17/D/43/1996, 15 November 1996, Committee Against Torture.

Committee also found that 'complete accuracy is seldom to be expected by victims of torture and . . . the inconsistencies that exist in the author's presentation of the facts do not raise doubts about the general veracity of his claims'.[202]

Other close approximations in the case law of both bodies appeared with regard to the probability that treatment contrary to Article 3 of the ECHR or Articles 1 and 16 of the CAT will be inflicted. For instance, in *Vilvarajah v United Kingdom*,[203] the Court considered that its

> examination of the existence of a risk of ill-treatment in breach of Article 3 at the relevant time must necessarily be a rigorous one in view of the absolute character of this provision and the fact that it enshrines one of the fundamental values of the democratic societies making up the Council of Europe. . . . It follows from the above principles that the examination of this issue in the present case must focus on the foreseeable consequences of the removal of the applicants to Sri Lanka in the light of the general situation there in February 1988 as well as on their personal circumstances.[204]

In a very similar language, the Committee found in *Aemei v Switzerland* that it had 'to determine whether the expulsion of Mr. Aemei (and his family) to Iran would have the foreseeable consequence of exposing him to a real and personal risk of being arrested and tortured'.[205] These are only a few examples of approximations between the two sets of case law which demonstrate that the reasoning of the CAT and the ECtHR is closely related; exploring all such approximations would, however, be beyond the scope of this volume.

4. Rationale of the Reasoning

The prohibition of torture and cruel, inhuman, or degrading treatment—enshrined in regional and international human rights instruments—strikes at the very heart of the protection of human rights. It is widely recognized among nations around the world, and the fact that it constitutes an absolute and a *jus cogens* norm is no longer considered to be controversial. Undeniably, the establishment of this norm has made important inroads into the criminal law of ECHR Contracting States. A number of states, preoccupied with terrorism, have shown some reticence towards the absolute nature of this prohibition.[206] There are also certain difficult interpretation issues associated with the application of the prohibition on torture and other ill-treatment. In fact, the distinction between torture and cruel, inhuman, or degrading treatment is still strongly influenced by the circumstances of each case and leads to variable results. Further, the definition of

[202] Ibid, para 10.3.

[203] *Vilvarajah v United Kingdom* (App Nos 13163/87–13165/87; 131447/87; 13448/87), judgment, 30 October 1991, Series A, Vol 215. See also ch VI, 2.1.4.

[204] Ibid, para 108.

[205] *Aemei v Switzerland* (n 199 above), para 9.5.

[206] Manfred Nowak, 'Challenges to the Absolute Nature of the Prohibition on Torture and Ill-treatment', 23 NQHR 674 (2005), 676.

cruel, inhuman, or degrading treatment is vague and leaves an important margin to the Court. These issues seem to have played an important role in the Court's approach to the activities of the CAT and Committee. Furthermore, the absolute character of the prohibition on torture and cruel, inhuman, or degrading treatment, which entails that states have a reduced margin of appreciation in this field, has left greater room for manoeuvre for the Court and is reflected in a higher level of reception in the case law. Further, in certain important areas where the Court did not have the opportunity, or chose not, to consider the CAT, its case law nonetheless converged with the standards set under this Convention. Overall, the Court has followed the open paradigm in this strand of its jurisprudence. The reception of international law is desirable in this context since both the CAT and the ECHR regulate human rights issues and have similar objectives. Moreover, the cases in which the CAT was considered did not represent a risk of weakening the protection provided for under the ECHR.

As regards the references to the CAT, it appears that the case law of the Strasbourg bodies has followed an even, albeit incomplete, circular development. While the Commission initially indicated that it would follow a purpose-oriented approach to the distinction between torture and other ill-treatment, the Court departed from this tendency and opted for an approach based on the severity of pain requirement. Thus, there was initially a difference in the approach used by the Commission and the Court; the Commission's approach seems to have been more protective of the individual, whereas the approach of the Court has been more restrictive and resorted to a narrower definition of torture. Later, when the CAT was enacted in 1984, its standards gradually penetrated the reasoning of the Court. The Court then integrated the definition of torture contained in Article 1 of the CAT into its case law. By including this definition, the Court also focused, in part, on the purpose of torture without, however, completely abandoning its initial approach. As a result, it has returned to some extent to the approach initially advocated by the Commission. Thus, as recent case law demonstrates, the Court seems to have chosen to follow a mixed approach in its case law.

In doing so, the Court appears to have been influenced by the uncertainties of the debate at the international level with regard to the distinction between torture and other ill-treatment.[207] The Court has reached a compromise position between the purpose-oriented and severity-oriented approaches, without taking a firm stand on either one. Its reasoning has contributed to the debate by demonstrating that taking a mixed approach may be advisable. In the context of the states' fight against terrorism, interrogation techniques are constantly evolving and often bordering on torture or cruel and inhuman treatment. Furthermore, the distinction between torture and inhuman treatment is difficult to measure and does not always depend on a sole criterion. In order to keep up to speed and to protect human rights efficiently, the Court has adopted a flexible approach which

[207] See nn 40 and 41 above and accompanying text.

it applies on a case-by-case basis. Most importantly, by using an approach based on the purpose and severity of pain, the Court has simply applied the requirements contained in Article 1 of the CAT.

Another strand of the Strasbourg case law concerned the coexistence of both bodies, the case law of the Committee, and the reports of the Committee and Special Rapporteur. The coexistence of case law has been largely unproblematic until now, in part because it has been scarce. Further, given that the cases were struck out of the list, the Court was not able to consider further its relationship with the Committee Against Torture. Nonetheless, due to the coherent legal set-up under both the ECHR and the CAT, no cases of litispendence should occur in the future. Moreover, applicants may still prefer to lodge a complaint before the ECtHR rather than the Committee because of better prospects of enforcement. Further, certain rights are better protected under the ECHR than under the CAT. It is yet to be seen, however, how the coexistence of the bodies will be articulated in practice. Until now, this strand of the case law marked by procedural and structural references has little to teach about the Court's tendency to refer to international law.

As regards the case law referring to the decisions of the Committee, the Court has not integrated them explicitly as part of its reasoning, but rather acknowledged that they constitute relevant sources of inspiration. Nonetheless, the lack of explicit acknowledgement does not seem to constitute a relevant factor here, as the Court seems to have followed the Committee's reasoning implicitly in its jurisprudence. Thus, there is an important convergence between its case law and that of the Committee. The Court has also referred to the reports of the Committee and Special Rapporteur as authoritative sources to back up its own findings. In some cases, however, it has preferred to rely on the findings of its regional counterpart, the European Committee for the Prevention on Torture, which reduced the need for reaching beyond the confines of the ECHR.

It must be recalled that the Committee Against Torture, as a UN treaty body, is plagued by the same problems common to all these institutions.[208] The ECHR, a regional instrument, is made up of a relatively homogeneous group of states with comparable economic, social, political, and legal cultures.[209] However, the CAT is an international treaty, and its Signatory States have diverse legal cultures. Despite this, the ECtHR was not reluctant to refer to its provisions, which have been adapted to all the existing countries and which could have a different meaning in different parts of the world. Moreover, the Court was not discouraged by the fact that European states constitute a minority of CAT members, and some of the Committee's case law may concern issues that do not arise in Europe. This behaviour is impressive in view of the fact that the Committee issues non-binding

208 See ch IV, 1.2 and 3, ch III, 6, and ch VI, 4.

209 Liz Hefferman, 'A Comparative View of Individual Petition Procedures under the European Convention on Human Rights and the International Covenant on Civil and Political Rights' (1997) 19(1) Hum Rts Qrtly 78, 84.

decisions and that it is not a purely judicial body. Further, the Court appears to have followed the Committee's case law implicitly. Its approach with regard to the CAT has been more courageous than that followed with regard to the ICCPR or the case law of the HRC, given that—facing the same difficulties—the Court has been more receptive.

Overall, it appears that the Court's behaviour with regard to the prohibition on torture and cruel, inhuman, or degrading treatment has been permeable and marked by a level of reception beyond average. This could be due in part to the fact that the prohibition against torture has been generally well-accepted and that Contracting States have a reduced margin of appreciation in this field. The Court may have felt less constrained and has made substantial references to the CAT, going even as far as directly incorporating certain standards into its case law. Thus, it has maintained standards which were similar to those set by the CAT and the Committee Against Torture. In view of the proliferation of instruments prohibiting torture, this approach is to be commended as it contributes towards the harmonization of cases relating to torture at the regional level. Finally, in light of the lack of unequivocal debate regarding the distinction between torture and other inhuman acts, the Court's reasoning should be commended for choosing an approach that maximizes the protection of ECHR human rights.

VI
Refugee Rights

1. Preliminary Observations

The number of persons seeking refugee status has dramatically increased as a direct consequence of the armed conflicts in Iraq, Afghanistan, and former Yugoslavia, the humanitarian crises in Sudan and other African countries, as well as the natural disasters prevalent on the Asian continent. The plight of their situation has given rise to numerous initiatives and interventions on the part of states and international organizations aimed at improving their living conditions. The work of the United Nations High Commissioner for Refugees (UNHCR), as the representative of the international community in matters relating to the protection of refugees, has been significant in this regard. In addition, some states have demonstrated their willingness to assist by providing financial and material aid, sending experts to countries in need, or granting asylum to persons who have been deprived of the possibility to enjoy life in their home country.

The substance of the responsibility of states towards non-nationals has, nonetheless, very complex overtones. As such, it raises new and interesting legal questions which need to be carefully evaluated and balanced against conflicting socio-economic considerations. There is no duty in traditional international law and in domestic immigration laws of most states to admit foreigners.[1] This standard originates from the principle of sovereignty or territorial supremacy, which entails that each state has exclusive jurisdiction over its territory. Thus, control by states over admission to and expulsion from their territory of foreigners has been regarded as a typically sovereign right. It has, however, been increasingly put under pressure and limited under contemporary international law as a result of the enactment of human rights and economic integration treaties.[2] Moreover, there has been a considerable shift in emphasis in according both nationals and foreigners equality of treatment.[3]

[1] Hélène Lambert, *The Position of Aliens in Relation to the European Convention on Human Rights* (Strasbourg: Council of Europe, Council of Europe Publishing, 2006), 11.

[2] Ibid.

[3] Andrew Drzemczewski, *The Position of Aliens in Relation to the European Convention on Human Rights* (Strasbourg: Council of Europe Press, 1993), 7–9.

States have the right to regulate the admission of foreigners into their territory and to have a comprehensive immigration policy that complies with their interests. However, a state's decision to expel someone may have serious consequences for refugees, asylum-seekers, and other non-nationals in need of protection. As a result, international and European human rights law attaches certain responsibilities to states' actions in this context. In the majority of ECHR Contracting States, four overlapping regimes regulate such responsibilities, namely the 1951 UN Convention on the Status of Refugees, the law of the European Union, the United Nations Convention Against Torture (CAT), and the ECHR. This chapter focuses on the 1951 Refugee Convention, but also considers briefly the relevant CAT articles.[4]

The role of the ECtHR in adjudicating complaints concerning refugee rights has been multifaceted. The Court, situated at the apex of the various international legal frameworks and sensitive national immigration policies, has had to consider two different types of interests with opposing aims, namely those of the state and those of the individual. This balancing exercise has often paid great deference to the state's decision, given that refugees' rights and immigration are fields where states have a wide margin of appreciation. In addition, many of the applications lodged have been rejected at the admissibility stage because the Court tends to give more weight to a government's assessment of the situation in a given country rather than to the fears of the applicant.[5] Furthermore, there is an extensive framework of EU legislation which concerns numerous asylum-related issues.[6] Significantly, this legislation regulates the situation of asylum-seekers in 25 to 27 of the 47 ECHR Contracting States (some EU Member States have decided not to be bound by these measures). Indicative of an authoritative consensus, such legislation is more binding and contains more effective enforcement mechanisms than the 1951 Refugee Convention and the 1984 CAT. Hence, the Strasbourg Court may have felt less compelled to refer to international law.[7] While the Court

[4] The CAT is considered in greater detail in ch V.

[5] Nuala Mole, *Asylum and the European Convention on Human Rights, Migration Collection* (Strasbourg: Council of Europe, Council of Europe Publishing, 2007), 38.

[6] Council Regulation (EC) 343/2003 of 18 February 2003 establishing the criteria and mechanisms for determining the Member State responsible for examining an asylum application lodged in one of the Member States by a third-country national [2003] OJ L50/1 (now also applicable in Denmark); Council Directive (EC) 2003/9 of 27 January 2003 laying down minimum standards for the reception of asylum seekers [2003] OJ L31/18 (Ireland and Denmark opted out); Council Directive (EC) 2003/86 of 22 September 2003 on the right to family reunification [2003] OJ L251/12 (Denmark opted out); Council Directive (EC) 2004/83 of 29 April 2004 on minimum standards for the qualification and status of third country nationals or stateless persons as refugees or as persons who otherwise need international protection and the content of the protection granted [2004] OJ L304/12 (Denmark opted out); Council Directive (EC) 2005/85 of 1 December 2005 on minimum standards on procedures in Member States for granting and withdrawing refugee status [2005] OJ L326/13 (Denmark opted out).

[7] Due to a lack of space, the relationship between EU law and the ECHR will not be considered in this work. The author focuses on the relationship between international law and the ECHR, and takes EU law into account only when this appears to be necessary. For further details

has followed the ECHR framework very closely and avoided reaching beyond its boundaries, there have nonetheless been interesting cases intertwined with international law in which it has had the chance to consider the 1951 Refugee Convention and the CAT. These cases are instructive as they demonstrate how the Court reasons and behaves in a field where states have typically had a wide margin of appreciation.

2. Case Law Referring to the 1951 Refugee Convention

The 1951 Refugee Convention and the 1967 Protocol relating to the Status of Refugees[8] were ratified by 45 of the 47 ECHR Contracting States,[9] and both instruments therefore enjoy wide approval at the European level. The 1951 Refugee Convention is the *lex specialis* of asylum in Europe, and the fact that it is a key international instrument is unquestioned.[10] At first, it may seem that, pursuant to the requirements enshrined in Article 53 of the ECHR,[11] the Court's case law should be replete with references to this treaty. The situation in reality is, however, quite different; the ECtHR has been circumspect in its approach and mentions the 1951 Refugee Convention infrequently. These references have further been limited by the fact that it has often been more beneficial for the applicant to resort to the ECHR instead of the 1951 Refugee Convention. Such a state of affairs has not, however, prevented the Strasbourg Court from referring occasionally to the relevant provisions of this instrument. The 1951 Refugee Convention has mainly appeared in three strands of the Court's case law, namely under Article 3 of the ECHR (prohibition of torture), Article 5 of the ECHR (right to liberty and security), and Article 8 of the ECHR (right to respect for private and family life).

As part of the case law falling under Article 3 of the ECHR, the ECtHR has explicitly recognized that the Convention grants greater protection to the applicant under certain circumstances. While some attention has been paid

regarding the relationship between EU law and the ECHR in the ECtHR case law, see *TI v United Kingdom* (App No 43844/98), decision, 7 March 2000, Reports 2000-III, 435; *Matthews v United Kingdom* (App No 24833/94), judgment, 18 February 1999, Reports 1999-I, 251; *Bosphorous Hava Yolları Turizm ve Ticaret Anonim Şirketi v Ireland* (App No 45036/98), judgment, 30 June 2005, Reports 2005-VI, 107; *Mendizabal v France* (App No 54431/99), judgment, 17 January 2006, not reported.

8 Protocol relating to the Status of Refugees, 606 UNTS 267, entered into force 4 October 1967.

9 This information was verified on 13 June 2010: United Nations Treaty Collection, Status, <http://treaties.un.org/Pages/ViewDetailsII.aspx?&src=TREATY&mtdsg_no=V-2&chapter=5&Temp=mtdsg2&lang=en>.

10 Mole (n 5 above), 10.

11 Article 53 of the ECHR provides that '[n]othing in this Convention shall be construed as limiting or derogating from any of the human rights and fundamental freedoms which may be ensured under the laws of any High Contracting Parties or under any other agreement to which it is a Party'.

to the question of whether refugee status had been granted in a given case, the Court has drawn clear boundaries between the 1951 Refugee Convention system and the ECHR. Furthermore, it has taken the view that the ECHR trumps other non-compliant international law provisions. The case law concerning Articles 5 and 8 of the ECHR has contained fewer references to the 1951 Refugee Convention and does not appear to exhibit any consistent trend in relation to the Court's approach to international law. In some cases, the Court has repeated the principles that were used in the case law under Article 3. The reasoning of the Court has also been conditioned by the wide margin of appreciation granted to the Contracting States. This deference of the Court has been particularly apparent in case law pertaining to Article 8, where the Court has even called on states to provide further guidance by legislative means. Nonetheless, the case law falling under Articles 5 and 8 has also been characterized by forceful and outspoken dissidences where more explicit references to international refugee law have been made.

2.1 Case Law Relating to Article 3 of the ECHR

2.1.1 A Comparison of the ECHR with the 1951 Refugee Convention

The aim of the 1951 Refugee Convention is to protect persons who qualify for the status of refugee. In order to be considered as a refugee, persons must meet four requirements: (1) they must have a well-founded fear of persecution; (2) the persecution feared must be based on one of five reasons (race, religion, nationality, membership of a particular group, or political opinion); (3) they must be outside their home country or country of habitual residence (if stateless); and (4) they must be unable to return, or, if owing to their fear, unwilling to avail themselves of the protection of that country.[12] The term 'well-founded fear of persecution' contains a subjective element of fear and the objective criterion of whether fear is well-founded.[13] As regards the source of persecution, the 1951 Refugee Convention does not mention whether the persecutor has to be an agent of a state or whether persons will also be protected from abuse by private actors. It is now accepted that the range of persecutors under the 1951 Refugee Convention includes the state, parties, or organizations controlling all or a substantial part of the state, and non-state actors, provided that they are unable or unwilling to provide protection against serious harm.[14] Article 33(1) of the 1951 Refugee Convention forbids States Parties to expel or return refugees to a country where they may be harmed

[12] Convention relating to the Status of Refugees, Art 1(2).

[13] United Nations High Commissioner for Refugees, *Handbook on Procedures and Criteria for Determining Refugee Status under the 1951 Convention and the 1967 Protocol relating to the Status of Refugees*, UN Doc HCR/1P/4/Eng/REV1, 1979 (re-edited), January 1992, Geneva, para 38.

[14] Guy S Goodwin-Gill and Jane McAdam, *The Refugee in International Law* (Oxford/New York, OUP: 2007), 99; United Nations High Commissioner for Refugees (n 13 above), para 65.

or persecuted (it does not mention extradition). This article enshrines the principle of *non-refoulement*, which lies at the heart of international refugee law.

This principle is, however, limited, as the 1951 Refugee Convention provides certain exceptions allowing for the return or expulsion of refugees. Article 1F provides that the Convention does not apply to a person with respect to whom there are serious reasons for believing that 'he has committed a crime against peace, a war crime, or a crime against humanity', 'he has committed a serious non-political crime outside their country of refuge prior to his admission to that country as a refugee', or 'he has been guilty of acts contrary to the purposes and principles of the United Nations'.[15] The UNHCR observed, however, that when applying this provision, the authorities must strike a balance between the degree of persecution feared and the nature of the offence committed.[16] If a person has a well-founded fear of persecution endangering his life, then the crime justifying his expulsion must be very severe. In addition, Article 33(2) of the 1951 Refugee Convention provides that a refugee may be expelled 'if there are reasonable grounds for regarding [him] as a danger to the security of the country in which he is, or who, having been convicted by a final judgment of a particularly serious crime, constitutes a danger to the community of that country'.[17] Moreover, Article 32(1) provides that expulsion of a refugee who resides lawfully in a country is allowed exceptionally on grounds of national security and public order.[18] Thus, there are substantive limitations to the prohibition against the return or expulsion of refugees.

The 1951 Refugee Convention does not provide for an international body to supervise its implementation. While Article 38 of the Convention provides that disputes between States Parties can be brought before the International Court of Justice, it does not establish a mechanism of individual complaint.[19] Nonetheless, given that most States Parties have implemented the Convention into their legislation, individuals can rely on its guarantees by initiating complaints at the domestic level. The problem with this course of action is that the criteria provided by the Convention are broad, and domestic courts from different states can have divergent interpretations of the same concept. Furthermore, while the Convention regulates many aspects of refugees' rights, the asylum procedure itself is still dictated by domestic law.

In this context, the ECHR appears to provide a more effective remedy to a person who will be expelled to a country where he or she is likely to be harmed as a result of torture or inhuman or degrading treatment, although it does not enshrine a right to asylum. The Convention is only concerned with individuals

[15] Convention relating to the Status of Refugees, Art 1F.
[16] United Nations High Commissioner for Refugees (n 13 above), para 156.
[17] Convention relating to the Status of Refugees, Art 33(2). [18] Ibid, Art 32(1).
[19] Ibid, Art 38.

who have been persecuted for at least one of the five reasons included in Article 1 (race, religion, nationality, membership in a particular social group, or political opinion), who have been granted refugee status, and who find themselves outside their country of nationality or habitual residence. These requirements are absent from the ECHR, which protects everyone residing in the jurisdictions of ECHR Contracting States, including failed asylum-seekers,[20] suspected terrorists,[21] criminals,[22] drug-traffickers,[23] and unaccompanied children.[24] Furthermore, Article 3 of the ECHR applies to a real risk of exposure to ill-treatment regardless of the reasons advanced for it.

Article 3 of the ECHR, listed as a non-derogable provision in Article 15(2) of the ECHR, has been interpreted by the ECtHR as an absolute ban on the forced removal of persons fearing torture and inhuman or degrading treatment in their home country.[25] It applies, therefore, even 'in times of war or other public emergency threatening the life of the nation'. Contrary to the 1951 Refugee Convention, the ECtHR has considered that Article 3 prohibits the return of persons independently of the undesirability or dangerousness of their conduct.[26] In addition, the Court has found, in line with the 1951 Refugee Convention, that the ECHR applies when the agents perpetrating the treatment are persons or groups of persons who are not public officials.[27] It must be shown, nonetheless, that the authorities are unable to obviate the risk of ill-treatment by providing appropriate protection.[28] The absolute character of Article 3 of the ECHR is far-reaching, as it also applies when the source of the risk of the prescribed treatment in the receiving country stems from factors which cannot engage the responsibility of public authorities either directly or indirectly.[29] Thus, in exceptional circumstances, it has even been found to apply to a person in the final stage of a disease (AIDS), lacking appropriate medical treatment and having no family in the receiving

[20] *Cruz Varas and others v Sweden* (App No 15576/89), judgment, 20 March 1991, Series A, Vol 201; *Vilvarajah and others v United Kingdom* (App Nos 13163/87–13165/87; 131447/87; 13448/87), judgment, 30 October 1991, Series A, Vol 215; *Vijayanathan and Pusparajah v France* (App Nos 17550/90; 17825/91), judgment, 27 August 1992, Series A, Vol 241-B.

[21] *Chahal v United Kingdom* (App No 22414/93), judgment, 15 November 1996, Reports 1996-V, 1831.

[22] *Ahmed v Austria* (App No 25964/94), judgment, 12 December 1996, Reports 1996-VI, 2195.

[23] *HLR v France* (App No 24573/94), judgment, 29 April 1997, Reports 1997-III, 745, para 40; *D v United Kingdom* (App No 30240/96), judgment, 2 May 1997, Reports 1997-III, 777.

[24] *Nsona v Netherlands* (App No 23366/94), judgment, 28 November 1996, Reports 1996-V, 1979.

[25] *Chahal v United Kingdom* (n 21 above); later forcefully reaffirmed in *Saadi v Italy* (App No 37201/06), judgment, 28 February 2008, not yet reported.

[26] *Chahal v United Kingdom* (n 21 above), para 80; *Saadi v Italy* (n 25 above), para 139.

[27] *Ahmed v Austria* (n 22 above).

[28] Ibid.

[29] *D v United Kingdom* (n 23 above), para 49.

country.[30] The 1951 Refugee Convention would not necessarily apply in these circumstances. Furthermore, the ECHR was found to be relevant in all the processes of removal and, in this way, it is more encompassing than the 1951 Refugee Convention; it applies not only to the return (*refoulement*) and expulsion[31] and deportation of foreigners,[32] but also to their extradition[33]—a process which is excluded from the 1951 Refugee Convention. Nonetheless, the scope of application of the ECHR is narrower than that of the 1951 Refugee Convention, as the ECHR only refers to torture and inhuman and degrading treatment and not to the five broad categories of persecution enshrined in the 1951 Refugee Convention. Both instruments, however, seem to have a comparably heavy burden of proof. The 1951 Refugee Convention requires a 'well founded fear of persecution'[34] and the ECHR calls for a real risk of torture or inhuman or degrading treatment.[35] The most important difference between the instruments seems to lie, however, in their method of enforcement. In contrast to the 1951 Refugee Convention, the ECHR provides an effective individual complaint mechanism before the ECtHR. Several requirements must be fulfilled, however, before an application is lodged with the Strasbourg Court. Pursuant to Article 35 of the ECHR, the applicant must first have exhausted all domestic remedies, and the complaint must be brought within six months of the date from which the final decision of a domestic court was given. It is very significant that all final judgments are binding on the respondent states. In contrast, the 1951 Refugee Convention does not provide, as noted earlier, for an international body which would supervise its enforcement.

Overall, the ECHR seems to offer a higher level of protection than the 1951 Refugee Convention in cases where torture or inhuman or degrading treatment could be inflicted upon the return or expulsion of a person to a receiving country. Despite this discrepancy, the 1951 Refugee Convention has found its way into the case law of the ECtHR in this particular context. This has mainly been due to the fact that the domestic case law was closely intertwined with the 1951 Refugee Convention, either because the Convention was invoked in domestic proceedings or because domestic legislation, implementing the instrument, referred to

[30] Ibid, para 53. It should be noted, however, that in subsequent cases lodged by applicants with AIDS, the Court found that they were inadmissible as they did not reach the gravity threshold of the *D v United Kingdom* case. See *Ndangoya v Sweden* (App No 17868/03), decision, 22 June 2004, not reported; *Amegnigan v The Netherlands* (App No 25629/04), decision, 25 November 2004, not reported; *SCC v Sweden* (App No 46553/99), decision, 15 February 2005, not reported; *N v United Kingdom* (App No 26565/05), judgment, 27 May 2008, not yet reported. See also Mole (n 5 above), 31.

[31] *Cruz Varas and others v Sweden* (n 20 above), paras 69–70.

[32] *Chahal v United Kingdom* (n 21 above).

[33] *Soering v United Kingdom* (App No 14038/88), judgment, 7 July 1989, Series A, Vol 161.

[34] Convention Relating to the Status of Refugees, Art 1(2).

[35] *Cruz Varas and others v Sweden* (n 20 above), paras 75–76.

it directly. On occasion, however, the Court has made statements concerning the Convention which have gone beyond the pure necessity of referring to this instrument.[36] In addition, the Court has made interesting statements concerning the scope of other international obligations of the Contracting States, UNHCR evaluations of an asylum claim, reports of the UNHCR and other organizations on the situation in a receiving country, the Court's own role within the international refugee law framework, and national refugee policies.[37] These case scenarios constitute an interesting example of the ECtHR's behaviour in a situation where it is faced with two sets of applicable legal provisions providing different standards of protection. Most interestingly, the Strasbourg Court has often stated explicitly that the ECHR grants greater protection to the applicant, but has still felt compelled to refer to the 1951 Refugee Convention which sometimes contains lower standards.

2.1.2 Extraterritorial Effect and the Limitations of the Examination

The first important development in this strand of case law was the recognition of the extraterritorial effect of Article 3 of the ECHR. In the *Soering v United Kingdom* judgment,[38] concerning the extradition of a person to a state where he could face the risk of being exposed to the death row syndrome, the Court held that Article 3 applied to exclusion measures of foreigners. Despite this finding, the Court stressed that:

> there is no question of adjudicating on or establishing the responsibility of the receiving country, whether under general international law, under the Convention or otherwise. Insofar as any liability under the Convention is or may be incurred, it is liability incurred by the extraditing Contracting State by reason of its having taken action which has as a direct consequence the exposure of an individual to proscribed ill-treatment.[39]

Thus, the Court circumscribed its responsibility and clarified that it only has a very specific role to play within the greater context of removal of foreigners. This declaration of intent could be viewed as an attempt on the part of the Court to situate itself within the international refugee law system.

In the *Soering* case, the Court also made an interesting comment about the application of the ECHR in a context where other international law instruments were relevant. Other sources, such as the 1951 Refugee Convention or the CAT, which specifically addressed the sending or return of persons to a country where they could face torture or other ill-treatment, were mentioned in the judgment.[40] The Court found nonetheless that other treaties

[36] *D v United Kingdom* (n 23 above). [37] *TI v United Kingdom* (n 7 above).
[38] *Soering v United Kingdom* (n 33 above).
[39] Ibid, para 91. [40] See also Mole (n 5 above), 19.

did not 'absolve the Contracting Parties from responsibility under Article 3 for all and any foreseeable consequences of extradition suffered outside their jurisdiction'.[41] The ECHR continued to apply in spite of the existence of other international law treaties. The Court further noted that '[t]he fact that a specialised treaty should spell out in detail a specific obligation attaching to the prohibition of torture does not mean that an essentially similar obligation is not already inherent in the general terms of Article 3 of the European Convention'.[42]

In most of the Article 3 cases relating to the return and expulsion of persons, the Court reiterated a standard set of principles before conducting a detailed analysis of the complaint. The Court observed that:

> Contracting States have the right as a matter of well-established international law and subject to their treaty obligation including Article 3, to control the entry, residence and expulsion of aliens.... Moreover, it must be noted that the right to political asylum is not contained in either the Convention or its Protocols. This is borne out by several recommendations of the Assembly of the Council of Europe on the right of asylum.[43]

It was also relevant for the Court whether a state had ratified the 1951 Refugee Convention.[44] Interestingly, in a few cases where the 1951 Refugee Convention was mentioned, domestic law applied in the respondent state referred directly to it.[45] The Court also referred to the national asylum policies, but these did not constitute the pivotal criteria in the finding of violation of Article 3 of the ECHR.[46] On the other hand, a state's knowledge and experience in dealing with a certain type of asylum-seeker was a relevant

[41] *Soering v United Kingdom* (n 33 above), para 86.

[42] Ibid, para 88.

[43] *Moustaquim v Belgium* (App No 12313/86), judgment, 18 February 1991, Series A, Vol 193, para 43 (similar wording); *Vilvarajah and others v United Kingdom* (n 20 above), para 102; *Ahmed v Austria*, para 38 (n 22 above); *Jabari v Turkey* (App No 40035/98), judgment, 11 July 2000, Reports 2000-VIII, 149, para 39; *TI v United Kingdom* (n 7 above); *Thampibillai v Netherlands* (App No 61350/00), judgment, 17 February 2004, not reported, para 59; *N v Finland* (App No 38885/02), judgment, 26 July 2005, not reported, para 158; *Salah Sheekh v Netherlands* (App No 1948/04), judgment, 11 January 2007, not yet reported, para 135.

[44] *Chahal v United Kingdom* (n 21 above), para 61; *Bahaddar v Netherlands* (App No 25894/94), judgment, 19 February 1998, Reports 1998-I, 250, para 25; *Jabari v Turkey* (n 43 above), 149, para 26; *TI v United Kingdom* (n 7 above); *Muslim v Turkey* (App No 35366/99), judgment, 26 April 2005, not reported, available only in French, para 42.

[45] *Ahmed v Austria* (n 22 above), para 28; *Bahaddar v Netherlands* (n 44 above), para 26; *TI v United Kingdom* (n 7 above); *N v Finland* (n 43 above), para 127; *Muslim v Turkey* (n 44 above), para 44; *Bonger v Netherlands* (App No 10154/04), decision, 15 September 2005, not reported; *Salah Sheekh v Netherlands* (n 43 above), para 42.

[46] *Bahaddar v Netherlands* (n 45 above), para 28; *Jabari v Turkey* (n 43 above), para 28; *Thampibillai v Netherlands* (n 43 above), paras 37–45; *Muslim v Turkey* (n 45 above), para 43; *Bonger v Netherlands* (n 45 above); *Salah Sheekh v Netherlands* (n 43 above), paras 47–79.

indicator.[47] While the Court tried to emphasize that Contracting States have a legitimate margin of appreciation in this context, many of its decisions and judgments have had an important impact on the domestic asylum system and policies. The Court has departed frequently from the motivations provided by the respondent governments, and has not hesitated to find violations of Article 3 of the ECHR on the basis of information provided by international organizations and NGOs.

2.1.3 Distinction Between the Instruments

The Court has clearly been conscious that the ECHR provides greater protection to an applicant who runs the risk of being tortured or mistreated upon his return or expulsion to a receiving country than the protection afforded by the 1951 Refugee Convention. In *Chahal v United Kingdom*,[48] the Court observed that, pursuant to Article 3 of the ECHR, 'the activities of the individual in question, however undesirable or dangerous, cannot be a material consideration. The protection afforded by Article 3 is thus wider than that provided by Articles 32 and 33 of the United Nations 1951 Convention on the Status of Refugees.'[49] The case concerned a Sikh applicant from India, who entered the United Kingdom illegally, and later brought his Indian wife, who gave birth to two children. He was granted an indefinite leave to remain in the United Kingdom and later became a leading Sikh militant. He was arrested on suspicion of involvement in a conspiracy to assassinate the Indian Prime Minister and moderate Sikhs in the United Kingdom. When the Home Secretary decided that he should be deported, the complainant applied for asylum. His application was rejected, and he lodged a claim with the ECtHR noting that his deportation would infringe Articles 3, 5(1), 5(4), 8, and 13 of the ECHR. Among other findings, the Court concluded, taking into account reports of the United Nations and Amnesty International, that his deportation would violate Article 3.[50]

[47] *Vilvarajah and others v United Kingdom* (n 20 above), para 114.

[48] *Chahal v United Kingdom* (n 21 above).

[49] Ibid, para 80. See also *Kashiyev and Akayera v Russia* (App Nos 57942/00; 57948/00), judgment, 24 February 2005, not reported, para 88, where the Court stated that '[e]ven in the most difficult circumstances, such as the fight against terrorism and organised crime, the Convention prohibits in absolute terms torture and inhuman or degrading treatment or punishment'.

[50] See also *Saadi v Italy* (n 25 above), where the Court reaffirmed the absolute nature of Art 3 of the ECHR, holding that the previously established test for *non-refoulement* was not subject to alteration or balancing on the basis of the perceived dangerousness of the individual concerned. See ch V, 2.1.2.3.

The observation that the ECHR affords greater protection than the 1951 Refugee Convention was repeated in other cases before the Court[51] and before the Commission.[52] This distinction may have been prompted by the Court's wish to justify the lack of reliance on the 1951 Refugee Convention in a case which is so closely intertwined with the Convention. As such, this statement seems to go beyond most of the references made by the Court in cases which truly required them. Here, the Court chose to provide further clarifications pertaining to international law on its own initiative. This, in turn, seems to have provided greater weight to its reasoning and arguments. Most importantly, however, it appears that by differentiating itself from the 1951 Refugee Convention, the Court also wanted to protect and not to weaken its own system. In fact, by incorporating certain lower standards from the 1951 Refugee Convention into the Strasbourg case law, the Court could have weakened the level of protection provided under the ECHR.

2.1.4 Granting of Refugee Status

In order to determine whether a person faces a real risk of ill-treatment, the Court has often considered whether or not he or she was granted refugee status, either by the UNHCR or by the governmental authorities. In *Ahmed v Austria*,[53] the Court found that the expulsion to Somalia of one of its nationals, who had been granted refugee status in Austria and had been sentenced thereafter to two-and-a-half years' imprisonment for robbery, would breach Article 3 of the ECHR. It was noted that Somalia was in a state of civil war and that fighting was going on between the different clans for the control of the country. The Court explained that it 'attaches particular weight to the fact that ... the Austrian Minister of the Interior granted the applicant refugee status within the meaning of the Geneva Convention'.[54] This finding seems to have been pivotal in the Court's reasoning, which led to a finding of violation of Article 3.

The *Vilvarajah and others v United Kingdom*[55] judgment presented a different case scenario from the one above, as the Court relied on a denial of refugee status to support its finding of non-violation under Article 3 of the ECHR. The case concerned five Tamils who fled Sri Lanka because of abuses by government forces, and sought asylum in the United Kingdom. Their claims were rejected, as the UK authorities deemed that they were victims of generalized violence, as opposed to individualized violence. They were deported to Sri Lanka, but returned when

51 *Ahmed v Austria* (n 22 above), para 41; *N v Finland* (n 43 above), para 159; *Saadi v Italy* (n 25 above), para 138.

52 *Chahal Family v United Kingdom* (App No 22414/93), report, 27 June 1995, not reported, para 104; *Paez v Sweden* (App No 29482/95), report, 6 December 1996, not reported, dissenting opinion of MM S Trechsel, I Cabral Barreto, N Bratza, and M Vila Amigó.

53 *Ahmed v Austria* (n 22 above), 2195.

54 Ibid, para 42.

55 *Vilvarajah and others v United Kingdom* (n 20 above).

their appeals against the rejection of their asylum application were successful. They reapplied for asylum and their claims were under consideration at the time of the judgment. The Court found that there was no breach of Article 3 as neither the background of the applicants nor the general situation indicated that 'their personal position was any worse than the generality of other members of the Tamil community or other young male Tamils who were returning to their country'.[56] Here, the Court seems to have been attentive to the Government's preoccupation that:

> [t]he consequences of a finding of a breach of Article 3 in the present case would be that all other persons in similar situations, facing random risks on account of civil turmoil in the State in which they lived, would be entitled not to be removed, thereby permitting the entry of a potentially very large class of people with the attendant serious social and economic consequences.[57]

The Court relied also on the fact that the UNHCR had been conducting a voluntary return of refugees programme since the end of December 1987 and that by August 1988 more than 23,000 Tamils had been voluntarily repatriated.[58] On the basis of this, the Court noted that there was an improvement in the political situation in the receiving State, and that the situation did not create a greater risk for the applicants than for other Tamils.

Interestingly, the Commission's evaluation of the situation was different as it noted that:

> the information coming out of that country was unclear. On the one hand the Office of the United Nations High Commissioner for Refugees (UNHCR) did not consider Tamils to be refugees for the purposes of the 1951 UN Convention relating to the Status of Refugees.... At the request of the Sri Lankan and Indian Governments, following their July 1987 Accord, it organised, from December 1987 onwards, a programme of voluntary repatriation of Sri Lankan Tamils, mostly from India.[59]

In addition, several partly dissenting members of the Commission[60] noted that they were

> not persuaded that the voluntary repatriation programme organised by the UNHCR was a clear indication of an appeasement in the general situation in Sri Lanka, given the fact

[56] Ibid, para 111. See, however, *Salah Sheekh v Netherlands* (n 43 above), para 148, where the Court observed that 'the applicant cannot be required to establish the existence of further special distinguishing features concerning him personally in order to show that he was, and continues to be, personally at risk.... It might render the protection offered by that provision illusory if,... the applicant were required to show the existence of further special distinguishing features.'

[57] *Vilvarajah and others v United Kingdom* (n 20 above), para 105.

[58] Ibid, paras 76 and 110.

[59] *Vilvarajah and others v United Kingdom* (App Nos 13163/87–13165/87; 13447/87; 13448/87), report, 8 May 1990, not reported, para 140.

[60] Mr Trechsel, Mr Ermacora, Mr Gözübüyuk, Mr Campinos, Mrs Thune, Mr Rozakis, and Mrs Liddy.

that this programme was not initiated by UNHCR, but was its response to the request of the Sri Lankan and Indian Governments and was limited to the voluntary repatriation of Tamils who were mostly in India.[61]

Thus, while the Commission considered that there was no violation of Article 3 of the ECHR, it seems that its evaluation of the situation may have been more thorough and careful than that conducted by the Court.

The reasoning of the Court in the *Jabari v Turkey* judgment[62] was also very attentive to the question of whether refugee status had been granted. In that case, it was decided that the deportation of an Iranian applicant with refugee status granted by the UNHCR to her home country would breach Article 3 of the ECHR. The applicant had been arrested in Iran on suspicion of having had intimate relations with a married man. She fled to Turkey, and tried to travel to Canada through France on a false passport. She was intercepted and returned to Turkey, where she was arrested for entering with a false passport. She applied for asylum, but the domestic authorities rejected her claim and ordered her deportation. Finally, the UNHCR granted her refugee status. The Court observed that it 'must give due weight to the UNHCR's conclusion on the applicant's claim in making its own assessment of the risk which the applicant would face if her deportation were to be implemented'.[63] This led the Court to find that there was a real risk of the applicant being subjected to treatment contrary to Article 3 of the ECHR if she were deported to Iran.

From this, it appears that a UNHCR or domestic granting of refugee status may have served the Court as a way of legitimating a decision intervening in the domestic legal system or impinging on the state's margin of appreciation. Similarly, a denial of refugee status by the UNHCR or the domestic authorities may have been used to buttress the reasoning of judgment finding no breach of Article 3 of the ECHR. It has been argued, however, that it is inappropriate for the Court to import standards of the UNHCR into the European Convention, because the criteria for refugee status under the 1951 Refugee Convention differ substantially from the notion of 'inhuman and degrading treatment' under the ECHR.[64] In effect, the Court could fail to fulfil its primary purpose under Article 3 of the ECHR to protect persons against the risk of torture or inhuman and degrading treatment because of its reliance on UNHCR standards requiring individuals to be singled out for persecution.[65] Undoubtedly, the Court must also be careful when importing standards from the 1951 Refugee Convention

[61] *Vilvarajah and others v United Kingdom* (n 59 above).

[62] *Jabari v Turkey* (n 43 above).

[63] Ibid, para 41.

[64] David Weissbrodt and Isabel Härtrieter, 'The Principle of Non-Refoulement: Article 3 of the Convention Against Torture and Other Cruel, Inhuman or Degrading Treatment or Punishment in Comparison with the Non-refoulement Provisions of Other International Human Rights Treaties' (1999) 5 Buff Hum Rts L Rev 1, 36.

[65] Ibid.

into its case law where these could afford a lower level of protection than that of the ECHR.

Recently, however, it seems that the new Court has been more careful with the appropriation of requirements from the 1951 Refugee Convention. In *Muslim v Turkey*,[66] an Iraqi applicant of Turkmen origin fled to Turkey and claimed asylum with the UNHCR as well as with the Turkish Government. The UNHCR rejected his request, but the Turkish authorities issued him with a temporary residence permit awaiting the possibility of his settling in a third country. He filed another application for asylum with the UNHCR, which was still pending at the time of the judgment. The Court found that the UNHCR's examination of the claim could give rise to a rejection under the 1951 Refugee Convention, but determined that this question was not relevant here.[67] The Court gave greater weight to the engagement of the Turkish Government not to expel the applicant as well as to the existence of a voluntary repatriation plan of Iraqis set up by the UN and backed by the Council of Europe.[68] The Court considered that the applicant had not proven that his personal situation could be worse than that of other members of the Turkmen minority and even, perhaps, of the other inhabitants of Northern Iraq.[69] Moreover, it added that a democratization process was underway in Iraq, which could lead to an improvement in the situation.[70] Thus, it was found that there was no risk of ill-treatment prohibited under Article 3 of the ECHR. While this evaluation of the situation can be questioned, it is important to note that the Court did not consider that a UNHCR determination of asylum was relevant here. This seems to have been the case, however, in the judgments cited earlier.

The Court was also more careful in the *NA v United Kingdom* case,[71] where it held unanimously that the expulsion of the applicant, an ethnic Tamil, to Sri Lanka would violate Article 3 of the ECHR. The applicant had been refused asylum in the United Kingdom, but this did not appear to have constituted a relevant ground in this case. The Court evaluated the situation in Sri Lanka on the basis of various independent human rights reports, underlining that in the past it had already attached importance to such documents.[72] It found the information provided by the UNHCR to be very useful but not decisive, as it was general and presented a broad survey of the varying risks to Sri Lanka's ethnic groups.[73] The Court considered that the evidence before it pointed to the systematic torture and ill-treatment by the Sri Lankan authorities of Tamils who would be of interest to them in their efforts to combat the Tamil Tigers. The Court found it acceptable to assess the individual risk of returnees on the basis of the list of risks provided by the respondent Government. Further, the Court assessed the applicant's situation on the basis of more recent information regarding Sri Lanka and

[66] *Muslim v Turkey* (n 44 above). [67] Ibid, para 74. [68] Ibid, para 71.
[69] Ibid, para 68. [70] Ibid, para 70.
[71] *NA v United Kingdom* (App No 25904/07), judgment, 17 July 2008, not yet reported.
[72] Ibid, para 119. [73] Ibid, para 121.

the deterioration of the security situation there. In addition, it took into account the cumulative approach to all possible risk factors identified by the applicant as applicable to the case. Thus, the Court's assessment of the situation was more critical, careful, and balanced than in its earlier case law.

2.1.5 International Obligations of the Respondent States

One of the most important references to international refugee law in the context of cases under Article 3 of the ECHR appeared in the *TI v United Kingdom* decision,[74] where the Court clearly demonstrated that multilateral international agreements regulating the allocation of asylum claims between two or more states could absolve them from their responsibilities under the ECHR. There, the Court considered the case of a Sri Lankan who was allegedly forced to work by the Liberation Tigers of Tamil Eelam (LTTE) until he escaped and was arrested by the Sri Lankan authorities on suspicion of being an LTTE member. He sought asylum in Germany, where his claim was rejected. He then went to the United Kingdom and claimed asylum there. The United Kingdom refused to examine the merits of his claim and attempted to return him to Germany in accordance with the Dublin Convention.[75] The applicant complained that his removal to Germany, from where he would be removed to Sri Lanka, violated Articles 2, 3, 8, and 13 of the ECHR. The ECtHR noted that, under the Convention, the Contracting Parties' obligations did not stop at protecting people from expulsion to states where they would risk torture or ill-treatment, thereby following the UNHCR 'safe third country' policy.[76] It was nonetheless decided that the applicant's claim was inadmissible because it was not proven that there was a real risk that Germany would expel the applicant to Sri Lanka in breach of Article 3 of the ECHR.[77]

In spite of this finding, the Court determined that the arrangements made by the Dublin Convention concerning the attribution of responsibility between countries for deciding asylum claims did not affect the UK's obligation under

[74] *TI v United Kingdom* (n 7 above).

[75] Convention determining the State responsible for examining applications for asylum lodged in one of the Member States of the European Communities ('Dublin Convention'), entered into force 1 September 1997—no longer in force, [1997] OJ C254/1. In 2003, this Convention was replaced by Council Regulation (EC) 343/2003 of 18 February 2003 establishing the criteria and mechanisms for determining the Member State responsible for examining an asylum application lodged in one of the Member States by a third-country national [2003] OJ L50/1.

[76] See United Nations High Commissioner for Refugees, *The 'safe third country' policy in the light of the international obligations of countries vis-à-vis refugees and asylum seekers*, London, July 1993; United Nations High Commissioner for Refugees, *Executive Committee Conclusions, International Protection*, EXCOM Conclusion No 85 (XLIX), 1998, para (aa). See also Mole (n 5 above), 45–49.

[77] It appears, however, that approximately two weeks after this decision another asylum-seeker was removed from the United Kingdom to Germany. In spite of the assurances provided by the German Government in *TI v United Kingdom* (n 7 above), the asylum-seeker was sent back to his country of origin. See Mole (n 5 above), 48.

the ECHR to ensure that an applicant is not exposed to treatment contrary to Article 3 of the ECHR.[78] Furthermore:

> [w]here States establish international organisations, or *mutatis mutandis* international agreements, to pursue co-operation in certain fields of activities, there may be implications for the protection of fundamental rights. It would be incompatible with the purpose and object of the Convention if Contracting States were thereby absolved from their responsibility under the Convention in relation to the field of activity covered by such attribution.[79]

The Court also took into account the UNHCR's comments when it found that, in spite of the Dublin Convention's laudable objectives, its effectiveness could be undermined in practice by the different approaches of the Contracting States with regard to the scope of protection afforded.[80]

The Court's views here are very important as they demonstrate how it portrays the ECHR within the international legal framework. For the Court, the ECHR trumps other incompatible international instruments and obligations contracted by the Contracting States. In this particular case, the Court found that where there are conflicting provisions, the conflict must be resolved in favour of the ECHR provision. This approach was followed again in *Bosphorous Hava Yolları Turizm ve Ticaret Anonim Şirketi v Ireland*.[81] However, in the *Bosphorous* case the Court held in addition that the protection of ECHR rights was 'equivalent' under the ECHR system and EU law. The application of this reasoning may nonetheless be circumscribed as it was used in the context of EU legislation rather than international instruments. It is possible that the Court will not use the same approach in certain areas of international law which do not reflect the same level of enforceability.

In the *TI v United Kingdom* case, the Court also made an interesting remark regarding its own role in relation to the 1951 Refugee Convention. The ECtHR observed that:

> it is not its function to examine asylum claims or to monitor the performance of Contracting States with regard to their observance of their obligations under the Geneva Convention on Refugees. On this basis, the fact that the German authorities exclude from consideration of asylum claims non-State agent sources of risk of ill-treatment and ill-treatment from individual officers prohibited by the laws of the country is not directly relevant. The Court's primary concern is whether there are effective procedural safeguards of any kind protecting the applicant from being removed from Germany to Sri Lanka.[82]

[78] *TI v United Kingdom* (n 7 above), 456–457.

[79] Ibid, 457; *Waite and Kennedy v Germany* (App No 53236/99), judgment, 18 January 1999, Reports 1999-I, 393, para 67.

[80] Ibid.

[81] *Bosphorous Hava Yolları Turizm ve Ticaret Anonim Şirketi v Ireland* (n 7 above), paras 150–156.

[82] *TI v United Kingdom* (n 7 above), 458. The Court reiterated this position in *Muslim v Turkey* (n 44 above), para 72.

This view was taken further in the more recent *Salah Sheekh v Netherlands* judgment,[83] where the Court had to establish the gravity of the situation in Somalia. It took into account various reports from the respondent Government, the UNHCR, and independent NGOs, and ensured that its review was independent. It was emphasized that:

> [i]t must be satisfied that the assessment is adequate and sufficiently supported by domestic material as well as by materials originating from other reliable and objective sources, such as for instance other Contracting or non-contracting states, agencies of the United Nations and reputable non-governmental organisations. In its supervisory task under Article 19 of the Convention, it would be too narrow an approach under Article 3 in cases concerning aliens facing expulsion or extradition if the Court, as an international human rights court, were to only take into account materials made available by the domestic authorities of the Contracting State concerned, without comparing these with materials from other reliable and objective sources.[84]

In all of the cases where the Court had to assess the situation in the receiving State, it relied on various UNHCR, UN, Council of Europe and NGO documents in order to evaluate the risk of a potential deportation or expulsion on a person.[85] It relied also on reports from non-Contracting States, such as the United States, but this was met on occasion with fervent criticism.[86] It follows, from these statements that, while the Court is prepared to consider various documents external to the ECHR system, it nonetheless draws clear boundaries between its own jurisdiction and the competencies of the UNHCR. It is evident that the Court's role is limited to the interpretation and application of the ECHR, but the Court sometimes feels the need to emphasize this point as a result of the expanding scope of international law.

[83] *Salah Sheekh v Netherlands* (App No 1948/04), judgment, 11 January 2007, not yet reported, para 135.

[84] Ibid, para 136.

[85] See, for example, in *Muslim v Turkey* (n 44 above), paras 48–51; *N v Finland* (n 43 above), paras 117–122; *Thampibillai v Netherlands* (n 43 above), paras 46–48; *TI v United Kingdom* (n 7 above); *Hilal v United Kingdom* (App No 45276/99), judgment, 6 March 2001, Reports 2001-II, 292, paras 38–46; *Jabari v Turkey* (n 43 above), paras 31–32; *HLR v France* (App No 24573/94), judgment, 29 April 1997, Reports 1997-III, 745, para 42; *Chahal v United Kingdom* (n 21 above), paras 49–60.

[86] *Said v The Netherlands* (App No 2345/02), judgment, 5 July 2005, Reports 2005-VI, 275, separate opinion of Judge Loucaides. In his separate opinion, Judge Loucaides stated the following: 'I cannot agree with the inclusion in the judgment...of the United States Department of State Country Report on Human Rights Practices in Eritrea as a reliable source of information on the human rights situation in that country. This is because I do not consider such reports to be credible sources of information on human rights in any part of the world. They are not prepared by an independent and impartial institution but by a purely political government agency, which promotes and expresses the foreign policy of the United States. Therefore, they cannot by definition be relied on as a neutral and impartial exposition of the facts mentioned therein. There is always an element of suspicion that such reports are influenced by political expediency based on US foreign policy with reference to the situation in the country concerned and that they serve a political agenda.'

2.2 Case Law Relating to Article 5 of the ECHR

2.2.1 A Comparison of the ECHR with the 1951 Refugee Convention

The 1951 Refugee Convention and the ECHR both explicitly allow states to detain asylum-seekers under certain circumstances. Overall, the 1951 Refugee Convention, together with the subsequent accompanying UNHCR documents, seems to adopt an approach to detention which is similar to that reflected in the ECHR and the ECtHR case law. There are some differences in both frameworks with regard to the type of detention review available and to the right to compensation for unjustified detention, the ECHR providing the higher level of protection in this regard. There is nonetheless a more fundamental difference between the systems which lies in the fact that the ECHR adds to the 1951 Convention an element that is lacking, namely the enforceability of rights and an international monitoring body.[87]

Refugees fearing for their lives and fleeing their country of origin rarely have time to fulfil the procedural requirements of immigration prior to their departure. While the 1951 Refugee Convention does not guarantee their admission in any given country, it nonetheless provides in Article 31(1) that:

> [t]he Contracting States shall not impose penalties, on account of their illegal entry or presence, on refugees who, coming directly from a territory where their life or freedom was threatened in the sense of article 1, enter or are present in their territory without authorization, provided they present themselves without delay to the authorities and show good cause for their illegal entry or presence.[88]

However, Article 31 does not exclude deprivation of or restrictions on the right to liberty pending the asylum procedure. Such measures are frequently imposed on asylum-seekers upon their arrival and are considered to be administrative measures rather than penalties.[89] Thus, pursuant to Article 31(2), it is possible to restrict the movement of asylum-seekers when necessary and until the status of the person concerned is regularized or until he or she obtains admission into another country.[90] Additionally, a state can exceptionally take provisional measures 'which it considers to be essential to the national security in the case of a particular person, pending a determination by the Contracting State that that person is in fact a refugee and that the continuance of such measures is necessary in his case in the interests of national security'.[91] The Revised UNHCR Detention

[87] Christos Giakoumopoulos, 'Detention of Asylum Seekers in Light of Article 5 of the European Convention on Human Rights' in Jane Hughes and Fabrice Liebaut (eds), *Detention of Asylum Seekers in Europe: Analysis and Perspectives* (The Hague/Cambridge, MA/Dordrecht: Martinus Nijhoff, 1998), 161, 181–182.

[88] Convention relating to the Status of Refugees, Art 31(1).

[89] Giakoumopoulos (n 87 above), 165.

[90] Convention relating to the Status of Refugees, Art 31(2).

[91] Ibid, Art 9.

Guidelines[92] and the Conclusion No 44 of the UNHCR Executive Committee[93] specify further that detention of asylum-seekers may be resorted to exceptionally and only if necessary to verify identity; to determine the elements on which the claim for refugee status or asylum is based; in cases where asylum-seekers have destroyed their travel and/or identity documents or have used fraudulent documents to mislead the authorities; and to protect national security and public order.[94] Further, Guideline 2 of the Revised UNHCR Guidelines provides that detainees should not be detained as a general principle.[95] It is also stated in the introduction to the Revised Guidelines that detention of asylum-seekers cannot be arbitrary. From this, it follows that the text of the 1951 Refugee Convention allows a limited form of detention, and that the supplementary documents specify and narrow down its scope by requiring that detention be applied on an exceptional basis.

Article 5 of the ECHR frames the detention in much more absolute and exceptional terms than Article 31(1) of the 1951 Refugee Convention.[96] Its aim is to prohibit arbitrary arrest or detention of any person who is subject to ECtHR jurisdiction, and not just to the detention of asylum-seekers.[97] It is not entirely clear how the notion of arbitrariness is to be defined, as the Strasbourg bodies have not yet determined specifically the consequences that it may entail. In addition, Article 5 of the ECHR provides that detention is permitted in the following situations:

(a) the lawful detention of a person after conviction by a competent court; (b) the lawful arrest or detention of a person for non-compliance with the lawful order of a court or in order to secure the fulfilment of any obligation prescribed by law; (c) the lawful arrest or detention of a person effected for the purpose of bringing him before the competent legal authority of reasonable suspicion of having committed an offence or when it is reasonably considered necessary to prevent his committing an offence or fleeing after having done so; (d) the detention of a minor by lawful order for the purpose of educational supervision or his lawful detention for the purpose of bringing him before the competent legal authority; (e) the lawful detention of persons for the prevention of the spreading of infectious diseases, of persons of unsound mind, alcoholics or drug addicts, or vagrants; (f) the lawful arrest or detention of a person to prevent his effecting an unauthorized

[92] United Nations High Commissioner for Refugees, Revised Guidelines on Applicable Criteria and Standards Relating to the Detention of Asylum-Seekers, UNHCR/IOM/22/99/Rev 1, UNHCR/FOM/22/99/Rev 1, Geneva, February 1999.

[93] United Nations High Commissioner for Refugees, *Executive Committee Conclusions, Detention of Refugees and Asylum-Seekers*, EXCOM Conclusion No 44 (XXXVII)–1986, para (b).

[94] Ibid, Guideline 3. [95] Ibid, Guideline 2.

[96] It should be noted that Art 2 of Protocol No 4, which governs the restrictions on freedom of movement, is of related interest to this section, given that asylum-seekers are often subjected to such measures. These measures will not, however, be analysed here due to lack of space: Protocol No 4 to the European Convention on Human Rights, securing certain rights and freedoms others than those already included in the Convention and in the First Protocol thereto, as amended by Protocol No 11, ETS No 46 (entered into force 2 May 1968).

[97] Goodwin-Gill and McAdam (n 14 above), 46.

entry into the country or of a person against whom action is being taken with a view to deportation or extradition.

A detention which is not for one of the purposes identified in Article 5 of the ECHR will be considered unlawful. As regards asylum-seekers, Article 5(f) is the most relevant and is resorted to by Contracting States in situations of expulsion, deportation, or extradition.

The frameworks of the 1951 Refugee Convention and the ECHR both enshrine the principle of lawfulness, which provides that detention may only be resorted to on grounds prescribed by domestic law. Article 5(1) of the ECHR stipulates that arrest or detention must be carried out 'in accordance with a procedure prescribed by law', which comprises both the substantive and procedural rules of national law.[98] In interpreting the principle of lawfulness, the ECtHR clarified that it also requires that 'any deprivation of liberty should be in keeping with the purpose of Article 5, namely to protect the individual from arbitrariness'.[99] Furthermore, this requirement takes into account the quality of the law (it must be precise and accessible) and requires it to be compatible with the rule of law. For the purposes of Article 5(1)(f), however, it is immaterial whether the underlying decision to expel can be justified under domestic law or the ECHR, as long as the detention is 'lawful'.[100] This would seem to require a lower level of protection than in other types of detention enumerated in Article 5(1). In a similar vein, Conclusion No 44 of the UNHCR Executive Committee provides that 'detention may be resorted to only on grounds prescribed by law'.[101] Guideline 3 of the Revised UNHCR Detention Guidelines also reiterates this requirement by referring to Conclusion No 44 and stating that detention must be 'clearly prescribed by a national law which is in conformity with general norms and principles of international human rights law'.[102] Thus, within these two legal frameworks, deprivation of liberty cannot occur in the absence of domestic legislation expressly authorizing it.[103]

Neither instrument provides any time limits with regard to the duration of the detention of asylum-seekers. Nonetheless, the Executive Committee in Conclusion No 44 '[r]ecognized the importance of fair and expeditious procedures for determining refugee status or granting asylum in protecting refugees and asylum-seekers from unjustified or unduly prolonged detention'.[104] Furthermore, the Revised UNHCR Detention Guidelines provide in Guideline 3

[98] *Amuur v France* (App No 19776/92), judgment, 25 June 1996, Reports 1996-III, 826, para 50.

[99] Ibid.

[100] *Chahal v United Kingdom* (n 21 above), para 112; See also Clare Ovey and Robin CA White, *The European Convention on Human Rights* (Oxford/New York: OUP, 4th edn, 2006), 148–149.

[101] United Nations High Commissioner for Refugees (n 93 above), para (b).

[102] United Nations High Commissioner for Refugees (n 92 above), Guideline 3.

[103] Giakoumopoulos (n 87 above), 174.

[104] United Nations High Commissioner for Refugees (n 93 above), para (c).

that if detention is 'judged necessary it should only be imposed in a non discriminatory manner for a minimal period'.[105] Article 5 of the ECHR does not contain any express limitation of the detention period for asylum-seekers, and the ECtHR has made some surprising comments in this field. In connection with the duration of the asylum and deportation proceedings in the *Chahal* case,[106] the Court found that '[i]t is neither in the interests of the individual applicant nor in the general public interest in the administration of justice that such decisions be taken hastily, without due regard to all the relevant issues and evidence'.[107] Although the applicant in the case had been detained in prison for over six years, the Court found that this delay did not infringe Article 5(1)(f) of the ECHR. Furthermore, in the *Kolompar* case,[108] the Court found that in spite of the unusually long period of detention (over two-and-a-half years), there was no violation of Article 5(1)(f) because the delay in detention was attributable to the behaviour of the applicant and not to the actions of the authorities.[109] The Court nonetheless emphasized in the *Chahal* and *Kolompar* cases that, while Article 5(1)(f) does not require domestic law to provide a time limit for detention pending a decision on deportation or extradition, proceedings are to be conducted with the requisite diligence.[110] Failing this, detention may cease to be permissible under Article 5(1)(f) and the Court may have to consider the length of time spent in detention pending deportation or extradition.[111] This lawfulness of detention is then assessed in accordance with the circumstances of each case.[112] Recently, the Court seems to have followed this principle closely and found violations of Article 5(1)(f), *inter alia*, with regard to a detention of undetermined length,[113] a detention of five years and 11 months,[114] a two-and-a-half-year detention,[115] and a two-month detention of a child in a centre for adults.[116] In general, these cases seem to indicate that there is a trend departing from the strict *Chahal* ruling.[117] Thus, while the ECHR and the 1951 Refugee Convention have phrased the requirement of reasonable delay in proceedings differently, they provide similar levels of protection.

[105] United Nations High Commissioner for Refugees (n 92 above), Guideline 3.

[106] *Chahal v United Kingdom* (n 21 above). [107] Ibid, para 117.

[108] *Kolompar v Belgium* (App No 11613/85), judgment, 24 September 1992, Series A, Vol 235-C.

[109] Ibid, paras 37–43.

[110] Ibid, para 36; *Chahal v United Kingdom* (n 21 above), para 113. See also *Bodrovskiy v Russia* (App No 49491/99), judgment, 8 February 2005, not reported, para 50. [111] Ibid.

[112] *Gordyeyev v Poland* (App Nos 43369/98; 51777/99), decision, 3 May 2005, not reported.

[113] *Nasrulloyev v Russia* (App No 656/06), judgment, 11 October 2007, not yet reported.

[114] *Erdem v Germany* (App No 38321/07), judgment, 5 October 2001, Reports 2001-VII, 15.

[115] *Singh v Czech Republic* (App No 60538/00), judgment, 25 January 2005, not reported.

[116] *Mubilanzila Mayeka and Kaniki Mitunga v Belgium* (App No 13178/93), judgment, 12 October 2006, not reported. See ch III, 4.4.

[117] See, however, *Gordyeyev v Poland* (n 112 above), where the Court considered that decisions with regard to asylum should not be made hastily, without due regard to all the relevant issues and evidence.

With regard to the conditions of detention of asylum-seekers, it appears that both systems do not differ substantially. Article 5 of the ECHR does not contain any detailed rights with regard to the detention of asylum-seekers. Nonetheless, Articles 2, 3, and 8 can be used by asylum-seekers to claim some of the essential rights pertaining to the conditions of detention. Article 3 of the ECHR (the prohibition on torture and inhuman or degrading treatment or punishment) has been successfully invoked by persons who claimed that they were subjected to inhuman detention conditions, such as overcrowding, inadequate heating, inadequate ventilation, inadequate sleeping and toilet facilities, insufficient food, insufficient recreation and contact with the outside world, and insufficient medical treatment.[118] The Court also stressed that under Article 3:

> the State must ensure that a person is detained in conditions which are compatible with respect for his human dignity, that the manner and method of the execution of the measure do not subject him to distress or hardship of an intensity exceeding the unavoidable level of suffering inherent in detention and that, given the practical demands of imprisonment, his health and well-being are adequately secured by, among other things, providing him with the requisite medical assistance....[119]

Thus, the Court expanded the meaning of Article 3 of the ECHR, and was able to fill in the gap in Article 5, which does not refer to conditions of detention.

As part of the framework of the 1951 Refugee Convention, the Executive Committee of the UNHCR stressed in Conclusion No 44 'that conditions of detention of refugees and asylum-seekers must be humane. In particular, refugees and asylum-seekers shall, whenever possible, not be accommodated with persons detained as common criminals, and shall not be located in areas where their physical safety is endangered.'[120] The Revised UNHCR Detention Guidelines reiterate that the conditions of detention for asylum-seekers should be humane and that respect be shown for the dignity of the person.[121] Further, they emphasize the need to screen all asylum-seekers at the outset of the detention to identify trauma or torture victims, to segregate men and women, children and adults within facilities (unless they are relatives), to use separate detention facilities to accommodate asylum-seekers, to allow asylum-seekers to make regular contact with and receive visits from friends, to allow asylum-seekers to receive appropriate medical treatment and psychological counselling, to allow asylum-seekers to conduct some form of physical exercise, to permit them to take further educa-

[118] See, for example, *The Greek Case (Denmark, Norway, Sweden and the Netherlands v Greece)*, report, 5 November 1969, 12 YB 1, 11; *Ilaşcu v Russia and Moldova* (App No 48787/99), judgment , 8 July 2004, Reports 2004-VII, 179; *Iovchev v Bulgaria* (App No 41211/98), judgment, 2 February 2006, not reported; *Price v United Kingdom* (App No 33394/96), judgment, 10 July 2001, Reports 2001-VII, 153; *Peers v Greece* (App No 28524/95), judgment, 19 April 2001, Reports 2001-III, 275; *Dougoz v Greece* (App No 40907/98), judgment, 6 March 2001, Reports 2001-II, 255.

[119] *Kudła v Poland* (App No 30210/96), judgment, 26 October 2000, Reports 2000-XI, 197, para 94.

[120] United Nations High Commissioner for Refugees (n 93 above), para (f).

[121] United Nations High Commissioner for Refugees (n 92 above), Guideline 10.

tion or vocational training, and to allow them to have access to basic necessities and to a complaints mechanism.[122] From this, it follows that both frameworks enshrine similar principles through the Strasbourg jurisprudence and the Revised UNHCR Detention Guidelines.

While both instruments, their additional soft law documents, and the relevant case law entitle the applicant to have the lawfulness of his/her detention reviewed, they concern different types and levels of evaluation. Pursuant to Article 5(4) of the ECHR, '[e]veryone who is deprived of his liberty by arrest or detention shall be entitled to take proceedings by which the lawfulness of his detention shall be decided speedily by a court and his release ordered if the detention is not lawful'. In addition, the ECHR requires this right to be practical and effective, and that the person concerned has the opportunity to avail himself or herself of it.[123] The scope of review required under Article 5(1)(f) still appears to be uncertain:[124] although the Court held in the *Chahal* judgment that it was not relevant whether the underlying decision to expel was justified, it also found that the domestic proceedings brought by the applicant did not comply with Article 5(4) because the courts were prevented from reviewing the decision to detain the applicant on grounds that national security was involved.[125] In fact, the court which conducts the review must be an independent judicial body providing certain types of guarantees specific to questions of deprivation of liberty.[126] In contrast to this, in Conclusion No 44 the Executive Committee of the UNHCR '[r]ecommended that detention measures taken in respect of refugees and asylum-seekers should be subject to judicial or administrative review'.[127] In addition, Guideline No 5 of the Revised UNHCR Detention Guidelines reiterates that asylum-seekers should be entitled 'to have the decision subjected to an automatic review before a judicial or administrative body independent of the detaining authorities'.[128] By excluding detention review by administrative authorities, it appears that the ECHR framework goes further than the documents specifying the requirements of the 1951 Refugee Convention.[129] The review by administrative authorities is not included under the ECHR, as the Strasbourg case law refers only to judicial review. Thus, the ECHR and the Strasbourg case law guarantee a higher level of detention review than the 1951 Refugee Convention.

Finally, in spite of the fact that both systems offer similar levels of protection, a very fundamental problem persists with regard to the lack of enforcement of the rights under the 1951 Refugee Convention. As already mentioned, the 1951 Refugee Convention does not provide for an individual complaint mechanism

122 Ibid.
123 Giakoumopoulos (n 87 above), 177.
124 Ovey and White (n 100 above), 152.
125 *Chahal v United Kingdom* (n 21 above), paras 130–132.
126 *Weeks v United Kingdom* (App No 9787/82), judgment, 2 October 1987, Series A, Vol 114, para 61.
127 United Nations High Commissioner for Refugees (n 93 above), para (e).
128 United Nations High Commissioner for Refugees (n 92 above), Guideline 5 (iii).
129 Giakoumopoulos (n 87 above), 178.

or an international monitoring body, and thus is dependent on the will of the Contracting States for its enforcement. Furthermore, the Convention contains general rights with regard to the detention of asylum-seekers; these are specified in subsequent documents which were adopted by the UNHCR. Naturally, the likelihood of being able to enforce such soft law documents is even lower than for the 1951 Refugee Convention. Thus, in this context, the ECHR offers, once again, a higher standard of protection by providing a specific enforcement mechanism and a more effective avenue through which to seek justice.

2.2.2 The Limited Number of References in the Case Law

Considering that the ECHR and the 1951 Refugee Convention frameworks offer similar levels of protection with regard to the detention of asylum-seekers, the use of and necessity for the Court to refer to the latter is considerably reduced. Again, this is due to the fact that the provisions of the ECHR are more effective than the requirements of the 1951 Refugee Convention because they can be enforced by the ECtHR. Furthermore, the case law of the ECtHR is clearly binding on the Contracting States, unlike the soft law instruments which were adopted after the 1951 Refugee Convention came into force. The possibility of enforcing the rights contained in the ECHR offers tremendous advantages in comparison to the system put into place by the UNHCR.

The absence of direct references to the 1951 Refugee Convention in this particular strain of the ECtHR's case law is due to the fact that the Court felt that, '[s]ubject, as always, to the rule against arbitrariness,... the State has a broader discretion to decide whether to detain potential immigrants than is the case for other interferences with the right to liberty'.[130] In many of these cases, the Court deferred to the discretion and determinations of Contracting States. Furthermore, the references to the 1951 Refugee Convention were limited by the fact that the Court had to assess the lawfulness of detention by reference to national law and not other external sources. In spite of this general trend, the 1951 Refugee Convention appeared nonetheless sporadically in a few ECHR cases where it was used in very different ways and gave rise to different results. The presence of these few references to the 1951 Refugee Convention can be explained in part by the fact that the cases were closely intertwined with asylum proceedings regulated by domestic law implementing the 1951 Refugee Convention requirements. Nonetheless, several of these references do not have significant precedential value, as they appeared in dissident opinions. Overall, there is no uniformity in the sporadic use of the 1951 Refugee Convention in these cases. It thus becomes very difficult to deduce the Court's underlying motive as part of this strand of the Strasbourg case law.

[130] *Saadi v United Kingdom* (App No 13229/03), judgment, 11 July 2006, not reported, para 44.

2.2.2.1 Intertwinement of Both Systems

The Court made an important reference to the 1951 Refugee Convention in the *Amuur v France* judgment,[131] which concerned refugees from Somalia who had travelled through Kenya and Syria to the Charles de Gaulle Airport in Paris. They were refused entry into France on grounds that they held false passports. Before being returned to Syria, the applicants were shuttled by the police between a hotel and the lounge of the airport for 20 days. They alleged breaches of Articles 3, 5, 6, and 13 of the ECHR. The Court rejected the respondent Government's argument that the detention measures did not amount to a deprivation of liberty because the applicants were free to return any time to Syria. It was noted with interest that France is also a party to the 1951 Refugee Convention.[132] As with other international instruments covered in earlier chapters, this ratification may have prompted and legitimated further references to the 1951 Refugee Convention. It was later emphasized that 'Contracting States have the undeniable sovereign right to control aliens' entry into and residence in their territory.... however... this right must be exercised in accordance with the provisions of the Convention, including Article 5.'[133] Conscious of the interplay between both legal frameworks in this field, the Court signalled that the fulfilment of obligations under the 1951 Refugee Convention is subject to a compatibility review under the ECHR.

Subsequently, the Court referred explicitly to Article 31 of the 1951 Refugee Convention,[134] reiterating that it must be complied with, when it stressed that:

> [h]olding aliens in the international zone does indeed involve a restriction upon liberty, but one which is not in every respect comparable to that which obtains in centres for the detention of aliens pending deportation. Such confinement, accompanied by suitable safeguards for the persons concerned, is acceptable only in order to enable States to prevent unlawful immigration while complying with their international obligations, particularly under the 1951 Geneva Convention Relating to the Status of Refugees and the European Convention on Human Rights. States' legitimate concern to foil the increasingly frequent attempts to circumvent immigration restrictions must not deprive asylum-seekers of the protection afforded by these conventions.[135]

The Court also observed that:

> Although by the force of circumstances the decision to order holding must necessarily be taken by the administrative or police authorities, its prolongation requires speedy review by the courts, the traditional guardians of personal liberties. Above all, such confinement

[131] *Amuur v France* (n 98 above). [132] Ibid, para 41. [133] Ibid.

[134] Guy S Goodwin-Gill, 'Article 31 of the 1951 Convention Relating to the Status of Refugees: Non-Penalization, Detention, and Protection' in Erika Feller, Volker Türk, and Frances Nicholson (eds), *Refugee Protection in International Law: UNHCR's Global Consultations on International Protection* (Cambridge/New York: Cambridge University Press, 2003), 205.

[135] *Amuur v France* (n 98 above), para 43.

must not deprive the asylum-seeker of the right to gain effective access to the procedure for determining refugee status.[136]

It was found that:

[i]n order to ascertain whether a deprivation of liberty has complied with the principle of compatibility with domestic law, it therefore falls to the Court to assess not only the legislation in force in the field under consideration, but also the quality of the other legal rules applicable to the persons concerned.... These characteristics are of fundamental importance with regard to asylum-seekers at airports, particularly in view of the need to reconcile the protection of fundamental rights with the requirements of States immigration policies.[137]

In these passages of the *Amuur* judgment, the Court was very conscious of the interaction between the legal frameworks in this situation, especially given that France had ratified the 1951 Refugee Convention. In a case closely intertwined with asylum proceedings, the Court also felt compelled to refer to both the ECHR and the 1951 Refugee Convention. Moreover, it seems to have used the 1951 Refugee Convention to bolster its reasoning, in which it found in favour of the applicant. In balancing the interests of the State and of the individual, the Court assessed whether the detention had fulfilled the standards of the ECHR and the 1951 Refugee Convention and emphasized that the applicants should not be deprived of their right to asylum in the process of detention, thus exceeding the requirements of the latter instrument.

2.2.2.2 Duration of the Asylum Proceedings and Domestic Decisions

As discussed earlier, the Court noted in relation to the asylum and deportation proceedings in the *Chahal v United Kingdom* judgment[138] that such decisions should not be taken hastily, without due regard to the issues and to the evidence.[139] A similar statement appeared in relation to asylum proceedings in the *Gordeyeyev v Poland* decision,[140] where the Court made a direct reference to the 1951 Refugee Convention, but took into greater account the findings of the domestic authorities with regard to the asylum determination of the applicant. The case concerned a Belarusian national who was extradited from Poland to Belarus on charges of forgery of documents. While he was in detention pending extradition in Poland, he applied for asylum submitting that he was a member of a Belarusian dissident organization and that he risked being ill-treated if returned to his country of origin. His request was rejected. Before the Court, he complained, *inter alia*, that his detention pending extradition was unlawful under Article 5(1)(c) and 5(1)(f) of the ECHR because it lacked legal basis in Polish law and was based on an incomplete extradition request.

[136] Ibid. [137] Ibid, para 50.
[138] *Chahal v United Kingdom* (n 21 above). [139] Ibid, para 117.
[140] *Gordyeyev v Poland* (n 112 above).

The Court found that the detention was legally justified and that the interpretation of domestic law was not arbitrary or unreasonable. It was further considered that:

> [h]aving regard to the issue to be determined in the asylum proceedings, i.e. whether the applicant had well-founded fears of being subjected to persecution within the meaning of the Geneva Convention Relating to the Status of Refugees and/or treatment contrary to Article 3 of the Convention, ... it was neither in the interest of the individual applicant nor in the general public interest in the administration of justice that such decisions should be taken hastily, without due regard to all the relevant issues and evidence.[141]

In assessing the length of the asylum proceedings, the Court observed that it paid significant attention to 'the fact that the applicant's request for asylum was rejected by the authorities as being entirely without substance'[142] and that 'the Minister of the Interior and Administration considered that the applicant's asylum claim amounted to an abuse of the relevant procedures'.[143] The Court further noted that the extradition proceedings were connected to the asylum claim. According to its view, 'the applicant should have been aware that by bringing his asylum claim he might contribute to the length of the extradition proceedings'.[144] It was pointed out that when the asylum proceedings were concluded, the question of extradition was determined without any significant delay. Thus, according to the Court, the extradition proceedings did not exhibit any lack of due diligence on the part of the domestic authorities under Article 5(1)(f). The complaint concerning this article was thus held to be manifestly ill-founded.

These findings seem to depart from the framework of the 1951 Refugee Convention, which requires a speedy determination of asylum proceedings. As already noted,[145] the Executive Committee of the UNHCR '[r]ecognized the importance of fair and expeditious procedures for determining refugee status or granting asylum in protecting refugees and asylum-seekers from unjustified or unduly prolonged detention'[146] in Conclusion No 44. While the Strasbourg Court uses the criteria of due diligence in order to assess the length of proceedings, the requirement that these decisions should not be taken hastily may give rise to results which depart from the rationale of the 1951 Refugee Convention.

Furthermore, the Court's finding that the state's determination of an asylum claim is relevant in the context of the duration of detention and asylum proceedings may unduly restrict the scope of the protection granted to asylum-seekers. As has been argued with regard to torture and degrading treatment above, the incorporation of UNHCR standards can restrict the scope of the ECHR because the criteria for a refugee status under the 1951 Refugee Convention differ substantially from that notion.[147] Similarly, the determination of refugee status

[141] Ibid. [142] Ibid. [143] Ibid. [144] Ibid. [145] See 2.2.1 above.

[146] United Nations High Commissioner for Refugees (n 93 above), para (c).

[147] See 2.1.4 above; Weissbrodt and Härtrieter (n 64 above), 36.

differs from the question of the length of detention and length of asylum proceedings. Thus, references to the 1951 Refugee Convention may restrict the rights of asylum-seekers in this context.

2.2.2.3 Right to Detain Asylum-seekers

In the *Saadi v United Kingdom* case,[148] the Grand Chamber relied on UNHCR soft law instruments to interpret for the first time the expression 'lawful... detention of a person to prevent his effecting an unauthorised entry' contained in Article 5(1)(f) of the ECHR. The *Saadi* case concerned an Iraqi doctor who belonged to the Iraqi Workers' Communist Party and who fled from his home country after having treated and helped to escape three fellow party members. He arrived at London Heathrow Airport where he claimed asylum, and was initially granted temporary admission. He was taken into detention for seven days at the Oakington Reception Centre as part of a fast-track procedure for determining asylum claims. He was given reasons for his detention of 76 hours after being taken in. Before the Court, he alleged that the respondent Government had infringed Articles 5(1) and (2) of the ECHR. In the Chamber and Grand Chamber judgments, the Court found that there was no violation of Article 5(1), but held unanimously that there had been a breach of Article 5(2).[149]

The UNHCR, intervening as third party in the case, was concerned that the Chamber judgment

> (1) assimilated the position of asylum seekers to ordinary immigrants, (2) considered that an asylum seeker effectively had no lawful or authorised status prior to the successful determination of the claim and (3) rejected the application of a necessity test to the question whether detention was arbitrary, permitted States to detain asylum seekers on grounds of expediency in wide circumstances that were incompatible with general principles of international refugee and human rights law.[150]

It was clarified that, '[i]n order to detain an asylum seeker under Article 5 § 1(f), there had to be something more than the mere absence of decision on the claim; the detention had to be necessary, in the sense that less intrusive means would not suffice, and proportionate to the aim pursued'.[151]

According to the UNHCR, the ECHR also had to be interpreted, like the Refugee Convention, in harmony with other rules of international law, especially human rights treaties. Further, ECHR rights had to be given a broad interpretation which would provide them with a practical and effective protection. Any limitations imposed on these rights would therefore have to be construed narrowly. The UNHCR submitted that, '[w]here a State admitted an asylum seeker

[148] *Saadi v United Kingdom* (App No 13229/03), judgment, 29 January 2008, not yet reported. See 2.4.2 below.

[149] *Saadi v United Kingdom* (n 130 above); *Saadi v United Kingdom* (n 148 above).

[150] *Saadi v United Kingdom* (n 148 above), para 54.

[151] Ibid, para 55.

to procedures, and the asylum seeker complied with national law, his temporary entry into and presence on the territory could not be considered as "unauthorised"; the grant of temporary admission was precisely an authorisation by the State temporarily to allow the individual to enter its territory consistent with the law'.[152] The UNHCR referred also to a decision of the Human Rights Committee where it was found that the detention of asylum-seekers cannot be used on a fact-insensitive blanket basis or purely for reasons of expediency or administrative convenience.[153]

When evaluating the claim under Article 5(1), the Court observed that 'it will, as always, be guided by Articles 31 to 33 of the Vienna Convention on the Law of Treaties'.[154] It reiterated that the ECHR had to be interpreted according to the ordinary meaning of its words in their context and in light of their object and purpose (Article 31(1) of the Vienna Convention on the Law of Treaties (VCLT)).[155] It then referred to Article 31(3)(c) of the VCLT and mentioned that it would also take into account any relevant rules and principles of international law applicable in relations between the Contracting States.[156] It was emphasized that Article 5 of the ECHR enshrines a fundamental human right, namely the protection of the individual against arbitrary state interferences with his right to liberty.[157] As an exception to this general rule, Article 5(1)(f) of the ECHR permits the detention of foreigners in an immigration context. The Court recalled that states have the 'undeniable sovereign right to control aliens' entry into and residence in their territory'.[158] As a result, they were 'permitted to detain would-be immigrants who have applied for permission to enter, whether by way of asylum or not'.[159] Deferring to the findings of the Court of Appeals, the House of Lords, and the Chamber, the Court held that, 'until a State has "authorised" entry to the country, any entry is "unauthorised" and the detention of a person who wishes to effect entry and who needs but does not yet have authorisation to do so, can be, without any distortion of language, to "prevent his effecting an unauthorised entry"'.[160]

The Court did not accept the UNHCR's suggestion that, as soon as an asylum-seeker surrendered to the immigration authorities, he could be considered to be making an authorized entry. According to its view, interpreting Article 5(1)(f) of the ECHR only to permit detention of 'a person who is trying to evade entry restrictions would be to place too narrow a construction on the terms of the provision and on the power of the State to exercise its undeniable right of control'.[161] Moreover, such an interpretation would 'be inconsistent with Conclusion No 44 of the Executive Committee of the United Nations High Commissioner for Refugees' Programme, the UNHCR's Guidelines and the Committee of Ministers' Recommendation..., all of which envisage the

[152] Ibid, para 56.
[153] Ibid, para 58; *A v Australia*, Communication No 560/1993, CCPR/C/59/D/560/1993, 30 April 1997, Human Rights Committee.
[154] *Saadi v United Kingdom* (n 148 above), para 61.
[155] Ibid, para 62.
[156] Ibid.
[157] Ibid, para 63.
[158] Ibid, para 64.
[159] Ibid.
[160] Ibid, para 65.
[161] Ibid.

detention of asylum seekers in certain circumstances, for example while identity checks are taking place or when elements on which the asylum claim is based have to be determined'.[162] Thus, the Court decided not to follow the UNHCR's interpretation of its own soft law instruments.

The Court went on to consider the meaning of 'freedom from arbitrariness' contained in Article 5(1)(f) of the ECHR. It found that:

> [t]o avoid being branded as arbitrary, detention had to be carried out in good faith; it had to be closely connected to the purpose of preventing unauthorised entry of the person to the country; the place and conditions of detention had to be appropriate, bearing in mind that the measure was applicable not to those who had committed criminal offences but to aliens who, often fearing for their lives, had fled from their own country; and the length of the detention should not exceed that reasonably required for the purpose pursued.[163]

The Court found that in the case at hand detention had been carried out in good faith and was closely connected to the purpose of preventing an unauthorized entry. In the Court's view, 'given the difficult administrative problems with which the United Kingdom was confronted during the period in question,... it was not incompatible with Article 5 § 1 (f) of the Convention to detain the applicant for seven days in suitable conditions to enable his claim to asylum to be processed speedily'.[164] Interestingly, the Court also mentioned that 'the provision of a more efficient system of determining large numbers of asylum claims rendered unnecessary recourse to a broader and more extensive use of detention powers'.[165] With regard to the complaint under Article 5(2) of the ECHR, the Grand Chamber held that a delay of 76 hours in providing reasons for detention was not compatible with the requirement that such reasons be given 'promptly' under this provision.

The Court's reasoning was criticized by partly dissenting judges.[166] According to their view, the Court's finding that states are permitted to detain would-be immigrants who have applied for permission to enter did not comply with prevailing international standards. It did not sit comfortably 'with the principle that asylum seekers who have presented a claim for international protection are *ispo facto* within the territory of a State, in particular for the purposes of Article 12 of the International Convention on Civil and Political Rights (liberty of movement) and the case-law if the Human Rights Committee, according to which a persons has duly presented an application for asylum is considered to be "lawfully within the territory"'.[167] Further, it was found that the Court should have followed the finding of the Human Rights Committee that Article 9 of the International Covenant on Civil and Political Rights (ICCPR) prohibits detention on grounds of administrative expediency.[168] However, the most important question for the

[162] Ibid. [163] Ibid, para 74. [164] Ibid, para 80. [165] Ibid.

[166] Ibid, joint partly dissenting opinion of Judges Rozakis, Tulkens, Kovler, Hajiyev, Spielmann, and Hirvelä. [167] Ibid.

[168] Ibid; *Van Alphen v The Netherlands*, Communication No 305/1988, CCPR/C/39/D/305/1988, 23 July 1990, Human Rights Committee.

partly dissenting judges was whether it was 'permissible today for the European Convention on Human Rights to provide a lower level of protection than that which is recognized and accepted in the other organisations'.[169]

The Court's reasoning coalesced around the lower end of international standards protecting asylum-seekers against detention. Using UNHCR soft law instruments, the Court evaded the ICCPR provisions and the case law of the Human Rights Committee. It appears to have considered that the UNHCR sources were more relevant in this case. While it could have granted greater protection to asylum-seekers, the Court chose to construe Article 5(1)(f) of the ECHR in a manner which was more agreeable with the states' interests. Indeed, the Contracting States have a wide margin of appreciation in this field, and the Court was undoubtedly influenced by this element in its reasoning. The partly dissenting judges rightly questioned the Court's findings: 'are we now to accept that Article 5 of the Convention, which has played a major role in ensuring controls of arbitrary detention, should afford a lower level of protection as regards asylum and immigration?'[170] The Court's interpretation of UNHCR soft law documents arrived at a result that was contrary to the UNHCR's submissions in the case. Moreover, the Court's reasoning seems to conflict with the case law of the Human Rights Committee,[171] as it allows the detention of asylum-seekers on grounds of expediency and administrative convenience.[172] It can be argued that the ECHR standards on the detention of asylum-seekers are lower than those prevailing at the international level.

2.2.2.4 International Obligations and the Right to Asylum

An interesting reference to the 1951 Refugee Convention, albeit not particularly binding, appeared in the jointly dissenting opinion of the Chamber judgment in the *Saadi* case[173] discussed above. Unlike the majority of the Court, Judges Casadevall, Traja, and Sikuta found that there was a violation of Article 5(1)(f) of the ECHR and referred, in this context, to the respondent State's international obligations within the ECHR framework. They recalled that:

> [u]nder international law, a State has the right, by virtue of its sovereignty, to control the entry and stay of foreigners on its territory. It is, however, equally well established that a State party to the Convention must be deemed to agree to restrict the free exercise of its rights under general international law to the extent and within the limits of the obligations which it has accepted under that Convention.[174]

[169] Ibid. [170] Ibid. [171] *A v Australia* (n 153 above).

[172] As already mentioned, the Court found that, 'given the difficult administrative problems with which the United Kingdom was confronted during the period in question,..., it was not incompatible with Article 5 § 1(f) of the Convention to detain the applicant for seven days in suitable conditions to enable his claim to asylum to be processed speedily': see *Saadi v United Kingdom* (n 148 above), para 80.

[173] *Saadi v United Kingdom* (n 130 above).

[174] Ibid, jointly dissenting opinion of Judges Casadevall, Traja, and Sikuta, para 2.

Thus, they reiterated that international obligations contracted into by states must comply or be harmonized with the ECHR. It was further found that the detention of the applicant was not carried out with a view to prevent him from making an unauthorized entry into a country, as is permitted by Article 5(1)(f).[175] Rather, it was considered that the true reason was not related to this provision, but 'purely based on administrative or bureaucratic grounds aiming to place the applicant in Oakington detention'.[176] According to the dissenting judges, the applicant had sufficiently shown that he would not try to enter the United Kingdom illegally.

The judges went to great lengths to reaffirm the importance and scope of the right to asylum by stating that:

> [t]he asylum procedure is legally recognized and prescribed by national law. It is a procedure which can last for anything from a few days to several years. The possibility of detaining an asylum seeker at any time during the asylum procedure on the ground that it was to 'prevent his effecting an unauthorised entry into the country' would represent great legal uncertainty for the person concerned. States which are parties to international instruments dealing with the legal status of asylum seekers and refugees (e.g. the 1951 UN Convention relating to the Status of Refugees, but also instruments in other systems, e.g. the European Union and the Council of Europe) are obliged to grant an asylum seeker admission to the territory (but not a residence permit) until the final decision in the asylum procedure is taken.[177]

This statement is meaningful as it appears to go further than the 1951 Refugee Convention and the ECHR by implying that a right of admission for asylum-seekers in a given country exists. Thus far, this right has been phrased in less-absolute terms as a non-penalization for asylum-seekers' illegal entry in a given country. As such, this dissident opinion expands the current scope of both texts with regard to the scope of the right to asylum.

2.2.2.5 Conflict of Norms: A Criticism

The 1951 Refugee Convention made another interesting appearance in Judge Pettiti's dissident judgment in the *Chahal v United Kingdom* case,[178] discussed

[175] Ibid, para 3. [176] Ibid, para 5.

[177] Ibid, para 4. In relation to the Contracting States' obligations, see also *Melnychenko v Ukraine* (App No 17707/02), judgment, 19 October 2004, Reports 2004-X, 1, para 64, where the Court considered that 'the applicant's reliance on the 1951 Geneva Convention as a legal argument is not of major impact, as it was not in force in Ukraine at the material time. However, . . . as a signatory State, Ukraine would have been bound, by virtue of the obligation flowing from Article 18 of the Vienna Convention on the Law of Treaties, to refrain from acts which might have defeated the object and purpose of the Geneva Convention pending its entry into force.' With this statement, the Court reminded Ukraine to follow its obligations under other international law instruments. This willingness to act as a *pseudo* guardian of other international treaties reaches beyond the traditional ECHR interpretation framework. The *Melnychenko* case is not considered in detail here due to lack of space and the specific focus taken in this chapter.

[178] *Chahal v United Kingdom* (n 21 above).

earlier.[179] There, the Court found that the six-year detention of the applicant in prison 'with a view to deportation' was compatible with Article 5(1)(f) of the ECHR and that the length of the asylum and judicial proceedings in the case was not excessive. While there were no references to the 1951 Refugee Convention in the majority's assessment of the complaint under Article 5 of the ECHR, the 1951 Refugee Convention was taken fully into consideration by Judge Pettiti. Unlike the majority, he found that there was a violation of Article 5(1) of the ECHR. In his view, the detention of Mr Chahal fell under the 1951 Refugee Convention, and needed to be considered in that light under Articles 3 and 5 of the ECHR. Although Judge Pettiti's reasoning does not have considerable precedential value, it nonetheless constitutes a very compelling example of how the Court may use international law in a situation where the ECHR allegedly conflicts with another international law instrument.

Strong words were used in this dissident opinion to stress that the *Chahal* case resembled the *Amuur* judgment,[180] where the Court ruled in favour of the applicants detained for 20 days in an international transit zone. According to Judge Pettiti, in the latter case 'the Court correctly identified the problem of administrative detention in the case of proceedings covered by the Geneva Convention of 1951, and within the province of the Office of the United Nations High Commissioner for Refugees'.[181] However, he criticized the fact that the majority judges in the *Chahal* case reviewed the applicant's detention from the point of view of ordinary detention under general domestic law rather than from the perspective of administrative detention under more specific international legislation.

In Judge Pettiti's view, there was a conflict between the ECHR and the 1951 Refugee Convention in the case:

> After his application for asylum as a political refugee had been refused, a deportation order was made on 25 July 1991 on the basis of the Geneva Convention. Mr Chahal's detention fell to be considered by the Court from that angle. There was therefore a confrontation between the Geneva Convention and the European Convention on Human Rights, which concern the same member States.[182]

It was further reiterated that:

> where an application is made for review, it must be heard expeditiously, as a matter of urgency. The organisation of review procedures is governed by the Geneva Convention and UNHCR resolutions. It is possible to petition the Commission on Human Rights of the United Nations in that regard. The European Court cannot review the procedures, but it can consider them under Articles 3 and 5 when a violation is alleged.

Thus, Judge Pettiti recognized that it would have been more appropriate to submit the case to another international body. However, his reasoning also implied

[179] See 2.1.3 and 2.2.1 above.

[180] *Amuur v France* (n 98 above).

[181] *Chahal v United Kingdom* (n 21 above), partly dissenting opinion of Judge Pettiti.

[182] Ibid.

that the ECtHR should have recognized the specificity of the situation and taken the 1951 Refugee Convention into greater consideration.

Judge Pettiti further criticized the majority for arguing that the duration of the proceedings was elongated because the applicant sought a review. Further, he found that a pending application for release could not constitute a ground for elongating detention where it was contrary to Article 5 of the ECHR. It was also clarified that:

> in international law under the Geneva Convention administrative detention differs from detention under the general law and must be enforced by measures such as an order for compulsory residence on administrative premises or in a hotel...or house arrest. The United Nations Covenants and the recommendations of the United Nations Sub-Committee on questions of human rights of all persons subjected to any form of detention or imprisonment must be heeded.

In this context, he strongly warned that '[t]he European Convention does not allow States to disregard their obligations under the Geneva Convention. The Court must be attentive to problems of potential conflicts between international inter-State instruments binding the member States of the Council of Europe.' It was also noted that '[u]nder the Geneva Convention, it is for each State to organise its appeal procedures in respect of matters arising under the Convention. The effectiveness of those procedures is reviewable by the UNHCR.' Further, '[a]dministrative detention under the Geneva Convention cannot be extended beyond a reasonable—brief—period necessary for arranging deportation'.[183] Finally, Judge Pettiti concluded that the applicant's detention resembled an indefinite sentence and that he was treated more severely than a criminal sentenced to a term of imprisonment.

Judge Pettiti's dissident reasoning is interesting for several reasons. First, it incorporates certain standards from the 1951 Refugee Convention into the ECHR framework, finding that the latter does not specifically deal with problems of administrative detention. Secondly, Judge Pettiti circumvents the ECHR and applies instead the 1951 Refugee Convention. While he signals that the Court is unable to review procedures falling under the 1951 Refugee Convention, he nonetheless applies them under the cover of Article 5 of the ECHR. Thirdly, he offers an interesting alternative to a situation where there is a conflict between international law and the ECHR by simply reaching out to the relevant part of international law. It appears that this was not a case where Judge Pettiti wished to expand the meaning of the ECHR by referring to the 1951 Refugee Convention. Rather, he preferred to resort directly to the most specific international instrument, finding that the ECHR was inadequate. He referred to the 1951 Refugee Convention in a very unconstrained and non-convoluted manner by simply

[183] Ibid. All the passages quoted in this paragraph and the preceding paragraph originate from Judge Pettiti's partly dissenting opinion.

referring to the relevant elements. His opinion remains nonetheless a dissident reasoning, and, as such, does not have precedential value.

2.3 Case Law Relating to Article 8 of the ECHR

2.3.1 A Comparison of the ECHR with the 1951 Refugee Convention

In the process of fleeing from their country of origin, refugees often run various risks and decide to leave certain members of their family behind. This decision is motivated by a number of factors pertaining to the need to protect young children, the uncertainty of obtaining asylum in another country, and the possibility that it will facilitate or speed up the asylum procedure. Even if they succeed in obtaining asylum, it is often difficult for them to be reunited with their loved ones in the new homeland. Furthermore, following admission, long-term and second-generation immigrants who commit offences or crimes often face deportation to their home country where their chances of rehabilitation are poor. In spite of this state of affairs, it needs to be reiterated that the right to family unity is a corollary of the right to asylum. The family constitutes a fundamental unit of society which is entitled to protection, and its role is entrenched in cultures and traditions across the globe.[184] For this reason, asylum-seekers, refugees, and other persons in need of protection should not be considered in isolation from their family. The loss of contact with their loved ones is a traumatic experience in most cases for asylum-seekers, for whom the family was the sole source of protection.

Although the 1951 Refugee Convention does not contain a specific provision on the right to family unity and family reunification, it grants certain rights to the refugee family in a number of contexts.[185] In addition, a number of soft law instruments adopted subsequently to the 1951 Refugee Convention under the auspices of the UNHCR enshrine the right to family unity.[186] The Conference of Plenipotentiaries, which adopted the final text of the 1951 Refugee Convention,

[184] Kate Jastram and Kathleen Newland, 'Family Unity and Refugee Protection' in Erika Feller, Volker Türk, and Frances Nicholson (eds), *Refugee Protection in International Law: UNHCR's Global Consultations on International Protection* (Cambridge: Cambridge University Press, 2003), 555, 556–557.

[185] Convention relating to the Status of Refugees, Art 4 (refugees' freedom with regard to the religious education of their children); Art 12(2) (respect for the rights attaching to marriage); Art 24 (right to the same family allowance and other social security benefits as nationals); para 2 of the Schedule annexed to the Convention (right to include children in the travel document of a parent or, exceptionally, of another adult refugee).

[186] Final Act of the United Nations Conference of Plenipotentiaries on the Status of Refugees and Stateless Persons, 189 UNTS 37, 1951, Section IVB on the Principle of the Unity of the Family; United Nations High Commissioner for Refugees (n 13 above), paras 181–188; United Nations High Commissioner for Refugees, *Executive Committee Conclusions, Family Reunion*, EXCOM Conclusion No 9 (XXVIII), 1977; United Nations High Commissioner for Refugees, *Executive Committee Conclusions*, EXCOM Conclusion No 15 (XXX), 1979; United Nations High Commissioner for Refugees, *Executive Committee Conclusions, Family Reunification*, EXCOM Conclusion No 24 (XXXII), 1981.

approved a recommendation that recognized that the unity of family 'is an essential right of the refugee'.[187] Furthermore, the recommendation urged the 'Governments to take the necessary measures for the protection of the refugee's family, especially with a view to: 1. Ensuring that the unity of the refugee's family is maintained particularly in cases where the head of the family has fulfilled the necessary conditions for admission to a particular country, 2. The protection of refugees who are minors'.[188] The UNHCR Executive Committee has repeatedly emphasized the importance of family reunion and has further clarified its scope. It has found, *inter alia*, that 'States should facilitate the admission to their territory of at least the spouse and minor or dependent children of any person to whom temporary residence or durable asylum has been granted'.[189] Furthermore, the Executive Committee has confirmed that the right to family unity of asylum-seekers who have been temporarily admitted pending arrangements for a durable solution should be respected.[190] It has also encouraged all states to enact legislation implementing the right to family unity for all refugees[191] and to give particular attention to the needs of unaccompanied refugee children pending reunification with their families.[192] The protection of the family, the right to family unity, and the right to family reunification are more firmly established in other international human rights law instruments.[193]

In contrast to the 1951 Refugee Convention, the ECHR provides for a qualified right to family life in Article 8(1). This provision stipulates that '[e]veryone has the right to respect for his private and family life, his home and his correspondence'. This right can be exceptionally limited by public authorities when it is required by domestic law and when it 'is necessary in a democratic society in the interests of national security, public safety or the economic well-being of the country, for the prevention of disorder or crime, for the protection of health or morals, or for the protection of rights and freedoms of others'. Despite the limitations they can impose, Contracting States have certain obligations towards persons protected by the ECHR and their discretion in these matters is also circumscribed.

[187] Final Act of the United Nations Conference of Plenipotentiaries on the Status of Refugees and Stateless Persons (n 186 above). See also United Nations High Commissioner for Refugees (n 13 above), paras 181–188.

[188] Final Act of the United Nations Conference of Plenipotentiaries on the Status of Refugees and Stateless Persons (n 186 above).

[189] United Nations High Commissioner for Refugees, *Executive Committee Conclusions*, EXCOM Conclusion No 15 (XXX), 1979.

[190] United Nations High Commissioner for Refugees, *Executive Committee Conclusions*, EXCOM Conclusion No 22 (XXXII), 1981.

[191] United Nations High Commissioner for Refugees, *Executive Committee Conclusions*, EXCOM Conclusion No 85 (XLIX), 1997, para x.

[192] United Nations High Commissioner for Refugees, *Executive Committee Conclusions*, EXCOM Conclusion No 88 (L), 1999, para (c).

[193] Universal Declaration of Human Rights, Art 16(3); International Covenant on the Economic, Social and Cultural Rights, Art 10(1); ICCPR, Arts 17(1), 23(1), and 24; United Nations Convention on the Rights of the Child, Arts 9 and 10(1).

Under Article 8 of the ECHR, the Court must balance two types of competing interests, namely the rights of individuals to a private and family life and the interests of the community. The Court has developed a three-prong test in order to assess the compatibility of interference with the rights included in Article 8. The Court first verifies whether there is interference with the right to family under Article 8(1). If such interference exists, the Court evaluates whether it is compatible with domestic law and whether it corresponds to one of the aims listed in Article 8(2). Once these elements are established, the Court then evaluates whether the intrusion can be justified as 'necessary in a democratic society, that is to say justified by a pressing social need and, in particular, proportionate to the legitimate aim pursued'.[194] Such an exercise is difficult to carry out as the Court must give preference to one interest over the other.[195] Furthermore, 'this is also the area in which the political or value-laden nature of the choice facing the court is most obvious, raising questions as to the legitimacy of judicial rather than democratic decision-making'.[196] It is thus not surprising that the Court has not established any firm criteria to determine whether a measure is necessary in a democratic society and has instead proceeded on a case-by-case basis. It has been acknowledged, however, that Contracting States have a wide margin of appreciation in the way they choose to comply with the Convention.

In addition, the Court has emphasized the traditional notions of state sovereignty by maintaining that states have a wide margin of appreciation in matters relating to immigration. It was found that:

> although the essential object of Article 8 is to protect the individual against arbitrary interference by the public authorities, there may in addition be positive obligations inherent in an effective 'respect' for family life.... However, especially as far as those positive obligations are concerned, the notion of 'respect' is not clear-cut: having regard to the diversity of the practices followed and the situations obtaining in the Contracting States, the notion's requirements will vary considerably from case to case. Accordingly, this is an area in which the Contracting Parties enjoy a wide margin of appreciation in determining the steps to be taken to ensure compliance with the Convention with due regard to the needs and resources of the community and of individuals.[197]

The Court has thus often exercised great deference with regard to the state's policy on asylum determinations. Nonetheless, the reasoning contained in this statement transcends to variable degrees the decisions and judgments handed down in this context.

[194] *Amrollahi v Denmark* (App No 56811/00), judgment, 11 July 2002, not reported, para 33; *Dalia v France* (App No 26102/95), judgment, 19 February 1998, Reports 1998-I, 91, para 52; *Mehemi v France* (App No 25017/94), judgment, 26 September 1997, Reports 1997-VI, 1971, para 3.

[195] Lambert (n 1 above), 428.

[196] James E Fawcett, *The Application of the European Convention on Human Rights* (Oxford/New York: OUP, 1969), 232–233.

[197] *Abdulaziz, Cabales and Balkandali v United Kingdom* (App Nos 9214/80; 9473/81; 9474/81), judgment, 28 May 1985, Series A, Vol 94, para 67.

The case law of the Court in the field of family reunion can be divided into two different strands: cases of foreigners wanting to enter into the territory of a Contracting State for family reunion purposes; and cases of removal of long-term immigrants who have committed crimes or offences resulting in their separation from family members.[198] As the first type of case involves wide-ranging obligations towards non-citizens on the part of the Contracting States, the Court has applied very strict criteria in order to determine whether family reunion can be allowed. In assessing the first prong of the test established under Article 8 of the ECHR, the Court has often tried to evaluate first whether there were obstacles preventing the persons concerned from returning to live in their country of origin with their family attempting to enter in an ECHR Contracting State. If this was possible, the Court usually found that there was no violation of Article 8. This approach was applied to persons who had the citizenship of the Contracting State,[199] persons who were long-term immigrants,[200] refugees,[201] and persons with a humanitarian status (or other temporary protection).[202] The Court seems to have been guided to a great extent by the margin of appreciation doctrine in this type of case.[203]

The Court became more lenient, however, following the *Sen v The Netherlands* judgment,[204] where it assessed the possibility of return for the applicants far less stringently than previously and where it found a violation of Article 8.[205] This trend seems to have continued until today.[206] In the second type of case relating to deportation and expulsion of long-term immigrants and second-generation foreigners, the Court did not conduct a verification of the possibility of return for the whole family to the country of origin. Thus, it had to make a careful assessment of whether the interference was 'necessary in a democratic society', and it applied the requirements of the three-prong test less restrictively. In the initial cases of the first type, the Court did not usually get to the analysis of this requirement. Thus, the assessment of the state's discretion in deportation and expulsion

[198] Lambert (n 1 above), 429.

[199] *Ahmut v The Netherlands* (App No 21702/93), judgment, 26 October 1996, Reports 1996-VI, 2017; *Joseph William Kwakye-Nti and Akue Dufie v The Netherlands* (App No 31519/96), decision, 7 November 2000, not reported.

[200] *Sen v The Netherlands* (App No 31465/96), judgment, 21 December 2001, not reported, available only in French.

[201] *Tuquabo-Tekle and others v The Netherlands* (App No 60665/00), judgment, 1 December 2005, not reported.

[202] *Gül v Switzerland* (App No 23218/94), judgment, 19 February 1996, Reports 1996-I, 159.

[203] Yutaka Arai-Takahashi, *The Margin of Appreciation Doctrine and the Principle of Proportionality in the Jurisprudence of the ECHR* (Antwerp/Oxford, New York: Intersentia, 2002), 68.

[204] *Sen v The Netherlands* (n 200 above).

[205] United Nations High Commissioner for Refugees, *Manual on Refugee Protection and the European Convention on Human Rights*, Regional Bureau for Europe, Department of International Protection, August 2003, updated August 2006, Part 2.3—Fact Sheet on Article 8, para 3.11.

[206] *Tuquabo-Tekle and others v The Netherlands* (n 201 above).

cases intensified as the Court took into greater account certain specific factors, such as the length of stay and the degree of integration of a person in the country of residence.[207]

The distinction between the two types of situation could be disappearing, as the Court has applied the requirements of Article 8 in some of the first types of case less stringently than previously. Further cases are necessary, however, to confirm a departure from this restrictive trend. A different approach would be beneficial as the distinction imposed by the Court appears to be artificial. There do not seem to be substantial reasons justifying the difference in treatment granted by the Court to arriving non-nationals and departing non-nationals. It could be argued that in the first type of case the obligation with regard to non-citizens imposed on the Contracting State is far greater than in the second type of case. It is also plausible that for this reason the Court showed greater deference in cases where more obligations were imposed and emphasized further the margin of appreciation granted to the Contracting States in these matters.

It remains, however, the case that the Court resorts to a limited right to family life and continues to emphasize that '[t]he duty imposed by Article 8 cannot be considered as extending to a general obligation on the part of a Contracting State to respect the choice by married couples of the country of their matrimonial residence and to accept the non-national spouses for settlement in that country'.[208] Thus, the ECtHR certainly does not require a general positive obligation of family reunion on the part of Contracting States, but does allow for family reunion under certain circumstances. Furthermore, in spite of the softening of the strand of case law concerning the entry of non-nationals into Contracting States, the Court's analysis remains very exhaustive, making it difficult for many to pass the threshold of the three-prong test.

Very few cases under Article 8 of the ECHR have related to refugees. Nonetheless, it can be argued that persons recognized as refugees under the 1951 Refugee Convention and persons who could suffer torture or ill-treatment in their country of return would be successful in their claim before the Court, as their removal would naturally constitute an obstacle to establishing a family life there or would be disproportionate to the aim pursued.[209] In such cases, however, it may become unnecessary to use Article 8. It is more beneficial for such persons to resort to Article 3 of the ECHR, which enshrines an absolute and unconditional guarantee against removal. As already discussed, this provision applies irrespective of a person's conduct or citizenship. It appears that for this reason so few refugee cases came before the Court under Article 8 and there were no references to the 1951 Refugee Convention. Nonetheless, Article 8 could be useful

[207] Arai-Takahashi (n 203 above), 68.

[208] See, for instance, *Abdulaziz, Cabales and Balkandali v United Kingdom* (n 197 above); *Cruz Varas and others v Sweden* (n 20 above), para 88; *Gül v Switzerland* (n 202 above), para 38.

[209] Lambert (n 1 above), 448.

for persons who would like to be reunited with their family members, who are internally displaced, and who would not suffer torture or ill-treatment if returned to their home country. The applications of such persons are, however, likely to fail given the temporary nature of their situation and the difficulty in establishing links with their country of refuge.[210]

The position of the ECHR with regard to family reunion seems to be shared by Contracting States that are also Members of the European Union. In 2003 a Council of Ministers' Directive on the right to family reunification[211] was adopted, which Member States had to implement by 3 October 2005. The Directive entitles third-country nationals holding a residence permit valid for at least one year and who have reasonable prospects of obtaining the right of permanent residence[212] or refugee status to be reunited with their families through the family reunification procedure.[213] Persons who are eligible under this procedure are the applicant's spouse and the legitimate, natural, and adopted children of the couple. In addition, Member States may authorize the reunification of unmarried partners, adult dependent children, and dependent ascendants.[214] The Directive does not apply to a person asking for the recognition of refugee status whose claim has not yet given rise to a final decision; a person authorized to reside in a Member State on the basis of temporary protection or applying for authorization to reside on that basis and awaiting a decision on his status; and a person authorized to reside in a Member State on the basis of a subsidiary form of protection in accordance with international obligations, national legislation, or the practice of the Member States or applying for authorization to reside on that basis and awaiting a decision on his status.[215]

It follows that the EU Directive on the right to family reunification offers a similar level of protection as the ECHR by excluding those benefiting from temporary protection in the state of refuge. Although the Directive entered into force long after the ECHR, it does represent the level of consensus that has been reached among the Members of the European Union. It is unlikely that in its upcoming cases the Court will attempt to break the consensus thus established, given that immigration is a field in which the States possess a wide margin of appreciation. Thus, the current level of protection at the European level will probably not reach the same level as that granted by the UNHCR Executive Committee.

The scarcity of refugee cases under Article 8 of the ECHR has translated itself into a lack of references under the 1951 Refugee Convention. As most refugee cases came before the Court under Article 3 of the ECHR, the Court has had few possibilities to refer to the 1951 Refugee Convention in the context of Article 8 of the ECHR. Due to certain specificities of the ECHR discussed above, it is more

[210] Ibid, 449–450.

[211] Council Directive (EC) 2003/86 of 22 September 2003 on the right to family reunification [2003] OJ L251/12.

[212] Ibid, Art 3(1).

[213] Ibid, Arts 9–12.

[214] Ibid, Art 4.

[215] Ibid, Art 3(2).

beneficial for asylum-seekers or refugees to use Article 3 of the ECHR instead of Article 8 under certain circumstances. The cases under Article 8 pertaining to family reunion mostly concern long-term immigrants, citizens, persons with humanitarian status, and persons with other types of protection. In this context, the Court nonetheless made several references to international law in an attempt to set clear boundaries to its jurisdiction. In addition, in a field where public interests were at stake, the Court's reasoning was conditioned by the wide margin of appreciation granted to Contracting States in this context. Thus, the Court's references rarely reached beyond the ECHR, and the Court paid much attention to the delineation of its competencies, sometimes even asking Contracting States to provide an answer to a question. The Court's circumspect and traditional approach has been met with criticism on the part of its own members. While there does not seem to be any significant consistency in the Court's scarce use of international law in this field, there does appear to be a well-established trend of deference to the States' decisions and policies.

2.3.2 Limitations of the Examination

The most prominent and recurring reference to international law used by the Court was the constant emphasis on the fact that Contracting States have, under international law, the sovereign right to control immigration into their country. The Court considered that 'as a matter of well-established international law and subject to its treaty obligations, a State has the right to control the entry of non-nationals into its territory'.[216] This statement was made in both strands of the Court's case law under Article 8 of the ECHR, namely those instances where non-nationals were trying to be reunited with their family and the return of non-nationals who had committed crimes or offences. In addition to this, the Court added in the latter type of case that Contracting States had the right to maintain public order in their country. As already mentioned, similar statements were made by the Court as part of the assessments under Article 3 of the ECHR. Thus, the Court justified the fact that Contracting Member States would have a wide margin of appreciation under the ECHR in matters falling under Article 8.

In *Berrehab v The Netherlands*,[217] the Court made an interesting statement with regard to its own role in the context of claims where a balance had to be struck between state and individual interests. The Dutch authorities had emphasized in that case that they pursue a restrictive immigration policy, but that certain

[216] See, for instance, *Abdulaziz, Cabales, and Balkandali v United Kingdom* (n 197 above), para 67; *Berrehab v The Netherlands* (App No 10730/84), judgment, 10 April 1987, Series A, Vol 138, paras 28–29; *Moustaquim v Belgium* (n 43 above), para 43; *Beldjoudi v France* (App No 12083/86), judgment, Series A, Vol 234-A, para 74; *Nasri v France* (App No 19465/92), judgment, 13 July 1995, Series A, Vol 320-B, para 41; *Gül v Switzerland* (n 202 above), para 38; *Ahmut v The Netherlands* (n 199 above), para 67.

[217] *Berrehab v The Netherlands* (n 216 above).

exceptions are allowed. While assessing whether the interference with Article 8 was necessary, the Court observed that 'its function is not to pass judgement on the Netherlands' immigration and residence policy as such. It has only to examine the interferences complained of, and it must do this not solely from the point of view of immigration and residence, but also with regard to the applicants' mutual interest in continuing their relations.'[218] Although this statement did not consistently appear in the Court's case law, it did seem to underpin most of the reasoning in the cases that fell under Article 8. Thus, the Court usually demonstrated great deference with regard to domestic immigration policies in these cases.

2.3.3 Criticisms of the Court's Approach

The Court's approach towards the margin of appreciation of Contracting States, however, gave rise to criticisms from its own judges. In *Gül v Switzerland*,[219] the Court considered the case of a Turkish national of Kurdish origin who fled to Switzerland where he applied for asylum based on his membership of a banned political party. His wife remained in Turkey with their two sons and joined him in Switzerland four years later. She gave birth to a daughter who was placed in a Swiss home. The applicant's request for asylum was rejected, but he, his wife, and his daughter were granted a permit on humanitarian grounds. The applicant then sought permission to bring his two sons from Turkey, but his request was refused on grounds that he did not have the means to provide for his family and that his older son was 18 years old. The applicant received invalidity benefits and his wife was undergoing medical treatment. Before the Court, the applicant complained that the refusal to allow his younger son to join him constituted a violation of his right to family life under Article 8. The Court considered that the applicants' right to residency in Switzerland did not give him a right to family reunion. Moreover, the majority considered that while it may have been difficult, the applicant and his wife could have returned to Turkey in order to be reunited with their children.[220] In addition, their son had more links with Turkey than with Switzerland. Thus, the Court found that Switzerland had not failed to fulfil the obligations arising under Article 8(1) of the ECHR.

Judge Martens, in his dissenting opinion, approved by Judge Russo, considered that the applicant's situation gave rise to a violation of Article 8 of the ECHR. As part of the assessment of Switzerland's obligations under this provision, he found that there was a time when the Court treated positive and negative obligations differently.[221] In his view:

> [t]he Abdulaziz, Cabales and Balkandali judgement is a striking instance.... Under the vagueness of the notion 'respect' in Article 8 the Court held that its requirements will vary

[218] Ibid, para 29. [219] *Gül v Switzerland* (n 202 above). [220] Ibid, para 42.
[221] Ibid, dissenting opinion of Judge Martens, approved by Judge Russo, para 8.

from case to case, thus creating for itself the possibility of taking into account when establishing whether or not there is a positive obligation, whether or not there is a consensus between member States, and moreover, a wide margin of appreciation for the State concerned. This approach has been rightly criticised both outside and inside the Court.[222]

While the Court's doctrine on this point has evolved, Judge Martens has nonetheless elucidated a mechanism in the Court's approach which is also implicitly replicated in its references to international law conditioned by the extent of the margin of appreciation possessed by states in a given area.

Judge Martens made another important comment with regard to the function of the Court in cases involving a conflict between state and individual interests. He found that 'the European Court has to ensure, in particular, that State interests do not crush those of an individual, especially in situations where political pressure—such as the growing dislike of immigrants in most member States—may inspire States authorities to harsh decisions'.[223] This concern is a particularly important one, as the Court may succumb to deference in such cases given the wide margin of appreciation given to states in this context. Thus, there may be few safeguards against political motivations on the part of states. As this comment also reveals, the cases under Article 8 of the ECHR are particularly sensitive and involve wide-ranging political and socio-economic interests.

Some dissenters have also criticized the majority for resorting to an unduly formalist and stringent interpretation of the ECHR. In *Ahmut v The Netherlands*,[224] the Court considered the case of a Moroccan national who migrated from his home country to the Netherlands leaving behind his wife and his five children. He later acquired Dutch nationality in addition to Moroccan nationality. His wife died in Morocco and the children were taken care of by their grandmother. He also requested a residence permit for his minor son visiting him in the Netherlands, but his request was rejected. Before the Court, the applicant complained that the Dutch authorities had violated his right to family life under Article 8 of the ECHR by refusing to grant his son a residence permit. The Court found that it was the applicant's conscious decision to live apart from his son and that he was not prevented from maintaining a degree of family life when moving to the Netherlands. Moreover, there was no obstacle for him to return to Morocco in order to be reunited with his son. According to the Court, Article 8 does not guarantee a right to choose the most suitable place to develop family life.[225] Thus, it was found that the Netherlands authorities had struck a fair balance between the applicant's interests and the country's interest in controlling immigration.

Judge Morenilla, in his dissenting opinion, disagreed with the majority and found that there was a violation of Article 8 in this case. In his view, the measures adopted by the Netherlands authorities were neither necessary nor proportionate

[222] Ibid. [223] Ibid, para 15. [224] *Ahmut v The Netherlands* (n 199 above).
[225] For further details regarding the Court's arguments, see ibid, paras 70–71.

to the legitimate aims included in Article 8(2).[226] Moreover, denying the applicant the right to be with his son, especially given the fact that his mother had died, was contrary to the ECHR and to the 'cogent reasons of humanitarian nature' enshrined in domestic legislation.[227] Judge Morenilla further clarified that:

> human rights are recognised in international instruments in the form of legal formulas imposing on national authorities positive or negative obligations to ensure the effective enjoyment of those rights and liberties. The juridical treatment of these provisions, their interpretation and application by the authorities—and, obviously by the courts—should in my view be in accordance with the humanitarian grounds for which they were established, avoiding excessive formalism. These humanitarian reasons are to me more 'cogent' than the opposite interpretation of the conventional text offered by the majority.[228]

Thus, in his view, the teleological interpretation of the ECHR should be less stringent and more in tune with the humanitarian needs of individuals.

A dissenting judge has also pointed out that international law is changing and that the ECtHR may be lagging behind. In *Nasri v France*,[229] the Court ruled that the deportation of an Algerian national who was convicted for gang rape would infringe Article 8 in the exceptional circumstances of this case. The applicant was deaf and mute since birth. He had lived most of his life in France with his family, he could not read or write, and he did not know any recognized sign language. He complained under Articles 3 and 8 of the ECHR, but the Court only found a violation under the latter. An interesting comment was made by Judge Morenilla, dissenting in part, with regard to the evolving nature of international law. He found, *inter alia*, that the applicant's deportation had to be considered as inhuman treatment under Article 3.[230] Moreover, he considered that the treatment of offenders on the administrative or criminal level should not depend on the national origin of their parents.[231] In his view:

> [a]ttention has been drawn . . . to the way in which international law has changed over the last few years, under the influence of recent developments in the human rights field, towards according equal treatment between aliens and nationals. This equality becomes more and more evident where the aliens are 'immigrants integrated' in the community where they work. . . . In any event, legal considerations or reliance on the traditional notion of State sovereignty cannot today serve as the basis for such treatment.[232]

Judge Morenilla criticized the Court for providing further evidence of its 'traditional circumspection' by confining itself to the assessment of the complaint under Article 8. Moreover, he found the Court too formalistic in so far as it classified the claim as an interference with the applicant's right to family life rather than his private life, a more general concept of which family life is only one element.[233]

[226] Ibid, dissenting opinion of Judge Morenilla, para 2. [227] Ibid.
[228] Ibid, para 3. [229] *Nasri v France* (n 216 above).
[230] Ibid, partly dissenting opinion of Judge Morenilla, para 1. [231] Ibid, para 3.
[232] Ibid, para 4. [233] Ibid, para 5.

2.3.4 *Duty of Contracting States*

In this strand of the Court's case law, the Court has paid tremendous deference to the margin of appreciation of Contracting States, stating that it is for them to decide certain immigration issues. In his separate concurring opinion in *Nasri v France*,[234] Judge Pettiti observed that several cases concerning the deportation of aliens were pending before the Court at that time; nonetheless, '[t]he European Convention [has] excluded from its substantive law the deportation of aliens by States (except collective deportations)'.[235] In his view, this problem was 'a matter for the member States of the Council of Europe, if they have the will to harmonise their policies in this field and cooperate, so as to take account of immigration flows and differences in the conditions applied with regard to the integration and family reunion by certain States with a view to strengthening the protection of families, rules that have not been adopted by others'.[236] In this statement, Judge Pettiti considered that this gap should be addressed by Contracting States through democratically established legislative mechanisms. Thus, more than in any other cases concerning non-nationals under Article 8, the deference of the Court was explicitly articulated.

2.3.5 *The Court's Conception of Its Own Role*

It is not surprising that as part of the case law under Article 8 of the ECHR, where Contracting States have a wide margin of appreciation, the Court felt compelled to reiterate that it has a limited role in the interpretation of international treaties. In *Slivenko v Latvia*,[237] the Court reviewed a case concerning a former Latvian resident of Russian origin and her daughter. The mother's father was an officer in the army of the Soviet Union and she was born in Estonia in 1959. Her family moved to Latvia with her when she was one month old. She married a Soviet officer and her daughter was born in Latvia. After Latvia regained its independence, the applicants were entered on the register of Latvian residents as 'ex-USSR citizens'. The first applicant's husband, who had been discharged from the army, applied for a temporary residence permit on the basis of his marriage to a permanent resident. His application was refused on the ground that he was required to leave Latvia in accordance with the treaty of April 1994 on the withdrawal of Russian troops which applied in particular to Russian officers in service on 28 January 1992. The three family members were forced to move to Russia. Before the ECtHR, they contended that their rights under Articles 5(1), 5(4), 8, and 14 of the ECHR were violated.

Under Article 8, the Court noted in its Grand Chamber judgment that the applicants' removal could be considered to have been conducted in accordance with the law. Taking into account the wider context of the constitutional and

[234] Ibid.
[235] Ibid, concurring opinion of Judge Pettiti (text inserted by author), 28. [236] Ibid.
[237] *Slivenko v Latvia* (App No 48321/99), judgment, 9 October 2003, Reports 2003-X, 229.

international law arrangements concluded after Latvia regained independence, the Court accepted that the treaty and its implementing measures had sought to protect the interests of national security. The Court further found that a scheme for the withdrawal of foreign troops and their families based on a general finding that their removal was necessary for national security was not incompatible with Article 8. Nonetheless, the implementation of such a scheme without any possibility of taking into account individual circumstances was contrary to this provision. According to the Court, the applicants were integrated into Latvian society and could not be regarded as endangering national security because they were part of the first applicant's family, whose father had retired in 1986 and had remained in the country. In all the circumstances, the applicants' removal could not be regarded as having been necessary in a democratic society under Article 8 of the ECHR.

The Court reiterated in this case that:

> it is primarily for the national authorities, notably the courts, to interpret and apply domestic law.... This also applies where international treaties are concerned; it is for the implementing party to interpret the treaty, and in this respect it is not the Court's task to substitute its own judgment for that of the domestic authorities, even less to settle a dispute between the parties to the treaty as to its correct interpretation. Nor is it the task of the Court to re-examine the facts as found by the domestic authorities as the basis for their legal assessment. The Court's function is to review, from the point of view of the Convention, the reasoning in the decisions of the domestic courts rather than to re-examine their findings as to the particular circumstances of the case or the legal classification of those circumstances under domestic law.[238]

This comment was made in the very specific context of the Latvian-Russian treaty on the withdrawal of Russian troops, which concerns only these two countries. The Court may, therefore, have been circumspect and tried to avoid commenting on the interpretation of this specific arrangement. In addition, the question of the withdrawal of Russian troops from Latvia is a politically sensitive issue for both Latvia and Russia, and the Court probably wanted to avoid interfering in this complex situation. It is plausible that if the treaty at stake in this case involved more ECHR Contracting States, the Court may not have felt the need to make such a statement.

3. Case Law Referring to the Convention Against Torture

In the context of the return of persons to a country where they may be harmed, the Convention Against Torture (CAT) differs in many respects from the 1951 Refugee Convention and resembles much more the ECHR. The main difference between these instruments lies in the fact that the CAT and the ECHR apply also

[238] Ibid, para 105.

to those who have not obtained the status of refugee, including failed asylum-seekers. However, the scope of protection under the CAT is more limited, as it only applies to persecution resulting in torture.[239] In fact, Article 3 of the CAT provides that '[n]o State Party shall expel, return ("refouler") or extradite a person to another State where there are substantial grounds for believing that he would be in danger of being subjected to torture'. Unlike the 1951 Refugee Convention, which only mentions expulsion and return, the CAT mentions in addition expatriation as one of the processes of excluding persons. This provision also applies to an indirect transfer to a third country from which the individual might be returned to a country where he could be subjected to torture.[240]

Article 1(1) of the CAT defines 'torture' as:

> any act by which severe pain or suffering, whether physical or mental, is intentionally inflicted on a person for such purposes as obtaining from him or a third person information or a confession, punishing him for an act he or a third person has committed or is suspected of having committed, or intimidating or coercing him or a third person, or for any reason based on discrimination of any kind, when such pain or suffering is inflicted by or at the instigation of or with the consent of a public official or other person acting in an official capacity. It does not include pain or suffering arising only from, inherent in or incidental to lawful sanction.

It follows from this provision that for an act to constitute torture it must be inflicted by an official. This requirement differs from the 1951 Refugee Convention and the ECHR, which envisage that non-state actors can also constitute a source of persecution.

The CAT also differs from the 1951 Refugee Convention in that the guarantee in Article 3—as under Article 3 if the ECHR—is absolute. Unlike the 1951 Refugee Convention, Article 2(2) of the CAT provides that '[n]o exceptional circumstances whatsoever, whether a state of war or a threat of war, internal political instability or any other public emergency, may be a justification for torture'. This provision should be interpreted as applying to all the provisions in the Convention, including Article 3, which aims to prevent torture in the country to which an individual could be returned.[241] It therefore appears that the 1951 Refugee Convention is more limited as it provides extensive exceptions for the exclusion of a refugee. Further, a substantial advantage of the CAT and the ECHR over the 1951 Refugee Convention is the existence of an individual complaints procedure. Article 17 of the CAT established the Committee Against

[239] Article 3 of the CAT would not be applicable to cruel, inhuman, or degrading treatment. See Manfied Nowak and Elizabeth McArthur, *The United Nations Convention Against Torture: A Commentary* (Oxford/New York: OUP, 2008), 574–575, para 76. However, see Art 16(2) of the CAT referring to expulsion and extradition, which would allow the application of the *non-refoulement* principle to cruel, inhuman, or degrading punishment on the basis of Art 3 of the ECHR and Art 7 of the ICCPR: Nowak and McArthur, ibid, 575, para 78. See also ch V, 3.1.

[240] *Mutombo v Switzerland*, Communication No 13/1993, UN Doc A/49/44, 27 April 1994, Committee Against Torture.

[241] Weissbrodt and Härtrieter (n 64 above), 16.

Torture and endowed it with the capacity to receive individual complaints relating to infringement of the Convention. As mentioned in previous chapters, the CAT was ratified by all ECHR Contracting States.[242] In order to bring a complaint before the Committee, the applicant must have exhausted all domestic remedies, unless such remedies are unreasonably prolonged or are deemed unlikely to bring effective relief to the victim.[243]

While refugee and migrant cases referring to the CAT have been analysed elsewhere in this work,[244] a few remarks in the context of this chapter must nonetheless be made. Although lacking any explicit references to the CAT, a very important judgment was issued by the Court in *Saadi v Italy*,[245] confirming a fundamental principle also contained in the CAT. In this case, the Court reaffirmed the absolute nature of Article 3 of the ECHR, holding that the previously established test for *non-refoulement* was not subject to alteration or balancing on the basis of the perceived dangerousness of the individual concerned. This case concerned a Tunisian national, married to an Italian woman, who was to be deported to Tunisia where he had been sentenced to 20 years' imprisonment for membership of a terrorist organization. This case clearly converges with the absolute nature of the prohibition on torture enshrined in the CAT.

Additional references in the Strasbourg case law concerned (1) the relationship between the Committee Against Torture and the Strasbourg bodies, (2) the Committee's case law, and (3) the reports of the Committee or of the Special Rapporteur.[246] The first type of cases were mainly procedural and explored the coexistence of the Committee and the Strasbourg framework. In these cases, there were few meaningful references which could teach us more about the reception process. The coexistence of case law has been largely unproblematic until now, in part because it has been scarce. Further, given that the cases were struck out of the list, the Court was not able to consider further its relationship with the Committee Against Torture. Nonetheless, due to the coherent legal set-up under both the ECHR and the CAT, no case of litispendence should occur in subsequent cases.

The second and third aspects of this jurisprudence were more substantive and involved more concrete sources of inspiration for the Strasbourg bodies. In most of the cases where the decisions of the Committee were invoked, the Court did not explicitly apply them but ruled in the same direction as the Committee, thereby maintaining the same standards in its reasoning. Further, in most cases where the parties relied on the reports of the Committee and the Special Rapporteur on Torture, the Court used them to buttress its reasoning. These reports also

[242] This information was verified on 13 June 2010: United Nations Treaty Collection, Status, <http://treaties.un.org/Pages/ViewDetails.aspx?src=IND&mtdsg_no=IV-9&chapter=4&lang=en>. See ch III, 4.5, and ch V, 1.

[243] CAT, Art 22(5)(b).

[244] See ch V.

[245] *Saadi v Italy* (n 25 above).

[246] See ch V, 3.

constituted important sources of information when the Court assessed the general situation in the receiving country. Overall, the Strasbourg bodies' findings appear to converge with the standards set by the Committee Against Torture and the findings of the Special Rapporteur on Torture. Thus, the reception level of the CAT in the Strasbourg cases was substantially higher than the reception level of the 1951 Refugee Convention. This difference in reception is due in great part to the fact that the CAT, unlike the 1951 Refugee Convention, offers a similar level of protection to the ECHR. The Strasbourg bodies therefore felt less inhibited in referring to the CAT than to the 1951 Refugee Convention.

4. Rationale of the Reasoning

The case law pertaining to the rights of refugees, asylum-seekers, and other persons in need of protection has been marked by the Court's variable deference to states' margin of appreciation. The Court's reasoning was grounded in the notion that states have been granted greater discretion in this field due to the fact that immigration control has a bearing on their sovereignty. Naturally, the definition of a national immigration policy has a clear impact on economic and social policies, and the choices which pertain thereto must factor in a wide array of socio-economic aspects. It therefore seems to follow that states need an important leeway in order to strike the right balance between competing interests and to establish an immigration policy which is viable in particular circumstances. Given also the fact that many states have acquired important experience in treating asylum requests, the Court may feel more at ease in leaving certain choices up to them. Nonetheless, this wide margin of appreciation has not been applied by the Court inflexibly; its intensity has varied from case to case, and according to the importance of the state interests at stake.

The Court's cautious balancing of state and individual interests appears to have had an impact on the Court's willingness to refer to international law. The Court has been circumspect and has avoided imposing any type of international law interpretation on the Contracting States, finding that it is a duty belonging to the implementing authority. In addition, ECtHR judges have not been willing to reach beyond the ECHR framework in order to provide answers to complex questions, leaving, and sometimes asking the Contracting States to decide, certain issues. In most part, the Court's consideration of the 1951 Refugee Convention remains limited to cases which were already intertwined with international law from the beginning. In addition, EU legislation pertaining to refugee and asylum-related issues represents an important benchmark for the Court with regard to the consensus that binds and prevails in the majority of the ECHR Contracting States. For this reason, the Court may have avoided references to other international instruments under which states have decided not to bind themselves to the same extent as under EU law.

The Court's reluctance to refer more frequently to the 1951 Refugee Convention could be rooted in the fact that this instrument significantly differs in membership and in territorial reach from the ECHR. The 1951 Refugee Convention binds a very diverse group of Contracting States and covers issues which appear in all existing countries. The ECHR, however, is composed of a relatively homogeneous group of states with comparable economic, social, political, and legal cultures.[247] Certain issues included under the 1951 Refugee Convention do not directly concern the ECHR Contracting States. Thus, the Strasbourg bodies probably felt inhibited relying on an instrument which is not specifically adapted to the European context. This general consideration may also have been relevant in other areas of the Strasbourg jurisprudence.[248]

Another important consideration in the Court's cautious reasoning has been the fact that, in the particular context of refugee rights, it is often more beneficial to rely on the ECHR than on the 1951 Refugee Convention; the ECHR framework provides a more effective enforcement mechanism, and often also grants greater protection to the applicant than the 1951 Refugee Convention. Furthermore, as already discussed with regard to cases under Article 3 of the ECHR, it is unjustified for the Court to incorporate certain standards from the 1951 Refugee Convention when these differ substantially from the assessment to be conducted under the ECHR. In the past, the Court has found the granting of refugee status relevant when assessing an application. Thus, if the applicant had a refugee status, the Court was more willing to find that his expulsion or deportation violated Article 3 of the ECHR than if he had not been granted such status. While taking into consideration a person's refugee status under Article 3 in cases of debatable relevance, this distinction in the Court's case law seems to be slowly effacing itself.

Most importantly, the Court was also brought to consider its own role as well as the place of the ECHR within the international refugee system. With regard to the former, the Court has set clear boundaries to distinguish and distance itself from the UNHCR system. Moreover, it has been demonstrated that the ECHR trumps other international instruments ratified by the ECHR Contracting States. In addition, in a case of conflict, conflicting provisions of international law binding on Contracting States have to be interpreted in conformity with the Convention. The ECHR is thus a benchmark against which the international engagements of the Contracting States have to be assessed. Interestingly, the dissenting ECtHR judges have also called on the states to respect their obligations under the 1951 Refugee Convention and to grant admission to asylum-seekers into their territory, thereby going further than the UNHCR standards require.

The Court's principled approach with regard to refugees, asylum-seekers, and other persons in need of protection was met with severe criticism by its own

[247] See also Liz Hefferman, 'A Comparative View of Individual Petition Procedures under the European Convention on Human Rights and the International Covenant on Civil and Political Rights' (1997) 19(1) Hum Rts Qrtly 78, 84.

[248] See ch III, 6; ch IV, 1.2 and 3; and ch V, 4.

members. It has been argued that the Court has misinterpreted the problem of administrative detention and that it should have made greater use of the 1951 Refugee Convention. According to one dissenting judge, the Court should also be more attentive to potential conflicts between international instruments binding Contracting States. Furthermore, it was found that the Court's reasoning was pervaded by traditional circumspection due to its reliance on the notion of state sovereignty. The Court was also criticized for proceeding on a case-by-case basis, in accordance with the states' consensus and margin of appreciation. The majority was warned that it must ensure that state interests do not defeat those of the individual, especially in situations of political pressure where the dislike of immigrants grows. Finally, it was also considered that the ECHR, being a human rights treaty, should be interpreted more in line with the humanitarian grounds for which it was established.

This chapter reveals that, in areas where there is a wide margin of appreciation granted to states, the Court tends to refer less to international law; the wide margin of appreciation overrides the need to refer to international law and the need to use evolutive interpretation. The Court proceeds on a case-by-case basis, probing whether a consensus exists among Contracting States. As is apparent from the case law reviewed, the Court has resorted to the widest margin of appreciation in cases relating to Article 8 of the ECHR, and it has been more attentive to individual needs in Article 3 of the ECHR. This could have been due to the fact that very important state interests were at stake in the case law relating to Article 8. The case law under Article 3 was far less controversial for the states to accept, and *ipso facto* there were also more references to international law in these instances. Overall, the survey of the case law reveals that the Court has leaned more towards the closed paradigm. In some areas, the reception of the 1951 Refugee Convention was not appropriate as it provided a lower standard of protection than the ECHR. It was therefore necessary to maintain a selective fragmentation in some areas covered by both frameworks. Thus, the Court has reaffirmed its self-sufficiency and independence vis-à-vis this special regime. It is yet to be seen how the ECtHR's approach to refugee and asylum-seekers' rights will evolve in times marked by a steady rise of xenophobia throughout Europe.

VII

State Immunity

1. Preliminary Observations

In a series of three judgments issued in November 2001, the Grand Chamber of the ECtHR had the opportunity to examine international state immunity law. The three cases concerned a very controversial area of state immunity, namely torture committed outside the forum state, a tort committed in the forum state, and employment relationships in an embassy. These themes are especially adapted to an analysis of the Court's reception techniques in international law, given that they are part of a sphere of law which is still in a state of flux. It is particularly useful to examine such situations, as they demonstrate how the Court reasons in challenging cases and how it resolves questions without a clear solution. They also indicate whether the Court contributes to the general debate in international law and whether it has an inclination to use international law to resolve issues at the European regional level.

The aim of this chapter is to evaluate the reasoning and reception techniques used by the Court in the three situations described above. The Court's references to international law in these cases were hermetic and grounded in traditional interpretation as well as pragmatic considerations. The Court was faced with a conflict between international legal rules and resolved this conflict on the basis of domestic law and state practice. Furthermore, its approach was marked by non-interventionism and deference to Contracting States.

The analysis of the Court's reasoning in this section will be four-fold. First, the current status of state immunity in international law will be analysed. Secondly, the three cases of the Court will be presented and the Court's reasoning evaluated. Thirdly, the rationale underpinning the Court's methodology will be assessed. Finally, it will be considered whether the Court's approach may have great implications on the European and international human rights legal system.

1.1 The Concept of Immunity

The concept of immunity refers to procedural rules which act as a barrier to the adjudication of disputes and arise at two stages in the case. At the jurisdictional stage, immunity can prevent a court from hearing a case, although it would otherwise have been able to hear it.[1] This type of immunity is generally called 'immunity from jurisdiction'. An immunity can also intervene at a later stage in the case, that is at the moment of the enforcement of the judgment.[2] This type of immunity is called 'immunity from enforcement'. It should also be noted that there are two types of immunity which can be granted to state officials. The immunity *ratione materiae* is granted for acts performed in an official capacity. It is also referred to as subject-matter or functional immunity, and continues to apply even if the official ceases his or her activities. The immunity *ratione personae* is granted to a limited category of officials who represent the state abroad, such as heads of state (these immunities are different from those granted to a state as an entity) or diplomats (these immunities are governed by the Vienna Convention on Diplomatic Relations[3] and the Vienna Convention on Consular Relations[4]). This section focuses on the immunity of jurisdiction of foreign states as applied by the European Court of Human Rights (ECtHR) with particular reference to its use of international law.

The immunity granted to a state as an entity is rooted in customary international law, and is premised on comity, international relations, and the principles of equality, non-intervention in the affairs of another state, and dignity.[5] The rule of state immunity was initially considered to be absolute, except when a state waived its rights and accepted the jurisdiction of the court.[6] This meant that the judiciary of the forum state would not be able to entertain a claim to which a foreign state was party.

From a historical point of view, the concept of immunity evolved over centuries to reach its current state. As governments became more and more active in commercial activities, individuals and other private entities which transacted with them attacked the doctrine of absolute sovereign immunity as fundamentally unfair in eliminating judicial recourse and favouring state companies. By the end of the nineteenth century, states began to differentiate between practices of states that were *acta jure imperii* and those that were *acta jure gestionis*. It was thought that foreign states were immune from jurisdiction in relation to their public or sovereign acts (*acta jure imperii*) but were not immune from jurisdiction for their private or non-sovereign acts (*acta jure gestionis*) including commercial activities. Thus, the doctrine of restrictive or limited state immunity was created, and in the period between the two World Wars both doctrines of absolute and restrictive state immunity coexisted. After the Second World War, the doctrine of

[1] Redress, *Immunity v Accountability: Considering the Relationship between State Immunity and Accountability for Torture and Other Serious International Crimes* (London: The Redress Trust, December 2005), 9.

[2] Ibid.

[3] Vienna Convention on Diplomatic Relations, 500 UNTS 95, entered into force 24 April 1964.

[4] Vienna Convention on Consular Relations, 596 UNTS 261, entered into force 19 March 1967.

[5] Redress (n 1 above), 9.

[6] Leandro De Oliveira Moll, 'Case Note: Al-Adsani v United Kingdom: State Immunity and Denial of Justice with Respect to Violations of Fundamental Human Rights' (2003) 4 Mel J Int'l L 561.

restrictive state immunity prevailed.[7] However, whether a rule of customary law on restrictive immunity exists is a disputed issue, due to the divergent approaches of states.[8]

1.2 Conventional Law

Extensive efforts were undertaken at the international level to develop multilateral treaties governing foreign sovereign immunity issues. Two international instruments were adopted which enshrine the principle of restrictive state immunity. The Council of Europe adopted the European Convention on State Immunity[9] ('Basle Convention') and an Additional Protocol that became effective in 1976. The Convention was ratified by eight states and signed by one state. Most recently, the United Nations, which had been working on state immunity issues for decades, finalized its own restrictive approach to state immunity through the UN Convention on Jurisdictional Immunities of States and Their Property.[10] The UN General Assembly passed the UN Convention on 2 December 2004 and the treaty was open for signatures until 17 January 2007. If widely adopted, the UN Convention may serve as a new international norm in the field of state immunity. At the time of writing, 21 countries have signed the Convention and seven countries have ratified it.[11]

The framers of these two Conventions avoided following the distinction between *acta jure imperii* and *acta jure gestionis*, given the multiple criteria that can be used in distinguishing them and the inherent difficulty of such a classification.[12] Instead, they listed each category of acts which constitute an exception to immunity. Generally, these exceptions include personal injury, damage to property, contracts of employment, commercial transactions, intellectual and industrial property, participation in companies, ships owned by a state, and ownership of property. These exceptions have, however, various restrictions and discussing all of them would be beyond the scope of this section. It suffices to mention that a major problem with regard to immunity remains, as the exception of personal injury enshrined in both Conventions implies that the act has to be committed in the forum state,[13] and therefore allows impunity. This means that victims who

[7] Ibid, 566. [8] Redress (n 1 above), 9.

[9] European Convention on State Immunity, CETS No 074, entered into force 11 June 1976.

[10] United Nations Convention on Jurisdictional Immunities of States and Their Property, Resolution A/RES/59/38, Doc A/59/508, adopted by the UN General Assembly, Fifty-ninth session, 2 December 2004, not yet entered into force.

[11] This information was verified on 13 June 2010: United Nations Treaty Collection, Status, <http://treaties.un.org/Pages/ViewDetails.aspx?src=TREATY&mtdsg_no=III-13&chapter=3&lang=en>. [12] De Oliveira Moll (n 6 above), 567.

[13] Article 11 of the Basle Convention provides: 'A Contracting State cannot claim immunity from the jurisdiction of a court of another Contracting State in proceedings which relate to redress for injury to the person or damage to tangible property, if the facts which occasioned the injury or damage occurred in the territory of the State of the forum, and if the author of the injury or damage was present in that territory at the time when those facts occurred.' Article 12 of the

have been abused in a foreign country and return to their homeland cannot institute court proceedings due to the lack of territorial connection.

1.3 International Practice

In addition to developments in conventional law, several precedents have indicated that the doctrine of state immunity is uncertain, given the divergence of views held regarding its scope. In the *Furundzija* judgment,[14] the International Criminal Tribunal for the former Yugoslavia (ICTY) signalled that the doctrine of state immunity is eroding and becoming less restrictive. The Court found in relation to the prohibition of torture that:

> [b]ecause of the importance of the values it protects, this principle has evolved into a peremptory norm or *jus cogens*, that is, a norm that enjoys a higher rank in the international hierarchy than treaty law and even 'ordinary' customary rules. The most conspicuous consequence of this higher rank is that the principle at issue cannot be derogated from by States through international treaties or local or special customs or even general customary rules not endowed with the same normative force.[15]

It would seem to follow from this bold and courageous statement that the prohibition of torture takes over the rule of state immunity, which is an ordinary rule of international customary law. The ICTY also added that 'the prohibition on torture imposes upon States obligations *erga omnes*, that is obligations owed towards all the other members of the international community, each of which then has a correlative right'.[16]

High hopes have also been raised by the creation of the International Criminal Court and the adoption of the Rome Statute[17] which stipulates that immunities do not bar the jurisdiction of the Court. In addition, the Rome Statute provides that torture, when committed as part of a widespread and systematic attack directed against a civilian population, constitutes a crime against humanity.[18] Although the International Criminal Court's jurisdiction is limited and the Court can only intervene when the domestic courts are unwilling or unable to do so, this development represents tremendous improvement for victims of human rights abuses.

UN Convention on Jurisdictional Immunities of States and Their Property stipulates in similar terms:

> Unless otherwise agreed between the States concerned, a State cannot invoke immunity from jurisdiction before a court of another State which is otherwise competent in a proceeding which relates to pecuniary compensation for death or injury to the person, or damage to or loss of tangible property, caused by an act or omission which is alleged to be attributable to the State, if the act or omission occurred in whole or in part in the territory of that other State and if the author of the act or omission was present in that territory at the time of the act or omission.

[14] *Prosecutor v Anto Furundzija*, judgment, ICTY, 10 December 1998, IT-95–17/1-T (1999) 38 ILM 317, para 153. [15] Ibid, para 153. [16] Ibid, para 155.

[17] Rome Statute of the International Criminal Court, 2187 UNTS 90, entered into force 1 July 2002, Art 27(2). [18] Ibid, Art 7.

Despite these positive developments, it should be remembered that the International Court of Justice observed in the *Democratic Republic of the Congo v Belgium* judgment,[19] quashing the international arrest warrant for a Congolese Minister of Foreign Affairs, that it is firmly established in international law that heads of state, heads of government, and ministers of foreign affairs are immune from jurisdiction in civil or criminal matters.[20] Pointing to its continued relevance, the Court's reasoning raises numerous doubts as to the exact scope of the doctrine of state immunity.

1.4 State Practice

Although state practice in this field has recently flourished, it is marked by a sharp division of views.[21] The existence of these conflicting opinions seems to be dependent on whether the country concerned has enacted legislation dealing with state immunity. Until now, it appears that only eight states have adopted such legislation, namely the United States, the United Kingdom, Singapore, Pakistan, South Africa, Canada, Australia, and Argentina.[22] In cases filed in Canada and in the United Kingdom, courts took notice of international law but resorted to their own laws on foreign state immunities and held that these prevail in cases of violation of a peremptory norm. However, in countries where no specific law has been enacted, such as Italy and Greece, courts have been willing to apply international law and to deny the application of immunities in relation

[19] *Arrest Warrant of 11 April 2000 (Democratic Republic of Congo v Belgium)*, 14 February 2002, ICJ Reports 2002, 182–236, para 51.

[20] In this case, a Belgian judge had issued an international arrest warrant against Mr Yerodia Ndombasi, the Congolese Minister of Foreign Affairs at the time, for war crimes and crimes against humanity allegedly perpetrated in the Democratic Republic of Congo since 1997.

[21] For a thorough summary of state practice regarding state immunities in contracts of employment and personal injury, see Susan Breau, 'Summary of the State Practice Regarding State Immunities in the Council of Europe/*Résumé sur la Pratique des États relative aux Immunités du Conseil de l'Europe*' in Gerard Hafner, Marcelo G Kohen, and Susan Breau (eds), *State Practice Regarding State Immunities/La Pratique des États concernant les Immunités des États* (Council of Europe, Leiden/Boston: Martinus Nijhoff, 2006), 177–199.

[22] Julie Gaudreau, '*Immunité de l'Etat et Violations des Droits de la Personne: Une Approche Jurisprudentielle*', Institut Universitaire des Hautes Etudes Internationales, HEI Publications, Etudes et Travaux, Papier no 05/01, March 2005, 17. See also Foreign Sovereign Immunities Act of 1976, 28 USC §§1330, 1602–1611, reprinted in (1976) 15 ILM 1398 (United States); State Immunity Act 1978, 20 July 1978 (ch 33), reprinted in (1978) 17 ILM 1123 (United Kingdom); State Immunity Act 1979, *Gazette of the Republic of Singapore*, no 19/1979, 193, reprinted in United Nations, *Materials on Jurisdictional Immunities of States and Their Property*, United Nations Legislative Series, UN Doc ST/LEG/SER.B/20, 28 (Singapore); State Immunity Ordinance 1981, VI of 1981, *The Gazette of Pakistan (Islamabad)*, 11 March 1981, 29 (Pakistan); Foreign Sovereign Immunity Act 1981, Republic of South Africa, *Government Gazette*, Vol 196, No 7849, 28 October 1981, 1 (South Africa); State Immunity Act, 1982, RSC 1985 (c S-18) (Canada); Foreign States Immunities Act 1985, No 196, *Acts of the Parliament of the Commonwealth of Australia passed during the year 1985*, Vol 2, 2696, reprinted in (1986) 25 ILM 715 (Australia); Inmunidad Jurisdiccional de los Estados Extranjeros ante los Tribunales Argentinos, Ley, 24.448, 31 May 1995, *Boletín Oficial*, 28 June 1995 (Argentina).

to violations of *jus cogens* norms.[23] Thus, the fact that codification took place in a given jurisdiction seems to have influenced the outcome of the decision. Overall, it appears that the practice of Contracting States with regard to state immunities in contracts of employment and personal injuries is slowly coalescing around the concept of limited immunity.[24]

1.4.1 National Decisions Based on International Law

In Italy, the Corte Suprema di Cassazione heard the *Ferrini v Federal Republic of Germany* case.[25] Mr Ferrini brought a civil claim for compensation for his capture and deportation from Italy to Germany by the German military during the Second World War for forced labour. He had attempted to bring a claim for compensation in Germany, but the courts refused it because it did not fall under the domestic statute. The Italian Court of First Instance and the Court of Appeal acknowledged that the violations amounted to war crimes but held that state immunity applied to German acts which were of a sovereign nature. The Corte Suprema di Cassazione rejected the lower court decisions finding that state immunity did not apply to violations of *jus cogens* norms. Following this decision, Germany has instituted proceedings against Italy before the ICJ claiming that its jurisdictional immunity as a sovereign state had been disregarded.[26] The ICJ's decision in this matter is awaited with impatience, as it would have an important bearing on the current state of international law.

In Greece, in the *Prefecture of Voiotia v Federal Republic of Germany* decision,[27] the prefect of Voiotia and survivors and relatives of the deceased brought a civil action against Germany in the Court of First Instance of Livadia in Greece. During the German occupation in 1944, Greek resistance fighters had attacked the German military which in return killed most of the civilian population in the village of Distomo, Greece. The Court found that Germany could not be granted immunity for war crimes, which could not be considered as sovereign acts. It was held that these violations of *jus cogens* norms constituted an implied waiver of immunity under international law, and Germany was ordered to pay compensation. Germany then appealed to the Areios Pagos (the Greek Supreme Court), arguing that it was entitled to immunity from jurisdiction. The Supreme Court held that the crimes carried out by the occupying power in violation of their sovereign power could not be granted immunity.[28] Unfortunately, when the survivors sought to enforce the judgment, they had to seek authorization from

23 Gaudreau (n 22 above), 17. 24 Breau (n 21 above), 177–199.

25 *Ferrini v Federal Republic of Germany*, Civil Chamber, Italian Supreme Court, 6 November 2003, No 5044.

26 International Court of Justice, 'Germany institutes proceedings against Italy for failing to respect its jurisdictional immunity as a sovereign State', Press release, 23 December 2008, <http://www.icj-cij.org/docket/files/143/14925.pdf> (last visited 13 June 2010).

27 *Prefecture of Voiotia v Federal Republic of Germany*, Case No 137/1997, Court of First Instance of Livadia, 30 October 1997.

28 *Prefecture of Voiotia*, Case No 11/2000, Greek Supreme Court.

the Greek Minister of Justice, who refused to authorize its execution. The victims and relatives of the deceased then initiated enforcement proceedings, in which the Greek Supreme Court ruled against them.[29] The case was then brought to the European Court of Human Rights, but it was found to be inadmissible.[30] Finally, the German Federal Court of Justice found that it was not obliged to recognize the decision of the Greek Supreme Court.[31]

1.4.2 National Decisions Based on Domestic Law

In the *Bouzari v Islamic Republic of Iran* case,[32] Mr Bouzari, an Iranian citizen, brought a civil claim against Iran in Canada. He owned a consulting firm that advised foreign investors seeking to develop oil and gas projects in the Persian Gulf. He was retained by a consortium of companies to act on a project for them. The project consisted of providing oil and gas drilling as well as exploration technology and pipeline and refinery construction to the National Iranian Oil Company (NIOC). The son of the then President of Iran offered his father's help in facilitating the project, in exchange for a $50 million commission. Bouzari alleged that, following his refusal to pay the commission, he was tortured in prison.

The Court of Appeal observed that it was not bound to apply a rule of universal jurisdiction to a civil action for torture committed abroad by a foreign state. The Court applied the 'real and substantial connection' test, established under Canadian common law, to determine whether there was a link between the case and Canada. It was also considered further that Mr Bouzari's claim did not fall under any of the exceptions to immunity provided in the Canadian State Immunity Act. Although the Court recognized the *jus cogens* status of the prohibition of torture, it held that no additional exception could be made to the application of state immunity in this case. It was also found that no state practice existed to demonstrate that a violation of a *jus cogens* norm entailed the non-application of state immunity. Either way, the Court further added that its domestic legislation would have priority over international rules in case of conflict.

In *Jones v The Kingdom of Saudi Arabia*,[33] the House of Lords ruled that three British men and one Canadian man, who claimed to have been tortured in Saudi Arabian jails after confessing to participating in a series of terrorist bombings in Riyadh (Saudi Arabia) in 2000 and 2001, could not sue Saudi officials responsible for their imprisonment in British courts because the officials were covered by state immunity. The House of Lords reversed a Court of Appeal judgment from

[29] Decision of the Greek Supreme Court, No 36/2000, 51 Nomiko Vima 856 (2003).

[30] *Kalogeropoulou and others v Greece and Germany* (App No 59021/00), decision, 12 December 2002, Reports 2002-X, 415.

[31] *Distomo*, Bundesgerichtshof (BGH), decision of 26 June 2003, III ZR 245/98, published in NWJ 2003, 3488.

[32] *Bouzari v Islamic Republic of Iran* (2004) 243 DLR (4th) 406, OCA.

[33] *Jones v The Kingdom of Saudi Arabia* [2006] UKHL 25.

October 2004 allowing the four men to bring lawsuits against the individual Saudi officials accused of torture, though not against the Saudi Government.

In his opinion, Lord Bingham of Cornhill adopted a methodology where he considered the 'balance currently struck in international law' between the prohibition of torture and state immunity. He quoted with approval the decision of the European Court of Human Rights in the *Al-Adsani* case[34] and recognized that the prohibition of torture has the status of a *jus cogens* norm.[35] Conducting a comparative analysis of the case law on the topic, he concluded that there was no rule in international law which allowed for universal civil jurisdiction for alleged torture. Furthermore, the Convention Against Torture and Other Cruel, Inhuman or Degrading Treatment or Punishment did not provide for universal civil jurisdiction, as it only required a private right of action when torture was committed in the forum state.[36] The UN Convention on Jurisdictional Immunities of States and Their Property provided no exception from immunity for civil claims based on acts of torture.[37] There was also no evidence that states had recognized or given effect to an international law obligation to exercise universal jurisdiction for breaches of *jus cogens* norms.[38] In his view, the UK 1978 State Immunity Act was consistent with the prohibition of torture in international law and its application did not infringe Article 6 of the ECHR.[39]

Lord Hoffmann issued a separate opinion where he considered the relevant sources of state immunity. He concluded that there was no requirement for a state to provide civil jurisdiction for acts of torture committed outside the forum state. There was also no breach of Article 6 of the ECHR if a state did not provide such jurisdiction.[40] In his view, the breach of a *jus cogens* norm did not automatically entail the denial of immunity to a foreign state. Furthermore, it was not for a national court to develop international law by unilaterally adopting a version of it which was not accepted by other states.[41] It was also considered that no exception could be read into the State Immunity Act.[42] Lord Hoffmann rejected the argument that torture or other breach of *jus cogens* norms could not attract immunity *ratione materiae* because it could not be an official act.[43] The three other Law Lords concurred with both opinions and dismissed Mr Jones' appeal.

In the *Ex p Pinochet (No 3)* case,[44] the House of Lords removed the immunity of Augusto Pinochet Ugarte, the former Chilean Head of State, from prosecution with respect to human rights abuses. It should be added, however, that the *Ex p Pinochet (No 3)* case only concerned a former head of state's *ratione materiae* immunity in criminal proceedings, and that the Law Lords considered that a

[34] *Al-Adsani v United Kingdom* (App No 35763/97), judgment, 12 December 2001, Reports 2001-XI, 79.
[35] *Jones v The Kingdom of Saudi Arabia* (n 33 above), para 1.
[36] Ibid, para 25.
[37] Ibid, para 26.
[38] Ibid, para 27.
[39] Ibid, para 28.
[40] Ibid, para 64.
[41] Ibid, para 63.
[42] Ibid, para 64.
[43] Ibid, para 84.
[44] *R v Bartle and Commissioner of Police for the Metropolis and others ex p Pinochet, R v Evans and another and Commissioner of Police for the Metropolis and others ex p Pinochet* [2000] 1 AC 147, HL.

serving head of state would be entitled to *ratione personae* immunity in criminal and civil proceedings.

The conflicting cases outlined in this section serve to indicate the extent to which domestic practice in the field of state immunity is in a state of flux. At the same time, it is also apparent that the doctrine of state immunities has barely started to evolve in a direction which is more favourable to human rights. Restrictive values protecting states are still strongly entrenched in the international as well as European legal systems.

2. The Strasbourg Case Law

2.1 Preliminary Observations

In its earlier case law, the Court considered the relationship between immunities and the right of access to a court (Article 6 of the ECHR) in the context of immunities granted to international organizations. In the decisions in *Waite and Kennedy v Germany*[45] and *Beer and Regan v Germany*,[46] the applicants, employed by foreign companies, were placed at the disposal of the European Space Agency (ESA) to perform services at the European Space Operations Centre in Darmstadt. When their contracts were not renewed, they instituted proceedings against the ESA, arguing that, pursuant to the German labour law, they had acquired the status of ESA employees. The ESA relied on its immunity from jurisdiction (contained in the ESA Convention[47]) which was upheld by the ECtHR. The Court denied that there had been a violation of the right of access to court, as enshrined in Article 6(1) of the ECHR. While in these cases the confrontation of the principles of immunity and access to court led the Court to adopt a restrictive approach, it was difficult to predict how this trend would develop in future cases involving other types of immunity.[48]

In 2001 the Court issued three judgments (*Al-Adsani v United Kingdom*,[49] *Fogarty v United Kingdom*,[50] and *McElhinney v Ireland*[51]) which concerned the

[45] *Waite and Kennedy v Germany* (App No 26083/94), judgment, 18 February 1999, Reports 1999-I 393.

[46] *Beer and Regan v Germany* (App No 28934/95), judgment, 18 February 1999, not reported.

[47] Convention for the Establishment of a European Space Agency, 1297 UNTS 161 (No 21524), entered into force 30 October 1980.

[48] It is worth mentioning that the applicants in *Waite and Kennedy v Germany* and *Beer and Regan v Germany* had an alternative means of redress (they could appeal to the ESA Appeals Body). This was not the case in the three judgments discussed here, where the applicants had no additional remedy available to them.

[49] *Al-Adsani v United Kingdom* (n 34 above).

[50] *Fogarty v United Kingdom* (App No 37112/97), judgment, 21 November 2001, Reports 2001-XI 157.

[51] *McElhinney v United Kingdom* (App No 31253/96), judgment, 21 November 2001, Reports 2001-XI, 37.

concept of state immunity and considered international law related to this subject. It had not ruled on the sovereign immunity of foreign states previously.

2.2 The *Al-Adsani v United Kingdom* Case

The *Al-Adsani v United Kingdom* decision concerned Sulaiman Al-Adsani, a British and Kuwaiti citizen, who returned to Kuwait in 1991 to defend his country against the Iraqi invasion. During the First Gulf War, he served in the Kuwaiti Air Force, and after the war, he stayed in Kuwait. He came into the possession of sex videotapes which implicated Sheikh Jaber Al-Sabah Al-Saud Al-Sabah. These videotapes were later circulated, after which the Sheikh and two others broke into Al-Adsani's house and imprisoned him in the Kuwaiti state prison. Al-Adsani allegedly signed a false confession and was released only to be arrested again several days later by the Sheikh. He was brought to the palace of the Emir of Kuwait's brother, where his head was repeatedly held underwater in a swimming pool containing corpses and closed in a small room where the Sheikh set fire to mattresses soaked in petrol. He was then treated in hospital for burns covering 25 per cent of his body.

Al-Adsani instituted civil proceedings in the United Kingdom for compensation against the Sheikh and the State of Kuwait in respect of physical and mental health injuries caused by torture in Kuwait in May 1991, as well as threats against his life and well-being made after his return to the United Kingdom on 17 May 1991. On 15 December 1992 he obtained a default judgment against the Sheikh. The Kuwaiti Government sought an order striking out the proceedings and the application was examined by the High Court on 15 March 1995. The High Court held that it was for the applicant to show on the balance of probabilities that the State of Kuwait was not entitled to immunity under the State Immunity Act 1978,[52] and decided that the State of Kuwait was not responsible for threats received by the applicant after 17 May 1991.[53] The proceedings against the State were struck out. Al-Adsani appealed to the Court of Appeal which held that he had not established that the State of Kuwait was responsible for the threats made in the United Kingdom and that the Kingdom of Kuwait was in any case entitled to immunity.[54] On 27 November 1996 Al-Adsani was also refused leave to appeal by the House of Lords and his attempts to obtain compensation from the Kuwaiti authorities through diplomatic means failed.

Al-Adsani lodged an application at European Commission of Human Rights on 3 April 1997 alleging that the English courts, by granting immunity from suit to the State of Kuwait, failed to secure enjoyment of his right not to be tortured and denied him access to a court, contrary to Articles 3, 6(1), and 13 of the

[52] State Immunity Act 1978 (1978) 17 ILM 1123.
[53] *Al-Adsani v Government of Kuwait and others* (1995) 103 ILR 420, QBD.
[54] *Al-Adsani v Government of Kuwait and others (No 2)* (1996) 107 ILR 536, CA.

ECHR. The European Court of Human Rights found by 9 to 8 that there was no violation of Articles 3 and 6.

2.3 The *Fogarty v United Kingdom* Case

In the second case, *Fogarty v United Kingdom*,[55] Mary Fogarty, an Irish citizen, was dismissed from her employment as administrative assistant at the US Embassy in London (Foreign Broadcasting Information Service). Fogarty initiated proceedings against the US Government in the North London Industrial Tribunal claiming that her dismissal resulted from discrimination based on sex and was contrary to the Sex Discrimination Act 1975. She claimed that her supervisor had persistently harassed her sexually, which led to her dismissal. The tribunal upheld her complaint and ordered the United States to pay her compensation.[56] The United States did not claim immunity during the proceedings.

While the case was still pending in the Industrial Tribunal, Fogarty applied for a one-year post as administrative assistant in a different department of the Embassy. This and subsequent attempts to obtain employment at the Embassy failed. She initiated a second action in the Industrial Tribunal claiming that the Embassy's refusal to re-employ her was a result of her previous successful sex discrimination claim. At this point, the United States claimed immunity under the State Immunity Act 1978, and Fogarty was advised against pursuing her claim further and that there was no further remedy in domestic law.

An application was then lodged with the European Commission of Human Rights on 8 July 1997. The applicant alleged that she had been refused access to a court and discriminated against contrary to Articles 6(1) and 14 of the ECHR. The ECtHR decided by 16 to 1 that there was no violation of Articles 6(1) and 14.

2.4 The *McElhinney v Ireland* Case

The last case, *McElhinney v Ireland*,[57] implicated an Irish police officer (*garda*), John McElhinney, who on 4 March 1991 accidentally drove across a British checkpoint barrier, and dragged a soldier on guard into Ireland. The soldier fired gun shots as he was carried away. When the car stopped, the soldier aimed his gun at McElhinney's head and pulled the trigger twice. The gun did not fire any shots because the trigger was blocked. While there was agreement as to these facts, many others were disputed. On 29 June 1993 McElhinney introduced a claim against the soldier and the British Secretary of State for Northern Ireland at the Irish High Court for damages suffered as a result of the incident. He was

[55] *Fogarty v United Kingdom* (n 50 above).

[56] The decision is not reported.

[57] *McElhinney v Ireland* (n 51 above).

informed by the solicitors of the UK Government that the Secretary of State for Northern Ireland bore no responsibility for the actions of the soldier who was under the authority of the Secretary of State for Defence. However, it was also added that the Secretary of State for Defence was entitled to immunity and could not be prosecuted. McElhinney substituted the defendant for the Secretary of State for Defence, and the Irish High Court ruled that McElhinney was not entitled to sue a member of a foreign government. McElhinney appealed and his appeal was rejected by the Irish Supreme Court on the basis of the sovereign immunity doctrine.[58]

McElhinney then lodged an application on 16 April 1996 against Ireland and the United Kingdom with the European Commission of Human Rights. He alleged that he was refused access to a court contrary to Article 6 of the Convention. The Court ruled by 12 to 5 that Article 6 applied but that there was no violation.

3. Analysis of the Court's References to International Law

3.1 A Common Reasoning

The three cases outlined above are characterized by numerous common threads, and the Court's reasoning in deciding them was similar. All applicants claimed that by applying the doctrine of immunity, domestic courts had denied them the right to access to a court in violation of Article 6(1) of the ECHR. Al-Adsani also alleged that his rights under Article 3 (prohibition of torture) had been violated and Fogarty claimed that her rights under Article 14 (prohibition of discrimination) had been infringed. In the three instances, the Court ruled that no violation had taken place.

The Court recalled briefly the relevant international law instruments on state immunity in the initial part of its decisions. It was observed that the Basle Convention had been signed and ratified by the United Kingdom (*Al-Adsani v United Kingdom* and *Fogarty v United Kingdom*) but not by Ireland (*McElhinney v United Kingdom*). In *Al-Adsani* and *McElhinney*, the Court referred to Article 11 of the Basle Convention, which provides that immunity cannot be claimed in relation to redress for injury to the person or damage to tangible property, if facts which gave rise to the injury occurred in the forum state, and if the author of the injury or damage was present at the time when these facts occurred. In *McElhinney*, the Court referred in addition to Article 31 of the Basle Convention, which states that immunities or privileges granted to the Contracting State in respect of actions performed by its armed forces on the territory of another state will not be affected by the provisions of the Convention. In *Fogarty*, the Court

[58] *McElhinney v Williams* (1995) 3 IR 382.

referred to Articles 5 and 32 of the Basle Convention. Article 5 provides that a state cannot claim immunity in proceedings which relate to a contract of employment between the state and individual when work is to be performed in the forum state. Article 32 provides additionally that the Basle Convention does not affect privileges and immunities relating to the exercise of functions of diplomatic missions and consular posts.

The Court's most recent source of international law was that cited in *Al-Adsani* and *McElhinney*, namely the 1999 Report on Jurisdictional Immunities of States and their Property[59] of the Working Group of the International Law Commission. The Working Group noted in its report that there had been civil claims for torture committed outside the forum state brought in domestic courts, especially in the United States and in the United Kingdom, against foreign governments. It was further observed that the domestic courts showed sympathy, but that the plea of state immunity generally succeeded.[60] The reliance on this evidence seems to be selective, as there were other more recent sources of international law available to the Court in 2001.

3.1.1 Analysis of Article 6(1) of the ECHR

3.1.1.1 Applicability of the Article

The Court found that Article 6(1) of the ECHR applied to all three cases and rejected the Governments' argument that the entitlement to immunity took over the rights contained in the ECHR.[61] The Court reiterated that Article 6(1) applied to disputes concerning the determination of civil rights and obligations recognized under domestic law. The Court then had to consider whether there was a dispute over civil rights in British and Irish law. The Court indicated in the *McElhinney* and *Al-Adsani* cases with regard to substantive content of the rights contested that the courses of action were well-established in domestic law. In the *Fogarty* case, the Court found that there were certain elements which were considered to be civil under the Court's jurisprudence.

In all three cases, the Court recalled that '[w]hether a person has an actionable domestic claim may depend not only on the substantive content, properly speaking, of the relevant civil right as defined under national law but also on the existence of procedural bars preventing or limiting the possibilities of bringing

[59] *Annex: Report of the Working Group on Jurisdictional Immunities of States and their Property*, Report of the International Law Commission on the work of its fifty-first session (3 May to 23 July 1999), Document A/54/10, A/CN.4/ SER. A/1999/Add.1 (Part 2), *Yearbook of the International Law Commission*, Vol 2, Part 2, 149.

[60] Ibid, Appendix, 172, paras 4–7.

[61] It has been suggested, however, that the Court's construction of the three applications raising issues under Article 6(1) cannot be commended. External constraints on the jurisdiction of a Contracting State do not seem to affect ECHR rights, but rather the applicability of the Convention as a whole under Article 1. See Emmanuel Voyiakis, 'Access to Court v State Immunity' (2003) 52 Int'l Comp LQ 297, 309 –310, 332.

potential claims to court'.[62] The Court also found that it would be inconsistent for the rule of law in a democratic society if a state would be able to remove a wide range of civil claims from the jurisdiction of its courts or confer immunity to a large group of persons. The Court was not willing to accept that a state would be able to extinguish a civil cause of action by conferring an immunity on to someone. In other words, it refused to recognize that an immunity might have priority over the rights enshrined in the Convention, and therefore considered that the granting of immunity must be scrutinized.

3.1.1.2 Violation of the Article

The Court then went on to analyse whether Article 6 had been violated, which gave rise to different interpretations on the part of the majority and of the minority. The majority claimed that the right of access to a court is not an absolute right and that it is subject to limitations imposed by national authorities, which enjoy a margin of appreciation. These limitations must conform to the Court's well-established two-pronged test, which is aimed at verifying the legality of restrictions imposed on the right of access to a court. First, the restriction must conform to a legitimate aim under the Convention and the Court's jurisprudence and, secondly, the restriction must be proportionate to the end it seeks to achieve.

3.1.1.2.1 Legitimate Aim In the majority's view, the granting of immunity by the respective Governments followed a clearly legitimate aim. In all three decisions, the Court noted that 'sovereign immunity is a concept of international law, developed out of the principle *par in parem non habet imperium*, by virtue of which one State shall not be subject to the jurisdiction of another State'.[63] It was found that 'the grant of sovereign immunity in civil proceedings pursues a legitimate aim of complying with international law to promote comity and good relations through the respect of another State's sovereignty'.[64]

Following this statement, the Court's reasoning and logic broke down and became circular. The Court did not look deeper into the aims pursued by the legislation but merely assumed that they conformed to international law. There is hardly any convincing evidence that states adopt their legislation on state immunity in belief of an international obligation.[65] The Court seems to have reasoned that since domestic law reflects international law then it is compliant with the Convention. Such an inference is not self-evident, and it should have been tested further. Judicial practice is usually hesitant to take domestic statutes on immunity

[62] *McElhinney v United Kingdom* (n 51 above), para 24; *Fogarty v United Kingdom* (n 50 above), para 25; *Al-Adsani v United Kingdom* (n 34 above), para 47.

[63] Ibid (italics in original).

[64] *McElhinney v United Kingdom* (n 51 above), para 35; *Fogarty v United Kingdom* (n 50 above), para 34; *Al-Adsani v United Kingdom* (n 34 above), para 54.

[65] Alexander Orakhelashvili, 'State Immunity and International Public Order' (2003) 45 GYIL 227 247.

as evidence of international legal rules.[66] Therefore, an enquiry should have been conducted in order to verify the status of international law on the topic and whether the restriction really complies with it. There was no evidence that the aim of international law in this field is to promote comity and good relations. It would have been possible to argue instead that the aim of international law in this field is to protect human rights, but the Court did not follow this direction. The Court's reasoning here seems to base itself on a restrictive view of international law, which is defined by reference to the domestic legal order.

3.1.1.2.2 Proportionality Test Subsequently, the majority applied the proportionality test in order to verify whether the restriction was proportionate to the aim pursued. It recalled that 'the Convention has to be interpreted in the light of rules set out in the Vienna Convention on the Law of Treaties, and that Article 31(3)(c) of that treaty indicates that account is to be taken of "any relevant rules of international law applicable in the relations between parties"'.[67] The Convention, including Article 6, could not be interpreted in a vacuum. It had to be interpreted, as far as possible, in harmony with other rules of international law of which they form part, including those on state immunity.[68] For the majority, it followed that 'measures taken by a High Contracting Party which reflect generally recognised rules of public international law on State immunity cannot in principle be regarded as imposing a disproportionate restriction on the right of access to court as embodied in Article 6 § 1'.[69] It was also reiterated that judges should be mindful of the ECHR's special character as a human rights treaty. This reasoning constitutes one of the Court's attempts to come to grips with systemic integration of various international legal rules contained in Article 31(3)(c) of the Vienna Convention on the Law of Treaties (VCLT).

3.1.2 The Court's Reasoning

The majority merely referred to state practice without really considering international law. It did not intend to rule on whether a rule of international law is itself a proportionate restriction for the purposes of Article 6 of the ECHR.[70] It rather sent a message to Contracting States that Article 6 will be applied in future cases in a way which gives them a wide margin of appreciation in relation to the extent of their obligations in international law and permits limitations on access to their courts.[71] The Court failed to confront the very nature of proportionality, which involves a balancing of interests of both parties. The stakes were high on both

[66] Ibid, 248.

[67] *McElhinney v United Kingdom* (n 51 above), para 36; *Fogarty v United Kingdom* (n 50 above), para 35; *Al-Adsani v United Kingdom* (n 34 above), para 55.

[68] Ibid.

[69] *McElhinney v United Kingdom* (n 51 above), para 37; *Fogarty v United Kingdom* (n 50 above), para 36; *Al-Adsani v United Kingdom* (n 34 above), para 56.

[70] David Lloyd Jones, 'Article 6 ECHR and Immunities Arising in Public International Law' (2003) 52 Int'l Comp LQ 463, 472.

[71] Ibid, 470.

sides, and the Court should have tested them in order to determine which side's interests were more compliant with the Convention. Instead, the Court used a hermetic argument which allowed it to shrug off any further questions.

In addition, the majority did not adequately address the distinctions between the application of state immunity in criminal and civil proceedings. In practice, it seems that this distinction does not really exist. It is true that certain differences exist regarding the rules for establishing and extending judicial competence with respect to domestic civil and criminal jurisdiction.[72] However, it is not clear to what extent the use of the rule on state immunity in one type of proceedings could be different in another type of proceedings. In using this type of argument, the Court should have justified the reasons for this distinction thoroughly, instead of assuming that the rule could be used in one instance and not in the other. It is still not clear why immunities cannot be applied in a criminal case while they can be applied in a civil case. It would be reasonable to assume that both types of situation can be treated analogically, but the Court did not explore this argument. The distinction is also problematic because the majority of judges failed to observe that an individual's responsibility does not translate into a state's responsibility, thereby blurring the lines between immunities granted to individuals and state immunity. It is curious that the Court did not prefer to make distinctions between individual immunities and state immunity, or immunities *rationae materiae* and *ratione personae*. In contrast to differentiation based on type of jurisdiction, the distinction based on type of immunity is commonly used. In this respect, the Court's approach does not contribute to the current stance in international law, but seems instead to complicate it further by introducing unjustified distinctions.

3.2 Differences in the Reasoning

3.2.1 The Reasoning of the Majority

3.2.1.1 The *McElhinney v United Kingdom* Case

From this point onwards, the reasoning of the majority differed in the three cases, as the Court considered the specific situations of the applicants. In *McElhinney v United Kingdom*,[73] the majority noted that there appeared to be a trend in international and comparative law towards limiting state immunity in relation to personal injury caused by an act or omission within the forum state. It considered that international instruments referred to 'insurable' personal injury (ie road traffic accidents, etc) 'rather than matters relating to the core area of State sovereignty such as acts of a soldier on foreign territory which, of their very nature, may involve sensitive issues affecting diplomatic relations between States

[72] De Oliveira Moll (n 6 above), 589.

[73] *McElhinney v United Kingdom* (n 51 above).

and national security'.[74] This view seems to be misleading, as the International Law Commission indicated clearly that the draft Article 12 extends beyond all insurable risk and is wide enough to contain international physical harm.[75] In addition, the word 'insurable' does not appear in any international or domestic legislation.[76]

The Court further noted that Ireland is not the only country to grant immunity for torts committed by *acta jure imperii*, and that the Supreme Court's decision conforms to the present state of development of international law. In relation to this finding, it should be noted that the *jure imperii* and *jure gestionis* dichotomy appears to be out of place in current state practice.[77] Although Ireland may not be the only state to rely on this distinction, most other states, such as the United Kingdom and the United States, have abandoned this test altogether and prefer to enact statutes providing explicit exceptions which allow the courts to take jurisdiction. This also seems to be the case with international legal instruments (ie the UN Convention on Jurisdictional Immunities of States and Their Property and the Basle Convention) which are based on an exceptions regime.

3.2.1.2 The *Fogarty v United Kingdom* Case

As in *McElhinney*, the majority in *Fogarty* noted that there appeared to be a trend in international and comparative law towards limiting state immunity in respect of employment-related disputes. However, with respect to cases relating to employment in a foreign mission or embassy, international practice is divided as to whom the state immunity applies (all staff or senior staff only) or if it applies at all.[78] Here again, the Court reasoned in quantitative terms, and observed that the United Kingdom is certainly not the only state to maintain such immunities and that it cannot be said that it does not conform to international standards.[79] In any case, the proceedings related to a recruitment process in an embassy and involved sensitive and confidential issues.[80] It was found that there was no trend which allows for the relaxation of state immunities rules in this field; the Court emphasized that the International Law Commission did not intend to exclude the application of state immunity with respect to recruitment at diplomatic missions.[81]

[74] Ibid, para 38.

[75] Xiadong Yang, 'State Immunity in the European Court of Human Rights: Reaffirmations and Misconceptions' (2003) 74 BYIL 333, 365.

[76] Ibid, 366.

[77] Ibid.

[78] *Fogarty v United Kingdom* (n 50 above), para 38.

[79] Ibid.

[80] Although there seems to have been no decision rendered in favour of a claimant in matters relating to recruitment at a diplomatic mission, this was not due to the confidential and sensitive nature of the information involved, but rather because the current law on state immunity requires the actual existence of an employment contract: Yang (n 75 above), 386.

[81] *Fogarty v United Kingdom* (n 50 above), para 38.

3.2.1.3 The *Al-Adsani v United Kingdom* Case

In *Al-Adsani v United Kingdom*[82] the majority opined that the UK State Immunity Act 1978 complied with the 1972 Basle Convention. It was noted that while the 1972 Basle Convention limits state immunity as traditionally conceived, it 'preserves it in respect of civil proceedings for damages for personal injury unless the injury was caused in the territory of the forum State'.[83] The majority then went on to consider Al-Adsani's argument that the prohibition of torture now constitutes a *jus cogens* norm which takes precedence over treaty law and other rules of international law. The Court seems to have agreed with only part of this statement. It emphasized that the prohibition of torture is one of the fundamental values of a democratic society and that there is a 'growing recognition of the overriding importance of the prohibition of torture'.[84] The Court referred to Article 5 (prohibition of torture) of the Universal Declaration of Human Rights,[85] Article 7 (prohibition of torture) of the International Covenant on Civil and Political Rights, and Articles 2 (obligation on part of state to prevent torture) and 4 (obligation to implement the offence of torture in domestic criminal law) of the Convention Against Torture and Other Cruel, Inhuman or Degrading Treatment or Punishment.

The majority further quoted a statement from the *Furundzija* judgment,[86] where the ICTY observed that the prohibition of torture has become a *jus cogens* norm. It also recalled that similar statements were formulated by other courts, namely in the *Ex p Pinochet (No 3)* decision.[87] The majority noted that, on the basis of the existing precedents, the prohibition of torture had attained the status of a peremptory norm. However, the case at hand did not concern 'as in *Furundzija* and *Pinochet*, the criminal liability of an individual for alleged acts of torture, but the immunity of a State in a civil suit for damages in respect of acts of torture within the territory of that State'.[88] The Court also found that none of the international legal instruments it had enumerated previously related to civil proceedings and state immunity.

The Court further considered that neither the amendment introducing an exception for civil claims for alleged acts of torture to the US Foreign Sovereign Immunities Act (FSIA)[89] nor the *Ex p Pinochet (No 3)* decision[90] provided 'a firm basis on which to conclude that the immunity of States *ratione personae* is no

[82] *Al-Adsani v United Kingdom* (n 34 above).

[83] Ibid, para 57.

[84] Ibid, para 60.

[85] Universal Declaration of Human Rights, adopted 10 December 1948, GA Res 217A (III), UN Doc A/810 (1948).

[86] *Prosecutor v Anto Furundzija* (n 14 above), para 153.

[87] *R v Bartle and Commissioner of Police for the Metropolis and others ex p Pinochet, R v Evans and another and Commissioner of Police for the Metropolis and others ex p Pinochet* (n 44 above).

[88] *Al-Adsani v United Kingdom* (n 34 above), para 61.

[89] Foreign Sovereign Immunities Act (1976), Pub L No 94–583, 90 Stat 2891.

[90] *R v Bartle and Commissioner of Police for the Metropolis and others ex p Pinochet, R v Evans and another and Commissioner of Police for the Metropolis and others ex p Pinochet* (n 44 above).

longer enjoyed in respect of civil liability for claims of acts of torture, let alone that it was not enjoyed in 1996 at the time of the Court of Appeal's judgment in the present case'.[91] In support of this, it was observed that the exception of the FSIA is limited in scope because an offending state must be designated as a state sponsor of acts of terrorism and the claimant must be a national of the United States. It is further limited in that after a judgment has been obtained, the property of a foreign state is immune from execution unless one of the statutory exceptions applies.[92] As regards the *Ex p Pinochet (No 3)* decision,[93] the Court noted that it only concerned the immunity *ratione materiae* from criminal jurisdiction of a former head of state, who was at the material time physically within the United Kingdom. The conclusion of the House of Lords did not affect the immunity *ratione personae* of foreign sovereign states from the civil jurisdiction in respect of such acts.[94] In the majority's view, it was not established in international law that there should be an exception to the application of the rule of state immunity in civil proceedings for damages of torture committed outside the forum state. However, this could be due to the fact that the majority relied on sources which support state practice granting states immunity from jurisdiction in civil claims for alleged torture committed outside the forum state.[95] It would have been possible, as demonstrated above, to take into account evidence which proves the contrary.

3.2.2 The Limited Contribution of the Majority

It can be argued that the three judgments above contributed to a certain extent to the international law on state immunity, given that they clarified the relation between the right of access to court and the law of state immunity.[96] It was found that as long as courts of the forum state conform to generally accepted standards relating to state immunity, the right of access to court under Article 6(1) of the ECHR will not be impaired.[97] The ECtHR was also the first international court to address the trumping effect of *jus cogens* over state immunity at the level of

[91] *Al-Adsani v United Kingdom* (n 34 above), para 63.

[92] Ibid, para 65. It should be noted that Congress passed the Anti-Terrorism and Effective Death Penalty Act (1996), Pub L No 104–132, 110 Stat 1214 in order to amend the Foreign Sovereign Immunities Act (1976), Pub L No 94–583, 90 Stat 2891. Section 221 of the Anti-Terrorism and Effective Death Penalty Act (1996) allows the bringing of civil suits for pecuniary damages against foreign states that cause death or personal injury through acts of torture outside the forum state. However, claimants must be US citizens and the defendant state must have been designated by the US Secretary of State as a sponsor of terrorism. It also allows the enforcement of a judgment against a state's property used for commercial activity in the United States.

[93] *R v Bartle and Commissioner of Police for the Metropolis and others ex p Pinochet, R v Evans and another and Commissioner of Police for the Metropolis and others ex p Pinochet* (n 44 above).

[94] Ibid.

[95] Katherine Reece Thomas and Joan Small, 'Human Rights and State Immunity From Civil Liability for Torture' (2003) 30 NILR 1, 13.

[96] Voyiakis (n 61 above), 331.

[97] Ibid.

international law.[98] In addition, the Court pronounced on three controversial exceptions from immunity. It was held that states are immune with respect to suits involving recruitment in a diplomatic mission, *jure imperii* acts of their armed forces in the forum state, and the jurisdiction of foreign courts in respect of violations of the *jus cogens* norm of prohibition of torture.[99] This development did not, however, contribute towards developing international human rights law, but rather towards supporting the traditional values underlying the doctrine of restrictive state immunity. Such an approach on the part of the ECtHR is not a step that should be welcomed or commended.

It has been argued that the Court's restrictive view of the prohibition of torture is not supported by human rights treaties.[100] While the Court recognized that Article 3 read in conjunction with Article 1 of the ECHR enshrines the duty to provide remedies for victims of torture, it considered that this right is limited to acts of torture committed in the forum state. The Court did not examine 'whether its restrictive construction of Article 3 is warranted in the light of "any applicable rule of international law" in terms of Article 31 § 3 (c) of the Vienna Convention, which in the case at hand could refer to the principles concerning torture in general international law'.[101] Article 3 of the ECHR does not seem to indicate that the prohibition of torture can be read in such a narrow fashion.[102] In addition, the Court's interpretation is neither supported by the plain meaning or the object and purpose of the ECHR.[103] It is especially contrary to Article 14 of the Convention Against Torture (CAT), which stipulates that '[e]ach State Party shall ensure in its legal system that the victim of an act of torture obtains redress and has an enforceable right to fair and adequate compensation including the means for as full rehabilitation as possible'.[104] In addition, Article 5 of the CAT prescribes that States Parties must take the necessary measures to establish their jurisdiction over torture.

The Court usually resorts to Article 31(3)(c) of the VCLT to support the Convention's effective operation and applicability where it is challenged.[105] However, in the *Al-Adsani* decision the Court referred to this article not to clarify what the ECHR means, but rather to determine to what extent it can be applied in the context of, arguably conflicting, rules of general international law.[106] It is possible that the Court was trying to import external rules to qualify the scope of the rights enshrined in the ECHR. Indeed, the Court did mention that the ECHR should be interpreted in harmony with other rules of international law, including those granting state immunity,[107] but instead it seems to have deferred

[98] Ed Bates, 'The Al-Adsani Case, State Immunity and the International Legal Prohibition on Torture' (2003) 3(2) HRLR 193, 221.
[99] Voyiakis (n 61 above), 331–332.
[100] Alexander Orakhelashvili, 'Restrictive Interpretation of Human Rights Treaties in the Recent Jurisprudence of the European Court of Human Rights' (2003) 14 Eur J Int'l L 529, 555.
[101] Ibid, 553–554.
[102] For further details, see ibid, 551–554.
[103] Ibid, 551–553.
[104] Ibid.
[105] Ibid, 556.
[106] Ibid.
[107] *Al-Adsani v United Kingdom* (n 34 above), para 55.

to them.[108] It is interesting to note that the Court did not refer to the *jus cogens* status of certain international law norms in the context of its interpretation.[109] Furthermore, it did not consider Article 31(3)(c) of the VCLT when interpreting Articles 1 and 3 of the ECHR. This provision was only considered in the context of the Court's interpretation of Article 6 of the ECHR.[110]

The Court's reasoning was in this part vague and not properly justified, as it was not clearly demonstrated how the rule of state immunity overrides the right of access to court. In *Al-Adsani*, the Court referred to the rules on state immunity as 'generally recognised rules of public international law', without ever illustrating how these rules acquired this generally recognized character.[111] The majority judges reached their conclusion without any proper examination of the relevant state practice and merely assumed that their arguments were correct. While many scholars consider that the rules on state immunity are part of customary international law, there is a lack of consensus and uniform state practice. Whether the Basle Convention constitutes general customary law needs be established on the basis of uniform state practice and *opinio juris*.[112] In addition, the Basle Convention only entered into force in eight states and the Convention on Jurisdictional Immunities of States and Their Property was not in force in any state. These legal instruments are weak authorities on which to base such bold assertions. Therefore, the Court's reasoning cannot stand, as it is not based on clear evidence and succinct argumentation. It could also be argued that the Court has failed to 'accord due importance to the nature of the ECHR as an instrument of public order establishing obligations of an objective nature, which go beyond the reciprocal commitment of individual contracting states'.[113]

In addition, the majority's opinion contained several contradictions. The majority judges recognized that the prohibition of torture had the status of a *jus cogens* norm and that it preceded other norms of international law. However, it was also accepted that—given the absence of an established rule of international law—the prohibition of torture would not have this status in civil proceedings. It is difficult to imagine that a *jus cogens* norm would change its status from one situation to the next and be selectively peremptory. Then, it would simply no longer be a peremptory norm. In addition, the Court distinguished the consequences of a *jus cogens* norm on the basis of the nature of the proceedings. According to its view, the *jus cogens* norm of prohibition of torture would only prevail in criminal proceedings. There is no established practice which would require the Court to change its approach to *jus cogens* in civil proceedings. Moreover, the standards applicable to civil and criminal cases when a conflict between the prohibition on torture and the rules on state immunity arises are not different.[114] Such a distinction is arbitrary and artificial. The Court failed to look at the very nature of a *jus*

[108] Orakhelashvili (n 100 above), 556.
[109] Reece Thomas and Small (n 95 above), 7.
[110] Orakhelashvili (n 100 above), 567.
[111] Ibid, 557.
[112] Ibid, 558.
[113] Ibid, 567.
[114] Ibid, 562.

cogens norm (its capacity to prevail over all other norms) and preferred to focus on its evidentiary aspect.[115]

3.2.3 The Different Reasoning of the Minority

3.2.3.1 The *Al-Adsani v United Kingdom* Case

It is interesting to note that the dissenting judges in the three cases at hand were much more sensitive to international law, although their reasoning contained several logical defects. This was especially the case in *Al-Adsani v United Kingdom*,[116] where Judges Rozakis and Caflisch wrote a common dissenting opinion, in which they were joined by Judges Wildhaber, Costa, Barreto, and Vajić. It was considered that the majority's opinion correctly found that the prohibition of torture is a *jus cogens* norm. Such a norm, in the event of conflict with any other rule of international law, always prevails. The dissenting judges explained that the rules on state immunity, derived from customary or conventional law, were not *jus cogens* norms and not hierarchically higher than any other rules. Therefore, the rules on state immunity had to be overriden by the prohibition of torture in international law. National law that is intended to give effect to the international rules on state immunity cannot be invoked as creating a jurisdictional bar, but has to be interpreted in light of the imperative precepts of *jus cogens* rules. While the majority accepted the fact that the prohibition on torture constitutes a *jus cogens* norm, it refused to draw the legal consequences of such an inference.

The minority's view is more compliant with international human rights law, but it is still problematic. The reasoning of the dissenting judges was unfortunately simplistic. As the exact scope of the trumping effect of the prohibition on torture is still disputed in international law, it would have been helpful if the minority had justified its reasoning further. There was virtually no analysis of the consequences of the finding put forward.[117] While it is true that the minority judges were only required to apply the law to the case before them and that it fell to the states to respond to a violation, the Court should nonetheless have spelled out the implications of its ruling, which departs from state practice.[118] In addition, given that their view could have important implications for Contracting States, it would have been appropriate to indicate the grounds on which they thought that Article 6 of the ECHR had been breached.

Further, the dissenting judges pointed out that the distinction made by the majority with respect to criminal proceedings, where *jus cogens* norms have an overriding effect, and civil proceedings, where they do not, is erroneous. First, it was considered that the English courts, when dealing with the applicant's claim, never resorted to the distinction made by the majority. Secondly, the minority observed that the distinction made by the majority between civil and criminal

[115] Ibid. [116] *Al-Adsani v United Kingdom* (n 34 above), para 65.
[117] Bates (n 98 above), 222. [118] Ibid, 223.

proceedings concerning the effect of the rule of the prohibition of torture was at odds with the very nature of *jus cogens* rules. It is not the nature of the proceedings which determines the effects of a *jus cogens* rule, but rather the character of the rule as a peremptory norm and its interaction with a hierarchically lower rule. Finally, it was concluded that the English courts should have entertained Al-Adsani's claim and that Article 6(1) had been violated.

The two other dissenting judges issued separate opinions. Judge Loucaides agreed with the joint dissenting opinion but added that 'it would be a travesty of law to allow exceptions in respect of civil liability by permitting the concept of State immunity to be relied on successfully against a claim for compensation by any victim of torture'.[119] His reasoning also differed from that in the joint dissent, as he considered that any form of blanket immunity, such as the one operating in this case, which does not allow the balancing of competing interests should be regarded as disproportionate. Judge Ferrari Bravo emphatically stated that 'the Court has unfortunately missed a very good opportunity to deliver a courageous judgment'.[120] In his view, the Court should have 'upheld the thrust of the House of Lords' judgment in *Regina v Bow Street Metropolitan Stipendiary and Others, ex parte Pinochet Ugarte (No 3)*... to the effect that the prohibition of torture is now *jus cogens*, so that torture is a crime under international law. It follows that every State has a duty to *contribute* to the punishment of torture and cannot hide behind formalist arguments to avoid having to give judgment.'[121]

3.2.3.2 The *McElhinney v United Kingdom* Case

In *McElhinney v United Kingdom*, five judges dissented. Judge Rozakis considered that the plea of sovereign immunity had lost much of its weight in view of the developments of international law. The majority had not carried out a proper balancing test of the interests of the foreign state and the affected individuals, as required by the proportionality test. He thought that the state interests were overridden by the right of the applicant to have access to a court. This was further reinforced by the existence of jurisdictional bonds between the applicant's case and Ireland.

Judges Caflisch, Barreto, and Vajić opined that the majority had misinterpreted customary international law on state immunity. It was argued that Article 11 of the European Convention on State Immunity and Article 12 of the former Draft Articles on Jurisdictional Immunities of States and Their Property (now the UN Convention on Jurisdictional Immunities of States and Their Property) represented the current position in international law. These provisions strongly

[119] *Al-Adsani v United Kingdom* (n 34 above), dissenting opinion of Judge Loucaides.

[120] Ibid, dissenting opinion of Judge Ferrari Bravo.

[121] Ibid (italics in original). It has also been argued that when the Court referred to the doctrine of state immunity, it failed to distinguish between sovereign (*jure imperii*) and non-sovereign (*jure gestionis*) acts and thereby resorted to an outdated theory of absolute immunity. See Orakhelashvili (n 65 above), 241.

suggested that there was no international duty to grant immunity for torts committed by other states in the forum state. Thus, it was found that there was no conflict between the doctrine of state immunity and the right of access to court. In this case, the latter right had been disproportionately breached, given that the applicant had been prevented from having access to Irish courts.

Judge Loucaides reiterated his opinion in *Al-Adsani*, where he considered that blanket immunities, such as the one granted in this case, were disproportionate. He found further that the ECHR was the *lex specialis* in the case, and as such it was the only instrument that should be taken into account: 'General principles of international law are not embodied in the Convention except insofar as reference is expressly made to them in the Convention (see, for example, Articles 15, 35 § 1 and 53 of the Convention and Article 1 of Protocol No 1).'[122] Therefore, there should be reluctance to accept restrictions on Convention rights derived from principles of international law, such as those on immunities, which are not even *jus cogens* norms.

3.2.3.3 The *Fogarty v United Kingdom* Case

In *Fogarty v United Kingdom*,[123] Judge Loucaides dissented, arguing that granting immunity with respect to damages claims for sex discrimination violated Article 6(1) of the ECHR, given the blanket nature of the immunity (the same argument as in *Al-Adsani* and *McElhinney*), the absence of an established rule supporting immunity, the fact that Fogarty's claim was an allegation of a human right violation (prohibition of discrimination), and the fact that there was no alternative remedy for the complaint. In his view, the fundamental consideration in this case was that access to court has been blocked without any examination of the nature of the claim and without a balancing of competing interests. He was the only dissenter in this case, with Judges Calfisch, Costa, and Vajić writing a separate concurring opinion. They argued that the exception to Article 11 of the former Draft Articles, which allows the granting of immunity in relation to recruitment, renewal of employment, or reinstatement of the individual (and where the person recruited will perform functions closely related to the exercise of governmental authority),[124] applied to the case. Thus, it was argued that the immunity granted to the United States should be maintained.

3.3 Further Considerations

It is interesting to note that neither the majority nor the minority of the Court considered the relationship between obligations *erga omnes* and *jus cogens* norms.

[122] *McElhinney v United Kingdom* (n 51 above), dissenting opinion of Judge Loucaides.
[123] *Fogarty v United Kingdom* (n 50 above).
[124] Currently Art 11(2)(c) of the UN Convention on Jurisdictional Immunities of States and Their Property.

It is possible that if both sides had considered the precise source of the *jus cogens* norm and its related status in international law, they could have avoided division in their approaches. Instead, it seems that they adopted an assumed source of the *jus cogens* norm without further argument, or avoided the fact that the source had a direct relevance to the question of legal effect.[125]

Judge Bravo was the only judge, in his dissent in *Al-Adsani*, to find that the effect of a *jus cogens* norm is the *erga omnes* obligation of every state to contribute to the punishment of torture.[126] States cannot hide, he argued, behind formalist arguments to avoid giving judgment. Judges Pellonpää and Bratza observed in their concurring opinion '[t]hat previous international practice does not support the conclusion that the *erga omnes* or *jus cogens* nature of the prohibition of torture has the consequence of obliging States to make their civil courts available for the victims of such violations is convincingly demonstrated by a study conducted by a group of distinguished international lawyers under the auspices of the British Branch of the International Law Association'.[127] The relationship between obligations *erga omnes* and *jus cogens* was considered in the *Furundzija* judgment,[128] which is probably one of the most progressive decisions on the meaning of the prohibition of torture. The fact that the European Court has not picked up on these issues indicates the level of discourse dominating the Court's majority opinions.

It should be pointed out that the disagreement among judges in the three cases reflects the disagreement that exists in international legal discourse regarding the scope of state immunities.[129] Further, the majority judgment in the *Al-Adsani* case is a fragile one, given the votes cast (9 to 8). This result may have been influenced by the uncertain situation of the doctrine of state immunity in international law. In view of these circumstances and divisions of views at the international level, it becomes more difficult to criticize the Court for misapplying or misinterpreting the relevant international instruments. Nonetheless, it could legitimately have been expected that the Court would take a different approach to this conflict of views, one which was more friendly to human rights. In the past decade, tremendous progress has been made in international human rights law with the recognition of the prohibition of torture as a *jus cogens* norm, and it could have been expected that the Court would elaborate further on the consequences of such a norm. In addition, given that certain courts have decided that *jus cogens* norms should precede rules on state immunities, the Court could have sided with them instead of setting a precedent convenient for Contracting States.

[125] Reece Thomas and Small (n 95 above), 8–9.
[126] *Al-Adsani v United Kingdom* (n 34 above), dissenting opinion of Judge Ferrari Bravo, 114.
[127] Ibid, concurring opinion of Judge Pellonpää joined by Judge Sir Nicolas Bratza, 110.
[128] *Prosecutor v Anto Furundzija* (n 14 above).
[129] Bernard H Oxman and Marius Emberland, 'Case note' (2002) 96 Am J Int'l L 699, 704.

Finally, it is interesting to note that when the *Prefecture of Voiotia v Federal Republic of Germany* case[130] reached the ECtHR in 2000, the Court did not modify its position in relation to the doctrine of state immunity. In a decision confirming the inadmissibility of the case,[131] the Court reiterated its view that granting immunity in relation to civil proceedings pursues a legitimate aim and that it is not a disproportionate restriction of the right of access to a court. Although the Court followed the *Al-Adsani* judgment closely, it could be argued that it went even further in this recent decision. In all likelihood, if the acts of torture in *Al-Adsani* had occurred in the United Kingdom, the Court would have lifted the state immunity.[132] In *Kalogeropoulou and others v Greece and Germany*, the relevant conduct had been committed in the territory of the forum state, which is a recognized exception to state immunity enshrined in both the 1972 Basle Convention and the 2004 UN Convention on Jurisdictional Immunities of States and Their Property.[133] Despite this, the Court found that there was no interference with the right of access to a court.[134]

It remains to be seen whether the position of the Court will change in upcoming cases. The Court may soon have another opportunity to pronounce itself on the topic, as the case of *Jones v The Kingdom of Saudi Arabia*[135] could find itself in its docket following the rejection of the victims' appeal by the House of Lords. Perhaps then, the Court will see that international law has evolved, as it announced in *Kalogeropoulou*: 'The Greek Government cannot therefore be required to override the rule of State immunity against their will. This is true at least as regards the current rule of public international law, as the Court found in the aforementioned case of *Al-Adsani*, but does not preclude a development in customary international law in the future.'[136]

4. Rationale of the Reasoning

The ECHR system is a complex framework, where many considerations, not only legal ones, come into play. The Court's restrictive approach is rooted in a juxtaposition of various intervening factors. Primarily, the Court is an international court with only a limited mandate to take judicial initiative.[137] Significantly, Judges Pellonpää and Bratza noted in their concurring opinion in the *Al-Adsani* case that 'when having to touch upon central questions of general international

[130] *Prefecture of Voiotia v Federal Republic of Germany* (n 26 above). See 1.4.1 above.
[131] *Kalogeropoulou and others v Greece and Germany* (n 30 above).
[132] Ibid.
[133] Kate Parlett, 'Immunity in Civil Proceedings for Torture: The Emerging Exception' (2006) 1 EHRLR 49, 57.
[134] *Kalogeropoulou and others v Greece and Germany* (n 30 above), 429.
[135] *Jones v The Kingdom of Saudi Arabia* [2006] UKHL 25. See 1.4.2 above.
[136] *Kalogeropoulou and others v Greece and Germany* (n 30 above).
[137] Bates (n 98 above), 120.

law, this Court should be very cautious before taking upon itself the role of a forerunner'.[138] These words are indicative of the Court's self-perception within the international legal system.

The Court's approach in the three cases discussed above is derived from an implicit and limited application of the concept of the margin of appreciation. More precisely, it arises from the fact that a ruling which gave precedence to the prohibition of torture over the doctrine of state immunity would be too difficult for the Contracting States to accept. Given that there is currently no consensus on this issue at the Contracting States level, the Court opted for a prudent approach. The margin of appreciation has also played a substantial role in the Court's consideration of the confrontation between the principles of immunity and access to court. When balancing state and individual interests, the Court adopted a restrictive approach and privileged the former over the latter. Thus, it was not willing to interfere in matters which it thought were part of the states' competence.

In addition, more practical policy considerations influenced the reasoning of the judges. For instance, in the *Al-Adsani* case, Judges Pellonpää and Bratza suggested that if the minority's view prevailed it would lead to a situation where 'those States which so far have been most liberal in accepting refugees and asylum-seekers, would have had imposed upon them the additional burden of guaranteeing access to a court for the determination of perhaps hundreds of refugees' civil claims for compensation for alleged torture'.[139] They added that the right of access to court entails the right to have a judgment executed. In their view, '[t]he acceptance of the applicant's argument concerning access to a court would thus have required a possibility of having judgments—probably often default judgments—delivered in torture cases executed against respondent States. This in turn would raise the question whether the traditionally strong immunity of public property from execution would also have had to be regarded as incompatible with Article 6.'[140] The judges preferred not to overburden the Contracting States by opening the floodgates and decided to limit the potential for filing similar claims in the future.

Further, given that the three judgments contained several political issues, the Court preferred to stay outside the political debate and to intervene only minimally. In fact, the majority considered only the bare essentials of the case without going into great detail and without extensively justifying its arguments. The Court's deference to the defendant state's position reveals that it preferred to leave politically sensitive and controversial issues to the discretion of the Contracting States. This way, it imposed upon itself a double auto-limitation by restraining the

[138] *Al-Adsani v United Kingdom* (n 34 above), concurring opinion of Judge Pellonpää joined by Judge Sir Nicolas Bratza, 110.

[139] Ibid, 107. [140] Ibid, 108.

spectrum of its duties and the potential role it could play in international law.[141] Whether it was motivated by caution or refused to innovate, its self-restraint also indicated that it was unwilling to contribute to the development of international law. Thus, the three judgments leave the Court's institutional competence impaired rather than empowered, and the Court's self-conception is therefore further limited. Its refusal to act as a source of inspiration within this framework may have serious repercussions in the years and cases to come.

While this kind of approach to international law is understandable, it is also highly problematic. As noted by Bates, 'it prevents the Convention from becoming a vehicle that can inspire legal systems to keep pace with public international law when, for whatever reason, the legal standards that body of law creates surpass State practice (domestic law) in terms of European common standard'.[142] It could be argued that the three judgments merely defer to state practice and encourage Contracting States to disregard international law.[143] However, giving states absolute discretion to legislate on this topic or waiting until they do so may be dangerous for the protection of human rights. States may be unwilling to change their legislation for political reasons, diplomatic considerations, or because they fear attracting torture victim asylum-seekers.[144] In proceeding this way, the Court entrenched a selected area of state practice, which appears to provide a lower level of protection than that granted by international law. Nonetheless, the jurisprudence of the Court should not impede domestic and international law from evolving.

The Court did take the needs of international legal policy briefly into consideration. As already mentioned, the Court issued the following statement: 'the grant of sovereign immunity in civil proceedings pursues a legitimate aim of complying with international law to promote comity and good relations through the respect of another State's sovereignty'.[145] While Articles 8 to 11 of the ECHR contain limitation clauses allowing states to restrict the right protected by referring to a legitimate aim, they do not mention comity or international obligations.[146] Article 6 of the ECHR does not contain any of the limitations found in Articles 8 to 11 and, arguably, allows even fewer limitations than those mentioned in these articles. The fact that the Court went beyond the existing limitations in Articles 8 to 11 indicates that it was willing to look beyond the European legal framework in order to reinforce the Contracting States' position.

Generally, the decisions of the ECHR comply with the current status of state immunity in international law. They are also what can reasonably be expected

[141] Gérard Cohen-Jonathan and Jean-Francois Flauss, '*Cour européenne des droits de l'homme et droit international général (2001)*' (2001) XLVII *Annuaire de droit français* 423, 445.

[142] Bates (n 98 above), 215. [143] Ibid. [144] Ibid, 216.

[145] *McElhinney v United Kingdom* (n 51 above), para 35; *Fogarty v United Kingdom* (n 50 above), para 34; *Al-Adsani v United Kingdom* (n 34 above), para 54.

[146] Orakhelashvili (n 65 above), 254.

from the Court under the current circumstances, as they reaffirm that the general rule or principle in international law is the application of state immunity, subject to several exceptions. They merely reflect the current status of international law which follows the doctrine of restrictive state immunity. From the foregoing analysis, it is possible to draw some conclusions in relation to the Court's methodology and approach to international law. The area of international immunity law is especially telling, as it indicates how the Court behaves in legally challenging situations where it must come up with concrete solutions. It also demonstrates further how the Court perceives itself in this context.

The Court resorted to a traditional approach to international law which closely ties in with the practice in some of the Contracting States. This approach seems to be very characteristic of the Court, which often defers to state practice. Moreover, the Court was influenced by the current situation of international state immunity law, which is in a state of flux. It was difficult for the Court to identify reliable authorities and sources of international law to reach its conclusion. Hence, it decided to adopt a traditional stance to a problem which necessitated some innovation.

Furthermore, the Court's methodology was vague and circular. When applying the test of Article 6(1) of the ECHR, the Court was not very thorough and assumed that the limitation to access to court was legitimate and proportionate. There was no balancing of the interests of both parties and no real testing of the claims. Arguably, Article 6 could now be applied to state immunity in a manner which gives an important margin of appreciation to states to act according to their own view of their international obligations.[147] This way, the Court is relieved from making complex determinations on the scope of immunity required by international law. Then, it is only in cases where the margin of appreciation is exceeded that the Court can proceed on the basis that international law does not require the grant of immunity.[148]

Perhaps the Court did not want to intervene in matters which arguably came under the state's discretion, and was reluctant to perform a judicial review of domestic legislation against international law. In comparison to other decisions of international courts and tribunals, the level of international discourse in the Court's decisions was very basic and traditional. There were hardly any innovative elements in the Court's reasoning. The Court seems to have paid little attention to the special nature of the ECHR, which is a human rights treaty. It seems to have accommodated the Contracting States, instead of the individual applicants. Such an approach is curious for an institution whose aim is to ensure that human rights are effectively protected.

[147] Lloyd Jones (n 70 above), 471.

[148] Ibid. It has been rightly pointed out, however, that this leads to the further question of 'whether a court applying Article 6 may hold a rule of international law to be disproportionate so that its application gives rise to an infringement of that provision'.

It appears that the Court's use of international law may have entrenched a restrictive interpretation of state immunity, instead of inspiring legal change.[149] The Court's stance is more restrictive than that found in the domestic decisions of some Contracting States (for instance, Italy and Greece). In all likelihood, most domestic courts will follow the decisions of the Court and the less-restrictive interpretation of state immunity may soon disappear. The *Al-Adsani* case was already cited with approval in the *Jones v The Kingdom of Saudi Arabia* case[150] mentioned earlier. What is more, the Court's decisions may have international repercussions, and may influence other domestic courts. For instance, the *Al-Adsani* majority opinion was cited in the Canadian *Bouzari* case, and no attention was paid to the minority opinion.[151] Thus, it is possible that states, other than the ECHR Contracting States, will follow the direction indicated by the Court. More importantly, the Court tried to use the technique of harmonization in the context of a conflict between international legal rules. In practice, however, the Court did not interpret the ECHR in light of relevant international law, but instead referred to international law *via* domestic law. In this way, it effectively relied on domestic law, which was the determining element of its interpretation. It is unfortunate that its reasoning was marked by an incoherent use of Article 31(1)(c) of the VCLT.

Although the Court usually employed the open paradigm, the level of reception of international law was moderate in this strand of its case law. It did not act as an innovator of international law and did not use the most progressive interpretations available. This approach seems to be rooted in the fact that the margin of appreciation granted to states with regard to their immunity is wide. Further, the general role of the Court is dependent on its institutional credibility and on the respect of the Contracting States. A closer look at the Court's jurisprudence reveals that it has followed the more restrictive possibility among those available in international law. In this way, it has attempted not to tamper with the states' discretion and the delicate balance which grounds its authority. Thus, the Court reinforced the role that Contracting States play in the ECHR framework in the context of state immunity.

149 Bates (n 98 above), 216.
150 *Jones v The Kingdom of Saudi Arabia* (n 33 above), para 18.
151 *Bouzari v Islamic Republic of Iran* (n 32 above), paras 68–69.

VIII

International Humanitarian Law

1. Preliminary Observations

The European Court of Human Rights has had several opportunities to apply the European Convention on Human Rights (ECHR) in the context of armed conflict. This application of the Convention is compelling in a study of the Court's reception techniques, as it intervenes in a field where there already exists a specific legal framework, namely international humanitarian law (IHL). IHL differs in many respects from European human rights law and both legal systems can sometimes come into conflict. The Court's approach in this field could also be distinguished from its stance in other areas of international law. Here, the Court preferred to create what may be viewed as its own approach[1] to armed conflict and has rarely resorted explicitly to the Geneva Conventions and the Additional Protocols. This occured despite the existence of an elaborate framework of law applicable to situations of armed conflict and the widespread approval among the ECHR Contracting States of IHL Standards. All 47 Contracting States to the ECHR have acceded to the four Geneva Conventions of 12 August 1949[2] and only three of these (Andorra, Azerbaijan, and Turkey) did not ratify the two Additional Protocols.[3]

The Court's approach in this area of its case law went against the prevailing trend in international practice which indicates that, in situations of armed conflict, IHL applies as *lex specialis* and supersedes human rights law. On the one hand, the application of the ECHR to situations of armed conflict is problematic, given that it is not specifically adapted to this context. On the other hand, resorting to the ECHR instead of IHL has several advantages that relate to the efficiency of the enforceability of human rights law. It is also interesting to note that the results achieved by the Court in its case law are similar to those ensuing from

[1] Anna Guellali, '*Lex specialis, droit international humanitaire et droits de l'homme: Leur interaction dans les nouveaux conflits armés*', 2007–3 RGDIP 539, 542.

[2] This information was verified on 13 June 2010: see IHL and Other Related Treaties, <http://www.icrc.org/IHL.nsf/(SPF)/party_main_treaties/$File/IHL_and_other_related_Treaties.pdf>.

[3] This information was verified on 13 June 2010. Ibid.

the application of IHL. Moreover, the Court's findings have specified further the right to life enshrined in IHL.[4]

The aim of this chapter is to analyse the Court's approach to a field of international law that has essentially been pre-empted by the existence of very specific rules. In the first part of this chapter, the purpose and status of IHL will be analysed. In the second part, the case law of the ECtHR referring to situations of armed conflict will be reviewed. In the third part, it will be seen that the Court has used an approach to situations of armed conflict which is based on the ECHR and on the indirect application of IHL (through the use of IHL vocabulary and reasoning). In the final part of this chapter, it will be considered why the Court has departed from international practice in this field.

2. International Human Rights and Humanitarian Law

2.1 Differences and Similarities Between the Systems

International human rights law (of which the ECHR is part) and IHL primarily distinguish themselves through the different objectives they strive to achieve. On the one hand, the aim of human rights law is to protect the governed from their governments. It essentially applies to a vertical relationship between unequal parties.[5] IHL, on the other hand, regulates the horizontal relationship between two equal parties confronting each other in an armed conflict.[6] The application of IHL is dependent on the existence of an international or non-international armed conflict, whereas the application of international human rights law in general, and the ECHR in particular, is dependent on whether a court has jurisdiction. Further, IHL applies for the duration of the hostilities, whereas international human rights law protects individuals at all times. Both systems also exhibit methodological and structural differences, which do not merely consist in distinct judicial approaches.[7] In addition, a certain unified conception is apparent from the structure of human rights law, whereas IHL is based on a more pragmatic, parcelled and categorized framework.[8]

[4] Gloria Gaggioli and Robert Kolb, '*L'apport de la Cour Européenne des Droits de l'homme au droit international humanitaire en matière de droit à la vie*' (2007) 17(1) SZIER 3. See also Guellali (n 1 above), 557–567; Yves Sandoz, '*Droit international humanitaire et droits de l'homme: mariage d'amour ou de raison?*' in Andreas Auer, Alexandre Flückinger, and Michel Hottelier (eds), *Les droits de l'homme et la constitution: Études en l'honneur du Professeur Giorgio Malinverni, Collection Genevoise*, (Geneva/Zurich: Schultess, 2007), 339, 342–344.

[5] Theodor Meron, 'The Humanization of Humanitarian Law' (2000) 94 Am J Int'l L 239, 240.

[6] Ibid. [7] Guellali (n 1 above), 557. [8] Ibid, 548.

A common thread nonetheless unites the systems in that they both aim to protect human dignity. The International Criminal Tribunal for the former Yugoslavia explained in the *Furudzija* judgment[9] that:

> [t]he essence of the whole corpus of international humanitarian law as well as human rights law lies in the protection of the human dignity of every person, whatever his or her gender. The general principle of respect for human dignity is the basic underpinning and indeed the very *raison d'être* of international humanitarian law and human rights law; indeed in modern times it has become of such paramount importance as to permeate the whole body of international law.[10]

2.2 The Interaction of Both Systems in Treaty Provisions

There is clear evidence of the interaction between the systems in various legal instruments. Article 72 of Additional Protocol I[11] confirms that the guarantees enunciated in Section III are additional to the provisions of the Fourth Geneva Convention 'as well as to other applicable rules of international law relating to the protection of fundamental human rights during international armed conflict'.[12] In fact, Article 75 of the same section protects an important number of basic human rights, including the prohibition of murder, torture, corporal punishment, mutilation, outrages upon personal dignity, taking of hostages, and collective punishments. It also contains an exhaustive list of procedural guarantees. In addition, the Preamble to Additional Protocol II states that 'the humanitarian principles enshrined in Article 3 common to the Geneva Conventions of 12 August 1949, constitute the foundation of respect for the human person in cases of armed conflict not of an international character'[13] and that 'international instruments relating to human rights offer a basic protection to the human person'.[14] The Fourth Geneva Convention contains numerous provisions protecting the rights of civilians in peacetime and in times of armed conflict, as well as in situations of total or partial occupation. Furthermore, the International Committee of the Red Cross study on international customary humanitarian law enumerates

[9] *Prosecutor v Anto Furundzija*, judgment, ICTY, 10 December 1998, IT-95–17/1-T (1999) 38 ILM 317 (1999).

[10] Ibid, para 183. See also Guellali (n 1 above), 573, where it was suggested that, regardless of which system is found to apply in a given case (IHL or human rights law), it should always comply with the imperative of protecting human lives. Furthermore, it seems that in general, international humanitarian law has been evolving and undergoing a process of 'humanisation'. For further information, see Meron (n 5 above), 242 *et seq.*

[11] Kenneth Watkin, 'Warriors Without Rights? Combatants, Unprivileged Belligerents, and Struggle over Legitimacy', Harvard Program on Humanitarian Policy and Conflict Research, Occasional Paper, Winter 2005, 69.

[12] Ibid.

[13] Ibid.

[14] Ibid.

a wide array of human rights in Rules 87 to 105[15] and draws on the jurisprudence of various international human rights bodies.[16] From the perspective of human rights law, Article 27(1) of the American Convention on Human Rights and Article 15(1) of the ECHR confirm the application of both instruments in times of war. Article 4(1) of the International Covenant on Civil and Political Rights (ICCPR) also implies that the Covenant remains applicable in wartime.

2.3 The Position of International Bodies: The Status of *Lex Specialis*

The fact that both systems can apply to various situations has been consistently recognized by the International Court of Justice (ICJ). In its advisory opinion, *Legal Consequences of the Construction of a Wall in the Occupied Palestinian Territory*, the ICJ considered that:

> [as] regards the relationship between international humanitarian law and human rights law, there are thus three possible situations: some rights may be exclusively matters of international humanitarian law; others may be exclusively matters of human rights law; yet others may be matters of both these branches of international law. In order to answer the question put to it, the Court will have to take into consideration both of these branches of international law, namely human rights law and, as *lex specialis*, international humanitarian law.[17]

The ICJ found in its advisory opinion, *Legality of the Threat or Use of Nuclear Weapons*,[18] that:

> the protection of the International Covenant of Civil and Political Rights does not cease in times of war, except by operation of Article 4 of the Covenant whereby certain provisions may be derogated from in a time of national emergency. Respect for the right to life is not, however, such a provision. In principle, the right not arbitrarily to be deprived of one's life applies also in hostilities. The test of what is an arbitrary deprivation of life, however, then falls to be determined by the applicable *lex specialis*, namely, the law applicable in armed conflict that is designed to regulate the conduct of hostilities. Thus whether a particular loss of life, through the use of a certain weapon in warfare, is to be considered an arbitrary deprivation of life contrary to Article 6 of the Covenant can only be decided by reference to the law applicable in armed conflict and not deduced from the terms of the Covenant itself.[19]

[15] Jean-Marie Henckaerts and Louise Doswald-Beck, *Customary International Humanitarian Law: Volumes 2, Part 1,* (International Committee of the Red Cross, Cambridge: Cambridge University Press, 2005), 299–383.

[16] See, in general, Heike Krieger, 'A Conflict of Norms: The Relationship Between Humanitarian Law and Human Rights Law in the ICRC Customary Law Study' (2006) 11 J Con & Sec L 265.

[17] *Legal Consequences of the Construction of a Wall in the Occupied Palestinian Territory*, advisory opinion, 9 July 2004, 2004 ICJ Reports 136, para 106 (italics in original).

[18] *Legality of the Threat or Use of Nuclear Weapons*, advisory opinion, 8 July 1996, 1996 ICJ Reports 226.

[19] Ibid, para 25 (italics in original).

In a similar vein, the UN Human Rights Committee confirmed that the ICCPR

> applies also in situations of armed conflict to which the rules of international humanitarian law are applicable. While, in respect of certain Covenant rights, more specific rules of international humanitarian law may be specially relevant for the purposes of the interpretation of Covenant rights, both spheres of law are complementary, not mutually exclusive.[20]

The notion of complementarity of the regimes was explained earlier:

> During armed conflict, whether international or non-international, the rules of international humanitarian law become applicable and help, in addition to the provisions in article 4 and article 5, paragraph 1, of the Covenant, to prevent the abuse of a State's emergency powers. The Covenant requires that even during an armed conflict measures derogating from the Covenant are allowed only if and to the extent that the situation constitutes a threat to the life of the nation.[21]

The UN General Assembly also reiterated that human rights continue to apply in situations of armed conflict:

> Bearing in mind the need for measures to ensure the better protection of human rights in armed conflicts of all types, ... Affirms the following basic principles for the protection of civilian populations in armed conflicts ...: 1. Fundamental human rights, as accepted in international law and laid down in international instruments, continue to apply fully in situations of armed conflict.[22]

Similarly, the Inter-American Commission on Human Rights affirmed that the American Convention on Human Rights and other international and regional instruments continued to apply in situations of armed conflict:

> the potential application of one does not necessarily exclude or displace the other [system of law]. There is an integral linkage between the law of human rights and humanitarian law because they share a 'common nucleus of non-derogable rights and a common purpose of protecting human life and dignity', and there may be a substantial overlap in the application of these bodies of law.[23]

In addition, the Commission emphasized that 'the provisions of conventional and customary humanitarian law generally afford victims of armed conflicts greater

[20] United Nations Human Rights Committee, General Comment No 31, Nature of the General Legal Obligation Imposed on States Parties to the Covenant, 26 May 2004, CCPR/C/21/Rev1/Add.13 (General Comments), para 11.

[21] United Nations Human Rights Committee, General Comment No 29, States of Emergency (Article 4), 31 August 2001, CCPR/C/21/Rev1/Add.11 (General Comments), para 3.

[22] United Nations General Assembly, Resolution 2675 of 8 December 1970 on Basic principles for the protection of civilian populations in armed conflicts, 1922nd plenary meeting, preamble.

[23] *Coard and others v United States*, IACommHR, Report No 109/99, Case No 10.951, 29 September 1999, para 39.

or more specific protections than do the more generally phrased guarantees in the American Convention and other human rights instruments'.[24]

Most importantly, the Commission ruled that its

> ability to resolve claimed violations of this non-derogable right arising out of an armed conflict may not be possible in many cases by reference to Article 4 of the American Convention alone. This is because the American Convention contains no rules that either define or distinguish civilians from combatants and other military targets, much less, specify when a civilian can be lawfully attacked or when civilian casualties are a lawful consequence of military operations. Therefore, the Commission must necessarily look to and apply definitional standards and relevant rules of humanitarian law as sources of authoritative guidance in its resolution of this and other kinds of claims alleging violations of the American Convention in combat situations. To do otherwise would mean that the Commission would have to decline to exercise its jurisdiction in many cases involving indiscriminate attacks by State agents resulting in a considerable number of civilian casualties. Such a result would be manifestly absurd in light of the underlying object and purposes of both the American Convention and humanitarian law treaties.[25]

Thus, from the international practice reviewed above, it appears that the prevailing consensus is that IHL supersedes the application of human rights law due to its status of *lex specialis*.[26] This practice can be contrasted with the case law of the ECtHR, given that the Strasbourg Court (as will appear below) went in the opposite direction and applied the ECHR directly (instead of IHL) to situations of armed conflict. Unlike the Inter-American Commission on Human Rights, the Court did not examine any consideration which might prevent it from exercising its jurisdiction. This is unusual, given that its regional counterpart decided to follow the rule established by international practice. Instead, the Strasbourg Court made very selective and implicit use of IHL, which gave rise to a reasoning that can be viewed as its own.

2.4 The Challenging of the *Lex Specialis* Rule by Academics

Despite its recognition in international practice, the validity of the *lex specialis* rule in the context of the relationship between IHL and international human rights law has been questioned by academics. It has been argued that there are many advantages in not following the current international practice. More specifically, it seems that the ECtHR has recently bypassed the application of the *lex specialis* principle of IHL in situations of armed conflict.[27] Instead, it directly

24 *Abella v Argentina*, IACommHR, Report No 55/97, Case No 11.137, Argentina, OEA/Ser/L/V/II.97, Doc 38, 30 October 1997, para 159.

25 Ibid, para 161.

26 For a detailed analysis of the application of *lex specialis*, see also Marco Sassòli, '*Le droit international humanitaire, une lex specialis par rapport aux droits humains?*' in Auer, Flückinger, and Hottelier (n 4 above), 375.

27 William Abresch, 'A Human Rights Law of Internal Armed Conflict: The European Court of Human Rights in Chechnya' (2005) 16 Eur J Int'l L 741.

applied human rights law to the conduct of hostilities in internal armed conflicts. The ECtHR's approach could be promising, as it has provided rules for the conduct of hostilities in internal conflicts, where IHL—accepted as legally binding—is inadequate and seldom obeyed.[28] With an approach that treats conflicts as law enforcement operations against terrorists, the ECtHR developed a methodology that may be more protective of victims and more politically viable than that of IHL.[29] This approach contributes to a stronger framework for the protection of rights, especially in armed conflict, and provides a powerful weapon in the enforcement of humanitarian law.[30]

According to several academics, the prevailing view is that human rights law and humanitarian law are complementary in the sense that they are both applicable in situations of international and non-international armed conflict.[31] There may be cases where both systems provide different solutions to a given problem, but this does not necessarily mean that IHL constitutes the *lex specialis*.[32] At times, human rights law will provide a more detailed and more specific rule than IHL in a given situation. In addition, there may not be sufficient evidence to demonstrate that IHL, as *lex specialis*, can displace human rights law in such circumstances.[33] Furthermore, the application of the *lex specialis* rule by the ICJ is by no means clear cut: it is conditioned by jurisprudential pragmatism and adapted to the circumstances of each case.[34] Moreover, in cases where IHL is applied as its content requires, human rights and humanitarian law norms often reveal a similar content.[35] In such cases, the protection granted by IHL norms does not prove to be lower than that provided under human rights law.[36] In a similar vein, it has also been suggested that the non-application of IHL by the Court did not have an impact on the solutions adopted by the Court in the cases before it.[37] In a case of armed conflict regulated by IHL as *lex specialis*, the Court did not apply a human rights rule which would be incompatible with a solution flowing from IHL.[38]

28 Ibid, 767.

29 Ibid.

30 Aisling Reidy, 'The Approach of the European Commission and Court of Human Rights to International Humanitarian Law' (1998) 324 IRRC 513, 529.

31 Sassòli (n 26 above), 395; Tom Hadden and Colin Harvey, 'The Law of Internal Crisis and Conflict: An Outline Prospectus for the Merger of International Human Rights Law, the Law of Armed Conflict, Refugee Law, and the Law on Humanitarian Intervention' (1999) 833 IRRC 119; Alexander Orakhelashvili, 'The Interaction between Human Rights and Humanitarian law: Fragmentation, Conflict, Parallelism, or Convergence?' (2008) 19 Eur J Int'l L 161, 181–182. See also Kenneth Watkin, 'Controlling the Use of Force: A Role for Human Rights Norms in Contemporary Armed Conflict' (2004) 98 Am J Int'l L 1, 34. Watkin considers that the two systems of law interact most closely in non-international conflict, situations of occupation, and the contemporary war on terrorism.

32 Sassòli (n 26 above), 395.

33 Orakhelashvili (n 31 above), 182.

34 Guellali (n 1 above), 547.

35 Orakhelashvili (n 31 above), 182.

36 Ibid.

37 Marco Sassòli, '*La Cour européenne des droits de l'homme et les conflits armés*' in Stephan Breitenmoser et al (eds), *Human Rights, Democracy and the Rule of Law, Liber amicorum Luzius Wildhaber* (Zurich: Dike, 2007), 709, 730.

38 Ibid.

Some incompatibilities and differences still remain between IHL and human rights law and it is necessary to eliminate them if both regimes are to complement each other.[39] For this purpose, a reformulation of several areas of human rights law, humanitarian law, refugee law, and the law on humanitarian intervention merging international human rights law and international humanitarian law would be beneficial. It has been argued, however, that the system of accountability developed in human rights law to regulate the use of force domestically cannot simply be transposed to the context of IHL.[40] As a result, both states and human rights supervisory bodies may have to readjust their understanding of the role that the mechanism of accountability under human rights law can play in improving the accountability framework of the use of lethal force in armed conflict.[41] Further, the 'incorporation of human rights principles of accountability can have a positive impact on the regulation of the use of force during armed conflict'.[42] Overall, these arguments indicate that the long-standing separation of both systems may have outlived its usefulness.[43]

It was also suggested that the *lex specialis* rule can be applied in general, but that several exceptions must be introduced where human rights law would override IHL. One of these exceptions is the international administration of a territory, which is not comparable to circumstances that prevail in peaceful democratic societies, but is closer to regular governmental activity than to combat operations. Another exception is a non-international armed conflict, where human rights law provides more specific rules than IHL. Further, non-international armed conflicts are closer to the regular sphere of application of human rights law, because they also concern the relation of the individual vis-à-vis his or her state.[44]

A more drastic alternative consists in formulating a whole new methodology with regard to the relationship between human rights and humanitarian law—the 'unified use of force rule'—which relies on the application of international human rights to IHL.[45] This new rule is considered to be legally and operationally required in light of the changing character of modern armed conflicts and IHL. It incorporates the absolute necessity threshold for the interpretation of the IHL rule that prohibits superfluous injury and unnecessary suffering as well as the proportionality rule. The 'unified use of force rule' is composed of three precepts:

First, military authorities may use force against combatants or mixed combatant-civilian targets only if there is no other alternative to inflicting injury and suffering for achieving

[39] Hadden and Harvey (n 31 above), 120. [40] Watkin (n 31 above), 34. [41] Ibid.

[42] Ibid. See, in general, Francisco Forrest Martin, 'Using International Human Rights Law for Establishing a Unified Use of Force Rule in the Law of Armed Conflict' (2001) 64 Sask L Rev 347.

[43] Hadden and Harvey (n 31 above), 133.

[44] For arguments in this paragraph, see Krieger (n 16 above), 265 and 274–275.

[45] See, in general, Martin (n 42 above); Francisco Forrest Martin, 'The Unified Use of Force Rule Revisited: The Penetration of the Law of Armed Conflict by International Human Rights Law' (2002) 65 Sask L Rev 405; Francisco Forrest Martin, 'The Unified Use of Force Rule: Amplifications in Light of the Comments of Professor Green and Paust' (2002) 65 Sask L Rev 451.

lawful objectives, both tactical *and* strategic. Second, if the means or method *per se* of such use of force is not illegal, the employed means or method must inflict only the *least possible* amount of suffering and injury. Third, suffering and injury may be escalated incrementally through the additional use of force by the original or another means or method of warfare only if at each incremental use, the use of such means or method is absolutely necessary for achieving the lawful objectives.[46]

From the above, it is clear that there is a debate in academic discourse, which considers that the present application of IHL as a *lex specialis* rule in situations of armed conflict is inadequate. This is due, in part, to the fact that human rights law provides a stronger enforcement mechanism in situations of armed conflict.[47] It could also be the case that IHL is not sufficiently elaborate with regard to certain situations of armed conflict and that human rights law provides more specific norms in these circumstances.[48] It has been argued that supplementing IHL with human rights law can have a beneficial effect on the protection of civilians and on the regulation of the use of armed force.[49] Finally, according to several academics, current practice does not support the application of IHL as a *lex specialis* rule and a new approach needs to be formulated in this context.[50]

These findings are useful in understanding the reasons which led the Court to apply the ECHR directly to situations of armed conflict. It seems that a mixture of these considerations have influenced the Court in adopting its approach. However, as will be seen, the main reason for the Court's behaviour appears to be rooted in political considerations surrounding the application of IHL and the fact that it would like the ECHR system to remain self-sufficient. In spite of the Court's tendencies, the practice reviewed earlier clearly demonstrates that IHL is considered by international bodies as having a *lex specialis* status where it provides a rule designated for a specific situation. It needs to be emphasized that the application of IHL in situations of armed conflict does not suspend the applicability of human rights law. Instead, it supersedes the continuously applicable human rights law and thus does not exclude it. In this sense, it appears to determine the interpretation of human rights law in situations of armed conflict.

3. References to IHL in the Strasbourg Case Law

The ECHR clearly applies in times of armed conflict. The actions or omission of Contracting Parties in an armed conflict can engage their responsibility within or outside their national territory.[51] This responsibility can also arise when, as a result

[46] Martin (n 42 above), 373 (italics in original).

[47] Abresch (n 27 above), 767; Reidy (n 30 above), 529.

[48] Krieger (n 16 above), 265.

[49] Abresch (n 27 above), 767.

[50] Hadden and Harvey (n 31 above), 119; Watkin (n 31 above), 34; Martin (n 42 above), 347.

[51] Reidy (n 30 above), 514. See, for instance, *Cyprus v Turkey* (App Nos 6780/74; 6950/75), decision, 26 May 1975, DR 2, 125, 136–137.

of military action, a state exercises effective control of an area outside its national territory.[52] In times of war or other public emergency, Contracting States can enter a derogation under Article 15 of the ECHR to limit their obligations under the ECHR.[53] In *Lawless v Ireland*,[54] a public emergency within the meaning of Article 15 was defined as a 'a situation of exceptional and imminent danger or crisis affecting the general public, as distinct from particular groups, and constituting a threat to the organized life of the community which composes the State in question'.[55] Any derogating measure must be consistent with other obligations under international law, including international humanitarian law.[56] Furthermore, Article 15(2) of the ECHR provides that '[n]o derogation from Article 2, except in respect of deaths resulting from lawful acts of war, or from Articles 3, 4 (paragraph 1) and 7 shall be made under this provision'. An act of war would appear to be lawful if it is consistent with the standards enshrined in IHL.[57]

In the past, the Court has examined the consistency of derogations against other international obligations, but has not invalidated them for this reason.[58] If a state does not enter a derogation, Article 53 of the ECHR provides an additional safeguard by requiring that '[n]othing in this Convention shall be construed as limiting or derogating from any of the human rights and fundamental freedoms which may be ensured under the laws of any High Contracting Party or under any other agreement to which it is a Party'. In those situations where no derogation is made, Articles 2, 3, 4, and 7 of the ECHR will fully apply. In spite of the possibilities available to examine IHL with regard to derogation under Article 15 of the ECHR, the Court and the Commission have not fully explored this opportunity due, in part, to the scarcity of cases where IHL could apply. Further, Contracting States have a wide margin of appreciation with respect to derogations entered under Article 15(1). State authorities are usually in a better position than the ECtHR to decide on whether there is an emergency and which measures should be adopted to remedy the situation.[59] Although states do not have an

[52] Ibid; see also *Loizidou v Turkey (Preliminary Objections)* (App No 15318/89), judgment, 23 March 1995, Series A, Vol 310, para 62; *Loizidou v Turkey (Merits)* (App No 15318/89), judgment, 18 December 1996, Reports 1996-VI, 2216, para 52.

[53] Reidy (n 30 above), 514.

[54] *Lawless v Ireland* (App No 332/57), report, 19 December 1959, Series B, Vol 1.

[55] Ibid, para 90.

[56] Reidy (n 30 above), 514. See also Pieter Van Dijk et al, *Theory and Practice of the European Convention on Human Rights* (Antwerp/Oxford: Intersentia, 4th edn, 2006), 1067–1068.

[57] Federico Sperotto, 'Law in Times of War: the Case of Chechnya', University of Denver, Human Rights and Human Welfare, Working Paper No 40, 20 August 2007, 5.

[58] Reidy (n 30 above), 514. See, for instance, *Lawless v Ireland* (App No 332/57), judgment, 1 July 1961, Series A, Vol 3, paras 40–41; *Ireland v United Kingdom* (App No 5310/71), judgment, 18 January 1978, Series A, Vol 25, para 222; *Branningan and McBride v United Kingdom* (App Nos 14553/89; 14554/89), judgment, 26 May 1993, Series A, Vol 258-B, paras 63–73; *Marshall v United Kingdom* (App No 41571/98), decision, 10 July 2001, not reported.

[59] Van Dijk et al (n 56 above), 1056–1057; *Ireland v United Kingdom* (n 58 above), para 207; *Branningan and McBride v United Kingdom* (n 58 above), para 43; *Aksoy v Turkey* (App No 21987/93), judgment, 18 December 1996, Reports 1996-VI, 2260, para 68.

unlimited power in this field, their wide margin of appreciation does constrain the Court's ability to review such derogations.[60]

3.1 The *Cyprus v Turkey* Case

In *Cyprus v Turkey*,[61] the Commission considered an application brought with regard to the invasion and occupation of part of the Republic of Cyprus by the Republic of Turkey on 20 July 1974, following a period of violence between Greek and Turkish Cypriots and an attempted Greek-sponsored coup. According to the applicant Government, Turkey, without a prior war declaration, invaded Cyprus and commenced military operations on Cypriot territory by means of land, sea, and air forces. By 30 July 1974, it had occupied a substantial area in the northern part of Cyprus. On 14 August 1974 Turkey extended its occupation to about 40 per cent of the territory of Cyprus by means of further military operations. The Government of Cyprus claimed that the Turkish armed forces had caused deprivation of life, subjected persons of both sexes and all ages to torture, inhuman, and degrading treatment and punishment, forced persons to work, displaced thousands of persons from their places of residence, and caused destruction of property and obstruction of free enjoyment of property. These acts were allegedly directed against Greek Cypriots only, due, *inter alia*, to their national origin, race, and religion. The Government of Cyprus relied on Articles 1 to 6, 8, 13, and 17 of the ECHR and Article 1 of Protocol No 1 as well as Article 14 in conjunction with the mentioned articles. The respondent Government maintained that the application was inadmissible given the non-existence of a properly constituted representation, failure to exhaust domestic remedies, and the abusive nature of the application.

The reference to IHL in this case appeared in the report of the Commission to the Committee of Ministers of 10 July 1976, where it considered, among other things, the detention and internment of persons during the conflict. The Commission explained that:

> both Cyprus and Turkey are Parties to the (Third) Geneva Convention of 12 August 1949, relative to the treatment of prisoners-of-war, and that, in connection with the events in the summer of 1974, Turkey in particular assured the International Committee of the Red Cross of its intention to apply the Geneva Conventions and its willingness to grant all necessary facilities for humanitarian action. In fact, ICRC delegates made regular visits to soldiers and civilians who had been granted prisoner-of-war status by the authorities on either side. They included, before the resumption of hostilities on 14 August 1974, 385 Greek Cypriots in Adana, who were visited by two ICRC delegates, one of them a doctor, 63 Greek Cypriots in Saray Prison in the Turkish part of Nicosia and 3,268 Turkish Cypriots in camps in Cyprus.[62]

[60] Van Dijk et al (n 56 above). 1056–1057.

[61] *Cyprus v Turkey* (App Nos 6780/74; 6950/75), decision, 26 May 1975, DR 2, 125.

[62] *Cyprus v Turkey* (App Nos 6780/74; 6950/75), report, 10 July 1976, (1982) 4 EHRR 482, 532, para 313. See also Jochen A Frowein, 'The Relationship Between Human Rights Regimes

As a result of this, 'the Commission has not found it necessary to examine the question of a breach of Article 5 of the European Convention on Human Rights with regard to persons accorded the status of prisoners of war'.[63]

With this last statement, it seems that the Commission recognized the special status of prisoners of war and the fact that the Third Geneva Convention provides the *lex specialis* rule in this situation.[64] This, however, is not mentioned anywhere explicitly in the report. The Commission merely explained that it would not examine the question of a breach of Article 5 of the ECHR.[65] It is possible that if the Commission had considered a violation of Article 5 due to the application of the Third Geneva Convention, it may not have been able to exercise its discretion in examining the question.[66] Thus, this ambiguous statement may have prevented it from relinquishing its jurisdiction in favour of another court.[67] Finally, the Commission's deference, although implicit, to the framework of IHL constitutes one of the most evocative references to this system of law. It is, however, an isolated event which was not pursued in the subsequent trend of the ECtHR's case law.

Finally, it is also interesting to note that two members of the Commission went even further than the majority with regard to the interpretation and application of IHL in their joint dissenting opinion. In the context of Article 15 of the ECHR, they considered that:

> the rules of international law concerning the treatment of the population in occupied territories (contained notably in The Hague Regulations of 1907 and the Fourth Geneva Convention of 12 August 1949) are undeniably capable of assisting the resolution of the question whether the measures taken by the occupying power in derogation from the obligations which it should in principle observe—by virtue of the European Convention—where it exercises (de jure or de facto) its jurisdiction, are or are not justified according to the criterion that only measures of derogation strictly required by the circumstances are authorised.... It follows that respect for these same rules by a High Contracting Party during the military occupation of the territory of another state, will in principle assure that the High Contracting Party will not go beyond the limits of the right of derogation conferred on it by Article 15 of the Convention.[68]

The two members of the Commission then continued and found that 'measures which are in themselves contrary to a provision of the European Convention, but which are taken legitimately under the international law applicable to an armed conflict, are to be considered as legitimate measures of derogation from the obligations flowing from the Convention'.[69]

and Regimes of Belligerent Occupation' (1998) 28 IYHR 1, 10; Krieger (n 16 above), 272; Hans-Joachim Heintze, 'On the Relationship Between Human Rights Law and International Humanitarian Law' (2004) 856 IRRC 789, 806.

[63] *Cyprus v Turkey* (n 62 above), para 313.
[64] Frowein (n 62 above), 10.
[65] Ibid.
[66] Ibid.
[67] Ibid.
[68] *Cyprus v Turkey* (n 62 above), para 6.
[69] Ibid, 564–565, para 7.

Thus, according to these two members, IHL instruments can be used in the application of Article 15 of the ECHR to derogations in situations of military occupation of a state. According to this stance, there seems be a presumption that if states comply with international law in adopting derogations, they automatically comply with the requirements of the ECHR. This not only demonstrates that IHL can be useful in the application of the ECHR, but also envisages that it can be used in order to determine whether a measure in derogation of the ECHR is lawful.[70]

3.2 The *Engel and Others v The Netherlands* Case

In *Engel and others v The Netherlands*,[71] the Strasbourg bodies considered an application referred by the European Commission of Human Rights and by the Government of the Kingdom of the Netherlands. The case originated in five applications against the Netherlands which were lodged with the Commission in 1971 by five Dutch nationals.

When submitting their applications to the Commission, all applicants were conscript soldiers serving in different non-commissioned ranks in the Netherlands armed forces. On separate occasions, various penalties had been imposed on them by their respective commanding officers for offences against military discipline. These penalties were different in the case of each serviceman involved in the case. The applicants had appealed to the complaints officer and finally to the Supreme Military Court which, in substance, confirmed the decisions challenged but, in two cases, reduced the punishment imposed.

The applicants complained that the penalties imposed on them constituted deprivation of liberty contrary to Article 5 of the ECHR, that the proceedings before the military authorities and the Supreme Military Court were not in conformity with the requirements of Article 6 (right to a fair trial) of the ECHR, and that the manner in which they were treated was discriminatory and in breach of Article 14 (prohibition of discrimination) read in conjunction with Articles 5 (right to liberty and security of person) and 6 (right to a fair trial) of the ECHR. Mr Engel also alleged a separate breach of Article 5 in connection with his provisional arrest and a breach of Article 11 (right to freedom of assembly and association) on the particular facts of his case. For their part, Mr Dona and Mr Schul contended that their interim custody had been in disregard of Article 5 and that the punishment imposed on them had contravened Articles 10 (right to freedom of expression), 11, 14, 17 (prohibition of abuse of rights), and 18 (limitations on permitted restrictions of rights) of the ECHR.

[70] Françoise Hampson, 'Using International Human Rights Machinery to Enforce International Law of Armed Conflicts' (1992) 32 MLLWR 119, 125.

[71] *Engel and others v The Netherlands* (App Nos 5100/71; 5101/71; 5102/71; 5354/72; 5370/72), judgment, 6 August 1976, Series A, Vol 22.

When considering the complaint under Article 5(1) read in conjunction with Article 14, the majority of the ECtHR made a brief, yet explicit, reference to IHL. As noted earlier, the applicants had complained that distinctions in treatment were made between servicemen. The majority of the Court found no breach under these provisions, and considered that the distinctions could have been dictated by a legitimate aim, namely the preservation of discipline by methods suited to each category of serviceman.[72] In this context, the majority also clarified that:

> [t]he hierarchical structure inherent in armies entails differentiation according to rank. Corresponding to the various ranks are differing responsibilities which in their turn justify certain inequalities of treatment in the disciplinary sphere. Such inequalities are traditionally encountered in the Contracting States and are tolerated by international humanitarian law (paragraph 140 of the Commission's report: Article 88 of the Geneva Convention of 12 August 1949 relative to the Treatment of Prisoners of War). In this respect, the European Convention allows the competent national authorities a considerable margin of appreciation.[73]

This explicit reference to IHL by the Court is limited for two reasons. First, Article 88 of the Third Geneva Convention was only used as a source of inspiration and was not directly relied on given that there was no armed conflict involved. Secondly, the majority reiterated that there was a considerable margin of appreciation left to the states in this field, and thus it used IHL to bolster the stance adopted by the respondent Government. Despite its limitations, this brief statement does demonstrate that the majority adopted a receptive attitude towards external legal sources to provide illustrations for its arguments. As will be seen, the Court's reasoning in this case remains puzzling, given that its subsequent case law is considerably less receptive to IHL.

3.3 The *Güleç v Turkey* Case

In the *Güleç v Turkey* case, the Court considered an incident where shots were fired from a tank at protesting demonstrators in the town of İdil in Şırnak Province on 4 March 1991. Two persons were killed, including Ahmet Güleç (the son of the applicant, Hüseyin Güleç), and 12 others were injured. The Government submitted that Ahmet Güleç was killed by members of the Kurdistan's Workers Party (PKK) positioned among the demonstrators, whereas the applicant argued that he had been shot by the security forces which opened fire on unarmed demonstrators.[74] The applicant filed a complaint with the Commission against the Republic of Turkey in which he relied on Article 2 of the ECHR.

[72] Ibid, para 72. [73] Ibid.

[74] *Güleç v Turkey* (App No 21593/93), judgment, 27 July 1998, Reports 1998-IV, 1698, paras 63–64.

Article 2 provides that:

1. Everyone's right to life shall be protected by law. No one shall be deprived of his life intentionally save in the execution of a sentence of a court following his conviction of a crime for which this penalty is provided by law.
2. Deprivation of life shall not be regarded as inflicted in contravention of this Article when it results from the use of force which is more that absolutely necessary:
   (a) in defence of any person from unlawful violence;
   (b) in order to effect a lawful arrest or to prevent the escape of a person lawfully detained;
   (c) in action lawfully taken for the purpose of quelling a riot or insurrection.

The ECtHR examined whether the State's use of force complied with Article 2(2). In this context, the Court considered that a balance had to be struck between the aim pursued and the means employed to achieve it.[75] It was noted that the security forces used very powerful weapons because they allegedly did not have truncheons, riot shields, a water cannon, rubber bullets, or tear gas. This was, in the Court's view, incomprehensible and unacceptable, given that the region was in a state of emergency and that disorder could have been expected. The Court ruled that the killing of Ahmet Güleç was not an absolutely necessary use of force and that it was disproportionate. It was also found that a thorough investigation into the circumstance of Ahmet Güleç's death was lacking.

Although IHL could have been applied in the case at hand, the Court preferred to resolve it on the basis of the ECHR. The judges noted that the situation reached the threshold of an emergency and that public disturbances were to be expected.[76] The judges could have considered instead that the hostilities had reached the threshold of common Article 3 to the Geneva Conventions.[77] The Court, however, followed an unusual course, and borrowed vocabulary originating from IHL while relying on the ECHR. It considered that the '[l]oss of life is unfortunately a frequent occurrence in south-east Turkey in view of the security situation there.... However, neither the prevalence of violent armed clashes nor the high incidence of fatalities can displace the obligation under Article 2 to ensure that an effective, independent investigation is conducted.'[78] Subsequently, the judges also observed that the armed forces had insufficient equipment and 'rules of engagement'.[79] Their vocabulary indicates that there could be some parallels between IHL and human rights law, especially with regard to the obligations laid down in common Article 3 to the Geneva Conventions and those characterized as non-derogable in Article 15 of the ECHR.[80] Furthermore, the Court's proportionality enquiry under Article 2 of the ECHR was an enquiry that could have been conducted under IHL, namely whether the incidental loss of civilian lives was excessive. The Court also seems to have come to terms with the inevitable loss of civilian lives during armed conflict and was preoccupied

[75] Ibid, para 71. [76] Ibid. [77] Heintze (n 62 above), 811.
[78] *Güleç v Turkey* (n 74 above), para 81. [79] Ibid, para 71.
[80] Heintze (n 62 above), 811.

with the fact that the investigation conducted was insufficient. If the Court had applied IHL, the next step in its enquiry would have been whether the loss of civilian lives was proportional to the military advantage gained. The Court was not, however, prepared to go this far.

3.4 The *Ergi v Turkey* Case

Mr Muharrem Ergi, a Turkish national, brought an application on behalf of himself, his deceased sister, Havva Ergi, and her daughter relying on Articles 2, 8, 13, 14, and 18 of the ECHR. The application concerned complaints relating to an incident on 29 September 1993 in which Havva Ergi was killed. On that day, the Turkish security forces set up an ambush in the vicinity of a village in order to capture members of the PKK. In crossfire between the security forces and members of the PKK, Havva Ergi was killed when standing on the veranda of her house. The applicant argued that the killing was a result of a retaliatory operation by the security forces, whereas the Government maintained that there had been a clash between the security forces and the PKK around the village and that the bullet did not originate from the military side.[81] The Commission considered that there was insufficient evidence to establish that the incident of 29 September 2003 had not been an ambush leading to a clash but had been a retaliatory measure. It was also unable to establish whether the bullet which killed Havva Ergi had been fired by the security forces. Nonetheless, it proceeded to examine whether the planning and conduct of the operation as well as the investigation complied with the requirements of Article 2 (right to life) of the ECHR.

In relation to the planning and conduct of the operation, the Court determined that:

> under Article 2 of the Convention, read in conjunction with Article 1, the State may be required to take certain measures in order to 'secure' an effective enjoyment of the right to life. In light of the above considerations, . . . the responsibility of the State is not confined to circumstances where there is significant evidence that misdirected fire from the agents of the State killed a civilian. It may also be engaged where they fail to take all feasible precautions in the choice of means and methods of a security operation mounted against an opposing group with a view to avoiding and, in any event, to minimising incidental loss of civilian life. . . . [It] must consider whether the security forces' operations had been planned and conducted in such a way as to avoid or minimise to the greatest extent possible, any risk to the lives of the villagers, including from the fire power of the PKK members caught in the ambush.[82]

The majority ruled that, in light of the failure of the authorities of the respondent State to adduce direct evidence of the planning and conduct of the ambush,

[81] *Ergi v Turkey* (App No 23818/94), judgment, 28 July 1998, Reports 1998-IV, 1751, para 77.
[82] Ibid, para 79.

it could be reasonably inferred that insufficient precautions had been taken to protect the lives of the civilian population.[83]

While the opinion of the majority did not explicitly refer here to the IHL framework, it made several implicit references to a number of provisions of this body of law. In interpreting the choice of means and methods to be used by the security forces in their operation in relation to Articles 1 and 2 of the ECHR, the majority seems to have relied on the vocabulary of Article 57(2)(a)(ii) of Additional Protocol I relating to precautions in attack.[84] This article requires the parties to the conflict to 'take all feasible precautions in the choice of means and methods of attack with a view to avoiding, and in any event to minimizing, incidental loss of civilian life, injury to civilians and damage to civilian objects'. Thus, the Court transposed a principle from IHL relating to international armed conflict into a situation of internal armed conflict. This principle had not been inserted into the IHL provisions pertaining to internal armed conflict, and it is not certain that it could have been applied, at the time of the judgment, as a customary rule.[85]

The Court further considered that, pursuant to Article 2 of the ECHR, the Government had to protect the civilian population not only from its own attacks, but also from the attacks of the PKK. This reasoning refers to the requirements of Article 58 of Additional Protocol I on the precautions against the effects of attacks,[86] which provides that:

> The Parties to the conflict shall, to the maximum extent feasible: (a) without prejudice to Article 49 of the Fourth Convention, endeavour to remove the civilian population, individual civilians and civilian objects under their control from the vicinity of military objectives; (b) avoid locating military objectives within or near densely populated areas; (c) take the other necessary precautions to protect the civilian population, individual civilians and civilian objects under their control against the dangers resulting from military operations.

Furthermore, the majority used the term 'civilians' throughout its opinion. Although it did not use the term 'combatants', it clearly distinguished between 'civilians' and security forces as well as members of the PKK.[87] Thus, it is clear in this case that the Court made an indirect reference to IHL by borrowing vocabulary specifically found in this field of law. In addition, it seems that the majority of the Court used reasoning inspired by IHL, as it considered whether there

[83] In addition, the Court ruled that the authorities failed to carry out an effective investigation into the circumstances surrounding Havva Ergi's death. It also found that there was no violation of Arts 14 and 18 nor any violation of Arts 13 and 25(1) of the ECHR. The applicant did not pursue his complaint on the basis of Article 8 in the Court, although he did claim that it had been violated before the Commission. The Court's reasoning in relation to these articles will not be examined here, as there were no references to IHL in these parts of the judgment.

[84] Gaggioli and Kolb (n 4 above), 5.

[85] Ibid.

[86] Nils Melzer, *Targeted Killing in International Law* (Oxford/New York: OUP, 2008), 385–386.

[87] Ibid, 386.

was a legitimate target, whether the attack on the target was proportional,[88] and whether the incidental loss of civilian lives outweighed the military advantage gained from the operation.[89]

Finally, the Court unanimously found that the respondent Government had not fulfilled the procedural requirement implicit in Article 2, read in conjunction with Article 1, which provides that an effective official investigation must be conducted when individuals have been killed.[90] According to the Strasbourg Court, this obligation is not confined to cases where it has been established that the killing was caused by a state agent.[91] By requiring a positive obligation to investigate in this context, the Court appears to have gone beyond the requirements of IHL. There seems to be no real equivalent to this obligation in IHL: while there is an obligation to investigate in some cases (ie prisoners of war,[92] civilian detainees,[93] etc), there is no such requirement with regard to internal conflict and there are no criteria to gauge the efficiency of an investigation.[94] The Court seems to have contributed to IHL by adding a further requirement which will be useful in protecting the lives of civilians and which will hold states accountable for their use of force.[95]

3.5 The *Özkan v Turkey* Case

The ECtHR considered an application filed by 32 Turkish nationals in April 2003.[96] The case concerned a military operation which took place on 20 February 1993 by the Turkish security forces against PKK members. Six gendarme teams carried out a search operation in the area of the Ormaniçi stream in order to apprehend PKK members. They noticed two men running towards the stream bed and fired two warning shots. The two men then ran towards the village of Ormaniçi, and shots were fired from the village. The security forces subsequently entered the village and responded with intense firing, which resulted in the killing of a girl child. The gendarme teams arrested many villagers, mistreated them, and detained them in inadequate conditions. The applicants alleged that there was a violation of Articles 2, 3, 5, 6, 8, and 25 of the ECHR. They later raised new complaints on the basis of other articles, but the Court considered that it had no jurisdiction in relation to these.

In relation to Article 2 (read in conjunction with Article 1) of the ECHR, the Court reiterated its reasoning from the *Ergi v Turkey* case[97] that a state must take

88 Hans-Joachim Heintze, 'The European Court of Human Rights and the Implementation of Human Rights Standards During Armed Conflicts' (2002) 45 GYIL 60, 74; Heintze (n 62 above), 810.

89 Reidy (n 30 above), 527.

90 *Ergi v Turkey* (n 81 above), para 82.

91 Ibid.

92 Convention relative to the treatment of prisoners of war, Art 121.

93 Convention relative to the protection of civilian persons in time of war, Art 131.

94 Gaggioli and Kolb (n 4 above), 9.

95 Ibid.

96 *Özkan v Turkey* (App No 21689/93), judgment, 6 April 2004, not reported.

97 *Ergi v Turkey* (n 81 above).

all feasible precautions in the choice of means and methods used during an operation to minimize incidental loss of civilian life.[98] It then considered that:

> at the material time there were serious disturbances in south-east Turkey involving armed conflict between the security forces and members of the PKK, that Ormaniçi was located near to the Gabar mountain chain, where in 1993 a number of PKK groups were staying and that the PKK was active in the region around Ormaniçi, . . . that the security forces' tactical reaction to the initial shots fired at them from the village on 20 February 1993 cannot be regarded as entailing a disproportionate degree of force. In so finding, the Court has also taken into consideration the fact that, apart from Abide Ekin, no civilians were injured as a result of the security forces' intensive firing. It therefore, accepts that, in the circumstances of the present case, the security forces' choice to open intensive fire on Ormaniçi in response to shots fired at them from the village was 'absolutely necessary' for the purpose of protecting life.[99]

Subsequently, the Court noted that 'once the security forces had taken control of Ormaniçi and had assembled its entire population in the village square, the security forces failed to make any attempt to verify whether there were any civilian casualties, which—given the amount and nature of the ammunition used by the security forces—was a realistic possibility'.[100] This led the Court to the conclusion that Turkey had violated the obligation to protect life in Article 2 of the ECHR, as it failed to protect the injured girl (who later died).[101]

Similarly to the *Ergi v Turkey* case, the Court seems to have referred here to the wording of Article 57(2)(a)(ii) of Additional Protocol I. It also distinguished between civilians, security forces, and PKK members.[102] From the statements above, it clearly appears that the Court enquired whether there was a legitimate target, whether the attack on the target was proportional, and whether the incidental loss of civilian lives outweighed the military advantage gained from the operation. The Court seems to have resorted to the principle of proportionality as enshrined in IHL, when it enquired whether the incidental civilian loss outweighed the military advantage gained from the operation. Furthermore, the concept of 'absolute necessity' was interpreted more liberally than in times of peace, which indicates that the Court was influenced by IHL in this context.[103] It considered that killing PKK members was justified to the extent that such force was required to achieve the legitimate purpose pursued. It is also interesting to note that the Court seems implicitly to have qualified the situation as a non-international armed conflict by stating that it was an armed conflict between the security forces and PKK members. From the above considerations, it transpires that the ECtHR has applied *sub silentio* an analysis used in the field of IHL within the framework of Article 2 of the ECHR.

[98] *Özkan v Turkey* (n 96 above), para 297; Melzer (n 86 above), 386.

[99] *Özkan v Turkey* (n 96 above), paras 305–306.

[100] Ibid, para 307.

[101] Melzer (n 86 above), 387.

[102] Ibid, 387.

[103] Ibid.

3.6 The *Isayeva and Others v Russia* Case

Medka Isayeva, Zina Yusupova, and Libkan Bazayeva complained about the indiscriminate bombing by the Russian Federation's military planes of civilians living in Grozny on 29 October 1999.[104] As a result of the bombing, Ms Isayeva was wounded and her two children and daughter-in-law were killed, Ms Yusupova was wounded and Ms Bazayeva's cars containing family possessions were destroyed. A criminal investigation into the bombardment confirming the applicants' version of the facts was suspended and reopened several times. The investigation was closed in 2004, given that the actions of the military pilots were found to be legitimate and proportionate in the circumstances. The applicants claimed that their relatives' and their own right to life as well as their right to protection from inhuman and degrading treatment had been violated. Ms Bazayeva complained, in addition, that the destruction of her cars containing the family's belongings infringed her property rights. The applicants relied on Articles 2, 3, and 13 of the ECHR and Article 1 of Protocol No 1. They also regarded the aerial bombardment as an indiscriminate attack on civilians, which could not be justified under common Article 3 to the Geneva Conventions of 12 August 1949.

A third party, Rights International (an NGO based in the United States), submitted written comments. The organization argued, referring to the Court's decision in *Banković and others v Belgium and 16 Other Contracting States*,[105] that the Court should take into account any relevant rules of international law in interpreting the Convention. The submission addressed the relevant rules of international law governing armed attacks on mixed combatant/civilian targets during a non-international armed conflict. It was submitted that the law of non-international armed conflicts as construed by international human rights law established a three-part test:

> First, armed attacks on mixed combatant/civilian targets were lawful only if there was no alternative to using force for obtaining a lawful objective. Second, if such use of force was absolutely necessary, the means or method of force employed could only cause the least amount of foreseeable physical and mental suffering. Armed forces should be used for the neutralisation or deterrence of hostile force, which could take place by surrender, arrest, withdrawal or isolation of enemy combatants—not only by killing and wounding. This rule required that States made available non-lethal weapons technologies to their military personnel. Furthermore, the authorities should refrain from attacking until other non-lethal alternatives could be implemented. Third, if such a means or method of using force did not achieve any of its lawful objectives, then force could be incrementally escalated to achieve them.[106]

[104] *Isayeva and others v Russia* (App Nos 57947/00; 57948/00; 57949/00), judgment, 24 February 2005, not yet reported.

[105] *Banković and others v Belgium and 16 Other Contracting States* (App No 52207/99), decision, Reports 2001-XII, 333.

[106] *Isayeva and others v Russia* (n 104 above), para 171.

The Government did not dispute that an attack had taken place, the fact that the applicant's two children had been killed, or the fact that the first and second applicants had been wounded. It was submitted, however, that the harm was unintended. In the Government's view, the attack was a legitimate use of force under Article 2(2)(a) of the ECHR, given that members of illegal armed formations had opened heavy fire. It was also argued that this constituted a threat to the pilots and civilians.

In assessing the lawfulness of the alleged violation under Article 2, the Court noted that:

> it is necessary to examine whether the operation was planned and controlled by the authorities so as to minimise to the greatest extent possible, recourse to lethal force. The authorities must take appropriate care to ensure that any risk to life is minimised. The Court must also examine whether the authorities were not negligent in their choice of action.[107]

The Court further found that its capacity to decide whether the attack was legitimate was hampered by the lack of information provided. More specifically, 'there was no reference to assessing and preventing possible harm to civilians who might have been present on the road or elsewhere in the vicinity of what the military could have perceived as legitimate targets'.[108] It was further explained that 'the documents submitted by the parties and the investigation file nevertheless allow the Court to draw certain conclusions as to whether the operation was planned and concluded in such a way as to avoid or minimise, to the greatest extent possible, damage to civilians'.[109] Again, as in *Ergi v Turkey*[110] and *Özkan v Turkey*,[111] the Court's opinion was replete with language drawn from IHL and more specifically from Article 57(2)(a)(ii) of Additional Protocol I.[112] The Court's main objective in conducting this enquiry was to minimize the incidental loss of civilian life.

The Court then found that:

> the situation that existed in Chechnya at the relevant time called for exceptional measures on behalf of the State in order to regain control over the Republic and to suppress the illegal armed insurgency. These measures could presumably include employment of military aviation equipped with heavy combat weapons. The Court is also prepared to accept that if the planes were attacked by illegal armed groups, that could have justified use of lethal force, thus falling within paragraph 2 of Article 2.[113]

By finding that the confrontation constituted an armed insurgency, the Court seems to have implicitly recognized that it was a non-international armed conflict.[114]

[107] Ibid, para 171. [108] Ibid, para 175. [109] Ibid, para 177.
[110] *Ergi v Turkey* (n 81 above). [111] *Özkan v Turkey* (n 96 above).
[112] See also Melzer (n 86 above), 387–389.
[113] *Isayeva and others v Russia* (n 104 above), para 178.
[114] Melzer (n 86 above), 388–389.

The Court further considered that the Government failed to produce evidence which would have justified the use of lethal force, but it nevertheless assumed 'that the military reasonably considered that there was an attack or a risk of attack from illegal insurgents, and that the air strike was a legitimate response to that attack'.[115] With this statement, the Court departed from the strict standard of 'absolute necessity' and opted for a standard of 'reasonable necessity'.[116] From this, it follows that pursuant to Article 2 of the ECHR it is lawful to use lethal force when there is a reasonable risk of attack. This liberal interpretation appears to be too extensive and not compliant with the wording of Article 2(2). Undoubtedly, IHL exerted an important influence on the reasoning of the Court in this passage.

This influence was also apparent when the Court examined the planning and conduct of the operation pursuant to Article 2. It did not find that 'the operation near the village of Shaami-Yurt was planned and executed with the requisite care for the lives of the civilian population'.[117] In fact, the authorities failed, among other things, to inform the air force of the 'safe passage' where civilians would be travelling by road[118] and to inform the civilian population of the probable arrival of rebels in the village.[119] They did not take all the necessary technical measures,[120] some members of staff were not aware of the civilian casualties until a year after the incident,[121] and the military used extremely powerful weapons on a short stretch of road filled with vehicles.[122] The failure on the part of the authorities to take precautionary measures constituted, according to the Court, a violation of Article 2 of the ECHR.

Once more, the Court resorted to vocabulary and reasoning which seem to have been imported directly from IHL. Such an approach allowed it to clarify further the content of IHL, given that it required the Government to warn the civilian population of the potential arrival of rebels.[123] In IHL, this duty only exists with regard to attacks and is rather weak, as it is only required on the part of states when the circumstances allow it.[124] The Court also required the Government to have an efficient information transmission system, which is not explicitly provided for in IHL. Finally, it was also found that the authorities had failed to carry out an adequate and effective investigation in violation of Article 2 of the ECHR into the circumstances of the attack.[125] Similarly to the *Ergi* case, the Court's reasoning exceeded the standards prevailing in IHL, which

115 *Isayeva and others v Russia* (n 104 above), para 181.
116 Melzer (n 86 above), 389.
117 *Isayeva and others v Russia* (n 104 above), para 199.
118 Ibid, para 189.
119 Ibid, para 187.
120 Ibid, para 188.
121 Ibid, para 191.
122 Ibid, para 195.
123 Gaggioli and Kolb (4 above), 5.
124 Ibid.
125 *Isayeva and others v Russia* (n 104 above), para 225. This reasoning was reaffirmed in recent cases concerning actions of the Russian military in Chechnya, where violations of Art 2 of the ECHR were found in respect of the failure to conduct an effective investigation: *Kashiyev and Akayeva v Russia* (App Nos 57942/00; 57945/00), judgment, 24 February 2005, not yet reported, para 166; *Estamirov and others v Russia* (App No 60272/00), judgment, 12 October 2006, not reported, para 95; *Elmurzayev and others v Russia* (App No 3019/04), judgment, 12 June 2008, not yet reported, para 111; *Atabayeva and others v Russia* (App No 26064/02), judgment, 12 June 2008, not yet reported, para 102.

contain several omissions with respect to the duty to investigate.[126] This case demonstrates once again that the Court's jurisprudence complements and fills in the gaps in the protection granted by IHL.

3.7 The *Isayeva v Russia* Case

In this case, the ECtHR examined Zara Isayeva's complaint regarding the indiscriminate bombing by the Russian air force of Katyr-Yurt, a Chechen village.[127] As a result of the bombing, civilians fleeing the village through what they thought was a 'safe passage' from fighting were killed and injured. Ms Isayeva lost her son and three nieces in this incident. A criminal investigation followed and confirmed Ms Isayeva's version of events. The investigation was later closed, given that the actions of the military were found to be justified. The applicant claimed that her relatives' right to life had been violated, that the investigation was ineffective, and that she had no access to a remedy. She based her complaint on Articles 2 and 13 of the ECHR. She also referred to the third-party submissions made in the case of *Isayeva and others v Russia*.[128] The Government suggested that the use of force was justified under Article 2(2)(a) of the ECHR, given the presence of a large group of armed fighters in Katyr-Yurt.

In reviewing the aspect of the complaint based on Article 2, the ECtHR repeated that '[t]he authorities must take appropriate care to ensure that any risk to life is minimised'.[129] This meant that the authorities had to take 'all feasible precautions in the choice of means and methods of a security operation mounted against an opposing group with a view to avoiding and, in any event, minimising, incidental loss of civilian life'.[130] As in the cases reviewed above, the Court drew heavily on the vocabulary of IHL.

In addition, it considered again that:

> the situation that existed in Chechnya at the relevant time called for exceptional measures by the State in order to regain control over the Republic and to suppress the illegal armed insurgency. Given the context of the conflict in Chechnya at the relevant time, those measures could presumably include the deployment of army units equipped with combat weapons, including military aviation and artillery. The presence of a very large group of armed fighters in Katyr-Yurt, and their active resistance to the law-enforcement bodies, which are not disputed by the parties, may have justified use of lethal force by the agents of the State, thus bringing the situation within paragraph 2 of Article 2.[131]

Thus, it could be argued that it perceived the situation, consistently with the *Isayeva and others v Russia* judgment, as a non-international conflict.

[126] Gaggioli and Kolb (n 4 above), 9. See 3.4 above.
[127] *Isayeva v Russia* (App No 57950/00), judgment, 24 February 2005, not yet reported.
[128] *Isayeva and others v Russia* (n 104 above), para 195.
[129] *Isayeva v Russia* (n 127 above), para 175.
[130] Ibid, para 176.
[131] Ibid, para 180.

Nevertheless, the Court shifted away from this analysis and considered subsequently that the situation at hand was not a military operation.[132] The Court stated that it

> considers that using this kind of weapon in a populated area, outside wartime and without prior evacuation of the civilians, is impossible to reconcile with the degree of caution expected from a law-enforcement body in a democratic society. No martial law and no state of emergency has been declared in Chechnya, and no derogation has been made under Article 15 of the Convention.... The operation in question therefore has to be judged against a normal legal background. Even when faced with a situation where, as the Government submit, the population of the village had been held hostage by a large group of well-equipped and well-trained fighters, the primary aim of the operation should be to protect lives from unlawful violence. The massive use of indiscriminate weapons stands in flagrant contrast with this aim and cannot be considered compatible with the standard of care prerequisite to an operation of this kind involving the use of lethal force by State agents.[133]

This passage seems to refute the earlier assumption and indicates that the Court viewed the situation as a law enforcement operation.

This impression is, however, misleading and confusing, given that the Court then returned to the approach used earlier in its reasoning. It continued to view the situation through the lenses of IHL by invoking language which was specific to this field of law. The Court distinguished between civilians and fighters and servicemen, emphasized the need to minimize civilian casualties, and enquired whether legitimate means and methods of combat were used. It then concluded that 'accepting that the operation in Katyr-Yurt on 4–7 September 2000 was pursuing a legitimate aim, the Court does not accept that it was planned and executed with the requisite care for the lives of the civilian population'.[134] It is possible that the Court viewed the situations from a mixed-perspective, that is from the perspective of a non-international conflict and a law enforcement situation.[135] It is nonetheless more plausible that the Court resorted to notions of IHL under the label of a law enforcement situation. Thus, the Court largely circumvented the application of IHL by referring to it *sub silentio*. It should be remembered, however, that the Court also contributed to IHL in this case by finding that the authorities failed to carry out an effective investigation.[136] As mentioned earlier, this finding exceeds the current requirements enshrined in IHL.[137]

3.8 The *Akkum and Others v Turkey* Case

In *Akkum and others v Turkey*[138] the Court considered an application filed by Turkish nationals with respect to three family members who had been found

[132] Melzer (n 86 above), 391.
[133] *Isayeva v Russia* (n 127 above), para 191.
[134] Ibid, para 200.
[135] Melzer (n 86 above), 391–392.
[136] *Isayeva v Russia* (n 127 above), para 224.
[137] Gaggioli and Kolb (n 4 above), 9. See 3.4 above.
[138] *Akkum and others v Turkey* (App No 21894/93), judgment (extracts), 24 March 2005, Reports 2005-II, 247.

dead following a military operation in Dicle (Diyarbakır), Turkey. One of the bodies found had been mutilated. The applicants alleged, *inter alia*, that their relatives were killed unlawfully by the security forces and that the authorities failed to carry out an adequate investigation into the killings. They relied on Articles 2, 3, 14, and 18 of the ECHR and Article 1 of Protocol No 1. The Turkish Government denied that soldiers were responsible for the killing of one of the relatives. They maintained that the two remaining relatives had been killed in crossfire between soldiers and members of the PKK and that it was not possible to determine who had actually shot them. The Court found that the Government had violated Articles 2, 3, and 13 of the ECHR and Article 1 of Protocol No 1. Turkey had also failed to fulfil its obligation under Article 38(1)(a) of the ECHR.

In its assessment, the Court first emphasized that it was of the utmost importance for the effective operation of the system of individual petition under Article 34 of the ECHR that states provide all the necessary facilities to make possible a proper and effective examination of applications.[139] The Court reiterated that, in proceedings relating to cases where an individual accuses state agents of violating his rights under the Convention, it is solely the respondent government which can, in certain circumstances, have access to information capable of corroborating or refuting the allegations.[140] Thus, a failure of the government to submit such information which was in their hands without a satisfactory explanation may not only give rise to the drawing of inferences as to the credibility of the applicant's allegations, but may also reflect negatively on the level of compliance by a respondent state with its applications under Article 38(1)(a) of the ECHR.[141] The Court observed that the Turkish Government had failed to provide a number of important documents, including a report and an operation plan. Thus, the Court found that Turkey had violated its obligation under Article 38(1)(a). Although this finding was made in the context of Article 38, it does not necessarily apply to Article 2. In fact, the refusal to provide crucial information does not automatically entail a violation of the right to life contained in Article 2. Nonetheless, it has recently been argued that a preliminary obligation for states to compile reports regarding the planning and results of a military operation could be deduced from this requirement.[142] As there is no similar obligation in IHL, the Court may have complemented this legal framework with a requirement that will facilitate the assessment of the legality of a military operation.[143]

In its evaluation of the facts, the Court deplored the lack of a thorough domestic investigation into the deaths, as well as the withholding of information by the Turkish authorities. The Court considered that it could draw inferences with regard to the credibility of the applicants' allegations and deduced that the death of one of the relatives was caused by soldiers. With regard to the remaining

139 Ibid, para 185. 140 Ibid. 141 Ibid.
142 Gaggioli and Kolb (n 4 above), 8. 143 Ibid.

relatives, the Court drew a parallel between the detainees, for whose well-being the State was held responsible, and the situation where people were found injured or dead in an area within the exclusive control of the State authorities.[144] In such situations, the events lie wholly or in large part within the exclusive knowledge of the authorities. The burden of proof is then reversed and it is for the state authorities to prove that the documents in their possession could not serve to corroborate the allegations of the applicants or to provide a satisfactory explanation of how the events occurred.[145] As the Government had failed to provide any argument in this regard, the Court found that it had failed to account for the deaths of the relatives and the mutilation of one of the bodies. In this context, the Court seems to have reached beyond the existing requirements of IHL; it made it possible to hold a state responsible for a violation of a right to life when persons found dead were under its control and when the state did not provide any explanation as to the circumstances of death.[146] This finding expands the existing IHL framework: it completes it by providing an obligation for states to account for the deaths caused by their military operations.[147]

3.9 The *Markovic and Others v Italy* Case

In the *Markovic and others v Italy* case,[148] the Court considered an application filed by 10 Serbs who were close relatives of people killed during the Kosovo conflict. The headquarters of Radio Televizija Srbije (RTS) in Belgrade were bombed by NATO on 23 April 1999 resulting in 16 deaths. The applicants had brought an action in damages in the Rome District Court, as they considered that Italy's involvement in the military operations had been more extensive than that of other NATO members. According to the applicants, Italy had provided major political and logistical support, including the use of its air bases by aircraft engaged in the strikes on Belgrade and the RTS. The applicants relied on Article 6 (right to a fair hearing) of the ECHR read in conjunction with Article 1. Following an application entered by the defendants for a preliminary ruling concerning the issue of jurisdiction, the Corte Suprema di Cassazione decided that Italian courts had no jurisdiction because Italy's decision to take part in the air strikes had been a political one and could not be reviewed by the courts. It is interesting to note that in domestic proceedings the applicants relied, among other provisions, on Additional Protocol I.[149]

The majority found that pursuant to Article 1 of the ECHR it had jurisdiction in the case, given that the applicants had already brought a civil action in Italy and that this established the required 'jurisdictional link' under the same

[144] *Akkum and others v Turkey* (n 138 above), 211. [145] Ibid.
[146] Gaggioli and Kolb (n 4 above), 8. [147] Ibid.
[148] *Markovic and others v Italy* (App No 1398/03), judgment, 14 December 2006, not reported. [149] Ibid, para 14.

provision.[150] It was also clarified that if civil proceedings were brought in the domestic courts, the state was required by Article 1 to secure in those proceedings respect for the rights protected by Article 6. Having thus found the application to be admissible, the majority of judges went on to enquire whether there was a violation of Article 6(1) taken together with Article 1. In that context, the majority made an express reference to Additional Protocol I,[151] where it considered its own role within the framework of interpretation of international law. It was found that:

> it is primarily for the national authorities, notably the courts, to interpret and apply domestic law. This also applies where domestic law refers to rules of general international law or international agreements. The Court's role is confined to ascertaining whether the effects of such an interpretation are compatible with the Convention.... Although it is not its role to express any view on the applicability of the 1977 Protocol or the London Convention, the Court notes that the Court of Cassation's comments on the international conventions do not appear to contain any errors of interpretation. There are two reasons for this: firstly, the statement that the 1977 Protocol regulates relations between States is true; secondly, the applicants relied on paragraph 5 of Article VIII of the London Convention, which concerns acts 'causing damage in the territory of the receiving State to third parties'... whereas the applicants' damage was sustained in Serbia, not Italy.[152]

It was found that there was no violation of Article 6.

With this affirmation the judges of the majority determined, on a rather ambiguous note, that it was not part of their role to interpret or to apply IHL. They then did the opposite by finding that the Corte Suprema di Cassazione's interpretation of Additional Protocol I was correct. This statement also constitutes an important affirmation of the Court's position with regard to the potential application of IHL in future cases and with regard to its role within the international legal system. In substance, however, the Court's commendation of the Corte Suprema di Cassazione's opinion was less impressive.

The Corte Suprema di Cassazione considered that:

> [w]hile the purpose of the provisions of international agreements governing the conduct of hostilities—the Protocol Additional to the Geneva Convention (Articles 35.2, 48, 49, 51, 52 and 57) and the European Convention on Human Rights (Articles 2 and 15 § 2)—is to protect civilians in the event of attack, they are rules of international law, and so also regulate relations between States. These same Treaties lay down the procedure for finding a violation and the sanctions in the event of liability (Article 91 of the Protocols and Article 41 of the Convention); they also designate the international courts and tribunals with jurisdiction to make such a finding. However, the legislation implementing these rules in the Italian State does not contain any express provision enabling injured

[150] Ibid, paras 54–56. It should be noted that Judges Costa and Rozakis wrote separate concurring opinions, whereas Judges Zagrebelsky, Zupančič, Jungwiert, Tsatsanikolovska, Ugrekhelidzie, Kovler, and Thór Björgvisson dissented.

[151] It was not invoked here by the applicants, but only at the domestic level.

[152] *Markovic and others v Italy* (n 148 above), paras 108–109.

parties to seek reparation from the State for damage sustained as a result of a violation of the rules of international law. The notion that provisions to that effect may implicitly have been introduced into the system through the implementation of rules of international law is at odds with the converse principle that has been mentioned which holds that protected individual interests are no bar to carrying out functions of a political nature.[153]

The majority opinion with regard to this interpretation remains traditional and more restrictive than the opinion of the commentary to the Additional Protocols.[154] While the judges considered that the Corte Suprema di Cassazione's interpretation was correct because Additional Protocol I governs relations between states, the commentary to the Additional Protocols is not so unequivocal. The commentary to Article 91 of Additional Protocol I provides that '[t]hose entitled to compensation will normally be Parties to the conflict or their nationals, though in exceptional cases they may also be neutral countries, in the case of violation of the rules on neutrality or of unlawful conduct with respect to neutral nationals in the territory of a Party to the conflict'.[155] It also adds that 'since 1945 a tendency has emerged to recognize the exercise of rights by individuals'.[156] Further, as Sassòli accurately points out, IHL corresponds to the traditional structure of international law in that it governs relations between states, but at the same time (often by the very same provisions) it also protects individuals against the state or other belligerent authorities.[157]

It should be mentioned, however, that the Commentary to the Fourth Geneva Convention[158] provides that:

> the Convention…does not apply to the relations of a State with its own 'nationals'. It conforms to the traditional conception of international law. A person is only a legal subject within a State and the provisions concerning the protection of civilians in time of war take no account of disputes which may exist between the State and its own citizens. That is a serious matter, in view of the arbitrary action of certain governments during the last world war.[159]

It clarifies further that:

> [i]t is possible that a doctrine which is today only beginning to take shape may acquire authority in international law tomorrow and one day provide the basis for establishing

[153] Ibid, para 18; *Presidenza Consiglio ministri c. Markovic and others*, Corte di Cassazione (Sezioni Unite), judgment no 8157, 5 June 2002, (2002) 85 *Rivista di diritto internazionale* 800, para 3.

[154] Yves Sandoz, Christophe Swinarski, and Bruno Zimmerman, *Commentary on the Additional Protocols of 8 June 1977 to the Geneva Conventions of 12 August 1949* (Geneva: International Committee of the Red Cross, 1987).

[155] Ibid, 1056, para 3656.

[156] Ibid, 1057, para 3657.

[157] Marco Sassòli and Antoine A Bouvier, *How Does Law Protect in War?, Cases, Documents and Teaching Materials on Contemporary Practice in International Humanitarian Law* (Geneva: International Committee of the Red Cross, 1999), 95.

[158] Jean S Pictet, *Commentary of the IV Geneva Convention Relative to the Protection of Civilian Persons in Time of War, Vol IV* (Geneva: International Committee of the Red Cross, 1994–1995).

[159] Ibid, 372–373.

the rights of the individual in relation to the State of which he is a 'citizen'. The Universal Declaration of Human Rights is doubtless as yet only a 'common standard of achievement for all peoples and all nations', but just as the protection afforded by the humanitarian Conventions applied first to the wounded and sick on the battlefield, and was then extended to prisoners of war and finally to civilians (with the exception of nationals), it may well end by covering the 'citizens' of a country themselves, and so embody in law the original guiding idea of the Red Cross, that suffering should be relieved wherever it exists, without political considerations of any kind, in the name of the respect due to the human person.[160]

It needs to be emphasized, however, that the Commentary to the Fourth Geneva Convention precedes the Commentary to Additional Protocol I and, therefore, the latter should have been followed by the Court as the most recent interpretation of IHL. Furthermore, with the increasingly more complex nature of modern armed conflict, it is no longer the case that IHL merely regulates relations between states. In recent times, armed conflicts have involved not only states, but also non-state actors or highly organized armed groups which become party to a conflict under IHL.[161] Thus, the ECtHR's interpretation of the applicability of the IHL with regard to states is questionable.

3.10 The *Korbely v Hungary* Case

In spite of warnings against interpreting IHL in the *Markovic* case,[162] the Court made extensive use of common Article 3 to the Geneva Conventions in the recent *Korbely v Hungary* judgment.[163] The application was brought to Strasbourg by a retired military officer who had participated in quelling a riot in Hungary during the failed 1956 revolution against the communist rulers. He was the captain of a 15-strong squad that killed a number of people, some of whom were armed. The applicant had been convicted in Hungary of multiple homicide constituting a crime against humanity and sentenced to five years' imprisonment. The judges at the domestic level had relied on common Article 3(1) to the Geneva Conventions. The applicant's conviction was based, *inter alia*, on the fact that one of the insurgents he had killed, Tamás Kaszás, was a non-combatant for the purposes of common Article 3. Relying mainly on Article 7 of the ECHR, the applicant submitted that he had been convicted in respect of an act which had not constituted a criminal offence at the time it was committed. The respondent Government argued that international criminal and humanitarian law applied in the case and that the domestic courts' interpretation of common Article 3 did not infringe Article 7 of the ECHR. The ECtHR concluded that the applicant's

[160] Ibid, 373.

[161] This could be the case, for instance, in the Israeli-Palestinian conflict where the military wing of Hamas could be perceived as being a party to an international conflict with Israel.

[162] *Markovic and others v Italy* (n 148 above).

[163] *Korbely v Hungary* (App No 9174/02), judgment, 19 September 2008, not yet reported.

acts did not satisfy all the elements of a crime against humanity and that there was a violation of Article 7 of the ECHR (no punishment without law) by 11 votes to 6.

The Court observed that it was not its role to seek to establish authoritatively the meaning of the 'crime against humanity' concept.[164] It also stated that it was not part of its role to resolve problems of interpretation of domestic legislation or domestic law referring to general international law or international agreements.[165] The majority of judges considered that the offence was defined with sufficient accessibility and went on to consider whether it was foreseeable that the act of which the applicant was convicted could be classified as a crime against humanity. It was further noted that murder within the meaning of common Article 3 could have provided a basis for a conviction for crimes against humanity committed in 1956.[166] In support of this, the Court referred to Article 6(c) of the Charter of the International Military Tribunal annexed to the London Agreement (8 August 1945),[167] Article 5 of the ICTY Statute (1993),[168] Article 3 of the ICTR Statute (1994),[169] and Article 7 of the International Criminal Court Statute (1998). However, additional requirements, not contained in common Article 3, needed to be fulfilled. These elements flowed from international law elements inherent in the notion of a crime against humanity at that time. For instance, in Article 6(c) of the Charter, which contains the primary formulation in force in 1956, crimes against humanity were referred to in relation to a war. In addition, an element of discrimination and persecution of an identifiable group of persons as part of state action or policy was required.[170] The Court considered, however, that the link with an armed conflict might no longer have been relevant by 1956. It was also found that the domestic courts had not determined whether the killing had met the requirement of a widespread or systemic attack on the civilian population.[171] Thus, it was held that it was open to question whether the constituent requirements of a crime against humanity had been met in the instant case.[172]

Common Article 3 to the Geneva Conventions affords protection to persons taking no active part in hostilities, including members of armed forces who have laid down their arms and those placed *hors de combat* by sickness, wounds, detention, or any other cause. The person killed, Tamás Kaszás, had been a leader of an armed group of insurgents who, after committing other violent acts, had taken control of the police building and seized the police officers' weapons. In

[164] Ibid, para 78. [165] Ibid, para 72. [166] Ibid, para 81.

[167] United Nations Charter of the International Military Tribunal—Annex to the Agreement for the prosecution and punishment of the major war criminals of the European Axis, 82 UNTS 379, 8 August 1945 ('the London Agreement').

[168] The Statute of the International Criminal Tribunal for the Former Yugoslavia (1993) 32 ILM 1192, adopted on 23 May 1993.

[169] The Statute of the International Criminal Tribunal for Rwanda (1994) 33 ILM 1602, adopted on 8 November 1994. [170] *Korbely v Hungary* (n 163 above), para 82.

[171] Ibid, para 84. [172] Ibid, para 85.

the Court's view, he could therefore not be regarded as a non-combatant in the sense of common Article 3. The Court found it crucial that Kaszás was secretly carrying a gun, which was not known to the applicant. Once it was known that he was armed, he had not tried to surrender in an apparent manner. He had embarked on an animated quarrel with the applicant, at the end of which he took out a gun with unknown intentions. It was during this action that he was shot. In these circumstances, the Court was not convinced that in light of the international law standards prevailing at the time, Kaszás could be said to have laid down his arms within the meaning of common Article 3. The Court also rejected the Government's argument that the applicant's conviction was not primarily based on his reaction to Kaszás drawing his handgun, but on his having shot, and ordered others to shoot, at a group of civilians.[173] Finally, the Court concluded that no conviction for crimes against humanity could reasonably be based on common Article 3 in light of the international standards prevailing at the time.

Judges Lorenzen, Tulkens, Zagrebelsky, Fura-Sanström, and Popović expressed a joint dissenting opinion with regard to the Court's finding of violation under Article 7 of the ECHR.[174] They considered that it was incorrect for the majority of judges to maintain that the domestic courts did not examine whether there had been a widespread and systemic attack on the civilian population. In their view, it was sufficient for the Supreme Court to observe that the central power of the dictatorship had employed troops against the population engaged in demonstrations and against the armed revolutionary groups that were forming.[175] It was also observed that the restraint and caution of the Court left open the question whether the act in respect of which the applicant was convicted could indeed constitute a crime against humanity. The dissenting judges criticized the majority for substituting their findings of fact for those of the Hungarian judicial authorities, which it explicitly mentioned it would not do.[176] It was further found that, in view of the complexity of reconstruing facts more than 50 years after they occurred, there was 'no reason to place more reliance on the conclusions reached by the Court than on those of the domestic courts. . . . the national courts were in a better position to assess all the available facts and evidence.'[177]

In a separate individual decision, Judge Loucaides agreed with the approach of the majority in respect of the crimes against humanity, but found it useful to add a number of comments on the issue. In his view, it was not clearly established at the time that crimes against humanity were part of customary international law, especially when they were not linked to acts of war.[178] Gradually, a connection between crimes against humanity and war activity was no longer considered to be a requirement for the establishment of such crimes. He cited Article 7 of the

[173] Ibid, para 91.

[174] Ibid, joint dissenting opinion of Judges Lorenzen, Tulkens, Zagrebelsky, Fura-Sanström, and Popović.

[175] Ibid, joint dissenting opinion, para 1.

[176] Ibid, joint dissenting opinion, para 2.

[177] Ibid.

[178] Ibid, dissenting opinion of Judge Loucaides.

ICC Statute as providing the relevant elements of crimes against humanity. In his view, the minimum elements of the offence were (1) murder, (2) committed against a civilian population, and (3) systematic or organized conduct in the furtherance of a certain policy. On the basis of these requirements, he found no difficulty in concluding that the activity for which the applicant was convicted constituted a crime against humanity.

Judge Loucaides disagreed with the majority's finding that the applicant's conviction was essentially focused on the reaction of the applicant to Kaszás. He accepted the Government's argument that his conviction was primarily based on his having shot, and ordered others to shoot, at a group of civilians. Therefore, Judge Loucaides did not see how it was possible to disregard the domestic courts' finding that the case against the applicant also concerned other civilians who were not armed. He emphasized that other insurgents were killed in the incident by the applicant's squad and that the applicant and the members of his group were armed with PPS-type 7.62-mm submachine guns and TT pistols. In his view, this random shooting with submachine guns, directed against unarmed civilians, other than Kaszás, could only constitute a crime against humanity. Unlike the majority, he also found that there was sufficient evidence that the shooting in question formed part of a widespread and systematic attack on the civilian population and that the Supreme Court had to address the question satisfactorily.

In comparison to its previous case law, the *Korbely* judgment constitutes an exception to the Court's usual approach to the IHL framework. In this case, the Court explicitly used common Article 3 to the Geneva Conventions as a starting point for its reasoning under Article 7 of the ECHR. The nature of the Court's analysis is rooted, however, in the fact that the case was closely intertwined with IHL. Common Article 3 to the Geneva Conventions constituted the basis of the conviction at the domestic level. Thus, the Court felt compelled by necessity to take into account the relevant international instruments. The Court's reasoning with regard to crimes against humanity was very cautious: the ECtHR observed that it was open to question whether the requirements for establishing that a crime against humanity was committed had been fulfilled. Its finding that, under international customary law, a nexus with an armed conflict might no longer have been relevant in 1956, was more courageous. While there is no longer a requirement for an armed conflict,[179] it does not appear to have been unequivocally established that this was the case in 1956. The Court also ventured into the slippery domain of active participation in hostilities. The question of 'direct participation in

[179] *Prosecutor v Dusko Tadić*, appeals judgment, 15 July 1999, IT-94–1, paras 249 and 251; *Prosecutor v Kunarac, Kovač and Vuković*, appeals judgment, 12 June 2002, IT-96–23&23/1, para 83.

hostilities' is an important concern in IHL, which was extensively studied by the International Committee of the Red Cross.[180] The Court has not really engaged with the uncertainties that pervade this vague and evolving field of IHL. Further, the Court initially observed that it was not part of its duty to establish authoritatively the meaning of the 'crimes against humanity' concept or to resolve problems of interpretation where domestic law refers to international agreements. It appears to have done the opposite by interpreting difficult factual questions as well as legal issues under the pertinent domestic and international legislation. Nonetheless, the ECtHR's approach remained cautious, as it did not provide an in-depth analysis of the concepts it had employed. Having been criticized for its previous references to IHL, the Court may have tried to improve on the approach it had previously used. It is yet to be seen, however, whether the Court will return to its tendency of referring to IHL *sub silentio*.

4. Analysis of the Reasoning Used in the Case Law

The ECtHR has not followed the prevailing consensus in international practice that IHL constitutes *lex specialis* in cases of armed conflict. Rather, it has based itself mostly on the ECHR in such situations. As mentioned earlier, it is interesting to contrast this situation with the Inter-American Commission on Human Rights, which has applied the provisions of IHL directly.[181] The Court's approach, however, has been based on the exclusive application of the Convention and the references to IHL have generally been made *sub silentio*. The Court has, nonetheless, been willing to apply a different standard of review with regard to cases occurring in situations or armed conflict by adapting the ECHR and rendering it more flexible. It is important to mention that applying human rights law in situations of armed conflict is problematic for the Commission and the Court because this is not the type of situation the Convention was really designed to deal with (in contrast to the IHL, which was).

The case law of the Court and the Commission is marked by an uneven and unstable evolution. In the initial phase, it appears that the Commission was willing to refer explicitly to the IHL framework. Then, the Court slowly started making indirect references to IHL, which became part of its approach in the framework of Article 2 of the ECHR. The Court was visibly less receptive to the

[180] International Committee of the Red Cross, *Interpretative Guidance on the Notion of Direct Participation in Hostilities under International Humanitarian Law*, Geneva, 2009, available at <http://www.icrc.org/Web/Eng/siteeng0.nsf/htmlall/p0990/$File/ICRC_002_0990.PDF> (last visited 13 June 2010).

[181] See *Coard and others v United States* (n 23 above); *Abella v Argentina* (n 24 above).

IHL framework than the Commission. In its subsequent case law, it signalled that it was not part of its role to examine the application of IHL. In recent times, however, it has not followed this indication and has referred explicitly to IHL provisions. Thus, it is uncertain how the Court will proceed in future cases involving armed conflict. It is hoped that no cases of this type will reach the Strasbourg Court.

Overall, the case law concerning IHL has generally appeared in areas where a non-international conflict was involved. Further, most cases containing references to IHL originated from Turkey and Chechnya, and involved the killing of civilians by the security or armed forces. They occurred in the context of an enquiry conducted under Article 2 of the ECHR, namely whether the use of lethal force was absolutely necessary. In this context, the Court drew heavily on IHL vocabulary and used an approach which seems to have been grounded in Article 57(2)(ii) and Article 58 of Additional Protocol I. In most cases, this was without any explicit reference to the IHL framework, to which body of law the Court resorted *sub silentio*. In only three cases did the parties invoke IHL, directly claiming that it had been breached.[182] Therefore, this does not seem to have been the decisive factor in the Court's consideration of IHL. It should be noted that this area of the Court's jurisprudence is circumscribed and constitutes a very limited interpretation of a particular aspect of IHL, namely the questions of precautions in attack and the loss of civilian life in the context of non-international armed conflict.

Although the Court's approach seems to have consolidated itself in the late 1990s, it is still highly imprecise and confusing. The Court used IHL on a very subtle basis in the cases concerning Turkey. In the *Güleç v Turkey* case,[183] the Court could have used IHL but only resorted to wording that is associated with this field of the law. Its approach no longer seemed to be based exclusively on the ECHR. Stronger references to IHL appeared in the *Ergi v Turkey*[184] and *Özkan v Turkey*[185] cases, although there was no explicit mention of the IHL framework. In those cases, the Court not only referred to the vocabulary inherent in IHL, but also used a type of reasoning which could have been associated with this body of law. It seemed to refer implicitly to the requirements of Article 57(2)(ii) of Additional Protocol I when it enquired whether an excessive loss of civilian life resulted from a military operation. Furthermore, the Court differentiated in both cases between civilians and parties to the conflict and,

[182] *Korbely v Hungary* (n 163 above); *Isayeva and others v Russia* (n 104 above); *Isayeva v Russia* (n 127 above). In *Isayeva and others v Russia*, a third party also made a submission where it was argued that the Court should apply the relevant provisions of IHL.

[183] *Güleç v Turkey* (n 74 above).

[184] *Ergi v Turkey* (n 81 above).

[185] *Özkan v Turkey* (n 96 above).

in *Özkan v Turkey*, seems to have qualified the situation as a non-international conflict.

This tendency to use the vocabulary and reasoning specific to the IHL framework repeated itself in the cases relating to the Chechen conflict. In *Isayeva and others v Russia*[186] and in *Isayeva v Russia*[187] the Court appears to have considered that the situation constituted a non-international armed conflict, and it distinguished civilians from fighters and servicemen. Furthermore, in *Isayeva and others v Russia* the Court followed the *Ergi* and *Özkan* cases by reiterating that incidental harm to civilians must be prevented. It was emphasized that the security forces must take the required precautions to spare civilian lives. In *Isayeva v Russia*, however, the Court followed this reasoning only in part, given that it also considered that the Chechen conflict was a law enforcement situation. It was not clear how the Court preferred to qualify the circumstances of the case. The Court's confusing reasoning indicates that its approach in this context is still imprecise and uncertain.

The Court's own view of its role within the international legal system seems to be conservative and traditional. As mentioned earlier, the majority of judges stated recently in *Markovic v Italy*[188] that it is not part of their role to consider the applicability of Additional Protocol I. Paradoxically, the Court did not, however, shy away from commenting on the Corte Suprema di Cassazione's interpretation of the same instrument. The foregoing analysis shows that, while the Court is attempting to limit its own institutional competence within the sphere of international law, it is nonetheless compelled to look beyond the immediate European legal architecture. Recently, the Court has been much more receptive than in its previous case law. In the *Korbely* case,[189] the Court explicitly used common Article 3 to the Geneva Conventions as a base for its reasoning. This exceptional approach appears to have been necessary due to the fact that the case was closely intertwined with this provision. It is an important departure from the previous jurisprudence, which was marked by indirect references to the IHL framework.

Another important point that emerges from the examination of the Court's case law is that the Court intends the ECHR framework to be self-sufficient and attempts to refrain from importing extraneous legal concepts as much as possible. As demonstrated earlier, this approach has not proved successful as the Court has consistently used vocabulary and concepts borrowed from IHL. Thus, in effect, the Court's intention seems to have given way to an unintended result; the ECHR system appeared, in these cases at least, to be porous, permeable, and adapted to the cross-fertilization of concepts. It could be that the Court's intention was relinquished in favour of more pragmatic considerations which required

[186] *Isayeva and others v Russia* (n 104 above).
[187] *Isayeva v Russia* (n 127 above).
[188] *Markovic and others v Italy* (n 148 above).
[189] *Korbely v Hungary* (n 163 above).

adaptation of the Convention to the context of armed conflict by using specific concepts of IHL.

5. Rationale of the Reasoning

Although IHL instruments benefit from a widespread acceptance in the ECHR Contracting States, the Court's resort to them has been very circumspect and marked by implicit references. In this strand of its case law, the Court has leaned towards the closed paradigm. This reluctance on the part of the Court to refer directly to IHL could be due to technical reasons, such as the lack of cases relating to derogations entered under Article 15 of the ECHR in the context of internal hostilities or armed conflicts.[190] It could also be explained by the numerous differences in the application of IHL and human rights law.[191] Moreover, it could be caused by the judges' lack of experience with IHL and the fact that they find themselves incompetent in this field.[192]

The Court's approach is also rooted, at least in part, in political reasons and in the need to avoid imposing its views upon the Contracting States. The explicit application of IHL to certain confrontations can be viewed as a stigmatization of the situation. States sometimes refuse to apply humanitarian law to non-international conflicts for reasons which are more political than legal.[193] For some, the application of IHL implies a tacit acknowledgement that another party exerts power in a sovereign state.[194] It could also be that the ambiguity in the scope of common Article 3 to the Geneva Conventions effectively allows states the opportunity to evade the responsibility to adhere to its provisions.[195] Furthermore, the recognition of the application of common Article 3 carries with it the fear of conceding that the government is unable to halt large-scale violence, that rebels have the international personality required to carry on diplomacy, or that rebels merit the prisoner of war status and immunity from criminal prosecution.[196] Acknowledging that Additional Protocol II applies could mean that a group other than the government exercises control over parts of the state's territory.[197] Furthermore, applying Additional Protocol I to a conflict could constitute a Government's admission that it is occupying a state against the will of the inhabitants.[198] Some states could also refuse to apply IHL to a non-international conflict by claiming that it would infringe the principles of sovereignty and non-intervention. Moreover, the difficulties involved in measuring the intensity of non-international armed conflicts render the classification complicated. Thus, despite the legal advantages of applying

[190] Guellali (n 1 above), 549. [191] Ibid, 549–550. [192] Ibid, 550.
[193] Abresch (n 27 above), 756. [194] Ibid.
[195] Anthony Cullen, 'Key Developments Affecting the Scope of Internal Armed Conflict in International Humanitarian Law' (2005) 183 Mil L Rev 66, 85.
[196] Abresch (n 27 above), 754. See also Cullen, ibid, 85–86. [197] Ibid. [198] Ibid.

IHL, certain states refuse to comply with its requirements because they consider that the political cost is too high.

In the ECtHR cases discussed above, it is unlikely that the respondent Governments would have welcomed the finding that IHL applies to the confrontations occurring in their territories. The Russian Government, for instance, refused to recognize the existence of an armed conflict in Chechnya, stating that the events occurring there constituted acts of terrorism.[199] Russia ratified the Geneva Conventions of 12 August 1949 on 10 May 1954 and the two Additional Protocols on 29 September 1989,[200] and these instruments should have been applied to the situation.[201] The conflict clearly reached the threshold of application of common Article 3 to the Geneva Conventions. Russia's leaders, however, tried to deflect international scrutiny away from the Chechen conflict by arguing that they were fighting terrorism.[202]

Similarly, the Turkish Government argued that there was no armed conflict with the PKK, and characterized the operations conducted by the security and armed forces as counter-terrorism measures.[203] Turkey ratified the Geneva Conventions of 12 August 1949 on 10 February 1954, but it never signed or ratified the two Additional Protocols. The conflict between the Turkish Government and the PKK does seem to fall under common Article 3 to the Geneva Conventions. The Turkish Government argued, however, that it did not constitute an armed conflict within the meaning of the Geneva Conventions. In the Government's view, this was because the PKK did not respect the rules of war, that its unilateral declaration of a 'cease-fire' had no effect on the organization's legal status, that it did not control territory in the sense of being able to conduct military operations and implement humanitarian law, and that its attacks occurred in Turkey and other states, which negated the concept of civil war or armed conflict.[204]

[199] Ibid; Human Rights Watch, *In the Name of Counter-Terrorism: Human Rights Abuses Worldwide—III. Country Studies: The Human Rights Impact of Counter-Terrorism in Ten Countries*, Briefing Paper for the 59th Session of the United Nations Commission on Human Rights, 25 March 2003, 18.

[200] International Committee of the Red Cross, Table of signatures, ratifications, accessions and successions, available at <http://www.icrc.org/ihl> (last visited 13 June 2010).

[201] It should be noted, however, that the Constitutional Court of the Russian Federation (Конституционный Суд Российской Федерации) recognized (on 31 July 1995) the applicability of Additional Protocol II with respect to the armed conflict in Chechnya and admitted that the Protocol was not duly respected because insufficient measures had been taken for national implementation of its provisions. This opinion was not shared by the Executive. See International Committee of the Red Cross, 'International Humanitarian Law—National Implementation: National Case Law', available at <http://www.icrc.org/ihl-nat.nsf/46707c419d6bdfa24125673e00508145/ac8db8b32b8a2a5d432564dc0048bda4!OpenDocument> (last visited 13 June 2010); Paola Gaeta, 'The Armed Conflict in Chechnya before the Russian Constitutional Court' (1996) 7 Eur J Int'l L 563.

[202] Human Rights Watch (n 202 above), 18.

[203] Abresch (n 27 above), 755.

[204] David Turns, 'At the "Vanishing Point" of International Humanitarian Law: Methods and Means of Warfare in Non-International Armed Conflicts' (2002) 45 GYIL 115, 133.

From the foregoing considerations, it appears that the political climate of the cases decided by the ECtHR was clearly heated and difficult to ignore. The Court's unwillingness to apply IHL directly to these cases can be explained, at least in part, by the fact that the Contracting States were opposed to the application of this body of law. As a consequence, the Court refrained from imposing its will on the Contracting States and preferred to respect their margin of appreciation in order to maintain its institutional credibility (to ensure that its decisions were respected by these States in the future). The Court's caution could also have been prompted by the uncertainty of certain IHL rules. This extremely sensitive area certainly required a considerable amount of political and legal dexterity in the manipulation of IHL concepts. Only in *Engel and others v The Netherlands*[205] did the political context not play a role in the Court's analysis. Given that there was no armed conflict, the Court did not hesitate to apply IHL together with the ECHR to this case of unequal treatment of different military ranks.

It should be reiterated and emphasized that, according to the International Committee of the Red Cross, 'the ascertainment whether there is a non-international armed conflict does not depend on the subjective judgment of the parties to the conflict; it must be determined on the basis of objective criteria'.[206] The Court's reasoning should also comply with this requirement. Interestingly, it was determined, albeit only implicitly, that the situation in Turkey and Chechnya reached the threshold of a non-international armed conflict. The lack of a more explicit acknowledgement of the application of IHL may have introduced further uncertainty as to the classification of the situation in these regions. The Court should therefore not defer to the views of the Contracting States involved in the conflict when determining the threshold reached in a given case.

Another important characteristic of the Strasbourg case law in this field is the distinct contrast between the approach adopted by the Commission and that used by the Court. The Commission used a more progressive, liberal, and receptive methodology in examining IHL issues. In this way, it almost embraced the approach which later became the dominant trend in international law and practice. In contrast to this, the ECtHR mainly resorted to the ECHR to resolve the cases at hand and referred to IHL indirectly by using the vocabulary and reasoning specific to this field of law. In this way, it circumvented international practice, which treats IHL as the *lex specialis* in situations of armed conflict. This approach cannot be characterized as being receptive to IHL. Most importantly, the Court explicitly announced recently that it will be non-receptive to and will not consider the applicability of IHL. Despite this, the Court's attitude does not seem to change the fact that its reasoning, albeit convoluted, did indirectly incorporate

[205] *Engel and others v The Netherlands* (n 71 above).

[206] International Committee of the Red Cross, Working Paper, 28 June 1999, available at <http://www.iccnow.org/documents/ICRCWorkPaperArticle8Para2e.pdf> (last visited 13 June 2010).

the relevant IHL norms relating to non-international armed conflicts and that thereby the Court has reached results similar to those that would ensue from a direct application of IHL. It is yet to be seen, however, how the Court's case law will evolve following the Court's more receptive approach and explicit use of IHL in the *Korbely* case.[207]

Overall, the Court has leaned towards the closed paradigm in this strand of its jurisprudence. It has, however, reduced to some extent the fragmentation between the ECHR and IHL by implicitly incorporating certain standards contained in the Geneva Conventions and Additional Protocols. It would have been more appropriate to acknowledge the sources of the Court's inspiration in these cases. Nevertheless, implicit references have also enabled the Court to harmonize the ECHR with some IHL standards. Furthermore, the lack of explicit reception and the reliance on the closed paradigm did not prevent the Court from making substantial contributions to the IHL framework by either expanding it or adducing additional requirements.[208] With regard to the precaution principle, the Strasbourg Court has required states to have an efficient information transmission system to warn pilots about the presence of civilians.[209] It has also required states to warn the civilian population of a probable arrival of rebels. With regard to the accountability of states, the Court found it essential to obtain a state's report regarding the planning and results of a military operation. It has also required states to conduct a thorough investigation into civilian deaths in the context of non-international conflicts. These findings have undoubtedly reinforced the IHL as well as the ECHR frameworks by providing further protection to the civilian population in the context of armed conflicts. Thus, it transpires from the foregoing analysis that both frameworks can complement each other and maximize the protection available.

[207] *Korbely v Hungary* (App No 9174/02) (n 163 above).
[208] Gaggioli and Kolb (n 4 above), 3. [209] Ibid.

Conclusion

1. Preliminary Observations

This study evaluates the approach that the Commission and the Court have taken to the reception of international law. Although exclusively aimed at applying and enforcing the ECHR, the jurisdiction of the Strasbourg bodies has become porous to international sources and influences. The previous chapters have evaluated the tendencies appearing in the permeation of six special regimes (child rights, refugee rights, civil and political rights, state immunity, international humanitarian law, and prohibition against torture) and two general regimes (the Law of Treaties and the International Court of Justice) into the Strasbourg case law. As such, they have defined with greater precision the level of reception of these sources in accordance with the interpretative approach chosen by the Strasbourg bodies. As part of this synthesis, it remains to be determined how the Court and the Commission have behaved overall with respect to the regimes chosen. One of the aims of this concluding chapter is to evaluate the cross-cutting factors which have had a bearing on the approach of the Strasbourg bodies. It will then be determined whether the ECHR system is integrated into the international legal order and how the Court perceives itself in this context. Further, it will be crucial to establish whether the Court and the Commission have the potential to reduce fragmentation of international law at the European level. Finally, as no legal regime is an island, the ECHR system has to be viewed in the context of its interactions with the outside world. For this reason, the behaviour of the Strasbourg bodies will be evaluated from a wider perspective, namely through the prism of fragmented international law.

In light of the content of the previous chapters, three basic aspects will be evaluated in this synthesis. First, the various factors which have played a role in the reception of international law will be explored. In this context, the aim is to list the most influential cross-cutting factors which appeared in the case law. Secondly, the influence of these factors will be evaluated from a comparative perspective. This will allow the reasons which have prompted the references to international law in the Strasbourg case law to be defined with greater precision. In this context, the research results obtained with regard to each regime will be compared and evaluated. Finally, it will be determined how the nature of the ECHR special regime has influenced the Strasbourg bodies' interactions with other regimes and the fragmentation of international law at the European level.

2. Cross-Cutting Factors: To Receive or Not to Receive?

The general interpretative frameworks outlined in the Introduction[1] to this work provide the basis for the Court's predisposition to international law, namely its willingness or reluctance to refer to each special and general regime. In addition, the Court and Commission have demonstrated that there are specific factors which have a bearing on the receptiveness of the Strasbourg bodies. They are the starting point which essentially determines whether references will occur in a given field. The factors listed below concern specific considerations pertaining to the nature of the relevant ECHR provisions, the nature of the international instrument considered, and the nature of the dispute and circumstances of the case. They have determined to a large extent the frequency and intensity of the Strasbourg bodies' references to international sources. As such, these factors have further defined and refined the approach already taken by the Court and Commission along the lines of the two interpretation frameworks. Furthermore, the reception process was never based on a single factor, and different factors were usually combined in the reasoning of the Strasbourg bodies.

2.1 International Law Invoked at the Domestic Level

In most cases evaluated in the preceding chapters, the reception of international law was facilitated by the fact that the relevant international legal sources were either invoked by the parties at the domestic level or were applied by the domestic courts in their judgments. Both bodies probably felt that under such circumstances the Contracting States would not contest their use of these external sources. The fact that international instruments had been previously invoked provided a rubber stamp and gave more confidence to the Court and the Commission. As these instruments were already part of the case, the Strasbourg bodies probably considered that they would not be criticized by Contracting States if they also referred to them. Such references were treated as a legitimate reliance on international law and increased the receptiveness of the Strasbourg bodies. Naturally, there were also cases with no apparent references to international law at the domestic level, where the Court or the Commission relied on international law in their reasoning. It is not possible, however, to determine with certainty whether any such international law references did not occur in the earlier phases of the case, namely during the hearings at the domestic level or in Strasbourg, without conducting further research into the relevant archives.

[1] See Introduction, 2.1 and 2.2.

2.2 Cases Intertwined with International Law

When cases were very closely intertwined with a certain international procedure, it became almost impossible for the Court or the Commission not to refer to international law. In those instances, the Commission and the Court behaved in a receptive manner, simply because international law had already been part of the legal reasoning or the parties' pleadings in the case. These references to international law were not surprising or impressive, as they were a necessary part of the reasoning. This occurred, for instance, in a specific category of cases which were intertwined with the Hague Convention on the Civil Aspects of International Child Abduction and the Hague Convention on Protection of Children and Cooperation in respect of Intercountry Adoption. The Hague Conventions were ratified by most ECHR Contracting States, and have become the *modus operandi* in matters which they regulate. Thus, the Court and the Commission did not have any choice other than to refer to the relevant international instruments. Thus, the Court felt confident enough to intervene in the domestic application of the Hague Convention on International Abduction, finding that the domestic courts had misinterpreted the instrument.[2]

The situation was also similar in refugee cases intertwined with domestic asylum proceedings.[3] These proceedings were often based on the Convention relating to the Status of Refugees, which *ipso facto* made its way into the decisions and judgments of the Strasbourg bodies. Moreover, the Court was prompted by the necessity to refer to international law in the *Bosphorous* case,[4] which was closely intertwined with a decision taken by the UN Security Council under the UN Charter (and a subsequent decision of the European Union).

There were also cases which required a reference as a condition for resolving the dispute at hand.[5] This occurred, for instance, in cases closely entwined with the International Covenant on Civil and Political Rights (ICCPR),[6] which were introduced before the Human Rights Committee (HRC) and the Court. These cases concerned the coexistence of both bodies, and the Court had to refer to the procedure undertaken before the HRC in order to reach a solution in the case. Another example of this category of case can be found in *Banković and others v Belgium and 16 Other Contracting States*[7] and *Ilaşcu v Moldova and Russia*,[8] where

[2] *Monory v Romania and Hungary* (App No 71099/01), judgment, 5 April 2005, not reported.
[3] See ch VI, 2.1–2.3, especially 2.2.3.
[4] *Bosphorous Hava Yolları Turizm ve Ticaret Anonim Şirketi v Ireland* (App No 45036/98), judgment, 30 June 2005, Reports 2005-VI, 107.
[5] Christos L Rozakis, 'The European Judge as Comparatist' (2005) 80(1) Tul L Rev 257, 275.
[6] See ch IV, 2.1.
[7] *Banković and others v Belgium and 16 Other Contracting States* (App No 52207/99), decision, Reports 2001-XII, 333, para 320.
[8] *Ilaşcu and others v Moldova and Russia* (App No 48787/99), judgment, 8 July 2004, Reports 2004-VII, 179, para 57.

the ECHR dealt with jurisdiction questions in relation to the principle of state responsibility in international law.

2.3 The Need to Harmonize a Provision with International Law

Another important factor having a bearing on the reception of international law at the ECHR level is the necessity to update the Convention's meaning. International instruments have been used as evidence of current human rights standards.[9] In fact, the Court has justified a particular interpretation of the ECHR by claiming that it is consistent with the treatment of the same issue under a different international treaty. This interpretation technique ensures that international human rights law develops consistently and that it constitutes a coherent branch of international law as 'human rights law', as opposed to a number of disparate treaty provisions.[10]

Harmonization has been used by the Commission and the Court to bring the ECHR in line with current standards in the area of child rights.[11] The ECHR contains very few explicit references to children and lacks any firm recognition of their rights. Moreover, little guidance was provided in the ECHR as to how these rights should be articulated. This situation has evolved over time, as the Court and the Commission have adapted the ECHR to changing domestic and international standards. As a result, the ECHR has become increasingly child-friendly.

The harmonization method was also used in cases concerning civil and political rights. For instance, in the *Groppera Radio AG and others v Switzerland* case[12] the Court attempted to harmonize Article 10 of the ECHR with Article 19 of the ICCPR. In that case, the Court held that licensing of broadcasting, authorized under Article 10(1) of the ECHR, had to fulfil the conditions laid down in Article 10(2) and could not be left entirely to a Contracting State's discretion. The Court supported this reasoning using Article 19 of the ICCPR[13] and its negotiating history, which do not contain any reference to licensing. According to the Court, this view confirmed the conclusion that Article 10(1) of the ECHR allowed states to control broadcasting by means of a licensing system, but it did not entail that licensing measures could be exempted from Article 10(2) requirements.

Similarly, in the *Riener*[14] and *Bartik*[15] cases, the Court attempted to harmonize Article 2 of Protocol No 4 with Article 12 of the ICCPR, both guaranteeing the freedom of movement. The Court referred to the ICCPR in an unhindered

[9] John Graham Merrills, *The Development of International Law by the European Court of Human Rights* (Manchester/New York: Manchester University Press, 2nd edn, 1993), 222.

[10] Ibid, 224.

[11] See ch III, 4 and 5.

[12] *Groppera Radio AG and others v Switzerland* (App No 10890/84), judgment, 28 March 1990, Series A, Vol 273. See ch IV, 2.2.2.

[13] *Groppera Radio AG and others v Switzerland* (n 12 above).

[14] *Riener v Bulgaria* (App No 46343/99), judgment, 23 May 2006, not reported. See ch IV, 2.2.9.

[15] *Bartik v Russia* (App No 55565/00), judgment, 21 December 2006, not reported. See ch IV, 2.2.9.

manner in those cases. This was due, in part, to the textual resemblance between Article 12 of the ICCPR and Article 2 of Protocol No 4 and to the fact that the former served as a basis to draft the latter. These references to the ICCPR served to support the Court's reasoning and to clarify further the meaning of the requirements under Article 2 of Protocol No 4.

The notion of harmonization has been seen by the ILC Study Group from the point of view of the systemic interpretation rule contained in Article 31(3)(c) of the Vienna Convention on the Law of Treaties (VCLT).[16] In this context, harmonization acquires a broader meaning which implies that treaties are part of the international legal system; they must be interpreted as being part of a whole and in accordance with the general principles of international law. Article 31(3)(c) has been read recently with renewed interest in the context of fragmentation and judicial interpretation of international law. It has been considered that systemic interpretation could be one of the possible ways to deal with the lack of unity and normative conflicts in international law.[17]

Systemic interpretation, as contained in Article 31(3)(c) of the VCLT, has also been applied by the Strasbourg bodies in their case law. As already indicated, these references have been scarce and problematic given that the Court and the Commission have not addressed the uncertainties inherent in this provision, applying it only in a mechanical manner. The Strasbourg bodies have resorted to Article 31(3)(c)[18] in cases where substantive issues of great importance for the protection of human rights presented themselves, such as state immunity, reservations, access to court, jurisdiction, and interim measures.[19] Some of the cases also concerned child abduction and adoption cases, and these were analysed in Chapter III.[20] It is possible that the Commission and the Court needed Article 31(3)(c) of the VCLT as a rubber stamp to legitimate its use of international law.

It is, nonetheless, puzzling that the Court has not resorted to this provision in other cases referring to international instruments. It can be argued that, in most cases where the Court incorporated international law into its reasoning, it could have resorted to this provision indirectly.[21] However, the references to Article 31(3)(c) do not exhibit any coherent trend in the Court's approach. The Court probably avoided citing this provision explicitly due to the interpretation problems it presents. As a result, any deductions on the basis of the Court's case

[16] United Nations General Assembly, *Fragmentation of International Law: Difficulties Arising from the Diversification and Expansion of International Law*, Report of the Study Group of the International Law Commission, finalized by Martti Koskenniemi, International Law Commission, 58th session, 1 May to 9 June and 3 July to 11 August 2006, UN Doc No A/CN.4/L.682, 13 April 2006, 25 and 206.

[17] See ch I, 2.4.

[18] Ibid.

[19] See ch I, 2.4.2.

[20] See ch III, 2.3.1 and 3.2.

[21] François Ost, 'The Original Canons of Interpretation of the European Court of Human Rights' in Mireille Delmas-Marty and Christine Chodakiewicz (eds), *The European Convention for the Protection of Human Rights: International Protection versus National Restriction* (Dordrecht/Boston/London: Martinus Nijhoff, 1992), 283, 288; Alastair Mowbray, 'The Creativity of the European Court of Human Rights' (2005) 5 HRLR 57, 59; Merrills (n 9 above), 69.

law regarding the operationalization of this rule in the context of fragmentation are difficult to make.

2.4 Use in the Drafting of the ECHR

When a provision to be interpreted was inspired by another international treaty dealing with the topic, the Court and the Commission have naturally turned to this instrument for guidance.[22] This allowed them to expand the meaning of the Convention in an uncontroversial manner. As mentioned in the preceding section, this interpretation technique was applied in the *Riener*[23] and the *Bartik*[24] cases, where the Court attempted to harmonize Article 2 of Protocol No 4 with Article 12 of the ICCPR (guaranteeing the freedom of movement). The Court referred to the ICCPR in an unhindered manner in those cases due to the textual resemblance between Article 12 of the ICCPR and Article 2 of Protocol No 4 and to the fact that the former served as a basis to draft the latter.

This interpretation mode was also used in the *Van der Mussele* case[25]—a representative example—where the Court analysed the meaning of 'forced or compulsory labour' which was included, albeit not defined, in Article 4 of the ECHR. As the *travaux préparatoires* were of little assistance, the Court turned to ILO Convention No 29. The Court considered that it was evident 'that the authors of the European Convention—following the example of the authors of Article 8 of the draft International Covenant on Civil and Political Rights—based themselves, to a large extent, on an earlier treaty of the International Labour Organisation, namely Convention No 29 concerning Forced or Compulsory Labour'.[26] Noting that there was a striking similarity between Article 4(3) of the ECHR and Article 2(2) of ILO Convention No 29, the Court considered that the definition of 'forced or compulsory labour' could provide a starting point for the interpretation of Article 4 of the ECHR.[27]

These types of references are perhaps the most natural and useful in seeking guidance with regard to the ECHR given that they originate from the instrument which inspired them. As such, they are more legitimate than other references and are bound to awaken less disagreement on the part of Contracting States if used. They also play an essential role in shedding further light on the ECHR provisions. Furthermore, they constitute an important means for the development of coherent case law in areas where several instruments may overlap. It should be noted, however, that few

[22] Merrills, ibid, 218. See with regard to domestic courts, Basil S Markesinis and Jörg Fedtke, *Judicial Recourse to Foreign Law: A New Source of Inspiration, University of Texas at Austin, Studies in Foreign and Transnational Law* (London: University College London Press, 2006) 135–137.

[23] *Riener v Bulgaria* (n 14 above).

[24] *Bartik v Russia* (n 15 above).

[25] *Van der Mussele v Belgium* (App No 8919/80), judgment, 23 November 1983, Series A, Vol 70. See ch III, 5.2.

[26] Ibid, para 32.

[27] Ibid.

of the instruments considered here have had a bearing on the creation of the ECHR framework, given that most of them came into force after the ECHR.

2.5 Uncertainty Regarding International Law

A factor which appears to have inhibited the Court's reception of international law is the uncertainty which pervades some of its areas. There are numerous issues which remain unsettled or which are still subject to international debate. Given the difficulties of reaching a universal agreement among non-homogenous states, international law is sometimes unable to provide precise and unequivocal answers. Further, due to the existence of divergent interpretations of certain international instruments, it may be increasingly difficult for the Court to rely on international law. When international law is unsettled or vague, it becomes more difficult for the Court to rely on it as an aid to interpretation. In fact, reliance on international sources defeats its initial purpose if it is unable to assist the Court.

The Court was often reluctant to engage with international law. This approach can be seen, for instance, in cases concerning internal conflicts, normally regulated by international humanitarian law (IHL). The Court did not explicitly refer in these cases to IHL instruments, but instead transplanted their vocabulary into its reasoning. This curious approach could be due, in part, to the uncertain nature of some IHL rules dealing with non-international conflicts. The Court bypassed these uncertainties by mechanically applying certain IHL rules and not acknowledging their sources.

The influence of unsettled international debate can also be seen in the Strasbourg case law concerning the constitutive elements of the definition of torture. The Court adopted a mixed approach to the distinction between torture and inhuman or degrading treatment.[28] This approach included purpose-oriented and severity-oriented components. While a number of commentators support the severity-oriented theory, others maintain that the distinction between torture and other inhuman acts is grounded in the purpose of the behaviour.[29] Thus, the practice and doctrine are not unequivocal with regard to the approach that should be adopted towards this distinction. Against this background, it becomes apparent why the Strasbourg case law has followed both approaches and has not taken a stand with regard to either one of them.

Another example of the impact of uncertainty in international law emerged in cases concerning state immunity. There is in practice disagreement as to the exact scope of the doctrine of state immunity.[30] Thus, it could be that the differences in opinion among judges in the ECHR cases dealing with state immunity[31] reflect

[28] See ch V, 2.1. [29] Ibid, 2.1.1. [30] See ch VIII, 1.3.

[31] *Fogarty v United Kingdom* (App No 37112/97), judgment, 21 November 2001, Reports 2001-XI, 157; *Mc Elhinney v United Kingdom* (App No 31253/96), judgment, 21 November 2001, Reports 2001-XI, 37; *Al-Adsani v United Kingdom* (App No 35763/97), judgment, 12 December 2001, Reports 2001-XI, 79.

the discord that exists in the international legal discourse.[32] In view of these circumstances and the debate at the international level, it becomes more difficult to criticize the Court for misapplying or misinterpreting the relevant international instruments.

Similarly, the Court's treatment of *jus cogens* norms in the cases on state immunity was influenced by the confusion originating from international law.[33] The majority of judges recognized that the prohibition on torture has the status of a *jus cogens* norm and that it precedes other rules of international law. However, it was also considered that, in the absence of an established international law rule, the prohibition on torture does not have this status in civil proceedings. The Court thus distinguished the consequences of a *jus cogens* norm on the basis of the nature of the proceedings. In its view, the *jus cogens* norm of prohibition on torture would only prevail in criminal proceedings. There is, however, no apparent requirement that the effect of a *jus cogens* norm should change according to the nature of the proceedings. Further, a *jus cogens* norm which changes from one situation to the next would not have a peremptory effect. It therefore seems that the Court's reasoning is contradictory. It must be specified, however, that the ECtHR was the first international court to address the effect of *jus cogens* over state immunity at the international law level.[34] The Court's treatment of this type of norm appears to have been influenced, in part, by the lack of precision and certainty in international law.

Although the Strasbourg bodies have incorporated the uncertainties of international law into some areas of their case law, there have also been instances where they have explicitly announced that unsettled international law is of no assistance to them. For instance, in the *Civil Service Unions* case,[35] the Commission found that the differences in language contained in international law instruments demonstrated that there was no settled view under international law as to the position of members of the administration of the state in respect of trade union rights. Thus, it was found that the international instruments invoked by the applicants could be discarded. This practice should, however, be contrasted with the Strasbourg bodies' application of Article 31(3)(c) of the VCLT, where they did not feel inhibited by the uncertainties relating to this provision.[36] The Court and the Commission seem to have applied this provision mechanically without fully engaging with its problematic aspects. There are, nonetheless, few explicit references to this provision in the Strasbourg case law. Moreover, they seem to be grounded in the necessity of the situation and the Strasbourg bodies' selectivity in applying the required sources.

[32] Bernard H Oxman and Marius Emberland, 'Case note' (2002) 96 Am J Int'l L 699, 704. See ch VIII, 1.3.

[33] See ch VIII, 3.2.1.3 and 3.2.2.

[34] Ed Bates, 'The Al-Adsani Case, State Immunity and the International Legal Prohibition on Torture' (2003) 3(2) HRLR 193, 221.

[35] *Civil Service Unions and others v United Kingdom* (App No 11603/85), decision, 20 January 1987, DR 50, 228. See ch IV, 2.2.1.

[36] See ch I, 2.4.

The uncertainty of international law inhibits its reception at the European level. The Court's use of international instruments is often justified by their utility; if international law cannot be of assistance, then it is often set aside by the Court. Uncertainty and vagueness are not novel problems in international law. As part of its references, the Court is bound to encounter this problem on a regular basis. An important aspect to keep in mind is not to deepen the existing divides or uncertainties in international law. Although the Court was not set up for this purpose, it should ideally try to contribute towards resolving these uncertainties. Such an approach would be particularly welcome from one of the most influential international human rights courts in the context of contemporary fragmented legal realities.

2.6 The Need to Fill in Gaps

In a number of cases, the Court addressed issues which were not explicitly regulated by the ECHR. Taking a bold approach, it has decided on occasion to fill such gaps on its own. Further, given that the ECHR was concluded almost 60 years ago, the Court often felt compelled to update its content through evolutive interpretation in certain important areas. This approach sometimes entailed reading into or finding implied rights in the Convention. Although it contributed to the protection of human rights, the Court's methodology was met with intense criticism, often from its own members, claiming that it was performing a legislative function.

The Court decided in *Golder v United Kingdom*[37] that the right of access to court was inherent in Article 6(1) of the ECHR. Using Article 31(3)(c) of the VCLT, the Court referred to Article 38(1)(c) of the ICJ Statute which includes, among the relevant legal sources, 'general principles of law recognized by civilized nations'. The Court considered that the principle whereby a civil claim must be capable of being submitted to a judge constituted a fundamental principle of law. Further, the prohibition of denial of justice was another such principle of international law. Thus, the Court found that Article 6(1) of the ECHR had to be read in the light of these principles and based itself, *inter alia*, on these principles to include a right which was not previously contained in the ECHR.

Another representative example of gap filling occurred in the *Mamatkulov* judgment.[38] The Grand Chamber held that interim measures acquired a binding character under the ECHR. The Court was influenced here, *inter alia*, by the *LaGrand (Germany v United States of America)* case[39] where the International Court of Justice (ICJ) found that interim measures had an obligatory character.

[37] *Golder v United Kingdom* (App No 4451/70), judgment, 21 February 1975, Series A, Vol 18. See ch II, 2.2 and ch I, 1 and 2.4.2.

[38] *Mamatkulov and Askarov v Turkey* (App Nos 46827/99; 46951/99), judgment, 4 February 2005, Reports 2005-I, 293. See also *Mamatkulov and Abdurasulovic v Turkey* (App Nos 46827/99; 46951/99), judgment, 6 February 2003, not reported. See ch I, 2.3 and 2.4.2 and ch II, 2.6.

[39] *LaGrand (Germany v United States of America)*, judgment, 27 June 2001, ICJ Reports 2001, 466.

Thus, it reversed previous case law on the topic,[40] which had established interim measures on the basis of Contracting States' practice. While in 1991 the old Court found that no power to order binding interim measures could be inferred from the ECHR, the new Court decided in 2003 and 2005 that such an inference was nonetheless possible. While it seemed like a radical innovation, the remedying of such omissions was a fundamental step for the preservation and strengthening of the ECHR machinery. The Court's approach has aided in ensuring that the provisions of the ECHR remain practical and effective. The cases mentioned above concern issues which are of crucial importance for the good functioning of the ECHR system. As a result, gap filling or remedying of omissions appears to occur mostly in cases where an update is necessary to preserve the efficiency of the ECHR.

2.7 Textual and Substantive Similarities

The Strasbourg bodies' willingness to refer to external sources was conditioned, in some cases, by the similarities that exist between the ECHR and other international instruments. These similarities were conducive to the reception of international law in situations where the Court and the Commission wanted to clarify or expand the meaning of the ECHR. Being unable to find guidance within their own jurisdiction, they turned to documents which most resembled the ECHR. Most similarities appeared within the ECHR and other international human rights regimes given that they cover similar areas and strive for the same goals. There were few similarities between the ECHR and the two areas of general international law discussed in this work.

From a substantive point of view, the ICCPR is most akin to the ECHR as it contains a similar catalogue of civil and political rights, provides for an individual complaint procedure, and has analogous aims. References to this instrument were therefore not unusual or unduly strenuous for the Strasbourg bodies. Further, there are several textual parallels between the ICCPR,[41] ILO Convention No 29,[42] and the ECHR framework, which have also made the reception process much easier. These textual resemblances are due in part to the fact that the three instruments have served in the drafting of the ECHR and its Protocols. Thus, the Court and the Commission have also been compelled to consider sources that have influenced the creation of the ECHR framework.[43]

2.8 More Specific Guidelines in International Law

The ECHR encompasses an extensive array of human rights. Its provisions are often vague and general, which naturally prompts the need on the part of the Court and the Commission to develop them. In this context, it was often

[40] *Cruz Varas and others v Sweden* (App No 15576/89), judgment, 20 March 1991, Series A, Vol 201.
[41] See ch IV, 2.2.9.
[42] See ch III, 5.2.
[43] See 2.4 above.

necessary for the Strasbourg bodies to use international instruments, as they were more specific and provided more guidance than the ECHR. This occurred in cases where the Court and the Commission wanted to harmonize the ECHR with international law, to put flesh on to ECHR provisions, as well as to remedy an omission. In these instances, the Court's methodology was also motivated by the specificity of the relevant international instrument. Thus, a general factor underlying many references appears to have been the lack of precision of the ECHR in certain areas and the corresponding need to seek guidance elsewhere. This occurred, for instance, in relation to the definition of torture, the adoption and abduction of children, treaty interpretation rules, as well as civil and political rights. Curiously, the Court's references to IHL—the *lex specialis* in the field of armed conflicts—were made *sub silentio* and the legal sources were not formally acknowledged in the Court's reasoning. However, this trend appears to have been the result of exceptional circumstances in the Strasbourg case law which can be explained on the basis of the controversial nature of the political issues involved.

2.9 The Need to Assess the Human Rights Situation in a Country

The Court has relied on reports originating from international organizations in expulsion cases under Article 3 of the ECHR when it has needed to evaluate the situation in the country receiving the applicant to be expelled. In fact, when the Court assesses the risk of mistreatment, it considers all the material placed before it or, if necessary, material obtained on its own initiative.[44] It is in principle for the applicant to provide evidence capable of proving that he/she would be exposed to a real risk of being subjected to treatment contrary to Article 3 of the ECHR. Further, the Court clarified in *Saadi v Italy*[45] that, in order to determine whether there is a risk of ill-treatment, it must examine the general situation in the receiving country. In the past, 'it has often attached importance to the information contained in recent reports from independent international human-rights-protection associations such as Amnesty International, or governmental sources, including the US State Department'.[46] While this material is not the only evidence to be taken into consideration in such cases, it provides relevant information as to the general situation and constitutes a good basis for the Court's evaluation. Thus, the possibility of using independent international reports has recently enhanced the Court's receptiveness of external sources.

[44] *HLR v France* (App No 24573/94), judgment, 29 April 1997, Reports 1997-III, 745, para 37; *Hilal v United Kingdom* (App No 45276/99), judgment, 6 March 2001, Reports 2001-II, 292, para 60; *Saadi v Italy* (App No 37201/06), judgment (Grand Chamber), 28 February 2008, not yet reported, para 128.

[45] *Saadi v Italy* (n 44 above). See ch V, 2.1.2.3.

[46] Ibid, para 131.

2.10 Political Issues and State Interests

The political climate has had a bearing on the level of reception of international law in certain cases. As the evaluation of the Strasbourg case law has demonstrated, the political issues and state interests can both enhance and inhibit the Strasbourg bodies' predisposition to consider international law. While the Court is an independent body which cannot be swayed by political considerations, it does not function in isolation from the context which surrounds it. The Court may feel the need to ensure that its authority is preserved, which requires it to take a pragmatic approach with regard to the standards set in its case law.[47] It remains vulnerable to criticism from Contracting States that it is not taking state practice into account. This aspect is of tremendous importance as the Convention's effectiveness is based on the states' cooperation in implementing the necessary changes into domestic law following a Court ruling.[48]

The Court's approach with regard to IHL may have been influenced by the circumstances surrounding the cases and the states' reluctance to have IHL applied to them.[49] The ECtHR's approach in those cases was based on the exclusive application of the Convention and the indirect references to IHL. In fact, the Court appears to have borrowed the IHL vocabulary and reasoning without acknowledging the source from which they originated. In the ECtHR cases considered, it was unlikely that the respondent Governments (Russia and Turkey) would have welcomed the finding that IHL applies to the confrontations occurring on their territories. Despite the legal advantages of using IHL, certain states refuse to comply with its requirements due to the political cost and stigmatization that it could entail. Being aware of these considerations, the Court may have chosen an approach which accommodates the political climate and the Contracting States' articulated interests.

As part of another political setting, the Court used a diametrically different approach to international law. With regard to the German Democratic Republic (GDR) cases concerning border policing,[50] the Court was overzealous in relying on international instruments. It applied the ICCPR when this instrument was ratified, albeit not implemented, by the GDR. The Covenant had a dubious status at the national level and could hardly be interpreted as invalidating the defences invoked by the applicants that existed under GDR law at the time. In addition, part of the acts committed by the applicants took place before the ICCPR had been ratified by the GDR. Thus, the application of the ICCPR provisions was strained and questionable. Behaving in a very open and receptive

[47] Bates (n 34 above), 213. [48] Ibid, 214. [49] See ch VIII, 5.

[50] *Streletz, Kessler and Krenz v Germany* (App Nos 34044/96; 35532/97; 44801/98), judgment, 22 March 2001, Reports 2001-II, 409; *K-HW v Germany* (App No 37201/97), judgment, 22 March 2001, Reports 2001-II, 495. See ch IV, 2.2.6.

manner, the Court simply applied the relevant ICCPR provisions without further consideration.

This approach could have been prompted, in part, by the fact that the case was intertwined at the domestic level with ICCPR provisions and that the German courts had previously referred to them. However, it seems to be more plausible that the Court was conscious of the political climate surrounding these cases. While the first individuals to have been tried in the reunified Germany were East German border guards,[51] the Germans soon grew weary of trials of those who merely carried out the orders and proceeded to try more important political figures. Given the unsatisfactory outcome of these trials, there was strong pressure to bring the remaining officials of the former GDR to trial. The attempt of the German courts to convict the applicants and the ECtHR's determination to respect their findings are apparent in the artificial and strained legal arguments used.

Thus, the political climate can exert an important influence over the Court's approach to international law, either by inhibiting or by prompting references. While it is difficult for ECtHR judges to ignore the context of a given case, reliance on international law must be conducted with care. A lack of justification or acknowledgement of the international sources used can be detrimental to the unity of international law. Undoubtedly, the Court finds itself at the apex of a delicate balance, but the political climate or states' interests should not impede it from referring to international law in a properly justified manner.

2.11 Advantages of using the ECHR

Another important reason which has discouraged the Court and Commission from referring to international law is the fact that reliance on the ECHR is sometimes more advantageous than other international instruments. The ECHR is clearly one of the most effective instruments to protect human rights at the European level; it contains an extensive catalogue of rights and has a strong enforcement mechanism. While a number of international instruments are more adapted to certain types of violation, the ECHR still contains certain provisions which grant more extensive protection to applicants. Further, the ECHR offers better prospects for enforcement than other international human rights instruments.

For instance, in the case of refugee rights, the Court has clearly been conscious that the ECHR provides greater protection to an applicant, who runs the risk of being tortured or mistreated upon his return or expulsion to a receiving country, than the protection afforded by the 1951 Refugee Convention.[52] In *Chahal v United*

[51] Adrienne Quill, 'To Prosecute or Not To Prosecute: Problems Encountered in the Prosecution of Former Communist Officials in Germany, Czechoslovakia, and the Czech Republic' (1996) 7 IICLR 165, 178–180.

[52] See ch VI, 2.2.3.

Kingdom,[53] a representative case, the Court found that, pursuant to Article 3 of the ECHR, 'the activities of the individual in question, however undesirable or dangerous, cannot be a material consideration. The protection afforded by Article 3 is thus wider than that provided by Articles 32 and 33 of the United Nations 1951 Convention on the Status of Refugees.'[54] It should be noted that the principle of *non-refoulement* under the 1951 Refugee Convention is limited, as Articles 32 and 33 of that Convention provide that a refugee can be expelled on grounds of national security and public order. As underlined by the Court, Article 3 of the ECHR is absolute and does not allow such exceptions.

This distinction between the two instruments may have been prompted by the Court's wish to justify the lack of reliance on the 1951 Refugee Convention in a case which was so closely tied in with this instrument. This statement exceeds the Court's usual references in cases intertwined with international law. By providing further clarifications pertaining to international law on its own initiative, the Court has given greater weight to its reasoning. More importantly, however, it appears that the Court was simply attempting to distance itself from the UNHCR network in order to ensure that certain human rights are better protected. The distinction between the ECHR and the 1951 Refugee Convention seems to have been prompted by the specificity of the ECHR and the necessity of rendering ECHR rights practical and effective.

It is thus not surprising that the Court differentiates the ECHR from other international instruments when these do not ensure the same level of protection or fulfil a different purpose. The Strasbourg bodies have been less receptive and have taken a divergent route when this was justified by the unique requirements of the legal regime within which they operate. For instance, with regard to the case law of the ICJ, the Court explicitly distinguished itself from that Court, finding in the *Loizidou* case[55] that, '[u]nlike international treaties of the classical kind, the Convention comprises more than mere reciprocal engagements between Contracting States. It creates over and above a network of mutual bilateral undertakings, objective obligations which in the words of the preamble benefit from a "collective enforcement".'[56] In this manner, the Court entrenched the special character of the ECHR and distanced itself from the ICJ's case law relating to the opposability of reservations. Thus, the Court's assessment of reservations differs from the ICJ's case law on grounds that the ECHR is a human rights treaty. The Court also wished to underline that the ECHR constitutes the *lex specialis* in this case.

[53] *Chahal v United Kingdom* (App No 22414/93), judgment, 15 November 1996, Reports 1996-V (No 22), 1831.

[54] Ibid, para 80. See also *Kashiyev and Akayera v Russia* (App Nos 57942/00; 57948/00), judgment, 24 February 2005, not reported, para 88, where the Court stated that '[e]ven in the most difficult circumstances, such as the fight against terrorism and organised crime, the Convention prohibits in absolute terms torture and inhuman or degrading treatment or punishment'.

[55] *Loizidou v Turkey (Preliminary Objections)* (App No 15318/89), judgment, 23 March 1995, Series A, Vol 310.

[56] Ibid, para 70. See ch II, 2.2 and 2.4.

2.12 Procedural and Substantive Law

In the Strasbourg case law there are differences in the level of reception of international procedural law and international substantive law. In this context, international procedural law refers to a treaty which sets up a given procedure to follow in order to resolve a dispute; international substantive law, on the other hand, refers to treaties granting concrete rights and obligations to states and individuals. By nature, procedural law is more neutral and does not usually refer to politically charged or controversial issues. Substantive law (especially human rights law) can, unfortunately, be a subject of intense disagreement among Contracting States. The level of reception in the Strasbourg case law has been higher where a case involved an international procedure than where it concerned substantive rights.

This may explain, in part, why the Strasbourg bodies felt less inhibited when referring to the Hague Convention on the Civil Aspects of International Child Abduction[57] and the Hague Convention on Protection of Children and Cooperation in respect of Intercountry Adoption.[58] Both of these instruments set out the procedure to resolve disputes regarding child adoption and abduction. These areas are not tremendously controversial and both treaties benefit from strong support from ECHR Contracting States. In these cases, the Court did not examine complex family questions but more practical aspects concerning the compliance with the ECtHR of decisions taken under the Hague Conventions.

Other references to international procedural law appeared in cases relating to the coexistence of the HRC and the ECtHR.[59] Some cases were introduced before both the Committee and the Court. The Court thus felt the need to refer to the proceedings under the First Optional Protocol in order to clarify its role vis-à-vis the Committee. The fact that certain cases were brought before both bodies enhanced reception, but the references which appeared in the case were not those meant to ensure that international law was harmonized and not fragmented. Rather, they were necessary in order to preserve and define further the coexistence of the bodies in order to avoid cases of litispendence.

While references to international procedural law enhance reception due to their uncontroversial nature, they are not as instructive as references to more substantive provisions. In the cases analysed here, the Strasbourg bodies referred to international law by necessity or due to the lack of controversy. References to substantive international law, such as other international human rights treaties, are usually a source of greater debate at the international level. It is as part of these references that the Court's self-perception in the international legal system can be assessed most satisfactorily. When relying on substantive rights enshrined in international instruments, the Court often has to make a deliberate choice to refer to a debated or controversial provision. This can, at times, compromise its

57 See ch III, 2. 58 Ibid, 3. 59 See ch IV, 2.1.

credibility and authority among Contracting States. References to international procedural law remain, nonetheless, an important part of a comprehensive assessment of the Strasbourg case law.

2.13 Ratification Record

In cases where the Strasbourg bodies referred to international human rights instruments, they also noted that the relevant instrument was ratified by the Contracting State implicated in the case or by a significant number of Contracting States. The Commission and the Court did not want to appear to be imposing additional obligations contained in external documents not approved by the Contracting States. The fact that most Contracting States had adhered to a given international instrument provided greater legitimacy to the Court's reference and greater authority to its reasoning. Consensus among Contracting States constitutes an important factor in maintaining the Court's institutional credibility and in ensuring that its decisions are implemented.

Occasionally, however, the Court was prepared to go further and to invoke the Convention on the Civil Aspects of International Child Abduction even when the state involved had not ratified it at the time of the judgment.[60] While this was particularly courageous, the Court appears to have resolved the matter on the basis of the ECHR. The Court has also invoked the ICCPR when this instrument was ratified, albeit not implemented, by the GDR in border-policing cases.[61]

In child rights cases, the Court has been considerably less receptive to the Convention on the Rights of the Child and the International Labour Organization Convention concerning the Prohibition and Immediate Action for the Elimination of the Worst Forms of Child Labour (ILO Convention No 182) than to the two Hague Conventions. As all four instruments were ratified by most ECHR Contracting States, it appears that the ratification record may not have constituted a dominant factor in the Court's approach. In this context, other elements have played an important role (ie the case was intertwined with international law, domestic law was invoked at the domestic level, similarity of language, and lack of guidelines in the ECHR).

2.14 Universal Reach of International Instruments

The unwillingness of the Strasbourg bodies to depart from the ECHR has been due, in part, to the fact that international instruments have a universal reach and are not specific to the European context. The instruments considered in this

[60] *Barjami v Albania* (App No 35853/04), judgment, 12 December 2006, not reported. See ch III, 2.3.2.

[61] *Streletz, Kessler and Krenz v Germany* (n 50 above).

work have been adapted to issues appearing in all countries, and can bear a different meaning in different parts of the world. Further, the ECHR Contracting States only represent a minority of the States Parties to the international treaties evaluated. As a result, some decisions handed down by the UN treaty bodies concern issues that do not arise in Europe. Furthermore, the UN treaty bodies have a quasi-jurisdictional nature and the ECtHR, rendering binding decisions, has been reluctant to refer to their non-binding conclusions.

Thus, the Court and the Commission have probably considered that referring to other international instruments and international case law would not necessarily contribute to the interpretation of ECtHR rights. The ECHR, a regional instrument, is made up of a relatively homogeneous group of states which have similar economic, social, political, and legal cultures.[62] However, the international treaties considered here apply to States Parties with very diverse backgrounds. While these considerations need to be taken into account, they should not dominate the judges' reasoning. It is important to reiterate that human rights have a universal value and are not merely a Western creation.[63]

2.15 Backgrounds of the Judges

One of the most important factors having a bearing on the tendency of the Commission and Court to refer to international law is the mentality or predisposition of the individual members or judges. It is beyond the scope of this work to analyse the judges' reasoning from a social sciences or multidisciplinary point of view using the required methodology. Such an approach would require taking into account different complex variables, such as psychological factors, ethnic backgrounds, political ideologies, societal perceptions, moral or religious beliefs. These factors play an important part in issues involving immigration, asylum, extradition, the death penalty, and the rights of homosexuals. It is regrettable that judicial mentality has not been studied at greater length and that its importance has been underestimated. This may be due to the fact that it is an area which is difficult to define in a satisfactory manner. It remains, however, that judicial mentality may be the most important inhibitor of the use of international material.[64]

Although inherently weak and unable to grasp the whole situation, certain remarks can still be made from a legal point of view. Several judges, including the former President of the Court, have written about the relation between international law and the ECHR.[65] Undoubtedly, the judges' extra-judicial writings and

[62] See ch III, 6; ch V, 4; and ch VI, 4.

[63] Rosalyn Higgins, 'Ten Years of the UN Human Rights Committee: Some Thoughts upon Parting' (1996) 6 EHRLR 574, 574.

[64] Markesinis and Fedtke (n 22 above), 173–174, 182.

[65] See, for instance, Luzius Wildhaber, 'The European Court of Human Rights and International Law' (2007) 52 Int & Comp LQ 217; Christos L Rozakis, 'The European Judge as Comparatist' (2005) 80(1) Tul L Rev 257; Ineta Ziemele, 'Case-Law of the European Court of Human Rights

speeches might help in understanding the breadth of their culture and willingness to look abroad for inspiration.[66] Another important aspect enhancing reception is the judges' educational and professional background. A survey of judges' CVs appearing on the Court's website demonstrates that 20 of the 46 ECtHR judges have work experience and/or have studied comparative and/or international law. This ratio represents 43.5 per cent of all judges.[67] Thus, it appears that less than half may have the required skills to deal with comparative and international law.

Familiarity with comparative law and comparative methodology is an important tool for supranational judges considering cases arising from one or more of the 47 Contracting States. It also serves as an important factor in establishing whether there is consensus on a given issue among Contracting States. Arguably, knowledge of comparative law is more helpful in the European regional context, and does not influence as such the reception of international law. It is submitted, however, that a judge's acquaintance with comparative law is an indication of his openness towards other legal systems and may also have a bearing on his predisposition to consider international legal sources.

Comparative law aside, the survey of judicial profiles demonstrates that 15 of the 46 judges, ie 32.6 per cent, have experience and/or training in international law. This ratio is much lower than that which concerns comparative law; it represents less than one-third of the ECtHR's judges. Thus, it is possible that more than two-thirds of the judiciary are less predisposed to consider international sources. Clearly, the discussion of international law requires not only that judges possess the required international law skills; the parties pleading before the Court also need to have adequate qualifications.[68] Judges and parties unfamiliar with international law may not be able satisfactorily to evaluate and apply the relevant international sources. Thus, the more regionally oriented background of ECtHR judges may have played an important role in the Court's recent leaning towards the closed paradigm.

2.16 Concluding Remarks

Overall, the Court referred to international law in cases most frequently where an international instrument had been invoked at the domestic level, the case was

and Integrity of International law' in Karel Wellens and Charo Huesa (eds), *L'influence des sources sur l'unité et la fragmentation du droit international* (Brussels: Bruyland, 2006), 187; Lucius Caflisch and Antônio Cançado Trindade, '*Les Conventions Américaine et Européenne des Droits de l'Homme et le Droit International Général*' (2004-I) 108 RGDIP 5.

[66] Markesinis and Fedtke (n 22 above), 173–174, 182.

[67] European Court of Human Rights, Composition of the Court, <http://www.echr.coe.int/ECHR/EN/Header/The+Court/The+Court/Judges+of+the+Court/> (last visited 13 June 2010).

[68] Helen Keller, *Rezeption des Volkerrechts, Max-Planck-Institut für ausländisches öffentliches Recht und Völkerrecht, Beiträge zum ausländischen öffentlichen Recht und Völkerrecht 160* (Berlin/Heidelberg/New York/Barcelona: Springer, 2003), 717 and 753.

intertwined with international law, an international instrument had been used in drafting the ECHR, gaps needed to be filled in the ECHR, and textual and substantive similarities existed between the ECHR and international law. It was also of important, albeit subsidiary, interest to the Court that there were more specific provisions of international law, there was a need to assess the situation in a country, the political climate and state interests favoured such a reference, and the use of the ECHR was more advantageous for the parties. The remaining factors analysed above featured less prominently and less frequently in the Court's case law, but did play an important role in shaping the Court's approach to international law. The factors appearing most frequently indicate that the Court's overall predisposition to consider international law has been careful and measured. It was situated within the realm of references which are necessary due to the nature of the case or due to the effective functioning of the ECHR. The Court seldom used international law when this was not necessary for the good functioning of the ECHR and desirable for the coherent operation of the international legal system. Its approach, therefore, was uncontroversial and within the realm of justified international law references.

3. Basic Characteristics of the Strasbourg Case Law

3.1 The Difference Between the Court and Commission

An important trend emanating from the Strasbourg case law is the marked difference in the international law approaches taken by the two Strasbourg bodies. In three of the areas covered in this work, the Commission has demonstrated itself to be more receptive and less self-centred than the Court. For instance, with regard to cases concerning IHL, the Commission was willing to refer explicitly to the IHL framework, whereas the Court contented itself with indirect references. The Commission used a more progressive and receptive methodology and treated IHL as *lex specialis* in armed conflicts; this later became the dominant trend in international law and practice.[69]

In cases relating to torture, it was apparent from the beginning that the Commission and Court took different approaches to the definition of torture and cruel, inhuman, or degrading treatment.[70] The reasoning used by the Court appears to have been based on the severity of treatment inflicted. The approach taken by the Commission, however, was based on the purpose element of the treatment, and thus was closer to the approach taken by the United Nations in the Convention Against Torture (CAT). The Commission tried to promote the protection of the individual, rejecting a too narrow construction favouring state sovereignty. The Court initially used a more restrictive interpretation of the

[69] See ch VIII, 4 and 5. [70] See ch V, 2.1, 2.1.1, and 4.

notion of torture and finally opted for a mixed approach based on the purpose and severity of the behaviour.

In child rights cases, the Commission used a more progressive and receptive approach to the Convention on the Rights of the Child (CRC) than the Court. Overall, there were fewer references to the CRC in the Court's case law and the statements made were less far-reaching.[71] On occasion, the Court preferred to rely on international instruments other than the CRC. This needs to be contrasted, however, with cases referring to the Hague Convention on the Civil Aspects of International Child Abduction, where the Commission was less receptive; it considered only a few cases regarding this instrument and found no violations in any of them. In contrast, the Court established a more elaborate case law and resorted to a more receptive approach in relation to the Hague Convention on International Child Abduction.

The difference in the level of reception in the Court's and the Commission's case law could perhaps be explained on the basis of their structural differences. Under the old system, the Commission's duty consisted in rendering decisions with regard to the admissibility of applications. If the application was declared admissible, the Commission went on to investigate the merits of the complaint and whether there was a violation of the Convention. The result of this investigation was a report which expressed the Commission's opinion as to whether there was a violation. These reports were not legally binding.[72] Final decisions in cases on which the Commission had reported were taken by the Committee of Ministers or the ECtHR. Although recognition of the Court's jurisdiction was voluntary, there was a clear expectation that Contracting Parties would accept it. Under the new system, the Commission and the Court have been replaced by a single permanent Court, which handles the admissibility and merits phases of the applications. The recognition of the Court's jurisdiction is obligatory for all Contracting States.

As part of this framework, the Commission may have been less insular and introverted than the Court because the opinions expressed in the reports were not binding. Although generally followed by the Court, the Commission's opinions had less weight than the judgments of the Court. The Commission probably felt less pressure to legitimize its references to international law than the Court. It was also less constrained by states' interests and the consensus prevailing at the domestic level. In contrast, the content of the Court's binding judgments was less far-reaching than the broader opinions expressed by the Commission. The references contained in the judgments were also more limited, as the Court had to be careful not to apply international law and not to impose additional international obligations on to Contracting States. As the Court is dependent on

[71] See ch III, 4.

[72] Clare Ovey and Robin White, *The European Convention on Human Rights* (Oxford/New York: OUP, 4th edn, 2006), 9.

the Contracting States for the implementation of the judgments, it was conditioned to some extent by their interests and the consensus that prevailed in their jurisdiction.

3.2 Referring to General Law versus a Special Regime

As part of this work, references to other special regimes and general international law were evaluated. The Strasbourg bodies referred to other special regimes in the case of child rights, torture, armed conflict, state immunity, refugee rights, and civil and political rights. References to general international law analysed in this work include the VCLT as well as the case law and Statute of the ICJ. Cleary, the Court and the Commission followed the special and general regimes dichotomy by emphasizing the special features as well as the different role and purpose of the ECHR. Thus, according to the Strasbourg bodies' view, the ECHR constitutes a special regime. The references considered in this work concerned (i) the relationship between a special regime and another special regime and (ii) the relationship between a special regime and general international law.

The interactions between the ECHR special regime and general international law were problematic. The references to the VCLT were infrequent and applied mechanically. Further, while some references to the ICJ's judgments and Statute appeared in the case law, they were limited by the Court's selectiveness and its finding that important differences existed between the ICJ and ECHR systems. It was initially envisaged that it would be easier for the Strasbourg bodies to rely on a general overarching regime than to refer to a specialized legal domain.[73] However, following an analysis and comparison of both types of regime, this hypothesis has now been refuted.

The level of reception was substantially higher with regard to the other special regimes than to general international law. In all likelihood, the ECtHR felt inhibited by the important differences that still exist between the ECHR and ICJ systems, and found that it was easier to refer to other specialized international human rights systems. These regimes are much closer to the ECHR than the ICJ framework, as they relate to a similar subject-matter. Further, the lack of receptiveness with regard to the VCLT could be explained, in part, by the generality and uncertainties inherent in Articles 31–33 of the VCLT.

The ECHR, as other special regimes, has its own specific objectives and applies its rules on a *lex specialis* basis. These objectives are closer to those of the other special regimes considered, given that both the ECHR and the special regimes concern human rights. It therefore becomes relatively easier—in the context of a single branch of international law, such as human rights law—for more specialized regimes to refer to one another due to their similarities. As a result, it may be easier to remedy the problem of fragmentation at the level of branches of

[73] See Introduction, 4.

international law, given that the interests of its components (ie special regimes) converge. Clearly, such a function-based approach would target certain localized problems more efficiently, which then have repercussions in wider spheres.

Problems may also arise when special regimes apply general international law, such as the VCLT, in order to reinforce their jurisdiction and the special nature of the relevant treaty. Pursuing this line of reasoning, they may deviate from standard interpretation and thereby weaken the authority of that interpretation to further their own interests and objectives.[74] This appears to have been a problem in the Court's case law when it referred to the VCLT. Attempting to avoid problematic interpretation issues, the Court applied Articles 31–33 of the VCLT in a selective and mechanical manner when a reference to international law needed to be legitimized. This approach may have deepened further the uncertainties relating to this instrument. Given the very influential nature of the Strasbourg case law, the Court may have entrenched a vague and circular interpretation of Articles 31–33 in the dialogue between international human rights courts. The Strasbourg bodies experienced similar dilemmas with regard to the ICJ's case law and Statute despite attempts to distance and differentiate themselves from this legal framework. In fact, the Court reached a different conclusion from the ICJ with regard to the opposability of treaty reservations. Thus, it reinforced the divide between the Convention and general international law.

3.3 Margin of Appreciation

The margin of appreciation is a general inhibitor to reception across the general and special regimes considered. It limits the Court's jurisdiction in a number of areas where Contracting States have more competence, and indirectly restrains the Court's ability to refer to international law. The Court is often prevented from moving beyond the consensus prevalent among Contracting States. Thus, this doctrine has played a prominent role in the Strasbourg bodies' approach to international law. Generally, the level of reception is closely related to the level of the margin of appreciation. However, some of the areas studied demonstrate that other considerations can have a greater bearing on the reception process.

In matters concerning IHL, where the margin of appreciation is generally high, the level of reception in the case law was low. In fact, the Court usually made indirect references to IHL by using language familiar to this area. In matters concerning state immunities, where Contracting States also have an important discretion, the Court has been moderately receptive to international law. Similarly, with regard to refugee issues, Contracting States have an important discretion given that immigration has a clear impact on economic and social policies. While the Court applied the margin of appreciation in a flexible manner in

[74] Martti Koskenniemi and Päivi Leino, 'Fragmentation of International Law? Postmodern Anxieties' (2002) 15 LJIL 553, 561–562.

this field, it was nonetheless reluctant to refer to international law. In the field of child rights, states have an important margin of appreciation with respect to family law and juvenile justice. In spite of this, the level of reception was high due to the fact that international child rights law is widely accepted among Contracting States.

In contrast, states do not appear to benefit from a significant margin of appreciation with regard to the rights contained in the ICCPR and the CAT. Both instruments contain fundamental human rights which have been accepted by most ECHR Contracting States. With regard to the ICCPR, the Strasbourg bodies were moderately receptive, and with regard to the CAT, the level of reception was generally higher. It therefore does not appear that the margin of appreciation played an important role in the reception of these instruments. In relation to the case law of the Permanent Court of International Justice and the ICJ, as well as the VCLT, the level of the margin of appreciation was less relevant. Both regimes often concern issues which are under the competence of the United Nations and not the ECHR Contracting States. Furthermore, the reception of both areas is more dependent on their inherent features (ie lack of compliance with the ECHR special characteristics) than on the margin of appreciation.

Finally, the three characteristics described above feature prominently in the Court's case law and give a better understanding of its use of international law. Due to structural differences, the Court's approach to international law was more limited than that used by the Commission. Unlike the Court's judgments, the views expressed by the Commission were not binding. Further, the Court's references to international law were conditioned by the nature of the regime to which it was referring: it was much easier for the Court to refer to a human rights special regime than to general international law. The resemblances between human rights special regimes facilitated such references. Further, the notion of margin of appreciation often inhibited the Court's non-mandated use of international law.

4. Comparative Analysis

4.1 Overview of the Factors' Influence

The factors analysed in the previous section have been included in two comparative tables[75] in order to provide a better overview of their influence on the reception process. The results in these tables have to be treated with caution, as they present a generalized view of the trends apparent in the Strasbourg jurisprudence. These generalizations were deduced on the basis of the majority of case law referring to a single regime. Clearly, there are numerous exceptions to each finding and they must therefore be qualified. These generalized findings constitute an

[75] See Comparative Tables 1 and 2 at the end of this chapter.

indication of the trends appearing in the reasoning of the Strasbourg bodies, rather than exhaustive documentation of their interpretation methods. The definition of the approach of the Court and Commission to international law is a difficult task, given that it has often been applied on an ad hoc and case-by-case basis. Furthermore, when assessing the Court's case law, it should be recalled that not all influential material is cited in the case law. For instance, some material may have been referred in argument or may have been part of a judge's general understanding but was not cited for various reasons in the judgment or decision. This work has excluded from its scope the assessment of these latent influences, but it is important to mention that they do exist. It is thus against this background that the comparative results have to be interpreted.

From the two comparative tables, it emerges that only one factor appeared in all eight regimes evaluated in this work; the fact that international law provided more specific guidelines than the ECHR was a general concern for the Strasbourg bodies, regardless of the area of international law relied on. This finding is not surprising as the Strasbourg bodies seldom refer, on their own initiative, to international law if it does not relate to a given case. Generally, they prefer to remain within the confines of the ECHR, which were clearly mandated by the Contracting States. As the use of international law is not explicitly provided for by the ECHR, the Strasbourg bodies do not wish to put their authority in jeopardy without any clear necessity emanating from certain deficiencies inherent in the ECHR.

The next most influential factor was the fact that international law was invoked at the domestic level. In all but one of the areas evaluated, most of the references to international law occurred in cases where international law had already been part of the domestic proceedings. It was only in case law referring to IHL that this element did not constitute a relevant consideration. In fact, there were few cases in which the parties or the domestic authorities had invoked IHL at the domestic level. It therefore appears that most international law references were rooted to some extent in pre-existing circumstances which fell outside the Strasbourg bodies' sphere of influence. This shows a lack of any initiative on the part of the Court or Commission to refer to international law.

Several other factors have played an important role in the reception of most regimes, namely the fact that the cases were intertwined with international law, that there were serious political or state issues at stake, and that there was a need to harmonize a provision with international law not covered by the ECHR. The fact that these factors dominated the case law could be explained on the basis that there were concrete necessities which could not be ignored if the ECHR system were to function adequately. Further, the fact that a case was intertwined with international law left little margin of manoeuvre and compelled the Strasbourg bodies to refer to the relevant international instrument. In addition, the universal reach of international instruments, the specificity and greater protection of the ECHR, as well as the uncertainty of international law played an important part in reducing the reception of half the regimes evaluated. The relevance of these factors is rooted again in the fact that some clear benefit could be derived from them in relation to the ECHR. With regard to less than half of the regimes, the following factors were relevant: the need to assess the factual situation, the procedural character of international law, textual similarity, substantive similarity, the ratification record, and the fact that an instrument was used in drafting the ECHR.

All of these factors were scattered across the special and general regimes with little logical order as to their concentration. Five of the 15 factors only appeared in cases referring to special regimes; these elements were the procedural character of international law, textual similarity, substantive similarity, the ratification record, and the use of an international instrument in the drafting process. It is not surprising that factors dealing with the similarities between the ECHR and another international instrument only had an impact on the reception of special regimes. Given that the ECHR is also a special regime, it has numerous characteristics in common with this category of sub-systems. This commonality has certainly facilitated the reception process. The remaining nine factors appeared with regard to both types of regime; these were factors associated with pre-existing and technical reasons as well as with the need to improve the ECHR. The presence of these factors in references to special and general regimes seems to be rooted, at least in part, in the fact that they were broad and influential independently of the nature of the international instrument considered. Finally, it is not surprising that the factor dealing with the more specific character and the better protection of the ECHR played a role in reducing the reception of both general regimes.

4.1.1 Pre-Existing and Technical Reasons

Factors concerning pre-existing or technical reasons appear to have played one of the most dominant roles in the Strasbourg jurisprudence. The fact that international law was invoked at the domestic level, the fact that the case was intertwined with international law, and the procedural character of international law are part of this category. The first two factors constituted in most cases the strongest bases for referring to international law in either special or general regimes. The prevailing tendency in the Strasbourg case law was that the Court and the Commission generally referred to international law once it had already been part of the legal reasoning or the parties' pleading. It was thus easier and more legitimate for them to rely on external sources which had previously been raised by the parties or domestic courts. Further, if international law was already part of the proceedings, the Court often had no other choice than to consider it. Nevertheless, the fact that international law had a procedural character constituted a relevant factor in only three of the six special regimes evaluated. This lower ratio was, however, incidental and rooted in the nature of the cases that came before the Strasbourg bodies. It is submitted that if more cases involving procedural international law had arisen, the Strasbourg bodies would probably have referred to them in a fairly uninhibited manner.

Thus, the pre-existing and technical reasons have had one of the most important influences on the reception of international law in the Strasbourg case law. The references prompted by them did not involve a substantial amount of discretion on the part of the Court and the Commission; they usually fell beyond their control, leaving little room for manoeuvre. The Court was also compelled to refer to international instruments, as this was sometimes required to reach a solution in such cases. As such, these references may say little about the Strasbourg bodies' own initiative and approach to international law. Rather, they demonstrate that the receptiveness of the Court is still to a greater extent circumstantial and involuntary. Clearly, such a mechanical reliance on external sources, deprived of a greater and more specific purpose, cannot on its own resolve complex dilemmas concerning the fragmentation of international law.

4.1.2 The Need to Improve and Update the ECHR

Another reason which had a dominant bearing on the Court's reception of international law was the need to improve and update the ECHR. The influence of this factor on the Strasbourg case law was comparable to that of the pre-existing or technical reasons. The need to harmonize an ECHR provision with international law, the need to fill gaps in the ECHR, and the availability of more specific guidelines in international law have played an important role in the Strasbourg bodies' interactions with the outside regimes. The latter factor had a bearing on the reception of all the regimes considered, whereas the others had an influence on most of them. Given that they came under their control, these factors required the Court and the Commission to use their discretion when deciding to reach beyond the ECHR confines. The references influenced by these factors were to some extent prompted by the Strasbourg bodies' willingness to use international law.

As such, these factors are very instructive in understanding the Strasbourg bodies' approach to international law. They indicate that the underlying motivation of the Court and the Commission in referring to international law was the need to reinforce the ECHR system and the protection of human rights at the European level. This functional approach is based on the fact that a clear benefit could be derived for the ECHR from the reliance on international law. Although the motivation behind these references could have been less self-centred, overall this tendency is encouraging as it indicates that the Strasbourg bodies used their discretion and were not solely dependent on the circumstances of each case. However, this statement needs to be qualified, as in many regimes the need to improve and update the ECHR often appeared in combination with other technical and pre-existing reasons. It is therefore difficult to determine which category of factors played a greater influence on the reception process in cases where they both appeared. Thus, the combination of pre-existing and technical reasons, as well as the need to reinforce the ECHR, provides the main ground prompting references to international law in the Strasbourg case law.

4.1.3 Common Ground Between the ECHR and International Law

The similarities between the ECHR and other international instruments played a less important role in the Strasbourg bodies' receptiveness to international law. The textual and substantive similarities, as well as the fact that an instrument was used during the drafting of the ECHR and/or its Protocols, were relevant in less than half of the regimes considered. This was not due, however, to the fact that the Court and Commission did not consider such similarities as relevant. On the contrary, when they emerged, these similarities constituted important points of reference and inspiration for the Strasbourg bodies. Their less-significant influence on the reception of international law in the Strasbourg cases is grounded in the fact that few of the instruments examined closely resembled the ECHR. Most of the UN Covenants considered entered into force after the ECHR and were more specialized than the Convention. There were also few similarities between the ECHR and the two areas of general international law examined. The Strasbourg bodies often picked up on these differences as they had to ensure that the international law differences did not weaken the level of protection provided by the ECHR. Thus, when a case involved an international treaty which substantially diverged from the ECHR, the Court and Commission explicitly tried to distance themselves from this instrument and abstained from receiving it in their case law.

4.1.4 Other Factors

The specificity and greater protection of the ECHR constitute important factors in the Strasbourg bodies' decision not to receive international law. In fact, they had a bearing on the reception of half the regimes evaluated. Naturally, the Court avoided reaching beyond the confines of the ECHR when this was not clearly useful or beneficial for its own system. Further, the Court appeared at times to have been overwhelmed by the universal reach of certain international treaties. The fact that they concerned a wider spectrum of issues and a more heterogeneous group of Member States may have discouraged the Court's references to these instruments. However, the main motivation behind these tendencies appears to have been the need to reinforce and not to weaken the ECHR system. Thus, the same reasons which prompted the Strasbourg bodies' references to international instruments also influenced their tendency to disregard international law. As such, the need to better protect ECHR rights constitutes a cornerstone of the Strasbourg reception process.

A substantial source of concern remains the uncertainty of international law. This has prevented the Court and the Commission from making more substantial references to both special and general regimes. The efforts on the part of these bodies to use international instruments were often impeded by dilemmas inherent in international law. As such, these problems were sometimes beyond their sphere of influence, and the state of references to international law was what could have been reasonably expected under the circumstances. Further clarification is especially needed with regard to the distinction between torture and other treatment, the effect of *jus cogens* norms, the scope of state immunities, various components of Articles 31–32 of the VCLT, and certain aspects of IHL. This would allow the Court to refer to the relevant international law in a less-inhibited manner.

An interesting finding of this study is that the ratification record (and the subsequent implementation of the relevant international instrument) has not always been an influential factor in the Strasbourg bodies' reasoning. While it was an important rubber stamp legitimating references to international law, the Court bypassed it in cases where it wanted to achieve a certain result or when an important issue was at stake. The ratification record appears to have been relevant in cases referring to four special regimes of all the regimes considered. It did not constitute, however, a relevant factor with regard to state immunity, IHL, and the two areas of general international law. This could be due to the fact that some of the rules belonging to these regimes were considered by the Court and the Commission to constitute customary international law. Overall, the ratification record is nonetheless a noteworthy factor in the Strasbourg bodies' reception of international law. Clearly, it is not the single decisive element in the reception process and usually appears together with other significant considerations. Finally, it was at times overridden by factors which seemed to be more important to the Strasbourg bodies.

4.2 Overview of the Cross-Cutting Issues and Results Analysis

4.2.1 General Trends

This section compiles the overall research results obtained through this study. As an aid to understanding the apparent trends, a comparative table at the end of this chapter provides a summary of the findings.[76] Similarly to the factor analysis above, the assessment of the research results is presented in the form of generalizations based on trends exhibited in the majority of the case law referring to a given regime. From the foregoing analysis, it appears that the rank occupied by the ECHR was higher with respect to seven of the eight regimes evaluated. This is not unusual given that the Court is exclusively charged with the application and enforcement of the ECHR (and not other international instruments). Exceptionally, the ECHR occupied a lower rank when the Court referred to the UN Charter and to the corresponding ICJ case law. The Court did not want to interfere with the UN's mission of maintaining peace and security; it thus applied the primacy principle contained in the UN Charter and found that it was

[76] See Comparative Table 3 at the end of this chapter.

incompetent to review the case.[77] Thus, according to the Court, the single international instrument which can override the ECHR is the UN Charter. Although this approach has been followed in a few recent cases,[78] it still remains to be seen how this trend will evolve in the future.[79]

The margin of appreciation granted to Contracting States has generally curbed the ability of the Strasbourg bodies to receive international law. Its scope was inversely proportional to the level of reception with respect to a given regime. Thus, when the margin of appreciation was lower, the reception level of international law was usually higher. This tendency, however, was not apparent with regard to the two general regimes considered, where the impropriety of reception overrode the importance of the margin of appreciation. In fact, the margin of appreciation doctrine was generally relevant with regard to four of the special regimes, where it ranged from moderate to wide. In addition, the margin of appreciation was more extensive in cases referring to special regimes than in cases relying on general international law. This aspect does not explain, however, the differences in the levels of reception between both types of regimes. Such variations in reception are grounded in the fact that most of the special regimes considered comply with the special characteristics of the ECHR.

This study further demonstrates that the Strasbourg bodies have leaned towards the closed paradigm in half the regimes evaluated. Further, the open paradigm was only relied on in cases referring to special regimes. This tendency is not tremendously encouraging, as it indicates that the Court has to some extent disregarded four of the regimes evaluated. As indicated in the Introduction to this work,[80] reliance on the closed paradigm is not conducive to reception and to the reduction of fragmentation. Nevertheless, it needs to be specified that the Strasbourg bodies have only leaned towards the closed paradigm in the reception of regimes which do not protect human rights to the same extent as the ECHR or which do not comply with its special features. Further, the jurisdiction of the Commission and Court has remained open towards the influence of human rights special regimes. Thus, their tendency to lean towards the closed paradigm may be justified in these cases. In addition, the Court and Commission have never fully embraced either end of the spectrum; even when they leaned towards the closed paradigm, they sometimes relied on the open paradigm. Being usually situated in the central part of the spectrum, the reasoning of the Strasbourg bodies has therefore never fallen into one of the extremes.

[77] See ch II, 2.7. *Berhrami and Behrami v France* and *Saramati v France, Germany and Norway* (App Nos 71412/01; 78166/01), decision, 2 May 2007, not yet reported.

[78] *Dušan Berić and others v Bosnia and Herzegovina* (App Nos 36357/04; 36360/04; 38346/04; 41705/04; 45190/04; 45578/04–45580/04; 91/05; 97/05; 100/05; 101/05; 1121/05; 1123/05; 1125/05; 1129/05; 1132/05; 1133/05; 1169/05; 1172/05; 1175/05; 1177/05; 1180/05; 1185/05; 20793/05; 25496/05), decision, 16 October 2007, not yet reported, para 29; *Kasumaj v Greece* (App No 6974/05), decision, 5 July 2007, not yet reported; *Gajic v Germany* (App No 36357/04), decision, 28 August 2007, not yet reported.

[79] See 4.3 below.

[80] See Introduction, 2.

The overall level of reception of international law in the Strasbourg case law ranged from low to moderate. It must be specified, however, that the reception of international law was appropriate in only four special regimes (civil and political rights, child rights, prohibition on torture, and state immunity). As a result, the actual level of reception in these areas ranged from moderate to high. As it was sometimes improper for the Strasbourg bodies to rely on international refugee law, IHL, and the two general regimes, the level of responsiveness to these regimes was significantly lower (ranging from low to moderate). Despite this modest reception record, the Court contributed to seven regimes, namely to all six special regimes and to one general regime. These contributions concerned the maximization of human rights protection, the provision of means for enforcement of certain international instruments, the reduction of fragmentation of international law, and the imposition of additional obligations on to states with regard to the protection of civilians under IHL.

Fragmentation between the ECHR and international law is apparent in the Strasbourg bodies' interactions with half the regimes considered, namely two special regimes (IHL and refugee rights) and two general regimes (VCLT and the ICJ framework). However, the divergences among the ECHR and certain other regimes are not always harmful. In fact, they should be especially maintained with regard to the VCLT and the ICJ framework. Harmonizing the Convention with general regimes could weaken the ECHR system and be detrimental to human rights protection. It is therefore not surprising that the Strasbourg bodies were more responsive to special regimes than to general international law. Most of the special regimes considered (civil and political rights, child rights, prohibition on torture, and state immunity) are well-adapted to being received in the ECHR framework, given that they concern the same subject matter and have analogous aims. This explains, in part, why the level of fragmentation between the ECHR and special regimes was lower than between the ECHR and general international law.

4.2.2 The Reception Scenarios

As part of the Strasbourg case law, there were numerous parallels in reception among the regimes evaluated. For instance, in cases where reception was appropriate, the Strasbourg bodies used the open paradigm and were moderately to highly receptive to international law. In this context, the case law of the Court generally converged with the regimes considered and no fragmentation between them and the ECHR appeared in the Strasbourg case law. This tendency occurred as part of the references to four special regimes, namely civil and political rights, child rights, state immunity, and the prohibition against torture. In all these regimes, the Strasbourg bodies also contributed to international law. The margin of appreciation was minimal to moderate in two of the four special regimes, namely civil and political rights and the prohibition on torture. It was moderate to wide with regard to the two remaining special regimes. The lower margin of appreciation facilitated the Strasbourg bodies' references to the ICCPR and the

CAT. It therefore emerges from these findings that child rights, civil and political rights, state immunity, and the prohibition against torture constituted similar reception scenarios. What is more, the reception of the prohibition against torture and civil and political rights gave rise to identical results. This pattern represents the optimal reception scenario in the Strasbourg case law, as it gives rise to high reception and begets little fragmentation of international law.

The second category of regimes exhibiting striking similarities is composed of IHL and refugee rights. The Strasbourg bodies relied on the closed paradigm in cases concerning these areas. Reception under both regimes was in some cases inappropriate and the level of incorporation of international law was low to moderate. The margin of appreciation was moderate to wide and this may have inhibited further references to these regimes. Despite the lower level of reception, the Commission and the Court nonetheless made a clear contribution to international law. Further, it appears that the Strasbourg case law still differs in some respects from IHL and international refugee rights. As already mentioned, this is not detrimental, given that harmonization of the ECHR with both of these regimes would weaken the protection of human rights at the European level.

The third category of comparable regimes includes the two areas of general international law analysed in this study, namely the VCLT and the ICJ framework. The Strasbourg bodies relied on the closed paradigm when referring to both of these general regimes. It was sometimes inappropriate for the Commission and the Court to incorporate certain aspects of general international law into their case law, given that they did not comply with the specific characteristics of the ECHR. The level of reception of the VCLT and the ICJ framework was thus low to moderate. Furthermore, substantial fragmentation remains between the ECHR and these two general regimes. It was necessary for the Court to differentiate the ECHR from the VCLT and the ICJ framework in order to better protect ECHR rights. Overall, this has deepened the already-existing discrepancies between the ECHR and these two general regimes. Although the Court appears to have contributed to the ICJ framework, it has also introduced further uncertainty with regard to rules contained in Articles 31–32 of the VCLT. The margin of appreciation does not appear to have played an important role in this reception process. The similarities in the reception patterns are grounded in the fact that both regimes are part of general international law and do not fully comply with the specific characteristics of the ECHR.

5. The Wider Context of the Strasbourg Reception Process

5.1 Interactions Between the ECHR and International Law

It is manifest that there are clear interactions between the ECHR special regime, other special regimes, and general international law. Further, certain discernable patterns appear in these relations. Overall, the Commission and the Court have leaned more towards the closed paradigm in their case law. As such, they have approached the end of the spectrum couched in constitutional terms rather than other international instruments. This general statement needs to be qualified, however, as the case law of both Strasbourg bodies has not focused only on one end of the spectrum. In the field of civil and political rights, child rights, state immunity, and the prohibition on torture, the Strasbourg bodies have been receptive and have leaned more towards the open paradigm. In addition, the factors analysed above[81] have allowed the situations in which the Court and the Commission referred to international law to be further circumscribed. These situations were generally prompted by the necessity and utility of an international law reference. In fact, the cross-cutting factors considered coalesced around the general need to improve and to reinforce the ECHR.

While both Strasbourg bodies have referred to international law to support a given conclusion or to provide further guidelines under the ECHR, they have not transgressed the boundary of references which are necessary for the reinforcement of the ECHR. In fact, the ECHR judicial policy was not motivated by the need to reduce fragmentation; such an aim would probably not have been legitimate under the current ECHR set-up. It appears that in the present context the only legitimate international law references are those which advance ECHR rights and not necessarily those which favour the unity of the international legal system. This limited notion of legitimacy represents an important obstacle to the reduction of fragmentation at the European level. Thus, if the legitimacy of international law were strengthened, the Court would probably feel less inhibited to make references aimed at anti-fragmentation.[82] Further, if the legitimacy of the Court as an anti-fragmentation body was specifically recognized by the Contracting States, the level of reception in the Strasbourg case law would certainly be higher.

Overall, the Strasbourg bodies' approach to international law has been marked by selectivity: references to international law have been cherry-picked, often to advance the aims and objectives of the ECHR and to reinforce the jurisdiction of the Court. This tendency has given rise to self-centred behaviour and a lack of awareness of the outside world on the part of the Strasbourg bodies. In this manner, the Court and the Commission have effectively insulated the ECHR special system and have not sufficiently reaffirmed the position that the international legal order constitutes a system. In the future, reliance on international law should become more functional in order to prevent the problem of fragmentation. Thus, further sensitization of ECtHR judges to this complex phenomenon

[81] See 2 above.

[82] For further information on the question of legitimacy of international law, see, in general, Mattias Kumm, 'The Legitimacy of International Law: A Constitutionalist Framework of Analysis' (2004) 15 Eur J Int'l L 907.

and to their role in this context is needed. It is imperative that judges integrate themselves into the greater legal order of which they are part.

The three types of fragmentation identified by the ILC Study Group[83] are present in the Strasbourg case law, namely fragmentation (1) through conflicting interpretations of general law, (2) through the emergence of special law as an exception to the general law, and (3) through conflict between different types of special law.[84] While the first type refers to effects of differing legal interpretations, the latter two denote genuine types of conflict where the law itself differs depending on the normative framework that is used to examine it. The first type of situation often involves a normative conflict where two institutions faced with similar facts interpret the law in different ways. The second type of divergence occurs when an institution makes a decision that deviates from how situations of a similar type have been decided in the past because the new case is an exception to a general rule. This could also apply to a whole regime of law which differs from a more general legal framework. The third case occurs when there is a conflict between different types of special law.

The first type of situation appeared when the Court departed from the ICJ's interpretation of the opposability of treaty reservations. This divergence was mostly due to the ECHR's special features and distinct character as a human rights treaty. The second type of fragmentation emerged when the Court differentiated the ECHR from general international treaties setting up reciprocal engagements between Contracting States. In this manner, the Court attributed itself a mandate to derogate from general international law, again on grounds of the special characteristics of the ECHR. With regard to the third type of fragmentation, it is apparent that there are still ample differences and potential conflicts between the ECHR and two special regimes, namely international refugee rights and IHL. Overall, the Convention fits well into the scenarios envisaged by the ICL Study Group and constitutes an optimal subject to study the phenomenon of fragmentation. Unfortunately, the ECHR system does not constitute, at least for now, a laboratory from which an eventual solution to this problem may emerge. Although there is willingness on the part of the ECtHR judges to receive international law, more sensitization is necessary to move beyond the current status quo of reception motivated by subjective needs and utility.

The previously established finding that the references used by international courts and tribunals reflect their willingness to maintain a certain independence and integrity vis-à-vis one another still holds true today.[85] The Court and

[83] See Introduction, 3.1.

[84] International Law Commission, Report of its fifty-sixth Session, 3 May to 4 June and 5 July to 6 August 2004, Supp No 10, Un Doc No A/59/10, 283–303; United Nations General Assembly (n 16 above), 30–34; International Law Commission, *Fragmentation of International Law, Topic (a): The function and scope of the lex specialis rule and the question of 'self-contained regimes': An outline*, Study Group on Fragmentation, Martti Koskieniemi.

[85] Nathan Miller, 'An International Jurisprudence? The Operation of "Precedent" Across International Tribunals' (2002) 15 LJIL 483, 499. See Introduction, 4.

Commission were reluctant to grant too much weight to international sources and rarely found them to be dispositive of the cases before them. These sources were treated as being persuasive rather than authoritative sources.[86] The Court usually did not attribute greater weight to international law than to the ECHR (except with regard to the UN Charter). Furthermore, the Court generally agreed with the decisions of other international tribunals and most international references constituted cases of positive reception. It appears, however, that the Court has explicitly distinguished itself from other international treaties, thereby entrenching the special characteristics of the ECHR in its case law. This came to be accepted with the increasing specialization of international law and the need to better protect human rights (which often differ in character from general international law).

Further, previous research demonstrated that the Court considers itself to be an integral part of the community of international courts and issues pronouncements on international law which generally converge with those of other international courts or tribunals.[87] On occasion, the Court has departed from the interpretation of international law used by others due to the special characteristics of the ECHR.[88] The core of this finding, applicable 10 years ago, still holds true to a greater extent today. Thus, it appears that the Court's approach to international law has not changed greatly in the last 10 years. Such a state of affairs is worrying considering that the face of international law has altered at a much faster pace. In order to keep abreast of these changes, the Court needs to adopt a more progressive and pragmatic approach to international law. It should, as it has done before, aim to achieve results which reach beyond the ECHR boundaries. Conscious of its authority in other special regimes, the Court has the potential of reducing fragmentation at the European and international levels. Moreover, guided by activism and benevolent liberalism,[89] it also possesses the right traits of character to overcome the obstacles that mark the current international legal scene.

5.2 An Approach Aimed at Self-Reinforcement

This study reveals that the Commission and the Court, by means of their constitutional aspirations and their tendency to lean towards the closed paradigm, have to a greater extent entrenched an approach which is not aimed at reducing fragmentation in their case law. The rationale of the international law references was not grounded in the need to enhance unity of the international legal system, but to preserve the special characteristics of the ECHR and to improve the functioning of the ECHR system. The Court and the Commission, as the

[86] Carl Lebeck, 'The European Court of Human Rights on the Relation between ECHR and EC-law: the Limits of Constitutionalisation of Public International Law' (2007) 62 ZöR 195, 215.

[87] Jonathan I Charney, 'Is International Threatened by the Multiple International Law Tribunals?' (1998) 27 *Recueil des Cours* 101, 216. See Introduction, 4.

[88] Ibid.

[89] Merrills (n 9 above), 249.

guardians of the ECHR, were focused on the functioning of their own system and jurisdiction. It is their lack of engaged interactions with other parts of the international legal system that has deepened the divide between the ECHR and international law.

While harmonization and systemic integration have been used by both bodies, they have mostly contributed to the ECHR system rather than to the international legal system as a whole. In order to reduce fragmentation significantly at the European level, the Commission and Court must use them in a more systematic manner with the specific aim of enhancing the unity of international law. There has been, however, little incentive for the Strasbourg bodies to reach beyond their own system and to partner up with other international courts or bodies. While certain central and eastern European constitutional courts have sided with the ECtHR against their national executive or legislature as a means to increase their authority,[90] the same incentive does not exist in the context of the relations between the Strasbourg bodies and other international courts or institutions. Although motivated by the common good, the Strasbourg bodies also sought to strengthen their own authority within the ECHR system. This could not, however, be accomplished by seeking further backing from international bodies. Instead, the extent of authority of the Strasbourg bodies lies in the hands of the Contracting States and it is their approval that they have usually sought. As a result of this lack of incentive to reach beyond their own jurisdiction, the Strasbourg bodies may also have been less receptive to international law.

For the moment, however, this approach does not appear to have caused tremendous legal difficulties. Some fragmentation has been observed between the ECHR and four of the eight regimes considered, namely two special regimes (refugee rights and IHL) and two general regimes (the VCLT and the ICJ framework). In this context, the maintenance of different standards was justified as the harmonization of the ECHR with these sub-systems could weaken European human rights protection. In addition, little fragmentation appeared in the Strasbourg case law referring to the remaining special regimes (civil and political rights, child rights, prohibition on torture, and state immunity); in most cases, the reasoning of the Strasbourg bodies converged with international standards, even without explicitly mentioning international instruments. There were, however, instances where the Strasbourg bodies interpreted international law differently from other bodies, introduced further uncertainty, and did not acknowledge the sources of their reasoning. These weaknesses should be kept in mind as they could resurface more often if no specific measures for the prevention of fragmentation are taken under the ECHR.

90 For further details, see Wojciech Sadurski, 'Partnering with Strasbourg: Constitutionalization of the European Court of Human Rights, the Accession of Central and Eastern European States to the Council of Europe, and the Idea of Pilot Judgements', 4 November 2008, Sydney Law School Research Paper No 08/135,16–25 and 38–41.

The moderate level of reception in the Strasbourg case law does not suggest that the Court is ready to confront the challenges lying ahead. It remains to be seen how the situation will evolve in the future when the international legal order becomes even more compartmentalized. In anticipation of this evolution, the Court should become less self-centred and acknowledge the necessity of reducing fragmentation at the European level. Furthermore, significant divergences in the context of a single branch of international law should not be tolerated. Thus, all special regimes subsumed under the branch of international human rights law—including the ECHR—should aim towards the approximation and convergence of their standards. If the status quo is maintained, the Court's approach aimed at self-reinforcement will inevitably entrench fragmentation in the Strasbourg case law. Thus, it is only with a method specifically aimed at anti-fragmentation that the unity of international human rights law can be maintained in the long run.

5.3 Insufficient Integration into the International Legal Order

The notion of an international legal system has been recognized by the Court, and the ECHR is clearly considered to be part of a greater whole. The Court has explicitly announced that it will resort to other relevant instruments when interpreting the ECHR (Article 31(3)(c) of the VCLT). This affirmation, however, was made on several occasions and did not confirm a consistent trend. It could be argued that the Court has resorted to this rule indirectly when referring to international law. However, this study takes the position that such references would need to be made more explicit before an assumption of this sort can be made. Further, addressing the rule of systemic integration contained in Article 31(3)(c) of the VCLT without paying further attention to its inherent uncertainties, as the Court and the Commission have done, does not provide a sufficient basis for any far-reaching conclusions with regard to the use of this rule. Deductions of this type would require the Court to take a firmer stand on the difficulties inherent in this method of interpretation. While it can be said that the Court has appropriated itself the concept of systemic interpretation and thereby confirmed the existence of an international legal system, it has not fully engaged with its components, apart from a few exceptions. Thus, the Court is not fully cognisant of the outer sub-systems and is not sufficiently integrated into the international legal order.

In addition, the international legal system as viewed by the Court and Commission does not seem to have a hierarchical structure. While the Court has recognized a form of constitutionalism based on the UN Charter, it appears that this finding may have been prompted by judicial restraint and the need to preserve the efficiency of the United Nations. In the Strasbourg case law, there is generally only one interaction between two legal systems, namely between the ECHR system and the international legal system. Beyond this distinction, there is no real demarcation between references to general international law and to international special regimes. General international law (apart from the UN Charter) and special regimes occupy the same rank in the Strasbourg case law, namely a status which is inferior to the ECHR. When a reference to international law is made, the Court does not seem to discriminate between one system and the other. Nonetheless, a certain order of references between special and general law should be established in order to provide greater certainty under the ECHR.

5.4 The Nature of the ECHR Special Regime

5.4.1 The ECHR's Constitutional and Regional Features

Although the ECHR is not a carbon copy of a domestic constitution, it does have a number of features which bring it closer to a constitutional instrument. Leaning more towards the closed paradigm, the Court and the Commission have reinforced the self-sufficiency of the ECHR system. In fact, the Strasbourg bodies' constitutional inclinations have limited the extent to which they can take international law into account.[91] Over time, the ECHR has thus become a special regime of the quasi-constitutional or auto-constitutional type.[92] According to the Strasbourg bodies, the ECHR is a constitutional instrument of the European public order.[93] The concept of European public order was mentioned when the Court found that the ECHR has a wider impact than ordinary international treaties instituting bilateral engagements between Contracting States; the ECHR is meant to reach beyond the scope of normal obligations under international treaties.[94] It is thus a network of mutual bilateral undertakings and objective obligations which, in the words of the Preamble, benefit from a 'collective enforcement'.[95] As part of this public order, the role of the ECtHR seems to point to something akin to public powers.[96]

The ECHR's constitutional standing is visible, *inter alia*, in the special method of interpretation followed by the ECtHR.[97] For instance, the Court developed the rule that an incompatible reservation may be severed from the body of the treaty and the reserving state may be held bound by the treaty, including the reserved provisions. This finding appears to be contrary to the voluntary char-

[91] Lebeck (n 86 above), 215.

[92] See Introduction, 3.3. See also Bruno Simma and Dirk Pulkowski, 'Of Planets and the Universe: Self-Contained Regimes in International Law' (2006) 17 Eur J Int'l L 483, 504; Andreas Fischer-Lescano and Günter Teubner, 'Regime-Collissions: The Vain Search for Legal Unity in the Fragmentation of Global Law' (2004) 25 Mich J Int'l L 999, 1014–1015.

[93] *Loizidou v Turkey (Preliminary Objections)* (n 55 above), para 75. See also Frowein, Jochen A, 'The Relationship Between Human Rights Regimes and Regimes of Belligerent Occupation' (1998) 28 IYHR 1, 39.

[94] Lebeck (n 86 above), 215.

[95] *Loizidou v Turkey (Preliminary Objections)* (n 55 above), para 70.

[96] Lebeck (n 86 above), 203.

[97] Erika De Wet, 'The Emergence of International and Regional Value Systems as a Manifestation of the Emerging Constitutional Order' (2006) 19 LJIL 611, 617.

acter of treaties and rules applicable to treaty reservations. However, the Court has justified this departure on the basis of the ECHR's special and constitutional character.[98] In this manner, it has granted the ECHR a rank which is superior to the relevant international law. Another important constitutional feature of the ECHR is the fact that its provisions have a peremptory effect, which means that Contracting States cannot choose to derogate from them on the basis of other international obligations.[99] They are prohibited from giving effect to public international law obligations if and to the extent that they are not compatible with human rights standards under the ECHR.[100]

The gist of the ECHR's constitutional nature was perhaps most aptly encapsulated in an opinion of Judge Lech Garlicki in *Öcalan v Turkey*.[101] Judge Garlicki accepted that the ECHR constituted an international treaty, but added that it 'represents a very distinct form of international instrument and—in many respects—its substance and process of application are more akin to those of national constitutions than to those of "typical" international treaties'.[102] According to his view, the ECHR should not be regarded as an ordinary treaty of public international law, but rather interpreted in a way which is analogous to how a domestic court would interpret a constitutional instrument.[103] This statement appears to articulate most explicitly the meaning of the ECHR's constitutional character. It could further be argued that the ECtHR should no longer be seen through the prism of international law given that it has evolved into a more developed body. The ECtHR's constitutional approach could in this context be to some extent justified, but it should nonetheless be complemented by a coherent approach to international law. While the ECtHR has reinforced itself, it does not operate outside the international legal order and it is necessary to take this fact into account. It is not, however, part of this study to prove or disprove the constitutional nature of the ECHR. It is sufficient to note that the ECHR displays certain important constitutional features which can be an obstacle to the Court's reception of international law.

Another important characteristic of the Court's special regime is its regionally oriented jurisdiction. Despite claims to internationalism, the ECHR can only be ratified by European states and is generally limited to the European territory. Some extraterritorial effect has, nonetheless, been attributed to ECHR provisions. Further, the Court's influential case law has an important spill-over effect into other domestic and international jurisdictions, which often turn to it for guidance. It remains, however, that the ECHR system comprises a group

[98] Ibid, 617–618; Lebeck (n 86 above), 202–203.
[99] De Wet (n 97 above), 617–618; Lebeck (n 86 above), 202.
[100] De Wet (n 97 above), 618; Christina Walter, '*Die Europäische Menschenrechtkonvention als Konstitutionalisierungporzess*' (1999) 59 ZaöRV 961, 980.
[101] *Öcalan v Turkey* (App No 46221/99), judgment, 12 May 2005, Reports 2005-IV, 131.
[102] Ibid, partly concurring and partly dissenting opinion of Lech Garlicki, para 3.
[103] Ibid, paras 3–4.

of relatively homogenous states with common interests and values. This apparent homogeneity ensures a more efficient and equitable implementation of the relevant norms. Further, the presence of a thick cultural community ensures the legitimacy of the regulations and that they are understood and applied in a coherent way.[104] It also provides the experienced and authoritative ECtHR with an opportunity to propose progressive interpretations and to become a forerunner of international law.

On the other hand, the regional nature of the ECHR can hinder the process of anti-fragmentation at the European level. It provides an opportunity for Contracting States with common values to entrench a certain interpretation of international human rights law which does not necessarily comply with that used by non-Contracting Parties to the ECHR. The regionalism of the ECHR can be viewed as a potential obstacle to the universal and unified character of international human rights. The geographical limitation of the ECHR can thus work as a double-edged sword in the context of fragmentation. However, the ECHR's regional character and its constitutional aspirations have until now hindered rather than enhanced anti-fragmentation.

In the context of the ECHR, the concept of 'self-contained regime' does not seem to be completely inadequate to designate the system that it encompasses. With a strong constitutional structure, the ECHR is still insular and self-sufficient. The constitutional features of the ECHR regime strongly advocated by the Court have on occasion been dented when it was necessary to look beyond its jurisdiction. As a general rule, the ECtHR has maintained a consistent position as to the auto-sufficiency of the ECHR regime by relying more on the closed paradigm. On a less-consistent basis, it has self-serviently referred to international law without providing a genuine justification. It has therefore maintained a certain link with public international law and other special international regimes, which has ensured that it has not entirely isolated itself. The Court has therefore not succeeded in creating a completely autonomous regime away from public international law. The ECHR can currently be characterized as a hybrid regime situated between a domestic constitutional model and an international special regime. It remains to be seen whether it will slowly evolve into a more porous sub-system which fits into a pluralist international legal order.

At present, the ECHR is not well-adapted to integrate the various international instruments available. In the long run, the development of a strong ECHR constitutional structure could entrench fragmentation in the Court's case law and limit the possibility of developing a unified and coherent international legal system. ECHR rights, having the character of peremptory norms, usually take precedence over international law. This weakens the force of the references made or inhibits them altogether, thereby compelling the Court to seek answers within the confines of the ECHR. Furthermore, extensive international law references or

[104] United Nations General Assembly (n 16 above), 106.

references aimed at reducing fragmentation may be considered illegitimate under the current ECHR constitutional set-up; they could be labelled as instances of 'judicial activism' and disapproved by the Contracting States. Until now, international law references have not been prompted by the need to reduce fragmentation but rather by the necessity to reinforce the ECHR system. Thus, structural difficulties seem to be impeding the development of functional references aimed at reducing fragmentation.

5.4.2 The ECHR's Conflict Resolution Rules

As the only provision of this type to be included in the ECHR, Article 53 sets up a limited conflict clause which provides that nothing in the Convention 'shall be construed as limiting or derogating from any of the human rights and fundamental freedoms which may be ensured under the laws of any High Contracting Party or under any other agreement to which it is a Party'. This provision has been understood to contain a simple principle, namely that the rights contained in the ECHR are minimum standards and that in case of a conflict between the ECHR and a national or international instrument concerning the same right, the most favourable provision to the applicant takes precedence.[105] However, Article 53 of the ECHR does not entitle the Court to incorporate and apply a more favourable provision included in an external instrument as part of its legal framework.[106] The aim of this provision is instead to ensure that the 'restrictions provided for in one instrument may not be invoked to limit the rights set out in the other'.[107] Unfortunately, the Strasbourg bodies have seldom relied on Article 53 when referring to external instruments and have provided little guidance as to its interpretation. Overall, Article 53 is much weaker and serves a much more limited purpose than the conflict clauses included in national constitutions or in certain international treaties,[108] which give them precedence over other legal instruments.

[105] Jan De Meyer, '*Brèves réflexions à propos de l'article 60 de la Convention européenne des Droits de l'Homme*' in Franz Matscher and Herbert Petzold (eds), *Protecting Human Rights: The European Dimension, Studies in honour of Gérard J. Wiarda* (Cologne/Berlin/Bonn/Munich: Carl Heymanns KG, 1988), 125; Emmanuel Décaux, 'Article 60' in Louis-Edmond Pettiti, Emmanuel Decaux, and Pierre-Henri Imbert (eds), *La Convention européenne des Droits de l'Homme : Commentaire article par article* (Paris: Economica, 1995), 903.

[106] De Meyer (n 105 above), 126.

[107] Council of Europe, *Problems Arising from the Co-existence of the United Nations Covenants on Human Rights and the European Convention on Human Rights: Differences as regards the Rights Guaranteed*, Report of the Committee of Experts on Human Rights to the Committee of Ministers, Doc H (70) 7, September 1970, 23, para 85.

[108] For instance, the ECHR lacks a provision similar to Art 307 of the Treaty establishing the European Community (EC Treaty) which gives absolute precedence to the EC Treaty over agreements that Member States have concluded between each other: Consolidated Version of the Treaty on the European Union and the Treaty establishing the European Community, 29 December 2006, [2006] OJ C321E/1. Another provision of this type is Art 103 of UN Charter, which provides that the Charter obligations of UN Member States prevail over conflicting obligations from another international treaty: Charter of the United Nations, Art 92.

Stronger, albeit no less unequivocal, conflict resolution rules were set up judicially by the Court. In most cases, the ECHR has been considered to be hierarchically superior to other conflicting norms of public international law. In the representative *Bosphorous* case,[109] the Court determined, *inter alia*, that state action taken pursuant to obligations flowing from membership in an international organization was presumed to be compatible with the ECHR as long as the substantive and procedural protection of human rights within the relevant international organization was equivalent to that of the ECHR.[110] The presumption of compatibility could be rebutted if, in the circumstances of a particular case, the protection of Convention rights was manifestly deficient. According to the Court, '[i]n such cases, the interest of international cooperation would be outweighed by the Convention's role as a "constitutional instrument of European public order" in the field of human rights flagrant denial or legal protection to the individual'.[111]

Nonetheless, a different conclusion was reached in *Berhrami and Behrami v France* and *Saramati v France, Germany and Norway*,[112] where the ECtHR declined to review the actions conducted by the United Nations in Kosovo and enforced the principle of the primacy of the UN Charter (Article 103) over conflicting international instruments (in this case, the ECHR). The Court's decision was grounded in the need to preserve the UN's effectiveness in fulfilling its mission, which consists in maintaining international peace and security. Thus, it was based more on the role of the United Nations and on recognizing the ECHR's place in international law than on ensuring that the ECHR was effective.

This finding, followed in subsequent case law,[113] is difficult to reconcile with the *Bosphorous* case, where the Court appears to have adopted a different approach based on a constitutional vision of the ECHR. In the *Behrami* case, however, the Court exercised self-restraint and applied the principle of primacy of the UN Charter (Article 103).[114] The Court preferred to give effect to an important conflict clause which ensures the smooth functioning of the UN system rather than embarking on an examination as to whether the UN system guaranteed an equivalent protection of human rights to the ECHR. As already mentioned, there are nonetheless numerous difficulties in its interpretation of this provision.[115] The Court felt that it was not competent to resolve disputes

[109] *Bosphorous Hava Yolları Turizm ve Ticaret Anonim Şirketi v Ireland* (n 4 above), 107. See ch II, 2.7.

[110] Ibid, paras 154–155.

[111] Ibid, para 156.

[112] *Berhrami and Behrami v France* and *Saramati v France, Germany and Norway* (n 77 above).

[113] *Dušan Berić and others v Bosnia and Herzegovina* (n 78 above), para 29; *Kasumaj v Greece* (n 78 above); *Gajic v Germany* (n 78 above).

[114] It appears unlikely that the Court wanted to rely here on a version of the international constitutionalism centred on the UN Charter.

[115] See ch II, 2.7.

pertaining to UN actions. Furthermore, it may have wanted to avoid opening the floodgates to other difficult and politically charged cases. The Court was also probably under much pressure and decided to defer to the existing international conflict clauses.

While a European public order superior to other international obligations appears to be emerging, this does not yet mean that ECHR rights trump all other conflicting international obligations.[116] Inevitably, the need to consider relevant international instruments involves balancing the different international obligations of Contracting States[117] and deciding whether the ECHR or the international obligation carries more weight. As is apparent here, the Court has not always approached the question of the ECHR's constitutional nature in a coherent fashion.[118]

The ECtHR is slowly developing its international identity and attempting to reaffirm its role on the international scene. While generally the Court has been self-serving and purpose-oriented, it has submitted here to the demands of international law and sacrificed its constitutional aspirations. The *Behrami* case[119] is very important for the institutional hierarchy issue upon which it touches. The Court has nonetheless not explained this relationship satisfactorily and has applied Article 103 of the UN Charter mechanically. This case has nonetheless raised to a higher level the discussion regarding the relationship between the ECHR and UN law. By recognizing the primacy of the UN Charter, the ECtHR may also have recognized that the ECHR is a sub-system of the international legal order which is subjected to higher regimes. This largely weakens the ECtHR's constitutional claims and indicates that its regime is not entirely autonomous. However, this was a rare, high-profile case where the Court was confronted with unusual questions. Its approach was therefore conditioned by factors which did not generally arise in other cases. Similarly to the European Court of Justice,[120] the ECtHR appears to pick and choose among international obligations without any coherent underlying justification.

Some commentators have viewed this ECtHR case as a manifestation of de Scelle's *dédoublement fonctionnel*. On this basis, they have argued that the Court has allowed itself 'to act on behalf of the UN legal order, aiming specifically at facilitating the realization of values stemming from that order'.[121] In this manner, the ECtHR has extended its enforcement machinery to the UN system, which does not possess an equivalent mechanism. It could thus be argued that in the

[116] De Wet (n 97 above), 626, 628–629. [117] Ibid, 626. [118] See also ibid, 628.

[119] Ibid.

[120] Gráinne De Búrca, 'The European Courts and the Security Council: Between Dédoublement Fonctionnel and Balancing of Values: Three Replies to Pasquale De Sena and Maria Chiara Vitucci' (2009) 20 Eur J Int'l L 853, 861.

[121] Pasquale De Sena and Maria Chiara Vitucci, 'The European Courts and the Security Council: Between Dédoublement Fonctionnel and Balancing of Values' (2009) 20 Eur J Int'l L 193, 210.

context of the war on terror further powers have been transferred from the state to the Security Council. The ECtHR has therefore cooperated with the Security Council, which was exercising powers delegated by states.[122]

From Scelle's perspective, international rules do not take precedence over national or special regimes. Instead, the international legal order is superior to national and special regimes.[123] As such, it naturally prevails over the legal orders under it, as it is an expression of a broader society. Due to a lack of concrete evidence as to the legal basis of the Court's reasoning, it could be argued that the Court has followed this theory implicitly. It is nonetheless difficult to pursue this argument further and to position the Court's reasoning in the context of a pluralist international legal order, where different legal systems clash and compete with one another.[124] Further, it is not possible to argue that it fits into a clear-cut dualist or monist approach to international law, given that it is not grounded in any meaningful institutional hierarchy of the international legal order. It is therefore burdensome to pinpoint more precisely the view of the international legal order that marked the Court's reasoning in the *Behrami* case.

The main trend dominating the Strasbourg jurisprudence confirms the ECHR's superior position as a constitutional instrument of European public order which can outweigh the interest of international cooperation.[125] Thus, the *Behrami* line of reasoning probably needs to be limited to its own specific circumstances and to be treated as an exception to the overall trumping effect of the ECHR. This view is also strengthened by the fact that the Court has rarely treated international law as being decisive. It has generally leaned towards the closed paradigm, thereby giving priority to ECHR provisions and reinforcing the constitutional side of the ECHR system. Although there is a general trend indicating that the ECHR is superior to international law, the conflict resolution rules set up by the Court remain uncertain and need to be specified further. More precisely, the situations in which international law is to be attributed a trumping effect should be established more clearly, so that the Court can adopt a more coherent approach to international law and to the problem of fragmentation.

5.5 Interactions Between Special Regimes

Overall, the interactions between the ECHR and other special regimes have been simplistic and disengaged. The approach of the Strasbourg bodies has generally been marked by deference, judicial restraint, and a lack of interference. They have rarely disagreed with other special regimes or distinguished themselves from their rules. They have done so on occasion in the interest of the Convention's special character and the need to reinforce the protection of its rights. Further, the

[122] Ibid, 211. [123] Ibid, 213.
[124] The contrary argument has been made with regard to the ECJ. See De Búrca (n 120 above), 857.
[125] De Sena and Vitucci (n 121 above), 629.

references to other special rules were mostly centred on the ECHR system with little administrative coordination and mutual supportiveness to seek regime-optimal outcomes.[126] These interactions were often selective, self-interested, and focused on the effectiveness of the ECHR system. Moreover, the dialogue between the different parts of the international judiciary and the Strasbourg bodies did not always work efficiently, as is especially apparent from the Court's interactions with the Human Rights Committee.[127]

In three of the special regimes analysed (refugee rights, international humanitarian law, and state immunity), it is difficult to define with precision the specific inter-regime relations. This is due in most part to the moderate responsiveness and reception of the relevant international instruments. In areas concerning state immunity and refugee rights, the ECHR's relation to the respective special regimes is difficult to deduce due to the variability and ambiguity of the Court's approach, as well as the insufficiency of references made. Further, the Court's willingness to distance itself from international refugee rights has not contributed to better relations with this special regime. The situation is also difficult to assess in relation to the ECHR's interaction with IHL due to its lack of acknowledgement of the international legal sources used. The Court seems to have been unwilling to recognize that inter-relations with the field of IHL existed. This approach has complicated the relationship between the ECHR and IHL even further.

In three additional areas characterized by a higher level of reception (child rights, civil and political rights, and prohibition against torture), there are more distinctive relations apparent in the case law. While these interactions remain embryonic and simplified, they have contributed more to the understanding of ECHR relations with other special regimes. In cases relating to child rights, the references were usually unproblematic and more audacious than usual. Moreover, they have allowed the Court to complement and to maximize the protection granted to children under the Convention. In cases relating to torture and inhuman or degrading treatment, the Court was generally responsive to the relevant international instruments and has used them selectively to support its interpretation of the ECHR. The Court was influenced in this regard by the uncertainties prevalent at the international level regarding the distinction between torture and other degrading treatment. The coexistence of the Committee Against Torture and the ECtHR does not seem to raise excessive problems. With regard to civil and political rights, there have been and there could be problematic relations between the Human Rights Committee and the ECtHR. The resemblance between the ECHR and the ICCPR allowed the Strasbourg bodies to rely on the latter when further guidance under the ECHR was required.

Thus, the situation with regard to the special regimes analysed is equally split, with one part of the regimes exhibiting few substantial interactions and the other evidencing a more elaborate relationship with the ECHR system. It remains the

[126] United Nations General Assembly (n 16 above), 252.

[127] See ch IV, 2.1.3.

case, however, that the status of the other special regimes is unclear under the ECHR. While the Commission and the Court have stated that it is legitimate to refer to other relevant international instruments, they have never clarified when and how this should be done. Naturally, the references to special regimes have often occurred when they provided a more specific rule and when the ECHR provided little guidance on a given issue. It is not clear, however, which rules should be applied in the event of a conflict between a special regime and the ECHR and how this conflict should be resolved. The Court has at times simply avoided applying certain conflict-resolution rules. For instance, it did not apply IHL as *lex specialis* in the context of cases relating to non-international conflicts.

The interactions between the ECHR and other regimes were prompted by the need to reinforce the former[128] rather than to ensure a smooth functioning of the latter. Moreover, the Court's lack of meaningful relations with other special regimes and the corresponding lack of an institutionalized approach to them could be due to the fact that these systems are different in nature from the ECHR. Unlike the ECHR, they apply to a non-homogenous group of states, they are universal in reach, they lack a strong enforcement mechanism, and they are weaker in the protection granted to individual applicants. The Court may not have found it practicable to entertain more enhanced interactions with other, different, international regimes. When differences appeared between the ECHR and an international instrument belonging to a special regime, the Court tried to distinguish itself and to distance itself from it to preserve the special ECHR character.

Clearly, further improvement is necessary in this area. The relations between special regimes should operate more on the basis of cooperation and mutual supportiveness in order to seek the most advantageous solutions. Moreover, the status of special regimes should be defined more precisely and the rules to resolve inter-regime conflicts established more clearly. Additional safeguards should be put into place in order to prevent bodies, such as the Court, from unilaterally resolving conflicts of norms originating from different regimes.[129] Finally, the dialogue and cooperation between the Court and other international courts should be improved in the interest of maintaining inter-regime coherence.

5.6 International Conflict Resolution Rules

The Court's use of international conflict resolution rules was meant to remedy fragmentation (as analysed by the ILC Study Group[130]) and should be

[128] See ch I, 2.2 and 3; ch II, 2.2, 2.4, and 3; and ch VI, 2.1.3 and 4.

[129] United Nations General Assembly (n 16 above), 252.

[130] See, in general, International Law Commission, Report of its fifty-sixth Session (n 84 above), 283–303; United Nations General Assembly (n 16 above).

improved in subsequent case law. Thus far, it has led on occasion to ambiguous or contradictory results. For instance, the Court's use of the *lex specialis* rule gave rise to certain problems in cases concerning non-international conflicts. In international practice, IHL constitutes the *lex specialis* applicable in the context of armed conflict, but the ECtHR has bypassed this practice in its case law.[131] Another problem arose when the Court and the Commission relied on the principle of systemic integration enshrined in Article 31(3)(c) of the VCLT. Although there are cases where the Strasbourg bodies have used this rule, they are insufficient to evidence any significant trend in their reasoning. Moreover, the Strasbourg bodies did not address the inherent difficulties of this provision and applied it in a mechanical manner.[132] The Court has also rendered the application of the *jus cogens* rule more ambiguous by precluding its trumping effect in certain situations. It recognized that the prohibition on torture has the status of a *jus cogens* norm but that—given the absence of an established rule of international law—it cannot precede other international rules in civil proceedings. This reasoning gives rise to the problematic conclusion that a *jus cogens* norm could be selectively peremptory.[133] The Court has also applied an international conflict clause, Article 103 of the UN Charter, in a manner which has been intensely criticized.[134] By giving effect to this rule, it has nonetheless preserved the effectiveness of the UN's mission and reduced the fragmentation of general international law.

Overall, the conflict resolution rules have been implemented in a disputable manner under the auspices of the Strasbourg bodies. When no specific hierarchy exists in international law and conflict resolutions rules are of no avail, there may be few alternatives left to ensure that fragmentation does not spread further. The approach of the Commission and Court in this context seems to have been based, in part, on comity in the interest of avoiding further conflicts with other special regimes and general international law. Such comity could also be seen as a consequence of the Court's growing constitutional structure and independent character. Given that there is no clear rule on hierarchy in the international legal system, it appears that a workable solution dictating mutual deference and respect between the different special orders has entrenched itself in the international judicial dialogue.[135] This practice was prompted by the need to maintain some kind of consensus between the different parts of the international judiciary. It has resulted, however, in further confusion about the status of international legal norms. In addition, it has not contributed to the certainty of the law or to the establishment of a hierarchy of norms.[136]

[131] See ch VIII, 3.
[132] See ch I, 2.4 and 3.
[133] See ch VII, 3.2.2. See also Alexandre Orakhelashvili, 'Restrictive Interpretation of Human Rights Treaties in the Recent Jurisprudence of the European Court of Human Rights' (2003) 14 Eur J Int'l L 529, 562.
[134] See ch II, 2.7.
[135] Lebeck (n 86 above), 231.
[136] Ibid, 234.

5.7 The Role of General International Law

This study has analysed the reception of two areas of general international law in the Strasbourg case law, namely the ICJ framework and the VCLT. While a few findings can be deduced from these areas, broad conclusions about the status of general international law under the ECHR are precluded due to the limited scope of this study. Further, it has been seen that it was easier for the Strasbourg bodies to refer to special regimes than to general international law. The difference in their approaches to both types of regime seems to be rooted in the fact that the ECHR and most of the special regime considered regulate the same subject matter. Overall, the Strasbourg bodies referred selectively to general international law when they wished to reinforce their reasoning or to improve the functioning of the ECHR system. Otherwise, they distanced themselves from general international law when it could deter the effectiveness of the ECHR. Their approach was conditioned to a large extent by the specific character of the ECHR, which is a human rights treaty comprising more than mere reciprocal engagements between Contracting States.

Another important area to examine in greater depth in future research is the Strasbourg bodies' relationship with general international law. It is important to test the extent of their reliance on this body of law. It remains unclear when the references made in this area should only be used as aids to interpretation and when they should constitute a residual application of general international law. This study has shown that the Court relied on rules of treaty interpretation in order to establish its own interpretative methodology and that it used ICJ decisions when complex, controversial, and important questions presented themselves. These references appear to constitute more than mere guides in interpretation. In fact, the Strasbourg bodies appear to have fallen back on certain aspects of general international law. However, the findings are not representative of all general international law. It needs to be determined how the Strasbourg bodies have behaved with regard to other general regimes. Another important issue to research further in this context is the ECtHR's latent reliance on general international law and its principles.

In an increasingly specialized legal environment, few institutions are left to speak the language of general international law in order to regulate relationships which reach beyond the pursuit of special interests and technical cooperation.[137] Naturally, it would be desirable to maintain a certain unity and coherence in the interpretation of general international law, which constitutes the background and default scenario of special legal regimes. However, this may not always be possible in the context of special regimes, such as the ECHR, which bear little resemblance to general international law. Thus far, it has been seen that the interpretation of certain aspects of general international law by the Strasbourg

[137] United Nations General Assembly (n 16 above), 255.

bodies has differed from that of other institutions. The Strasbourg bodies have maintained that this distinction is necessary to preserve the special character of the ECHR. It remains to be seen how the situation will evolve in the future and whether it will be possible to prevent any further differences between the ECHR and general international law. The outcome of this evolution may depend to a large extent on whether the Court's constitutional features are strengthened.

6. Future Research

A number of issues relating to the fragmentation of special regimes remain uncertain. For instance, the very notion of self-contained (special) regimes remains vague in spite of the tremendous research efforts carried out by the ILC Study Group and academics.[138] An important question emerging from this study is how special regimes with strong constitutional or institutional structures should be integrated into the international legal system. In this context, further guidelines should be formulated in relation to the application of the VCLT to the different types of special regime. It remains unclear how strong constitutional regimes are to incorporate the international rules on conflict resolution contained in the VCLT. Should their constitutional features be accommodated as part of this process? Which rank should be attributed to other special and general regimes? A differentiated and contextualized approach needs to be taken to each special regime given that there is no single model available. As this work has shown, the ECHR is a very particular regime which presents its own problems with regard to fragmentation. A generic panacea for anti-fragmentation is therefore bound to fail in this specific context. Finally, it is crucial to examine in greater depth the concepts of regional constitutionalism and special regime constitutionalism as possible threats to the unity and coherence of international law.

As part of future research, further attention should also be paid to the greater European context of the Strasbourg case law. The phenomenon of fragmentation at the European level is more complex than in other special regimes. European fragmentation has now probably reached multi-levelled proportions due to the presence of complex interactions between domestic law, EU law, the ECHR, other special regimes, and general international law. The ECtHR, being one of the relevant actors, can only resolve the fragmentation problem in cooperation with other bodies. Further, the analysis of the reception of international law in the Strasbourg case law constitutes only one aspect of the reduction of fragmentation at the European level. Other aspects are not considered here due to the limited scope of this work; they need nonetheless to be explored in future research.

[138] Ibid, 65–99. See Introduction, 3.3. See also Simma and Pulkowski (n 92 above), 504; Fischer-Lescano and Teubner (n 92 above), 1014–1015.

Possible solutions to European fragmentation must be adapted to its specific environment. A coherent approach to international law and anti-fragmentation would need to accommodate the ECHR's and the Court's inherent constitutional features. Although it has not precluded the development of an anti-fragmentation reasoning, the Court's constitutional predisposition has not exactly fostered the expansion of this practice. If the ECHR mutates into an even stronger constitutional system, the establishment of anti-fragmentation case law may become difficult. It is from its international and constitutional characteristics that the future of the Court's anti-fragmentation technique will be drawn. It will probably remain a mixture of both constitutional and receptive approaches, which will compete in the Court's reasoning and reinforce themselves with time. It must be kept in mind, however, that a strong constitutionalist approach could defeat anti-fragmentation. Thus, as part of a mixed approach to anti-fragmentation, the constitutional component should not outweigh the receptive element. Ideally, a balance between the two should be sought or more emphasis should be placed on reception.

In addition, it needs to be kept in mind that an effective strategy to reduce fragmentation can only be carried out in an area or branch of international law where the different special regimes have similar aims and interests.[139] Bodies originating from different legal regimes and having diverse missions tend to interpret international law in divergent ways; for instance, the World Trade Organization may apply the VCLT in a way which differs from the ECtHR. As a result, it is reasonable to require that bodies originating from the international human rights branch interpret international instruments in a uniform manner. It may not be appropriate, however, to require that all existing special regimes interpret general and specialized international law in the same way given that there are important differences in their aims and missions. In the context of the ECHR, it is therefore necessary to ensure that the Court relies on international law in a manner which is consistent with the interpretation of the other bodies included in the international human rights branch. Any future research concerning European approaches to anti-fragmentation would need to take these specific considerations into account.

7. Further Improvement at the ECHR Level

The ever-expanding scope of international law gives rise to numerous potential overlaps and conflicts between special and general regimes. Most international judicial bodies usually operate in isolation, without explicit regulation of their jurisdictional interactions and with little regard for the jurisprudence of other international courts. Forum shopping and multiple litigations have become

[139] See also Koskenniemi and Leino (n 74 above), 561–562.

frequent in the institutionally fragmented international law of human rights. Such a state of affairs is highly detrimental to the coherence and effective protection of human rights. In the context of the ECHR, the fragmentation of international law has not yet given rise to legal difficulties, but its negative influence is starting to be felt. Thus, various preventive measures should be taken in order to ensure that this problem will not further damage the ECHR system.

In the upcoming years, further efforts should be put into improving judicial cooperation between the ECtHR and other international bodies. This could mitigate the possibility of conflicting rulings and would improve the coordination between the various special regimes. There is currently no established mechanism allowing the Court to verify whether a decision has already been handed down in a case before it. However, the Research Division of the ECtHR's Registry has been expanded due to the increasing need to consider non-ECHR material. It is charged with studying questions relating to comparative and international law, and prepares reviews of the case law of the Court and other bodies. Judicial cooperation should be intensified under the auspices of this unit; it could take the form of requests for information, expert advice, transfers of litigation, or recognition of rulings from another body. This would improve administrative coordination, mutual legal assistance, and the possibility of finding optimal regime solutions between the ECHR and other counterparts of the international legal system.

Another important improvement to the status quo would be to provide further judicial training on various problems affecting international law. As seen earlier,[140] less than half of the ECtHR judges have training and/or work experience in comparative and/or international law. Further, even when judges have such training and/or experience, it is important to provide them with continued education to ensure that they stay abreast of the different changes intervening at the international level. For instance, extensive training should be provided to ECtHR judges on how to use the VCLT as a possible tool for resolving conflicts of norms. In addition, further emphasis should be placed on the requirement of prior international law training and experience when choosing judges for the Court. In the current fragmented legal world, judges have acquired additional duties which consist of ensuring that the application of international law is coherent and unified. ECtHR judges should therefore possess the required skills in order to anticipate potential fragmentation problems. In this context, doubts as to the legitimacy of international law references aimed at reducing fragmentation should be dispelled since they constitute necessary steps in the evolution process of the ECHR and the international legal order.

As fragmentation has a clear impact on regional frameworks, more attention should be paid to this problem in the context of international law references used by the Court. Further sensitization of ECtHR judges is necessary in order to eradicate cherry-picking and selectivity in their approach to international law.

[140] See 2.14 above.

It must be ensured that they are no longer centred on their own system and that they fully embrace their international responsibilities. International law-friendly approaches may soon become insufficient to ensure the coherence and unity of international law at the European level. Then, proactive approaches aimed at the systemic integration of international law, and especially of international human rights law, in the context of the ECHR, will be needed. Undeniably, judicial interpretation cannot on its own eradicate the phenomenon of fragmentation. Further institutional coordination and state intervention is necessary in order to remedy this deep-rooted problem. Judges nonetheless play a fundamental part in redressing international law problems when legislative action is impossible or inadequate. Thus, in the words of John Donne, it is clear that no judge, no legal regime is an island, entire of itself; every judge, every sub-system is a piece of the international legal order, a part of the main.[141]

[141] John Donne, *The Major Works including Songs and Sonnets and Sermons* (Oxford/New York: Oxford University Press, 1990), 344.

Comparative Table 1: Factors

Factors \ Areas	Civil and political rights	Child rights	Refugee rights	Prohibition on torture	State immunity	IHL	Law of treaties	ICJ
International law invoked at the domestic level	X	X	X	X	X		X	X
More specific guidelines in international law	X	X	X	X	X	X	X	X
Cases intertwined with international law	X	X	X		X		X	X
Need to harmonize with international law	X	X		X	X		X	X
Use in the drafting of the ECHR and/or Protocols	X	X						X
Need to fill in gaps	X	X		X			X	X
Political issues and state interests			X		X	X	X	X
Universal reach of the instrument	X		X				X	X

Comparative Table 2: Factors

Factors / Areas	Civil and political rights	Child rights	Refugee rights	Prohibition on torture	State immunity	IHL	Law of treaties	ICJ
Need to assess the factual situation			X	X		X		
Procedural and substantive law	X	X	X					
Textual similarity	X	X						
Substantive similarity	X		X	X				
ECHR more specific and advantageous			X			X	X	X
Ratification record	Sometimes ignored	Sometimes ignored	X	X				
Uncertainty in international law				X	X	X	X	

Comparative Table 3: Cross Cutting Issues and Results

Factors / Areas	Civil and political rights	Child rights	Refugee rights	Prohibition on torture	State immunity	IHL	Law of treaties	ICJ
Regime type	Special	Special	Special	Special	Special	Special	General	General
Rank occupied by the ECHR	Higher	Higher	Higher	Higher	Higher	Higher	Higher	Lower
Margin of appreciation	Minimal	Moderate to Wide	Wide	Minimal to Moderate	Wide	Moderate to Wide	Minimal	Variable
Open/closed paradigm	Open	Open	Closed	Open	Open	Closed	Closed	Closed
Appropriate/ inappropriate reception	Appropriate	Appropriate	Sometimes inappropriate	Appropriate	Appropriate	Sometimes inappropriate	Sometimes inappropriate	Sometimes inappropriate
Level of reception	Moderate to High	High	Low to Moderate	High	Moderate	Low	Low to Moderate	Low to Moderate
Contribution to international law	Clear contribution	Clear contribution	Clear contribution	Clear contribution	Debatable contribution	Clear contribution	No	Debatable contribution
Fragmentation in interactions in the case law	No	No	Yes	No	No	Yes	Yes	Yes

Bibliography

Books and Articles in books

Allen, Trevor RC, *Constitutional Justice: A Liberal Theory of the Rule of Law* (Oxford/New York: Oxford University Press, 2001).

Amr, Mohamed Sameh M, *The Role of the International Court of Justice as the Principal Judicial Organ of the United Nations, Legal Aspects of International Organisation* (The Hague/London/New York: Kluwer Law International, 2003).

Arai-Takahashi, Yutaka, *The Margin of Appreciation Doctrine and the Principle of Proportionality in the Jurisprudence of the ECHR* (Antwerp/Oxford/New York: Intersentia, 2002).

Bedi, Shiv RS, *The Development of Human Rights by the Judges of the International Court of Justice* (Oxford/Portland, OR: Hart Publishing, 2007).

Blair Johann, *The International Covenant on Civil and Political Rights and its (First) Optional Protocol: A Short Commentary Based on Views, General Comments and Concluding Observations by the Human Rights Committee* (Frankfurt am Main/Berlin/Bern/etc: Peter Lang 2005).

Bossuyt, Marc and Olivier Lins, '*La prise en considération de la jurisprudence de Strasbourg par le Comité des droits de l'homme des Nations Unies*' in Gérard Cohen-Jonathan and Jean-François Flauss (eds), *Le rayonnement international de la jurisprudence de la Cour européenne des droits de l'homme, Droit & Justice 64* (collection directed by Pierre Lambert) (Brussels: Bryulant/Nemesis, 2005), 83.

Boulesbaa, Ahcene, *The U.N. Convention on Torture and the Prospects for Enforcement, International Studies in Human Rights* (The Hague/Boston/London: Martinus Nijhoff 1999).

Breau, Susan, 'Summary of the State Practice Regarding State Immunities in the Council of Europe/*Résumé sur la Pratique des États relative aux Immunités du Conseil de l'Europe*', in Gerhard Hafner, Marcelo G Kohen, and Susan Breau (eds), *State Practice Regarding State Immunities/La Pratique des États concernant les Immunités des États* (Council of Europe, Leiden/Boston: Martinus Nijhoff, 2006), 168.

Cassese, Antonio, *International Law* (Oxford: Oxford University Press, 2nd edn, 2005).

Collected edition of the 'travaux préparatoires' of the European Convention on Human Rights, Preparatory Commission of the Council of Europe, Committee of Ministers, Consultative Assembly, 11 May to 8 September 1949 (The Hague: Martinus Nijhoff, 1949), Vol I.

Collected edition of the 'travaux préparatoires' of the European Convention on Human Rights: Recueil Des Travaux Préparatoires de la Convention Européenne Des Droits de L'Homme (Council of Europe, Dordrecht/Boston/Lancaster: Martinus Nijhoff, 1985), Vol I.

Crawford, James, *International Law as an Open System* (London: Cameron May, 2002).

Danelius, Hans, 'Protection Against Torture in Europe and the World' in Ronald St J Macdonald, Franz Matscher, and Herbert Petzold, *The European System for the Protection of Human Rights* (Dordrecht: Martinus Nijhoff, 1993), 267.

Décaux, Emmanuel, 'Article 60' in Louis-Edmond Pettiti, Emmanuel Decaux, and Pierre-Henri Imbert (eds), *La Convention européenne des Droits de l'Homme: Commentaire article par article* (Paris: Economica, 1995), 897.

Degan, Vladimir, *Sources of International Law* (The Hague/Boston/London: Martinus Nijhoff, 1997).

De Meyer, Jan, '*Brèves réflexions à propos de l'article 60 de la Convention européenne des Droits de l'Homme*' in Franz Matscher and Herbert Petzold (eds), *Protecting Human Rights: The European Dimension, Studies in honour of Gérard J. Wiarda* (Cologne/Berlin/Bonn/Munich: Carl Heymanns KG, 1988), 125.

Drzemczewski, Andrew, *The Position of Aliens in Relation to the European Convention on Human Rights* (Strasbourg: Council of Europe Press, 1993).

Evans, Malcolm D and Rod Morgan, *Preventing Torture: A Study of the European Convention for the Protection of Torture and Inhuman or Degrading Treatment or Punishment* (Oxford: Clarendon Press, 1998).

Fawcett, James E, *The Application of the European Convention on Human Rights* (Oxford/New York: Oxford University Press, 1969).

Freeman, Michael, 'Taking Children's Rights More Seriously' in Philip Alston, Steven Parker, and John Seymour (eds), *Children, Rights and the Law* (Oxford: Clarendon Press, 1992), 52.

Giakoumopoulos, Christos, 'Detention of Asylum Seekers in Light of Article 5 of the European Convention on Human Rights' in Jane Hughes and Fabrice Liebaut (eds), *Detention of Asylum Seekers in Europe: Analysis and Perspectives* (The Hague/Cambridge, MA/Dordrecht: Martinus Nijhoff, 1998), 161.

Golsong, Heribert, 'Interpreting the European Convention on Human Rights Beyond the Confines of the Vienna Convention on the Law of the Treaties?' in Ronald St J Macdonald, Franz Matscher, and Herbert Petzold (eds), *The European System for the Protection of Human Rights* (Dordrecht/Boston/London: Martinus Nijhoff, 1993), 147.

Goodwin-Gill, Guy S, 'Article 31 of the 1951 Convention Relating to the Status of Refugees: Non-Penalization, Detention, and Protection' in Erika Feller, Volker Türk, and Frances Nicholson (eds), *Refugee Protection in International Law: UNHCR's Global Consultations on International Protection* (Cambridge/New York: Cambridge University Press, 2003), 205.

— and Jane McAdam, *The Refugee in International Law* (Oxford/New York: Oxford University Press, 2007).

Goy, Raymond, *La Cour internationale de justice et les droits de l'homme, Droit et justice 36, Collection dirigée par Pierre Lambert* (Brussels: Nemesis/Bruylant, 2002).

Greer, Steven, *La marge d'appréciation: Interprétation et pouvoir discrétionnaire dans le cadre de la Convention européenne des Droits de l'Homme,* Dossiers sur les droits de l'homme no 17 (Editions du Conseil de l'Europe, 2000).

Haraszti, György, *Some Fundamental Problems of the Law of Treaties* (Budapest: Akadémiai Kiadó, 1973).

Hencknaerts, Jean-Marie and Louise Doswald-Beck, *Customary International Humanitarian Law: Volumes 1–3* (International Committee of the Red Cross, Cambridge: Cambridge University Press, 2005).

Higgins, Rosalyn, 'The International Court of Justice and Human Rights' in Karl Wellens (ed), *International Law: Theory and Practice, Essays in Honour of Eric Suy* (The Hague/Boston/London: Martinus Nijhoff, 1998), 691.

Human Rights Watch, *In the Name of Counter-Terrorism: Human Rights Abuses Worldwide—III. Country Studies: The Human Rights Impact of Counter-Terrorism in Ten Countries*, Human Rights Watch Briefing Paper for the 59th Session of the United Nations Commission on Human Rights, 25 March 2003.

Inglese, Chris, *The U.N. Committee against Torture: An Assessment* (The Hague/London/Boston: Kluwer Law International, 2001).

Jastram, Kate and Kathleen Newland, 'Family Unity and Refugee Protection' in Erika Feller, Volker Türk, and Frances Nicholson (eds), *Refugee Protection in International Law: UNHCR's Global Consultations on International Protection* (Cambridge: Cambridge University Press, 2003), 555.

Kälin, Walter and Jörg Künzli, *Universeller Menschenrechtsschutz* (Basel: Helbing & Lichtenhahn/Nomos, 2008).

Kellberg, Love, 'The Case-Law of the European Commission of Human Rights' in Antonio Cassese (ed), *The International Fight Against Torture: La lutte internationale contre la torture* (Baden-Baden: Nomos, 1991), 119.

Keller, Helen, *Rezeption des Volkerrechts, Max-Planck-Institut für ausländisches öffentliches Recht und Völkerrecht, Beiträge zum ausländischen öffentlichen Recht und Völkerrecht 160* (Berlin/Heidelberg/New York/Barcelona: Springer, 2003).

— and Alec Sweet Stone, *A Europe of Rights* (New York/Oxford: Oxford University Press, 2008).

Kilkelly, Ursula, *The Child and the European Convention on Human Rights* (Dartmouth/Aldershot/Brookfield/Singapore/Sydney: Ashgate, 1999).

—, 'The Impact of the Children's Convention on the European Convention on Human rights' in Deirdre Fottrell (ed), *Revisiting Children's Rights: Ten Years of the UN Convention on the Rights of the Child* (The Hague: Kluwer Law International, 2000), 87.

Lambert, Hélène, *The Position of Aliens in Relation to the European Convention on Human Rights* (Council of Europe, Strasbourg: Council of Europe Publishing, 2006).

Letsas, George, *A Theory of Interpretation of the European Convention on Human Rights* (Oxford: Oxford University Press, 2007).

Macdonald, Ronald St John and Douglas M Johnston, *Towards World Constitutionalism: Issues in the Legal Ordering of the World Community* (Leiden: Martinus Nijhoff, 2005).

Markesinis, Basil S and Jörg Fedtke, *Judicial Recourse to Foreign Law: A New Source of Inspiration, University of Texas at Austin, Studies in Foreign and Transnational Law* (London: University College London Press, 2006).

Matscher, Franz, 'Methods of Interpretation of the Convention' in Ronald St J Macdonald, Franz Matscher, and Herbert Petzold (eds), *The European System for the Protection of Human Rights* (Dordrecht/Boston/London: Martinus Nijhoff, 1993), 63.

McGoldrick, Dominic, *The Human Rights Committee: Its Role in the Development of the International Covenant on Civil and Political Rights* (Oxford: Clarendon Press, 1991).

Melzer, Nils, *Targeted Killing in International Law* (Oxford/New York: Oxford University Press, 2008).

Merrills, John Graham, *The Development of International Law by the European Court of Human Rights* (Manchester/New York: Manchester University Press, 2nd edn, 1993).

Mole, Nuala, *Asylum and the European Convention on Human Rights, Migration Collection* (Council of Europe, Strasbourg: Council of Europe Publishing, 2007).

Nowak, Manfred, 'The Interrelationship Between the Covenant on Civil and Political Rights and the European Convention on Human Rights' in Stavròula Vassilouni (ed), *Aspects of the Protection of Individual and Social Rights* (Hestia: Marangopoulos Foundation for Human Rights, 1995), 131.

Nowak, Manfred and Elizabeth McArthur, *The United Nations Convention Against Torture: A Commentary* (Oxford/New York: Oxford University Press, 2008).

Orrego Vicuña, Francisco and Christofer Pinto, *The Peaceful Settlement of Disputes: Prospects for the Twenty-First Century*, Preliminary Report Prepared for the 1999 Centennial of the First International Peace Conference (The Hague, 1999).

Ost, François, 'The Original Canons of Interpretation of the European Court of Human Rights' in Mireille Delmas-Marty and Christine Chodakiewicz (eds), *The European Convention for the Protection of Human Rights: International Protection versus National Restriction* (Dordrecht/Boston/London: Martinus Nijhoff, 1992), 283.

Ovey, Clare and Robin CA White, *The European Convention on Human Rights* (Oxford/New York: Oxford University Press, 4th edn, 2006).

Pérez-Vera, Elisa, *Explanatory Report* (The Hague Conference on Private International Law: HCCH Publications, 1982).

Pictet, Jean S, *Commentary of the IV Geneva Convention Relative to the Protection of Civilian Persons in Time of War, Vol. IV* (Geneva: International Committee of the Red Cross, 1994–1995).

Redress, *Immunity v. Accountability: Considering the Relationship between State Immunity and Accountability for Torture and Other Serious International Crimes* (London: The Redress Trust, December, 2005).

Rodley, Nigel S, The *Treatment of Prisoners under International Law* (Oxford/New York: Oxford University Press, 2nd edn, 1999).

Sandoz, Yves, '*Droit international humanitaire et droits de l'homme: marriage d'amour ou de raison?*' in Andreas Auer, Alexandre Flückinger, and Michel Hottelier (eds), *Les droits de l'homme et la constitution: Études en l'honneur du Professeur Giorgio Malinverni, Collection Genevoise* (Geneva/Zurich: Schultess, 2007), 339.

—, Christophe Swinarski, and Bruno Zimmerman, *Commentary on the Additional Protocols of 8 June 1977 to the Geneva Conventions of 12 August 1949* (Geneva: International Committee of the Red Cross, 1987).

Sassòli, Marco, '*Le droit international humanitaire, une lex specialis par rapport aux droits humains?*' in Andreas Auer, Alexandre Flückinger, and Michel Hottelier (eds), *Les droits de l'homme et la constitution: Études en l'honneur du Professeur Giorgio Malinverni, Collection Genevoise* (Geneva/Zurich: Schultess, 2007), 375.

—, '*La Cour européenne des droits de l'homme et les conflits armés*' in Stephan Breitenmoser, Bernhard Ehrenzeller, Marco, Sassòli, Walter Stoffel, and Beatrice Wagner Pfeifer, *Human Rights, Democracy and the Rule of Law, Liber amicorum Luzius Wildhaber* (Zurich: Dike, 2007), 709.

— and Antoine A Bouvier, *How Does Law Protect in War?, Cases, Documents and Teaching Materials on Contemporary Practice in International Humanitarian Law* (Geneva: International Committee of the Red Cross, 1999).

Schwebel, Stephen M, 'Human Rights in the World Court' in Raghunandan Swarup Pathak and Romaa Prasad Dhokalia (eds), *International Law in Transition, Essays in Memory of Judge Nagendra Singh* (Dordrecht/Boston/London: Martinus Nijhoff, 1992), 267.

Sinclair, Ian, *The Vienna Convention and Law of Treaties, Melland Schill Monographs in International law* (Manchester: Manchester University Press, 1984).

Toma, Ramona, *La réalité judiciaire de la Cour européenne des droits de l'homme: Activisme et retenue judiciaires* (Baden-Baden: Nomos Verlagsgesellschaft, 2003).

United Nations High Commissioner for Refugees, *Handbook on Procedures and Criteria for Determining Refugee Status under the 1951 Convention and the 1967 Protocol relating to the Status of Refugees*, UN Doc HCR/1P/4/Eng/REV.1, 1979 (re-edited) (Geneva, 1992).

Van Bueren, Geraldine, *The International Law on the Rights of the Child, International Studies in Human Rights* (Dordrecht/Boston/London: Martinus Nijhoff, 1995), Vol 35.

Van Dijk, Pieter and Godefrious JH Van Hoof, *Theory and Practice of the European Convention on Human Rights* (The Hague/London/Boston: Kluwer Law International, 3rd edn, 1998).

—, Fried Van Hoof, Arjen Van Rijn, and Loe Zwaak, *Theory and Practice of the European Convention on Human Rights* (Antwerp/Oxford: Intersentia, 4th edn, 2006).

Villiger, Mark E, 'Articles 31 and 32 of the Vienna Convention on the Law of Treaties in the Case-Law of the European Court of Human Rights' in Jürgen Bröhmer (ed), *Internationale Gemeinschaft und Menschenrechte: Festschrift für Georg Reiss zum 70. Geburtstag am 21. Januar 2005* (Cologne: Carl Heymann, 2005), 317.

—, *Commentary on the 1969 Vienna Convention on the Law of Treaties* (Leiden/Boston: Martinus Nijhoff, 2009).

Yourow, Charles Howard, *The Margin of Appreciation Doctrine in the Dynamics of European Human Rights Jurisprudence, International Studies in Human Rights* (The Hague: Martinus Nijhoff, 1996), Vol 28.

Ziemele, Ineta, 'Case-Law of the European Court of Human Rights and Integrity of International law' in Karel Wellens and Charo Huesa (eds), *L'influence des sources sur l'unité et la fragmentation du droit international* (Brussels: Bruylant, 2006), 187.

Articles

Abi-Saab, Georges, 'Fragmentation or Unification: Some Concluding Remarks' (1999) 31 NYUJ Int'l L & Pol 919.

Abresch, William, 'A Human Rights Law of Internal Armed Conflict: The European Court of Human Rights in Chechnya' (2005) 16 Eur J Int'l L 741.

Akehurst, Michael, 'The Hierarchy of the Sources of International Law' (1974/1975) 47 BYIL 273.

Bates, Ed, 'The Al-Adsani Case, State Immunity and the International Legal Prohibition on Torture' (2003) 3(2) HRLR 193.

Benvenisti, Eyal, 'Margin of Appreciation, Consensus, and Universal Standards' (1999) 21 NYUJ Int'l L & Pol 843.

Bodeau-Livinec, Pierre, Buzzini, Gionata P, and Villalpando, Santiago, 'Agim Behrami & Bekir Behrami v. France; Ruzhdi Saramati v. France, Germany & Norway. Joined App. Nos. 71412/01 & 78166/01' (2008) 102 Am J Int'l L 323.

Caflisch, Lucius and Cançado Trindade, Antônio, '*Les Conventions Américaine et Européenne des Droits de l'Homme et le Droit International Général*' (2004-I) 108 RGDIP 5.

Canor, Iris, 'The European Courts and the Security Council: Between Dédoublement Fonctionnel and Balancing of Values: Three Replies to Pasquale De Sena and Maria Chiara Vitucci' (2009) 20 Eur J Int'l L 870.

Charney, Jonathan I, 'Is International Threatened by the Multiple International Law Tribunals?' (1998) 27 *Recueil des Cours* 101.

—, 'The Impact on the International Legal System of the Growth of International Courts and Tribunals' (1999) 31 NYUJ Int'l & Pol 697.

Cohen-Jonathan, Gérard and Flauss, Jean-Francois, '*Cour européenne des droits de l'homme et droit international général (2001)*' (2001) XLVII *Annuaire de droit français* 423.

Combacau, Jean, '*Le droit international: bric-à-brac ou système?*' (1986) 31 *Archives de philosophie du droit* 85.

Cullen, Anthony, 'Key Developments Affecting the Scope of Internal Armed Conflict in International Humanitarian Law' (2005) 183 Mil L Rev 66.

Cullen, Holly, '*Siliadin v. France*: Positive Obligations under Article 4 of the European Convention on Human Rights' (2006) 6 HRLR 585.

De Búrca, Gráinne, 'The European Courts and the Security Council: Between Dédoublement Fonctionnel and Balancing of Values: Three Replies to Pasquale De Sena and Maria Chiara Vitucci' (2009) 20 Eur J Int'l L 853.

De Oliveira Moll, Leandro, 'Case Note: Al-Adsani v United Kingdom: State Immunity and Denial of Justice with Respect to Violations of Fundamental Human Rights' (2003) 4 Mel J Int'l L 561.

De Sena, Pasquale and Vitucci, Maria Chiara, 'The European Courts and the Security Council: Between Dédoublement Fonctionnel and Balancing of Values' (2009) 20 Eur J Int'l L 193.

De Vos, Christian, 'Mind the Gap: Purpose, Pain, and the Difference Between Torture and Inhuman Treatment' (2007) 14(2) Hum Rts Brief 4.

De Wet, Erika, 'The Emergence of International and Regional Value Systems as a Manifestation of the Emerging Constitutional Order' (2006) 19 LJIL 611.

Dominicé, Christian, 'Methodology of International Law' in Bernhardt, Rudolf (ed) (1997) 3 EPIL 354.

Dupuy, Pierre-Marie, 'The Danger of Fragmentation or Unification of the International Legal System and the International Court of Justice' (1999) 31 NYUJ Int'l L & Pol 791.

—, '*L'unité de l'ordre juridique internationale. Cours général de droit international public*' (2002) 297 *Recueil des Cours* 9.

Eissen, Marc-André, 'The European Convention on Human Rights and the United Nations Covenant on Civil and Political Rights: Problems of Coexistence' (1972–1973) 22 Buff L Rev 181.

Evans, Malcolm D, 'Getting to Grips with Torture' (April 2002) 51 Int'l Comp LQ 365.

Fischer-Lescano, Andreas and Teubner, Günter, 'Regime-Collisions: The Vain Search for Legal Unity in the Fragmentation of Global Law' (2004) 25 Mich J Int'l L 999.

French, Duncan, 'Treaty Interpretation and the Incorporation of Extraneous Legal Rules' (2006) 55 Int'l Comp LQ 281.

Frowein, Jochen A, 'The Relationship Between Human Rights Regimes and Regimes of Belligerent Occupation' (1998) 28 IYHR 1.

—, 'General Course: The European Convention on Human Rights as the Public Order of Europe' (1990) I Collected Courses Academy Euro L 267.
Gaeta, Paola, 'The Armed Conflict in Chechnya before the Russian Constitutional Court' (1996) 7 Eur J Int'l L 563.
Gaggioli, Gloria and Kolb, Robert, '*L'apport de la Cour Européenne des Droits de l'homme au droit international humanitaire en matière de droit à la vie*' (2007) 17(1) SZIER 3.
Gaudreau, Julie, '*Immunité de l'Etat et Violations des Droits de la Personne: Une Approche Jurisprudentielle*', Institut Universitaire des Hautes Etudes Internationales, HEI Publications, Etudes et Travaux, Papier no 05/01, March 2005.
Goodman, Micah, 'After the Wall: the Legal Ramifications of the East German Border Guard Trials in United Germany' (1996) 29 Cornell Int'l LJ 727.
Guellali, Anna, '*Lex specialis, droit international humanitaire et droits de l'homme: Leur interaction dans les nouveaux conflits armés*', 2007–3 RGDIP 539.
Hadden, Tom and Harvey, Colin, 'The Law of Internal Crisis and Conflict: An Outline Prospectus for the Merger of International Human Rights Law, the Law of Armed Conflict, Refugee Law, and the Law on Humanitarian Intervention' (1999) 833 IRRC 119.
Hafner, Gerhard, 'Pros and Cons Ensuing from Fragmentation of International Law' (2004) 25 Mich J Int'l L 849.
Hampson, Françoise, 'Using International Human Rights Machinery to Enforce International Law of Armed Conflicts' (1992) Vol XXXI—1–2–3–4 MLLWR 119.
Hefferman, Liz, 'A Comparative View of Individual Petition Procedures under the European Convention on Human Rights and the International Covenant on Civil and Political Rights' (1997) 19(1) Hum Rts Qrtly 78.
Heintze, Hans-Joachim, 'On the Relationship Between Human Rights Law and International Humanitarian Law' (2004) 856 IRRC 789.
—, 'The European Court of Human Rights and the Implementation of Human Rights Standards During Armed Conflicts' (2002) 45 GYIL 60.
Helfer, Laurence R and Slaughter, Anne-Marie, 'Toward a Theory of Effective Supranational Adjudication' (1997) 107 Yale LJ 273.
Higgins, Rosalyn, 'Ten Years of the UN Human Rights Committee: Some Thoughts upon Parting' (1996) 6 EHRLR 574.
—, 'The ICJ, the ECJ, and the Integrity of International Law' (2003) 52 Int'l Comp LQ 1.
—, 'A Babel of Judicial Voices? Ruminations from the Bench' (2006) 55 Int'l Comp LQ 791.
Kilkelly, Ursula, 'The Best of Both Worlds for Children's Rights? Interpreting the European Convention on Human rights in the Light of the UN Convention on the Rights of the Child' (2001) 23 Hum Rts Qrtly 308.
Klabbers, Jan, 'Constitutionalism Lite' (2004) 1 Int'l Org L Rev 31.
Koskenniemi, Martti, The Fate of Public International Law: Constitutional Utopia or Fragmentation, Chorley Lecture 2006, London School of Economics, 7 June 2006, available at <http://www.helsinki.fi/eci/Publications/MKChorley%20Text-06a.pdf> (last visited 10 January 2009).
— and Leino, Päivi, 'Fragmentation of International Law? Postmodern Anxieties' (2002) 15 LJIL 553.

Krieger, Heike, 'A Conflict of Norms: The Relationship Between Humanitarian Law and Human Rights Law in the ICRC Customary Law Study' (2006) 11 J Con & Sec L 265.
Kumm, Mattias, 'The Legitimacy of International Law: A Constitutionalist Framework of Analysis' (2004) 15 Eur J Int'l L 907.
Lambert, Hélène, 'The European Court of Human Rights and the Right of Refugees and Other Persons in Need of Protection to Family Reunion' (1999) 11 IJRL 427.
Lebeck, Carl, 'The European Court of Human Rights on the Relation between ECHR and EC-law: the Limits of Constitutionalisation of Public International Law' (2007) 62 ZöR 195.
Linderfalk, Ulk, 'On the Interpretation of Treaties: The Modern International Law as Expressed in the 1969 Vienna Convention on the Law of Treaties', Law and Philosophy Library 83, Springer, 2007.
Lloyd Jones, David, 'Article 6 ECHR and Immunities Arising in Public International Law' (2003) 52 Int'l Comp LQ 463.
Martin, Francisco Forrest, 'The Unified Use of Force Rule Revisited: The Penetration of the Law of Armed Conflict by International Human Rights Law' (2002) 65 Sask L Rev 405.
—, 'The Unified Use of Force Rule: Amplifications in Light of the Comments of Professor Green and Paust' (2002) 65 Sask L Rev 451.
McLachlan, Campbell, 'The Principle of Systemic Integration and Article 31(3)(c) of the Vienna Convention' (2005) 54 Int'l Comp LQ 279.
Meron, Theodor, 'The Humanization of Humanitarian Law' (2000) 94 Am J Int'l L 239.
Miller, Nathan, 'An International Jurisprudence? The Operation of "Precedent" Across International Tribunals' (2002) 15 LJIL 483.
Mowbray, Alastair, 'The Creativity of the European Court of Human Rights' (2005) 5 HRLR 57.
Nakan, Winston P and Atkins, Lucie, 'The International Law of Torture: From Universal Proscription to Effective Application and Enforcement' (2001) 14 Harv Hum Rts J 87.
Nowak, Manfred, 'What Practices Constitute Torture?: US and UN Standards' (2001) 28 Hum Rts Qrtly 809.
—, 'Challenges to the Absolute Nature of the Prohibition on Torture and Ill-Treatment' (2005) 23 NQHR 674.
Orakhelashvili, Alexander, 'State Immunity and International Public Order' (2003) 45 GYIL 227.
—, 'Restrictive Interpretation of Human Rights Treaties in the Recent Jurisprudence of the European Court of Human Rights' (2003) 14 Eur J Int'l L 529.
—, 'The Interaction between Human Rights and Humanitarian law: Fragmentation, Conflict, Parallelism, or Convergence?' (2008) 19 Eur J Int'l L 161.
—, '*R (on the application of Al-Jedda) v Secretary of State for Defence*' (2008) 102 Am J Int'l L 337.
Oxman, Bernard H and Emberland, Marius, 'Case note' (2002) 96 Am J Int'l L 699.
Parlett, Kate, 'Immunity in Civil Proceedings for Torture: The Emerging Exception' (2006) 1 EHRLR 49.
Phuong, Catherine, 'The Relationship Between the European Court of Human Rights and the Human Rights Committee: Has the "Same Matter" Already Been "Examined"?' (2007) 7/2 HRLR 385.

Pitea, Cesare, 'Rape as a Human Rights Violation and a Criminal Offence: The European Court's Judgment in M.C. v. Bulgaria' (2005) 3 J Int'l Crim Just 447.

Pronto, Arnold, '"Human-Rightism" and the Development of General International Law' (2007) 20 LJIL 753.

Rao Sreenivasa, Pemmaraju, 'Multiple Judicial Forums: A Reflection of the Growing Strength of International Law or Its Fragmentations' (2004) 25 Mich J Int'l L 929.

Quill, Adrienne, 'To Prosecute or Not To Prosecute: Problems Encountered in the Prosecution of Former Communist Officials in Germany, Czechoslovakia, and the Czech Republic' (1996) 7 IICLR 165.

Quint, Peter, 'The Border Guard Trials and the East German Past—Seven Arguments' (2000) 48 Am J Com L 541.

Reece Thomas, Katherine and Small, Joan, 'Human Rights and State Immunity From Civil Liability for Torture' (2003) 30 NILR 1.

Reidy, Aisling, 'The Approach of the European Commission and Court of Human Rights to International Humanitarian Law' (1998) 324 IRRC 513.

Reineke, Fred, 'Treaty and Non-Treaty Human Rights Agreements: A Case Study of Freedom of Movement in East Germany' (1986) 24 Colum J Transnat'l L 647.

Rodley, Nigel S, 'The Definition(s) of Torture in International Law' (2002) 55 CLP 467.

—, 'Human Rights and the Humanitarian Intervention; the Case-Law of the World Court' (1989) 38 Int'l Comp LQ 321.

Rozakis, Christos L, 'The European Judge as Comparatist' (2005) 80(1) Tul L Rev 257.

Roth, Brad, 'Retrospective Justice or Retroactive Standards? Human Rights as a Sword in the East German Leaders Case' (2004) 50 Wayne L Rev 37.

Rouillard, Louis-Philippe F, 'Misinterpreting the Prohibition on Torture Under International Law: The Office of Legal Council Memorandum' (2005) 21 Am U Int'l Rev 9.

Sadurski, Wojciech, 'Partnering with Strasbourg: Constitutionalization of the European Court of Human Rights, the Accession of Central and Eastern European States to the Council of Europe, and the Idea of Pilot Judgements', 4 November 2008, Sydney Law School Research Paper No 08/135.

Sands, Philippe, 'Treaty, Custom and the Cross-Fertilization of International Law' (1998) 1 YHRDLJ 85.

Sari, Auriel, 'Jurisdiction and International Responsibility in Peace Support Operations: The Behrami and Saramati Cases' (2008) 8 HRLR 151.

Schulz, Andrea, 'The 1980 Hague Child Abduction Convention and the European Convention on Human Rights' (2002) 12 TLCP 355.

Silberman, Linda, 'Interpreting the Hague Abduction Convention: In Search of a Global Jurisprudence' (2005) 38 UC Davis L Rev 1049.

Simma, Bruno and Pulkowski, Dirk, 'Of Planets and the Universe: Self-Contained Regimes in International Law' (2006) 17 Eur J Int'l L 483.

Sperotto, Federico, 'Law in Times of War: the Case of Chechnya', University of Denver, Human Rights and Human Welfare, Working Paper No 40, 20 August 2007.

Spjut, Robert J, 'Torture Under the European Convention on Human Rights' (1979) 73 Am J Int'l L 267.

Tomuschat, Christian, 'International Law: Ensuring the Survival of Mankind on the Eve of a New Century, General Discourse on Public International Law' (2001) 281 *Recueil des Cours* 63.

Turns, David, 'At the "Vanishing Point" of International Humanitarian Law: Methods and Means of Warfare in Non-International Armed Conflicts' (2002) 45 GYIL 115.

Von Bogdandy, Armin, 'Constitutionalism in International Law: Comment on Proposal from Germany' (2001) 47 Harv Int'l L J 223.

Voyiakis, Emmanuel, 'Access to Court v. State Immunity' (2003) 52 Int Comp LQ 297.

Walshand, Michael and Savard, Susan, 'International Child Abduction and the Hague Convention' (2006) 6 Barry L Rev 29.

Walter, Christina, '*Die Europäische Menschenrechtkonvention als Konstitutionalisierung-prozess*' (1999) 59 ZaöRV 961.

Watkin, Kenneth, 'Warriors Without Rights? Combatants, Unprivileged Belligerents, and Struggle over Legitimacy', Harvard Program on Humanitarian Policy and Conflict Research, Occasional Paper, Winter 2005.

—, 'Controlling the Use of Force: A Role for Human Rights Norms in Contemporary Armed Conflict' (2004) 98 Am J Int'l L 1.

Watson, William, '*Behrami v. France*: Constructive Blue Helmets Protect KFOR Nations From Accountability' (2008) 16 Tul J Int'l & Comp L 575.

Weissbrodt, David and Härtrieter, Isabel, 'The Principle of Non-Refoulement: Article 3 of the Convention Against Torture and Other Cruel, Inhuman or Degrading Treatment or Punishment in Comparison with the Non-refoulement Provisions of Other International Human Rights Treaties' (1999) 5 Buff Hum Rts L Rev 1.

Whitlock, Craig, 'Terrorism Financing Blacklists at Risk: Global System Faces Multiple Challenges', *Washington Post*, 2 November 2008, A1.

Wildhaber, Luzius, 'The European Court of Human Rights and International Law' (2007) 52 Int & Comp LQ 217.

Yang, Xiadong, 'State Immunity in The European Court of Human Rights: Reaffirmations and Misconceptions' (2003) 74 BYIL 333.

Yaseen, Mustafa Kamil, '*L'interprétation des traités d'après la Convention de Vienne sur le Droit des Traîtés*' (1976/3) 151 *Recueil des Cours* 1.

Zemanek, Karl, 'The Legal Foundations of the International System' (1997) 266 *Recueil des Cours* 62.

Index